SOCIOLOGY
BRIEF EDITION

SOCIOLOGY

BRIEF EDITION

Beth B. Hess
County College of Morris

Elizabeth W. Markson
Boston University

Peter J. Stein
William Paterson College

In Collaboration with Karen Theroux

MACMILLAN PUBLISHING COMPANY
New York

MAXWELL MACMILLAN CANADA
Toronto

Editor: **Bruce Nichols**
Production Supervisor: **Katherine Evancie**
Production Manager: **Nick Sklitsis**
Text and Cover Designer: **Eileen Burke**
Cover Photograph: **Tony Savino/SIPA Press**
Photo Researchers: **Fred Courtright** and **Chris Migdol**
Illustrations by **Publication Services, Inc.**

This book was set in 10/11 ITC Garamond Book by
Ruttle, Shaw & Wetherill, Inc. and was printed and
bound by R.R. Donnelley and Sons Company. The
cover was printed by Phoenix Color Corp.

Macmillan Publishing Company
866 Third Avenue, New York, New York 10022

Macmillan Publishing Company is part of
the Maxwell Communication Group of Companies.

Maxwell Macmillan Canada, Inc.
1200 Eglinton Avenue East
Suite 200
Don Mills, Ontario M3C 3N1

Library of Congress Cataloging-in-Publication Data

Hess, Beth B.
  Sociology / Beth B. Hess, Elizabeth W. Markson, Peter J. Stein
  in collaboration with Karen Theroux.—Brief ed.
     p.   cm.
  Includes bibliographical references and indexes.
  ISBN 0-02-354431-7 (paper)
  1. Sociology. I. Markson, Elizabeth Warren. II. Stein, Peter J. III. Title.

Copyright acknowledgments begin on page 515,
which constitutes an extension of the copyright page.

HM51.H46 1992
301—dc20   91-7543
              CIP
Printing: 2 3 4 5 6 7   Year: 2 3 4 5 6 7 8

PREFACE

In the many years we have taught introductory sociology, we have found that what our students want, above all, is to discover a sociological perspective and to apply their insights to the social and personal issues they face in everyday life. From the instructor's point of view, we sought to craft a book that was comprehensible, accurate, and shaped by a guiding vision, yet adaptable to individual teaching styles. About 12 years ago we set out to write an introductory textbook that would provide a clear framework for understanding society and present material in a current and readable format. We wanted to be careful to neither mystify nor patronize our readers. In short, we sought to develop a text that was accessible to students and stimulating to instructors.

Our book, *Sociology*, now in its fourth edition, has been well received by instructors and students and has been used at several hundred community colleges, four-year colleges, and universities in the United States and other countries.

We realize that the diversity of teaching styles, sociological orientations, and academic calendars means that a comprehensive text cannot meet every instructor's needs. A number of colleagues have suggested their preference for a core text for shorter courses or for a book that can be supplemented with paperbacks and is more compatible with their own teaching styles.

Thus, in collaboration with Karen Theroux, we have developed *Sociology: Brief Edition* to provide an informative, readable, and timely overview of the fundamental ideas of sociology. Although the core structure and approach of this book reflects our coverage in the more comprehensive *Sociology*, fourth edition, we have not included some chapters and sections; we have added new sections and reorganized some of the material. The present book can be used alone to provide an introduction to the field of sociology or may be supplemented with other readings.

The authors of *Sociology: Brief Edition* bring to the task over 70 years of collective teaching experience at community colleges, four-year liberal arts colleges and universities, and graduate programs. We have enjoyed working together and have strengthened our friendship through this project. Karen Theroux, who joined us for this project, has written extensively on a number of social and educational issues and served as editor of *Forecast*, a Scholastic publication. We hope you enjoy reading and learning from our book.

CONTENT

Sociology: Brief Edition provides, in 12 chapter and 2 essays, an overview of the basic ideas, issues, and research of both classical and contemporary sociology. The first chapter introduces the student to the study of society and the research process from its beginning in theory to the evaluation of findings. Part I examines the *self in society* in four chapters. We focus on the cultural context consisting of values, rules, behaviors, and products; the social structures that embody culture; socialization, the process through which culture is internalized; and conformity, deviance, and crime. Part II consists of three chapters detailing *social differences and inequality.* We examine general principles of stratification and the consequences of inequality; the importance of gender in the distribution of power, prestige, and property; the social construction of human sexualities; and race, ethnicity, and religion as determinants of social rank. Part III consists of three chapters examining *the institutional spheres* of courtship, marriage, and the family; economic and political systems; and educational and religious systems. Part IV explores *social change* through the broad current of cultural and social change, and collective behavior and social movements. Two essays focus on major contemporary issues: health care and an aging population; and popular culture: mass media, popular music, and sports.

Throughout the book there is a constant focus on structural factors and a balance among the major theoretical perspectives of sociology. Interesting and timely examples are used in the text to clarify theories and concepts that are not always readily comprehended by introductory students. Although many examples come from North American culture, considerable use of comparative material from other cultures is made including the Soviet Union, Eastern Europe, South Africa, Asia, Central America, and such traditional societies as the Pintupi, Tasaday, Trobriand Islanders, Ik, and !Kung.

FEATURES

Sociology: Brief Edition retains a number of highly praised features from *Sociology,* fourth edition, all designed to make the text as "user friendly" as possible:

Chapter Outlines and Openers.   Each chapter opens with a quick overview of the chapter's content and a series of interesting and timely items to spark the interest of the reader and to introduce themes in the body of the chapter.

Marginal Definitions.   The universally praised glosses of key terms reinforce concepts as they are presented in the body of the text. Students report that these highlighted definitions are very useful for chapter review.

Social Policy Issues.   Each chapter contains a Social Policy Issue, which helps students understand how sociology relates to societal priorities and life choices. Some of the issues examined include the minimum wage debate, homelessness, child care, racism, freedom of speech, abortion, and the link between religion and the government.

Vignettes.   Autobiographical vignettes are written by sociologists who explain how they became interested in their recent sociological research and how they go about "doing sociology." The vignettes acquaint students with various styles of sociological research and provide evidence about how sociologists practice their craft. Some issues covered in the vignettes are child care in the United States and Sweden, the Civil Rights Movement, corporate political behavior, the death penalty, the link between democracy and bureaucracy, men's changing roles, middle-class African-Americans, education as a process of change, and everyday sociology.

Summaries. Numbered summaries at the end of each chapter help students review the material.

Suggested Readings. Brief descriptions of interesting, current, and important books cover the topics discussed within each chapter.

Illustrations. Photographs, charts, tables, and graphs expand the learning process for students and make the book more appealing. They are designed to help readers understand concepts presented in the text and to see how such ideas relate to their own lives.

SUPPLEMENTS

Sociology: Brief Edition is supported by a full package of instructional materials.

- The *Instructor's Manual with Test Questions* has been prepared by Thomas and Sandra Dunn of Western Kentucky University. The *Instructor's Manual* benefits from many helpful suggestions of colleagues who have used the parent text and includes chapter summaries, teaching objectives, key concepts and names, discussions of various teaching approaches, and an extensive bibliography of film and media resources.
- A *Computerized Test Bank* is available for the IBM PC, XT, AT, and all compatibles.
- A student *Study Guide* was prepared by Ellen Rosengarten of Sinclair Community College (Dayton, Ohio), who brings to the task substantial experience as an undergraduate instructor. The *Study Guide* provides chapter outlines, definitions, sample test questions, and other learning devices such as glossary terms and exercises for the student.
- A *Transparency Set* includes 40 full-color overhead transparencies to accompany lectures.
- A *Computer Simulation,* "Famine Relief in the Desert Horn," describes a situation in which students must involve themselves in decision-making processes that illustrate their underlying sociological perspectives. Using the format of interactive fiction, the program simulates a famine-relief effort. Students must mobilize resources to distribute surplus U.S. grain to the fictitious famine area of the Desert Horn. The software is accompanied by an *Instructor's Manual,* which shows how to use the simulation to discuss concepts such as power, authority, networking, and impression management. The *Manual* has been written by Christina Spellman, a creative teacher and writer.

ACKNOWLEDGMENTS

We have had the benefit of extremely supportive Macmillan colleagues. Our thanks go to our acquisition editor, Bruce Nichols, who provided strong support throughout the project; the production supervisor, Katherine Evancie, whose diligence, hard work, and cooperative style moved the project along swiftly and smoothly, and Chris Migdol, whose efforts as our photo editor livened up the pages of the text.

We also gratefully acknowledge our debt to the many colleagues who reviewed earlier editions of *Sociology* as well as the current *Brief Edition,* including

David P. Aday, Jr., *College of William and Mary*
William R. Aho, *Rhode Island College*
Robert Allegrucci, *Wichita State University*
Angelo A. Alonzo, *Ohio State University*
William R. Arnold, *University of Kansas*
Donald R. Bailey, *Francis Marion College*
Alan Bayer, *Virginia Polytechnic Institute*
Susanne Bleiberg-Seperson, *Dowling College*
Audie Blevins, *University of Wyoming*
Janet Carlisle Bogdan, *Le Moyne College*
Selma K. Brandow, *Trenton State College*
Ervin G. Bublitz, *Winona State University*
William Bruce Cameron, *University of South Florida*
Walter F. Carroll, *Bridgewater State College*
John B. Christiansen, *Gallaudet University*
Robert A. Clark, *Whitworth College*
John K. Cochran, *University of Oklahoma*
Samuel Cohn, *University of Wisconsin–Madison*
Gerry R. Cox, *Fort Hays State University*
John H. Curtis, *Valdosta State College*
M. Herbert Danzger, *Herbert H. Lehman College*
Susan Dargan, *Framingham State College*
Ralph O. David, *Pittsburg State University*
David L. Decker, *California State University–San Bernardino*
William DiFazio, *St. John's University*
Lois C. Dilatush, *Metropolitan State College*
John R. Dugan, *Central Washington University*
Richard L. Dukes, *University of Colorado–Colorado Springs*
Isaac W. Eberstein, *Florida State University*
Jackie Eller, *Middle Tennessee State University*
J. Rex Enoch, *Memphis State University*
William Feigelman, *Nassau Community College*
Craig J. Forsyth, *University of Southwestern Louisiana*
Jesse J. Frankel, *Pace University*
Clyde W. Franklin, II, *Ohio State University*
Richard J. Gigliotti, *University of Akron*
Henry F. Gilmore, *Albany State College*
Judith Bograd Gordon, *University of New Haven*

Whitney Gordon, *Ball State University*
James W. Grimm, *Western Kentucky University*
Gerard J. Grzyb, *University of Wisconsin–Oshkosh*
Elaine J. Hall, *University of Connecticut*
Judith Hammond, *East Tennessee State University*
Donald W. Hastings, *University of Tennessee*
Jacqueline Hill, *Purdue University–Calumet*
Christine A. Hope, *College of Charleston*
Gerald Hughes, *Northern Arizona University*
Jeanne Humble, *Lexington Community College*
Anne S. Jenkins, *Cheyney University*
Daniel Johnson, *Virginia Commonwealth University*
Janis Johnson, *Immaculata College*
Ann Jones, *Northern Illinois University*
Dennis Kalob, *Loyola University*
Ali Kamali, *Upsala College*
Michael Kimmel, *State University of New York–Stonybrook*
Joseph A. Kotarba, *University of Houston*
Joan Krenzin, *Western Kentucky University*
Peter A. Kuo, *Chaminade University of Honolulu*
Michael Kupersanin, *Duquesne University*
Paul L. Leslie, *Greensboro College*
Barry B. Levine, *Florida International University*
Janet Huber Lowry, *Austin College*
Dale A. Lund, *University of Utah Gerontology Center*
Joan Luxenburg, *Central State University*
Mary Ann Maguire, *Tulane University*
Kooros M. Mahmoudi, *Northern Arizona University*
William T. Markham, *University of North Carolina–Greensboro*
Patricia Yancey Martin, *Florida State University*
Ron Matson, *Wichita State University*
E. Doyle McCarthy, *Fordham University*
Patrick McNamara, *University of New Mexico*
Ruth P. Miller, *John Carroll University*
Lynn D. Nelson, *Virginia Commonwealth University*
David O'Donnell, *University of Wisconsin–Superior*
John E. Owen, *Arizona State University*
Robert S. Palacio, *California State University–Fresno*
Philip J. Perricone, *Wake Forest University*
David M. Petersen, *Georgia State University*
Dretha M. Phillips, *Roanoke College*
Margaret E. Preble, *Thomas Nelson Community College*
Meredith D. Pugh, *Bowling Green University*
Claire M. Renzetti, *St. Joseph's University*
R. P. Rettig, *Central State University*
Pamela Richards, *University of Cincinnati*
Ron Roberts, *University of Northern Iowa*
Edward Sabin, *Towson State University*
S. Frederick Seymour, *Northern Illinois University*
Henry M. Silvert, *Yeshiva University*

Ida Harper Simpson, *Duke University*
Paul Sites, *Kent State University*
H. Lovell Smith, *University of Maryland*
Rina Spano, *Caldwell College*
Steven Stack, *Auburn University*
Suzanne Staggenborg, *Indiana University–Bloomington*
Charles E. Starnes, *Oregon State University*
Phillipa Stevens, *Marymount University*
Henry Stewart, *University of Richmond*
Don Swenson, *University of Notre Dame*
Nancy Thalhofer, *Eastern Michigan University*
Robert Tillman, *Wheaton College*
Charles M. Tolbert, II, *Florida State University*
Susan D. Toliver, *Iona College*
Steven L. Vassar, *Mankato State University*
Joseph Ventimiglia, *Memphis State University*
Bruce H. Wade, *Spelman College*
Edward J. Walsh, *Pennsylvania State University*
Sarah A. White, *J. Sargeant Reynolds Community College*
Timothy Wickham-Crowley, *Georgetown University*
Eric Woodrum, *North Carolina State University*
Diane Zablotsky, *University of Maryland*

We wish to thank our colleagues at the County College of Morris, Boston University, and William Paterson College for their many insightful and helpful comments and suggestions.

This edition is dedicated to our spouses, children, and grandchildren: Laurence Hess, Emily and Gary Robinson, and Gary, Jr., Ritchie, and Amy Robinson; Ralph, Alison, and David Markson; Michele Murdock and Michael Murdock-Stein.

Beth B. Hess
Elizabeth W. Markson
Peter J. Stein

— ABOUT THE AUTHORS —

Beth B. Hess is professor of sociology at County College of Morris, where she has had extensive experience in teaching introductory sociology. A graduate of Radcliffe College and Rutgers University, she has published several textbooks in social gerontology, becoming a Fellow of the Gerontological Society of America in 1978. Most recently, her work has focused on issues of concern to women, including papers on public policy and older women; a book on the New Feminist Movement, *Controversy and Coalition* (coauthored with Myra Marx Ferree; Twayne, 1984); *Women and the Family: Two Decades of Change* (coedited with Marvin B. Sussman; Haworth, 1984); *Analyzing Gender: A Handbook of Social Science Research* (coedited with Myra Marx Ferree; Sage, 1987); and the fourth edition of *Growing Old in America* (with Elizabeth W. Markson; Transaction, 1990). Beth Hess has devoted much time and energy to professional organizations. She chaired the Behavioral and Social Science section of the Gerontological Society of America, as well as the Journal and Publications Committee of the Society for the Study of Social Problems. She has been president of the Association for Humanist Sociology, president of the Eastern Sociological Society and president of Sociologists for Women in Society. Currently, she serves as secretary of the American Sociological Association.

Elizabeth W. Markson is research associate professor of sociology and associate director, Gerontology Center, at Boston University. She is also adjunct associate professor of sociomedical sciences and community medicine at Boston University School of Medicine. Markson received her B.A. degree at Bryn Mawr College, her Ph.D. in sociology from Yale University, and postgraduate training in family therapy at the Kantor Family Institute. She has worked in both applied and academic settings over the past 20 years and has contributed to various scholarly journals. Her books include *Older Women* (winner of the 1984 Books of the Year Award from the *American Journal of Nursing*), *Public Policies for an Aging Population* (with Gretchen Batra), and, most recently, *Growing Old in America,* fourth edition, (with Beth B. Hess). She has been active in various professional organizations and has served on the executive boards of the Society for the Study of Social

Problems and the Northeastern Gerontological Society, as well as being chair of the Youth, Aging, and Life Course, and Family Divisions of the Society for the Study of Social Problems.

 **Peter J. Stein** is professor of sociology at William Paterson College. He received his B.A. degree at the City College of New York and his Ph.D. in sociology from Princeton University. Stein has taught a number of undergraduate and graduate courses over the past 20 years including Introduction to Sociology, Marriage and the Family, Social Problems, Sociology of Adulthood, History of Social Theory, and Sociology of Sports. His published articles focus on work and family roles, corporate human resource policies, dual-earner couples, and single adults. His books include *Single; Single Life: Unmarried Adults in Social Context; The Family: Functions, Conflicts and Symbols* (with Judy Richman and Natalie Hannon); and *The Marriage Game: Understanding Marital Decision Making* (with Cathy Greenblat and Norman Washburne). He has been active in various professional organizations and has served as vice president of the Eastern Sociological Society, chair of the Family Division of the Society for the Study of Social Problems, and on the Council of the Sex and Gender section of the American Sociological Association. He recently served as chair of ASA's Committee on Teaching.

BRIEF CONTENTS

CONTENTS

1

THE SOCIOLOGICAL PERSPECTIVE

PART I
SELF IN SOCIETY

2

CULTURE

PART II
SOCIAL DIFFERENCES
AND INEQUALITY

6

SOCIAL STRATIFICATION

ESSAY

B

HEALTH CARE AND AN AGING POPULATION

PART III
INSTITUTIONAL SPHERES

9

COURTSHIP, MARRIAGE, AND THE FAMILY

10

ECONOMIC AND POLITICAL SYSTEMS

11

EDUCATIONAL AND RELIGIOUS SYSTEMS

PART IV
MODERNIZATION: SOCIAL MOVEMENTS AND SOCIAL CHANGE

12

SOCIAL CHANGE: MODERNIZATION AND SOCIAL MOVEMENTS

VIGNETTES

SOCIOLOGY
BRIEF EDITION

1

The Sociological Perspective

We begin by defining sociology and its special subject matter. Chapter 1 locates sociology in historical context and describes the ideas of the theorists and researchers who established this field of study. The second section of the chapter moves from the question of *what* sociologists study to *how* they seek answers to these questions. Scientific and nonscientific factors are identified, sources of information described, and ethical dilemmas discussed. A brief section on data analysis helps students to read tables, graphs, and other figures.

Only humans can go on a diet, commit suicide, transform sexual attraction into a love relationship, or organize days into weeks. Why? Because there is one crucial difference between humans and animals: We are able to reflect on our own actions and to control bodily impulses by creating rules that govern the behavior of people in groups. Such self-consciousness and flexibility are the product of millions of years of human evolution in which the powerful inner drives and impulses that trigger most animal behavior have been gradually brought under the control of our uniquely sophisticated brain.

The content of the human mind consists of ideas and rules that members of any collectivity (set of people) create to bring order and predictability to their shared lives. This is the significance of the seven-day week, conceived many thousands of years ago by the ancient Hebrews to separate their religion from those based solely on natural means of marking time. Although the seven-day week is an absolutely artificial construct with no relationship to any naturally recurring phenomena—either of the moon or sun or Earth—notice how quickly we adapt to this rhythm and act differently on different days. Note, also, the importance of a day off, not only for oneself but for bringing people together in families and in religious observance.

WHAT IS SOCIOLOGY?

Sociology is the study of human be-havior as shaped by group life.

Sociology is the study of human behavior as shaped by group life, including both collective forces (group constructions) and the ways in which people give meaning to their experiences (self-reflections). This means that the individual is not the appropriate unit of analysis for understanding behavior because human beings do not—cannot—exist in isolation from others.

We cannot predict how individuals will act in a group simply on the basis of what we know about each person. When we interact with others, we create a level of reality—that of the collectivity, whether it be 2 people or 200. This larger unit has characteristics that refer only to the group and not to any specific member: a particular size, rules of behavior, a division of labor, a way of dealing with conflict, and so forth. These are the **social structures** that we examine throughout the course.

Social structure is the ordering of be-havior and social re-lationships in a rela-tively predictable way.

It is impossible to predict the significance of an event or behavior without knowing the meanings created within that collectivity. What, for example, makes a baked good a birthday cake? The candles themselves are meaningless; they stand for something only because we, members of a particular collectivity, have decided that a candle marks the passage of a year and that it can transform an ordinary cake into a special treat.

Yet at the same time that our behavior is influenced by existing structures of thought and action, we are continually changing and modifying those structures. It is, remember, precisely the flexibility of humankind that is our unique heritage.

HUMAN FLEXIBILITY

Relative to body size, the human brain is larger than that of other animals, with more pathways and specialized parts that permit more complex cognitive processes. Although other animals can be taught to control some of their reactions, humans rely entirely on *learned* responses.

In a model of instinctual behavior, the organism (body) experiences the arousal of some deep drive (impulse) that then leads to a specific tension-reducing act, all as one unbroken chain of behavior, as the figure below shows.

A moment's thought should lead you to the conclusion that this is *not* how humans behave; if they do, we remove them from the community, to prisons or asylums, precisely because they cannot control themselves. Human behavior, in contrast, is mediated by the reflexive mind, which allows us to interpret how we feel and then to select the appropriate actions to reduce the tension of drive arousal. (See figure below.)

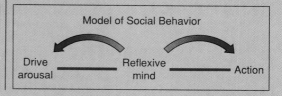

Model of Instinctual Behavior

Drive arousal → Action

Model of Social Behavior

Drive arousal — Reflexive mind — Action

Sociology and the Other Social Sciences

Human behavior and group life can be studied from a number of perspectives in the *social* sciences (as distinguished from the natural sciences, such as biology or physics). Sociology differs from history, economics, and political science in that it focuses less exclusively on only one aspect of social life or a limited set of events. We examine the *totality* of collective experience, including a historical dimension, economic and political structures, and such other products of human interaction as beliefs and values, rules regulating sexuality and family life, patterns of learning, health care practices, and music, art, and play.

The difference between sociology and psychology is the most difficult to explain to introductory students. Americans tend to believe that their actions flow directly from individual needs or motivations. This belief reflects a psychological perspective that views behavior as determined by a person's mental and emotional states.

In contrast, the sociologist begins with the *situation* in which the behavior takes place. In the sociological perspective, behavior is seen as being largely influenced by the context in which it occurs.

To illustrate the basic difference between these approaches, let us take the example of the statistical link between mental depression and unemployment. A psychiatrist might call for a massive mental health effort to treat the depressive symptoms of the unemployed so that they could then seek out and maintain steady employment. A sociologist would argue that mental symptoms are more likely the result rather than the cause of being unemployed. The solution, therefore, is not more mental health clinics, but more jobs.

The Sociological Imagination

The concept of "the sociological imagination," or way of looking, is based on a distinction between "personal troubles" and "public issues." **Troubles** are private matters, limited to aspects of daily life of which a person is directly aware. By contrast, **issues** are factors outside one's personal control caused by crises in the larger system—such as business cycles, wars, or university policies—that ultimately affect daily life.

Sociologists study how private troubles are transformed into social issues. For example, to be out of work is to experience great personal troubles. But when large numbers of people are unemployed it becomes a public issue.

The sociological imagination also directs attention to three key questions: (1) How are activities patterned in a given society? (2) Where is that society located in human history? And (3) what kinds of men and women are produced in that society? The answers to these questions are not the same from one place or time to another.

The Sociological Perspective

As you begin the study of sociology, you will need to learn a number of important terms and to understand certain key concepts that are the tools used to assess and solve social problems. Thus far, we have identified several characteristics of the **sociological perspective:**

- A concern for the *totality* of social life.
- An emphasis on the *context,* or setting, of human actions.
- A recognition that *meaning* is a social product assigned arbitrarily by members of a collectivity.
- A focus on the *collectivity* rather than isolated individuals.
- A focus on the *interaction* among individuals or collectivities, which shapes social life.

The term **collectivity** refers to several types of social unit: (1) an *aggregate,* or a simple collection of individuals who are in the same place at the same time, as in the example of people waiting for a train; (2) a *category,* or people who share a distinctive characteristic, such as all children or all Asian-Americans, and (3) a *group,* or people linked by shared goals and a sense of unity, based on direct or indirect contact over an extended period. Such groups range from a dating couple to a family to all members of a given society.

A perspective is a way of looking; and a sociological perspective is based on the assumption that for a given collectivity there is a *collective reality* that can be studied in its own right.

Personal troubles are private matters, limited to aspects of daily life of which a person is directly aware.

Public issues are factors outside one's personal control and are caused by crises in the larger system.

The **sociological perspective** focuses on the totality of social life, the context of social interaction, the individual as part of a collectivity, and interaction among individuals as collectivities.

A **collectivity** is a set of people that can be as unconnected as an aggregate or as closely linked as a group.

Social Facts

As members of categories and groups make decisions, they produce **social facts,** patterned regularities that describe the collectivity rather than its separate parts. For example, although individual women bear children, the sum of these separate acts is a birthrate that is a property of the society as a whole.

Birthrates are important evidence that human behavior is not guided solely by biological drives or necessity. In the United States more children are born in late August and early September than at any other time of the year—in both the South and the North (so it is not a matter of climate). Given that the Christmas and New Year's holidays in our society are associated with reunions and reconciliations, is it any wonder that the birthrate peaks some nine months later?

Emile Durkheim on Social Facts.   The great French sociologist Emile Durkheim laid the groundwork for modern sociological theory when he held that *social facts must be explained by other social facts*—by reference to the social structure rather than to individuals or their bodies or minds. Durkheim (1897) demonstrated this principle in his study of European suicide rates, which varied consistently from one country to another and by subgroups within a given area—differences that could not be explained by climate, religious doctrine concerning suicide, or biological factors. How can we explain that suicide rates are lower in Catholic than in Protestant communities, among the married than the unmarried, and among parents compared to people without living children?

The common factor, according to Durkheim, was **social integration,** the degree to which a person is part of a larger group. Marriage, parenthood, and the communal emphasis of Catholicism (in contrast to Protestantism's focus on the individual) are ties that bind one person to others. Therefore, if we want to predict the likelihood of suicide, information on psychological states will be less useful than knowledge about people's enduring social ties.

The goal of sociologists is not to predict what any given individual might do, but the **probability,** or the statistical likelihood, of certain events. Sociological predictions best apply to aggregates, categories, and groups, and less to individuals.

Social Facts and Reification.   While recognizing social facts, we must be careful not to talk about "society" as if it were a person. All too often, even in professional articles, one reads that "society does this" or "says that"; this is the logical fallacy of **reification,** or treating an abstract concept as a concrete object. Because societies are composed of people engaged in patterned behaviors, we must always specify just who and what we are talking about when we speak of "society."

Social Facts and Subjective Reality.   Thus far, we have discussed social facts as collective characteristics resulting from many individual acts. Another type of social fact is the *meaning* that people give to their shared experiences. People make sense of their experiences through conversations with others.

Together we define what is real and not real, good or bad, true or false. Notice how often you look for information from other people about whether or not someone is "nice" or a rock group is "good." By reinforcing our own

Social facts are patterned regularities that describe the collectivity.

Social integration refers to the degree to which a person is part of a larger group.

Probability refers to the statistical likelihood of a given event.

Reification is the logical fallacy of treating an abstract concept as a concrete object.

Subjective reality is developed through social interaction and refers to the ideas and feelings we have about ourselves and the world.

impressions with the perceptions of others, we develop our ideas and feelings about ourselves and the world—our **subjective reality**—through social interaction.

EARLY SOCIOLOGICAL THEORY

The Importance of Theory

A **theory** is a set of logically related statements that explain an entire class of events.

The study of society begins with some general ideas of how social life is organized and how membership in various collectivities affects life choices and chances. A **theory** is a set of logically related statements that explain an entire class of events. Without a theory to guide us, pieces of information remain unconnected items that tell us little about larger patterns.

Sociologists have used a number of theoretical frameworks, or *models,* to explain the same sets of social facts. Each theory, by focusing on a limited segment of the larger social context, represents a special way of viewing the world and directs our attention to different aspects of society.

The Roots of Sociology

Sociology as the *systematic* study of people in social units has its roots in Europe in the late eighteenth century—the Age of Enlightenment. This period followed the collapse of the old medieval order based on unquestioned obedience to royalty or religious authorities.

For many Enlightenment thinkers, faith in the divine was to be replaced by reliance on human reason and scientific analysis. The discovery of the individual and of society were major breakthroughs in intellectual history; new ideas—democracy, self-consciousness, social system—were brought into the common language.

The **sociology of knowledge** is the study of the way in which the production of knowledge is shaped by the social context of thinkers.

Sociology emerged at a particular historical moment in response to a need for certain types of information. According to the **sociology of knowledge,** what we want to know and what we study are themselves social products, shaped by the historical context of thinkers.

Enter Sociology—Comte (1798–1857) and Martineau (1802–1876). Auguste Comte, often called the founder of sociology, coined the word *sociology* from the Latin *socius* (companion, with others) and the Greek *logos* (reason, study of). The field of sociology would be distinguished by (1) its subject matter—society as something other than the sum of individual actions; and (2) its methods—careful observation, objective measurement, and comparison (the scientific method).

Positivism sees science as value free and totally objective.

Comte believed in **positivism**—the idea that all science, including the scientific study of society, must be value free and objective. The ideal of objectivity, however, was often violated by Comte and others who assumed that their own values—those of white, Western, educated men—represented a timeless standard of truth.

At the same time that Comte was laying the foundations for sociology, an Englishwoman, Harriet Martineau, was making systematic observations of social patterns in England and the United States for her book *Society in America.* However, Martineau is best known not for her original work but as the English translator of Comte.

The liberalizing trends of the Enlightenment, with their emphasis on individual freedom and economic justice, were soon challenged by the counter-Enlightenment and the restoration of antidemocratic ruling groups ("elites"). The three giants of classical sociology—Marx, Durkheim, and Weber—attempted to resist these forces of traditionalism.

Karl Marx (1818–1883).   Observing the first fruits of the Industrial Revolution in Europe in the mid-nineteenth century, Marx was appalled by the miserable conditions of ordinary workers and by the vast inequality between the few who controlled the land, factories, educational institutions, and political offices, and the many who had only their labor to sell in a market crowded with other unorganized workers. For Marx, social order was always open to question because it is based on exploitation and conflict.

Marx developed a complex theory of history and society that has greatly influenced modern sociology. The theory is based on several concepts: (1) *Organic Totality*—the concept of society as an organism similar to the human body, with each part performing a distinct function; (2) *Importance of the Economic Sector*—the concept that the basic division in society is that between owners and nonowners of the **means of production** (tools, land, factories, information, wealth), and that this ownership extends to the realm of **ideas;** and (3) *Historical Change Through Conflict*—the concept of a process of continual struggle between the owners and the nonowners, set in motion by built-in strains within the economic system. This conflict can end only when members of the society as a whole own the means of production.

> The **means of production** refers to the tools, land, factories, information, and wealth that form the basis of a society.
>
> Ownership of means of production by the ruling class extends to **ideas** as well as things.

Emile Durkheim (1855–1917).   Durkheim, like Comte, viewed society as a reality in its own right. Individual members of society are born, live, and die, but a certain pattern to their experiences exists independently. Individual lives are played out in a society with a pre-existing set of rules governing, for example, family life or economic activity.

Durkheim was very concerned with establishing sociology as a separate academic discipline, hence his emphasis on the uniqueness of society and the impossibility of reducing it to the study of individuals. As a consequence, Durkheim was also a pioneer in the use of **social statistics**—official records and systematic observations—to deduce social facts. As for beliefs and ideas, Durkheim saw these, too, as reflections of society, of a social reality shared by members of the group.

> **Social statistics** refer to official records and systematic observations from which social facts can be deduced.

Max Weber (1864–1920).   Although his life span overlaps that of Durkheim, the concerns of Max Weber (pronounced "Veybear") were closer in many ways to those of Marx. Weber's optimism about the liberating potential of human reason was balanced by a pessimistic realization of its limits: As science uncovers the laws of nature, some of the wonder and mystery of existence is destroyed. Weber saw that technology and modern organizations could become a new type of prison (an "iron cage") replacing the faith and fantasies that helped people to survive in the past.

American sociologists have been influenced by Weber's discussion of the place of one's own value judgments in sociological analysis. Weber could see the necessity for value-free research as well as the danger of being without any concern for the uses to which one's knowledge is put. Weber also insisted on the importance of *Verstehen* (German for "insight")—the ability to imagine the world as other people might see it.

> *Verstehen* is the ability to see the world as it might be experienced by others.

Social Policy and Sociology

How valuable to government policymakers is the work of sociologists? The answer to this question depends on what kinds of information politicians want. The policy objectives of Republican leaders are very different from those of Democrats, and each can pick and choose the research that supports their philosophical goals. For example, political conservatives have no difficulty finding scholars who claim that welfare programs create poverty, whereas political liberals can muster ample evidence to the contrary.

Not only do political considerations determine how and to what extent sociologists influence government (public) policy, but through their control of research money the policymakers themselves can influence what gets studied and who does the studying. In general, the level of funding for sociological research is high during Democratic administrations and low during Republican ones. This is so because sociology tends to focus on social problems and processes of change, a liberal rather than a conservative agenda. Nonetheless, there is also great diversity within the ranks of practicing sociologists.

Sociologists have contributed to debates on various issues of social policy, whether on one side or the other, or on both. Throughout this book we will highlight many such issues, which you as an informed citizen will be asked to vote on and which will help form your personal value system. ■

MODERN SOCIAL THEORY

The following section explains the three dominant contemporary theoretical perspectives: (1) functional analysis, (2) the conflict model, and (3) interpretive sociologies, which include symbolic interaction, dramaturgy, and ethnomethodology. We will also look at two more recent theoretical perspectives: humanist social theory and feminist sociology.

The Functional Perspective

Functional analysis examines the relationship between the parts and the whole of a social system.

The central focus of **functional analysis** is the relationship between two levels of social reality: the whole (the society, any group) and its parts (area of activity, members of the group). What do the parts contribute to the maintenance of the whole? How does the structure of the whole affect the parts? How do the various parts mesh?

Institutional spheres are major areas of social activity.

Society as a whole is composed of parts that we call **institutional spheres,** or areas of social activity: the economy, political system, marriage and family life, educational processes, and beliefs and rituals that unify its members. The specific content of these spheres varies from one society to another and will change over time in any one society; but each essential task—each function—must be performed if the whole group is to survive from one generation to another.

Talcott Parsons (1902–1979).   The American sociologist Talcott Parsons is the best-known theorist of functional analysis. He began with the concept of a **social system** composed of interdependent parts, each of which must perform an essential function for the maintenance of the totality. The parts are linked by "exchanges" that facilitate task performance. For example, Par-

A **social system** is a totality composed of interdependent parts.

WOMEN IN THE DEVELOPMENT OF AMERICAN SOCIOLOGY

The founders of American sociology were also products of their time. Many came from a strongly religious Protestant background, with its emphasis on individual responsibility and the obligation to do good in this world. And many were women associated with the University of Chicago in the early part of this century: Jane Addams, Charlotte Perkins Gilman, Marion Talbot, Florence Kelley, Edith Abbott, Alice Paul, Elsie Clews Parsons, Leta Hollingworth, Jessie Taft, Alice Hamilton, Emily Greene Balch, and Sophonisba Breckinridge. These women called themselves "sociologists," and most were members of the American Sociological Society (later, Association). Many were doing high-level quantitative research (urban mapping, consumer surveys, time budgets) at a time when the fashion among their male colleagues at Chicago was for anthropological-type studies of criminals and other unusual people. But as sociology became a recognized discipline and various universities sought to "upgrade" their prestige, women were discouraged from entering the field. Of the 82 presidents of the American Sociological Association, only four have been women, beginning with Dorothy Swaine Thomas in 1952.

sons's (1955) functional analysis of the American family in the 1950s emphasizes the division of labor between husband and wife, which he saw as necessary for family stability and social order. This model portrays the husband as the family's representative to the world of work, whereas the wife provides emotional support to the family unit. The children's education is highly supportive of the parents and of the existing social order. Thus, each part maintains the others and all combine to preserve the system over time.

Robert K. Merton (b. 1910) and the Refinement of Functional Theory.
Merton's work focuses on "theories of the middle range," which are applications of functional analysis to a limited set of social patterns. Merton examines the *predictable impact* of social structure on human action. For example, if immigrants need help in dealing with government agencies where no one speaks their language or appears to care much about them, the situation is ripe for politicians to help the powerless in return for their votes. This is a social system explanation for the rise of political machines in American cities between 1880 and 1920.

Merton made the distinction between **manifest** and **latent functions.** Manifest refers to "open, stated, or intended goals"; latent refers to "unexpected and unintended consequences." Recognition of multiple consequences leads also to the realization that not all behavioral patterns or aspects of social systems are functional; that is, they do not contribute to the maintenance of a society or group. Some patterns may actually reduce the capacity of a system to adapt and survive; these are therefore considered **dysfunctional.**

Criticism of Functional Analysis.   Critics claim that attempts to explain everything with a single model usually tell us little about anything in particular

Manifest functions are open, stated, and intended goals.

Latent functions are unexpected and unintended consequences.

Dysfunctional patterns reduce the capacity of a system to adapt and survive.

The functional perspective focuses on how components of a society function for social cohesion. For example, this totem, being carved by Tsimishian Indians of British Columbia, Canada, symbolizes the group's identity and helps unify the tribe.

because the theory is too abstract, too removed from the level of individual experience.

The second target of criticism of functional theory is the conservative bias of its focus on harmony, stability, and social order. Disharmony and conflict, critics say, can be seen as temporary problems in an otherwise healthy system, and not necessarily as signals that the system itself is flawed.

Third, as Parsons's analysis of the American family suggests, what seemed clear in the 1950s is less so today. In his eagerness to find functionality, Parsons overlooked sources of strain within the family, both between parents and children and husbands and wives.

From the perspective of a sociology of knowledge, it is not difficult to see why American sociologists working between 1945 and 1960 would have taken such an optimistic view. These were years of great economic growth, social stability, and what appeared to be widespread value consensus. For many sociologists, however, the conflicts of the 1960s exposed the limitations of the functional model. Nonetheless, functional analysis remains an important theoretical tool.

The Conflict Perspective

Conflict theory examines disagreement, hostility, and struggles over power and resources in a group.

As its name indicates, **conflict theory** focuses on disorder, disagreement, and open hostility among individuals and groups and on lack of harmony among system parts. From this point of view, struggle over power and resources is

The conflict perspective focuses on the sources of disagreement and hostility between groups with different amounts of power. Labor strikes, such as this one between the Communication Workers of America (CWA) and the NYNEX telephone company, pit workers against management.

normal, and harmonious relationships require explanation. Conflict can be minimized in periods of economic prosperity, as in the 1950s, but will be intensified during economic downturns, as in the 1930s.

From this perspective, sociologists examine (1) sources of tension among people and groups with different amounts of power, (2) techniques of conflict control, and (3) ways in which the powerful maintain and enlarge their influence. For example, a conflict perspective on the American family would focus on power inequality between parents and children and between husbands and wives.

The conflict question is: Who benefits from any given social arrangement? For example, where a functionalist would explain police violence as necessary to restore order, a conflict theorist would note that such violence is most often directed against the least powerful members of the society.

Both the functional and conflict models, however, share a tendency to examine social structure at an abstract level and to seek general rules about the nature of social systems. This emphasis on society as a whole is referred to as **macrosociology** (*macro* = large). In contrast to macrosociological perspectives, many sociologists have examined human interaction at the personal, face-to-face level to see how people actually interpret their life and create meaning. This emphasis on smaller, less abstract units of analysis is called **microsociology** (*micro* = small).

Macrosociology focuses on society as a whole or on social systems at a high level of abstraction.

Microsociology focuses on smaller units of social systems, such as face-to-face interactions.

The Interpretive Perspective

Microsociology is characterized by a diversity of approaches that share a focus on human interaction as the starting point of sociological understanding. These are often called **interpretive** models because they focus on the processes whereby people make sense of and give meaning to the events of daily life. Included under this heading are symbolic interaction, dramaturgy, and ethnomethodology.

Interpretive sociology focuses on processes by which people make sense of daily life.

Symbolic interaction views social systems as products of interaction and the meanings that people give to their situations.

The Symbolic Interaction Perspective.   The **symbolic interaction** model incorporates two essential features of social life: (1) the reflexivity of the human mind, which allows us to think and communicate in *symbols,* and (2) the fact that we become fully human only in association with others.

The symbolic interaction model asks: How do people make sense of their world, influence one another, and define themselves? We interpret our experiences through our daily interactions with other humans. The world "out there" must be filtered through individual minds and reaffirmed through individual choice (volition). For example, the patterns that we call "the American family" exist only because individual men and women decide to get married, have children, and conduct themselves according to the expectations of others. Yet our idea of "family" has changed dramatically over the past 200 years.

The social patterns that we think of as outside ourselves and that limit (constrain) behavior are themselves a product of microlevel chains of behavior. Thus the rules of social order are always subject to change and modification; there is an element of uncertainty and flux to social life.

Humans are not simply reactors to structural demands; they are active creators of meaning. Meanings are constructed in collaboration with others and may, over time, take on a reality of their own (to form what we call social structure); nonetheless, that reality depends ultimately on microlevel interactions. It is the *interplay* of individual consciousness and existing structures that has fascinated contemporary interpretive sociologists.

Locating sociology in the details of everyday life, in ongoing interactions and encounters, is also the goal of the *dramaturgical analysis* of Erving Goffman (1959, 1983) and the *ethnomethodology* of Harold Garfinkel (1967).

The **dramaturgical approach** sees social interaction as a series of minidramas.

Goffman's work is called **dramaturgical** because social interaction is viewed as a series of minidramas in which actors present images of themselves, attempt to manipulate the reactions of other people (the audience), protect

The symbolic interaction perspective focuses on how people interact with one another. Here employees of a department store in Tokyo, Japan, greet customers. Would you expect to see this much deference displayed in your favorite American store?

their identity, and develop rules that guide behavior in daily encounters. We play many different parts, depending on the context, and at each performance some aspect of our identity is at risk.

Uncertainty and risk also characterize Garfinkel's **ethnomethodology,** a concept that refers both to the subject matter and the means for gaining information about it. Because so much of what we do takes place without conscious awareness, the researcher must dig below the level of "taken-for-granted" reality to discover the basic meaning of social action.

Ethnomethodology involves probing beneath the "taken-for-granted" reality.

For example, why do men hold doors open for women? Considering that the other types of people for whom doors are held open are children, the elderly, or the disabled, might not the deeper meaning of the custom be a reinforcement of women's powerlessness? An ethnomethodologist would test this possibility by asking probing questions designed to uncover unspoken assumptions.

NEWER DIRECTIONS IN SOCIOLOGICAL THEORY

The three major sociological perspectives try to answer the basic question: How is society possible? If we return to the example of unemployment, a functionalist would link changes in the skills needed in the economic system to different rates of unemployment among workers. A conflict analyst would note that it is not so much lack of skill as lack of social power that determines unemployment rates. In contrast, interpretive studies would explore the meaning of unemployment to the individual and how one's relationships are affected. As different as these perspectives are, they are all sociological, because they all focus on interaction—among individuals, between collectivities, or across major areas of activity.

Humanist Sociology

Rejecting the positivist position that social science can—or should —be value free, humanist sociologists believe that one should become actively engaged in social change. Their concern for social justice rather than social order has led most humanist sociologists to the interpretive perspective, with its emphasis on the human capacity to resist and change social structures. But because various collectivities control different resources, the most powerful of them will be able to impose their meaning, creating oppressive structures that must be actively resisted.

Feminist Sociology

Concerns similar to those of the humanists have motivated feminist scholars, who claim that positivism has produced a world view that separates the researcher from the objects of study and imposes an interpretation of reality that is basically Western, white, male, and middle-class onto the lives of others. Until recently, most research either left women out or assumed they shared the same perceptions as men, or, if they held different views, were somehow morally or mentally deficient. Over the past two decades, feminist sociologists

TABLE 1-1   Models of Social Theory

	Functional Model	Conflict Model	Interpretive Model
Nature of Society	Integrated, interrelated social structures that together form a system	Competing groups and collectivities seeking to secure own ends	Interacting individuals, groups, and social networks
Basis of Interaction	Consensus on values; shared goals	Power, conflict, constraint	Shared meanings via shared symbols
Focus of Study	Social order and how society is maintained	Social change and conflict	Development of adaptation to group
Level	Social structure	Social structure	Interpersonal
Social Change	Orderly, moderate change	Change in power relationships and social structures	Changed meanings and symbols

(both male and female) have filled the knowledge gap and confronted the biases in research and theory.

Today women hold many of the highest offices in American sociological organizations; feminist scholars have formed a professional society, Sociologists for Women in Society, and in 1987 launched a scholarly journal, *Gender & Society.* Many feminist sociologists rely on interpretive techniques whereas others prefer macrosociological models; both groups agree on the importance of gender as an element of social structure.

Reductionist Challenges to the Sociological Perspective

Reductionism involves reducing social life to individual behavior or biology.

Biological determinism is based on the belief that genetic factors explain differences in human behavior.

Sociobiology is the study of the inheritance of genetically determined behaviors.

The sociological emphasis on the structural level of reality has periodically been challenged by theorists of **reductionism,** who attempt to explain social facts by reference to biology or individual behavior.

Biological determinism is a common form of reductionism espoused by students of animal behavior, who claim that humans are simply apes with more brains and less hair. These scholars believe that basic genetic and physiological elements account for behavioral differences between the sexes or among various ethnic and racial categories.

Sociobiology is the most technical theory to date of the inheritance of genetically determined behavior. Just as Darwin traced the evolution of physical characteristics, sociobiologists claim that certain kinds of behaviors—for example, aggression, male sexual dominance, female nurturance—have maximized the survival of the animals or human beings that display them. Therefore, through reproduction over hundreds of thousands of years, these behaviors actually become encoded in the genetic material of the species.

All the supporting evidence for this theory has come from animal studies; its applicability to human behavior is thus far unproven. Even if the biological roots of human behavior could be accurately identified, this would only explain very general patterns and not variations from one society or from one time period to another.

From a sociology-of-knowledge perspective, this type of belief fits the general climate of political and social conservatism of the past two decades and its emphasis on the self. Sociobiology can be used to justify inequality by suggesting that sex and racial differences in achievement reflect genetic and not social factors.

Other examples of individualistic reductionism are the **exchange** and **rational-choice** theories, which adopt an essentially economic model of behavior: People tend to do that which brings the most benefits at the least cost.

Critics of this model point out that people do not always act out of their own self-interest, nor do they always have the same resources at their disposal or similar levels of knowledge about costs and benefits. *Any* action can be explained by saying that it must have had some value to that person.

At the microsocial level, however, an exchange perspective can be very illuminating: Ask yourself what a given individual expects to gain from a particular course of action and what the behavior costs in time and energy, in self-respect, and in other goals not pursued.

Whatever the direct effects on behavior of biology, rational calculations, or even body chemistry, each person lives in a web of social relationships and in a historical context that can modify the expression of any impulse. This is the essence of the sociological imagination.

Exchange and **rational-choice** models adopt an essentially economic model of cost and benefit to explain people's behaviors.

DOING SOCIOLOGY

- In the late 1970s American women were urged to undergo "natural childbirth" in order to enjoy the advantages of an immediate bonding with their infants. By the mid-1980s, the original researchers admitted that no studies could confirm the existence of a crucial bonding period immediately following birth.
- Although most Americans believe that high-level executives are under extraordinary occupational stress, recent statistics clearly indicate that job-related stress and the symptoms of heart disease are most common among people who do physically demanding, heavily supervised work.
- In 1986 interesting data on the probability of marriage among well-educated women contained in an unpublished paper by researchers at Yale and Harvard Universities was presented to the press. Magazines were quick to feature cover stories claiming that an unmarried, 40-year-old, college-educated woman had a better chance of being killed by a terrorist than of finding a mate.

These are only three examples of how "commonsense" explanations are influenced by what Americans want to believe. Most Americans will probably continue to hold these beliefs even though scientific proof is either lacking altogether or actually points to an opposite conclusion. The mother–infant bonding study, for example, was rushed into print before the authors could see if the effects lasted beyond infancy. The early studies of job-related stress depended on information from heart disease specialists, who rarely receive visits from low-income workers.

The case of the marriage data illustrates several points: (1) the difficulty of accurately translating complex statistics into understandable material for

SOCIOLOGY, SOCIAL CHANGE, AND YOU

Kathryn (Grzelkowski) Gaianguest

Kathryn Gaianguest (Ph.D., Indiana University) has returned to academia to teach, to write, and to develop training programs in sociological practice for students who want to work in non-academic settings. She is now an associate professor of sociology at the University of Maine, where she maintains her focus on sociological practice as a member of the American Sociological Association's Committee on Sociological Practice, the Society for Applied Sociology, and the Association for Humanist Sociology. In addition, she has been involved in presenting policy-setting proposals to the Commission on Maine's Future and in research on new policies for services for homeless adolescents.

Many of you have come to this class in introductory sociology because it is required for your major. Some of you signed up because you're curious about sociology and others because it filled a slot in your schedule. You, as a class and as individuals, are therefore very diversified in your interest in, commitment to, and involvement with sociology. We can apply a sociological perspective to help us understand the effects of your diversity. For example, we can predict that this course will have different meanings for each of you—that some topics will be more relevant than others, that some ideas will illuminate a personal relationship or help you understand why you and others feel dependent and depersonalized in certain environments (e.g., in school, or through discrimination), or will give you a way to interpret issues that you have found puzzling in the past. Whatever meanings sociology will carry for you, I have a challenge for you as you begin your personal journey through this semester. At the end of each chapter and each exam will you exhale a sigh of relief, say "Now that's behind me" and forget about this investment in your educational career? Or will you take something of sociology away with you to draw from and apply to your own life situations?

Throughout my career I have tried to combine sociological knowledge with active efforts for change in everyday life. After a few years of teaching, I moved into the public and private nonprofit sectors where I practiced sociology for ten years as (1) a director of an agency advocating services for children with special needs; (2) a chief planner in a state department of mental health, mental retardation, and corrections; (3) academic director of a private nonprofit, off-campus learning program for college students; and (4) consultant to a public defender's office. During this time I consciously chose to "put sociology to work" and to build humanistically oriented relationships within institutions and communities.

The premise of a humanistic approach is that people can feel that they have control over their own lives. Therefore, the humanist approach has led me to develop specific sociologically grounded action proposals for social change such as (1) moving mental health patients from 20-bed wards in an institution to 5-person group homes in the community, that is, to "normal" family units that can provide personalized support; (2) using evidence in a murder trial from the defendant's family life and community experiences in challenging the application of the death penalty; (3) working with local grass-roots organizations to consolidate their marketing power against price-setting by local home heating oil distributors; (4) developing community self-help organizations to decrease dependency on large-scale, outside organizations; and (5) using a classroom format where students take as much control as possible over their own learning, including shared decision making in the requirements for the course and the method(s) of grading.

In all of these fairly diverse areas my sociological knowledge has also assisted me in implementing these approaches. For example, in the case of the price-setting problem mentioned previously, we could anticipate from our studies of power relationships that the oil distributors would tighten their efforts to maintain fixed prices at a high-profit level and that trying to use the courts would be simply beyond the financial means of this relatively poor community. But our analysis also told us that the community had two sources of power: (1) the numbers of people purchasing fuel (but feeling powerless as individuals) and (2) some independent oil companies within reasonable distance of the community. Once people in the community agreed to work cooperatively and to purchase fuel through a newly established Fuel Buying Collective, it was economically possible for an outlying oil company to bid on the contract at a lower price than

the coalition of local distributors. Furthermore, the success of cooperative action energized the community to search for new ways of empowering its members. So from this initial action, further social change emerged.

This semester you will read about some ways in which social organizations can strip people of their sense of control. You will also learn about social structures—community, schools, work environments, churches, and families, for example—that appear to meet our life-support needs yet which perpetuate inequality, conflict, and social injustices. Throughout this semester you will discover how sociologists address these issues in social policies and social change.

As someone who has combined sociology with many different aspects of work, I challenge you to ask the following questions as you read each chap-

ter this semester: "So what?" and "What now?" Ask yourselves: "Can sociology be useful to me in the future? How can I *use* what I have learned throughout this semester in my family, at work, in my community? How can I apply sociological perspectives to making informed decisions related to the environment, to government policies both at home and abroad, and to fulfilling interpersonal relationships?"

Just as each of you has a different attitude toward sociology coming into this course, so each of you can realize different applications of sociology to your lives and the world around you. From the examples I have given, you can see that sociology is not just scientific research, but a living discipline. Put it to work for you in your everyday life, and in those areas where you seek social change.

popular consumption; (2) the media's immediate and uncritical acceptance of research that carried the names of prestigious schools; and (3) the public's desire to believe that women who do not marry "on time" because they are pursuing a career will somehow be punished by remaining single forever.

We must, therefore, carefully examine what we take for granted, what kind of evidence is gathered to support a given conclusion, and the possibility that what is accepted as "science" is not always impartial.

WHY WE DO RESEARCH

Because much of sociology deals with everyday life, personal observation and experience might seem to be the most accurate sources of information. But our ideas about what is natural and obvious are precisely what must be examined.

People often assume a cause-and-effect relationship that is actually open to question and that requires careful study. They also continue to hold certain beliefs despite evidence to the contrary. Moreover, regardless of the accuracy of a given assumption, those who believe it will act as if it were true. This is the sociological concept of the **definition of the situation**: *What people believe to be real is real in its consequences*. If, for example, it is thought that most people who receive welfare are too lazy to work, there will be little

Definition of the situation is a concept indicating that what people believe to be real is real in its consequences.

support for increasing welfare benefits as the cost of living rises. In fact, children compose 40 percent of federal welfare recipients, their mothers another 20 percent, with the remainder elderly, blind, or disabled.

WAYS OF KNOWING: SUBJECTIVE AND OBJECTIVE

Subjective knowledge derives from an individual's own frame of reference.

Human beings arrive at knowledge in both *subjective* and *objective* ways. **Subjective knowledge** comes from the individual's own frame of reference. Some things may be a matter of *faith;* others appear to be based on personal *observation;* and still other pieces of knowledge are matters of *intuition,* a gut feeling. Although for researchers in the interpretive tradition these subjective modes of knowing are important data, they tell us little about the broader social systems affecting behavior.

Furthermore, people may not always apply common sense even when it is accurate. For example, how many people practice effective study or health habits, or always drive within speed limits? There have also been occasions when the prevailing sociological opinion has been wrong and when the commonsense perception has been more accurate. For example, some sociologists have announced the end of political extremism and the decline of religion in modern life. Recent evidence on these issues, however, indicates that ordinary people probably knew better than the "experts."

The dominant trend in contemporary American sociology is to reject commonsense explanations in favor of more *objective* modes of knowing and the analysis of social facts at the macrolevel. Much recent social research attempts to copy the techniques of such natural sciences as chemistry or physics, even though the scientific method itself has frequently been marred by conflicts, prejudice, and errors.

The Scientific Method

Scientists aim for objectivity by being aware of how their own attitudes, expectations, and values might affect their research. To minimize the influence of these factors, researchers use data-gathering techniques that provide safeguards against simply fulfilling their own expectations. But no method can totally eliminate researcher bias. For example, in one experiment, students were told that their lab animals were smarter than others; this group's rats ran the maze faster than did identical animals whose human managers expected them to be a bit slow.

How much more difficult is it, then, to measure human beings and their ever-changing thought processes? Just asking someone a question for the first time can subtly influence that person's answer to the same question at a later date. If a researcher asks your opinion of a breakfast food or a presidential candidate, you must stop and think, which will affect your opinion the next time you are questioned.

The **scientific method** consists of objective observations, precise measurement, and full disclosure of results.

Ideally, a scientist follows a set of procedures to ensure accuracy and honesty throughout the research process. The **scientific method,** in contrast to faith, common sense, and intuition, involves (1) objective observations,

The scientific method involves objective observations, precise measurements, and full disclosure of research results. What kinds of questions do you think this researcher in the People's Republic of China is asking?

(2) precise measurement, and (3) full disclosure of research techniques and results. These permit others to replicate, verify, or confirm studies and findings.

Precise measurement is used in an attempt to achieve objectivity. Research *instruments* such as questionnaires, checklists, and interview forms allow different observers to obtain similar information. One can thus compare or combine research results for more than one observation at a time.

Deciding what to measure is the researcher's first problem. Abstract concepts such as marital satisfaction, student activism, or religiosity cannot be measured directly. But **empirical referents,** observable acts used as evidence of the abstract concept, can be measured and counted. Researchers have used such empirical referents as attendance at services (an objective measure) or feelings about the importance of religion (a subjective referent) to study religiosity. (See Figure 1-1.)

Problems can arise in the use of empirical referents. One concerns **reliability**—the measuring instrument's ability to yield the same result on re-

Empirical referents are items that can be measured and counted.

Reliability refers to whether the measuring instrument yields the same results on repeated trials.

FIGURE 1-1   The relationship between abstractions and empirical referents.

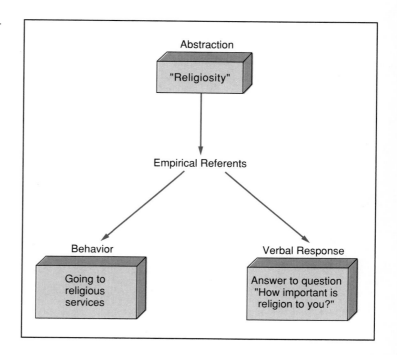

Validity refers to whether the measuring instrument is really measuring what it was designed to.

Replication involves repeating a specific study often with different types of respondents in various settings and at other times.

A **sample** is a selection from the entire population of interest.

peated trials. Reliability is tested by having different researchers use the same instrument in various settings and time periods. Another problem is **validity**—the instrument's ability to measure what is was designed to measure. Validity is tested by using another set of questions that show the same response pattern. The instrument's accuracy is tested by **replication**—repeating a specific study using the same research instruments to measure different types of respondents in various settings and at other times. Finally, for the greatest possible assurance of precise and objective results, the instrument must be used with the appropriate collectivity or **sample,** a manageable number of persons selected from the entire population of interest. When research is complete, researchers have a scientific duty to make full disclosure, meaning that research materials are fully available to colleagues.

THE SCIENCE IN SOCIAL SCIENCE

Researchers have had varying success in using the scientific method to explore social life. Every study is somewhat flawed due to the essential changeability of human beings, problems of reliability and validity, and the impossibility of total objectivity. These difficulties have led some sociologists to suggest that the use of the term *social scientist* implies an exactness that cannot be supported. But many sociologists still prefer to be thought of as social scientists because science is associated with numbers, and Americans tend to equate numbers with precision and accuracy.

Qualitative research relies primarily on interpretive description rather than statistics.

Quantitative research utilizes the features of scientific objectivity, including complex statistical techniques.

Furthermore, the use of statistics ("hard" data) is associated with intellectual toughness, in contrast to ideas or impressions ("soft" data). Numbers are seen as masculine, verbal descriptions as feminine, and in almost all societies masculinity is highly valued and associated with power. As a consequence, **qualitative research,** which depends on interpretive descriptions, is frequently ignored by the leading journals, which favor the complex statistical techniques of **quantitative research.** However, both qualitative and quantitative research share the goals of gathering data that test theoretical models, that can be repeated by other researchers, and that improve our ability to predict social behavior. Sociology benefits from both types of data, and neither can be fully understood without the other.

THE RESEARCH PROCESS

Five major steps make up the research process (see Figure 1-2).

1. Selecting and framing the research question.
2. Choosing the appropriate time frame and method.
3. Collecting the data.
4. Analyzing the data.
5. Drawing conclusions and reporting the findings.

Each step involves choices, sometimes dictated by the researchers' theoretical model, and sometimes by practical considerations such as the availability of subjects, funding, and the time needed to do the work.

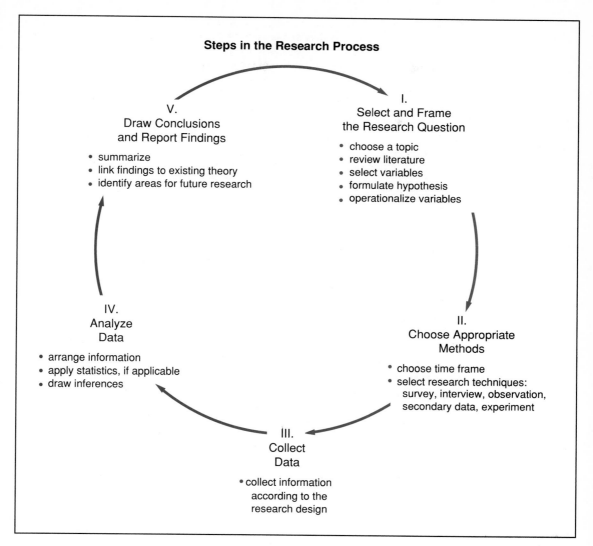

Steps in the Research Process

V.
Draw Conclusions
and Report Findings

• summarize
• link findings to existing theory
• identify areas for future research

I.
Select and Frame
the Research Question

• choose a topic
• review literature
• select variables
• formulate hypothesis
• operationalize variables

IV.
Analyze
Data

• arrange information
• apply statistics, if applicable
• draw inferences

II.
Choose Appropriate
Methods

• choose time frame
• select research techniques:
  survey, interview, observation,
  secondary data, experiment

III.
Collect
Data

• collect information
  according to the
  research design

FIGURE 1-2

What to Study

Deciding what to study may be the most nonscientific step of all, for two reasons: (1) the researcher's own bias or interests and (2) the research agenda of funding sources. The more complex the research design, the greater financial support necessary for data gathering and analysis. Researchers are, therefore, increasingly dependent on grants from foundations, private research firms, corporations, and government agencies. As a result, studies are targeted to what the funding organizations want to know more about. Even so, American scholars still enjoy relative freedom in selecting research topics.

Sociologists are interested in many aspects of social life—what people do for relaxation, how and why some people become street performers, how public spaces are used, how people respond to accidents. What questions interest you in this scene?

Variables are factors that differ from one person or collectivity to another or that change over time.

Constants are characteristics that do not change from one person or time to another.

Hypotheses are specific statements derived from a theory about relationships among variables.

In choosing an aspect of social life to study, most sociologists act on their interest in the link between one social fact and another: for example, between the nature of a job and work-related stress. These related social facts are **variables** (factors that differ from one person or collectivity to another or that change over time), in contrast to **constants** (characteristics that do not change from one person or time to another).

Research begins with a *theory*—a conceptual model of how social life is constructed: If the world works the way the researcher thinks it does, how would the variables of interest (nature of job and work-related stress) be linked? The untested answer to this question, an informed guess, is called a **hypothesis.** A hypothesis is a specific statement derived from a theory about relationships among variables: "If variable X (nature of the job) changes in a certain way, then Y (work-related stress) will also change in a predictable way." This statement is then tested with evidence gathered from systematic studies of job characteristics and workers' health.

Before undertaking a research project, it is important to conduct a *search of the literature* (using a computerized reference bank) to find out what is already known about the topic, and to clarify the research question. It is possible that a topic has been so thoroughly researched that further study is pointless. More likely, the literature will reveal inconsistencies that further research could reconcile. That research will attempt to find a correlation between or among variables. **Independent variables** have the greatest impact, come first in the chain of events, are relatively fixed, and are thought to affect other variables; **dependent variables** are assumed to be influenced by changes in the independent variables.

Designing the Study

In general, the research question dictates the appropriate method for gathering data to test hypotheses. Much depends on whether the information must come from a large number of people or from a particular subgroup; whether or not the topic is sensitive; and on whether follow-up studies will be needed to measure change.

Time Frames.   Cross-sectional studies take place at one time only. Like snapshots, they focus on how different kinds of people behaved or responded at a given moment. In contrast, several cross-sectional studies conducted at different times are like a moving picture, and provide information on process and changes.

Panel or **longitudinal studies** follow a group of respondents over time. The disadvantage of this approach is that it is not always easy to keep track of people for long periods; those who remain in the study could be quite different from those who drop out, thus reducing the accuracy of the findings.

Surveys.   Large-scale social **surveys** (or **polls**) are designed to yield information from a large number of respondents. Because it is usually impossible to question each member of the population of interest—all voters, for instance—a more manageable number, or *sample,* can be considered representative of the larger population when selected through random sampling. **Random sampling** gives all possible respondents an equal chance of being chosen. Common *random selection* techniques include pulling names from a rotating drum or using a computer to generate telephone numbers.

The survey researcher presents this sample with a pretested set of questions designed to tap the relevant variables. This can be done by mail, telephone, or personal visits, each of which has pros and cons in terms of cost, time, and response rate. In any survey, the amount and quality of information gathered depends on the respondents' willingness to answer. Regardless of this limitation, much information can be gathered from many people in a short time, and if the sample is randomly selected, the findings can be generalized to the larger population.

Loading the Questions.   To evaluate the findings of survey data, however, it is important to look closely at the way in which the questions are worded. Questionnaires prepared by organizations with a specific goal, such as political parties, labor unions, or business associations, often contain "loaded" questions designed to produce certain responses. For example, a labor-oriented group working against tax breaks for business circulated a questionnaire with the following question: "Do you agree or disagree that large corporations

Independent variables have the greatest impact, come first in the chain of events, are relatively fixed, and affect dependent variables.

Dependent variables are influenced by independent variables.

Longitudinal studies follow a group of respondents over time.

Surveys or **polls** yield information from a large number of respondents.

Random sampling occurs when all possible respondents have an equal chance of being chosen.

should start paying their fair share of taxes before there are any increases in any taxes that ordinary working and middle-income Americans pay?"

The wording of a loaded question is usually more subtle, acting as a "red flag" that brings particular feelings to the surface. For example, a random-sample survey by a government agency found that the phrase "public welfare" headed the list of services that respondents would cut most severely. But most people in the same survey would also place "aid to the needy" (another term for public welfare) ahead of support for colleges, parks, and highway repair.

Intensive Interviews.   Sometimes, a large representative sample is not necessary, especially if one is conducting exploratory, or pilot, research before designing a larger study, or if one is seeking intimate information. In these circumstances, a small and nonrepresentative sample is sufficient. Often, one or two carefully selected cases can provide information on processes that are not easily visible to an observer but are thought to have universal application.

Observation and Participant Observation.   Survey and interview data can tell us only what people say they do. How can we study what people actually do? Observation is time-consuming and limited in the number of people and occasions that can be studied. In addition, observers can disrupt the activity being examined.

In **participant observation**, the researcher becomes part of the interaction under study.

Participant observation, whereby the researcher can become part of the interaction under study, eliminates many of these barriers. However, it may take a long time before the participant observer is fully accepted. It is also impossible to measure the extent to which the participant observer has subtly changed the group and its interactions.

Secondary Analysis.   Surveys, interviews, and observations all generate original data—new information. Yet libraries are stocked with material that has already been gathered and can be reused. **Secondary analysis** refers to the use of information collected by others. Bear in mind that using available data, although often a great saver of time and money, has disadvantages. The data are sometimes incomplete or may have been biased by the original researcher.

Secondary analysis involves the use of data collected by others.

Official data are collected by government agencies.

Official data are available from the United States government, which produces many volumes of information every day. In fact, the United States Government Printing Office is the world's largest publisher. Of special value are the census data gathered from American households every ten years, as well as yearly or monthly random sample surveys on employment, income, family characteristics, housing, voting, and so forth. Although the U.S. Bureau of the Census and other government agencies have a tradition of being protected from political interference, various administrations can influence what topics are covered and how often certain kinds of data are published.

Historical records such as documents, papers, and letters identify relationships among variables over time and space.

Historical records such as letters, archives, and other papers can also be used as a basis for secondary analysis. These records are used mainly for comparing relationships among variables that are relatively constant and those that are modified as a society changes over time, such as family relationships and rules of inheritance.

Content analysis makes use of books, newspapers, magazines, and everyday items for a careful counting of how often particular images, words, or ideas appear. From the analysis, the researcher can test hypotheses about values or social change. For example, one recent analysis of ashtrays, cookie jars, greeting cards, and household items produced between 1890 and 1960 shows little change in negative stereotyping of African-Americans right up to the 1960s. (Note: In this text, the terms African-American, Latino, and Native American are used unless specific data using other terminology are cited.)

Comparative studies offer a powerful means for testing the universality of relationships among variables by comparing different societies. Data banks containing this information are available to researchers interested in **cross-cultural comparisons.** A favorite topic for comparative study is the generality of sex-linked behaviors. Some researchers, finding a fairly similar division of labor across many societies, have concluded that basic biological and personality differences between men and women account for the universality of male dominance. More recently, scholars have examined the comparative literature for information specifying the conditions under which the power differences between men and women are minimized or exaggerated.

Content analysis counts the number of references to a given item in a sample of publications.

Cross-cultural comparisons examine relationships among variables in different societies.

A natural disaster, such as the 1989 earthquake in the San Francisco–Oakland area of California, can provide unique opportunities for field research. What sort of information do you think sociologists would look for?

Experiments come closest to the scientific ideal of control over variables.

Experiments.   Of all the described research methods, experiments are the closest to the scientific ideal. However, the control over variables that is the essence of the experimental design makes this method least appropriate for sociologists. In everyday life such control over people or situations is impossible because behavior is typically influenced by the interpretations that people bring to the situation and then modify during the interaction. Yet experimental research, however artificial, can clarify relationships that are not easily identified in everyday observation. (See Figure 1-3 for a classic experimental design.)

The following steps outline the classical experiment:

1. Subjects are assigned to two groups that are as similar as possible in all factors likely to affect results.
2. Members of both groups are measured on the dependent variable—the attitude or behavior the researcher thinks will be influenced by introduction of the independent variable.
3. The independent variable, or *causal factor,* is introduced to *one sample only,* now the *experimental group* (E). The sample from which the factor is withheld becomes the *control group* (C).
4. At a later date, members of the experimental and control groups are again measured on the dependent variable and changes compared between Time 1 and Time 2. Group differences on the dependent variable can then be attributed to manipulation of the independent variable.

Laboratory experiments are carried out in such a way that the researcher can control all extraneous elements. This degree of control is, of course,

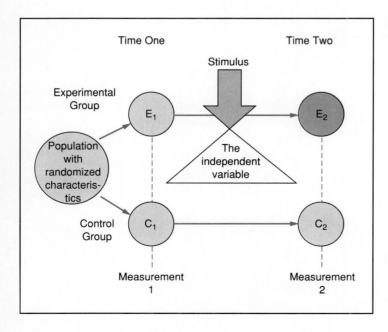

FIGURE 1-3   Classic experimental design.

impossible to maintain in the real world. Social psychologists have, however, developed the method of the **field experiment,** in which the researcher can manipulate some aspects of the real-world environment and then observe the reactions of unaware ("naive") subjects. The television program "Candid Camera" is composed of a series of such field experiments.

There are also **natural experiments,** in which the same population is measured before and after an event that is assumed to change the situation, such as a natural disaster or a new law. Studies of the effect of capital punishment often compare murder rates in a state before and after the passage of death penalty legislation.

> **Field experiments** are conducted in the real world.
>
> **Natural experiments** involve measuring the same population before and after a natural event that is assumed to change the situation.

ANALYZING THE DATA

Numbers alone rarely permit adequate testing of hypotheses. The many pieces of data must be arranged so that groups or variables may be compared. Sociologists today are trained in **statistics,** numerical techniques for the classification and analysis of data.

> **Statistics** are numerical techniques for the classification and analysis of data.

Percentages

The simplest and most important statistic is the **percentage,** or how many of a given item there are in every one hundred, often referred to as the *proportion.* Percentages allow researchers to compare groups of different sizes. How easily can you tell which is the larger proportion—25 out of 300 cases or 30 out of 400? The use of percentages simplifies such a comparison: 8.3 percent versus 7.5 percent—the larger number, 30, is actually a smaller part of its total.

> A **percentage** indicates how many of a given item there are in every one hundred.

Rates and Ratios

Rates.   Like percentages, **rates** are the number of times a given event occurs in a population on a base other than 100—birth- and death rates, for example. The birthrate can be computed on the basis of the whole population: In January 1989 the birthrate was 14.9 per 1,000 Americans. A more informative statistic would be based on the population of females between the ages of 15 and 44: In January 1989 the birthrate was 63 per 1,000 women of childbearing ages (down from a high of 118 in 1960).

> **Rates** are the number of times a given event occurs in a population, on a base other than 100.

Ratios.   A **ratio** compares one subpopulation to another, such as males to females or suicides to homicides. For example, the proportion of males to females, or the sex ratio, varies over time and with age. In the United States today, among people under 14, there are about 104 males for every 100 females, but because male death rates are consistently higher than those for females, at age 85+ there are only 40 men for every 100 women.

> A **ratio** compares one subpopulation to another.

Measures of Central Tendency

Three of the most common statistics are single numbers that summarize an entire set of data. These **measures of central tendency** are:

Measures of central tendency are single numbers that summarize an entire set of data.

The **mean** is an average.

The **median** is the midpoint of an entire set of cases.

The **mode** is the single most common category of cases.

- **Mean:** An arithmetical average—the total of all scores divided by the number of respondents.
- **Median:** The *midpoint* of an entire set of cases, with 50 percent of cases above and 50 percent below that number.
- **Mode:** The single most common category of cases—the answer given by the largest number of respondents.

When you evaluate statistics, remember that numbers become meaningful only when placed in an interpretive context. For example, the fact that 13.5 percent of all Americans in 1987 were officially designated as poor does not tell us very much unless we know how the poverty level is defined, and how it compares with other times and places.

SOCIAL POLICY ISSUE

To Tell or Not to Tell?

Suppose that you, the researcher, have data that you do not want to disclose because you think it may be used against people with whom you are in sympathy. Some researchers do not publish; others try to minimize negative outcomes by interpreting the findings as narrowly as possible.

There are a number of cases in which sociologists have published very controversial reports—for example, Daniel Patrick Moynihan (1965) on the African-American family, and James Coleman (1975) on school desegregation. The Moynihan study was widely interpreted as blaming the educational and economic failures of many urban African-American males on their being raised in female-headed families. Coleman's report claimed that court-enforced school desegregation, especially involving cross-town busing, was responsible for "white flight" to the suburbs. Both studies have been refuted by other sociologists, who have also raised what they consider the ethical issue of a more general responsibility of social scientists not to increase racism in our society.

The counterclaim that a researcher has an obligation, in the name of impartial science, to report findings even when they go against prevailing views, was forcefully made by Coleman, who also noted that younger researchers are often afraid to publish findings that might arouse hostility among colleagues.

As a researcher, how would you deal with data that could upset your colleagues and be used by politicians you dislike? ■

Presenting the Data

Sociologists communicate with one another by publishing in professional journals, by reading papers at professional meetings, and by circulating copies of research reports among friends and colleagues. Social scientists have tried to copy the natural sciences in creating a cumulative base of knowledge on which most researchers can agree, but with only limited success. Each new study appears to refute an earlier conclusion or to be open to a variety of theoretical interpretations.

When reporting their findings, social scientists may overemphasize small differences because these achieve a statistical significance. Such data also promote the **particularistic fallacy,** which assumes that a correlation that exists at the level of the collectivity also exists at the level of individuals.

In other cases, sociologists tend to underemphasize their findings because there are many exceptions to every statement. Thus, we often use such words as *many, most, typically, in general, perhaps, may, could,* and other terms that allow leeway in predictions to avoid giving the impression that the study of human behavior is more precise than it is.

> The **particularistic fallacy** occurs when a correlation at the collective level is applied to individuals.

Tables and Figures

Perhaps the most important part of a research report is the presentation of data in tables, charts, graphs, or diagrams.

Reading Tables.   A **table** consists of columns and rows of figures arranged to clarify relationships among variables. A table should, in most cases, convey information at a glance more readily than detailed descriptions. (See Table 1-2.)

> **Tables** consist of rows and columns of figures arranged to clarify relationships among variables.

To interpret a table, start by carefully reading the title, the headings, and the footnotes. Only then will you understand the numbers in each part of the body of the table (called *cells*). In Table 1-2, for example, the title tells you that the cell numbers are the percentages in 1988 of people in the United States age 65 and over who were either single, married, widowed, or divorced.

The cells show the extreme difference between older men and women in the likelihood of their being married rather than widowed. Over half of all elderly women are widowed, whereas over three-fourths of older men have a living wife. What explains these differences by sex? One clue is the higher death rate of males than of females of all ages. Another is that women typically marry men older than themselves.

TABLE 1-2   Marital Status of Persons 65 Years Old and over in the United States, 1988 (in percents)

	Male	Female
Single	4.6	5.3
Married	77.7	41.5
Widowed	13.9	48.7
Divorced	3.9	4.5

Source: U.S. Bureau of the Census, *Current Population Reports,* P-20, No. 437, 1989, p. 9.

Charts and Graphs.   Tables are only one way of presenting data. Graphics can be more powerful. For example, the data in Table 1-2 could be expressed either in *bar graphs* or in *pie-shaped diagrams,* as shown in Figure 1-4.

Deception

Each research method contains some elements of deception. This is most obvious in experimental and observational studies in which it is important that the people being observed are unaware of the goals of the research. But even the simplest survey questionnaire invades the respondents' privacy for a hidden purpose.

Ethics in Experiments.   All experiments involve the manipulation of human subjects, either by placing them in false situations or by exposing some but not others to a given stimulus. Suppose that you were testing a new program to curb drug abuse; how would you justify choosing some adolescents for the new program while leaving others untreated?

Another dilemma revolves around how much the researchers need to tell in order to secure "informed consent" from research subjects. Many laboratory-type experiments today are conducted with "captive audiences," such as inmates of institutions and college students, who may risk losing parole or getting a lower grade if they refuse to take part in a research project.

FIGURE 1-4   Marital status of people 65 years old and over in the United States: 1988. (Source: U.S. Bureau of the Census, *Current Population Reports*, P-20, No. 437, 1989, p. 9.)

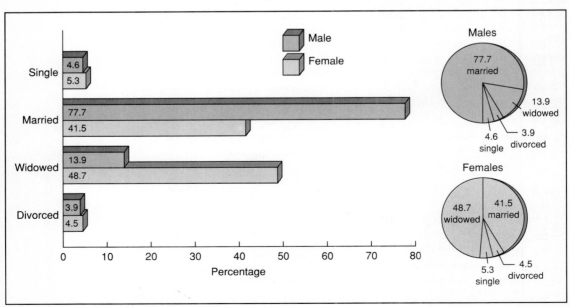

Other studies rely on volunteers who are paid for their time and who therefore might feel obligated to act in a certain way.

Correction of Research Abuses and Misuses.   In response to ethical questions, professional social science organizations have tightened their codes of ethics regarding research on human subjects. Most institutions of higher education now have review committees that oversee research on people conducted by faculty or students. These regulations are designed to ensure that no harm will result from subjects' participation.

Government funding is typically regulated by "peer-review" panels of scholars who judge the quality of research proposals. Because peer-review panels are typically drawn from leading figures in a field, there is a tendency to approve projects that support existing conceptual models, as well as a temptation to help friends and colleagues. In addition, heads of government agencies can "stack" the peer panels with people known to favor administration goals.

Respondent Bias.   Respondents as well as researchers can practice deception. Research subjects are not always aware of, or forthcoming about, what they really think or do. Researchers should recognize four potential problems: (1) misinformation—when respondents' idea of the "truth" is incorrect; (2) evasions—intentional withholding of information; (3) lies—designed to mislead the questioner; and (4) fronts, or shared lies about settings—establishments such as massage parlors claiming to be health spas or banks that exist to launder money.

Some kinds of respondent bias are unintentional, as in the general tendency of people to give socially acceptable answers, or to be yea-sayers or nay-sayers no matter what the issue. Within all these limits, however, the sociological enterprise continues to produce studies that enlarge our understanding of social structures and the people who compose them.

SUMMARY

1. This chapter defines the field of sociology: the study of human behavior as shaped by group life.

2. The concept of the sociological imagination is based on a distinction between personal troubles and public issues.

3. The sociological perspective focuses on the totality of social life, the context of human behavior, and the group level of reality.

4. Emile Durkheim identified social facts, which are patterned regularities of behavior that characterize the collectivity.

5. While Auguste Comte tried to uncover the basic laws of social life, Karl Marx understood history as the struggle to end the oppression of the powerless by the powerful.

6. For Max Weber, the modern age held both the liberating potential of human reason as well as the possibility that technology and modern organizations could lead to a new "iron cage."

7. The functional perspective focuses on the relationship between the parts and the whole of a social system.

8. The conflict perspective focuses on disagreements, hostility, and struggles over power and resources in a society.

9. The interpretive perspective, which includes symbolic interaction, dramaturgy, and ethnomethodology, focuses on how people interact with each other.

10. Included among new directions in social theory are humanist sociology and feminist sociology.

11. The structural emphasis of sociology has been challenged by biological determinism and individualistic reductionism.

12. Sociologists test their theories through research, using a variety of methods to collect many types of subjective and objective information.

13. The scientific method involves objective observation, precise measurement, and full disclosure of research methods and results.

14. Research methods that may be used include cross-sectional studies; large-scale social surveys; interviews; observations; secondary analysis of available data; and/or experimental design.

15. Groups of respondents and variables are compared by using statistics such as percentages, ratios, and measures of central tendency.

SUGGESTED READINGS

Alonso, William, and Paul Starr, eds. *The Politics of Numbers.* New York: Russel Sage Foundation, 1987. The generation of statistics in the arena of public policy.

American Sociological Association. *Careers in Sociology.* ASA, 1722 N. Street NW. Washington, DC: 1991. Send for your free copy.

Bart, Pauline, and Linda Frankel. *The Student Sociologist's Handbook.* 4th ed. New York: Random House, 1986. A useful guide for undergraduate and graduate students in sociology.

Bradburn, Norman, and Seymour Sudman. *Polls and Surveys: Understanding What They Tell Us.* San Francisco: Jossey-Bass, 1988. A comprehensive overview of public opinion research and its uses.

Collins, Randall, and Michael Makowsky. *The Discovery of Society.* 4th ed. New York: Random House, 1988. An articulate account of the historical and contemporary development of sociological theory.

Deegan, Mary Jo. *Jane Addams and the Men of the Chicago School, 1892–1918.* New Brunswick, NJ: Transaction Books, 1988. A study of the political relationship between University of Chicago male sociologists and their colleague Jane Addams.

Denzin, Norman K. *Interpretive Interactionism.* Newbury Park, CA: Sage, 1989. A detailed discussion of a developing sociological perspective.

Etzkowitz, Henry, and Ronald Glassman, eds. *The Renaissance of Sociological Theory: Classical and Modern.* Itasca, IL: Peacock, 1990. A comprehensive collection of the latest developments in sociological thought.

Fishman, Walda Katz, and C. George Benello, eds. *Readings in Humanist Sociology: Social Criticism and Social Change.* Bayside, NY; General Hall, 1986. A collection of the best articles from *Humanity and Society,* the Journal of the Association for Humanist Sociology.

Kennedy, Robert E. Jr. *Life Choices: Applying Sociology.* 2d ed. New York: Holt Rinehart & Winston, 1988. A very useful paperback that answers the question, "What can I get from studying sociology?"

Leiberson, Stanley. *Making It Count: The Improvement of Social Research and Theory.* Berkeley, CA: University of California Press, 1985. A critique of contemporary quantitative research in the social sciences.

Rossi, Peter, James Wright, and Andy Anderson, eds. *Handbook of Survey Research.* Orlando, FL: Academic Press, 1985. A state-of-the-art handbook on various aspects of survey research.

Smith, Dorothy E. *The Everyday World as Problematic: Feminist Sociology.* Boston: Northeastern University Press, 1987. Smith argues that sociology's standards of objectivity and rationality reflect the subjectivity of men.

Whyte, William Foote, with Kathleen King Whyte. *Learning from the Field; A Guide from Experience.* Beverly Hills, CA: Sage, 1984. Prominent sociologists draw on their participant observation.

SELF IN SOCIETY

The four chapters of Part I cover the processes whereby members of human groups create worlds of meaning and patterns of behavior that meet their personal needs and permit the collectivity to survive over time. We begin, in Chapter 2, with the study of *culture,* an enveloping context of thinking, feeling, and acting that is created, maintained, and changed through human interaction. Chapter 3 introduces the concept of *social structure,* the patterned relationships through which culture is expressed.

Socialization, the subject of Chapter 4, refers to the process through which rules of behavior—culture and social structure—are learned. Socialization also involves the emergence of self-concept, ideas about who and what kind of person we are. Although the goal of socialization is conformity to expectations, none of us is so thoroughly socialized that variations in thought and behavior do not occur.

Nonconformity, or *deviance,* and one particular form of deviance, *crime*, are the subjects of Chapter 5, with special attention to the functions, dysfunctions, and social control of behaviors that violate the rules.

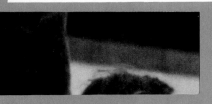

2

Culture

Imagine that during a nuclear attack your classroom has been miraculously transported to a deserted island and that you and your classmates have forgotten all that you knew before the explosion. How do you communicate with one another? Find food? Divide tasks and keep order? Pair off to reproduce new members of the group in a way that minimizes jealousy and conflict? How do you teach the newborn what you have learned and instill a sense of shared responsibility for one another?

These are the essential problems of survival for any collectivity and its individual members. Because human beings are not biologically or psychologically preprogrammed for any one set of responses, each group must work out its own solutions, depending on the resources at hand and the results of trial-and-error attempts to control themselves and their environment. This is the process whereby humans create *culture* and *social structure*. Culture consists of those ways of thinking, believing, and behaving that order our lives. Only collectivities that can create and maintain a viable culture will survive over time. No human group is without culture, and no two cultures are exactly the same.

THE EVOLUTIONARY BASIS OF CULTURE

The need for culture is an outcome of the 2 to 3 million years of human evolution during which a number of important changes in the body took place, beginning with the shift to an upright posture. Standing on two feet allowed the front paws to develop into hands that could ultimately make tools. A shift to a more varied diet led to changes in the structure of the jaw, leaving more room for brain growth. The placement of the human head at the top of the spinal cord freed space for the development of a voice box in the throat. Major changes in the female reproductive system transformed human sexuality into a predominantly social relationship. Throughout this entire chain of bodily changes, the brain itself became increasingly complex in order to process new types of information and to guide responses.

At the same time, because of the narrowing of the birth canal, the human infant had to be born when its head and shoulders could fit through it, thus before the nervous system matured—which means long before any fixed responses could be coded into the human brain. The helplessness of the human infant also makes its survival dependent on the ability of other humans to care for it over a period of many years.

Human behavior, as noted in Chapter 1, is characterized by *flexibility* and *adaptability;* it is not determined by instinct. Born without any preprogrammed behaviors, human beings must *learn* how to interpret and respond to the world around them. The same evolutionary process that made learning necessary also provided the necessary equipment for the task: a uniquely complex brain coupled with the ability to utter a large number of very different sounds. The result is the human capacity to create languages of great variety and sophistication through which members of a given group share knowledge, communicate feelings, and build on the accumulated wisdom of the collectivity—its culture.

The Emergence of Culture

Culture began to replace physical evolution as the means of adapting to the environment more than 2 million years ago, when the first prehumans stood upright. It appears that the basic group of *prehumans* consisted of a female and her children, who survived by **foraging**—picking readily available foods, such as fruits, nuts, and berries, and eating them on the spot (Calvin, 1985). At various times the mother-child unit would be joined by one or more of the adult males who followed them around and who were selected as mates on the basis of their willingness to share food and help with the young (Strum, 1988; de Waal, 1989).

> **Foraging** involves picking readily available foods for immediate consumption.

By 400,000 years ago, populations that could be labeled "human" appeared and spread rapidly from Africa to southern Europe and across Asia. Called *Homo sapiens*—the thinking people—they were characterized by relatively complex brains, skeletons very similar to ours, and a set of simple stone tools. In most bands of *Homo sapiens,* containing two or three dozen members linked by relatively stable bonds of kinship and affection, foraging was replaced by **gathering,** whereby foods were stored and preserved for later use. Because fire had by now been discovered, it is also likely that both women and men trapped small animals and birds. Between 100,000 and 75,000 years ago, a more "modern"-looking *Homo sapiens* appeared, and by 40,000 years ago, this new population, *Homo sapiens sapiens*, was the dominant species, from which *all* living humans are descended.

> **Gathering** involves transporting, storing, and preserving readily available foods.

DESCRIBING CULTURE

Culture is often called the blueprint for living of those who share a given territory and language, feel responsible for one another, and recognize their shared identity. The culture of such a group (or society) consists of: (1) solutions to the problems of survival, (2) the ideals and values that shape rules of conduct, and (3) tools and other human-made objects (**artifacts,** or material culture). People become functioning members of their society as they learn and participate in the culture.

> **Culture** is the map for living of those who share a territory and language, feel responsible for each other, and recognize their shared identity.
>
> **Artifacts**, or material culture, consist of tools and other human-made objects.

Another way of looking at culture is to examine the way in which it shapes how people experience the world and express meaning (Swidler, 1986). (See also the box, "The Cultural Construction of Pain.") Because the human central nervous system develops within a social setting, there can be no human nature independent of culture, and there will be as many "human natures" as there are cultures (Geertz, 1973).

Symbols and Language

The key to culture and cooperation is the evolution of the human capacity for using symbols. A **symbol** is a sound, object, or event that signifies nothing in and of itself, but only the purely arbitrary meaning that members of a group attach to it. For example, a straight line—|—stands for the number "one" only for people using the Arabic numeral system. When joined at right angles by an intersecting line, it will be recognized by Christians as the sign of the cross, with all the emotional attachments that this symbol evokes.

> A **symbol** is a sound, object, or event that is given meaning by members of a group.

THE CULTURAL CONSTRUCTION OF PAIN

A classic study of responses to pain among American hospital patients found that people suffering from the same physical condition showed very different reactions, depending on their religious and ethnic background. Both Jewish and Italian patients tended to be much more emotional than the "old Yankees" who usually kept a "stiff upper lip" and cried only when they were alone. Yet, although the Jewish and Italian patients were similarly open and vocal about their pain, they were motivated by different concerns: the Italians by the immediate experience of discomfort, the Jews by worry over the long-term effects of their illness. Thus, though all patients were exposed to similar levels of pain, their cultural backgrounds had shaped different ways of recognizing and reacting to signals from their bodies.

Source: Zborowski, 1952.

The most important symbol system is language itself—a set of sounds and gestures whose significance depends on the common understanding of those who use them. *All human communication is symbolic,* through words and actions whose meaning is socially defined. Although the languages spoken by members of other cultures may seem strange to our ears, just as ours does to them, all human languages are of equivalent value and truthfulness and represent the crowning achievement of evolution: the capacity for reflexive thought.

Animals can be taught the meaning of certain gestures (such as the raised hand for "stay") and to answer to the sound that stands for their name. A few chimpanzees, after many years of training, have mastered some elements of Standard American Sign Language, and one or two have even produced new (untaught) gestures. But such abilities are extremely limited when compared to an average two-year-old human's seemingly endless flow of words, phrases, and untaught concepts. Furthermore, whereas apes (and other animals) may communicate effectively among themselves, they have not created cultures

Body movements, gestures, and facial expressions all send messages without the use of language. What messages are being conveyed here?

that extend across entire groups or that grow more complex over time (Premack, 1986).

Nonverbal Communication

Not all communication is through speech. Gestures, facial expressions, and body movements are all ways of sending messages. The study of nonverbal (unspoken) communication is called **kinesics** (Birdwhistle, 1970).

Kinesics is the study of nonverbal communication.

As with spoken language, the meaning of the gesture depends on the culture. The interpretation of some gestures may vary widely from one society to another, whereas other gestures, such as a smile, seem to have much the same meaning in any culture. Within a society a given gesture can have different meanings depending on the context; saluting an officer on a military base is a sign of respect; saluting one's parents may symbolize disrespect.

Language and Perception

It is through language that members of any society learn to *structure percep-tion.* That is, we see, interpret, and understand the world through the screen of culture embodied in our language:

> Human beings do not live in an objective world alone . . . but are very much at the mercy of the particular language which has become the medium of expression for their society. The "real world" is to a large extent unconsciously built up on the language habits of the group. *No two languages are ever sufficiently similar*

THE SYMBOLIC SIGNIFICANCE OF WORDS

Words have an evaluative dimension. Some signify "good" qualities, and others have "bad" overtones. The use of value-laden words to arouse emotion and structure thought is most obvious in politics.

The conflict over reproductive rights in the United States over the past 15 years illustrates the profound symbolic power of words. Those who seek to limit a woman's reproductive options call themselves "pro-life," which automatically makes their opponents "anti-life" (or its equivalent, "pro-death"). They refer to "unborn children," so that abortion is equated with the taking of life. These words immediately evoke strong negative images.

Their opponents, seeking equally powerful positive symbols, speak of "choice," the "right to privacy," and "voluntary termination of a pregnancy," calling on the traditions of individualism and freedom from government control, which are also highly valued in our society. The material symbol of the coat hanger, signifying the lengths that women would go to in the absence of legal and safe medical options, is designed to focus attention on potential physical harm to the woman. Thus, each side has sought to manipulate public opinion through linguistic constructions.

to be considered as representing the same social reality. The worlds in which different societies live are distinct worlds, not merely the same world with different labels attached. (Sapir, 1949, p. 162; emphasis added)

There are cultural variations in the perception of such basic aspects of the world as time, space, and color. For example, the Hopi Indians of the southwestern United States have no words to express past, present, or future time because the Hopi way is timeless, in contrast to the clock-based culture of European societies (Landes, 1983).

Vocabularies are also useful for understanding aspects of the environment that are important for group survival. For example, gatherers of thousands of years ago likely had words for hundreds of particular types of plants because survival depended on knowing exactly what was edible or usable in some way. Although they may know little about plants, American teenage males can typically identify scores of different types of automobiles because part of their masculine image is to be aware of the subtle differences among car models.

As descendants of the original *Homo sapiens sapiens,* all 5.1 billion inhabitants of our planet share a common physical and mental structure. The differences in thought and behavior are attributable to culture: the socially constructed beliefs and rules by which people live in human groups.

CULTURAL DEVELOPMENT: FROM SIMPLE TO COMPLEX

All known cultures—of the past and of the present—can be arranged along a line (a continuum) representing degrees of difference between the *most simple* and the *most complex* in terms of technology, the knowledge base, social structure, and material artifacts. As shown in Figure 2-1, a society's adaptation to its environment (its **mode of subsistence**) provides an economic base able to support a certain size population (Lenski and Nolan, 1983; Johnson and Earle, 1987).

As more techniques for adaptation are discovered, a division of labor results, with some people performing certain tasks and others doing different

Mode of subsistence refers to the way in which a group adapts to its environment through the production of goods and services.

FIGURE 2-1   A continuum of cultural change. (See also Lenski and Lenski, 1989.)

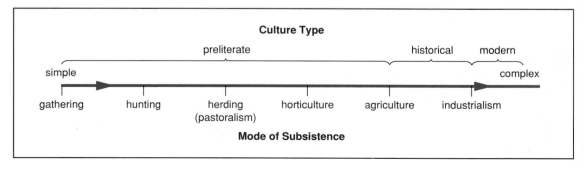

types of work. The more elaborate the division of labor, the greater the differences among people and consequent inequality among subgroups within the society.

Types of Cultures and Societies

In the discussion of culture types we will use the terms *simple* and *preliterate* in place of such value-laden words as *primitive* or *uncivilized.* There are no "uncivilized" people, only those whose cultures are relatively simple. **Preliterate** means without written language and correctly describes most preagricultural societies, although the spoken language can be very elaborate, containing a range of sounds not found in our language. Agricultural societies are referred to as **historical** because some written record has been left. **Modern** societies are those that have entered the industrial era.

> **Preliterate** societies do not have a written language.

> **Historical** societies have left written records.

> **Modern** societies are those that have entered the industrial era.

For most of our evolutionary past, humans lived in small bands of between 20 to 60 persons who subsisted by *gathering,* and where both women and men tended their young, shared the fruits of their labor, remained united by bonds of blood and marriage, and typically made decisions as a group. With the introduction of *hunting,* perhaps as early as a half-million years ago, a division of labor took place in which young males specialized in the hunt while the women continued to forage and gather, prevented by childbearing from being away from the campsite for long periods or distances.

Hunting added new knowledge, tools, and skills to the group's culture base, eventually including how to cook and store meat and how to use other parts of the animals for clothing, weapons, and new tools. Hunting societies were often organized into tribes of several families, in which women gathered for their own kinfolk, whereas meat from the hunt was usually distributed among all who share the campsite. Sharing the results of the hunt linked individuals and families in relationships of giving and receiving (Testart, 1987). By 32,000 years ago, some hunting-gathering societies had grown very

The different agricultural technologies of Ethiopia and Idaho illustrate the existence of both traditional and modern modes of subsistence in the contemporary world. How efficient is each of these agricultural methods?

large, with semipermanent base camps, relatively elaborate tool kits, and objects of art such as beads and ceramics (Price and Brown, 1985; Headland and Reid, 1989).

Herding (or pastoralism) added such specialties as the care and breeding of animals, and *horticulture* (simple farming) involved learning about plants, how to prepare land, and when to harvest crops. Each of these modes of subsistence was more complex than the preceding one.

The introduction of *agriculture,* some 10 to 12 thousand years ago, marked a major shift in social and cultural development. More systematic than horticulture, agriculture involved plowing furrows and irrigating crops, thus ensuring a more dependable food supply. A surplus in good seasons would lead to new adaptations such as trading with other societies and building storage facilities. The need for record keeping produced number systems and writing to keep track of who owned what.

The size and permanence of agricultural communities tended to produce increasingly complex political structures in which power was centralized in chiefs and a ruling elite (including religious and military leaders) who superseded the authority of family heads and who passed their positions on to their own children. The informal exchanges and sharing of goods and services found in less complex societies were replaced by a market system where value was determined by the impersonal mechanisms of supply and demand. Agricultural societies were held together by formal laws and the interdependencies created by an ever-expanding division of labor, which also created new forms of social, political, and economic inequality.

These key characteristics of preliterate and historical societies are shown in Table 2-1, which greatly simplifies the enormous variety of cultures and social structures within each type. These culture types are also called *preindustrial* to distinguish them from the profoundly different culture and social structures that emerged with the Industrial Revolution of the past two centuries. Beginning in Western Europe and spreading throughout the world, *industrialization* is associated with rapid increases in knowledge, technology, and material culture. The United States is located at the most complex end of the continuum illustrated in Figure 2-1, along with the nations of Europe, the Soviet Union, Japan, Australia, and Canada.

Today more than 3,000 distinct societies are located at all points along this continuum, each with its unique history of contact with other groups, of environmental pressures, and of changes from within that produce a culture like that of no other society. Thus, there are no "pure," simple societies that can be said to represent fully the way of life of the earliest human groups, although it is certainly possible to make educated guesses about what types of behavior would have maximized the chances of survival over time.

ANALYZING CULTURE

Culture is an *abstraction;* few of its elements can be seen or touched; we can only describe what people do and the explanations they give for their conduct. Culture provides a blueprint or framework for social arrangements that regulate daily life and that meet personal and collective needs.

TABLE 2-1 Types of Preindustrial Societies

Type	Size	Mode of Subsistence	Specialization of Labor	Political Structure	Economic Distribution	Degree of Inequality	Integrating Mechanism
Band	20–60 people in one place	Gathering	Very little	Informal, based on skill	Communal sharing	Very low	Kinship (blood and marriage)
Tribe	Hundreds in several residential groups	Hunting Herding Horticulture	Slight, on basis of age and sex	Informal, family- and residence-based	Redistribution of group's goods	Minimal	Residential groups and cross-cutting task groups
Chiefdom	500 to several thousand in large communities	Agriculture and other specializations	Moderate	Chiefs and other recognized leaders	Gift exchange (reciprocity)	Relatively high	Centralized leadership
Early state	Many thousands in cities and towns	Intensive agriculture and professional crafts	Extreme	Formal, legally structured, usually hereditary	Market exchange	Marked political and economic divisions	Monopoly of force by political and religious leaders

THE TASADAY: FROM LEAVES TO LEVIS?

In the mid-1960s the anthropological world was startled to learn of the accidental discovery of a band of two dozen people, isolated in the rain forests of the Philippines, who had maintained an astonishingly simple way of life. All the elements of culture were there: gathering as a mode of subsistence; shared decision making among all adults; strict rules about who could mate with whom; and an elaborate set of beliefs explaining how they came to the caves and what the future holds (Nance, 1982).

The appearance of the Tasaday was hailed as a major clue to the culture of the earliest human groups. Long before the tools and technology of the hunt were invented, small bands of gatherers similar to the Tasaday must have spread across Africa and Asia. In these groups both women and men probably performed the same tasks—finding food and tending children—with minimal differences in social power on the basis of gender. Such bands could not survive without high levels of cooperation and food sharing. Because of their noncompetitive way of life,

the Tasaday had no words for enemy, war, or hostility.

Since the 1960s, however, many changes have taken place among the Tasaday, so much so that when revisited recently by journalists from the West, they were discovered wearing Levi's and T-shirts, using modern tools, and adopting the customs of a nearby hunting tribe. This radically changed life-style has led some observers to suggest that the original discovery was a public-relations gimmick of the government of the former dictator Ferdinand Marcos to make him appear a protector of the powerless.

Other anthropologists who have recently visited the band, however, conclude that what has happened is a textbook example of cultural change through contact with more complex societies (Mydans, 1988; Nance, 1988). Such culture contact has become so widespread that we do not expect a similarly isolated group to be discovered; but if one should, the chances are that its culture would be similar to that attributed to the Tasaday.

Cultural Universals and Cultural Variability

Certain types of arrangements are found in every culture. These are the **cultural universals,** or basic social *institutional spheres* shown in Table 2-2. The necessary elements of individual and collective survival, when organized into institutional spheres, become the society's economic system, its political structure, its family system, its educational processes, and its belief system.

Cultural universals are basic elements found in all cultures.

The *content,* the specific details of the institutional spheres, and the ways in which these traits are linked together will be different from one society to another, shaped by geography and history. These processes account for **cultural variability,** the astonishing variety of customs, beliefs, and artifacts that humans have devised to meet universal needs. For example, although the need for orderly reproduction has led to rules regulating courtship and marriage in all societies, these can range from a communal ceremony among individuals who may never live together, to arranged marriages and child brides, to the seemingly hit-or-miss choices of contemporary Americans.

Cultural variability reflects the variety of customs, beliefs, and artifacts devised by humans to meet universal needs.

TABLE 2-2   Cultural Universals

Universal Needs	Group Response (Institutional Spheres)
• Adaptation to the environment; food, shelter	• Economic activity: production and distribution of goods and services
• Maintenance of order; rule enforcement; dispute settlement; protection and defense	• Political behavior; lawgiving; policing; defending; judging
• Orderly reproduction and recruitment of new members	• Marriage and family rules
• Training new members in the ways of the group	• Training and education
• Constructing beliefs that relieve anxiety and make members feel responsible for one another.	• Belief systems

Ethnocentrism and Cultural Relativism

In comparing different cultures, we tend to evaluate the customs of others in the light of our own beliefs and values. Members of all cultures assume that their own design for living is the best and only correct way. Often, the name chosen for the society means "the people," implying that those not sharing the culture are not "people," but outsiders, or "them."

Ethnocentrism is the belief that one's own culture is the best and therefore the standard by which other cultures are consequently judged.

The belief that one's own culture is the only true and good way, as well as the tendency to judge other cultures by those standards, is called **ethnocentrism** (*ethno* = race, group, people; *centric* = revolving around). This certainty about the rightness of one's beliefs and behaviors reinforces the tendency to conform and to defend one's society.

Ethnocentrism becomes *dysfunctional* (reduces the adaptability of a social system) when beliefs in one's superiority lead to hostility and conflict. If other people are judged less than human, they can be treated differently from those who are "like us." In American history each different ethnic, religious, or racial group was at some point considered inferior to white Anglo-Saxon Protestants, and therefore deserving less than equal treatment.

The social scientist strives to observe all cultures objectively. Aspects of culture should be understood in terms of the meanings attached to them in a given society and not by the standards of another culture. The attempt to

Nationalism and patriotism are natural results of ethnocentrism, the belief that one's own culture is the best and the tendency to judge other cultures by those standards.

understand the world as seen by members of other societies is called **cultural relativism.** Value judgments based on one's own culture are replaced, as far as is possible, by an appreciation of the values of other cultures. The social scientist does not ask if cultural elements are good or bad according to some absolute measure, but rather why the element exists, how it is sustained, and what purpose it serves in that culture. Above all, we must avoid the tendency to think of people in simple societies as being less evolved or intelligent than are members of modern industrial societies.

Cultural relativism involves an effort to understand the world as seen by members of other societies.

Is Modernization Good for You?

SOCIAL POLICY ISSUE

During the 1960s and 1970s, it was assumed that the industrialized world could best help developing nations in three ways: (1) to increase food production by introducing modern farming techniques and machinery; (2) to build up cash reserves by growing a few crops for trade in the international market rather than engage in small-scale diversified farming for one's family or village; and (3) to provide a source of low-paid labor for light manufacturing.

Although such policies were clearly designed to help the economies of the industrialized nations, it was also thought that modernization would bring benefits to the less-developed societies: political and economic stability, higher income for individuals, a demand for improved education, democratic political institutions, and eventually greater equality between men and women. The directors of agencies for international economic development were not only ethnocentric in their faith in the superiority of modern institutions, but they also looked at the world through a male perspective. Men would be trained for the new roles and taught the new farming techniques, with the expectation that benefits would filter down to wives and children (Blumberg, 1988). In actuality, none of these positive effects has occurred, providing a textbook case of latent consequences that overwhelm manifest functions (see Chapter 1). Cash crops reduce economic stability because they are linked to a world market in which the value of crops can plummet overnight, as in the case of sugar and coffee in the 1980s. Starvation is common because the cash crop replaced the varieties of food previously grown. The introduction of mechanized farming has driven small farmers off the land, and because few other jobs are available, large numbers of unemployed men drift into the major cities. Democratic institutions have not taken root; indeed, civil wars are more intense and widespread than ever.

In addition, the position of women within these societies has greatly deteriorated (Ward, 1984). When plow agriculture is introduced into a horticultural society, for example, women's role in food production and local markets is lost, along with the independence and power that came from these activities (Boserup, 1970). The shift of economic power from women to men is often accompanied by higher birthrates, further confining women to household labor and child care (Ember, 1983). Furthermore, in those countries where light manufacturing plants have been built, employers tend to prefer women workers because they can be paid less and given longer hours. This does not translate into personal power, however, as the women remain under control of their impoverished husbands and fathers (Tiano, 1987).

Clearly, economic development as currently practiced has had a pro-

STUDYING WOMEN IN DIVERSE CULTURES

Esther Ngan-Ling Chow

Esther Ngan-Ling Chow is currently a professor of sociology at American University. She is the author of several articles on Asian-American women and women of color. She is coediting Women, the Family, and Policy: A Global Perspective *(with Catherine White Berheide) and is the author of a Chinese textbook,* Sociology of Gender.

In *The Sociological Imagination,* C. Wright Mills points out that the central task of sociology is to understand personal biography and social structure and the relationships between the two. My experience as a Chinese-American sociologist clearly illustrates how my work in sociology is closely related to sociocultural contexts where I have lived. My multicultural background allows me to integrate the cultures of the East and the West, thus broadening my sociological perspective and enriching my intellectual understanding of the impact of sociocultural change on social relationships.

Cultural pluralism has shaped most of my academic career. When I was an undergraduate majoring in sociology and minoring in economics at the Chinese University of Hong Kong, many courses were taught by both Chinese and Western professors, and they used both Chinese and English textbooks. My first major project was a study of how industrialization in the larger society transformed social organization and human life in a Chinese rural village. As a participant-observer, I witnessed a mixed form of village economy shifting from an agricultural base to a wage-labor system. Many men, particularly young ones, began to work for wages in the city. Although some women still labored side by side with their men in the field, other women, older people, and children engaged in home-based handicraft work for nearby factories. This project allowed me, for the first time, to see how changes at the macrolevel of economic development affected social life at the microlevel.

As a graduate student at the University of California at Los Angeles, my understanding of social processes was transformed by the radical movements of the 1960s. I became increasingly critical of traditional classroom knowledge as the civil rights movement, the women's movement, and the anti–Vietnam War demonstrations brought important social issues to the surface for public debate and intellectual scrutiny. In particular, issues of racism, sexism, and poverty made me aware that social inequality in the United States was broader and more deeply embedded in the social structure than I originally thought. This linking of sociological knowledge with social reality has shaped the research questions I ask as a sociologist.

According to Mills, individuals can understand their experience by locating themselves in a particular historical period and can know their chances in life only by becoming aware of other individuals in similar circumstances. Indeed, sociology has taught me to rethink my life as a Chinese-American woman and to identify with those who are placed in similar life situations. In my studies of Asian-American women, I have focused on the intersection of race/ethnicity, gender, and class, the central organizing principles of social life and the bases of unequal treatment. These processes are complicated for Asian-American women by potential conflict between their two cultural heritages. For example, Asian-American women are frequently stereotyped as being submissive, passive, quiet, exotic, and weak. But my research revealed their struggle to resist, both passively and actively, such stereotypes. Within the family, however, men continued to make all the important decisions for their wives and children. My findings helped raise the consciousness of the women I studied, suggesting how the quality of their life could be improved.

Furthermore, my interest in gender inequality as a global

phenomenon led me to raise questions about how women's power varies cross-culturally. For example, I used survey data from 1,130 families collected in the People's Republic of China (PRC) to examine the effects of the government's attempts to reduce birthrates. I compared only-child and multiple-child families and found no substantial differences in the household division of labor and child-care responsibilities. Regardless of the number of children, many tasks were shared, but women still shouldered the major child-rearing duties. Chinese women are caught in a tug-of-war between the government trying to limit childbearing and a male-dominated family tradition encouraging fertility. Gender equality appears a distant goal, but control over reproduction is an essential first step.

This research adds to the growing body of knowledge about women in very different cultural and social contexts. Not only feminist scholarship, but sociology in general, benefits from a cross-cultural perspective. This is how we escape our ethnocentric blinders and expand our understanding of the world.

foundly negative impact on women of developing nations and has done little to improve the economic well-being of their children or even that of most men in the society. To reduce world hunger and political instability, the industrial nations must become less ethnocentric, promoting policies that take existing social and cultural realities into account, and considering the well-being of women as well as men. If you were director of economic assistance to such countries, how would you go about achieving these broader goals?

Ideal and Real Culture

Within any society, the observer must distinguish **ideal culture** from the actual beliefs and practices that guide everyday life. When asked to describe our culture, we are likely to give an answer based on ideals rather than actuality. Ideals are not always easily realized in everyday life. In our society, for example, the ideal of religious tolerance is frequently violated by attacks on atheists and by attempts to deny tax exempt status to "cults."

Ideal culture reflects the highest virtues and standards of a society.

Every culture provides examples of the gap between what ought to be and what is. Few members of any society can consistently maintain ideal standards of behavior. Thus, **real culture,** how people actually behave, often includes justifications for actions that fall short of our highest goals. The excuses still being used to deny equality to African-Americans suggest the power of immediate pressures over ideal expectations. The "strain toward consistency" between the real and ideal adds a dynamic tension to culture and society.

Real culture refers to actual behavior.

Norms and Values

Rules of conduct are part of the learned tradition of any group. Rules of behavior are called **social norms.** These are both *prescriptions,* which are definitions of the acceptable (just as a physician's prescription specifies the contents of a medication), and *proscriptions,* which are definitions of acts that are not acceptable (taboos).

Social norms are rules of behavior.

Some norms are more important than others. For example, rules involving behavior that is essential to group well-being ("Thou shalt not steal") are typically of greater weight than rules of personal hygiene ("Brush your teeth"). Many norms are simply a matter of taste; others allow little leeway. Yet behaviors considered essential in one society may not be in another. Coloring one's face is optional in America but is essential in Hindu societies, where such markings indicate social position.

Classifying Norms.   Following the original classification of William Graham Sumner (1906), we distinguish several types of norms.

Folkways.   Those approved standards of behavior passed on from one generation to the next as "the way we do things" are called **folkways.** Generally, folkways cover activities that are not essential to group survival. Eating with knife and fork, for example, is an American folkway, and is somewhat different from the way Europeans use the same utensils. Yet seemingly trivial folkways do express cultural themes, such as an obsession with personal cleanliness in the case of reliance on deodorants and mouthwash, or male dominance in the case of opening doors for women.

> **Folkways** are approved standards of behavior passed on from one generation to the next.

Violations of folkways are typically handled informally, through words and gestures of disapproval. These responses of others are called **sanctions.** Norms are enforced through positive sanctions that encourage conformity and negative sanctions that withhold such approval. The more important the norm, the stronger the sanctions.

> **Sanctions** refer to reactions that convey approval or disapproval of behavior.

Mores.   **Mores** (always in the plural and pronounced "more-ays") are norms that cover moral and ethical behavior, and thus are more crucial to social order and more severely enforced than folkways. For example, the obligation to help a relative, to respect authority, and to maintain community standards of decency are moral rules that bring public condemnation and scorn on the violator. These reactions, though still informal, are powerful shapers of behavior. But the mores of one historical period may not be the same at another date. For example, it was the duty of a Puritan parent to beat the evil out of a child, whereas today the same behavior would be considered abusive.

> **Mores** are norms that cover moral and ethical behavior.

Laws.   Generally, norms that are formally adopted and that govern behavior most essential to group survival are called **laws,** and they apply to all members of the society. Laws are enforced by *formal sanctions,* exercised by officials specifically charged with maintaining order: police, judges, and keepers of prisons and asylums.

> **Laws** are norms that govern behavior considered essential to group survival.

Sumner saw *customary laws* as crystallizations of traditional practices. They make clear just what is acceptable and the cost of disobedience. *Enacted law,* in contrast, can represent a departure from custom and may even go against previously accepted behaviors, as in the case of Prohibition in the United States. Although all laws are designed to ensure public order, they often reflect the ideal culture, setting standards that not everyone can meet. A prime example of such laws are the Ten Commandments of the Hebrew Bible, a minimal set of rules necessary for social order: obey authority, minimize jealousy and violence within the society, give honest testimony, and respect property. In general, from a functional perspective the norms of any society are derived from basic ideas about good and bad, right and wrong. These general concepts are called **values.**

Values.   Central beliefs about what is important form a standard against which the norms can be judged. Specific rules such as "Thou shalt not kill" reflect both a respect for human life and the group's need to avoid the internal feuding that could follow a murder. There are, however, exceptions even to universal values. Killing innocent people is approved in wartime (indeed, medals are given to superior killers), and death itself may be the penalty for killing under other circumstances.

Each culture embodies concepts of ultimate good, virtue, beauty, justice, and other abstract qualities that are thought to be reflected in the norms. Yet the link between values and norms is not always direct or consistent. For example, the norms—folkways, mores, and laws—that governed race relations in the United States until the 1960s could hardly be reconciled with American values such as equality and justice.

Rituals.   **Rituals** are culturally patterned ways of expressing some central value or recurring concern of the collectivity. Among the most universal rituals are common ceremonies that reinforce the unity of the society and that help individuals get through some major transition in their lives (Wuthnow, 1987; Kertzer, 1988). For example, most societies have highly ritualized courtship and mating patterns that are taught to each generation of young people. Birth, death, and the transition from childhood to adulthood are typically marked by elaborate rituals such as baptisms, funerals, and confirmation ceremonies.

Public ceremonies that mark some change in a person's position in the society are known as **rites of passage** (Van Gennep, 1909/1960). Initiation ceremonies in adolescence (puberty) are among the most common. The precise ceremony varies from culture to culture: Plains Indian boys are left on a mountainside to have a vision; at age 13, Jews recite the Holy Scriptures during a Bar/Bat Mitzvah; and in the Andaman Islands, a dance is held in honor of the boy who is soon to become a man as his back and chest are ritually scarred.

> **Values** are the central beliefs of a culture that provide a standard by which norms are judged.

> **Rituals** are culturally patterned ways of expressing central values and recurring concerns.

> **Rites of passage** are the ceremonies marking important changes in a person's position in the group.

In recent years, more minorities and women have gained access to the rites of passage formerly denied them by restrictive social institutions such as the military.

CULTURE IN EVERYDAY LIFE: EATING

Eating, a simple and universal human activity, is everywhere surrounded by rules, rituals, values, symbols, and taboos. The personal act is transformed into a social event. There are typical foodstuffs for each society: Americans are great consumers of meat, the French of wine, the Tasaday of tadpoles, and the Eskimo of seal blubber. A set of values and beliefs develops around these foods; special utensils and behaviors are required; the food has a "meaning" conferred by the group. One need think only of the Thanksgiving turkey in the United States to realize that we are not speaking of unusual customs of preliterate tribes. At this feast the nation's earliest settlers are remembered; the ideal family is sentimentalized; and the eaters are expected to give thanks to God. In sum, patriotism, family loyalty, and religion are reinforced in this version of the worldwide custom of celebrating the harvest. In other societies the end of the growing season is an occasion for excesses—overeating and overdrinking, as well as sexual freedoms not otherwise permitted. These releases of energy reward the hard work during the harvest and prepare people for the relatively quiet months ahead while also legitimating a short period of norm breaking.

Within a society, some people are distinguished from others by what and how much they eat. Different food taboos exist for men and women, or for children and adults. The well-off have different diets from the poor, and in some societies strangers are served food different from that eaten by the natives. Women and children are frequently forbidden to eat with the adult males of the group, and women are typically expected to eat last and least. You can gain some insights into the relative power and prestige of the members of your own family by observing what happens at the dinner table.

In each society, the ritual and its symbolism are different—a cultural variable. The function of ritual everywhere is to reinforce collective values, to relieve anxiety about the unknown, and to bring human drives and emotions under the control of the group through time-honored ceremonies.

Subcultures

We have defined *culture* as responses to the conditions of existence, that is, as adaptive solutions to the problems of survival and the effects of history. If subgroups within a society have unique experiences and different needs and opportunities, then we would expect great diversity in life-style among these subgroups. Such variations in values, beliefs, norms, and behaviors are called *subcultural adaptations,* or **subcultures.**

Subcultures consist of variations in values, beliefs, norms, and behavior among societal subgroups.

Subcultures appear whenever access to the general culture is different for some members of a society. As all but the most simple societies have division of labor, specialization, and differences in power and prestige, subgroups can be identified in almost every society. The more complex the culture and the more diverse the population, the greater the probability that a society has subcultures.

Subcultures are variations on general cultural themes that permit members of the subgroup to survive under conditions different from those faced by the dominant group. In America, racial, ethnic, and religious minorities have constructed subcultural adaptations to their situation. Keeping some of their Old World customs and language permitted the first generation of immigrants to survive the abrupt change to American ways. For Asian-Americans, African-Americans, and Latinos, language, skin color, or cultural distinctiveness still provoke discrimination. As long as this is so, the need for subcultural adaptations and supports will remain strong.

There are also some subgroups whose members prefer to remain relatively isolated from mainstream institutions in order to preserve their unique life-styles. One thinks immediately of the Amish, who have been able to maintain traditional farming communities in the midst of industrialized America, and of some Orthodox Jews who have set themselves apart even from other Jewish groups. Such subcultures are preserved by minimizing contact with the "outside" world, especially in the education of their children, which takes place totally within the community.

Boundary Maintenance.   Members of subgroups can protect themselves from outsiders by creating and reinforcing group boundaries. This is the function of special languages, or **jargons.** Just as doctors, lawyers, and sociologists talk to one another in a specialized vocabulary that identifies group members while confusing patients, clients, and other "outsiders," so also do members of gangs or religious minorities have secret handshakes, special clothes, and other signs of recognition, as well as a jargon that cannot be understood by others. In some societies, where women experience a very different reality from that of men, women have a private, special language (e.g., Shibamoto, 1987, in the case of Japan). American teenagers have a way of talking and dressing that sets them apart from both children and adults. Such barriers generate solidarity among the in-group and protect against invasion by out-groups.

Jargons are special languages of subgroups/subcultures.

Countercultures.   Some subcultures also contain elements of clear opposition to the values and beliefs of the larger society (Yinger, 1982). A **counterculture** provides an oppositional life-style for those who cannot or will not conform to the dominant norms, such as, the beatniks of the 1950s, the flower children of the 1960s, the members of the 1970s drug scene, and various other cultural dropouts. Similarly, those who live in communes or religious communities cut off from the larger society exemplify a way of life very different from that of the mainstream. Those in opposition to the existing social patterns tend to seek out others who share their views and who will reinforce their rejection of mainstream values and behaviors.

Countercultures represent oppositional life-styles for those not conforming to the dominant norms.

The Value System of the United States

What can one say of a society in which the rock star Madonna and Mother Teresa, a nun who ministers to the most impoverished peoples of the world, both appear on a list of "most admired women," along with Oprah Winfrey, Jacqueline Kennedy Onassis, and Nancy Reagan? Clearly, there is little agreement on the qualities that Americans value most.

Possibly, no country containing dozens of religious, racial, and ethnic minorities could have a "standard culture," one clear set of values and ap-

Cultural heteroge-neity refers to the existence of many different subcultures and subgroups in a society.

proved behaviors. **Cultural heterogeneity** (the existence of many different subgroups) is an invitation to subcultural development in America. But there is a set of general values and beliefs that are shared by most members of the society. *Nationalism* and *patriotism*, as the natural outgrowth of ethnocentrism, are powerful factors in all societies as a form of social cement that can unite otherwise different segments of the population. This is the function of national anthems, colorful inauguration ceremonies, and national holidays.

Core Values.   Robin Williams, Jr. (1970), presents a list of 15 dominant value orientations representing a conception of the good life and the goals of social action—what might be called the **American ethos:**

The **American ethos** is a set of core values guiding the beliefs and behaviors of Americans.

1. *Achievement and success* as the major personal goals.
2. *Activity and work* favored above leisure and laziness.
3. *Moral orientation,* that is, absolute judgments of good/bad, right/wrong.
4. *Humanitarian motives* as shown in charity and crisis aid.
5. *Efficiency and practicality,* a preference for the quickest and shortest way to achieve a goal at the least cost.
6. *Process and progress,* a belief that technology can solve all problems and that the future will be better than the past.
7. *Material comfort* as the American Dream.
8. *Equality* as an abstract ideal.
9. *Freedom* as a person's right against the state.
10. *External conformity,* the ideal of going along, joining, and not rocking the boat.
11. *Science and rationality* as the means of mastering the environment and securing more material comforts.
12. *Nationalism,* a belief that American values and institutions represent the best on earth.
13. *Democracy* based on personal equality and freedom.
14. *Individualism,* emphasizing personal rights and responsibilities.
15. *Racism and group-superiority themes* that periodically lead to prejudice and discrimination against those who are racially, religiously, and culturally different from the white northern Europeans who first settled the continent.

This is a bewildering list, combining political, economic, and personal traits, some of which actually conflict with others. As our history shows, equality is an uneasy partner of beliefs in racial superiority, whereas nationalism often limits the exercise of freedom. The coexistence of such contradictory values accounts for a certain vitality as well as divisions within American society. Furthermore, the content and the importance of any set of value orientations change over time.

For example, the dominant values proposed by the founders of America in the 1780s included such virtues as moderation in eating and drinking, cleanliness, chastity, silence, and thriftiness (Benjamin Franklin, 1784/1970)—ideal behaviors not always found at the top of a contemporary list. But there are some values that have endured: the centrality of work, performance as a measure of personal worth, punctuality, individual responsibility, and a commitment to justice. These continuities reflect the underlying strength of a particular value system that emerged in Western Europe in the sixteenth

What values are admired in the Nobel Peace Prize winner, Mother Teresa, and the successful trend-setting entertainer, Madonna?

century, originally described by Max Weber as "the Protestant Ethic," but which is now simply called the **work ethic.** The behaviors supported by the work ethic allowed the emerging merchant class to accumulate wealth, to keep its profits, to claim a wide area of personal freedom, and generally to lay the foundation of modern capitalism.

Central to this ethic are the following concepts:

Work as a "calling." A *calling* is a sacred task. In most societies throughout history, work has been something people did to survive. To regard physical labor of whatever type as a divine duty is a powerful motive for producing more than what is required just to survive. So strong is the work ethic in our society that even enjoyment of leisure must be presented as an extension of work-related meanings; it must be earned and must present challenges to be overcome (Lewis, 1982).

Success as a sign of grace: If work is a sacred task, there must be some way of distinguishing those who perform well from the lazy and the careless. Success in one's chosen occupation seems a clear and simple sign of divine favor.

Individuals as monitors of their own state of grace. The Protestant revolt against the Catholic church was primarily an attempt to do away with the

The **work ethic** refers to a set of beliefs that emerged in Western Europe in the sixteenth century and are associated with the rise of modern capitalism.

layers of religious authority that interfered with a person's direct communion with God. In this view, the individual alone was responsible for his or her own fate. The Protestant symbol was the lonely pilgrim, overcoming the terrors and temptations of earthly life, always anxious and never certain that God's will was being done. Inner fears of eternal damnation served to regulate social behavior.

As Weber notes, although these ideas provide a motivational basis for working hard, striving for success, and accumulating private profits, they were also used to justify other characteristics of early capitalism. How else to persuade people to labor 12 to 14 hours a day in filthy factories for barely subsistence wages except by convincing them that they are doing God's will? And how else to reassure the owners that they are not exploiting workers except to suggest that their success is a sign of grace? Furthermore, failure must reflect a personal flaw, some lack of moral virtue *within the individual.*

Originally, the early Protestants and our Puritan pilgrims stressed *simplicity of life-style* or *wordly asceticism.* Vulgar displays of wealth were scorned. Clearly, this concept would be extremely important in the early stages of modern economic development, where the practice of denying pleasure is a precondition for the accumulation of capital required to begin new businesses.

Just as surely, however, the continued success of profit-making businesses depends on increasingly higher levels of demand for products. Although worldly asceticism may be important for generating start-up money, a lot of other people must be willing to part with their earnings in order to buy what is being produced. Thus, a "culture of materialism," based on owning and consuming goods and services, is essential to the later stages of industrial capitalism (Mukerji, 1983).

The culture of materialism is based on the meanings given to the accumulation of worldly goods—as symbols of the "good life" and of the owner's prestige, as the deserved rewards for hard work, and as a means of providing security for one's children. The American economist Thorstein Veblen (1899) used the term **conspicuous consumption** to refer to lavish displays of wastefulness designed to impress others with one's ability to throw away money, a thought that would surely shock our Puritan forebears and that also produces some ambivalence today.

Conspicuous consumption is the open display of wastefulness designed to impress others.

The values enshrined in the original work ethic and the changes that have been made over the past three centuries form the basis of the American emphasis on individualism, achievement, progress, personal morality, and public charity only for the "worthy poor." As we see in Part III of this book, the work ethic is still used to justify and maintain great inequality in our society.

Cultural Hegemony.   In the perspective of conflict theory, values and norms are not neutral; they do not affect all members of a group in the same manner. On the contrary, what is considered good and true and fair benefits some people and not others. Ideas, no less than things, are cultural artifacts—creations of the group and of its most powerful members. The concept of **cultural,** or **ideological, hegemony** refers to the control over the production of values and norms that is exercised by those who are in a position to create and enforce rules of conduct. It is achieved by defining a reality in which the ruling class seems to have some natural or inevitable right to be in charge (Gramsci, 1959, 1971; Sassoon, 1982).

Cultural, or **ideological, hegemony** refers to control over the production of values and norms by those in power.

WILL THE REAL CLASS OF 1992 PLEASE STAND UP!

From its annual survey of entering college students, the American Council on Education reports that the class of 1992, compared to previous classes, is more concerned with using education as a means to a well-paying job. Twenty-two percent, the highest since the survey was begun in 1965, described themselves as politically conservative, and unusually high majorities supported the death penalty and mandatory drug testing by employers. However, on other issues—environmental issues, abortion, disarmament, and consumer protection—the students overwhelmingly supported liberal positions.

In part, the trend toward conservatism may reflect the Reagan administration's cutbacks in federal financial assistance for students from low-income and minority families, so that the incoming class comes from wealthier, more conservative households.

Sources: American Council on Education, Survey of the Class of 1992, January 1989; Hoge, Hoge, and Wittenberg, 1987, pp. 500–519.

Changing Values?   But what about caring, openness, cooperation, and community? Didn't the 1960s produce another set of values, at least for young adults? There is evidence that the strength of the work ethic has diminished recently. Much has been written about young, well-educated, upwardly mobile professionals—"yuppies"—whose devotion to work is modified by considerations of personal fulfillment, family, and enjoying the good life.

There is no question, either, that the 1960s left a legacy of openness to new experience; a concern for the environment and its preservation; support for the civil rights of women, racial minorities, and homosexuals; and a strengthened desire for peace. But "traditional" values of nationalism, individual competition, and materialism are very much alive. One of the most sociologically fascinating characteristics of the 1980s has been the fierce backlash against the ideals of the 1960s. Public opinion polls once more show strong support for the military as well as increasing opposition to further gains for women, homosexuals, and African-Americans.

It is too early to tell whether these backlash trends are the last gasp of the old ethic or its bedrock strength. We can say, however, that there are two competing value orientations today, no longer clearly associated with age. The youngest as well as the oldest adults appear more traditional than do people in their thirties and forties.

Traditional	New Rules
Individualism	Involvement/commitment
Competition	Cooperation
Achievement	Self-fulfillment
Patriotism	Tolerance
Work	"Good life"

To some extent, this value split reflects a basic dualism that runs throughout our culture. It remains to be seen which set of values—traditional or new rules—dominates the decades ahead.

SUMMARY

1. Culture, often called a blueprint for living, is the means by which people adapt to the environment.

2. Culture influences the way people experience the world and express meaning.

3. All human communication is symbolic, through words and actions, whose meaning is socially defined. Language is the most important symbol system, but nonverbal communication is also symbolic.

4. Cultures can be arranged along a continuum from simple, preliterate hunting-and-gathering bands that had no written language, to agricultural societies using writing. Industrial societies have entered the modern era and utilize a complex technological base.

5. Cultural universals are basic elements found in all cultures. Cultural variability refers to the specific customs, beliefs, and artifacts that humans devise to meet those universal needs.

6. Ethnocentrism refers to the belief that one's own culture is the only true and appropriate way of living.

7. Cultural relativism is the attempt to observe all cultures objectively and understand the world as seen by members of that society.

8. Social norms are prescriptions (do's) and proscriptions (taboos, dont's) derived from the central values of the culture; they guide behavior. Folkways, mores, and laws are three types of norms.

9. The more complex and heterogeneous the society, the more likely it is to have subgroups. Countercultures represent alternative life-styles for those not conforming to the dominant norms.

10. The American value system is rooted in the Protestant work ethic. Robin Williams, Jr., has identified 15 sometimes contradictory core values that guide behaviors of Americans.

11. From the perspective of conflict theory, values are not neutral but reflect control over the production of values and norms by those in power.

12. American society is currently characterized by tension between traditional and new rules and values.

SUGGESTED READINGS

Benedict, Ruth. *Patterns of Culture.* Boston: Houghton Mifflin, 1934. A statement of the need to view culture as an integrated whole, reflected in all aspects of social structure and personality.

Gitlin, Todd. *The Sixties: Years of Hope, Days of Rage.* New York: Bantam, 1987. An account of the 1960s in the United States, in particular of the many movements for social change in that decade.

Hall, Edward. *The Silent Language.* Garden City, NY: Doubleday, 1959. An anthropologist describes how nonverbal communication conveys cultural values.

Harris, Marvin. *Good to Eat: Riddles of Food and Culture.* New York: Simon and Schuster, 1986. A fascinating collection of examples of unusual cultural practices.

Kephart, William. *Extraordinary Groups: The Sociology of Unconventional Life-Styles.* 3d ed. New York: St. Martin's Press, 1987. Examinations of the Amish, the Oneida Community, the Father Divine Movement, the Gypsies, the Shakers, the Mormons, and the modern communes.

McCracken, Grant. *Culture and Consumption: New Approaches to the Symbolic Character of Consumer Goods and Activities.* Bloomington: Indiana University Press, 1988. The complex interaction between culture and consumption in Western society since the sixteenth century.

Melbin, Murray. *Night as Frontier: Colonizing the World after Dark.* New York: Macmillan, 1986. Examination of life at night as a release from conformity.

Schwartz, Barry. *George Washington: The Making of an American Symbol.* New York: Macmillan, 1987. Using Durkheim's concept of collective representations, the author examines Washington as a "symbol."

Zerubavel, Eviatar. *The Seven Day Circle: The History and Meaning of the Week.* Chicago: University of Chicago Press, 1989. A fascinating sociological account of how the week originated and how it shapes our lives.

A

Popular Culture: Mass Media, Popular Music, and Sports

Popular culture consists of what people do in their leisure time and the products designed for mass consumption.

Popular culture consists of products designed for mass consumption. It can also be described as whatever people do when they are not at work or asleep, that is, in their *leisure* time. A big business in America, popular culture has two aspects: (1) the human impulse to play, be creative, and let one's imagination roam (Biesty, 1986), and (2) the needs of an advanced capitalist economy to generate new markets and to reap profits (Rojek, 1989).

POPULAR CULTURE IN MASS SOCIETY

As a species, humans have benefited from their impulse to play and to create things of beauty (artistry). Leisure-time activities lessen personal anxiety and relieve tension. For the collectivity, the production of things that give pleasure to others brings members together.

These individual and collective benefits become very important in modern societies, where leisure time is often defined as the pause that refreshes weary workers. Because play is an end in itself, we say that it is *expressive*. It is done to express or satisfy certain human needs. Work, on the other hand, is a means to another goal; it is *instrumental*. Popular culture, therefore, is seen as an expressive outlet that balances the demands of instrumental obligations and duties.

Popular culture has a unifying function, in that elements that are produced and distributed across the nation via radio, television, magazines, and newspapers create a **mass culture**, which promotes common values and attitudes in large, heterogeneous (mixed) societies.

Although the terms *popular* and *mass culture* suggest something that emerges out of the personal creativity of "the people," conflict theorists note that the production of culture, like any other activity, is socially structured. How the **production of popular culture** is controlled is a major concern of conflict theorists. From TV and radio programs to sports events and art exhibits, mass culture is manufactured in the same way as any product. "Gatekeepers" and "tastemakers" form a cultural elite whose social position permits them to impose their standards of goodness and beauty.

It can also be said that leisure time is not truly "free time," because of the extent to which it is allocated and structured by political and economic forces (Rojek, 1989; Wilson, 1988). The times and places in which leisure activities occur, as well as what facilities are available to which populations—for instance, a sandlot or a golf course—depend in part on the decisions and actions of employers and politicians.

Mass culture refers to elements of popular culture that are produced and distributed through the mass media.

Control over the **production of popular culture** is a major concern for sociologists in the conflict tradition.

Mass Culture: Themes and Variations

In a society as mixed as ours in terms of race, religion, ethnicity, education, and income there will be great differences in the expressions of popular culture. Popular culture in America also show great variation by region.

Mass culture has traditionally been attacked for appealing to the lowest levels of taste and existing only for profit (Denisoff and Wahrman, 1983; J. Blau, 1986). But contemporary students of popular culture point out that throughout most of Western history both ordinary citizens and the wealthy and powerful enjoyed many of the same pastimes and entertainments, such as Shakespearean plays and classical operas.

Most sociologists focus on structural aspects of the production of culture: organizations, markets, industries, distribution chains, and other systems that determine what is finally produced and offered to the public (Ryan, 1985). In this view, popular culture is the outcome of a three-way interaction among (1) the objects produced, (2) the profit-making producers and distributors of those objects, and (3) the social groups that consume them.

THE MASS MEDIA

Like any other facet of culture, popular culture is learned and shared within families, peer groups, and particular subcultures. But by far the most important element in the spread and homogenization of popular culture is the existence of mass media in modern societies. *Media* is the plural of *medium*, which

Mass media are channels of communication in a mass society, primarily the print and electronic media.

means a channel through which something is carried (transmitted). The term **mass media** refers to the agents of communication in a mass society: (1) the print media—books, magazines, and newspapers; and (2) the electronic media—television, radio, and recordings.

The two most common leisure activities of Americans are watching television and reading newspapers. Ninety-nine percent of American households have at least one radio, and 89 percent have at least one television set, which is watched for an average of seven hours a day. More than half of all households receive cable television and about 60 percent are also equipped with video cassette recorders (VCRs).

The mass media employ more than a million workers and account for tens of billions of dollars in payrolls as well as over $100 billion in print and electronic advertising. The mass media—in content as well as advertisements—play a crucial role in raising the level of demand for goods and services that is so essential for the continued growth of our economic system.

Influences of the Mass Media

Throughout much of the world, media are owned and operated by government agencies. In the United States the media are privately owned, profit-making enterprises, only minimally controlled by government. The diversity of American media and their separation from the state have long been considered essential to the First Amendment guarantee of free speech. Yet most media are businesses run for profit and are subject to various pressures: (1) the political agenda of their owners, (2) the power of advertisers, (3) special interest groups, (4) and attitudes of the general public.

The trend over the past two decades is for small and relatively independent newspapers, radio stations, and local TV outlets to be absorbed by larger nationwide organizations. A handful of "media goliaths" now determine the content and editorial policies of a majority of American newspapers, magazines, and book publishing companies. For example, between 1981 and 1986, the number of corporations controlling most media shrank from 46 to 29 (Bagdikian, 1988), and another dozen mergers have taken place since then.

Effects of the Mass Media.   Criticism of the mass media is based on the assumption that what people see and hear strongly affects their attitudes and behavior. However, the research evidence is unclear. Most studies have examined potential negative effects on children of viewing televised violence. Although early government-sponsored reviews found qualified support for the idea that televised violence is linked to aggressive behavior among some children, other studies have found that any such effect is very weak and temporary (Cullingford, 1984; Gunther, 1985). And while it appears that the act of watching television takes time away from reading and social interaction, some researchers have found that TV viewing can stimulate cognitive development among children (Tripp and Hodge, 1986). Television viewing, however, may have more subtle long-term effects that cannot yet be measured. For example, troubling messages about race and gender appear consistently in programming and commercials watched by children and adults.

The media have their strongest effect in setting the agenda—the list of topics that come to the attention of the consuming public. By their choice of

A dramatic example of the way in which the media can set the public agenda occurred when a local station aired a video tape filmed by a bystander in a suburb of Los Angeles showing a group of police officers beating a black motorist with nightsticks and kicking him as other officers looked on. The tape was broadcast nationally, setting off a national debate about excessive police force and racism on the part of some police officers. What evidence do we have about police behavior?

what to cover and for how long, newspapers, television, and magazines define what is real and important. Nonetheless, the majority of readers and viewers are not passive sponges but active selectors of what they see and read. Media influence is strongest where people have no other means to find out what is happening in the world (Grabner, 1984; Cundy, 1989).

POPULAR MUSIC

Like other products of our mass culture, popular music is an industrial product packaged for profit. The industry itself is dominated by a few conglomerates (Denisoff, 1986; Frith, 1987). Because listeners today can tape their own copies of favorite songs, record companies have only a limited amount of time to make money from a recording. The trend, therefore, is to limit expressive freedom and turn the artists themselves into profit-making commodities through live concerts, posters, T-shirts, and talk-show appearances (Frith, 1987). Even music television, which originally opened the way for variety and experimentation, has come under the control of the conglomerates and has evolved into one more medium of promotion.

Music and Social Themes

The history of music in our culture is linked to social protest. From "Yankee Doodle" to "We Shall Overcome," songs have symbolized resistance to authority and hopes for change (Dunaway, 1987). The music of African-Americans especially created a separate sound to express both the pain of oppression and the possibility of liberation. The tradition continued in this century from labor movement songs to the music of the Civil Rights and antiwar movements of the 1960s (Garofalo, 1987).

But with only a few exceptions, today's protest music appears self-centered and pessimistic about change, more designed to let off steam than to bring people together (Holden, 1989). Hard rock, punk rock, and heavy metal all test the limits of culturally permissible sound and lyrics and give voice to the insecurities of white working-class youth in the form of a howl of rage. The protest form of urban African-American male teenagers—rap or hip hop—is a unique musical form combining the ghetto game of rapping (contests of exaggeration and boasting) with the beat of punk and hard rock and a touch of Caribbean rhythm. In terms of lyrics, African-American rap and white heavy metal music share a profound fear and hatred of women and homosexuals (Leland, 1989).

Despite their powerful sounds and images, there is very little evidence that song lyrics or music videos have direct consequences for the vast majority of audiences. However, alarmed citizen groups have pressured record companies to label products that might be offensive, which may actually have boosted sales.

The record industry, like any other American business, is stratified by race. African-American men have been able to find jobs in the production end of the business, but with the exception of Motown, a minority-owned and -operated company, most important managerial posts continue to be held by whites. The situation for women of any color is even less promising, and the sexism of the lyrics often extends to the treatment of women as performers. Women have found greatest acceptance in blues and country music, in which they often sing of unrequited love.

SPORTS

Sports are important leisure activities in all societies—a source of entertainment and an expression of cultural values and themes. Sports differ from play in that they are organized by sets of rules. In this sense, sports can be distinguished from nonorganized athletic activities such as hiking, fishing, and jogging. Sports are not spontaneous expressions of the human impulse to play but rather a form of structured social behavior with values, norms, statuses, and roles.

As with other institutions in modern industrial society, sports are characterized by increasing specialization of roles (for example, baseball's "designated hitter"), bureaucratic organization (NCAA, NFL, etc.), quantification ("stats"), secularization, and gradual equality of opportunity (Guttmann, 1978). Sports also reflect and reinforce important social and cultural themes. For Americans, sports embodies the values of work, competition, manliness, and commercialism.

Amateur Sports in the United States

By definition, amateurs are not paid to perform; playing the game is its own reward. Once only the affluent could afford to play without compensation, but today amateur athletics in the United States are associated with working-

The annual Super Bowl game, watched by more Americans than any other event, combines professional sports with popular music. The 1991 game was played during the Persian Gulf war, and Whitney Houston, a popular recording star, brought the house down with her patriotic rendition of the National Anthem. What are some of the other ways in which mass media and sports are linked?

class activities organized at the community level, such as bowling clubs and softball leagues.

Sports are also closely tied to the American educational system. College athletic programs have become big business, not only self-supporting but often money-making for the rest of the school (Hart-Nibbrig and Cottingham, 1986). The pressure to field a winning team has become intense, often taking precedence over such concerns as the intellectual development of athletes. A number of scandals involving recruitment of athletes and illegal acceptance of funds have raised questions about colleges' academic integrity.

Universities today are multimillion-dollar enterprises, with buildings and grounds to maintain, faculty and staff to pay, and thousands of students to house and feed. As student fees cover only a small part of these costs, institutions of higher education have been forced to look for other sources of income: allocations from state legislatures, alumni donations, and payments for television sports events (close to $150 million worth in 1990). Teams with winning records can enhance all three sources of income.

As college-level sports become a multibillion-dollar business, the interest of fans, recruiters, and television networks is increasingly drawn to high school contests (Eskenazi, 1989). Yet playing sports detracts from the time that could be spent improving grades and ensuring admission to college (Stein and Hoffman, 1981). In addition, the probability of being able to cash in on athletic skills is very low. The odds of a man becoming a professional athlete are 4 in 100,000 for whites, 2 in 100,000 for African-Americans, and 3 in 100,000 for Latinos (Leonard and Reyman, 1988).

Professional Sports

Professional sports in America have become thoroughly industralized. Ball players are bought and sold like any other property and moved from one city to another; players profit from high annual salaries (baseball players in 1990

65

College athletic programs, especially football and basketball, have become big business. Yet many of the Division I college athletes never graduate, and only a small number make it to the professional leagues. Should colleges be responsible for graduating their athletes?

earned an average of $580,000). Television networks offer hundreds of millions of dollars to sports leagues for broadcast rights but earn the money right back by charging advertisers hundreds of thousands of dollars for half- or one-minute commercials. Team owners make money not only from ticket sales and concessions (parking, food), but also through tax writeoffs and subsidies.

One disturbing aspect of American professional sports is the growing level of violence. A number of contributing factors have been cited: cultural acceptance of violence as a means of resolving disputes, the sense of masculine honor, fear of defeat, media coverage that appears to glorify or legitimize violence, an apparent weakening of the norms of civility among spectators, ready availability of beer, sports betting, and the physical discomforts and ugliness of many arenas and stadiums (Goldstein, 1983; Smith, 1983; Hazelton, 1989). To some extent, both players and spectators set sports apart from other activities and give it a morality of its own, where aggressiveness is part of the game (Bredemeier and Shields, 1985). For the player, violence is a form of self-protection. Yet injuries have become more frequent and severe in recent years due to such factors as the heightened level of competition, use of steroids in weight-training, lighter equipment and the adoption of artificial playing surfaces.

Sports and Stratification

Social class is an important determinant of who participates in various types of sports. Activities that require expensive equipment or private facilities and extensive coaching—tennis, golf, sailing, skiing, polo, competitive swimming, and ice skating—are mostly enjoyed by the relatively affluent. In contrast, low-income and minority athletes are more likely to take up boxing, wrestling, track, basketball, or baseball—sports that can be practiced in a variety of places with relatively open access.

The dramatic expansion of professional sports and the impact of the Civil Rights Movement have provided opportunities for minority players, but the road to athletic glory for African-Americans has been long, lonely, hard, and very ugly (Ashe, 1989; Hoose, 1989). The growing number of minorities on the field and in the front office has led some researchers to conclude that commercialization will bring desegregation because success depends on selecting top talent regardless of race. The extremely high salaries of today's superstars may give an inaccurate impression that major changes are also occurring in the overall distribution of wealth, power, and prestige in America. But sports is not a source of real power in society. Power in America resides in Wall Street and Congress and corporate boards, not in Yankee Stadium or on a Las Vegas stage. Minority-group members can achieve fame and fortune in sports and entertainment precisely because the major stratification hierarchies—in government and in business—are not disturbed.

Attempts to broaden opportunities for women in sports have been deeply resented and resisted. Title IX Legislation enacted in the 1970s dramatically improved opportunities for girls and women. But since the courts permitted a narrower interpretation of this law in 1984, colleges and universities are no longer under an obligation to provide equal opportunity to female athletes. Despite the relative lack of strong federal enforcement or of peer and parental encouragement for women's sports, the idea of gender equity in sports has slowly made its way into the public consciousness, and the performances of female athletes have continued to improve dramatically. Women may remain far less likely than men to earn millions of dollars as professionals, but it is no longer an impossibility. Still, if sports and other aspects of popular culture are true reflections of the deeper structures of a society, it is clear that the goal of gender and racial equity remains a distant vision.

SUMMARY

1. Popular culture—what people do in their free time—keeps people informed and entertained, reinforces values, and brings people together.

2. The conflict perspective focuses on who controls production of culture and whose values and power are maintained.

3. Popular culture in America is transmitted through mass media, especially television and newspapers.

4. United States media are privately owned, profit-making enterprises. The current trend is toward increasingly centralization of media ownership.

5. Popular music is a profit-making product; the industry, as with other businesses, is stratified by race and gender.

6. Sports, both amateur and professional, express strongly held values regarding work, manliness, and violence.

7. Scandals and illegal activities have focused attention on college athletic programs.

8. The trend toward commercialization has made sports more democratic but also more prone to inequalities of race, social class, and gender.

9. Lack of encouragement, and of enforcement of Title IX Legislation, block full participation by women in sports. However, sports equity has become more acceptable and the performances of women athletes have improved substantially.

SUGGESTED READINGS

Berger, Arthur Asa, ed. *Television in Society.* New Brunswick, NJ: Transaction Books, 1986. Essays concerning violence and television, mass media values, and elite controls.

Chandler, Joan M. *Television and National Sport: The United States and Britain.* Urbana and Chicago: University of Illinois Press, 1988. A cross-cultural study of live telecasts of baseball, football, cricket, soccer, and tennis.

Coakley, Jay J. *Sport in Society: Issues and Controversies.* 4th ed. St. Louis: C. V. Mosby, 1989. The sociology of sports.

Deegan, Mary Jo. *American Ritual Dramas: Social Rules and Cultural Meanings.* Westport, CT: Greenwood Press, 1989. An examination of American participatory social rituals.

Denisoff, R. Serge. *Inside MTV.* New Brunswick, NJ: Transaction Books, 1988. This history of MTV explains how music videos promote movies and albums.

Fine, Gary Alan. *With the Boys: Little League Baseball and Preadolescent Culture.* Chicago: University of Chicago Press, 1987. The socialization of young boys through organized sports and the informal activities.

Gitlin, Todd, ed. *Watching Television: A Pantheon Guide to Popular Culture.* New York: Pantheon Books, 1987. Essays on the cultural importance of television.

Gray, Herman. *Producing Jazz: The Experience of an Independent Record Company.* Philadelphia: Temple University Press, 1989. The organization and social relations of a small but renowned jazz recording company.

Kaplan, E. Ann. *Rocking around the Clock: Music Television, Postmodernism, and Consumer Culture.* New York: Methuen, 1987. A study of MTV as a "television apparatus."

Mandle, Jay R., and Joan D. Mandle. *Grass Roots Commitment: Basketball and Society in Trinidad and Tobago.* Parkersburg, IA: Caribbean Books, 1988. How basketball has become a game for economically deprived communities in Trinidad.

Ruck, Bob. *Sandlot Seasons: Sport in Black Pittsburgh.* Urbana: University of Illinois Press, 1987. The history of sports in one African-American community.

Smith, Ronald A. *Sports & Freedom: The Rise of Big-Time College Athletics.* New York: Oxford University Press, 1988. The evolution of individual sports and the NCAA bureaucracy.

Staudohar, Paul D. *The Sports Industry and Collective Bargaining.* Ithaca, NY: ILR Press, 1986. Sports as a business that employs workers and includes contract bargaining, salary negotiations, drug use, and violence.

Stebbins, Robert A. *Canadian Football: The View from the Helmet.* London: University of Western Ontario Centre for Social and Humanistic Studies, 1987. What football means to individual players.

3

Social Structure, Groups, and Interaction

"Before the disaster, the neighbors, we could look out and tell when one another needed help or when one was sick or something was disturbing that person. . . . If the lights was on late at night, we knew that something unusual was going on and we would go over. . . . People would just know what to do. . . . I don't think there was a better place in the world to live. . . . You'd just have to experience it, I guess, to really know. It was wonderful" (Erikson, 1976, p. 190).

These comments, made by residents of Buffalo Creek, West Virginia, describe the close social bonds among the 5,000 residents of this mountain mining area. These relationships were suddenly shattered when a makeshift dam, holding 132 million gallons of dirty water used in the mining of coal, gave way after several days of heavy rain. Within a few hours, Buffalo Creek was flooded; 4,000 town residents were homeless, and 125 people lay dead in the mud. The once relatively secure, close-knit mining community had been reduced to rubble. The survivors of the flood were so deeply shocked by these events that they withdrew into themselves emotionally, feeling alone and helpless. Not only had the flood destroyed property, life, and people's sense of well-being, but it also disrupted the *social structure*, the bonds and relationships that had given the residents a sense of community. As one survivor commented, "We did lose a community, and I mean it was a good community . . . now everybody is alone. They act like they're lost" (p. 196). Or as Erikson put it, "While both 'I and you' continued to exist physically, 'we' no longer exist as a connected pair or as linked cells in a communal body" (p. 154).

Social structure comprises the patterns of social interaction through which culture is enacted. It may be useful to think of social structure as the bones of a society and culture as the flesh covering the bones. A key concept in sociology, social structure has several components: systems, norms, statuses, roles, interactions, and groups.

Most social behavior is orderly and predictable. A society comes into being and continues to survive because underlying patterns allow its members to know what they should be doing and to predict the behavior of others. Without this element of predictability, our lives would be chaotic. Imagine what it would be like if you never knew how anyone would act toward you: If each time you stretched out your hand you got a different response, ranging from a handshake to a jab in the mouth, you would soon tire of handshaking. That does not happen because we have rules of behavior, or **norms,** that define acceptable behavior in specific situations.

Predictability of behavior is possible because each **status,** or position that we occupy in a social system, is characterized by rights and duties. In each status, certain things are expected of us (duties). A **role** is the expected behavior associated with a particular status (Linton, 1936).

Social structure comprises the patterns of social relationships within which behavior is carried out.

Norms are rules of behavior that define acceptable conduct.

Status is a position in a social system and is characterized by certain rights and duties.

Role is the expected behavior associated with a particular status.

THE IMPORTANCE OF SOCIAL STRUCTURE

The concept of social structure is particularly hard for Americans to grasp. We value individualism and support the idea that goals are achieved through individual effort rather than by luck or group action. Most of us are only dimly aware of the ways in which our values, beliefs, attitudes, and behavior are patterned to produce various relationships. When we try to explain behavior or situations, we tend to seek causes *within* ourselves rather than look to external sources. For example, studies have shown that, despite the feminist movement and expansion of opportunities for females, women remain disproportionately employed in nonexpert, poorly paid jobs, whereas the more important positions are held by white men. Many Americans have interpreted this finding as indicating that something "in" women—lack of initiative or lack of job commitment, for example—makes them less interested in success than men.

An alternative explanation is that opportunities for women have been restructured in new ways that lock women into nonexpert, low-paying jobs. Throughout the world, hiring practices block opportunities for advancement. Women's positions within the social structure of the workplace rather than inborn traits determine how far they can advance.

COMPONENTS OF SOCIAL STRUCTURE

From a *conflict theory* perspective, the most important aspect of any society is how economic production is organized. This is another example of how a macrolevel issue affects one's personal situation and thus further illustrates the sociological imagination (see Chapter 1). In every society most people work, but only a few control their labor and what they produce. These social arrangements of production, in which some control the labor of others, provide the basis for social structure. Social structure thus reflects such social relationships of production as employer-employee or boss-worker. Among the Mundurucu of Brazil, for example, a transition in their economy—from one based on the trade of wild rubber through a barter system to one based on digging for deposits of gold—had far-reaching effects on Mundurucu social relationships. Communality and cooperation were replaced by a growing emphasis on the monetary worth of work and ability to amass cash (Burkhalter and Murphy, 1989).

In more complex societies, such as the United States, the placement of men and women in the process of production influences their behavior. The corporate executive and the assembly-line worker have different vested interests. From a conflict viewpoint, relative power over the modes of production generates interests based on social position that in turn pattern relationships and social interaction (Porpora, 1987).

Social Systems

A useful concept for understanding how a structure of social relationships is put together and how it works is the social system. A **social system** represents a particular arrangement of statuses and roles that exist apart from the people occupying the statuses and performing the roles (Linton, 1936). From a *functionalist* perspective, a social system (Parsons, 1951) consists of elements with mutually dependent parts joined in a more or less stable manner through time. Change or movement in one part affects the other parts.

For example, your own family could not be described as a whole in terms of each member's unique personality and physical attributes. Every family is more than its individual members; it is an entity unto itself as well. Each

A **social system** represents an arrangement of statuses and roles that exist apart from the people occupying them.

family has a division of labor for household tasks, such as buying groceries, balancing the checkbook, taking out the garbage, and deciding how money should be spent. The family as a unit also makes its own rules, which govern behavior among its members. Moreover, each family has developed a history of its own with symbols, ranging from shared possessions and family photos to favorite places to go or ways of spending time together. These are not features of each individual but patterns developed from the *interaction* of family members and their particular way of presenting themselves to the outside world. Each social system, like your own family, has qualities that refer only to the system as a whole. The effects of being a part of a system cannot be fully understood without reference to the system as a whole.

Micro- and Macrosystems.   Sociologists speak of a microlevel or *microsystem* when referring to face-to-face interaction, that is, to the behavior of people in relationships, such as a particular family, a group of friends, or students in a dormitory. The macrolevel or *macrosystem* is a social system at a higher level of abstraction, such as *the* American family system rather than any given family or the economic system rather than the workers at the local McDonald's. However, each macrosystem contains the lower ones.

Status.   Distinct from the individual who occupies it, status represents one's position in a social structure and in a social system. Statuses are the building blocks in social structures. All of us occupy many statuses because each of us participates in a number of social systems. (Student, worker, daughter or son, and so forth).

Statuses are always linked; that is, each of us is socially assigned to a status and occupies it in relationship to other statuses. For example, the classroom is composed of two status categories: teacher and student. Without referring to any particular person, we can speak of teacher and student as abstract types. We have, in other words, mental maps of status systems that are populated by particular people. You yourself fill the status of student in various classrooms with different teachers, but in each case there are patterned regularities. The structuring of classroom behavior will exist as an arrangement of statuses long after you leave the school.

The classroom, whether in elementary school or in college, is a social system consisting of statuses and roles. How do these statuses and roles change as we advance in the educational system?

Ascribed and Achieved Status.   Some social positions are based on characteristics that are relatively unchangeable or over which a person has no control. Age, sex, and race, for instance, are not easily changed (although some people may try to disguise them). These are **ascribed statuses** and are often associated with positions that are occupied regardless of effort or desire. To be a certain age is to be able to do some things and not others. In some societies, the social position of one's parents determines the course of one's life, whether as prince or pauper.

In contrast, **achieved statuses** are positions occupied by choice, merit, or effort. Becoming a husband or a wife in our society today is an achieved status. We choose to marry. So, increasingly, is parenthood a matter of choice. One can make many decisions about what kind of work to do or how long to go to school. Still other statuses are filled through election or appointment. Generally, the more complex the society, the more likely are statuses to be occupied through achievement rather than ascription.

Although each of us occupies a number of social statuses, some statuses may be more important than others. The most socially important status is called a **master status** inasmuch as it affects almost every aspect of our lives. It is the status with which we are most identified. A master status has a generalized symbolic value, so that people automatically assume that a person with that status possesses a set of other traits associated with it. For example, a nun may occupy a series of both ascribed and achieved statuses: daughter, sister, aunt, teacher, female, age 35, white, social activist, and so forth. But her master status is likely to be that of nun; it is the most visible and most likely to affect others' responses to her in social interaction. If this nun decides to participate in an antinuclear protest and is arrested, it is unlikely that news headlines would read "Aunt Arrested in Demonstration." What would be considered newsworthy is her master status—nun.

If each of us made a list of all the statuses we occupy, the result would be what Merton (1968) has termed our **status set.** Our statuses within a set may be *consistent*—related so that one position tends to reinforce assumptions about other statuses. Or they may be *inconsistent*—leading to disapproval or to anxiety (as may be the case with a military psychiatrist who owes an obligation both to his patients and to the military system).

Role.   The concept of role, as noted, refers to the expected behaviors of anyone who occupies a specific status, whether ascribed or achieved. There are no roles without statuses or statuses without roles (Linton, 1936). Combined, status and role are ways of organizing individual behavior into the predictable patterns that make social life possible. For example, the status of student calls for a range of behaviors, or **role prescriptions,** very different from those of a teacher. Think how surprised we would be if a teacher came to class and proceeded to vacuum the room, or if students danced in the aisles. Such inappropriate behavior would destroy the *social system* of the classroom.

Although the concepts of status and role may sound confusing at first, we all occupy statuses in every situation throughout each day. Each time we interact with other people, our behavior is shaped by the role requirements of our position in that particular social structure, which we simply take for granted. Just as we learned to talk in sentences long before we had a course

---

Ascribed statuses are based on characteristics over which a person has little or no control, such as sex, age, race, and ethnicity.

Achieved statuses are positions occupied as a result of choice, merit, or effort.

Master status is the most important status occupied and the one that affects almost every aspect of a person's life.

A **status set** consists of all the statuses occupied by a person.

Role prescriptions are norms for permissible and desirable behavior of the occupant of a status.

in vocabulary or grammar, we learned the elements of social structure without being aware of them.

Roles are organized into *sets* that center on a specific status. Any status involves a person in a number of social relationships. For example, the status of student contains several role sets: student/instructor, student/student, student/administrator, student/janitor. Notice how differently you enact the student role when relating to other students, your equals, compared to interaction with instructors, status superiors, or with janitors and other service staff defined as status inferiors.

The flexibility that each of us has in playing a given role, however, is limited by one's multiple statuses. For example, everyone is either male or female and of a certain age: thus, every other status is influenced by age and gender status. For example, middle-aged adults usually occupy more statuses than the very young or the very old and thus are in more complex role sets. The multiple roles of parent, spouse, employee, son or daughter, and member of civic and religious associations influence one's performance in any one status.

Multiple statuses offer several advantages: (1) the resources and knowledge acquired in one role can be useful in other roles; (2) the impact of any one role loss is reduced by having alternative sources of identity and support; and (3) competing demands can offer an acceptable excuse for failure to meet the highest expectations in a particular role.

More often, however, multiple statuses lead to conflict and strain.

Role Conflict.   In any relationship, after a person's role becomes established, he or she is expected to behave in a certain fashion appropriate to that role. Sometimes when we occupy several different statuses, the role obligations required by one status contradict or compete with those required by another. This situation creates **role conflict,** when two or more of a person's statuses have incompatible demands and expectations. Role conflict is the theme for many novels and television dramas where the heroine or hero is caught between competing obligations, such as when the ace reporter uncovers a story implicating a close friend.

Role conflict occurs when two or more of a person's statuses have incompatible demands and expectations.

Some roles are designed to prevent conflict. For example, physicians are generally not permitted to operate on members of their own family; officers and enlisted personnel in the military are socially segregated in housing, dining rooms, and in clubs; and some businesses prohibit dating between managerial and line workers. Yet the social distance created by such separation often has negative consequences; in the military, for example, loyalty and willingness to take orders might be diminished. To avoid this type of tension, "bridge" positions or statuses are created, such as the noncommissioned officer, the factory foreman, or the academic counselor. In turn, however, occupants of these bridge statuses are likely to experience role conflict, caught as they are between competing demands.

Role strain results from contradictory demands and expectations built into one status.

Role Strain.   Just as competing expectations within the same role can produce role conflicts, so multiple roles can produce role strain. **Role strain** results from contradictory demands and expectations built into one status (Goode, 1960). A current case in point is the employed mother of young children. As a full-time worker she is paid to devote 35 or 40 hours to her job, while as a mother she is expected to care for her children. Even where day care is available, a mother is "supposed" to stay home with a sick child. She is also typically responsible for the bulk of housework, or the care of older relatives. Juggling these multiple roles is very likely to produce role strain (Pleck, 1985; Hoch, 1989).

One way to reduce role strain is to reinterpret or redefine roles. Multiple roles themselves do not necessarily lead to role strain; what is crucial is the amount of time, energy, and commitment required by each role. One might choose to comply with those expectations that carry more severe penalties for nonconforming—a kind of cost-benefit analysis of the amount of time and energy associated with each role versus the rewards or benefits. Thus, the working wife might delegate part of her role to another person in the system, as when her husband agrees to take turns caring for a sick child, or when an adult sibling assists in caring for the sick parent. The success of this strategy, however, depends on mutual agreement among members of the role set involved.

CONTEXT OF SOCIAL INTERACTION

Definition of the Situation

To a large extent our behavior is determined not only by our statuses and role sets but by the **definition of the situation,** a stage of deliberation and examination during which we define and interpret the social context in which we find ourselves, assess our interests, and select specific attitudes or behaviors accordingly (Thomas, 1927). Behavior in a role therefore is not merely a response but an active effort to define and interpret the social context.

Defining New and Unusual Situations.   Although no society leaves potentially troubled encounters to chance, what about a situation that has never occurred before? How do we know how to behave? *Anomie* is a French word that means "lack of rules," or normlessness. Emile Durkheim (1897/1966) applied it to situations in which norms are absent, unclear, or confusing—that is, in which no clear normative guidance is offered to the role players. For a group to be unified, it must develop a set of norms to regulate behavior. The norms include a clearly defined code of what is expected in the situation.

When the situation itself dissolves or is destroyed, as it was in the Buffalo Creek disaster, the norms disappear as well. Because people are rule-making and rule-following creatures, they cannot tolerate anomie. We all attempt to create norms to impose meaning and order on anomic situations. In England early in World War II, for example, when people first streamed into air-raid shelters, no clear norms existed; after all, no one had ever spent night after night sleeping and living underground. But soon, codes of appropriate conduct were developed, and typical divisions of labor emerged. Families occupied the same places each night; there were acknowledged leaders, jokesters, comforters, and other role players. Within days, a social system of the air-raid shelter had been constructed; order replaced anomie.

If behavior is a response to the situation as perceived by those in it, then varying situations are likely to produce variation in behavior. This point is

Definition of the situation is the process by which people interpret and evaluate the social context to select appropriate attitudes and behaviors.

Anomie refers to situations in which norms are absent, unclear, or confusing.

During World War II, the London underground (subway) was used as a bomb shelter during night-long raids on the city by Germany. British citizens developed new norms and behaved in an orderly manner despite the otherwise anomic situation.

particularly well illustrated by the work of the social psychologist Stanley Milgram (1965), in a set of now classic experiments. Unknowing subjects were told that as part of a study of learning they would be required to give electric shocks to people who answered questions incorrectly. The experiment was manipulated in several ways. In some situations the subject saw the "learner" (actually a paid assistant) going into the learning room, or could hear the learner's presumed reaction to the electric shock; in others the experimenter stood over the subject or gave orders via headphones or a public-address system. It was found that the subjects' willingness to inflict pain was affected not by their background or by any psychological trait, but by the experimental situation itself. That is, when the instructor stood over the subject, it was difficult not to obey; when the authority figure was not present, the subjects were less likely to administer the shocks. The key point here is that people are strongly influenced by the situations in which they find themselves and by the interpretations that they give to those situations.

GROUPS

Thus far, we have focused primarily on elements in the social structure, such as status and role, and on the context of social interaction. Yet a society also comprises the sum of people who are connected to one another in some patterned way, that is, who live in groups. Throughout our lives we belong to a variety of groups, each of which can influence our actions and our very ideas about ourselves.

A **group** is characterized by a distinctive set of relationships, interdependence, a feeling that members' behavior is relevant, and a sense of membership.

The term *group* is deceptively simple; it is used in everyday conversation to refer to many things. In sociology, however, a **group** has the following characteristics: (1) a distinctive set of social relationships among the members; (2) interdependence among various people; (3) a feeling that the behavior of each member is relevant to other members; and (4) a sense of membership, or a "we" feeling. Groups are highly varied, ranging from the members of a family to the workers in an office, from patient and doctor to children attending a summer camp. The membership may be stable or changing, but groups share two common elements: (1) *mutual awareness* of the other members of the group and (2) *responsiveness to the members,* so that actions are shaped in the context of the group.

Group Characteristics

Primary Groups.   In sociology a basic distinction is made between small and close-knit groups on the one hand, and large, impersonal groups on the other. Charles Horton Cooley (1864–1929) introduced the term **primary group** to describe groups in which the members have warm, intimate, personal ties with one another. Calling the primary group "the nursery of human nature," Cooley saw it as the source of a person's earliest and most nearly complete sense of social unity. The family is our first primary group. Primary groups involve an identity of goals among the members, who share a similar world view and strive for shared goals. Because of their close ties, each person in the primary group is concerned with the welfare of others (Cooley, 1902; 1909).

> A **primary group** is a small group in which members have warm, intimate personal ties with one another.

Belonging to a primary group is thus an end in itself; relationships among members are valued in their own right, rather than as means to another goal, and are called **expressive.** Because contacts are usually enjoyable, primary groups are relatively permanent. Face-to-face contacts, spontaneous interaction, involvement with the whole of oneself rather than just a part, and intensity of relationships are hallmarks of the primary group. Table 3-1 summarizes some of these characteristics.

> **Expressive** behavior is valued in its own right.

Secondary Groups.   Unlike primary groups, **secondary groups** are characterized by few emotional ties among members and by limited interaction involving only part of the person. Formal relationships replace the spontaneity of the primary group. All members share one common interest, but otherwise their goals are different, their contacts with one another relatively temporary,

> **Secondary groups** are characterized by few emotional ties and by limited interaction.

TABLE 3-1   Comparison of Primary and Secondary Groups

Structural Characteristics	Processes	Sample Relations	Sample Groups
Primary Groups			
Physical proximity	Whole person relationships	Husband–wife	Family
Small number of members	Spontaneity	Close friends	Neighborhood
Long duration	Informal social control	Close work group	Work team
Shared norms and values Shared goals	Expressive behavior	Parents–children	"Gang"
Secondary Groups			
Large number of members	Segmented role relationships	Student–teacher	College freshmen
Limited sharing of norms and values	Formality	Officer–subordinate	Army
Limited shared goals	More formal social control	Boss–worker	Corporation
No physical proximity necessary	Instrumental behavior		Alumni association
Contacts of limited duration			

Instrumental behavior is a means to some other goal.

and their roles highly structured. Indeed, interaction is **instrumental behavior,** because it is a means to some other end not an end in itself. For example, participation in voluntary neighborhood associations is primarily encouraged by the goals of getting positive results and improving the neighborhood (Wandersman et al., 1987).

Primary groups are often formed within secondary settings. Ties formed in voluntary organizations, for example, are likely to be formed among people similar in status, and larger groups promote the tendency of people in friendship pairs to be similar (McPherson and Smith-Lovin, 1987). Moreover, primary groups may influence the larger social system. For example, studies of the behavior of combat soldiers during World War II showed that the average American soldier was driven neither by patriotism nor hatred of the enemy but rather by loyalty to his buddies (Stouffer et al., 1949; Shils, 1950).

Gemeinschaft **and** *Gesellschaft.*   The difference between primary and secondary groups is echoed in the distinction made by German sociologist Ferdinand Tönnies (1853–1936) between *Gemeinschaft* (community) and *Gesellschaft* (society). *Gemeinschaft* exists in communities with many primary-group relationships, united by common ancestry or geographic closeness. In the *Gesellschaft,* relationships are more businesslike and limited. The major social bonds are voluntary, based on a rational self-interest in achieving a particular goal, and characterized by instrumental behavior. In general, the development of modern societies can be seen as a progressive replacement of the *Gemeinschaft* by the relationships of the *Gesellschaft.* Yet *Gemeinschaft* bonds do not disappear altogether. We continue to seek acceptance and emotional support in family ties and friendship circles.

Gemeinschaft refers to small, traditional communities, characterized by primary-group relationships and intergenerational stability.

Gesellschaft refers to contractual relationships, wherein social bonds are voluntary, based on rational self-interest, and characterized by instrumental behavior.

Conversely, the intense personal nature of the small community is often perceived as stifling of individuality, personal freedom, spontaneity, and creativity. Thus, young people have typically sought independence in the more impersonal structures of the wider society.

Gemeinschaft communities, characterized by primary group relationships and intergenerational stability, still exist. In some small towns like Stafford, Vermont, people meet to discuss issues of mutual concern and to participate in the political life of their community on a very direct basis.

In-Groups and Out-Groups. **In-groups** are ones to which "we" belong; **out-groups** are ones to which "they" belong. The amount of hostility directed toward out-groups is related to the degree of in-group closeness. Such hostility is closely allied to *ethnocentrism,* or the belief that one's own group is best, and that it is the standard against which all other groups should be measured.

Strong in-group and out-group feelings reinforce competition. This may be clearly seen at any athletic event, where the fans root fiercely for their team, sometimes insulting the other side or even destroying property. The members of the in-group are more likely to see their team's defeat as being caused by *external* factors, such as unfair referees, rather than poor playing on their own side. The strong "we" feeling of the in-group permits its members to interpret events in a way that supports their existing beliefs and that justifies continued membership.

> **In-groups** are the primary or secondary groups to which a person belongs. **Out-groups** are ones to which a person does not belong.

Reference Groups. Thus far, we have discussed groups to which people belong. There is, however, one specific type of group to which a person need not belong, but that nonetheless influences identity, norms, and values. This is the **reference group,** which provides a *checkpoint,* or *standard,* against which one may measure one's own status and role performance (Hyman, 1942). Reference groups are often those in which a person *aspires to gain or maintain acceptance.* The athlete on a Little League team may have the Boston Red Sox as a reference group. College students may aspire to membership in sororities, fraternities, or other campus groups.

> A **reference group** exerts a strong influence on one's identity, norms, and values, whether or not one actually belongs to that group.

GROUP STRUCTURE AND PROCESSES

Social groups are the building blocks of social structure. Differing widely in size, purpose, and membership, groups nonetheless share several structural elements and processes that affect their functioning.

Group Structure

Group Formation and Membership. Group membership is a circular process: The more people associate with one another, the more they come to share common norms and values, and the more they tend to like one another (Homans, 1950). This process strengthens group ties through shared activities, friendships, norms, and values. This is not an accidental process, for we gravitate toward groups that reinforce our values and our beliefs out of a *need for consensus* that lessens conflict over correct behavior (Newcomb, 1943). When people are caught in value differences among groups to which they belong, they generally resolve their discomfort by selecting the group that offers the most immediate rewards of affection, approval, companionship, and participation. In high school and college, many students are caught between competing groups, such as the family and peers; to reconcile the differences in norms and values between them, some rebel against the family and align more closely with their peers.

Perhaps because we participate daily in groups, it seems that what goes on is spontaneous and random. In even the most relaxed and unstructured groups, however, established patterns of interaction develop in which the

A **sociogram** identifies interaction patterns in studying group structure.

members are ranked in relationship to one another. Group structure has been studied through the **sociogram** (Moreno, 1934). Researchers using the sociogram ask all the members of a group to name those people with whom they would like to work, play, go on a date, and so forth; the choices are then plotted. For example, Figure 3-1 shows the responses of ten students who were asked with whom they would like to spend free time. Mary was the most popular: Six people wanted to spend free time with her. She, however, chose only three of those who chose her. As you look at the sociogram, you will also notice that there were several friendship groupings: Les and Paul; Bob and Pat; and Mary, Donnie, Ali, and Alex. In contrast, Joanie seemed to be a loner, as she neither chose anyone nor was chosen. Although sociograms help describe the structure of the group, asking people with whom they would like to spend time and asking them with whom they actually do spend their spare time may produce very different results. One set of questions taps ideal friendship choices, the other elicits information about actual patterns of interaction. How questions are phrased is thus very important in analyzing the data derived from sociograms.

Group Size.   The size of a group is an important aspect of structure that influences interaction within the group and the statuses and roles available (Simmel, 1950). Remember that primary groups are always relatively small.

The **dyad**, or two-person group, is intimate, exchanges significant amounts of information, and presents great possibilities for total involvement and conflict.

The smallest unit of sociological analysis is the **dyad**, or two-person group, such as a dating couple. The dyad is characterized by (1) intimacy and a high exchange of information, so that "two can feel as one"; (2) the greatest opportunity for total involvement by each member, but also the greatest possibility of conflict; and (3) joint responsibility. The dyad is extremely fragile, for either person can destroy it by leaving, by withdrawing affection or other needed resources, or by lack of concern for common problems of the dyad (Gupta, 1983).

The **triad**, or three-person group, is more stable than the dyad, with a greater division of labor.

The **triad**, or three-person group, is typically more stable than the dyad. Although the triad usually has less affection and intimacy than the two-person group, it does have a more complex division of labor and more interdependence among the three members. Two members can unite against one member, but the coalitions generally shift, so that unity is maintained and no one person dominates the triad.

The number of possible combinations of role partners and of roles that may be played in a group increases far faster than the group size. The very fragility of the dyad is caused by the fact that only one interaction or set of

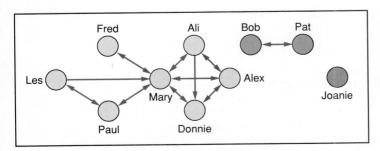

FIGURE 3-1 Sociogram of student choices of the person with whom each would like to spend free time. (Mutual choices are indicated by double arrows and one-way choices by arrows pointing from chooser to chosen.)

The dating couple, one example of a dyad, can provide a setting for intimacy, exchange of information, good times, and involvement. But dyads are also fragile, with either partner being able to break up the couple.

roles is possible at one time. That number quadruples, however, in a triad. As the size of the group increases, the number of possible combinations increases dramatically. In a group of six people, 15 dyads are possible. Clearly, the interactions of a group are closely related to its size.

Social Networks. Group membership provides numerous benefits throughout our lives. The sum total of one's group memberships and relationships is often described as a **social network.** Social networks may consist of tightly knit, primary-group relationships and/or looser, secondary-group memberships. Each of us has a social network, characterized by degree of closeness or distance to other members of our network, although composition of our social networks may change throughout our lives.

A **social network** comprises the sum total of one's group memberships and relationships.

Social networks provide valuable sources of social support; people with closely knit social networks are likely to experience less stress and to be more able to cope with crisis than those with few resources on which to call. A growing body of literature within the past decade has indicated that the support provided by one's social network is an effective buffer against a variety of social, psychological, and physical stressors throughout the life course (House, 1987; Lin and Ensel, 1989).

Table 3-2 lists those groups to which one is most likely to belong at different points in life. In parentheses are groups that are open to at least some people at a given stage in their life.

Group Interaction Processes

Behavior in groups is neither spontaneous nor unstructured. Rather, established interaction patterns evolve even in the most relaxed and unstructured groups. The term **interaction processes** refers to the ways in which role partners agree on the goals of their interaction, negotiate how to reach the goal, and distribute resources. Although each interaction has elements of

Interaction processes refer to the ways in which partners agree on their goals, negotiate behaviors, and distribute resources.

TABLE 3-2   Typical Patterns of Group Membership through the Life Course

Stage in Life Course	Primary-Group Membership	Secondary-Group Membership
Infancy	Family	None
Preschool	Family Playmates	Distant relatives Neighborhood Church
School	Family Close friends/peers	Student-teacher Classroom/school Distant relatives Neighborhood Church Hobby groups/sports
Adolescence	Family Close friends/peers Work groups	School Part-time/summer work group
Young adult	Family of birth Close friends Lover/spouse Family through marriage and parenthood Work groups	Formal work organization Professional/union group Church Neighborhood Hobby/sports/special-interest groups
Middle-aged adult	Family of birth Close friends Lover/spouse Family of marriage Work groups	Formal work organization Church Neighborhood Civic groups Hobby/sports, etc. Parent groups
Old age	Lover/spouse Children Close friends	Church Neighborhood Civic groups Special-interest groups
Very old age	Lover/spouse Close friends Children	Church Neighborhood Civic groups

uniqueness, role partners can interact only in certain ways. These processes can be placed on a continuum, ranging from very willing and positive exchanges of goods, services, or feelings to forced responses. As long as two or more role partners are involved, their potentially conflicting needs and resources must be taken into account.

As groups form, members enact different roles that make up the role structure of any group. Role structures describe the division of labor in social relationships and differ in content and complexity. Two basic role types are particularly important in sociological analysis: *instrumental roles* and *expressive roles* (Bales, 1950). **Task, or instrumental, roles** are oriented toward accomplishing tasks, ranging from pumping gas at a gas station to attempting to win a tennis match. In a classroom situation, for example, the role of the teacher is primarily instrumental: to ensure that students learn certain materials and to maintain control of the class. In contrast, **expressive roles** involve

Task, or **instrumental, roles** are oriented toward specific goals.

Expressive roles are oriented toward the expression and release of group tension.

the expression and release of group tension and emotion through laughter, joking, argument, and other informal actions that maintain group harmony. Even in relatively unstructured social situations, such as a party, essential instrumental and expressive roles are played; some people organize refreshments, provide the music, or make sure that people meet one another (instrumental roles), and others break self-consciousness and encourage expression of feelings with clowning and horseplay (expressive roles).

The Dramaturgical View of Interaction.   Each of us attempts to define a situation in ways in which interaction is made predictable. And each of us has a vested interest in presenting ourselves to others in ways that produce the results most beneficial to us. From the **dramaturgical** view developed by Goffman (1959), all role partners may be usefully viewed as actors who perform roles in a physical setting, or stage (see Chapter 1). Together, the roles we play make up a *social script.* When we interact with others, we present a front: our physical appearance, conduct, and definition of the situation. Then we rely on cues from others to orient ourselves to the roles we shall perform.

The **dramaturgical** view of interaction sees all role partners as actors performing roles in a social setting or on a stage.

As in the theater, interaction has a **frontstage,** where certain roles are performed, and a carefully separated **backstage,** where role players are freed from the pressures of public performance. We can see the usefulness of this model in analyzing interaction in a restaurant. Before customers arrive, restaurant personnel set up tables, prepare food for cooking, and play a variety of backstage roles. They also play frontstage roles among themselves—friend, boss, and so forth. When customers arrive, the dining room staff is frontstage in its interaction with customers—taking orders, being polite, and providing services. When dining room staff go into the kitchen, however, they are both backstage (complaining about the customers) and frontstage (dealing with kitchen personnel). As Goffman has noted: "The . . . current round of activity of a given performer typically contain[s] at least a few facts which, if introduced during the performance, would discredit or at least weaken the claims about self that the performer was attempting to project. . . . When such facts are introduced, embarrassment is the usual result" (1959, p. 209).

Frontstage interaction occurs in full view of the public. **Backstage** interaction is free of public performance constraints.

In other interactions, the social script is unclear, and role players must negotiate the interaction. Each gives off cues that the other may accept or reject. Once the script is agreed on, ambiguity is reduced. As Goffman concluded his analysis of the dramaturgical model: "The key factor in this structure is the maintenance of a single definition of the situation, this definition having to be expressed, and this expression sustained in the face of a multitude of potential disruptions" (1959, p. 254).

Principles of Exchange.   Elements of exchange also characterize how people interact. In each exchange, one has to give something up to get what one wants. Ideally, a person has a surplus (goods, energy, affection, approval) to exchange for some desired object (love, money, attention) that another person can provide. What is considered a fair exchange depends on each person's own history, needs, resources, and other sources of supply.

Principles of exchange govern relationships among people as they bargain for desired goods and services.

For example, when a group of hunters among the Bushmen of the Kalahari Desert in South Africa make a big kill, the food they bring home is divided among their kin, with the expectation that when someone else makes a kill the debt will be repaid. Whether an exact balance is ever reached is not as important as the norms of reciprocal exchange being maintained. In certain parts of France today, two strangers who share the same table at lunch may eat their meals separately and silently. However, each diner pours a glass of wine from his or her own carafe into the other's glass. This exchange establishes a social relationship, ensuring the comfort of both parties during the brief lunch encounter. Similarly, gift-giving on such religious holidays as Christmas and Hanukkah, although criticized as destroying the sacred meaning of these occasions, is a basic way of establishing and strengthening social relationships (Schudson, 1986).

Some participants in exchange have more power than others to define the terms. The importance of value received in the exchange model can be illustrated by patterns of selecting husbands and wives. In many societies, marriage is based on exchanges between families: a cow or land in exchange for a bride or groom. The goal is to demonstrate the bargaining power and position of the entire family, and young people have little power to choose their marriage partner. In India, parents place newspaper ads that stress a groom-to-be's family background, education, and earning capacity, and the parents of potential brides advertise their daughter's beauty, cooking abilities, and good manners.

Coercion is the use of force to induce compliance.

Short of **coercion** (the use of force), interaction processes are characterized by some degree of willingness to follow the norms. Cooperation, competition, and compromise are all *modes of exchange,* and the rules of the game are agreed on by the participants for each interaction.

Competition results when situations are defined as ones in which scarce resources are unequally distributed.

Competition.   When individuals or groups define the situation as being one in which scarce resources will be unequally divided, **competition** results. Usually, the competition is framed as a test of some recognizable quality that is unevenly distributed among persons and groups, such as talent, skill, physical attractiveness, intelligence, strength, or courage. Competition is basically social in that the people involved agree to the rules of the game. There is a shared belief even among losers that the competition is either necessary or fair, or both. The costs of the competition, for both winners and losers, are often personal strain and tension.

Cooperation is the sharing of resources in order to achieve a common goal.

Cooperation.   **Cooperation** occurs when people agree to pool their resources and efforts to reach a common goal. Cooperation involves consid-

Competition is social because the participants agree to the rules of the game. What are the rewards and costs of competition, in sports and in life? What happens when the rules of the game are broken?

ering others. The welfare of the group comes before that of each member, although people must perceive that their needs are being met. From an exchange perspective, cooperation is the basis of social order and the most social mode of interaction.

Compromise. **Compromise** is a cooperative effort to minimize the all-or-nothing aspects of competition. Here again, there is a basic agreement among the group members on principles and their shared meanings of fairness. People or groups mutually give up extreme demands and settle for a limited goal. The essence of compromise is that all parties appear to receive some benefits important to them.

Compromise involves giving up extreme demands to achieve limited goals.

Conflict. **Conflict** occurs when parties try to meet their needs by destroying or disabling their opponents. Unlike the other modes of interaction, conflict does not assume approval of the social order. Conflict occurs precisely because such support has been withdrawn, and aims to defeat and replace those who make and enforce the rules.

Conflict occurs when parties try to destroy or disable their opponents.

Over the past two decades, groups in opposition to official policy have used conflict effectively because of the presence of television cameras and the media's need to present exciting images on the home screen each evening. The antiwar, gay rights, civil rights, Gray Panthers, and women's movements have all used the media to force viewers to face issues and to take sides. The viewers, though, have not always sided with the activists. Gay rights activism gave rise to a backlash crusade against homosexuals, the women's movement produced STOP-ERA and antiabortion demonstrations, antinuclear groups have activated significant pronuclear lobbies, and the civil rights movement has given new life to the Ku Klux Klan. Conflict presentation, whether in the small group or on a national scale, tends to create extremes of opinion, leading to more conflict and even violence, but often, also, to major change in the social system.

Conflict Reduction. Each side in a conflict assumes that its goals are correct. This sense of rightness permits people to engage in behavior that might not be acceptable in other situations. Because societal and personal conflict can disrupt social bonds, several ways of reducing conflict are available: (1) *cooptation,* (2) *mediation,* and (3) *ritualized release of hostility.*

Groups opposing governmental or corporate policies have used various methods to express their protests. Here, members of Greenpeace, an organization concerned with environmental protection, demonstrate their strong opposition to offshore drilling for oil by American corporations. How effective are such demonstrations?

THE SOCIOLOGY OF EMOTIONS

Arlie R. Hochschild

Arlie Russell Hochschild is professor of sociology at the University of California at Berkeley. She is the author of The Managed Heart: Commercialization of Human Feeling *(1983), which has won several awards. Her most recent volume (with Anne Machung) is* The Second Shift: Working Parents and the Revolution at Home *(1989).*

I think my interest in how people manage emotions began when my parents joined the U.S. Foreign Service. At the age of 12, I found myself among many guests and looking up at their smiles; diplomatic smiles can look different when seen from below than when seen straight on. Afterwards I would listen to my mother and father interpret various gestures. The tight smile of the Bulgarian emissary, the averted glance of the Chinese consul, and the prolonged handshake of the French economic officer, I learned, conveyed messages not simply from person to person but from one country to another.

As a graduate student at Berkeley some years later, I was excited by the writings of C. Wright Mills, especially his chapter in *White Collar* called "The Great Salesroom." Mills argued that when we "sell our personality" in the course of selling goods or services we engage in a seriously self-alienating process, one that is increasingly common among workers in advanced capitalist systems. Mills seemed to assume that in order to sell personality, one need only have it. Yet simply having personality does not make one a diplomat, any more than having muscles makes one an athlete. What was missing was a sense of the active emotional labor involved in the selling. This labor, it seemed to me, might be one part of a distinctly patterned yet invisible emotional system—a system composed of individual acts of "emotion work," social "feeling rules," and a great variety of exchanges between people in private and public life.

My search led me to the works of Erving Goffman and to his analysis of how we try to control our appearance even as we unconsciously observe rules about how we ought to appear to others. But Goffman does not tell us how a person acts on feeling—or stops acting on it, or even stops feeling.

I would define feeling, like emotion, as a sense, like the sense of hearing or sight. In a general way, we experience it when bodily sensations are joined with what we see or imagine. Like the sense of hearing, emotion communicates information. From feeling we discover our own viewpoint on the world.

We often say that we *try* to feel. But how can we do this? Feelings, I suggest, are not stored "inside" us, and they are not independent of acts of management. Both the act of "getting in touch with" feeling and the act of "trying to" feel may become part of the process that makes the thing we get in touch with, or the thing we manage, *into* a feeling or emotion. In managing feeling, we contribute to the creation of it.

I believe that when we try to feel, we apply latent feeling rules. We say, "I shouldn't feel so angry at what she did," or "Given our agreement, I have no right to feel jealous." Feeling rules are standards used in emotional conversation to determine what is rightly owed and owing in the currency of feeling. Through them, we tell what is "due" in each relation, each role. In interaction we pay, overpay, underpay, play with paying, pretend to pay, or acknowledge what is emotionally due another person.

Now what happens when the managing of emotion comes to be sold as labor? What happens when feeling rules, like rules of behavioral display, are established not through private negotiation but by company manuals?

As a matter of tradition, emotion management has been better understood and more often used by women as one of the offerings they trade for economic support. Especially among dependent women of the middle and upper classes, women have the job (or think they ought to) of creating the emotional tone of social encounters: expressing joy at the Christmas presents others open, creating the sense of surprise at birthdays, or displaying alarm at the mouse in the kitchen. Gender is not the only determinant of skill in such managed expression and in the emotion work needed to do it well. But men who do this work well have slightly less in common with other men than women who do it well have with other women.

Similarly, emotional labor affects the various social classes differently. If it is women, members of the less advantaged gender, who specialize in emotional labor, it is the middle and upper reaches of the class system that seem to call for it most. And parents who do emotional labor on the job will convey its importance to their children to prepare them with the skills they will need for the jobs they will probably get.

In general, working-class people tend to work more with things, and middle-class and upper-class people tend to work more with people. More working women than men deal with people as a job. Thus, there are both gender patterns and class patterns to the civic and commercial use of human feeling.

Source: Excerpted from Arlie Russell Hochschild, *The Managed Heart: Commercialization of Human Feeling,* Berkeley: University of California Press, 1983.

Cooptation occurs when the members of the dissenting group are absorbed by the dominant group; as a result, the ideas of the opposition filter into the mainstream, so that there is no longer a need for confrontation. An example of the first form of cooptation would be to appoint consumer activist Ralph Nader to the Federal Trade Commission. An example of the second was extending the vote to women.

Cooptation occurs when members of a dissenting group are absorbed by a dominant group.

Mediation, or the use of a third party to resolve the issues, often occurs in labor-management conflicts within the small group, and more recently in divorce mediation. (This is another reason why the triad is more stable than the dyad; the dyad has no one to mediate disputes [Simmel, 1950].)

Mediation refers to the use of a third party to resolve issues.

A **ritualized release of hostility** is used by some societies and groups to contain conflict. Anthropologists have reported carefully controlled, ritualized warfare among groups within a society or between neighboring societies (Dirks, 1988). Regional conflicts in America are often displaced onto athletic teams: North–South football games, for example, become an occasion for waving the Confederate flag.

Ritualized release of hostility occurs when hostility is expressed under controlled situations.

The Sociology of Emotions. Although classical sociological theorists as diverse as Durkheim, Marx, and Weber were aware of the importance of emotions as motivating forces for social cohesion, only recently have sociologists emphasized the ways in which such emotions as love, hate, jealousy, anger, guilt, and sympathy are socially constructed, exchanged, and maintained.

The **sociology of emotions** demonstrates that emotions are socially constructed, exchanged, and maintained.

Through the process of socialization, each of us acquires a kind of grammar or set of **feeling rules** that shape how, when, with whom, and where an emotion is expressed (Hochschild, 1979). Children are taught to interpret their feelings, judge which emotions are appropriate, and modify their behavior to match these feeling rules (Pollak and Thoits, 1989); they are also taught to suppress certain feelings (Leavitt and Powers, 1989). Display of any emotion thus has a feedback loop that affects our power and intimacy in relationships with others.

Feeling rules shape how, when, with whom, and where emotion is expressed.

Emotions are also constructed within a cultural and historical context.

The American concept of love, for example, has changed greatly over the past 150 years. As home and workplace became increasingly separate during the nineteenth century, love became defined in expressive rather than instrumental terms, with women responsible for nurturance—"a family duty blueprint," wherein women were expected to devote their life to husband and children. Most recently, an "interdependence blueprint" of love has developed, which emphasizes mutual support and equal responsibility of both men and women for loving (Cancian, 1987).

How we manage emotion itself varies, of course. We can give, withhold, reject, expect, fake, or "work on" our emotions (Hochschild, 1983). Consider a dating relationship. If, after several dates that were mutually enjoyed by both, one partner announces to the other, "I love you," that person probably has reason to believe that the feeling will be returned. Regardless of the accuracy of this reading, the announcement will affect the course of the relationship. If a shared "grammar" exists, one partner can usually expect his or her feelings to be returned because it is likely that each has similar perceptions of the situation. Sharing the same "grammar," however, also allows the role partners to "play the game" instead of really meaning it.

Emotion is thus an interactive exchange. People build up "feeling currencies," which others hold on account, ready to give in the future (Hochschild, 1983). Sympathy, for example, is guided both by feeling rules and the structure of relationships, with the size of one's sympathy account in a group varying according to past conformity to sympathy norms within the group (Clark, 1987). People who overinvest or underinvest in at least some types of emotions may face closed accounts.

Throughout our lives we learn to change or eliminate emotions considered inappropriate to specific roles and situations. For example, emotion management is a taboo topic for discussion in the medical school curriculum. Yet to manage their feelings about physical contact with the human body, medical students learn a set of unspoken emotion rules, including transforming the patient or procedure into an object of analysis, joking, avoiding human contact, or empathizing with patients (Smith and Kleinman, 1989). Learning to manage emotions is a sometimes costly, dehumanizing process that affects other aspects of our lives.

Shared emotions, however, provide a basis for social cohesion, as they unite us in common interests (Durkheim, 1984; Scheff, 1988). Moreover, emotions are linked to physical bodies in a dynamic fashion: The social situation triggers individual emotions and interchanges; these in turn feed back into our bodies on a physiological basis. Much of the research on stress, for example, has indicated that a situation perceived as stressful triggers very specific physiological responses.

Formal organizations are social structures characterized by formality, ranked positions, large size, relative complexity, and long duration.

FORMAL ORGANIZATIONS

Formal organizations are an important part of the social system because everyone spends so much time in them; only preschool children and adults who work at home are exempt from being "organization people." Formal organizations (sometimes called *complex organizations*) are characterized by

- Formality
- Ranked positions
- Large size
- Relative complexity
- Duration longer than that of the memberships composing them

Examples of complex or formal organizations include such different units as football teams, local school systems, colleges, hospitals, businesses, and government agencies. Formal organizations are larger and more structured than small groups. A clear-cut division of labor follows an organizational blueprint. Role behavior stems primarily from one's status in the organization and is typically less flexible than in informal groups.

The formal organization is an effective and efficient mechanism for doing a large job or many tasks. In any group, as division of labor and the complexity of tasks increase, the degree of organization and the size of the group also increase. For example, the one-room schoolhouse of the past was much like a small, relatively informal group. A modern school is a formal organization in which various teachers specialize in particular fields, students may move from one classroom to another, and both students and faculty are accountable to the principal, who, in turn, is accountable to a higher level of centralized authority, the superintendent.

The sum of formal organizations within a society form **social institutions,** or institutional spheres, that is, the interdependent parts of the society as a whole, such as family and its economy. (See pp. 45–46 for a discussion of institutional spheres.)

A **social institution** is a cluster of systems, values, norms, statuses, and roles that develop in response to basic needs.

Bureaucracy

One type of formal organization common in modern societies is the **bureaucracy.** First described by Max Weber (1922), the bureaucracy is a specific type of organization, characterized by impartiality, rationality, and efficiency, whose purpose is to accomplish large-scale administrative tasks involving many people. Weber's description of the bureaucracy is an *ideal type*—the purest form of the bureaucracy—and has the following characteristics:

The **bureaucracy** is a formal organization characterized by rationality and efficiency.

1. A clear-cut division of labor attached to statuses in the organization, with a high degree of specialization for each status position.
2. A hierarchical delegation of power and responsibility, with each lower status under the control and supervision of a higher one.
3. A consistent set of rules and regulations for specific situations or tasks to assure uniform performance.
4. Impartiality, whereby status occupants are to perform their tasks without bias or favoritism.
5. Employment based on stated qualifications and employees protected against unreasonable dismissal.
6. Records kept of all transactions.

The Bureaucracy at Work: Positive Features.   The positive aspects of the bureaucracy include a division of labor that promotes efficiency, and clear and specified chains of command and expectations for workers, and that

Among the negative features of bureaucracy are the seemingly endless rules, regulations, and paperwork. Where do you think your file is?

discourages favoritism and petty rivalries in promotion. In a complex society such as the United States, the simplicity of the *Gemeinschaft* organization (such as the mom-and-pop store) is inappropriate for producing automobiles, breakfast cereals, or large crops of wheat, or for ranching or treating a heart attack victim. Modern tasks and knowledge are too complex for any one person to master all aspects of even a single specialty, such as farming, manufacturing, or hospital administration.

The relative security of a person's position within the bureaucracy may be a hidden strength. Research comparing people in high-ranking positions in bureaucratic organizations with those in smaller, nonbureaucratic systems found that the bureaucrats were more creative and had more varied interests, perhaps because the large corporations had the "pick of the crop" of college graduates, or because the relative security of the bureaucratic organization frees executives to explore new ways of doing things without immediate fear of job loss or demotion (Kohn, 1971).

The Bureaucracy at Work: Negative Features.   Most Americans have had personal experience with one or more of the negative aspects of the bureaucracy: inefficient communication, buck passing, red tape, and needlessly complex regulations. In 1987, for example, "simplified" income tax forms turned out to be more confusing than the barely understandable ones that they replaced. An even more simplified form was ultimately issued. Such complexity and wordiness reflect the nature of bureaucratic organization. A bureaucracy has rigid written rules specifying appropriate behavior for all possible events. Yet these rules sometimes create problems, rather than solve them. Because they are difficult to detect, the problems tend to be perpetuated.

Rewarding incompetence has also been noted by Professor Lawrence Peter, coauthor of *The Peter Principle* (1969). With tongue firmly in cheek, Peter developed a new science: hierarchiology, or the study of how people rise to their level of incompetence within a bureaucracy. This is the Peter Principle:

Early in life, I faced the problem of occupational incompetence. As a young schoolteacher, I was shocked, baffled, to see so many knot-heads as principals, inspectors, and superintendents. I questioned older teachers. All I could find was that the knot-heads . . . had been capable (once) and that was why they had been promoted. Eventually, I realized the same occurs in all trades and professions . . . a competent employee is eligible for promotion, but incompetence is a bar to promotion. So an employee's final position must be one for which he is incompetent! (p. 8)

Another negative feature of bureaucracy that has flourished is Parkinson's Law: Work expands to fill the number of hours allotted to it (Parkinson, 1957). A third feature—that "officials beget officials"—can be seen in many colleges and universities, where the number of deans and assistant deans has grown at a higher rate than that of faculty positions.

The inflexibility and impersonality of the bureaucracy has been widely criticized. Yet few of us would want our personal qualities or beliefs, such as skin color or religion, to be made a factor in our dealings with it. Impersonality can actually guarantee equal treatment.

Is the Bureaucracy a Threat to Democracy?

SOCIAL POLICY ISSUE

Since about 1900 bureaucracies have been expanding as businesses and governments have become larger and more complex. Although Weber viewed the bureaucracy in a complex society as both rational and efficient, he also hoped that the power of the bureaucracy would be restrained by elected officials responsible to the citizenry.

Critics of bureaucracy, however, have argued that the very nature of bureaucracy allows it to overwhelm democratic processes (Glassman, Swatos, and Rosen, 1987). Myths of infallibility and indispensability protect the bureaucracy from outside criticism and from accountability to the larger society.

Bureaucracies, once created, are often difficult to control because of their complexity and ability to amass information. It may also be argued that the more rational a bureaucracy becomes, the more it becomes dehumanized and fails to serve the very mission for which it was created. Thus, organizations specifically created to deliver services to the public may undermine individual rights and civil liberties. The ability of the CIA, the FBI, the police, and credit agencies to gather, computerize, retrieve, and use confidential information is generally unrestrained by law (Bohme and Stehr, 1986; Glassman et al., 1987). Decision making by both public and private health and welfare agencies may not always serve the supposed beneficiaries. For example, during the 1960s, the power of "street-level" Boston Housing Authority bureaucrats, despite judicial efforts to ensure open housing, resulted in blatant racial segregation in public housing (Pynoos, 1986).

Even more difficult to control in a democratic society are hidden bureaucracies whose actions may not be known either to the general public or to members of Congress, or, presumably, the president and vice president, as in the case of the undercover operations of the CIA in Nicaragua and Iran during the 1980s (Marshall, Scott, and Hunter, 1987).

Although bureaucracy curbs political corruption and lessens the likelihood of favoritism in hiring and promotions, the difficulty of controlling its hidden and visible actions poses a dilemma. What sociology-based policy recommendations would you make to ensure that governmental and business bureaucracies can be monitored through democratic checks and balances? ■

Informal Groups and Impersonality within the Bureaucracy

Weber described bureaucracy as an "iron cage" in which people often feel trapped by rational, impersonal arrangements over which they have no control and which seem to defy all possibilities of flexibility and change. Although the formal structure of the bureaucracy is impersonal, its goals of rationality and discipline are rarely fully realized. Changes in rules, communication patterns, and official leadership lag behind daily events, and rules must be general enough to allow for new situations.

Informal primary groups develop within bureaucracies to meet personal needs.

Impersonal patterns of relationships within the bureaucracy give rise to **informal primary groups** of members of work teams. This kind of informal structure may either reinforce the purpose of the organization (as the primary group in the military usually does) or work against its goals. Workers develop tactics to manipulate events and turn them into opportunities to satisfy their own needs. For example, in some organizations, workers fulfill their own needs on company time by using scraps to make goods for themselves, writing personal correspondence, and so forth (de Certeau, 1984).

Today's bureaucracies are becoming less formal. In the military, for example, there has been a tendency for patterns of authority to change: from direct orders with no questions asked to persuasion and group agreement about what is to be done (Janowitz, 1980). Hierarchy has also been altered by technical change. Expanding use of professional "experts" who operate in cooperative work groups has enhanced communication and work efficiency. Changing social values, too, have altered organizational structures. For example, some feminists have turned from bureaucracy to egalitarian and participatory structures as more rational forms of social organization for shelters for battered women (Rodriguez, 1988).

Although no single remedy for the impersonality of bureaucratic organization is generally accepted, flexible organizational styles and leadership patterns are constantly evolving. In situations of rapid social change, the emphasis on control within the traditional bureaucracy may be giving way to modifications that encourage creativity and less rigid structures (Rothschild and Russell, 1986).

SUMMARY

1. Social structure describes the patterns of social interaction, including systems, statuses, roles, interaction, and groups, through which behavior is carried out.

2. A status is a position in a social system, linked to other statuses by norms that provide rules and guidelines for behavior.

3. Role refers to a set of behaviors expected of a person in a given status.

4. Social systems represent specific arrangements of statuses and roles composed of interdependent parts.

5. From a functional perspective, social systems consist of elements with mutually dependent parts that remain stable over time.

6. From a conflict perspective, the most important aspect of social structure is the organization of a society's economic production.

7. Microsystems refer to face-to-face interaction, such as a specific family, while macrosystems refer to social systems at a higher level of abstraction, such as the American family system.

8. Statuses may be acquired at birth (ascribed) or gained through one's own efforts (achieved). Modern societies place more importance on achievement than on ascription.

9. Most of our daily activities are structured by the demands and possibilities of the roles we perform. The number of roles we perform may cause strain; the diverse expectations of role partners may lead to conflict.

10. Guidelines for role expectations lessen the anxiety of normlessness, or anomie, as people define their situations and develop appropriate rules of behavior.

11. Groups are collections of people tied together by a distinctive set of shared relationships. Groups may be primary or secondary.

12. Groups have characteristics of their own, including size, division of labor, and interaction involving elements of exchange, cooperation, competition, and conflict. In-group solidarity is often enhanced by directing hostility toward out-groups.

13. Emotions are interactive processes, governed by a set of rules and characterized by exchange processes.

14. Groups are also the building blocks of larger systems, termed *organizations*. The sum of the organizations in any one sector of society form institutions.

15. In modern societies, small groups are often overshadowed by formal organizations.

16. Positive aspects of bureaucracy include a division of labor that promotes efficiency and the discouragement of favoritism. Its negative features include buck passing, red tape, and needlessly complex regulations. The debate as to whether bureaucracy is a threat to democracy continues.

SUGGESTED READINGS

Bellah, Robert N., Richard Madsen, Anne Swidler, William Sullivan, and Steven Tipton. *Habits of the Heart: Individualism and Commitment in American Life.* Berkeley: University of California Press, 1985. An examination of individualism and commitment as well as the shift from "communities of memory" to more "transient life-style enclaves" focusing on self-interest.

Erikson, Kai. *Everything in Its Path: Destruction of Community in the Buffalo Creek Flood.* New York: Simon and Schuster, 1976. An account of what happened when the dam burst at Buffalo Creek.

Glassman, Ronald M., William H. Swatos, Jr., and Paul L. Rosen. *Bureaucracy against Democracy and Socialism.* Westport, CT: Greenwood Press, 1987. Fourteen essays presenting the problems faced by democracy and communism in relation to bureaucracy.

Hochschild, Arlie. *The Managed Heart: Commercialization of Human Feeling.* Berkeley: University of California Press, 1983. The management of emotions and of emotional labor in the workplace.

Kanter, Rosabeth Moss. *Men and Women of the Corporation.* New York: Basic Books, 1977. How the corporation's own structure, chain of command, and promotion system affect the behavior of employees.

Merton, Robert K. *Social Theory and Social Structure.* 2d ed., rev. and enl. New York: Free Press, 1968. Analysis of social structure in the field of sociology.

Rothschild, Joyce, and J. Allen Whitt. *The Cooperative Workplace: Potentials and Dilemmas of Organizational Democracy and Participation.* New York: Cambridge University Press, 1986. An important study of social change, based on extensive research in various worker cooperatives.

4

The Social Self

If human infants are born without any preprogrammed responses to the social world, without knowing a particular language or way of organizing mental images, how do they become functioning, say, Tasaday or Pintupi or Americans? If such abilities are automatic consequences of physical growth, then children could be raised by any creature who fed them, as by the wolves and apes of folklore. Even today the weekly tabloids at supermarket checkouts regularly proclaim the discovery of yet another *feral* (wild or untamed) child raised by animals. But in fact human infants cannot be guided to normal childhood by any but other human beings. Indeed, even infant monkeys require contact with mature monkeys in order to become effective adults capable of living in a group (Harlow and Harlow, 1977).

Human *physical* as well as social development does not unfold automatically. The newborn *(neonate)* becomes a human being through interaction with others who can teach the language and culture of the group into which she or he is born, who will encourage the infant to walk and talk, see that the child is fed and protected, and offer affection, support, and security. Furthermore, with each new situation and its role demands, the individual must be taught the appropriate behaviors. This learning process is called **socialization**—the transmission of culture by speech and gesture. At the same time, through the very same interactions, we learn about our "self" and develop a sense of who and what kind of person we are.

> **Socialization** is the lifelong process whereby one internalizes culture and develops a sense of self.

Socialization is a dual process: As we internalize the way of life of our society we also develop an identity. Both behavior and self are learned, and socialization provides the link between culture and social structure. Socialization is also *lifelong*—as long as there are new roles and conditions to which one must adapt, humans must depend on their ability to learn how to respond.

SOCIALIZATION

The Effects of Extreme Isolation

Most sociology textbooks begin the discussion of socialization by asking what would happen to an infant who was deprived of all contact with humans. Because such events are probably very rare, assessing the effects of extreme isolation is difficult. A second problem is that a lack of proper physical and mental development could be caused not by extreme isolation but by a birth defect that led the parents to reject the infant in the first place. The classic study, involving only two cases of extreme isolation, was published more than 50 years ago (Davis, 1940), and very few have been reported since.

A more recent example is Genie who was 13 when discovered in 1970. From the time she was 20 months old, she had been kept in a small room, spoken to by no one, and often severely beaten by her father (Curtiss, 1977; Pines, 1981). When found, she could neither talk nor walk; she was not toilet-trained and could not chew food, even though she had apparently been a normal baby at birth. Under the care of trained professionals, she was taught how to eat and walk and take care of herself. Slowly, also, she began to talk, but only one or two words at a time. Unlike other children, Genie never experienced the rapid development of language that follows the two-word stage, and her measured IQ remained below average. It seems that there is a

Socialization is the process by which we learn how to behave in society and to develop a sense of self. Physical contact and a nurturing environment between parents and their children provide a baseline of trust necessary for socialization.

critical period in childhood for developing the capacity for language. Without human contact at that point, a child may lose the opportunity to become fully human.

In adulthood, too, extreme isolation has severe consequences. Solitary confinement is a cruel and unusual punishment precisely because we need contact with others to maintain a sense of reality, including our own identity. People who are placed in solitary confinement lose their sense of time—that's why they are often portrayed as trying to keep track of days by marking scratches on the wall—and ultimately come to doubt every aspect of their lives. Among prisoners in Nazi concentration camps in the 1940s, for example, the most isolated men and women experienced the most extreme losses of self-awareness and mental stability (Rose, Glazer, and Glazer, 1979).

Reality is socially constructed, so without others to help us define reality we risk "losing our senses," which is the reason why social isolates are so vulnerable to mental problems. The human capacity for social life and our great need to be with other people are the basis of socialization and have roots in the evolutionary development of *Homo sapiens.*

The Evolutionary Bases

As we have discussed in Chapters 1 and 2, humans differ from other animals, including our primate relatives, in our reliance on learning rather than instinct. Not only *must* we learn, but, thanks to our reflexive mind and capacity for language, we *can* learn. The human infant is born at a less developed stage than any other animal young; it cannot take care of itself and remains helpless for several years. Hence, one crucial biological basis for socialization is the extraordinary vulnerability of the human neonate.

Physical Helplessness.   You may have observed newborn kittens or puppies that, within weeks, can get around on their own and even be parted from their mother. In contrast, those animals closest to us on the evolutionary scale, the great apes, have newborns in a manner similar to that of humans—typically one at a time, several years apart—that are relatively helpless and cling to the mother.

The human being is, at birth, a bundle of potentials, unguided by instinct, but capable of learning any language and culture, and totally dependent on its social environment. The infant's mind matures while he or she is being fed and cared for by others. The term *helpless* in this context refers only to physical dependency; the newborn's brain is actively recording sensations, processing information, and organizing experience.

Dependency.   This physical dependence on others is an essential precondition to learning. Because the brain and the nervous system are developed at the same time that an infant is being fed and cared for, a basic sensitivity to the expectations of others is built into our earliest experience. This dependence never leaves us, although the objects may shift—from parents to friends to lovers and even to one's own children.

Each society has evolved some relatively stable unit to care for helpless young, typically a group centered on the mother (this is also true of apes). Having carried the infant and given birth to it, the mother is the obvious person to care for it. Her movements are restricted by her weakened condition after childbirth and the need to breast-feed. Though there is no maternal (mothering) instinct, there are many reasons why women behave maternally: the sheer helplessness of the newborn being one, and the mother's own emotional and physical investment in the product of her body being another. But because of very high maternal death rates in most societies throughout history, there is an evolutionary advantage to the human infant's ability to relate to any adult nurturer, and to nonrelatives' willingness to care for other people's offspring.

The newborn becomes especially sensitive to cues from its care givers. Over time, the infant discovers that it, too, contributes to the interaction: a wail brings attention, a gurgle thrills an audience, and whining can bring harsh words. An *interdependence* develops between infants and care givers, although overwhelming power resides in the adults, who can provide or withhold what the infant needs for survival.

Emotional Needs.   Nurturance for physical survival is only one need of the infant. We propose that three other responses from others are essential for well-being across the life course: affection, approval, and some assurance that one is who one claims to be **(validation of self).** A similar set of needs was suggested by W. I. Thomas (1923) in terms of "four wishes"—for new experience, mastery, recognition, and security.

Validation of self requires assurance that one is who one claims to be.

In infancy, this need for others is physically based. In later years, the ties are almost purely emotional, built on the model of the earliest dependency. The cases of Genie and other isolated children are clear evidence of the need for human contact if one is to *become* a human being. Continued interaction is required if one is to *remain* a stable person and, often, to remain alive and healthy. For example, a longitudinal study of the residents of one county in California showed that people without social and community ties were more likely to die in the nine-year follow-up period than were those with many links to other people (Berkman, 1985).

Individual Differences.   Although all newborns have undeveloped potential, they are not, of course, identical. Some will learn faster than others, will be musical, will be tall or short, will be calm or fidgety, and so on through a lengthy list of traits that have some *genetic component.* But genetic tendencies do not automatically produce behavior—they only increase the likelihood that one response will occur rather than another. Tendencies develop within social structures and can be stifled or encouraged.

Even people born with a great talent—for music, or mathematics, or a sport—need support and encouragement to realize their potential. The environment of the home and the availability of trained instructors are crucial factors for becoming exceptionally skilled. Because almost everyone has a special talent, we have to look to these social factors to explain why some young people develop the desire to excel and why others do not.

THE SOCIALIZATION PROCESS

Every newborn can learn any culture, speak any language, and organize experience in different ways as it matures. A function of primary (early) socialization is to present a single world of meaning as the only possible way to organize perceptions (Berger and Luckmann, 1966). At the microlevel, this information is given through direct training for social roles.

Learning One's Place

When people occupy a particular status, they must learn the appropriate role behavior. Role learning involves several elements: information, opportunities to rehearse, feedback from role partners, and social supports.

Information.   At some point the learner must be given guidance for adequate role performance. The military recruit receives detailed descriptions from a drill instructor; mothers-to-be can attend child care classes; children are prepared in advance for kindergarten.

Rehearsal.   Knowing what to do is one thing; doing it is something else. Most performances benefit from practice. Opportunities for trial-and-error learning under relatively safe conditions are usually given to people just entering a role—for example, the "honeymoon" period for newlyweds, political newcomers, and first-year college students. When the honeymoon ends, the role incumbents are expected to fulfill the obligations of the new status in maintaining the social system as a whole.

Another form of rehearsal is called **anticipatory socialization,** which is practice in advance of assuming a role. Thus, children play sex-typed roles, high school seniors begin to act like college students, employees expecting a promotion dress more carefully, and older adults take up the hobbies they intend to pursue in retirement. Somewhat related to anticipatory socialization

Anticipatory socialization involves rehearsing prior to assuming a role.

Success in mastering a role depends on the social support of people who are willing to train the learner. In the case of teaching swimming to young children, patience helps a lot.

Modeling is the copying of characters of admired people.

is the behavior called **modeling,** or copying the characteristics of admired people. Parents, movie stars, and sports figures are common role models for children.

Feedback.   Role performances take place before an audience of role partners who transmit messages regarding the performance. **Positive sanctions** are those reactions indicating that the role is well played. **Negative sanctions** involve open criticism or at least the withholding of approval. Depending on the importance of the sanctioner, people will modify their behavior in order to receive positive feedback.

Positive sanctions indicate approval of role performance.

Negative sanctions convey disapproval of role performance.

Social Supports.   Success in a role often depends on the help of people who are willing to train the learner and to tolerate role rehearsals. A growing body of research has documented the crucial importance of supportive social networks throughout life, but especially in old age (e.g., House, 1987; Litwak and Messeri, 1989). People who have many friends tend to cope with role changes such as retirement and widowhood more successfully than do those who are isolated.

Subcultural Differences

In the United States, many important subcultural differences are apparent in both the content and style of childhood socialization. To the extent that ascribed statuses such as race, religion, and ethnicity are associated with certain marriage or employment patterns, parents will raise their children to meet these expectations. Achieved statuses such as parental income and education are also powerful indicators of socialization goals and techniques. But of all subcultural differences the most crucial appears to be *parental occupation.*

Parental Occupation.   Although it is linked to income, education, race, religion, and ethnicity, parental occupation exerts a strong and independent effect on the socialization experience, as is shown in the work of Melvin Kohn and his associates over two decades, in the United States and elsewhere (e.g., Kohn et al., 1990).

The major occupational distinction is between those jobs that involve dealing with (a) people and/or ideas, or with (b) machines and other inanimate objects. The first type of work is associated with "white-collar" occupations, where solving problems and manipulating symbols are the key to success. These tasks tend to be nonrepetitive and loosely supervised, allowing room for *autonomy* (self-direction). In contrast, most "blue-collar" jobs require being on time, following instructions, heavy supervision, and little if any leeway for creativity. As a consequence, white-collar parents encourage their children to be intellectually curious, flexible, and self-controlled, even when this challenges parental authority. Blue-collar parents, however, place a high value on displays of respect for authority and on obedience, punctuality, conformity, and technical skills.

In this way, social-structural variables (the nature of one's work) affect parental values, which, in turn, influence socialization practices and, ultimately, personality traits of the child. For example, in both Poland and the United States, fathers whose occupations call for self-direction place a high value on personal responsibility in their offspring, whereas men whose work is heavily supervised tend to value conformity in their children (Slomczynski et al., 1981). Similar findings have been reported for women located in different sectors of the labor force (Spade, 1983).

These differences are also reflected in disciplining techniques. Parents in highly supervised work tend toward physical punishment of children, whereas those in self-directed work favor a more psychological approach, especially the threat of the withdrawal of affection. As described in Table 4-1, the two patterns have been labeled *traditional* and *modern*.

The distinction between traditional and modern can be illustrated by the parents' reactions to a child who has broken a neighbor's window. "Traditional" parents are likely to spank the child for destroying property and to worry about the expense of replacing the window. The "modern" parent tends to focus on the child's state of mind, with the goal of teaching the child self-control rather than fear of being caught and punished.

Spoil the Rod and Spare the Child?

SOCIAL POLICY ISSUE

The issue of *corporal* (bodily) *punishment* in our schools reflects conflicting strands in American culture. On the one hand, there is a tradition of concern for the welfare of children, which has surfaced at various historical moments: in colonial Massachusetts in the 1660s, in the child reform movement of the 1880s, and today with regard to child abuse in the family (E. Pleck, 1987; Gordon, 1988). On the other hand, legislation to protect children from their care givers conflicts with other important values such as the privacy of the family from government intervention and the right of parents to discipline their children.

American parents, however, appear to be relatively tolerant of strict discipline outside the home, even to the point of allowing corporal punish-

TABLE 4-1   Two Patterns of Child Rearing

"Traditional" or Status-Centered	"Modern" or Person-Centered
1. Each member's place in the family is a function of age and sex status.	Emphasis is on selfhood and individuality of each member.
2. Father is defined as boss and more important as agent of discipline: he receives "respect" and deference from mother and children.	Father more affectionate, less authoritative; mother becomes more important as agent of discipline.
3. Emphasis on overt acts—*what* child does rather than *why*.	Emphasis on motives and feelings—*why* child does what he or she does.
4. Valued qualities in child: obedience, cleanliness.	Valued qualities in child are happiness, achievement, consideration, curiosity, self-control.
5. Emphasis on "direct" discipline: physical punishment, scolding, threats.	Discipline based on reasoning, isolation, guilt, threat of loss of love.
6. Social consensus and solidarity in communication; emphasis on "we."	Communication used to express individual experience and perspectives; emphasis on "I."
7. Emphasis on communication from parent to child.	Emphasis on two-way communication between parent and child; parent open to persuasion.
8. Parent feels little need to justify demands to child; commands are to be followed "because I say so."	Parent gives reasons for demands—e.g., not "Shut up" but "Please keep quiet or go into the other room; I'm trying to talk on the telephone."
9. Emphasis on conforming to rules, respecting authority, maintaining conventional social order.	Emphasis on reasons for rules; particular rules can be criticized in the name of higher rational or ethical principles.
10. Child may attain a strong sense of social identity at the cost of individuality, poor academic performance.	Child may attain strong sense of selfhood but may have identity problems, guilt, alienation.

Source: Skolnick, 1987, p. 387.

ment in the schools. The United States is one of only five modern societies that still permits school personnel to hit students, and only nine states have specifically forbidden the practice (Miller, 1987). Spanking and paddling are common in the southern United States, and verbal abuse of school children is found throughout the country (Hentoff, 1988).

Experimental studies by psychologists suggest that physical punishments can influence behavior only under limited conditions: when administered predictably and immediately, and in proportion to the offense (Penner, 1986, pp. 205–206). For long-lasting behavior change the most powerful techniques are not punishments but the selective giving or withholding of rewards including affection and approval (Bee, 1989).

Furthermore, physical disciplining has several negative consequences. When it is applied inconsistently, the message is lost; when it is applied harshly, respect for authority is eroded. Above all, corporal punishment is counterproductive in the control of aggression because the hitter is showing that aggression pays off. It is very difficult to ask children to control themselves when you have just lost your temper. Parents who wish to raise children who are guided by internalized norms rather than fear of external authorities might want to question school policy as well as their own responses. You might want to examine the psychological literature for information on effective *nonphysical* disciplining techniques in preparation for your own experience in parenting. What characteristics do you wish to encourage and how can these traits be instilled through primary socialization? (See pages 61–63.) ■

Historical Change.   Have parental values changed over the past few decades? There is scattered evidence that differences in socialization patterns on the basis of parents' job characteristics have narrowed. The overall trend is toward encouraging independence rather than conformity in one's children, with the shift toward valuing autonomy strongest among Catholic parents, reflecting long-term changes in the cultural context of Catholic family life in America (Alwin, 1984).

Agents of Socialization

If culture is learned, there must be regular channels of transmission. The people and organizations charged with the task of teaching rules and roles are called **agents of socialization.** Chief among these are parents, peers, teachers, and the media.

Agents of socialization are people and organizations responsible for teaching rules and roles.

Parents.   The first and most important agents of socialization are the people who care for infants—usually the biological parents. In the earliest months and years, information from these nurturers, conveyed by both words and

Agents of socialization help new generations learn various aspects of culture. In some cases, learning can be fun. Who are the important agents of socialization in your life?

gestures, make up the child's basic understanding of the world. The child learns the culture as it is interpreted by the socializers. And the desire for continued contact with care givers, combined with a fear of losing their affection and approval, motivates the infant to become particularly sensitive to their wishes.

Many of these cues are *nonverbal,* expressed in how one is touched or spoken to, played with or held. These impressions are crucial for establishing trust between the child and its socializers. The *quality* of these early interactions is as important as the quantity and content. Especially important is the ability to *empathize,* to put yourself in the place of the other. Empathetic parents and care givers teach the child to imagine the feelings of others.

Parents have great potential power. The culture is *internalized* (brought into the mind of the child) through parental expectations. These early learnings are the foundation of later development, and the guilt caused by failure to live up to parental expectations of success is an important motivator of performance throughout adulthood.

In a simple society, parents can probably teach the growing child everything necessary to function as an adult. But in rapidly changing, complex societies, where knowledge becomes quickly obsolete, other agents of socialization become important: friends, teachers, and the mass media. Although parental controls are weakened in complex societies, many attitudes are transmitted from one generation to another. Such similarity may be the result of direct parental socialization or the product of **reciprocal socialization,** whereby children modify their parents' view of the world. Some continuity is also the result of similar occupational statuses (Glass et al., 1986).

Peers.   Another powerful source of information and socialization is the friendship group of **peers.** Whereas parents are the child's superiors, peers are equals; and whereas the greater power of parents makes some kinds of learning difficult, one can deal with one's peers on a level of equality—tease, insult, rehearse roles, tolerate mistakes, and so on.

Children need friends in order to learn how to take turns, share, fight fairly, deal with adults, and prepare for the next stage of growth. At school the peer group provides vast stores of important knowledge about how to handle authority, manipulate the system, act in and out of school, and approach members of the opposite sex. Even in adulthood, peer groups are important agents of socialization—to marriage, parenthood, retirement, and widowhood. But the adolescent peer group has received the most popular and scientific attention.

Adolescent Peer Group.   For several decades, American parents and other adults have looked with amazement and anxiety at the friendship groups of young people between ages 13 and 18. Parents fear the power of the group as a challenge to family values and as a rival for the teenager's loyalty.

Yet the adolescent peer group is necessary for young people in their journey from dependence to independence, from childhood to adulthood. The peer group helps adolescents to prepare for adult roles by tolerating one another's attempts to construct an identity. In a society where people achieve adult statuses primarily by choice or merit, the young person needs the peer group in order to learn how to meet objective ("universalistic") standards of

Through **reciprocal socialization** children modify their parents' view of the world.

Peers are equals and an important source of information and socialization.

performance, in contrast to the ascribed, unequal, and individualized ("particularistic") criteria of the family. (See Figure 4-1.)

The process whereby the peer group operates as an agent of socialization parallels that described for infant socialization. Peers to some extent replace parents as sources of affection, approval, and validation, and friends are emotionally bound to one another through fear of rejection. But adolescents still need parental support. Parents remain important socializers to basic values and long-term goals (e.g., finances, education, and career), whereas peers have the most influence on immediate life-style choices, such as appearance, sexual behavior, and leisure activities (Sebald, 1986). Because the major task of adolescence in modern society is precisely to outgrow dependence on one's parents, the strength of the adolescent peer group simply reflects the difficulty of achieving independence.

FIGURE 4-1 The adolescent peer group is a medium for the transition from childhood to adult statuses.

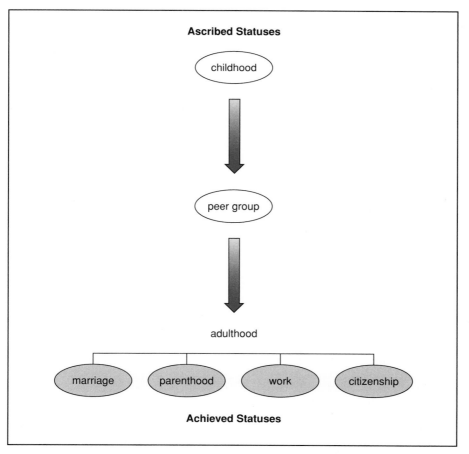

Teachers.   Much formal socialization today is in the hands of professionals. Teachers, from nursery school on, receive pay for being agents of socialization. Ideally, a teacher has both special knowledge and the skills needed to transmit it. Teachers are also role models for responsible adulthood and for the importance of education. Some may even convey the excitement of learning itself.

Mentors are teachers who act as guides and sponsors.

In high school and college, many young people form especially close relationships with particular instructors, who become their **mentors** (guides and sponsors). By devoting time and energy to one's students rather than to one's own career advancement, mentors can influence career decisions and open the door to advanced training. Without such a sponsor, many students fail to achieve their full potential.

The Media.   The mass media—print and electronic—produce information as well as entertainment. Many people learn about politics, form a vision of

WHO'S THAT WOMAN IN THE APRON?

In a content analysis of prize-winning picture books for preschool children in the 1960s, researchers (Weitzman et al., 1972) found that stories about boys far outnumbered those about girls and that boys were portrayed as larger, smarter, and more active than girls. Adult men were also pictured as competent and engaged in important business, whereas the women remained in the background, dependent and nurturant reactors to the adventures of boys and men. Furthermore, the imbalance between male and female characters was even greater when animals rather than humans were portrayed.

More recently, researchers (Grauerholz and Pescosolido, 1989) have examined children's literature from 1900 to 1984. Overall, for the entire period, male characters outnumber female ones by almost 3 to 1, especially among animals, where the ratio is 6 to 1. Among adults, men were four times as likely as women to be central characters. And while the ratio of male to female children fluctuated over the 84 years, the proportion of male adults and animals increased steadily, even while the number of women authors of children's literature also increased.

Contrary to expectations, the researchers did not find that the portrayal of girls and women as central actors increased during the 1940s, when women were engaged in nontraditional employment during World War II. Rather, the numbers of girls and boys in book titles and as main characters appeared closer to equal at the beginning of the century and again in the late 1970s and early 1980s. In the 1900 to 1920 period, this was because children were most often shown in large groups, so that some girls were included. With the emphasis on individualism and heroism of the decades between 1920 and 1970, boys and men became central figures in all forms of American literature, including books for young people. The increase in representations today of girls as active and adventuresome reflects a growing awareness of broad-based social change in gender expectations. But when adults and animals are involved, the roles remain as traditional as ever.

Sources: Weitzman et al., 1972, pp. 1125–50; Grauerholz and Pescosolido, 1989, pp. 113–25.

the good life, and develop attitudes toward others from their exposure to newspapers, radio, television, magazines, and books.

FORMATION OF THE SELF

Transmission of culture is only one aspect of socialization. While people process information about their culture and role expectations, they also learn about their *self.* **Self-identity** is an organization of perceptions about who and what kind of person one is. Humans are not born with such knowledge. It is learned and developed gradually through precisely the same socialization experiences by which the culture is internalized.

Self-identity is an organization of perceptions about who and what kind of person one is.

Self-concept as a central component of personality has, for the most part, been studied from the interpretive perspective. For it is through language, the symbol system of culture, and in the intimacy of face-to-face interaction, that messages about the self are conveyed. How the individual interprets and evaluates this information is central to the social construction of identity.

James, Cooley, and the Social Self

Only gradually does the infant come to distinguish itself from its nurturer. It is, of course, impossible to question a newborn (or even a young child) about its feelings and perceptions. Social scientists can only imagine how it must feel to be an infant. Without more certain knowledge, they have devised this scenario:

It appears that the newborn is totally absorbed in the nurturer-infant system. But the human mind is reflexive, and at some point the infant begins to perceive itself in contrast to the overwhelming other. As the care giver coos and murmurs, addressing a "you," the infant dimly begins to differentiate (separate) itself, to see itself as being that "you." This is what is meant when the sociologist speaks of the human mind as able to see itself as an object; the infant can reflect on the "you," that is itself, an "I."

The Social Self.   The concept of a *social self* was introduced by the psychologist William James (1842–1910), who stated that a person has as many social selves as there are others who recognize that person and carry an image of him or her in their minds. The self, therefore, is rooted in social interaction. People are linked to society through their very self-concept: I am the one who acts and believes and feels in a manner guided by the norms of my society.

The Looking-Glass Self.   Building on James's concept of the social self, Charles Horton Cooley (1864–1929) proposed that the self is composed of a basic self-feeling that is then shaped and given specific content through interactions with important others.

Cooley is best known today for his image of the **looking-glass self.** Just as a mirror reflects a reverse image, one's perception of oneself is never direct. Rather, we see ourselves reflected back in the reactions of others. According to Cooley, our ideas of our self come from (1) our imagining how we appear

The **looking-glass self** suggests that we see ourselves reflected back in the reactions of others.

to other people, (2) how we think they judge our appearance, and (3) how we feel about all this. Our sense of self is more like a process than a fixed object; it is always developing as we interact with others, whose opinions of us are ever-shifting. For example, a child who hears only positive feedback from parents may be confused later when a teacher's reactions indicate unsatisfactory performance. We can see, then, that the primary group would be the crucial location for both socialization and personality development.

But not all reflected images influence the self-process. A person actively manipulates the reactions of others, selects which cues to follow, and judges the relative importance of role partners. In general, we tend to accept impressions that reinforce a basic identity and to resist those that do not.

George Herbert Mead and the Self Process

George Herbert Mead's (1863–1931) view of human society was based on the ability of human beings to use symbols to communicate, to create rules, and to adjust their behavior to the expectations of others. A person can do all these things by developing a "self" that can reflect on its own behavior through interaction with others. Society is the constantly changing sum of all these ongoing activities. Society is also in our minds, through internalized rules, roles, and relationships.

Taking the Role of the Other.   If, as Cooley proposed, we learn about ourselves by imagining how we appear to other people, then the reflexive mind not only sees itself as an object but can see into the minds of others. For Mead, this imaginative leap is central to the development of self-concept.

Mead, following Cooley, noted that our first socialization experiences take place within a primary group, where we learn the shared meanings of our culture. We are able to guess what others are thinking precisely because we have a common language and standards for role performance. The child learns by precept (being told how to behave) and practice (trial and error and then feedback). This learning takes place through language, both verbal and nonverbal. Mead used the word **gesture** for a symbol that is shared by group members and thus made part of a role performance.

A **gesture** is a symbol whose meaning is shared by group members.

Significant Other.   Particularly important to the formation of self are those specific people whose approval and affection are especially desired. Parents at first, then peers, role models, and lovers, can all become **significant others,** with special power to shape one's perceptions. Even children can become significant others, as only they can validate an adult's identity as a "good parent."

Significant others are people whose affection and approval are particularly desired.

Generalized Other.   As we learn to take the role of the other, not only do we assume the viewpoint of significant others, but we also internalize the cultural norms for anyone in a given status. Mead's **generalized other** refers to these expectations of the society at large. The individual learns both *particular standards* of acceptable behavior (from significant others) and the *universal norms* that apply to the role (from the generalized other).

The **generalized other** reflects societal standards of acceptable behavior in the role.

Because of the human need for approval and affection, our significant others have a very strong influence on our attitudes, perceptions, and behavior.

Stages of Role Taking.   Learning to take roles, according to Mead, develops by stages. At first, the child *imitates* others in its immediate environment, primarily family members. This type of activity is relatively disorganized and spontaneous, but it allows the child (up to age three) to differentiate itself from others by becoming another person for a moment or two. Even an imaginary playmate extends the child's role-taking experience.

According to Mead's developmental theory, at ages three and four the child expands its repertory to playact such roles as doctor, letter carrier, fire fighter, in addition to family-based roles. This **play** is actually very serious because the child is learning to take the role of the other in a variety of situations.

> **Play** expands a child's ability to take the role of another.

When children enter school and the society of age peers, they are exposed to even higher levels of generalization. At these ages, organized **games,** with their rules, structure, and specialized role partners, become the means by which one learns increasingly complex forms of role taking. The ability to internalize an entire web of role behaviors is carried into adulthood.

> **Games** are characterized by rules and structure.

The Emergence of Self.   Learning to take the role of the other is only one part of the *process of self.* If internalization were all that was necessary for the formation of the self-concept, individual behavior would exhibit little novelty or spontaneity. But the self is dynamic, always in the process of formation, ever capable of change. Mead distinguished between two aspects of self: the **"I"** and the **"me."** The "I" is the more spontaneous and creative element, reflecting on and responding to the "me," which is the socialized self composed of the internalized attitudes of others. This dialogue produces an *organization of perceptions* that forms the self-concept and guides behavior at any one time.

> The **"I"** is the creative spontaneous part of the self, whereas the **"me"** consists of the internalized attitude of others.

For example, you are constantly engaged in conversations with yourself in which part of your self is longing to be free of reading assignments and homework, whereas the other part is reminding you of the expectations of your teacher and the college. Sometimes the "I" will win out, and you will put the books aside in favor of a night out with your friends, and at other times the "me" will triumph because you do have long-range goals that require passing exams and earning a diploma. But Mead saw no necessary conflict between the "I" and the "me," as both are needed to form the social self.

Goffman and the Presentation of Self

Many sociologists view the self as a reflection of the cluster of roles being performed by people at any point in the life course. For Erving Goffman (1922–1983), identity is actually a series of *self-presentations,* that is, the impressions that we present to others. The self, then, always risks being rejected, and every encounter becomes a minidrama in which we "manage" the impression we give so that others will accept who we claim to be. We construct a presenting self as the "real me" in order to influence the reactions of role partners and to control the situation.

A **virtual self** awaits us in each role we perform.

In this view, a self exists for every situation. Goffman wrote of a **virtual self** (or possible self) that awaits us in every role—what society expects of a person in that role. Whatever our innate tendencies and abilities, each role offers an opportunity to become a particular type of person. But some possible selves are not very appealing to our self-image. For example, many homemakers reject the identity offered by that role, and students who have part-time employment at fast-food counters will resist being thought of as "hamburger helpers." Therefore, there may be a gap between self-image and the virtual self-in-the-role.

Role distance is the space placed between the self and the self-in-the-role.

Role Distance.   Goffman used the term **role distance** to describe the space that a person can place between the self and the self-in-the-role. People use several distancing techniques to warn others not to take them as the virtual self implied in the role. For example, students who have temporary jobs—busboy, waitress, cashier, stock clerk—probably let others know that they are on their way to better things. Role distance protects the self and offers some freedom for the expression of personal style. Other situations, however, offer little choice but to become the self-in-the-role.

The Mind as Jailor.   In a well-publicized experiment, Philip Zimbardo and his colleagues (1973) found that the line between the self and the self-in-the-role can be erased under some circumstances. After answering an ad in local and campus newspapers to participate, for $15 per day for two weeks, in "a study of prison life," 21 average, middle-class, college-age men, carefully screened for physical health, emotional maturity, and respect for the law, were accepted. The experimenters randomly assigned the subjects to the status of either prisoner or guard in a "mock prison."

Deindividualization is the process of removing a person's civilian identities.

Every step was taken to make the prison as realistic as possible. Both prisoners and guards were **deindividualized,** or "depersonalized," through the typical prison processes of removing their civilian identities. The prisoners wore uniforms and had to ask the guards for permission for most normal activities. The guards also had their uniforms: khaki, with nightsticks, hand-cuffs, whistles, and reflector sunglasses.

Neither group was given much formal instruction in how to play its role, yet within days each person had *disappeared into the appropriate role.* The guards quickly learned to enjoy unchecked power, and the prisoners began to act in ways that encouraged the guards' dehumanizing treatment. The researchers were amazed at the speed and ease with which the assigned roles and the definition of the situation controlled behavior.

One prisoner was released after a day and a half due to extreme depression. On each of the next three days, another prisoner developed similar symptoms and was released. A fifth man broke out in a psychosomatic rash. By the end of six days, the entire experiment was called off, so transformed had these "normal, healthy, educated young men" become. What caused the transformation? The experimenter concluded:

> the subjects' abnormal social and personal reactions are best seen as a product of their transaction with an environment that supported the behavior that would be pathological in other settings, but was "appropriate" in this prison. Had we observed comparable reactions in a real prison, the psychiatrist undoubtedly would have been able to attribute any prisoner's behavior to character defects or personality maladjustment, while critics of the prison system would have been quick to label the guards as "psychopathic." This tendency to locate the source of behavior disorders inside a particular person or group underestimates the power of situational forces. (Zimbardo et al., 1973, p. 41; see also Zimbardo, Ebbesen, and Maslach, 1977)

OTHER VIEWS OF HUMAN DEVELOPMENT

Guided by Mead's model, more recent scholars have expanded our understanding of how social environments affect people's self-image. It is also possible that people at different ages organize self-concept differently. Not only is the self-concept an intricate system of abilities, tendencies, and identities formed and reformed over the life course, but it is also an active agent in selecting, interpreting, and shaping its own environment (Rosenberg and Kaplan, 1982).

The concept of the social self has been criticized for being too narrowly focused on role and interaction. In a classic essay, Dennis Wrong (1961) criticized what he called the "oversocialized" view of self, or personality, which overlooks the biological and emotional components of behavior. The purely sociological model cannot easily account for impulsive acts or the range of individual differences within groups of people who have been socialized similarly.

Other critics object to the extreme emphasis on flexibility and change, arguing that some aspects of self are relatively stable across the life course. Indeed, recent research indicates that some personality traits do not change greatly with age: friendliness, anxiety level, and openness to new experience (Costa et al., 1987). In contrast, feelings of satisfaction and well-being and of connectedness to others show little stability across time and are strongly influenced by experiences.

Until the development of the field of the sociology of emotions (see Chapter 3), the two major aspects of personality development that had not been integrated into sociological models were the **affective** (having to do with feelings) and the **cognitive** (having to do with how people think and process information). The study of these factors has been left largely to psychologists and social psychologists. Many of these ideas have influenced sociological research and theory.

Affective factors refer to feelings and emotions.

Cognitive factors refer to how people think and process information.

Sigmund Freud and the Control of Impulse

The Austrian physician Sigmund Freud (1856–1939) is best known as the founder of psychoanalysis, which involves both the study of the unconscious motivations and the treatment of symptoms of emotional distress. Although many of his concepts reflect the culture of educated European society of the late nineteenth century, several of Freud's insights remain enduring contributions to sociology. Most important are the conflict between the individual and society, the construction of self as a social/psychological process, and the role of ego defenses.

The Conflict between Self and Society.   In the essay *Civilization and Its Discontents* (1930/1962), Freud explores, from a psychological perspective, much the same assumption that underlies sociology in general: that social life is impossible unless and until human beings can control their behavior. Culture, remember, consists of norms that govern conduct, but human beings are also biological organisms with drives and desires. Therefore, a dynamic tension exists between the individual and the need for social order: the individual strives to satisfy basic urges, but cannot survive without the support of others; yet the social order depends on members of a collectivity being able to forgo instant gratification. Society—or, as Freud called it, civilization—is based on the control of impulse. Socialization is the process of renouncing (giving up) instant pleasure.

Stages of Development.   According to the Freudian model, these renunciations of instant pleasure take place in a series of emotionally stressful episodes in infancy and childhood. First, we must give up the all-embracing comfort of being fed and cuddled as we are weaned from the breast or bottle. As infants, we can do little except cry a lot, repress anger in the unconscious part of the mind, and learn that rules are made by others, and life will be full of hard knocks.

Then we must learn to control our bladder and intestines—to become toilet trained—with all the anger brought on by this loss of freedom. As children, we now confront a powerful social system "out there," eventually give up the struggle for control of our body, and deposit another residue of anger into the unconscious. Finally, still in childhood, we must deal with strong and disturbing sexual feelings of either attraction or dislike, originally directed toward our parents. The resolution of this crisis involves renunciation of sexual gratification within the family, the **repression** of unacceptable impulses (placing them below the level of consciousness), and a redirection of sexual feelings toward members of the opposite sex who are not relatives.

Repression involves the placing of unacceptable impulses below the level of consciousness.

Notice that while Freud emphasizes processes within the child's mind (*psyche*), these events take place in a social context, in interactions with adults who represent the wider society. Social/psychological development does not unfold automatically. The powerful bonds that link the child to its nurturers are used to manipulate guilt feelings, so that fear of losing affection and approval motivate the child, and then the adult, to conform to the expectations of significant others.

But unlike the individual in Cooley's and Mead's theories of the social self, Freud's child does not necessarily achieve harmony within the group. Those repressed feelings can bubble up from the unconscious at any time, causing the mental disturbances that require the services of the psychoanalyst. The fear of losing control leads us to develop protective mechanisms called **ego defenses.**

The Role of Ego Defenses.   The Freudian psyche has three aspects: (1) The *id,* consisting of impulsive desires; (2) the *superego,* consisting of internalized norms, often called the conscience; and (3) the *ego,* which links the self to the real world, mediating the drives of the id and the control of the superego.

Ego defenses are techniques for dealing with impulses that are unacceptable to the self and that could endanger social solidarity. Defenses include denial, repression, blame, displacement of anger onto socially acceptable objects, and rationalization (finding acceptable reasons for thinking or doing the unacceptable). Ego defenses protect us against our worst impulses. Furthermore, such defenses are essentially social because they are used to sustain relationships. Because we must depend on one another, loss of self-control would have collective as well as personal consequences (Swanson, 1988). And because the Freudian self is always somewhat discontent, unable completely to satisfy the body's desires, the ego must constantly be protected from challenges to one's image of what it is to be a good person.

> Ego defenses protect the self-image.

Erikson and Ego Development

In the decades since Freud's death, the idea of *psychosocial development* has been taken up by scholars who depart from Freud in two major respects. First, Freud's emphasis on the childhood years has proved too limiting; personal growth takes place throughout life. Second, the Freudian emphasis on instinctual desires has also been questioned. The newer theories are more concerned with the ego as an organized set of self-perceptions. The most influential of these post-Freudian theories of life stages and **ego development** is that of Erik Erikson.

> Ego development involves the possibility of change and growth across the life course.

Erikson extended the stages of personality growth and change to cover the entire life course, a series of challenges that require reorganization of the ego. Erikson (1964) described the following eight stages:

- *Stage 1.* From experiences with nurturers, the infant develops a sense either of *basic trust* or of *mistrust.*
- *Stage 2.* In the first three years of life, the child learns and practices all

kinds of new skills, emerging with a feeling either of *autonomy* (self-regulation) or of *doubt* and *shame* over its abilities to cope with events.

- *Stage 3.* The four- to five-year-old's success in exploring the environment and in dealing with peers can lead to a sense of *initiative* and self-confidence; failure can produce feelings of *guilt.*
- *Stage 4.* Between the ages of six and thirteen, the focus shifts from family to school, where the child can develop the self-concept either of *industriousness* or of *inferiority.*
- *Stage 5.* In adolescence, the developmental task is *identity formation,* and failure to create a firm sense of self leads to *confusion* about one's identity.
- *Stage 6.* The great challenge of young adulthood is to establish stable love relationships, and the outcome is *intimacy* or *isolation* and loneliness.
- *Stage 7.* Citizenship, work, and family formation are the primary tasks of mature adulthood, and they lead to *generativity,* in contrast to the *self-absorption* and *stagnation* of those who do not contribute to the well-being of others.
- *Stage 8.* Even the end of life poses a developmental challenge: finding continuity and meaning in one's life—*integrity*—or being unable to break out of isolation and self-absorption, giving way to *despair.*

Erikson's eight stages are best understood as descriptions of the characteristics of the very best or the very worst outcomes. Few people go through these precise experiences at just the right ages. Most of us meet life's expected and unexpected challenges with varying degrees of success and failure.

Although Erikson's model is presented as basically psychological, note

Older adults do not have to lead lives of isolation and despair. A strong sense of self, built in part on sharing with one's peers, produces an integrity that can carry through the full course of a lifetime.

that his transition points coincide with major changes in the person's *social* environment and the sequence of status changes, for example, from infant to child, from child in the family to student, from student to worker, from nonmarried to married, from nonparent to parent, and from fully involved in family and community to retirement.

Central to Erikson's model is the concept of **ego identity,** a sense of continuity and sameness in the self across time and in different situations. Symbolic interactionists have long been fascinated by the question of how, if identities are socially constructed, people are able to maintain an image of continuity of the self when roles are constantly changing. Working in the area of overlap between sociology (collective realities) and psychology (internal meanings), a growing number of social psychologists are mapping out the ways in which the self is both product and producer of group processes (Weigert et al., 1986). For example, how can people accept the reality of being divorced (acknowledgment of failure) while maintaining a positive image in their own eyes and those of friends? Most divorced people construct a "story"—an ego defense—that places blame on the former partner and justifies their own behavior, and also protects against full recognition of the disapproval of friends or relatives (Gerstel, 1988).

Ego identity refers to a sense of continuity and sameness in the self-concept across time and situations.

Piaget and Cognitive Development

The concept of **cognitive development** refers to changes over time in how we think as both mind and body mature. The major figure in this field was Jean Piaget (1896–1980), a Swiss psychologist, who based his theories on observations of children at play and their answers to his questions. From his effort to see the world from their point of view, Piaget concluded that children of different ages had very different understandings of what they were doing.

Cognitive development refers to changes over time in how we think.

Not only were there age-related shifts in the complexity of thinking, but Piaget also found changes in **moral reasoning,** that is, the way in which children evaluated situations. As the mind is able to deal with increasingly complicated information, so also does the child learn to handle such abstractions as ideas of fairness and justice. In the games of marbles that Piaget observed over and over, very young children accepted the rules absolutely. Slightly older children were more flexible, modifying the rules to meet unexpected situations. At a more advanced age, youngsters realized that the rules existed only because the players agreed to them, and that the rules could be changed radically and entire new games invented. Notice how these observations tie into Mead's ideas about the importance of games, as well as support the basic sociological point that *rules and roles are socially constructed.*

Moral reasoning involves the application of standards of fairness and justice.

Although Piaget saw cognitive development as age related, he did not claim that the process was automatic; a child's thinking becomes more complex only when confronted with real-life experiences that encourage such thought. You probably know adults whose rigid thinking resembles that of a Piagetian three-year-old. And as the cases of isolated children mentioned at the start of this chapter remind us, environmental stimulation, trial-and-error attempts to master the task of daily living, and supportive feedback from others are all essential to cognitive growth.

LEARNING FROM CHILDREN

Barrie Thorne

Barrie Thorne is Streisand Professor with a joint appointment in the Program in the Study of Women and Men in Society and in the Sociology Department at the University of Southern California. She coedited Language, Gender, and Society *(with Cheris Kramarae and Nancy Henley) and* Rethinking the Family: Some Feminist Questions *(with Marilyn Yalom). She is now writing a book on children's gender arrangements in elementary schools.*

Our research topics sometimes seem to choose us as much as we choose them; there is rich and complicated interplay between living one's life and doing sociology. My first large research project—a participant-observation study of the draft resistance movement of the late 1960s—grew out of my opposition to the Vietnam War and my interest in learning about, and making, political change. I was a draft counselor and helped organize antiwar demonstrations, combining the involved consciousness of a political activist with the more detached outlook of a sociological observer—an uneasy, but provocative mix.

Participating in the radical movements of the late 1960s put me at the origins of the contemporary women's movement. I joined an early consciousness-raising group and became a feminist, a transformation of self and social context that, in turn, shaped the questions I asked as a sociologist. In the early 1970s feminists in many academic fields began to ask "Where are the women?" That relatively simple question led us to see gaps and distortions in traditional knowledge. For example, at that time, sociologists rarely studied housework, the wage gap between men and women workers, or relations of mothers and daughters; and their views of rape echoed the victim-blaming of the surrounding society. Feminists created a new specialty, the sociology of sex and gender, and we showed that attention to gender may alter basic ways of thinking about core sociological topics such as inequality, work, social organization, and families.

I had taken a Ph.D. comprehensive exam in sociolinguistics in 1967, but it was not until the women's movement alerted me to issues of gender that I noticed the absence of research on women's patterns of talk and communication. In the early 1970s I worked with feminist colleagues to create a new cross-disciplinary area of research: the study of gender and verbal and nonverbal communication.

In my research on communication patterns I was especially interested in studies that found differences in the ways men talk with men, and women with women (several studies, for example, found that women used more mutual head-nodding and "mm hm"'s to indicate that they were listening). I was curious about the dynamics of gender separation and possible differences in the ways women bond with other women, and men with men.

By that time, however, my attention had begun to shift from women and men to boys and girls. I had a four-year-old son who took me into the worlds of children in parks, in our neighborhood, and in day care centers. I noticed a striking fact: even preschool-age children tend to divide by gender; boys play more often with boys, and girls with girls. As a sociologist, I knew such patterns are not "natural," but are socially organized. And as a feminist and a mother, I wondered about the effects of gender separation on children's daily experiences and on their present and future gender relations.

I decided to become a participant-observer in an elementary school and, with a special eye for gender, to find out how children and adults construct their daily worlds. I gained access to a combined fourth-fifth grade classroom in a working-class school in California. During the school day I essentially tried to hang out, observing and taking notes in the classroom, the lunchroom, the hallways (where I discovered the intricacies of lining up and defining "cuts"), and on the playground, where I roamed and recorded descriptions of the complex arrangement of activities and groups.

Analyzing the notes I had taken over eight months in the first school and three months in a similar school in Michigan, I found recurring patterns from which I mapped the complexities of children's gender arrangements. Elementary schools are crowded environments and girls and boys share the same formal curriculum; they sometimes interact in relaxed ways. But they also spend a great deal of time in separate groups, occasionally dramatizing gender boundaries with games such as "chase and kiss" (also known as "girls chase the boys/boys chase the girls"), but some children do cross gender boundaries and participate in activities of the other gender. I also found complex interactions between gender and minority status. For example, in the California school, when seating was divided by gender, other boys repeatedly maneuvered two nonbilingual Hispanic boys into sitting next to girls, a position the boys saw as contaminating.

Erik Erikson once wrote, "Children bring up their parents as much as parents bring up their children." That adage describes my experience not only as a parent, but also as a researcher. I was often surprised by the perceptiveness and social competence of children; they create their own complex cultural worlds. My surprise alerted me to adult biases. As adults, we often assume children are incomplete versions of ourselves; we define ourselves by our being, but children (seen as the targets of "socialization") by their becoming. We tend to ignore children, assuming that their daily actions are trivial and worthy of notice only when they seem to be cute or irritating. And we may assume that we already know what children are "like," both because they are a familiar part of our environment and also because we were children ourselves at one time.

Adults find it difficult to take children seriously because of the ways our society organizes age divisions. We locate children in families and age-graded schools, excluding them from public life. Children are relatively powerless, although their subordination is extremely complex; treating them like adults may result in their exploitation (this is much truer of younger than older children; note the enormous diversity glossed by the singular term, *the child*). My relatively modest empirical study led me to these much larger concerns. It finally occurred to me that the question, Where are the children? may be as compelling as the earlier question, Where are the women? We have far to go in understanding children as social actors in varied institutions. To meet that challenge, we will have to wrestle more fully with the complex politics of childhood.

Kohlberg, Gilligan, and Moral Development

Inspired by Piaget's work, Lawrence Kohlberg has spent several decades conducting longitudinal and cross-cultural studies of "the child as moral philosopher." In essence, Kohlberg (1981) proposed that, given the necessary experience and stimulation, children go through a sequence of six stages in their ability to handle moral problems.

Between the ages of four and ten, the child's sense of good or bad is linked to obedience to those in positions of power, based on fear of punishment. In adolescence, conformity to the rules is accompanied by the belief that the existing social order is right and true and deserves to be defended. But with the appropriate moral education, older children and young adults can reach the two highest stages of reasoning, in which considerations of community welfare, general rights, and universal ethical principles—such as justice, equality, and the dignity of individuals—become the guides of action and self-judgment.

Although cross-cultural studies show striking similarities in the early stages of reasoning among children in other complex societies, Kohlberg has been criticized for an ethnocentric bias in defining the highest good as essentially the values enshrined in the work ethic, most particularly an emphasis on individual rights. This might explain why Kohlberg's model fails to capture the moral reasoning involved in the principle of collective or common good that characterizes many modern societies (Snarey, 1988).

The major criticism of Kohlberg's work, however, is that he based his theory on data from boys and men. When Kohlberg discovered early in his work that girls did not make judgments in the same way as boys, he simply assumed, as did Freud and Piaget before him, that females were somewhat deficient in moral reasoning, and he proceeded to construct a model of "human development" from the male experience. While teaching with Kohlberg, the psychologist Carol Gilligan noticed that many women students were dropping his course, and she decided to find out why.

In a Different Voice.   Gilligan's research showed that girls and women brought a set of values to their moral judgments different from men's (Gilligan, 1982; Gilligan et al., 1989). For example, in one of Kohlberg's dilemmas, respondents are asked whether or not a man named Heinz should steal a medicine he cannot afford to buy to save the life of his dying wife. Males approached the problem in terms of abstract standards of right or wrong, saying, for example, that laws must be followed without exception because they ultimately protect all members of the society. In contrast, girls and women wondered about the consequences to Heinz, his wife, their children, and the entire web of family relationships, seeking an alternative that caused the least harm to everyone.

According to Kohlberg's scoring system, the girls' answer would rank at about Stage 3, whereas the boys' would be at Stage 6. But, Gilligan asks, by what standard is an "ethic of care" a lower level of moral development than an "ethic of rights"? or separation a higher value than connectedness? Are these not just two different ways to approach a moral dilemma, with the male pattern rated higher by male researchers? If such gender differences are not innate, but the product of socialization and of life experiences, then they are changeable. If men were to raise children, they would think in terms of attachments, and if women had to spend their lives competing for occupational status, they would think in terms of individual rights. And, indeed, several recent studies find minimal differences in cognitive development in girls and boys in modern societies (Greeno and Maccoby, 1986; Snarey, 1988). In other words, the two ways to resolve moral dilemmas have to do with role rather than with inherent sex differences.

The theories discussed in this section—of ego development, psychosocial stages, cognition, and moral reasoning—are all concerned with processes within the individual, prompted by events in the social environment. Another area of psychological research on learning is concerned more with observable behavior than with the inner workings of the psyche.

Behaviorism concentrates on the study of observable activity as opposed to reported or inferred mental and emotional processes.

B. F. Skinner and Behaviorism

Behaviorists concentrate on observable and measurable actions. The behaviorist who most influenced sociologists is B. F. Skinner (1904–1990). Skinner has claimed that all behavior is shaped by the manipulation of rewards: When an action is rewarded, it is likely to be repeated; when it is not rewarded, it is less likely to be repeated. If a change in behavior is desired, the easiest way to achieve it is to change the conditions under which a reward is available. The sociological implications of Skinner's experiments, conducted on pigeons and lab animals and applied to humans, have been spelled out by Homans (1961) and are one source of contemporary exchange theory and rational choice theory. These implications are best understood by the concept of the *Skinner Box.*

Skinner Boxes.   Skinner achieved some notoriety many decades ago by tending his infant daughter for part of the day in a completely controlled environment that became known as the **Skinner Box.** (The child, incidentally, not only survived but thrived.) The concept of the environment as a box has important sociological applications. Although humans, unlike pigeons, construct their own environments, they, like pigeons, respond to the rewards in their social world and base later actions on a knowledge of what happened before. Social structures can be thought of as Skinner Boxes, in which people act within a system of rewards received and withheld.

The **Skinner Box** is a completely controlled environment.

Behavior Modification.   These principles have been applied to cases in which extreme behavior change is desired by authorities. Prisons and mental hospitals, because they are environments that can be thoroughly controlled 24 hours a day (total institutions), have been prime sites for experiments in *behavior modification.* All rewards are withheld until the inmate performs the actions desired by custodians, *regardless of the person's internal state (drives, motives).*

Critics of behaviorist models claim that these models overlook the importance of the role of human interpretation (meaning) and the social context of behavior. This approach also suits the political climate of the times, providing a "cost-effective, reductionist, rational decision-making stereotype of the modern individual" (Denzin, 1986). Although the behaviorist approach no longer dominates American psychology, Skinner's principles still guide people attempting to create communities that encourage sharing and caring (Rohter, 1989). Many contemporary behaviorists, however, take into account a step between the presentation of a stimulus and the response of the individual (as in Figure 4-2), which brings the theory in line with the thrust of the symbolic-interaction perspective.

SOCIALIZATION ACROSS CULTURES AND THE LIFE COURSE

The Cultural Factor

As described in Chapter 2, each culture is a selection of traits from the range of human possibilities. Some cultures, such as ours, place high value on individualism; others, such as the People's Republic of China, emphasize obligations to the group. Fearlessness is admired in some societies, cautiousness in others, and so on down the long list of human traits. Also, usually one type of personality is desired for females, another for males; one set of traits

FIGURE 4-2 A contemporary behaviorist's modification of the classical stimulus-behavior model.

for children, another for adults, and another for the elderly. This variety of personality styles is possible because each culture, through its symbol system, creates a particular way of thinking, reinforces certain emotions, and shapes the self-image of its members. The cultural blueprint also determines socialization practices that produce the desired personality types.

What is "normal" for one society may be considered crazy or "sick" in another. In one of the early classics of cultural anthropology, Ruth Benedict (1934) described the inhabitants of the island of Dobu as being deeply mistrustful of one another but especially of close family members—behavior that would be considered "paranoid" in our society, where one is supposed to love and trust one's parents or spouse. In contrast to Dobuans, the Zuni Indians of the southwestern United States are socialized to a personality style of noncompetitiveness and cooperative sharing—a way of life equally strange to most Americans. Although many of Benedict's details have been challenged by later studies, the major point remains intact: different socialization practices and experiences produce different types of people. Culture, more than human nature, shapes our personalities (Shweder and LeVine, 1985).

Adult Socialization

Socialization in childhood cannot prepare a person for the many different roles of adulthood in a modern industrial society. Just think of the major role changes of early adulthood: graduation from school, entry into an occupation, marriage, parenthood, community and civic involvements. These changes, in addition to *socialization* (learning the new role), require **desocialization** (learning to give up a role) and **resocialization** (learning important new norms and values). Each major role change carries with it the potential for a reorganization of the self.

How many times have you said of someone, "He's changed since he got married," or "That job certainly made a new person of her"? These are not new people, of course, but the same people undergoing important role transitions. Their way of life has been altered and so, accordingly, has their view of themselves and their way of dealing with others.

The transitions of middle and late life have often been thought of as "crises." It was long assumed, for example, that women in midlife are especially vulnerable because they have lost their mother role, and that men in retirement are particularly unhappy at the loss of the worker role. Research, however, does not bear out these predictions, which are based on assumptions about the necessity of parenting to women and of work to men. In fact, most women actually enjoy their freedom from child rearing, particularly if they are employed (Coleman and Antonucci, 1982); many men look forward ea-

Desocialization is learning to give up a role.

Resocialization is learning important new norms and values.

gerly to retirement, and those who can afford it are leaving the labor force at increasingly earlier ages.

Most role transitions in adulthood are fairly predictable and can be eased by anticipatory socialization and by the existence of coping skills. It also helps if one's friends are going through similar status changes. In other words, the popularity of books and articles on the so-called midlife crisis for both men and women greatly exaggerates the effects of the changes that are taking place (Markson, 1989). Most transitions are relatively gradual and not especially stressful. (It is the unexpected, "off-time" transitions, such as early widowhood, that are difficult to handle [Neugarten and Hagestad, 1983].) Moreover, the very process of aging changes from one age group to another because of the effects of historical change (Riley, 1985). There is also evidence that as people mature they become more sure of themselves and develop positive self-images (Gove et al., 1989).

If the self were as fixed as some wish to believe, there would be no point in going to a therapist, or engaging in any of the self-improvement schemes that so characterize this society. Paradoxically, Americans believe in the ability to change themselves, while still clinging to a belief in stable personality traits. There is evidence to support both views: Some traits are relatively unchanged over time, and these give us a sense of identity; yet we can always improve on other traits and come closer to an ideal self.

Reflections on the Nature of the Child

Each culture and historical era has its view of the essential nature of the child. The Puritans assumed that children were little savages who needed to have evil impulses beaten out of them; Americans in the 1940s and 1950s believed that childhood experiences left an indelible mark on adult personality; and, since the 1960s, it has become fashionable for adults to overcome these childhood limitations and discover the "real me" through "self-improvement" therapies.

Professional opinion has also undergone historical change, from an emphasis on fixed traits to a fascination with the idea of biologically determined stages of development, and finally, today, to a recognition of the essential changeability and flexibility of childhood *and* adult personality. Furthermore,

Research indicates that as people mature they become more sure of themselves and develop positive self-images. These retirees are touring Vermont on their bikes. What do you think you'll be doing when you're their age?

according to the child psychologist Jerome Kagan (1984, 1989), we should pay less attention to what parents "do" to children than to the meanings that children place on what happens to them. This formulation comes close to the symbolic-interactionist emphasis on the person as an active interpreter of experience. Kagan also proposes that there are no *general* cognitive abilities, only ways of reacting to specific situations; that is, the behavior cannot be understood without consideration of the context. Thus, the earlier debates over the relative effects of nature (biology) versus nurture (socialization) have been replaced by a more complex understanding of the interplay between individual tendencies and the social environment.

SUMMARY

1. This chapter traces the development of humans in the social context. Human behavior is learned through the process of socialization, the transmission of the culture of the society and subgroups into which one is born.

2. People assume roles by acquiring the necessary information, being aware of the reactions of others, and receiving social support for role performance.

3. In the United States the major agents of socialization are parents, peers, teachers, and the media.

4. Socialization practices vary among different subcultures, particularly parental occupation. Two major patterns of child rearing are the traditional, or status-centered, approach and the modern, or person-centered.

5. Socialization also involves the development of self. Charles Horton Cooley proposed that the looking-glass self is shaped and developed as we see ourselves reflected back in the reactions of others.

6. George Herbert Mead stressed the capacity to take the role of the other as being crucial to the development of the self; Goffman proposed the concept of self-presentation, management of the impression we present to others.

7. Sigmund Freud focused on the conflict between human drives and the requirement of social life, termed *civilization*.

8. The Freudian self is characterized by a dynamic interplay of the id, the ego, and the superego.

9. Erik Erikson expanded Freud's model, emphasizing ego development in the eight stages of the life course.

10. Another area of socialization concerns cognitive development, which refers to changes over time in how people process information. Jean Piaget was the pioneer in observational studies of children.

11. Lawrence Kohlberg built on Piaget's work to describe stages in moral development—how people make judgments about right and wrong.

12. Carol Gilligan has developed an alternative theory based on the different experiences of females and males.

13. Behaviorism, the last psychological model of learning, focuses on observable activities. The behaviorism of B. F. Skinner is based on the manipulation of rewards without regard to the internal states of people.

SUGGESTED READINGS

Adler, Patricia A., and Peter Adler, eds. *Sociological Studies of Child Development: A Research Annual.* Vols. 1–3. Greenwich, CT: JAI Press, 1986, 1987, 1988, 1989. Useful articles dealing with the study of children and child development from a sociological perspective.

Bandura, Albert. *Social Foundations of Thought and Action: A Social Cognitive Theory.* Englewood Cliffs, NJ: Prentice-Hall, 1986. Bandura's social cognitive theory, which focuses on the socially based reciprocity among the environment, the person, and behavior in understanding thought and action.

Elkin, Frederick, and Gerald Handel. *The Child and Society.* 5th ed. New York: Random House, 1988. An overview of the socialization process.

Erikson, Erik H. *Childhood and Society.* New York: Norton, 1986. The interplay between personality and the social environment during the socialization process in several cultures.

Graff, Harvey J., ed. *Growing Up in America: Historical Experiences.* Detroit: Wayne State University Press, 1987. Socialization experiences from the colonial period to the present.

Hewitt, John P. *Dilemmas of the American Self.* Philadelphia: Temple University Press, 1990. Stability and change in the American social character and identity.

McAdoo, Harriette Pipes, and John Lewis McAdoo, eds. *Black Children: Social, Educational, and Parental Environments.* Newbury Park, CA: Sage, 1985. The socialization experiences of African-American children.

Riley, Matilda White, with Bettina J. Huber, and Beth B. Hess, eds., *Social Change and the Life Course.* Vol. 1, *Social Structures and Human Lives.* Newbury Park, CA: Sage, 1988. Useful essays on aspects of the life course.

Schooler, Carmi, and K. Warner Schaie, eds. *Cognitive Functioning and Social Structure over the Life Course.* Norwood, NJ: Ablex, 1987. The interplay between changes in intellectual functioning and changing social statuses and roles occupied across the life span.

5

Deviance and Crime

- Don is a 20-year-old honor student who plans to major in chemistry. He and two classmates have recently begun to use his parents' basement as a "home laboratory" to manufacture a synthetic drug that they say is "better and purer" than "ecstasy" (DMT) and are developing a thriving business among other college students.
- Evelyn is a college junior majoring in special education. A straight-A student and president of the junior class, she has recently become engaged to her high school sweetheart, Adam, who is majoring in computer science. They expect to marry after they graduate and have agreed not to have sex until their honeymoon. Neither Evelyn nor Adam smokes, drinks, or does drugs.

What do these people have in common? They are all engaged in **deviant behavior.** To deviate means to depart from the normal, the approved, or the expected. Whereas deviance is associated with criminals and the mentally ill, it can also describe the acts that are more ambitious, industrious, heroic, or righteous than generally found or expected.

Deviant behavior violates generally held norms.

The sociological study of deviance, however, has been almost entirely concerned with *socially disapproved* deviation from the norms, in part because we are fascinated by stories of people who break the rules. Social order everywhere depends on people doing what is expected of them by others. But every time a group establishes a norm—a rule of acceptable behavior—another category of actions is automatically created: unacceptable behavior, or deviance. Doob (1971) commented that when the circus was invented, so also was the sideshow. The major function of the sideshow is to reassure viewers of their own normality while ridiculing people who depart from the expected. In this way, conformity is reinforced and anxiety over the unusual is relieved.

Sociologists are primarily concerned with the process whereby behaviors come to be defined as either deviant or normal. The sociology of deviance focuses on a series of interrelated questions: (1) How are social norms established? (2) In what circumstances do violations of the norms occur? (3) What social groups are likely to be involved with different types of deviance? (4) How do others respond to nonconforming behavior? and (5) Who has the power to define normal and abnormal?

CONFORMITY AND DEVIANCE

As we saw in Chapter 2, norms vary widely across cultures and through historical time. In complex societies, normative agreement becomes very problematic because of the great number of competing values. For example, people who wish to conserve our natural resources will oppose business interests seeking to expand industrial development—and both can appeal to widely accepted value systems. Legalized abortion is strongly supported by those who value women's rights but just as fiercely opposed by others who claim to represent the interests of the unborn. Given the extreme diversity of interests within a complex society, how do some norms become more important than others?

Sociological research shows that the relative power of competing groups determines which standards of right and wrong become *the* norms for the group. By studying definitions of deviance in any group, we learn what powerful people find threatening. It is tempting for those who make the rules to see violators of norms as people who suffer from some personal problem—a sickness of mind or body, or some deep moral flaw—that makes them unable to conform. Yet, from the sociological point of view, deviant behavior differs not in its basic nature but only in content from what is called conformity. Indeed, the processes whereby deviant and nondeviant roles are constructed and performed are quite similar.

Issues of deviance and conformity become defined as *social problems* through the same interplay of competing power groups as in the definition of the norms themselves. Those who feel most strongly or who have the most at stake in terms of immediate self-interest tend to win out over people less well organized or less fervent or less personally affected. What comes to be called good or bad conduct is the outcome of struggle among those who have the power to shape and define cultural products.

Consider the case of marijuana. Use of marijuana, like any drug, varies by time and place. For example, in India, a country with strong religiously grounded objections to alcohol use, one form of marijuana known as "bhang" is actually prescribed by custom and religion. A liquid form of marijuana mixed with fruit, bhang is expected to be served openly at weddings. By contrast, in the United States, where marijuana is classified as an illegal substance, liquor is freely available to wedding guests. Yet the current definition of marijuana as a *social problem* is relatively recent; in the early 1900s marijuana was commonly used in over-the-counter medications available in any pharmacy. It was also widely prescribed by physicians for a variety of medical conditions—from headaches and excessive menstrual bleeding to epilepsy, ulcers, and even tooth decay. Nor did the medical or scientific community feel that users developed symptoms of addiction or tolerance to marijuana (Clinard and Meier, 1985).

How did marijuana become defined as a dangerous drug? The answer would seem to lie in vested-interest groups. In 1930 the Federal Bureau of Narcotics (FBN) was established as a separate agency to enforce drug laws. Once created, FBN officials began to look for areas in which it could become involved. Marijuana was one such area. Working in collaboration with the Treasury Department, whose interest was largely financial, the FBN became a "moral entrepreneur" (manager), vigorously enforcing existing laws while also promoting additional antidrug legislation. More restrictions on the sale and use of "dangerous" substances were essential to the survival and growth of the bureau, whose budget was dependent on the amount of drug behavior to be regulated. In the 1930s the FBN conducted a major media campaign to convince Americans that marijuana was an extremely dangerous drug. In time, the bureau's definition became the public reality.

Yet attempts to discourage behavior by defining it as a social problem are not always successful. By 1970 survey data showed that 42 percent of college students had smoked pot at least once, and in 1972 a presidential commission declared marijuana use a nationwide threat to the health and morals of American youth. By this time, the drug had become firmly established in the public mind with the youth movement of hippies, campus radicalism, changing sexual norms, and protest against the Vietnam War. Mar-

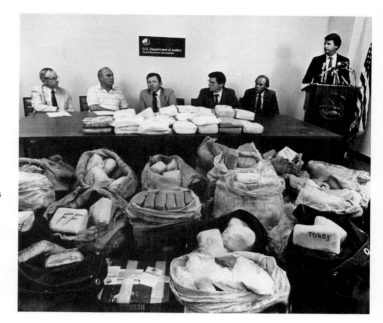

Despite periodic drug busts, such as this one in Miami, and despite pronouncements by the U.S. government about wars on drugs, 25 million Americans use cocaine, including crack, regularly, spending about $50 billion annually on their habits. Why is the war on drugs not being won?

ijuana became a symbol of social disorder, and control over its use was elevated to a crusade for law and order. The government's "war on drugs," however, keeps falling victim to other powerful interests, including the conduct of foreign policy, foreign trade, and military considerations. It is doubtful that the United States will say "no" to drugs, with the illegal drug industry being driven by powerful political and economic forces, and an estimated 25 million Americans using coke and crack regularly and paying $50 billion per year for drugs (Gorriti, 1989, pp. 70–76; Skolnick, May 23, 1989, p. A-17; Inciardi, March 15, 1987, p. 1ff; Cockburn, September 11, 1986, p. 31.)

STRUCTURING CONFORMITY

Many years ago in American society (and in some societies today) deviants were thought to be possessed by devils. In Puritan America, for example, people who deviated from the norms were believed to be witches who had made a contract with the Devil and should be imprisoned or killed. The deviant of today is thought to need psychiatric help or punishment (or both). In either case, the deviant has upset ongoing relationships within a system by behaving unpredictably.

How Norms Develop

Norms develop through social interaction and represent a kind of negotiated reality that shapes individual perceptions and behaviors. Even in situations without established norms, members of the group will quickly construct rules that relieve uncertainty and provide guidelines for behavior.

In the 1950s, Solomon Asch, a social psychologist, performed a now-classic experiment that illustrates how conformity is structured. In this study, which involved estimates of the length of lines (see Figure 5-1), naive subjects were teamed with confederates of the investigator who had been instructed to give wrong answers. Three-fourths of the naive subjects conformed at least once to the wrong answers. Only one-fourth trusted their own perceptions. In other words, most of the naive subjects accepted the norms of the group, even though the norms contradicted their own experience.

This study highlights three important factors that shape conformity for all of us. First, in a situation in which we are in the minority, we are likely to distort our perceptions to reduce the uncertainty of the situation and to feel more comfortable. Second, group pressure may distort judgment, so that each of us doubts his or her own perceptions when others do not agree with us. And last, each of us may decide to agree, even if unconvinced, that our feelings or perceptions are incorrect.

But life is not lived in a laboratory, and complete agreement with all norms is unlikely. Conformity and deviance may be thought of as the opposite ends of a continuum of behavior. Any person's position on the continuum will probably vary from one norm to another and from one social situation to the next.

Strength of Norms

As we discussed in Chapter 2, some norms are more important than others. In most complex societies, rules that involve behavior essential to the group's well-being ("Honor thy father and thy mother") typically carry more weight than rules of personal hygiene ("Brush your teeth twice a day"). In the United States, deviation from the norm of having only one husband or wife at one time can be prosecuted. People who refuse to acknowledge introductions or who do not say thank you may be considered snobs, but not public menaces deserving punishment. The complexity of industrialized society guarantees that only those norms considered most important to the group will be severely sanctioned.

Proscriptive norms govern forbidden conduct. **Prescriptive norms** dictate what is expected.

Norms may also be either **proscriptive** ("thou shalt not") or **prescriptive** ("thou shalt"). Sociologists have observed that deviations from proscriptive norms are more likely to be severely punished than violations of prescriptive norms.

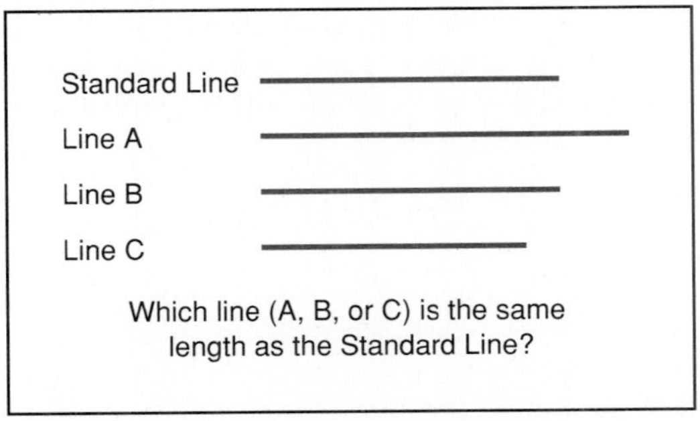

Standard Line ———————————

Line A ———————————

Line B ———————————

Line C ———————————

Which line (A, B, or C) is the same
length as the Standard Line?

FIGURE 5-1 In the Asch experiment, naive subjects were asked whether line A, B, or C matched the standard line on the top. (Source: Adapted from Asch, 1956.)

We are so constantly surrounded by rules we have internalized through socialization that they appear to be the "right and proper way of doing things" (Sumner, 1909/1940). Yet all norms are essentially arbitrary; what is defined as normative, and therefore what is defined as deviance, changes over time. It also varies from society to society. At one time or another, all of the following activities were defined as criminal deviant acts (some punishable by death): printing a book, claiming that the earth is round or not the center of the universe, performing an autopsy on a dead human body, not attending church, and boxing. There is no one eternal or universal standard of behavior.

Conversely, some behaviors that are harshly condemned in our society today were considered relatively normal in the last century. Opium-based narcotics, for example, were widely available in nonprescription syrups that were even advertised in family magazines. The original Coca-Cola contained a small amount of cocaine to endow it with medicinal properties. It is possible that a higher percentage of Americans were addicted to these "cures" in the nineteenth century than at the present.

DEFINITIONS OF DEVIANCE

In the early 1960s, a study of acceptance of various nonconforming behaviors found that marijuana users were ranked with prostitutes among the least tolerated deviants (Simmons, 1969). Since that time, attitudes toward marijuana and other drug use have changed markedly. By 1987, as Table 5-1 shows, 36 percent of high school seniors admitted to researchers that they used marijuana or hashish, 10 percent indicated they used cocaine (excluding crack), and 6 percent said they used hallucinogens such as LSD, mushrooms, and related "designer" drugs.

Use of drugs—or at least admitting to using drugs—changes over time, however. Researchers at the Survey Research Center at the University of Michigan combined the senior-year data and follow-up data from all cohorts

TABLE 5-1 Are More Teenagers Saying No to Drugs?

	Percent of High School Seniors Who Say They Use Drugs												
	Class of 1975	1976	1977	1978	1979	1980	1981	1982	1983	1984	1985	1986	1987
Marijuana/ hashish	40.0	44.5	47.6	50.2	50.8	48.8	46.1	44.3	42.3	40.0	40.6	38.8	36.3
Hallucinogens	11.2	9.4	8.8	9.6	9.9	9.3	9.0	8.1	7.3	6.5	6.3	6.0	6.4
Cocaine[a]	5.6	6.0	7.2	9.0	12.0	12.3	12.4	11.5	11.4	11.6	13.1	12.7	10.3
Heroin	1.0	0.8	0.8	0.8	0.5	0.5	0.5	0.6	0.6	0.5	0.6	0.5	0.5
Alcohol	84.8	85.7	87.0	87.7	88.1	87.9	87.0	86.8	87.3	86.0	85.6	84.5	85.7

Note: Percentages based on students who said they used drugs at least once within 12 months of when they were surveyed.

[a] Figures on crack use not available.

Source: Institute for Social Research at the University of Michigan.

of high school seniors studied. The findings indicated that between 1975 and 1985 marijuana use rose sharply among all the high school seniors after graduation but that use began to decline among all age groups thereafter. Cocaine use also increased very sharply after age 18 among the class of 1976 seniors, but, unlike marijuana use, coke use continued to increase. Later graduating classes were more likely to use coke while still in high school, perhaps because of its increased availability, acceptability, and lower price. And, since 1983, an increasing proportion of high school seniors have reported smoking crack. Doing drugs has become less statistically deviant among college students.

Trends in drug use illustrate a major sociological concept proposed by Emile Durkheim: Deviance is measured by the *societal reaction* to an act or life-style that violates popular or institutional norms (Durkheim, 1893/1960).

SOCIAL FUNCTIONS OF DEVIANCE

Durkheim further proposed that deviance, rather than being destructive or evil, is necessary to societal well-being. Durkheim pointed out that crime is a necessary part of all societies because it fulfills the important service of generating *social cohesion* in opposition to it. Union in mutual anger creates what Durkheim termed the *public temper,* a feeling shared by members of a group and belonging to no one person in particular. Through such group consensus, social order is reinforced. This process is well illustrated by the public temper created in the United States by reports of the mistreatment of the 52 persons held hostage in Iran for 14 months in 1979–81.

Boundary setting occurs when shared norms and values set the limits of acceptable behavior.

When deviants are identified and punished, members of the society are united in a common morality that strengthens their own belief system. Thus, deviance has a dual function: *unification of the group,* and **boundary setting** (Durkheim, 1960), the process by which shared norms and values are established within social groups such as the family, the school, the workplace, a professional association, a religious organization, one's hometown, or the entire society. Within these groups, boundaries are placed at the outer limits of acceptable behavior, so that people's actions are limited and made relatively stable and predictable. Kai Erikson (1966) suggested that people learn boundaries through **confrontation.** Often, the nature of this confrontation is public, as in demonstrations for gay rights or against family planning clinics, in which support and opposition are tested.

Confrontations test the limits of acceptable behavior.

Deviance as a Safety Valve

Some deviance serves as a **safety valve** for disruptive tendencies.

Some deviance, however, is permitted in most societies as a **safety valve,** or a way of releasing frustration, tension, or anger. One example is the current attitude toward prostitution in the United States. Illegal in most states, prostitution nonetheless continues to exist, with only occasional raids and arrests by the police and media crusades. Why is this so?

Prostitution: Who Benefits?   Many sociologists have argued that prostitution continues to be more or less tolerated—although condemned—because it fills certain functions for society. Through prostitution, sexual outlet is permitted to men—but not to women—without threatening either family stability or myths about female sexuality. Moreover, prostitution is a convenient way for many men to have sexual intercourse in a situation that allows them to explore new, sometimes unconventional sexual practices in a manner in which they, as employer, maintain control. Many people see a positive value in prostitution, although official morality opposes it. Others view prostitution as not only immoral but criminal. Feminists object to its exploitation of women.

Prostitution today is a multimillion-dollar business, controlled by men, involving male pimps and other employees as diverse as lawyers, law enforcement personnel, and a cast of thousands, including madames, organized crime figures, and corporate leaders. It has its own status system, from $1,000-a-night call girls who entertain executives—often to help a business make a deal—to poorly paid streetwalkers (Miller, 1986). Wherever she may work, the prostitute is a key person within a social network and must call on others for referrals, services, income, and protection (see Figure 5.2). Often an

This young runaway turned to prostitution to survive the streets, while Sydney Barrows, called the "Mayflower Madam" because her ancestors were among the original colonists, established a high-class brothel as a business enterprise. Whereas streetwalkers are regularly arrested and jailed, Ms. Barrows made an out-of-court settlement and published a book of memoirs, which has generated a great deal of income.

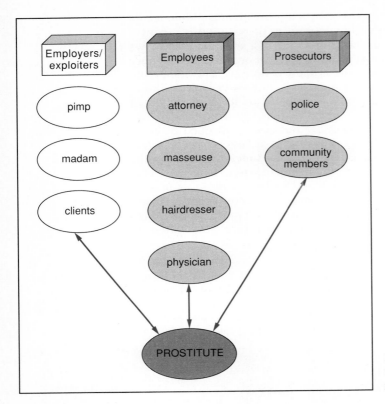

FIGURE 5-2 The social network of the prostitute. (Source: Adapted from M. R. Laner in Bryant, 1974.)

employee of a pimp who manages her career, the prostitute, in turn, produces jobs for others. Her very existence also provides employment for those charged with maintaining and enforcing laws against prostitution (for example, the vice squad of a police force). Prostitution is part of a larger pattern of deviance creating employment and promotion opportunities for agents of social control. Its success as a business highlights some basic values of our society.

Expressing Discontent

Another function of deviance is the expression of discontent with existing norms. The youth revolt of the 1960s, for example, involved primarily middle-class youths who openly rejected the values of success and conformity popular in the 1950s. As products of a relatively wealthy society engaged in the Vietnam War, the students who rejected conventional behaviors were not only testing boundaries but also searching for something beyond the boundaries. Note, also, the closing of ranks among other segments of the society in opposition to the young: hardhats and college administrators, many parents and politicians created a public mood of shared moral indignation at such supposed ingratitude.

Violation of norms may indicate a flaw in the social system itself. For example, the civil rights activists of the 1960s violated many local norms of conventional behavior and tested the law itself with their nonviolent attempts to gain equal access to seats on buses and at lunch counters. Similarly, many groups of school teachers and university professors, formerly unlikely to violate conventional norms and disrupt campus and classroom routines by striking, increasingly tend to do so in protests against administration policies.

Continued boundary testing can often promote social change as definitions of deviance are liberalized. But when severe boundary crises occur, members of the community begin to punish activities that were ignored before the crisis. European witch hunts conducted from the fourteenth through the seventeenth centuries occurred during a time of demographic and economic upheaval to mobilize public opinion on the side of dominant church elites precisely when their power was weakening (Ben-Yehuda, 1985). Women were targeted as witches both because of their lack of access to legitimate social power and their visibility in new social roles—midwife is one such example—that challenged traditional social patterns and beliefs.

The example of Puritan New England also shows that what is defined as deviant behavior depends on the social and political context and reflects the biases of those in power. The people most likely to be condemned for witchcraft in New England were poor middle-aged women, usually single or widowed, who had a reputation for nagging or annoying their neighbors (Demos, 1983). As Erikson noted, those people who most fear witches are also most likely to find them in their midst.

Principled Challenges to the Norms

Principled challenges are deliberate attempts to confront the norm setters. The challenge is seen as having a moral aspect and is most often an attempt to reform or change a particular part of the society without changing the basic social or normative structure. These protests usually occur when conventional, legitimate means of bringing pressure either have failed or have moved too slowly.

> **Principled challenges** are deliberate attempts to confront the norm setters.

For example, within the past several years, there have been dozens of protests against the building and use of nuclear power plants. In the 1960s and the early 1970s, opposition to nuclear power centered in established groups that used the normal channels of publicity and lawsuits (Barkan, 1979). These lawsuits have been slow, costly, and uncertain, leading some people to mount their own principled challenge to nuclear power. In May 1977, 14,000 people occupied the construction area of Seabrook, New Hampshire, and were arrested. Suddenly, national publicity was directed toward the movement and its goals. Protests have continued, and the construction of nuclear plants has been halted, partly as a result of these actions.

SOCIAL CONTROL

The term **social control** refers to the planned or unplanned processes by which people are taught, persuaded, or forced to conform to norms. Because the survival of any social group depends on most of its members behaving in

> **Social controls** are techniques for getting people to conform.

a predictable manner most of the time, rewards for conformity and negative sanctions for deviant behavior are a crucial aspect of all social systems.

Social controls can be either informal or formal. *Informal mechanisms* include expressions of approval or disapproval by significant others. Socialization is every group's first defense against deviance; a person's conscience is the most effective and least expensive form of social control. But few people are so self-controlled that they do not deviate from the norms at some time or another. Informal cues from significant others—a raised eyebrow, a slap on the wrist, the silent treatment — are usually sufficient to limit further deviance.

Formal agents of social control are people in social roles specifically devoted to norm enforcement.

When informal sanctions are not effective, **formal agents of social control** are called on. Formal agents are people in social roles specifically charged with enforcement of the norms. In our society these are mental health professionals, law enforcement and criminal justice personnel, welfare workers, and, often, religious leaders, who attempt to curb deviant behavior and reinforce conformity through various rewards and punishments. As a last step in the process of social control, people whose behavior is so unpredictable or unacceptable that it threatens social order are simply removed from the community.

Repressive control systems use extensive power to restrain many behaviors. **Restrained** control systems involve less intense use of power over fewer behaviors.

Although all societies have networks of informal and formal controls, there are variations in the leeway allowed for acceptable role performance and in the severity with which deviation is punished. Currie (1968) identified two basic types of formal control systems: **repressive** and **restrained.** In repressive systems, the agents of social control have extraordinary power to detect and restrain a wide range of forbidden behaviors, such as the Republic of South Africa's enforcement of laws that limit the movements of the country's majority black population or the violent repression of student protest in mainland China in 1989.

In contrast, restrained systems of social control are characterized by limits on the invasion of personal privacy, as well as by greater tolerance of variation in conformity to the norms. Sweden and the United States, for example, have relatively restrained systems of formal controls.

THEORIES OF DEVIANCE

Why do they do it? This is the first question that most Americans ask about any type of deviance. Several theories attempt to explain why people deviate from the expected, each of which reflects a particular value position with distinct consequences for controlling deviance and for dealing with nonconforming people.

Biological and Psychological Theories

Biological Theories.   There is a very old belief that something is basically wrong with the deviant person. Numerous biologically based explanations for deviant behavior have been proposed since the nineteenth century. More sophisticated attempts to discover biological explanations for deviant behavior have been made during the twentieth century. One such classification was proposed by Sheldon (1949) who classified all people according to three body types: endomorph, ectomorph, or mesomorph (see Figure 5-3). According to this theory (based on earlier work by Kretschmer [1925]), endomorphs are soft and fat and prone to manic depression and alcoholism; ectomorphs are thin and small-boned and prone to schizophrenia; and mesomorphs are muscular, big boned, and prone to criminal activity, alcoholism, and manic depression. Theories based on body type, however, have produced contradictory findings.

More influential at the present is the hypothesis that abnormal chromosomal patterns may be linked to deviant and antisocial behavior. A number of studies have suggested that there is a greater than expected frequency of men with XYY chromosomal patterns in prison and in mental hospitals. Normally, males have an XY chromosomal pattern and females have an XX pattern. However, biological explanations for deviance are incomplete.

Psychological Theories.   The belief that deviant behavior results from some kind of moral flaw or mental problem in a person remains as popular today as during biblical times. By the nineteenth century, physicians and reformers had begun to identify certain types of people as "moral imbeciles"—those who violated social norms even though their reason and intellect were un-

FIGURE 5-3   Three basic body types described by Sheldon. Can you identify the different body types shown? How complete is the theory of body type?

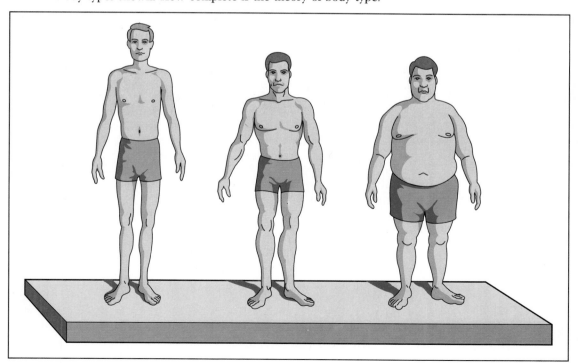

impaired. With the growth of the mental health movement during the nineteenth century, such terminology was considered too unscientific, and a set of categories, including *psychopath, sociopath,* and, most recently, *antisocial personality* took their place. The concept of antisocial personality, currently a psychiatric diagnosis (American Psychiatric Association, 1987), is convenient in that it bridges both biological and psychological theories. According to the *Diagnostic and Statistical Manual of Mental Disorders III-R* (1987), published by the American Psychiatric Association, "Antisocial personality disorder is five times more common among first-degree biologic relatives of males with the disorder than among the general population . . . [but] adoption studies show that both genetic and environmental factors contribute to the risk of this group of disorders" (p. 344). Yet this diagnosis has come under attack as incomplete and as a circular argument because characteristics are listed for the diagnosis after people have committed antisocial acts.

Deviant behavior is also attributed to effects of negative childhood experiences resulting in imperfect "ego" strength or internal control over behavior. Although most of us have had some negative experiences in childhood, not all of us become full-fledged deviants. What is more likely is that people who commit certain types of deviant acts learn behaviors. that differ from middle-class norms.

Sociological Theories

Although sociologists note what psychologists, psychiatrists, and biologists say about the origins of deviant behavior, the *social act* is our major concern. Explanations of deviance must be examined both within the context of the society where the behavior occurs and within the framework of social interaction. Deviant behavior as well as the behavior of those who attempt to control it occur within a *social context.*

Various sociological approaches to the study of deviant behavior have been proposed. Sociological theories of deviance, most of which complement each other, are concerned with why deviance exists in every known human society; how people become deviant; and what mechanisms for social control are used to limit and punish obvious violations of important social norms. Akers (1977) has suggested that sociological theories of deviance may be grouped under two general headings: structure and process. The major emphasis of structural theories is on the macrosocial level and concerns explanations of the differences in type and amount of deviant behavior among people occupying various social statuses. Process theories focus more on the microsocial level; that is, how individuals are socialized into deviant behavior. No single theory of deviance, however, is exclusively concerned with structure or process.

Structural Approaches to Deviance.   *Functional theory* is a structural approach that directs attention to how elements of social structure and behavior *maintain* the stability or the relative equilibrium of societies or groups. Thus, much behavior that we label deviant actually reflects the cultural values of the society in which it occurs—even if only by offending agreed-upon standards of behavior. As Erikson (1966) stated, "The thief and his victim share a common respect for the value of property; the heretic and inquisitor speak much the same language and are keyed to the same religious mysteries; the traitor and the patriot act in reference to the same political institutions" (p. 22). Deviance reinforces the authority of the norms, sometimes strengthening them.

Erikson proposed that the proportion of deviants in the population is likely to stay relatively constant over time. In his studies of Puritan New England, Erikson observed that although the *number* of convictions varied from year to year the offender *rate* remained fairly constant. The relative stability of offender rates reflects definitions of deviance that roughly match the capacity of the social control mechanisms of the community. Only so many people can be processed at a time without overtaxing the courts and the jails.

When a community's or a society's resources for controlling deviance are overwhelmed by too many violators, social change is likely to occur, and the boundaries of conformity are likely to be redefined. This is indeed what happened in New England. When the witch trials threatened to overwhelm the community's capacity to punish witches, the trials for witchcraft ceased. Something similar is occurring today as our prison system has been severely strained by public demands to "lock 'em up and throw away the key."

Another structural approach proposed to explain deviant behavior is that of *anomie*. Anomie describes the disorganization that exists in individuals or society when norms are conflicting, weak, or absent. When we have been socialized to the norms and goals that govern behavior within a particular culture but are denied access to the means of reaching those goals, anomie may result. Assuming that the goal in American society is to be rich or successful, people in less powerful statuses who are systematically denied the opportunity to achieve wealth or success by legitimate means will seek alternative ways to achieve the goal. Robert Merton (1957) proposed five ways in which a person may adapt to the gap between the means and the goals of a culture.

As Table 5-2 shows, only one of several adaptive mechanisms conforms to both the culturally determined goals and the legitimate means of achieving them. The *innovator* will seek new and probably illegitimate means of acquiring wealth and success, for example, racketeering. The *ritualist* is resigned

TABLE 5-2   Merton's Typology of Individual Modes of Adaptation to Cultural Means and Goals

Individual Mode of Adaptation		Accepts Cultural Goals	Accepts Institutionalized Means of Attainment
	Conformity	Yes	Yes
	Innovation	Yes	No
Other Adaptations	Ritualism	No	Yes
	Retreatism	No	No
	Rebellion	No/but seeks to replace with other goals	No/but seeks to restructure means of attainment

Source: Adapted from Merton, 1957, p. 140.

to fate, recognizes that fame and fortune are out of reach, and tends to overconform to the rules for good conduct. The bureaucrat who is more concerned with keeping a job than with upward mobility or achievement is a type of ritualist. The *retreatist*, however, rejects both the means and the goals of the society and drops out—into drug use, mental illness, alcoholism, or life as a street person. Finally, the *rebellious* rejects both means and goals while seeking social change. Political radicals, members of some religious cults, and followers of alternative life-styles (some of which were popular in the late 1960s) all reject conformity and adopt new goals and means.

Those who are denied access to or who reject the legitimate means and goals of their society also tend to turn away from former peer and reference groups and to seek out new ones that accept and reward their nonconforming behavior.

Albert Cohen (1955) expanded anomie theory, suggesting that both delinquent and law-abiding behavior depend largely on one's sociocultural environment and social interaction. **Delinquent subcultures** develop primarily among poorer juveniles who are relatively unskilled at competing in a middle-class world. When they enter school, they are measured by middle-class norms that have not before been emphasized in their socialization.

Delinquent and criminal subcultures originate in the differences between aspirations and blocked opportunity structures.

Delinquent or criminal subcultures have their roots in the lack of fit between culturally learned aspirations among poor youth and the limited possibilities of attaining success. Three types of delinquent subcultures may arise from *blocked opportunity structure* (Cloward and Ohlin, 1960). Each of these subcultures stresses a different career pattern and source of gratification: for the criminal, property and wealth; for the conflict-oriented, violence; and for the retreatist, complete withdrawal from both deviant and conformist pressures. All three subcultures can be found today in any major American city.

Conflict theorists also focus on macrosocial explanations. The roots of conflict lie in the tension between the few who control the means of production and who also have great political influence, and the mass of powerless citizens. Power is used to enact and enforce laws supporting the interests of the owners against those of the less powerful. The small groups (elites) who control the economic and political systems set the policies that define legal as well as cultural conformity. Ruling groups must continually create the impression that the established system is serving the interests of all segments of the population. This is the ultimate goal of "cultural hegemony": to convince the powerless that their needs are being met. As the French author Anatole France once wrote, "The law in its majestic equality forbids rich and poor alike to beg in the streets, steal bread, and sleep under bridges."

As for the criminal justice system, conflict theorists tend to view the administration of justice as rigged against the poor, members of minority groups, and others who might challenge the legitimacy of the *status quo*. From the perspective of conflict theorists, civil rights marchers in the 1960s broke laws because they considered that order unjust, and today's environmentalists lie down in front of bulldozers to protect public land rather than out of any death wish. However, the formal forces of social control have been employed against the protesters.

Process Approaches to Deviance.   The labeling perspective emphasizes the formation and application of social definitions. The basic premise of

labeling theory is that deviance is not a personal quality and is not created by deviants' acts. Instead, deviance is created by group definitions and reactions. It is the emphasis on the *process* of defining a person's behavior that has given this approach its name. Deviance is not a quality of behavior itself but is created in the interaction between the person who commits the act and those who respond to it (Becker, 1973). A key point in labeling theory is that declaring someone deviant may result in a self-fulfilling prophecy and reinforce the behavior. As Becker argued:

> deviance is not a quality of the act the person commits, but rather a consequence of the application by others of the rules and sanctions to an "offender". . . . Whether an act is deviant, then, depends on how other people react to it. (Becker, 1973, pp. 8–9, 11)

Although labeling theory developed in the 1950s, its roots go back to earlier symbolic-interactionist studies of juvenile delinquency (Tannenbaum, 1938) and to the concept of cultural relativism. Deviance is an interactive process between those who violate a norm (or who are believed to have done so) and others who interpret and react to the violations. For example, smoking cigarettes is increasingly regarded as deviant behavior—so much so that some cities, such as Cambridge, Massachusetts, have passed laws to prohibit smoking in any public building. Anyone who smokes *in public buildings* in Cambridge runs the risk of being labeled as a law breaker and a hazard to general health and well-being.

Is labeling as important in defining deviance as some sociologists have suggested? Or are deviant labels the result of deviant behavior? Some analysts (Chauncey, 1975; Cockerham, 1979; Gove, 1975, 1979) have suggested that deviant labels are a result, not a cause, of deviant behavior. Others, like Scheff (1966), have proposed that labeling is the single most important cause of a deviant career.

Yet, as recent work has pointed out, labeling can have not one, but several, effects, including (1) creating deviant behavior; (2) maintaining deviance; and (3) affecting other areas of life, including jobs, family relationships, and friendships. There is evidence that, although a label may or may not directly affect the specific behavior to which it is attached, the interaction resulting from the label definitely affects other areas of life (Link, 1983). A label of mental illness, for example, puts people at a higher risk of job loss and rejection by potential mates, as well as generally undermining their ability to cope.

Edwin Sutherland (1939) was particularly interested in how one type of deviance, criminal behavior, is learned, and he proposed the theory of **differential association,** which may be summarized as follows:

1. Criminal behavior is learned in social interaction with others and has no unique biological or genetic basis.
2. It is within *primary groups* that one learns motives and techniques for committing crimes, reasons for conforming to or violating particular rules, and what behavior is permissible in which situation.
3. A person becomes a criminal when definitions favorable to the violation of law outweigh the unfavorable ones.
4. The differential associations most likely to result in criminal behavior are frequent, long-lasting, and intense and occur relatively early in life.

Labeling theory emphasizes the process of defining a person's behavior as deviant.

The theory of **differential association** states that deviant behavior is learned in primary groups and involves the same learning processes as nondeviant behavior.

5. Learning criminal behavior is the same as learning any other behavior. Thus, there is no value or need pattern unique to criminals as opposed to noncriminals. A person becomes criminal when the reinforcement for lawbreaking is stronger than the reinforcement for remaining law-abiding.

Social learning theory states that both deviant and conforming behaviors are learned through reinforcement.

More recently, **social learning theory** has modified Sutherland's concept of differential association. Social learning theory draws on the "law of operant behavior," which says that behavior is conditioned by the environment in which it occurs and the interactions that reinforce or discourage that behavior (Jeffery, 1978; Burgess and Akers, 1968; Akers, 1977). It is the substance and direction of learning that shapes conformity or deviance.

The process of social learning occurs as follows: (1) Depending on a person's past history, the same stimulus or event may reinforce behavior in one person but not another; (2) criminal behavior is reinforced for some people through a variety of positive reinforcers, such as respect from peers or acquisition of material rewards. (For example, the inner-city teenager who makes several hundred dollars selling crack and is able to buy designer sneakers and a stereo and show off to friends is more likely to receive positive reinforcement for his actions and continue to deal dope than a youth of the same age who receives a generous allowance from affluent parents.) Punishment for deviant behavior is not necessarily effective unless it occurs near the time of the occurrence of the deviant act. Delayed punishment may create avoidance and escape behaviors rather than normative conduct.

DEVIANT CAREERS AND NONCAREERS

Primary deviance is behavior that violates a norm.

Secondary deviance results from the social responses to primary deviance.

Lemert (1967) has described two types of deviance that relate to the development of a deviant career. **Primary deviance** originates within the person and is behavior that violates a norm but may either be undetected or excused by others. **Secondary deviance** results from the social responses a person receives to a primary deviance. For example, although a person who sees visions or hears voices is unusual, if these perceptions occur only in private and are offset by satisfactory performance in other roles, the deviation may be undetected or excused for any length of time. If, however, the same person in the company of others holds a conversation with the voices or offers a chair to an invisible creature, he or she is likely to suffer social consequences. Indeed, the questionable behavior could become intensified precisely because others have come to expect it. The deviant is so labeled, then, by others.

A **stigma** is a morally undesirable label that tends to be generalized to other undesirable characteristics as well.

How does a deviant career begin for some and not for others? According to labeling theory, there are several steps in the process. First, the rule breaker is caught and publicly labeled. Second, once tagged, a person's new label is treated as a *master status trait* (see Chapter 3). The person's other identities and roles are virtually ignored. Third, once a person is perceived as deviant, nothing about her or him is trusted or taken for granted, and the deviant trait seems to color that person's entire being in the eyes of others. A **stigma**, or "sign of moral blemish," attaches to a characteristic that differs from the normal or the normative in a society. Those with this label are treated as if they bear a mark of disgrace. Thus, the person is *stigmatized,* as others withdraw their acceptance and distort that person's real identity to fit stereotypical expectations (Goffman, 1963). In turn, the stigmatized person internalizes part or all of the views of the labelers about the stigma, altering his or her self-concept in the process. As Millman commented about obesity, a generally stigmatized category in our society:

> While most people have a clearer self-image and pretty well know what to make of other people's behavior, the fat person is too self-conscious and too marginal. . . . She reasonably comes to doubt her judgments about social conditions. . . . The fat individual often finds it easier to give up, to abandon a world that doesn't want her anyway. . . . Everything in her privatized life takes on an illicit or furtive quality. . . . So does she come to feel embattled with her environment. (p. 82)

The last step in a deviant career involves seeking out others who share the stigma. With others who are also stigmatized, the deviant at last finds a supportive peer group. Not only is she or he socially accepted in this group, but a particular world view that explains and supports the stigmatized behavior is created and maintained. This supportive network is called a **deviant subculture.**

Deviant subcultures are supportive peer groups and networks for deviants.

In these subcultures, people may try to redefine the stigma in order to counter the majority's perspective on the particular attribute. There are, for example, groups of overweight people who are not devoted to weight loss. Instead, they are supportive of the larger body type and the idea that being heavier is beautiful and, perhaps, healthy. These support groups are essential for individuals trying to redefine themselves. These groups may even be one of the first steps toward making changes in the majority's point of view.

Eccentric Behavior

Some types of deviant behavior do not bring extreme stigmatization. A person may be simply considered an "oddball," or **eccentric.** Eccentrics, like deviants, are recognized rule breakers and are observed and defined by others as being unusual. Eccentrics may be tolerated for several reasons: (1) They are viewed as unimportant oddities (for example, punks), (2) they are members of an in-group that protects them (for example, drunken politicians), or (3) they are protected by their position, wealth, or knowledge (for example, Michael Jackson).

Eccentric behavior is not viewed as disruptive or threatening to the social order.

Fame and fortune may protect one from stigma and from being locked into a deviant career even when public labeling has occurred. In 1974, then president Richard Nixon and much of his staff were forced to resign because of the Watergate scandals. Several were charged with and convicted of serious crimes. Yet their conviction and imprisonment did not ruin their lives, nor were they tracked into criminal careers. Many turned to lecturing and writing, several of them earning hundreds of thousands of dollars, and Nixon has become an "elder statesman."

Petty and Institutionalized Evasions of the Norms

Petty (trivial, minor) **violations** of the norms are often ignored until they threaten social order. Charging personal expenses to a business account, failing

Petty violations of norms are trivial and minor violations of rules.

to report all taxable income, parking illegally, and using another student's notes are common petty violations.

Although such rule breaking carries the risk of negative sanctions, the petty normbreaker is generally not concerned with the consequences. The rule itself may seem stupid or inconvenient. Breaking these rules may even be justified as fair compensation for an imagined or real loss ("It's OK to cheat on your taxes; the government takes too much anyway").

Institutionalized **evasion of norms** occurs within organizations as a permanent official part of the system and may be tolerated because it helps get the job done.

Institutionalized evasion of norms often occurs within an organization as a permanent, unofficial part of the system. Such evasions may be tolerated because they actually help to achieve the goals of the organization. For example, executives at A. H. Robins Pharmaceutical Company purchased the rights to market an intrauterine contraceptive device (IUD), the Dalkon Shield, in 1971. Shortly thereafter, they learned that the device was both ineffective and dangerous. Yet the product continued to be advertised and marketed, and the physician who developed it continued to receive royalties. By 1974, Robins was forced by the government to withdraw it from the market. Nevertheless, the company continued to sell the device abroad. Only in 1984 did Robins recall all shields still in use. Meanwhile, numerous users had experienced unwanted pregnancies, miscarriages, and chronic inflammation of the pelvis. At least 33 women had died. Many women sued the company that failed to inform them or their physicians of the hazards.

In this illustration, institutional deviance in the form of suppression of information allowed the company to fulfill its corporate purpose: to make a profit through the sale of a device prescribed by physicians. The deviant behavior of corporate executives conformed to the profit norms of the corporation.

Mental Illness as a Social Process

Mental illness is **re-sidual deviance** that is less easily identified than more obvious norm violations.

To the sociologist, mental illness is **residual deviance;** it is less obvious and more difficult to define than, say, murder, treason, or bigamy and therefore is not easily classified. Diagnoses of mental illness tend to reflect the norms of the times. In the nineteenth century, physicians considered both masturbation and homosexuality symptoms of mental pathology. Today, neither is regarded as indicating a mental disorder. It is, however, interesting to note that, whereas the American Psychiatric Association voted to drop homosexuality from its list of mental illnesses, a new illness has been added: habitual tobacco use. This is a good illustration of the importance of contemporary norms in defining mental illness.

Psychiatrist Thomas Szasz (1987) has proposed that the concept of mental illness has been extended to convert the problems of everyday living into illness. Much mental illness, according to Szasz, is a set of symptoms or a role rather than actual disease. Szasz maintains that psychiatry does not treat the mind as medicine treats the body, for whereas physicians manage *disease,* psychiatrists manage *people.*

How does behavior become labeled as mental illness? Obviously, people may see, hear, or experience the unusual for many reasons: genetic, family, and stress factors; drugs; infection; malnutrition or extreme exhaustion; or deliberately altered states of consciousness. Consider alcohol: Drinking in moderation is generally culturally approved in American society. But the line between "normal" and "problem drinking" is thin. Alcohol dependence is classified as a mental illness by American psychiatrists and as an illness by groups such as Alcoholics Anonymous.

Most alcoholics tend to resist defining themselves as problem drinkers for as long as possible. Similarly, members of a family or other close-knit group are reluctant to shift their definitions of a person's behavior from "normal" to "sick"—whether the label is alcoholism or some other mental disorder. It is when a behavior becomes disruptive or threatening to others that one is most likely to be labeled as mad. For example, during the 1950s, "madwives" hospitalized for schizophrenia were often full-time, working- and middle-class housewives and mothers whose marriages were characterized by economic dependence and powerlessness. Often isolated from adults other than their spouses, their behavior became increasingly strange and progressed toward a crisis leading to institutionalization (Warren, 1987). Once hospitalized, the women's powerlessness was intensified through an authority coalition between her husband and her physician.

Tracking the Patient's Career.   According to Erving Goffman (1961), the change in self-concept involved in the process of becoming a mental patient is recognized by the person experiencing it only after the fact. A large role in determining who will actually become a mental patient is played by **career contingencies:** the occupation and income of the rule breaker, the visibility of the rule breaking, the availability of psychiatric or psychological treatment within the geographic area, and the type of norms that are broken. People who are admitted to psychiatric wards or mental hospitals are usually put there because their behavior, though not illegal, disturbs others who can no longer tolerate it. Thus, a **circuit of agents** is needed to define someone as a mental patient. Such circuits include both *informal social-control agents,* such as family members, friends, and neighbors, and more powerful *formal agents,* or *gatekeepers,* representing the community, such as the police, the clergy, social agencies, and physicians.

Once in the hospital, other social processes lead to further changes in the self-concept. Stripped of outside roles and everyday possessions, such as clothing or pens and paper, patients find that all information about them is recorded and shared by the staff, who discredit any attempts made by the patient to maintain a positive, private, respectable self-concept. Instead, one is asked to face up to one's illness. Patients respond in different ways, but the end result is that the self is no longer private. A new self, adapting to the situation, is gradually reconstructed, but unlike the old self, it "is not a fortress but a small open city" (Goffman, 1961).

Shedding the label of mental patient is not easy. In the media, the former mental patient who commits an offense is immediately identified as a *mental patient,* although she or he occupies other statuses and roles. "Mental patient" becomes the person's master status trait, and others expect behavior that is unpredictable, unpleasant, and perhaps violent. Like other stigmatized people, those labeled as mentally ill risk being locked into a deviant role unless they conceal their stigma.

Today, as increasing numbers of people once in mental hospitals have been released to the community (**deinstitutionalized**), they have found that the label of "mental patient" affects their quality of life. For example, some

Career contingencies involve a series of social factors that determine outcomes for people by opening up or closing off certain options.

A **circuit of agents** includes both informal networks and formal agents.

Deinstitutionalization involves the release of mental patients into the community.

former mental patients live in special community residences for the mentally ill that are simply mini-institutions, where little effort or money is invested in "normalizing" their behavior (Markson, 1986).

Homelessness as a New Deviant Career?

Although reliable statistics are currently impossible to obtain, it is clear that a large number of Americans are homeless. Estimates of the number of homeless vary widely: the 1984 Department of Housing and Urban Development (HUD) estimate put the figure at 250,000 to 500,000 nationwide; in 1987 the National Coalition for the Homeless put it at 2 to 3 million and increasing by an average of 25 percent yearly.

The deinstitutionalization of mental hospital patients more than a decade ago cannot account for the current numbers of "street people." Nor is the allegation that most homeless are mentally ill supported by recent research (Snow, Baker, and Anderson, 1988; Piliavin, Westerfelt, and Elliott, 1989). The homeless population in the United States and in other nations comprises at least three groups: the chronic, or traditionally, homeless; the deinstitutionalized; and the "dishoused," or new, homeless: families, young people, and ethnic minorities unable to find affordable housing (Doolin, 1986; Friedrichs, 1988; Burt and Cohen, 1989). Homelessness is not confined to urban areas. In prosperous suburbs with rising housing costs, families who earn the minimum wage or live on fixed incomes cannot afford apartments or houses.

According to estimates based on a survey of 23 American cities, the fastest growing segment of homeless people is composed of unemployed or underemployed families with children, accounting for an estimated 30 to 40 percent of the unhoused. More than 40 percent of the homeless are minorities (National Coalition for the Homeless, 1987; U.S. Senate, 1988). In some cities, veterans of the Vietnam War and other wars are estimated to compose one-third of the homeless (U.S. Senate, 1988). Estimates provided by personnel at homeless shelters suggest that the percentage of people age 50 and over using shelters ranges from 14 to 28 percent, as many as one-fourth of whom are age 60 and over. Street outreach surveys have reported much higher proportions of homeless older people: as high as 50 percent.

Homelessness among people of all ages derives from a number of factors, including unemployment, social service and disability cutbacks, personal crises, and lack of affordable housing. Most of the homeless for whom information is available are no longer able to find housing due to skyrocketing rents, elimination of single-room-occupancy (SRO) hotels, and a shrinking stock of affordable housing. During recent years no new funds for construction of public housing have been provided. At the same time, low-income housing is being converted into expensive condominiums with government subsidies to the owners. The number of people on waiting lists for low-income public housing continues to grow. Nor are shelters for the homeless readily available, and the demand far exceeds the supply.

What policies have benefited the homeless? To date, the federal government has maintained that homelessness is a local problem and that the federal role should be limited to making surplus housing and food available. In 1987, Congress passed the Homeless Assistance Act, providing emergency funds to

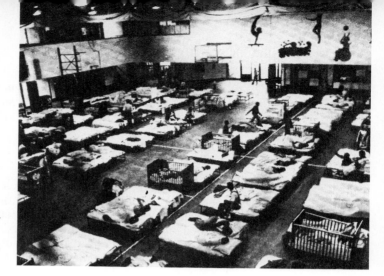

The homeless population is comprised of at least three groups: the chronically homeless, the deinstitutionalized, and the new homeless or "dishoused," who are families, young people, and ethnic minorities not able to find affordable housing.

state, local, and nonprofit organizations to convert buildings for use as emergency shelters and transitional housing and offering surplus federal property for housing, as well as funds for a variety of social services. Yet many aspects of this legislation require that the state, local government, or private nonprofit agency match federal funding from other sources: not an easy task in an era of fiscal constraint. Some community organizations have practiced "Greyhound therapy," whereby homeless people are given a one-way ticket to another city. Other community leaders have proposed ordinances to detain the homeless, by force if necessary, in shelters or to place them in long-term institutions.

One spokesperson for the homeless summed up the policy dilemmas posed by homelessness in the United States by noting that homeless people have become a commodity, leading to the development of new growth industries to treat the "individual pathologies" of the homeless while ignoring their most basic needs for housing and income maintenance (Friedrichs, 1988). After evaluating the various solutions for homelessness, what sociology-based policies would you advocate for your home community? ■

LAW, CRIME, AND THE CRIMINAL JUSTICE SYSTEM

What do the following have in common: a gunman firing a semiautomatic rifle on a California schoolyard; a member of Congress from New York City extorting $1.8 million dollars in corporate stock; a Boston street gang shooting a 19-year-old security guard in a case of mistaken identity?

The common denominator is that they are illegal or criminal acts. As these examples indicate, there can be more than one cause of crime or criminality—a point of particular interest to sociologists. Every society has its rules as well as its deviants and agents of social control. The amount of crime in any society depends on two factors: first, the range of conduct controlled by law; and second, the effectiveness of agents of social control. How does crime differ from other types of deviance? Only a few acts arouse such strong feelings that they are forbidden by law. People who commit illegal acts are targets of formal and official sanctions, including arrest, prosecution, and punishment.

THE ROLE OF LAW

In modern societies the *law* of the state or province is the formal code of rules enforcing conformity. In simple societies, these are matters of custom and informal sanctions. Social norms become laws when their violation is controlled by action exercised in a socially approved, predictable way by impersonal agents of the people empowered to act as accuser and judge.

Criminal law provides sanctions against conduct believed to be against the interests of the society or the state.

Civil law provides sanctions against violations of the interests of private people.

A difference is usually made between **criminal** and **civil law.** Conduct believed to be against the interests of the society or the state is sanctioned under *criminal law.* Conduct against the interests of private people is punishable under *civil law.* This distinction is not as neat as it sounds. For example, consider the act of assault, which is directed against a specific person but which is also a threat to the public interest. Assault, therefore, involves both a criminal and a civil violation of law (Quinney and Wildeman, 1977).

The criminal law is one set of rules and regulations in society. It overlaps norms of the family, the church, and other institutional spheres. Many criminal behaviors were so defined before the days of Moses in the Bible. Others, like dope pushing, airline hijacking, and income tax evasion, are relatively new additions. What is a crime in one time and place is not necessarily a crime in another. For example, before the American Civil War, slavery was legal in many states. Today, not only is slavery against the law, but anyone treating another person as a slave is likely to go to prison.

There has probably never been a society without crime. What varies is the definition of crime, which is largely a result of which groups have sufficient power to enact their norms into law. The concept of crime as a wrong against society is very old, although punishment was often left to the injured person or her or his family rather than to agents of the state. Retaliation, or "an eye for an eye," was an early and exact form of social control. This rule, although bloody, ensured that the punishment would be no greater than the harm done and was actually a first step in creating the balance scales of justice. With the rise of nation-states, the right to punish wrongdoers was taken away from the individuals and their families and became a state monopoly. When sanctions are applied universally to all who commit a given act, we can speak of the *rule of law.*

How Norms Become Laws

The **social injury model** sees laws as a means of protecting members of the society.

At least three ideas have been proposed to explain how norms become laws: (1) *social injury,* (2) *consensus,* (3) *conflict.* The **social injury model** is based on the commonsense idea that all laws are passed to protect people in a particular society. But this approach fails to answer two questions. First, what is harmful behavior? Second, who decides what is harmful?

The **consensus model** is based on the belief that norms become laws because they reflect a general agreement about appropriate behavior. Conflicts typically revolve around relatively unimportant issues. The consensus model is a *functionalist* explanation, based on the work of Emile Durkheim.

In contrast to the functional model, **conflict** theorists propose two major approaches to explain the establishment of laws. The first is the *economic view*, stemming from the work of Karl Marx. According to Marx's view of crime, those who own the means of production, for example, capitalists in the United States, also control the political process. They use this power to enact and enforce laws supporting their own economic interests and to check the interests of the lower classes. Laws also benefit the upper strata in the labor market, as when certain lower-class behaviors are designated as illegal and unwanted surplus workers are removed from the labor force and sent to jail. To commit a crime is often to impose power upon others, whereas to be punished for a crime is to be subject to the power of others (Hagan and Palloni, 1986). At the same time, crime creates jobs for other members of the community: judges, lawyers, legal scholars, crime-detection experts, and some psychologists, psychiatrists, and sociologists.

Quinney (1977) and other contemporary conflict theorists have argued that the government uses its power to control lower-class people's opposition to their enforced poverty. In this view, most laws are enforced because they reflect the political, economic, and ideological interests of specific power groups (for example, laws against loitering or defacing property). Control of crime may also be a profitable financial investment. As Quinney and Wildeman (1977) suggested, "A major part of the law and growing social-industrial complex is what we can call the 'criminal justice–industrial complex.' That industry finds it profitable to invest in crime is one of the final contradictions of the capitalist system" (pp. 117–18). Investment in the criminal justice system includes prisons, guards, police staffs, lawyers, judges, social workers, and others.

A variation on this theme is proposed by **culture conflict** theorists who stress differences in *values*. From this viewpoint, when the community has competing factions and custom can no longer maintain conformity, law is imposed by the most powerful interest group. Table 5-3 summarizes the types of criminal behavior explained by each of these three theoretical views. Any

The **consensus model** is a structural/functional model based on the idea that norms become laws because they reflect customs and general agreement about appropriate behavior.

Conflict models assume that laws serve the interests of the dominant class.

The **culture conflict model** stresses value differences and a belief that the laws reflect the values of the most powerful groups.

TABLE 5-3 A Model of Theoretical Perspectives as They Relate to Types of Criminal Behavior

Behavior	Explained by Theoretical Perspective		
	Social Injury	Consensus (Functionalist)	Conflict
Dreaded by most (for example, murder)	Yes	Yes	Yes
Threat to many vested-interest groups (for example, power-elite groups)	No	Yes	Yes
Threat to special-interest groups (for example, nuclear plant sit-in)	No	No	Yes

given system is the outcome of the interplay of consensus, conflict, and the need for order.

CRIME IN THE UNITED STATES

Crime in the Streets

Street crimes are actions that directly threaten people or property.

Fear of crime is widespread in the United States. Although fear of crime has decreased since the 1970s, by 1985, 32 percent of all adults still felt "uneasy" walking their own streets (Harris, 1985). Most feared are **street crimes**; that is, acts directly threatening one's person or property. African-Americans are more frightened of crime than whites, the poor more afraid than the middle or upper classes, and inner-city residents more fearful than suburbanites. Elderly women, who are most apprehensive, are the least frequent victims, while young men, who are least afraid, are the most frequent victims (U.S. Department of Justice, 1988; Moore and Trojanowicz, 1988).

Those at greatest risk of violent crime are unmarried African-American men between the ages of 20 and 24 (U.S. Department of Justice, 1988). Only slightly more than half of all violent crimes were committed by someone unknown to the victim; males were more likely to be victimized by strangers than were females. People who have heard about others' victimizations are almost as afraid as actual victims (Moore and Trojanowicz, 1988). Indeed, fear of crime seems to be most strongly associated with physical decay of the neighborhood, panhandling, prostitution, drug use, and teenagers loitering on street corners (Skogan, 1986).

Contrary to popular opinion, most violent crimes committed in the United States involve victims and offenders of the same race (U.S. Department of Justice, 1988). About 46 percent of violent crime occurs between 6:00 A.M. and 6:00 P.M., with crimes committed by offenders known to the victims more likely to occur during the daytime (U.S. Department of Justice, 1988).

Uniform Crime Reports are compiled by the FBI from city, state, and county police information.

Measuring Crime. In the United States, two major data sources are used to determine the extent of crime. The first is the *Uniform Crime Reports,* compiled by the Federal Bureau of Investigation from monthly and yearly information submitted by city, state, and county police units. Eight categories, selected because they are regarded as among the most serious law violations, form the basis of the FBI Crime Index: (1) murder nad nonnegligent man-slaughter, (2) forcible rape, (3) robbery, (4) aggravated assault, (5) burglary, (6) larceny, (7) motor vehicle theft, and (8) arson. Not included in the index are confidence games, embezzlement, forgery, and other nonviolent crimes. As you can see in Table 5-4, which summarizes rates per 100,000 population for 1987, among these **index crimes**, those involving property—particularly larceny/theft and burglary—are most commonly reported. Index crimes are those most often committed by the poor and powerless.

Index crimes include murder, forcible rape, robbery, and aggravated assault.

Although the *Uniform Crime Reports* are widely used by the police and the mass media, they have two major shortcomings: (1) Not all crimes are reported to the police, and (2) The data reported by various local units are not always comparable.

Nonetheless, the data do roughly indicate the number of crimes considered most serious by officials and the types of activities in which law enforcement agencies are engaged. Because of their unreliability, however, they are not very useful in the assessment of changes in the volume of crime.

To add to the information provided in the *Uniform Crime Reports,* the Department of Justice conducts a ***National Crime Survey*** of close to 50,000 randomly selected households. Twice a year the adults in these households are interviewed about any incidents in which they have been the victims of crime, whether reported or not. These data on victimization give a more accurate picture of the amount of crime than do the official reports, but there is no way to tell the extent to which respondents conceal, exaggerate, or minimize their experiences.

Typical data from the victim survey are shown in Table 5-5. As you can see, Latinos and African-Americans are more likely than non-Latinos and whites to experience serious violent crime, burglary, and motor vehicle theft. Single parent families, households with five or more residents, and people in cities run higher risks of victimization than people who live in suburbs or rural areas (Smith and Jarjoura, 1989). In addition, interview data from the *National Crime Survey* suggest that most crimes are not reported.

Homicide.   Homicide ranks as the second leading cause of death for 18- to 24-year-olds in the United States. The typical homicide victim in the United States is a young African-American male. Homicide victims and their killers are most likely to come from the same racial or ethnic background. The victim and killer are likely to know each other as well: In 1986 only 18 percent of the homicides reported to the police in the United States were known to be committed by a stranger (U.S. Bureau of Justice Statistics, 1988).

Some criminologists claim that the homicide rate could be decreased by

The ***National Crime Survey*** is based on samples of U.S. households and businesses.

TABLE 5-4   Rates of Selected Crime Index Offenses per 100,000 Population in the United States, 1987

Crime	Rate per 100,000
Larceny/theft	3,081
Burglary	1,330
Motor vehicle theft	529
Aggravated assault	351
Robbery	213
Forcible rape	37
Murder/manslaughter	8

Note: Arson, the eighth index crime, is not included in the table inasmuch as rates per 100,000 were not calculated. During 1987, 84,371 cases of arson were committed according to FBI reports: 55 percent of them involved the malicious burning of a building; 28 percent the burning of a motor or other vehicle; and the remaining 17 percent "other."

Source: *Statistical Abstract of the United States 1989,* pp. 166, 174.

TABLE 5-5   Percent of Households Touched by Crime, by Selected Characteristics, 1987

Percent of households touched by	Annual Family Income				Place of Residence[a]			Race of Household Head			Ethnicity of Household Head	
	Low	Medium		High							Non-	
	Under $7,500	$7,500–$14,999	$15,000–$24,999	$25,000 or more	Urban	Suburban	Rural	White	Black	Other	Non-Hispanic	Hispanic
Any NCS crime	23.9%	22.7%	24.0%	26.9%	28.6%	24.2%	18.5%	23.9%	27.8%	25.0%	24.0%	30.1%
Violent crime	6.3	5.2	4.3	4.1	5.8	4.1	3.7	4.4	5.8	5.3	4.5	6.1
Rape	.2	.1	.1	.1	.1	.1	.1	.1	.2	.1	.1	.1
Robbery	1.6	1.1	.8	.7	1.6	.7	.5	.8	2.2	1.2	.9	1.8
Assault	4.8	4.3	3.4	3.5	4.3	3.4	3.3	3.7	3.8	4.0	3.7	4.3
Aggravated	1.8	1.6	1.3	1.2	1.8	1.1	1.3	1.3	1.7	2.0	1.4	1.7
Simple	3.4	3.0	2.4	2.5	2.9	2.6	2.3	2.6	2.4	2.5	2.6	3.2
Total theft	14.9	14.9	17.4	20.1	19.2	17.7	13.0	17.2	16.8	16.4	17.0	20.0
Personal theft	8.6	8.8	10.8	14.0	11.9	12.0	8.0	11.2	9.6	11.3	10.9	12.4
Household theft	8.2	7.8	8.3	8.2	9.9	7.4	6.2	7.7	9.4	7.4	7.8	10.7
Burglary	7.3	5.6	4.7	4.8	6.3	4.7	4.3	4.8	7.9	6.0	5.1	6.8
Motor vehicle theft	1.0	1.3	1.5	1.8	2.2	1.5	.6	1.4	2.3	2.0	1.5	2.4
Serious violent crime[b]	3.5	2.7	2.2	2.0	3.5	1.8	1.8	2.2	3.8	3.3	2.3	3.5
Crimes of high concern[c]	9.8	7.9	6.9	7.0	9.4	6.8	5.6	7.0	10.4	8.8	7.2	10.2

Note: Detail does not add to total because of overlap in households touched by various crimes.

[a] These estimates are not comparable to estimates for place of residence prior to 1986 because of changes in geographic classification.

[b] Rape, robbery, or aggravated assault.

[c] A rape, robbery, or assault by a stranger, or a burglary.

Source: U.S. Department of Justice, 1988a, Tables 3 and 4.

restrictions on the sales of handguns, which were used in large percentages of recent murders, rapes, and robberies (U.S. Department of Justice, 1988). Yet the evidence that gun ownership is a cause of criminal violence remains controversial. According to a 1982 national survey, the typical handgun owner is male, white, Protestant, middle-class, and Southern (*Society*, 1982)—neither the typical homicide victim nor offender.

Other sociologists refer to a *subculture of violence* in the United States in which physical aggression is the norm (Wolfgang and Ferracuti, 1967). Poor young males, especially in ethnic groups stressing masculine honor, are more likely to learn to solve arguments through violence than are young people from middle-class homes. Yet, there is an element of blaming the victim in the theory of subcultural violence. The high rates of homicide among young African-American males, and to a lesser extent, young African-American females, indicates unbearable levels of frustration and blocked opportunity (Crutchfield, 1989).

Property Crimes.   The number of crimes against people is relatively small compared to the number of **property crimes.** In 1987, more than 3 million burglaries, almost 6 million larceny/thefts, and about 1 million motor vehicle thefts were reported to the police. To prevent such victimization, about one-third of American homes and two-thirds of our workplaces have some type of crime prevention device.

> **Property crimes,** such as burglaries, larceny, and theft, are much more prevalent than crimes against people.

Property crimes are most likely to be reported to police when they take place in large cities and least likely to be reported when they occur in rural areas. The relationship between population size and the probability of victimization is in part due to the anonymity that the city provides.

Sociologists are also examining whether variations in the probability of victimization by age group, marital status, social class, and place of residence can be partly explained by patterns of *normal* activity. That is, as more people spend more time outside the home—at work or at leisure—they are at greater risk of becoming victims, especially if these "routine activities" take place where there are motivated offenders relatively unsupervised by agents of social control (Messner and Blau, 1987; Stahura and Sloan, 1988). There is also evidence that crimes such as grand larceny and burglary are most frequent in communities where there are marked differences in levels of economic power and income.

Female Criminals

Until recently, very little had been written about the female offender. Considerably fewer women than men have been arrested and imprisoned. In 1987 women accounted for only about 18 percent of those arrested in the United States, and only 5 percent of prisoners.

Several theories have sought to explain the relative lack of female criminals. These include the idea of the female offender as a biological or psychological oddity, rebelling against the natural passivity of her sex. It has also been proposed that differences in the types and patterns of crimes by women result from gender socialization. Adler (1979) commented that we all go crazy or criminal along well-worn, gender-linked paths. We cannot understand the female (or for that matter, male) offender except in the context of her or his social role. The types of crimes in which women have been involved include prostitution, larceny (primarily shoplifting), vagrancy, and domestic violence—all linked to gender role.

Has the women's movement changed the nature of female criminality? U.S. data show a gradual increase in the proportion of women arrested within the last decade. The increase, however, has been almost entirely accounted for by greater female participation in such minor property crimes as larceny, fraud, and forgery. As women are probably no more or no less moral than men, this change appears to reflect increased opportunities to commit such acts. In addition, women who are arrested for criminal activity rarely express feminist sentiments. On the contrary, the few crimes of violence committed by women are closely tied to their roles as mothers, wives, and lovers. For example, one of the few studies of women who have been convicted of embezzlement and fraud found that most were motivated by the need to support their families (Zeitz, 1981). In contrast, men convicted of embezzlement or fraud tended to be motivated by desires for prestige or to cover mistakes.

Organized Crime

Organized crime is committed by members of formally structured groups operating outside the law.

The simplest definition of **organized crime** is continued organized endeavors to accumulate wealth in defiance of the law. Organized crime has three major characteristics: (1) its members supply goods and services not otherwise available, such as loans, gambling, and narcotics; (2) in order to carry out illegal activities without interference, they bribe and otherwise corrupt public officials and others in positions of power; and (3) violence is used to enforce agreements.

Organized crime is as much a part of the American scene as apple pie (Block and Chambliss, 1981). When immigrants found that the streets of urban America were not paved with gold, and when discrimination and prejudice limited their access to legitimate economic opportunities, illegal activity provided a ready, if crooked, ladder of social mobility. In the United States during the late nineteenth century, organized crime was dominated by the Irish and Germans. By the turn of the century, Eastern European Jews had emerged as gang leaders, and by the late 1920s, Italians had begun to displace the others in organized crime.

If organized crime provides a ladder of social mobility, then African-Americans and Latinos, as the minorities most likely today to be excluded from legitimate opportunity structures, should have become increasingly involved in organized crime. Limited evidence suggests that this is true, although the African-American and Latino operations remain primarily in narcotics, gambling, protection, and extortion. As white ethnic criminals move into legitimate businesses, their low-prestige illegal activities are handed over to other racial and ethnic groups.

For obvious reasons, the amount of money amassed and invested by organized crime is unknown. With their wealth, crime syndicates can manipulate the value of shares on the stock market, control prices of retail goods, evade regulation of the quality of goods produced, avoid paying income taxes, secure government contracts without competitive bidding, and influence trade unions.

Crimes in the Suites: White-Collar and Organizational Crime

White-collar crime is a term coined by Edwin Sutherland (1949) to describe those crimes committed by respectable, high-status people in the course of their employment. **Organizational crime** refers to illegal actions undertaken by legitimate corporations and their officials—bribery, price-fixing, and tax evasion—for corporate rather than personal advantage.

For example, if you have ever made a copy of a videotape, record, music cassette, or computer program without authorization from the holder of the copyright, you have committed a white-collar crime. If, in the course of normal business activity, you have approved the production of an automobile with a known defect, you have committed an organizational crime.

White-Collar Crime.   White-collar crime, like any other crime, is caused by the coincidence of three necessary conditions: motivation, neutralization of social controls, and opportunity (Coleman, 1985). The bank executive who embezzles funds, the physician who performs unnecessary surgery, the businessperson who pads expenses, the teacher who conceals a second source of income from the Internal Revenue Service, and the promoter of fraudulent land schemes are all white-collar criminals.

The extent of white-collar crime in the United States is unknown because the crimes are extremely difficult to detect, often have no identifiable victims, and involve fairly complex financial dealings.

White-collar crime, like any other kind of crime, is defined differently from one instance to another. Changes in social norms have redefined many professional behaviors. Technology, the mass media, and economic prosperity have created the possibility of new forms of white-collar crime, such as using a computer to falsify bank accounts. The increasing complexity of modern society both widens the white-collar criminal's options and narrows the risk of detection. To the average victim of white-collar crime, the means of redress are so technical, lengthy, and expensive that most find it easier to ignore the crime than to fight.

Organizational Crime.   Organizational crimes differ from white-collar crimes in that they are not committed for personal gain but in one's role as an employee or a corporate decision maker. For example, the executives of Lockheed, Exxon, and some 200 other American firms who regularly bribed agents of foreign governments in defiance of U.S. law were corporate criminals, acting to fulfill organizational rather than purely personal goals.

In addition, organizational crimes may be punished under civil, criminal, or administrative law (Schwartz and Ellison, 1982). Although its officers and employees may be jailed, a corporation cannot be put behind bars (Clinard and Yeager, 1980). In general, businesses and corporations that break the law

White-collar crimes are illegal activities committed by individuals of high status, usually by nonviolent means, in the course of their employment for their own benefit.

Organizational crimes are carried out in one's role as employee to achieve corporate goals.

are handled by government regulatory agencies, such as the Environmental Protection Agency, the Food and Drug Administration, and the Federal Trade Commission. The complex legal procedures surrounding the control of organizational crime, plus the attention given to street crime in the media, have perpetuated the image of "real crime" as being homicide, burglary, larceny, or other individual acts against people or their property.

Dishonest schemes in the corporate world take many forms, most of which are difficult to detect or to prove. These range from petty frauds to stock swindles. Some common scams include bid rigging, insider trading, stock manipulation, corporate tax fraud, franchise fraud, and bankruptcy fraud.

Although some people have argued that it is only natural for businesses or agencies to attempt to get an advantage or to protect their own interests, these acts unnecessarily threaten the health, the economic well-being, and the lives of far more people than do murder, robbery, or rape. According to one estimate, the cost of corporate crime is more than ten times greater than the combined crimes of larceny, robbery, burglary, and auto theft committed by individuals (Spence, 1989). Greater resources, however, are spent detecting and prosecuting crime in the streets than crime in the suites. A study by Etzioni (1985), focusing on *Fortune* magazine's 1984 list of America's 500 largest industrial corporations over the 1974–84 period, indicated that 62 percent of the corporations were involved in one or more illegal incidents, and the top 100 corporations in the United States accounted for more incidents than all the others combined.

Because corporations cannot go to jail, the stiffest penalty, other than jailing its officials, is a fine. A $25,000 fine for a corporation whose annual revenue is several billion is hardly a stiff penalty. Furthermore, a stiff fine may be reduced if a donation that is tax deductible is made to worthwhile causes. Since the early 1980s the federal government has intensified its attack on organizational crime. The Racketeer Influenced and Corrupt Organizations Act (RICO), which was passed in 1970 to control organized crime, has now been extended to include other businesses. The Bank Security Act of 1970 requires banks and brokers to report most cash and foreign currency transactions of $10,000 or more, and the Comprehensive Crime Control Act, passed in 1984, gave authorities new weapons to prevent fraud against banks.

Crimes related to environmental or safety regulations, however, have not been a significant target. Rather, the attack has focused on defense procurement, money laundering, and bank and securities fraud. Because of the large stakes involved in the stock market, the Federal Securities and Exchange Commission has focused on criminal use of insider information—privileged data used by executives to trade stocks for their own as well as corporate benefit.

The billions of dollars spent by the Department of Defense on weapons since 1980 have been accompanied by such practices as cost overruns, rigged bids, kickbacks, duplicate billing, falsified documents, security breaches, and outright bribery. In 1985, 45 of the nation's top 100 defense contractors were under active criminal investigation; others settled their cases; and for still others the evidence was too difficult to pursue. The complexity of the government agencies and the low salaries paid to workers charged with overseeing the vast military program almost invite abuse. The sociological point is that corruption and corporate crime in the defense industry has more to do with the structure of the situation than with the personalities of the individuals involved.

The Profit Motive

The tragic explosion of the space shuttle *Challenger* in 1986 shocked many Americans. But engineers from Morton Thiokol Incorporated, the subcontractor for the solid-fuel booster rockets, were aware that the synthetic rubber seals between the rocket's joints could fail in cold weather. In the trade-off between profits over safety, pressure from corporate users and from NASA in favor of launching won out, and warnings by the engineers were ignored.

The Thiokol case illustrates a lack of corporate accountability. The corporate structure itself is oriented toward profit and away from liability and thus is almost a standing invitation to irresponsible conduct (Mintz, 1985). Moreover, within the corporate structure the usual constraints on behavior, such as religion, conscience, and criminal codes, are relaxed. But is the person who assaults people from an office chair any less a criminal than the one who accosts them in an alley?

Neither Thiokol nor NASA is alone in lacking corporate accountability. By the early 1930s, for example, there was reliable evidence that workers in the asbestos industry were developing incurable lung disease; by the 1960s, studies showed that asbestos was a danger to anyone who came in contact with it. Yet the industry's largest company, Manville Corporation, had systematically concealed these findings. When, ultimately, juries began to award

The tragic deaths of six American astronauts and a civilian teacher in the Challenger explosion revealed the power that profit motive and political pressure hold over human life. Which model of society helps us to understand the supremacy of profit?

compensation for injury and damage, Manville Corporation filed for bankruptcy (Brodeur, 1985).

Because organizational deviance has not been much reduced by laws or regulation from outside, or by policing from within, we must conclude that the benefits outweigh the costs of such activity. Organizational crime, like any other, provides goods and services at a profit to the organization. Unless the demand for such benefits declines or alternative sources are found, such activities will continue.

Crimes without Victims

Crimes without victims violate moral standards, but those involved are willing participants.

Crimes without victims are sometimes known as *vice,* or *crimes against morality,* and are believed to endanger the moral fiber of society. Yet moral standards in complex societies are mixed and constantly changing. Because those involved in such offenses as pornography, prostitution, gambling, drug use, and sex acts between consenting adults have themselves chosen to be participants, many people have argued that these acts should be decriminalized.

Victimless crimes are also likely to lead to the corruption of law enforcement personnel. For example, if a police officer is told to get rid of the prostitutes on Forty-second Street in New York City, where there are more prostitutes than the officer can arrest at one time, what criteria will he or she use: appearance, skin color, personal feelings? If someone pays the officer to leave some "girls" alone and enough women can still be arrested to please the superior officers, is any harm done? In all these ways, the ideal of equal treatment under the law is systematically and regularly violated.

Gambling. Arguments against gambling include its links to organized crime, the bribery of government officials, and the destruction of family life. Although it is impossible to know how many people engage in illegal gambling, the desire to try to get something for almost nothing is widespread. Of the millions who could have been caught, there were less than 25,000 gambling arrests in 1989.

Although gambling is considered sinful by many, churches have for many years conducted Bingo games to raise needed funds. State governments prefer to run off-track betting parlors or establish lotteries than to raise taxes. From a sociological perspective, state lotteries are dysfunctional in a number of ways: bettors are victimized by exceedingly poor odds of winning, and social values are eroded. Because of the very low chance of winning and the relatively low payoff for most games, legal gambling has not crowded out such illegal operations as the "numbers game," which operates on the same principle but with a better payoff and tax-free winnings.

Drug Use. Few issues have received as much attention as drug use; several recent public opinion polls indicate it is the number one concern of the American people. Supporters of tougher laws argue that the users are victimized by their dependence on drugs. The link between drug use and street crimes has also been cited as a reason for maintaining strict drug laws. Much of this relationship disappears, however, if the social status of the user is taken into account. In other words, whereas many poor criminals are drug users, many middle-class users do not commit crimes.

Most research evaluating the impact of drug use has been poorly designed, and data on the effect of marijuana, heroin, cocaine, and other substances have been politicized both by those who support a tighter control of drugs and by those who support decriminalization or legalization. What is clear is that the illegal drug market is a primary source of income for organized crime.

The 1989 "War on Drugs" declared by President Bush, with its emphasis on law enforcement rather than on education and rehabilitation, may, according to some critics, do little to help addicts: "Given the sheer diversity of narcotics and the ease with which new materials can be synthesized . . . punitive regulation cannot ultimately succeed" (*Nature,* 1989).

JUVENILE DELINQUENCY

Juveniles may come to the attention of the law enforcement system for three reasons: (1) they have committed a crime, (2) they are neglected or abused, or (3) they have committed a **status offense.** A status offense is an act that would not be considered a violation of the law if committed by an adult—for example, being a truant from school, violating curfew laws (staying out late at night), using alcohol or tobacco, or running away from home.

Because there is some disagreement on the age at which one ceases to be a juvenile, the upper limits to this category fluctuate. To make matters more complex, a different age could apply in cases involving adoption or failure to support a child or for "persons in need of supervision" (PINS). Even the minimum age at which the death penalty may be imposed shows considerable variation among states, from a low of 10 years to a high of 18 years of age.

Many of the differences in the age at which one is considered adult reflect long-established norms as well as the efforts of various interest groups. For example, "age of reason," a term used by lawyers to describe the age at which a child is capable of acting responsibly, has commonly been defined as seven years. In general, according to legal tradition, a child between ages 7 and 14 is assumed to be incapable of committing a crime although evidence to the contrary can be offered. Variations in laws regulating minimum age for marriage reflect beliefs about sexuality, family formation, and ability to support and care for children as well as regional and subcultural differences.

Who is arrested as a juvenile delinquent? Data consistently indicate that American males are three times more likely than females to be arrested. Although more white than nonwhite young people are arrested, African-Americans and Latinos are disproportionately represented among the arrested. That children from low-income and working-class homes have higher rates of arrest than those from higher-income homes could reflect either a real difference in delinquent activity, fewer financial or family resources, or the tendency for police and other authorities to label poor youth as lawbreakers. If reported,

Juveniles come to the attention of law officials because they have committed a crime or status offense or been neglected or abused.

A **status offense** is an act that would not be considered a violation if committed by an adult.

Children from low-income and working-class homes have higher rates of arrest than those from higher income homes. Why is this so?

offenses by those with more resources are typically dealt with informally before any charge or arrest is brought.

THE JUVENILE COURT SYSTEM

The **juvenile court system** is separate from the adult system and was designed to protect children and adolescents from the stresses of labeling and severe punishment.

There are two separate court systems in the United States, one for juveniles and one for adults. The **juvenile court system** was specifically designed to keep children and adolescents from undergoing the stress of adult courtroom procedures and the effects of labeling. The emphasis is on treatment rather than punishment. Over the past 20 years, however, the U.S. Supreme Court has acted to restrict the informality of the juvenile-justice system with the goal of greater uniformity in the ideology, resources, and decisions of judges (Mahoney, 1987).

Today, although each state has its own pattern of juvenile justice, every defendant has the following legal rights: (1) to know the nature of the charges, (2) to have legal counsel, (3) to question witnesses, and (4) to avoid self-incrimination. In every state, appeal procedures have also been established.

TABLE 5-6 Persons Arrested, by Charge, Sex, and Age: 1987

Represents arrests (not charges) reported by 10,616 agencies (reporting 12 months) with a total 1987 population of 202 million as estimated by FBI

Charge	Total (1,000)	Male	Under 15 years	Under 18 years	18–24 years	25–44 years	45–54 years	55–64 years	65 years and over
						Percent Distribution			
Total arrests	**10,796**	**82.3**	**5.2**	**16.5**	**31.1**	**44.7**	**4.8**	**2.1**	**.8**
Serious crimes	2,266	78.4	10.9	29.1	29.8	35.6	3.3	1.5	.8
Murder and nonnegligent manslaughter	17	87.5	1.2	9.5	34.3	47.1	5.4	2.2	1.4
Forcible rape	31	98.8	5.3	15.7	29.2	48.4	4.3	1.7	.6
Robbery	123	91.9	5.8	22.4	38.1	37.7	1.3	.3	.1
Aggravated assault	302	86.7	3.7	12.8	28.3	50.6	5.3	2.1	.9
Burglary	375	92.1	12.7	35.2	34.2	28.8	1.3	.3	.1
Larceny-theft	1,257	68.9	12.9	30.9	27.6	34.7	3.7	2.0	1.2
Motor vehicle theft	147	90.3	9.6	39.9	33.3	25.1	1.3	.3	.1
Arson	15	86.3	25.4	40.5	22.3	31.3	3.9	1.7	.4
All other nonserious crimes	8,529	83.3	3.6	13.2	31.5	47.1	5.2	2.2	.8

Source: *Statistical Abstract of the United States 1989*, p. 173.

These rights, however, do not extend to status offenses such as truancy, running away, or unmanageability.

During 1987 about 1.3 million delinquency cases, or about 44 cases per 1,000 population ages 10 to 17 in the United States, were disposed of by juvenile courts. Over three-quarters of these cases involved males (*Statistical Abstract, 1989,* p. 182).

What are the juveniles in custody like? According to a survey by the Department of Justice, 12 percent were age 14 or younger; about 61 percent were between the ages of 15 and 17, and the remainder were 18 or older. Forty-one percent were African-American; 19 percent were Latino. More than half reported that a family member had been imprisoned in the past, and more than half lived primarily in a single-parent family (U.S. Department of Justice, 1988). Clearly those juveniles represented a sample of the most economically disadvantaged members of their age group.

THE POLICE AND LAW ENFORCEMENT

The **police** in every society have the right to use coercive force to control behavior.

Police in every society are people who have been given the general right to use coercive force to control behavior (Klockars, 1985; Bagley, 1985). As formal agents of social control, police are empowered by the state to detect and limit criminal behavior. As informal agents, they make on-the-spot decisions about which offenses and offenders will receive attention, how they will be processed, and with what offense they will be charged.

The police are enforcers of rules rather than definers or moral entrepreneurs. Enforcers do not necessarily have any personal stake in the law to be upheld. In contrast, moral entrepreneurs are crusaders with a heavy investment in the social control of behavior that they consider morally offensive (Becker, 1973). As enforcers, police are bureaucrats whose duties are defined by their position within a complex organization.

Actual police work, however, is extremely complex. Police bureaucracies are unique in many respects. The status of police officer requires not only conformity to organizational rules but also initiative and risk taking on the job. Police on the street must be ready to use coercive force in unexpected situations; detectives solve crimes only if citizens provide them with enough clues; and the basic bureaucratic police structure is deeply divided between workers and bosses who have different interests and beliefs (Reiner, 1985). Street police, for example, believe that police in management positions have little, if any, understanding of what work on the beat is like (Reuss-Ianni, 1983).

The individual officer's status is thus unclear. Connected in part to civilian life, to a bureaucratic organization, and to the criminal world, the police often are not well liked in the community. Their spouses and children are cut off from most of the officer's life; there are high rates of family violence and marital problems.

Police Corruption

Corruption refers to acts that violate public trust and involve deliberate support of illegal activity. Tendencies toward corruption are built into the law

The police in every society are people who have been given the general right to use coercive force to control behavior. Whose interests and rights are served by the police?

enforcement system (Kelling et al., 1988). Police work often requires reliance on informants, entrapment (luring someone into committing an offense), and other forms of trickery. Such tricks may range from the radar trap and unmarked car of the highway patrol to the undercover work of an agent infiltrating the Ku Klux Klan. Also, the tension between administrators and front-line personnel within law enforcement bureaucracies encourages patrol officers and detectives to pursue their own personal versions of police work so that they become moral entrepreneurs rather than enforcers (Punch, 1985). Because the police have the power to arrest offenders, lawbreakers often offer bribes. In police slang, those who accept small bribes or engage in minor forms of misconduct are "grass eaters"; those who receive large payments or gains from organized crime are "meat eaters." The opportunities for corruption exist; it only remains for someone to take them.

ADULT COURT SYSTEMS

The judicial process has three principal participants: the **prosecutor** (district attorney), the **defense attorney,** and the **judge.** Many others, including the defendant, appear in supporting roles. The prosecutor represents the interests of society and any injured parties; the defense attorney represents the accused; and the judge personifies the law and impartial justice.

Although one cornerstone of the American legal system is the right to a jury of one's peers, most cases are settled by guilty pleas or by the release of the suspect as a result of a lack of solid evidence. Of the few cases that go to

The three major parties in the criminal justice system are the **prosecutor**, the **defense attorney**, and the **judge**, each representing different interests.

trial, the majority of accused people choose to appear before a judge without a jury.

The judicial process in the United States is complicated by several parallel court systems. Not only are there separate systems for adults and for juveniles, there is also one set of courts for federal offenses and another for violations of state laws. As noted earlier, there are civil as well as criminal wrongs. In addition, each system has lower and higher courts, with the latter hearing appeals from the former, and above all the layers and separate systems sits the Supreme Court, which can hear appeals from all the lower benches if a constitutional issue or federal/state conflict is involved. The very complexity of the system, while often a source of frustration and annoyance, is designed to ensure that the scales of justice are not overbalanced by the state.

Processing the Criminal

Just as the judicial court system is complex, so is processing the person accused of a crime. At every step in the process, decisions are made that influence the fate of the suspect. For example, African-Americans arrested for homicide are more likely to be charged with first-degree murder when the victim is white than are either African-Americans or whites arrested for the murder of someone of the same race (Radelet, 1981; 1985). After being arrested and charged with a crime, the suspect who cannot afford bail money or is denied bail by the judge goes to jail to await trial. During this time, the accused might be advised to plea-bargain ("cop a plea"), that is, plead guilty to a lesser charge. **Plea bargaining** is a controversial, behind-the-scenes negotiation (Maynard, 1984) between the prosecution and the accused to reduce the charges if the defendant pleads guilty.

Plea bargaining is a negotiation between the prosecution and the accused to reduce the charges if the defendant pleads guilty.

Traditionally, judges have been given considerable leeway in sentencing, including open-ended or indeterminate sentences (three to six years, for example) with parole boards responsible for deciding an offender's actual release date. Within recent years, this system has been attacked as inconsistent and unfair. Critics claim that both social class and race, for example, affected sentencing so that poor people and African-Americans are more likely than others to receive stiffer sentences for similar crimes (Kleck, 1981; Unnever, 1981; Nakell and Hardy, 1987).

More conservative critics argue that sentences are too short and that parole boards release prisoners too early. As a result, federal district courts and some states now have set determinate, or fixed, sentences for certain types of crimes, designed to stiffen penalties and reduce racial, social-class, and geographic disparities.

Punishments and Crime

Will harsher penalties reduce the volume of criminal activity in the United States? Because only about 1 percent of the criminal acts committed lead to imprisonment, the chances of avoiding arrest and conviction are very high. The vast majority of crimes go unreported. Of reported crimes, perhaps 85 percent are unsolved. For every 100 arrests, an average of 4 cases go to trial, and about 30 percent of these result in an acquittal. And for every 100 persons sentenced, only 71 spend any time in jail or prison.

Yet, when it comes to allocating money for the criminal justice system, most of the public and their legislators favor harsher sentences and building more jail cells. In the past, the single most important factor in determining the size of a prison population has been the number of cells available: the more cells available, the more people sentenced to prison (Nagel, 1980). Since 1979, with the opening of 138 new state prisons and the renovation and expansion of numerous others, nearly 5.4 million square feet of state prison space has been added. Not surprisingly, given both an increase in determinate sentencing, in prison space, and in public pressure for longer prison terms, the inmate population has grown.

The Debate over the Death Penalty

Throughout human history, some deviance has been considered so disruptive of social order that the offenders have been banished or executed. **Capital punishment** is another term for the death penalty (from the Latin *capo,* head). Until 1967 in the United States, capital punishment, by firing squad, hanging, or the electric chair, was an accepted part of our criminal justice system. In 1967 the Supreme Court heard a challenge to the death penalty on the grounds that it was (1) "cruel and unusual punishment" and therefore forbidden by the Eighth Amendment to the Constitution, and also (2) that because the execution rate for African-American offenders was ten times higher than that for whites, the "equal protection" clause of the Eighteenth Amendment was violated. The Court banned capital punishment in existing cases because it was being applied in an arbitrary manner, leaving open the possibility of reinstating the death penalty if the states could set uniform standards.

In the following years, one state after another enacted death penalty legislation designed to meet the Court's test of fairness. But no executions took place until after 1976, when the Court upheld the revised legislation in three separate cases. Capital punishment was once more the law of the land. As you can see in Figure 5-4 on page 166, the number of death-row inmates began a steep rise. After lengthy appeals, 25 people, almost half of whom were African-American, were put to death in 1987. The number of people executed has also risen sharply in each subsequent year. Close to 40 states now have capital punishment statutes and almost 2,000 persons, almost all men, disproportionately African-American, and all convicted of murder, are under sentence of death. The last major challenge to the death penalty—again based on violation of equal protection—was turned back by the Supreme Court, on a five-to-four vote, in early 1987. In 1989 the Supreme Court also ruled that juveniles and mentally retarded people could be executed.

Only the Republic of South Africa, among all modern industrial nations, has joined us in approving capital punishment. Popular support for the death penalty is based on two beliefs: (1) that it deters crime and (2) that the state is justified in seeking retribution for a serious crime.

Capital punishment is another term for the death penalty.

STUDYING THE DEATH PENALTY

Michael L. Radelet

Michael L. Radelet is an associate professor of sociology at the University of Florida. He is the author of two dozen studies on the death penalty, including one that documents more than 300 cases in which people convicted of homicide were later found to be innocent (Bedau and Radelet, 1987).

In 1979, when I arrived in Florida after seven years of studying medical sociology, I had no interest in, knowledge about, or opinions concerning the death penalty. But when a friend told me that the National Association for the Advancement of Colored People (NAACP) was collecting records to see if the death penalty in Florida was being applied with a racial bias, I volunteered to analyze their data. It sounded quick and easy, exactly what new professors need if they hope to earn tenure, and I naively thought the results might show no racial disparities.

One of the strongest attractions of sociology is that through it one gets to learn about some very interesting groups. People on death row are one such group, and because I did not want to be accused of being an ivory-tower intellectual, I began to write to one of the condemned men. Later I visited him, and I did so 20 more times until he committed suicide a year later. For the next four years, I paid monthly visits to another inmate, who was executed in 1985. Since then I've worked with attorneys, as a paralegal, on a hundred more cases, and I have gotten to know dozens of condemned inmates and their families.

More than anything else, it was these families that made me take a stand opposing capital punishment (Radelet, 1989). Their agony, coupled with the data showing strong racial bias in the administration of the death penalty (Radelet, 1981), far outweighs in my mind any justifications for the death penalty. Prisoners suffer, and given that in most states the alternative to the death penalty is life imprisonment without parole, eliminating the death penalty will not mean that murderers will go unpunished. Furthermore, the death penalty usually hurts the prisoner's family as much as the prisoner himself. Imagine how you would feel if your son were about to be executed. The death penalty doesn't help families of homicide victims—it simply increases the number of innocent families who mourn the loss of a loved one.

Given this perspective, my involvement in capital punishment quickly grew beyond the purely academic. In the last few years I have had to sprinkle the ashes of one dead inmate in Africa, deliver the worldly goods of another to his family in Canada, store the inherited possessions of three or four more in my closets, sit with a half dozen families while their loved one was meeting his maker, and visit with a few inmates in the hours before their executions. Holding the hands of mothers while their sons are being executed and being the recipient of bulk discounts at local funeral homes has only strengthened my abolitionist commitment.

Does publicly standing opposed to the death penalty violate ethnical principles about "objectivity"? I don't think so. As I see it, objectivity is not the same as neutrality, and *not* to shout out at what one sees as a moral outrage is in itself a moral outrage. After all, when I lecture about racism in my sociology courses, I do not feel obliged to give equal time to the Ku Klux Klan. Sociologists must have informed perspectives, but these perspectives need not be "neutral."

Others, of course, see the death penalty differently. That, too, is part of the excitement that sociology has to offer, as part of what we teach is the ability to argue issues from several different perspectives. But it seems to me that on an issue such as capital punishment, one's position, pro or con, is less important than simply taking a stand, learning how to defend it, and respecting the opinions of those who differ. What annoys me most are people who are apathetic or who take a position without bothering to learn anything about it.

Sociology is a discipline that teaches compassion for the powerless. There are lots of relatively powerless people who need help—the homeless, the poor, the elderly, victims of racism or sexism, migrant farm workers, battered women and children, prisoners, and, yes, even death row inmates, to name a few. Sociology can teach compassion for those less fortunate, the value of making a commitment to make things better, and the competence to make one's voice heard—no matter what stand one takes on an issue.

Sources: Bedau, Hugo Adam, and Michael L. Radelet, "Miscarriages of Justice in Potentially Capital Cases," *Stanford Law Review* 40 (1987): 21–179; Radelet, Michael L. "Racial Characteristics and the Imposition of the Death Penalty," *American Sociological Review* 46 (1981): 918–27; Radelet, Michael L., ed., *Facing the Death Penalty: Essays on a Cruel and Unusual Punishment* (Philadelphia: Temple University Press, 1989).

Opponents of the death penalty note that most studies show no statistically significant murder-rate reduction as a result of the use of capital punishment (Bailey, 1980; Archer, 1984; Bowers et al., 1984). Moreover, because most murders are crimes of passion committed against members of one's own family or friends, it is difficult to estimate how many would have been avoided through rational calculation about the punishment.

People who support retribution view executions as a visible means of redressing (balancing out) a social wrong. Nonetheless, there are some people, such as sociologist Michael Radelet, who continue to argue that executions in the United States are ineffective, arbitrarily applied, cruel and unusual punishment. Moreover, one recent study documents approximately 300 cases in which innocent people were executed (Bedau and Radelet, 1987).

Prisons and Jails

Close to 1.5 percent of the adult population of the United States is under some form of supervision by the criminal justice system. The great majority—two-thirds—are in the community under probation. Close to 550,000 are in state or federal prisons; another 120,000 are serving their short-term sentences in local jails; and 260,000 are out of prison on parole (Bureau of Justice Statistics, 1989). These numbers are all-time highs and represent a political response to the public perception that crime is out of control.

The history of prisons or incarceration (from the Latin "to place behind walls") in America has been influenced by two opposing philosophies, both of which can be derived from our Protestant value system: **rehabilitation** and *punishment*. To rehabilitate means to return to a previous state, and is based on a belief in the power of repentance and salvation. Punishment rests on the dual assumptions that evil must be painfully removed from the sinner and that victims must be avenged. As it is almost impossible to punish and rehabilitate at the same time, the meaning of incarceration in our society has fluctuated between these two principles.

Rehabilitation means restoration to a former state.

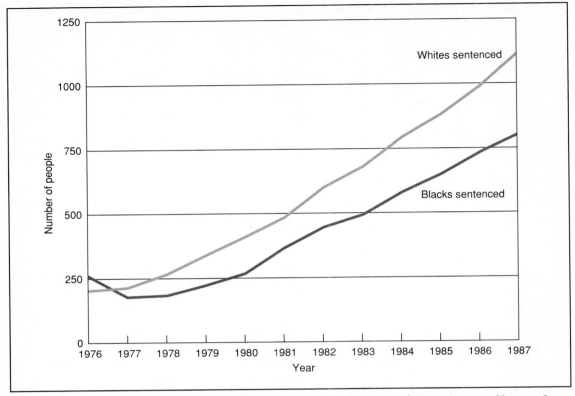

FIGURE 5-4   Prisoners under sentence of death, 1976–1987, by race. (Source: *Statistical Abstract of the United States 1989.*)

Total institutions, such as prisons and jails, control and monitor all aspects of inmates' lives.

Prisons as Total Institutions.   Prisons and jails are **total institutions** (Goffman, 1961) in which diverse human needs are handled by a bureaucratic organization that promotes group living. All activities are closely scheduled and predictable, based on the needs of the institution and its staff. Inmates are stripped of their preprison identities. They are put in uniforms, shaved (if they are males), given a number, and subjected to other ceremonies of degradation and depersonalization.

Total institutions are all designed to resocialize and change people and their sense of themselves (Goffman, 1961). Every total institution is a *mini-society* for its residents, and all prisons, from the maximum-security walled prison of Sing Sing in New York State to the minimum-security prison farm of Chino, California, share certain characteristics: (1) restriction of personal freedom, (2) limited choice of work, (3) impersonality, (4) social distance between prisoners and prison officers and guards, and (5) organization as primarily a single-sex setting.

These structural aspects of the prison give rise to a subculture among inmates that includes such rules for behavior as playing it cool, doing one's own time, not getting involved, being tough, never informing on fellow inmates, and not sympathizing with officials or accepting their word.

Both staff and inmates must adjust to the requirements of institutional order. Prison norms are, however, inconsistent with rehabilitation, because exposure to prison norms limits both the opportunity to learn skills for legitimate success in the outside world and prisoners' contact with their families.

Prison Conditions Today.   Lack of privacy, the brutality of guards and other inmates, loss of contact with families, boredom, poor food and medical care, increasing rates of AIDS caused by needles shared among addicts, and persistent daily discomforts have turned many American prisons into "jungles." With the current overcrowding of U.S. prisons, few funds can be devoted to educational and job-training programs. Lacking the skills necessary to become stable citizens, half of all prisoners will be back in prison at some time in their lives. The term used to describe a repeat offender is *recidivist,* literally "one who has fallen again."

In contrast to the belief that certain people have a tendency, or **predisposition,** to act in certain ways, is the **situational view,** which ascribes certain kinds of behavior to the social situation and the particular statuses and roles assigned to people.

The **predispositional view** assumes that there is a tendency among certain people to act in certain ways.

The **situational view** assumes that the social situation and statuses and roles assigned to people produce certain kinds of behavior.

Against the background of the mock prison experiment (described in Chapter 4), such events as prison riots become more understandable. One of the most savage prison riots in U.S. history occurred in the New Mexico State Penitentiary in 1980, leaving 33 inmates dead and 80 injured, as well as $82 million worth of damage to the prison. As analyzed by Useem (1985), the New Mexico riot illustrates how structural characteristics affect inmate and guard behavior. Between 1970 and 1975 the prison had a rehabilitation strategy based on job training and employment placement. In 1975 funds for these activities were cut back in favor of increasing the inmate population. Inmate violence increased as the men felt cheated by the authorities. With more than 1,100 men in a space designed for 850, tempers flared, and the prisoners split into warring subgroups. Prison violence will undoubtedly increase as overcrowding continues.

Jails.   Local jails house three different populations: those being held between arrest and arraignment (having a judge decide whether or not the accused should be held for trial); those awaiting trial (usually only people unable to raise bail money or who have been denied bail) or on trial; and those convicted and serving terms of less than one year or waiting to be transferred to a prison.

From a sociological point of view, the jail, even more than the prison, demonstrates the subtle uses of the criminal justice system as an agency of social control. Most of its inmates have not yet been convicted of any crime but are there because they offend the public's sense of appropriate behavior (Irwin, 1985). They have drunk too much, been rowdy in public, talked back to a police officer, or were suspected of doing drugs or selling sex. In addition, the question of who remains in jail and who is sent home with a promise to appear in court is usually answered on the basis of social status and resources.

Alternatives to Prison

According to recent estimates, even if the United States spends $10 billion in building new facilities, prisons will still be more than 20 percent over capacity in the year 2000 (Petersilia et al., 1987). There are a number of solutions to overcrowding. Some, such as additional smaller and more secure prisons, are very expensive to build and staff, and are probably not cost-effective in reducing recidivism. Others, used successfully in Europe, include (1) small correctional facilities in which inmates can gain work experience and income from which taxes can be deducted to pay the cost of their incarceration; (2) homelike surroundings that inmates may decorate as they choose, and in which they may wear civilian clothing and engage in activities to reinforce a noncriminal identity; and (3) short-term visits home or extended visiting from relatives, particularly spouses and children.

Throughout the United States, alternative programs are on the rise. Parole is the most common, featuring intensive supervision of probationers, daily reporting to probation officers, random drug tests, performance of community services, house arrest, and electronic monitoring. By 1988 officials in 33 states used electronic monitoring devices to supervise nearly 2,300 offenders who had been convicted of a wide range of criminal violations (Schmidt, 1989). Such programs are economically attractive, as offenders usually must have jobs and pay for all or part of the cost of their own supervision. Yet probation and similar alternatives have been criticized both by civil liberties groups as intruding into offenders lives and by conservatives as being too soft on criminals (Hudson, 1987).

SUMMARY

1. In every society, some behaviors become defined as appropriate standards of role performance.

2. Once norms are developed, conformity is encouraged and enforced by agents of social control.

3. Norms set boundaries for acceptable behavior and at the same time define deviance—behavior that goes beyond the boundary.

4. A deviant is defined by others as needing attention by agents or agencies of social control.

5. In complex societies, the relative power of competing groups determines which norms become the guiding norms for the society.

6. The norms of a society structure conformity and deviance. This has been studied in the laboratory and in various social settings.

7. From a functional perspective, deviant behavior is seen as functionally necessary. Deviance mobilizes support for community values and clarifies boundaries between the accepted and the unacceptable.

8. Social controls—techniques used to make people conform—use both informal mechanisms and formal agents specifically assigned to norm enforcement.

9. Theories on individual causes of deviance, based on biological differences and psychological theories, have not been able to establish any clear relationship between biology, early childhood experiences, or mental states and acts of nonconformity.

10. Sociological theories of deviance focus on the social context of the act, and take into account both structure and process.

11. The conflict perspective focuses on the use of power to enforce the laws supporting the interests of powerful interest groups.

12. Some types of deviance, considered odd or eccentric and not threatening to the social order, are tolerated, as are petty and institutionalized evasions of norms.

13. Mental illness can be seen as a residual deviance, behavior that is variously defined depending on the people and circumstances involved. As a social process it involves labeling, stigmatization, internalization, career stages, and treatment.

14. Every society has rules considered so important to social order that their violation is severely sanctioned. In simple societies customs and informal sanctions are used; in modern societies rules are formalized into laws.

15. Criminal law punishes conduct violating the interest of society or the state. Civil law punishes conduct violating the interest of private citizens.

16. The social injury, consensus, and conflict models represent three different explanations of how norms become laws.

17. Contrary to popular belief, most violent crimes occur between members of the same race.

18. Several theories, sometimes contradictory, have been proposed to explain why far fewer women than men have been arrested or imprisoned.

19. Organized crime—attempts to gain wealth illegally—may be used as a way out of the poverty of urban ghettos.

20. Although most attention in the United States has been focused on street crime because it is violent, in terms of money involved and lives affected, white-collar and organizational crime is far more prevalent.

21. Crimes without victims, or vice crimes, rather than posing a moral threat to society are likely to lead to corruption.

22. Juveniles come to be identified by the law when they commit a crime, are neglected or abused, or commit a status offense. They are processed by the juvenile court system.

23. The criminal justice system involves the prosecutor, the defense attorney, and the judge, each representing different interests. Most offenders avoid being brought to trial, and very few are ultimately sentenced to prison.

24. Prison life is extremely dehumanizng and most ex-convicts eventually return to crime. Overcrowding often leads to prison violence.

SUGGESTED READINGS

Akers, Ronald. *Deviant Behavior: A Social Learning Approach.* 4th ed. Belmont, CA: Wadsworth, 1989. A text that stresses a social learning approach to understanding deviance.

Archer, Dane, and Rosemary Gartner. *Violence and Crime in Cross-National Perspective.* New Haven: Yale University Press, 1984. Crime and violence in 110 countries based on a cross-cultural comparison.

Caputi, Jane. *The Age of Sex Crime.* Bowling Green, OH: State University Popular Press, 1987. The increasing incidence of serial murders of women by men.

Carpenter, Cheryl, Barry Glassner, Bruce D. Johnson, and Julia Loughlin. *Kids, Drugs, and Crime.* Lexington, MA: Lexington Books, 1988. The link between adolescent drug use and criminal activity.

Cullen, Francis T., William J. Maakestad, and Gray Cavender. *Corporate Crime under Attack: The Ford Pinto Case and Beyond.* Cincinnati: Anderson, 1987. The events of a 1973 collision involving a Ford Pinto and the death of the car's owner and the prosecution that ensued.

Denzin, Norman K. *The Alcoholic Self; The Recovering Alcoholic; Treating Alcoholism: An Alcoholics Anonymous Approach.* Newbury Park, CA: Sage Publications, 1987. A powerful statement about American society and a social theory of alcoholism in this award-winning trilogy.

DiIulio, John J. *Governing Prisons: A Comparative Study of Correctional Management.* New York: Free Press, 1987. How correctional institutions can be managed so as to reduce violence and foster pride among correctional workers.

Douglas, Jack D., and Frances Chaput Waksler. *The Sociology of Deviance: An Introduction.* Boston: Little, Brown, 1982. A comprehensive look at the sociological approaches to deviance.

Erikson, Kai. *Wayward Puritans.* New York: Wiley, 1966. A historical analysis of the ways in which deviant behavior was created and dealt with in Puritan New England.

Erickson, Patricia G., Eduard M. Adlaf, Glenn F. Murray, and Reginald G. Smart. *The Steel Drug: Cocaine in Perspective.* Lexington, MA: Heath, 1986. Historical and contemporary problems associated with the use of cocaine.

Ermann, M. David, and Richard J. Lundman. *Corporate and Governmental Deviance: Problems of Organizational Behavior in Contemporary Society.* 3d ed. New York: Oxford University Press, 1987. Origins, patterns, and reactions to corporate and government deviance.

Hope, Marjorie, and James Young. *The Faces of the Homeless.* Lexington, MA: Heath, 1987. The growing population of the homeless in the United States.

Kenney, Dennis Jay. *Crime, Fear, and the New York City Subways: The Role of Citizen Action.* New York: Praeger, 1987. The role of the citizen action group, the Guardian Angels.

Los, Maria. *Communist Ideology, Law and Crime: A Comparative View of the USSR and Poland.* New York: St. Martin's Press, 1988. Criminality and criminal law in the Soviet Union and Poland under communism.

Marx, Gary T. *Undercover: Police Surveillance in America.* Berkeley: University of California Press, 1988. Undercover police work, effects on involved targets, extraneous parties, and the agents themselves.

Miller, Eleanor M. *Street Women.* Philadelphia: Temple University Press. Social networks supporting prostitution and significant ethnic differences among black and white prostitutes' careers.

Plant, Martin A., David F. Peck, and Elaine Samuel. *Alcohol, Drugs, and School-Leavers.* London: Tavistock, 1985. Young people's use of alcohol and drugs in Britain and the effectiveness of alcohol education classes and films.

Radelet, Michael L., ed. *Facing the Death Penalty: Essays on a Cruel and Unusual Punishment.* Philadelphia: Temple University Press, 1989. A probing examination of those living on death row and their families.

Ridlon, Florence V. *A Fallen Angel: The Status Insularity of the Female Alcoholic.* Lewisburg, PA: Bucknell University Press, 1988. The consequences of societal responses in shaping deviant outcomes: a report on female alcoholics.

Spitzer, Stephen, and Andrew T. Scull, eds. *Research in Law, Deviance and Social Control: A Research Annual.* Vol. 9. Greenwich, CT: JAI Press, 1988. Deviance, explored through historical and contemporary examples of mass panics and the AIDS epidemic.

SOCIAL DIFFERENCES AND INEQUALITY

The three chapters in Part II describe how achieved characteristics, such as skill and income, and ascribed characteristics, such as sex, race, religion, and ethnicity (nationality background), lead to judgments of social worth and unequal treatment within the society. *Stratification systems* are formed when people are placed in categories that are ranked from high to low on the basis of such traits. In all societies more complex than a gathering band, stratification is a key element of social structure, affecting people's life chances and choices.

Assuming that any social system has a limited supply of valued resources—goods and services, honor, affection, power over others— sociologists ask how these resources are distributed. The study of stratification examines the links between personal differences and social inequality. In Chapter 6, we discuss general principles of stratification, the consequences of structured inequality, and opportunities for upward or downward movement. Chapter 7 examines the importance of sexuality and of gender in the distribution of power, prestige, and property in social systems. Chapter 8 covers race, religion, and ethnicity as determinants of social rank.

6

Social Stratification

Who should be saved? Although many people might need a heart transplant, the supply of healthy hearts available for this purpose is extremely limited. If you were the hospital administrator with final say, and only five of the following eight persons could be chosen, whom would you choose, and why?

- A 50-year-old Asian-American male minister
- A 40-year-old white female homemaker
- A 30-year-old white male homosexual physicist
- A 25-year-old white male Marxist professor
- A 16-year-old African-American student
- A 60-year-old Latina female physician
- The 55-year-old governor of the state
- The 20-year-old disabled son of wealthy parents

Each of these descriptions contains a mix of ascribed and achieved characteristics, some of which are valued more highly in our society than others. This mental exercise is designed to make you aware of your standards of judgment.

When we rank some kinds of people as more deserving than others, we create a **stratification system.** The essence of stratification is captured in one sentence from George Orwell's novel *Animal Farm* (1945): "All the animals are equal here, but some are more equal than others." Is it always necessary that some people be more equal than others? What are the bases and the consequences of inequality?

Stratification systems rank some individuals and groups as more deserving than others.

PRINCIPLES OF STRATIFICATION

In all societies there are three kinds of valued resources: (1) **power**—the ability to impose one's will on others; (2) **prestige**—respect from others; and (3) **property**—wealth, whether measured in land, green paper rectangles, beads, oil, or yams. And in all societies more complex than simple gathering bands, these resources are unequally distributed among individuals and groups.

Because people who differ in their ascribed and achieved traits are evaluated differently, a **social hierarchy** is formed. A hierarchy is a set of ranked statuses from highest to lowest. Because the most- and least-valued characteristics are likely to be relatively rare, status hierarchies tend to be diamond-shaped, narrower both at the top and at the bottom (see Figure 6-2, p. 185). Once such a hierarchy is formed, people at different levels, or *strata* (plural; the singular is *stratum*), can claim differing amounts of power, prestige, and property.

Although it is possible to imagine a society in which all members are equally valued and equally treated, the human experience appears to be that once a group's economy involves a division of labor beyond gathering, some tasks are considered more important than others, and the people who do different kinds of work are likely to be differentially (unequally) rewarded.

Among the many tribes of Western New Guinea, for example, the degree of inequality increases with the complexity of the economic base. The Baruya are divided into three classes: the "great men," who are warriors, the "big

Power is the ability to impose one's will on others. **Prestige** refers to respect given by others. **Property** refers to wealth owned.

A **social hierarchy** is a set of ranked statuses.

men," who have the most crops, and the "little people," who are women, children, and men with few economic or social resources. The neighboring Duna are even more stratified because in shifting from simple to complex horticulture they are able to produce a surplus of crops, which leads to greater divisions within the tribe. And wherever intensive agriculture has been introduced, sharp divisions emerge between a few "big men" producers or traders and a large "peasant" class of farm workers (Strathern, 1982).

THEORETICAL PERSPECTIVES

The universality of stratification systems is typically explained and justified by theories of human nature and/or collective needs.

The Functional Theory of Stratification

The *functional perspective* seeks to explain social structures in terms of the consequences of a given arrangement: "What happens because such and such a system exists?" The functional analysis of stratification, in the classic formulation of Davis and Moore (1945), goes like this: Not all persons have the same abilities. Some will have more of those qualities needed and valued by members of a given society at a particular historical moment, such as strength, hunting skills, artistry, wisdom, or ambition. On the other side of the stratification equation is the fact that desired rewards are always limited in quantity, whether naturally or artificially (if everyone can have it, it loses its value as a symbol of superior performance). Thus, if skills are unequally distributed within a population, it is in the interests of group survival that those with the most ability use it for the well-being of all. In return, such persons deserve greater rewards—in admiration, command, or material goods—than do those with less important talents.

Meritocracy refers to a hierarchy based on ability and credentials.

Functionalists believe that stratification processes produce a hierarchy of talent, called a **meritocracy**—the rule of the most worthy or deserving. From a functional perspective, therefore, some forms of inequality are inevitable, beneficial to society, and a powerful motive to performance. This point of view is currently popular among writers on the political right as an explanation of inequality on the basis of race and sex (e.g., Goldberg, 1986). The

The functionalist and conflict perspectives differ in their explanations of how people gain power. How would each perspective explain why most business executives are men?

functionalist position has been challenged by generations of sociologists, who point out the potential dysfunctions of a system that could breed resentment over blocked opportunity. Moreover, inequality appears to be as much due to scarcity of top slots as to unequal abilities, and many top positions are inherited rather than earned (Tumin, 1953; Heller, 1987).

Conflict Theories of Stratification

In contrast to the functional approach, the conflict perspective, as described in Chapter 1, explains social structure as the outcome of struggles over scarce rewards. Those already in power are able to make the rules that set limits on competition. In addition, as Karl Marx pointed out, the dominant ideas of any society are those of its dominant strata. This insight—that ideas are also social products—has been expanded by conflict theorists into the concept of ideological hegemony (Gramsci, 1959/1971; Sassoon, 1982). *Hegemony* means sphere of influence or control, and *ideological hegemony* refers to the control of cultural symbols—beliefs, values, ideals of justice, and so forth (Bourdieu, 1985). Because those who own or control the media, educational institutions, and other sources of information come from the higher strata, they are likely to promote definitions of reality that justify their own success. Conflict explanations of inequality focus on *structural* rather than personal variables. Structural variables include the distribution of occupations in a society, past and present hiring practices, labor markets, the degree of unionization, the organization of the workplace, and the diversity of firms and businesses in a community. These are characteristics of social systems, not of individuals, and they play an important part in creating and maintaining inequality among various groups of workers.

A Unified View

The functional and conflict perspectives need not be considered mutually exclusive (Lenski, 1966; Milner, 1987). The functional model could account for the origins of stratification systems, which are then maintained by the mechanisms of control studied by conflict theorists. Thus, people with unusual ability or luck can amass great power and wealth at a particular historical period. Once established, they seek to pass these advantages to their children, even in societies with a declared ideological commitment to equality of opportunity, such as the Communist nations of Eastern Europe before 1990 (Szelenyi, 1987). The transmission of social status advantages is possible because members of subsequent generations are unequal in social position from the beginning. As in a footrace, some runners will be naturally faster, but others will have been provided with better equipment, training, and a head start.

DIMENSIONS OF SOCIAL STRATIFICATION

The term **social stratification,** then, refers to hierarchies of statuses that reflect the unequal distribution of power, prestige, and property in a given society. To some extent, anyone in a high position knows that one dimension

Social stratification refers to hierarchies of statuses based on unequal distribution of power, prestige, and property.

of high status can be used to secure the other types of advantages. But Max Weber (in Gerth and Mills, 1946) emphasized the need to consider three separate ways of ranking, even though they cannot always be separated in real life:

1. *Class* refers to people at the same economic level, who may or may not become aware of their common interests and form social classes.
2. *Status groups* are based on the degree of prestige (not necessarily class position) of their members, who tend also to share a common life style.
3. *Parties* are political groupings that may or may not express class interests.

Before coming to conclusions about the stratification system of any society, let us explore the distribution of power, prestige, and property in the United States today.

Power

Authority refers to socially legitimated power.

Power, defined by Max Weber as the ability to impose one's will on others, is a social resource that is unequally distributed in almost every relationship, group, and society. **Authority** refers to power that belongs to a socially recognized status (e.g., the position of president, police officer, or parent) and is, therefore, considered legitimate by other members of the society. People who hold important government positions tend to come from the upper half of the wealth and education hierarchy. Few people leave public office poorer than when they entered, and very few of the poor have ever run for office or been appointed to high posts. Thus, position on one hierarchy can be used to gain status in another—wealth to gain power, and power to gain wealth.

Other forms of legitimate power in everyday life include the control that parents exercise over children, that of husbands over wives in most societies, of employers over employees, and of teachers over students. But not all power is considered legitimate; for example, leaders of organized crime enjoy great economic and political power while operating outside of the law.

Influence is the ability to persuade others to follow one's will.

Influence can be defined as the ability to persuade others to follow one's will and is based less on occupying a particular social status than on interpersonal skills. Influential people often also possess unique talents or knowledge, or they may be close to people in authority.

Authority refers to power residing in a socially recognized status. In a historic moment, two persons with great authority met: Pope John Paul II and President Mikhail Gorbachev of the Soviet Union. This was the first time a political leader of the Soviet Union had had an audience with the Pope.

Prestige

Prestige (or status honor) depends on the respect given by others. In modern industrial societies, prestige is based largely on occupation and income, especially if the occupation requires a long period of training (see Table 6-1). Although a distinction is made between the economic rewards of an occupation and its value to the society, both considerations enter into prestige rankings, so that agreement on a person's social value becomes a justification for economic inequality (Hope, 1982). Prestige judgments are also influenced by whether women or men dominate the occupation, with "women's work" typically rated lower.

But the link between occupational prestige and income is not perfect: college professors, whose prestige rank is quite high, tend to have incomes only slightly above the national average. Conversely, low-rated garbage collectors or dockworkers often benefit from relatively high union-negotiated wage scales. Furthermore, many people in low-prestige jobs maintain a sense of self-worth through their relationships with family members and coworkers, or through their mastery of whatever skills are required for that occupation (Walsh and Taylor, 1982).

In other cases, generally low-ranked occupations associated with illegal drugs bring very high rewards in terms of income and power, and successful criminals could be figures of prestige in their local communities. Generally, however, the distribution of respect within modern societies is related to training, skills, and income. In turn, people in high prestige occupations have the power to impose their particular version of justice and order on the society as a whole (Goode, 1978).

Property

Every society has certain items that signify material success. In the United States, we measure wealth by counting the monetary value of everything owned by household members, including houses, cars, stocks and bonds, savings accounts, life insurance policies, and retirement accounts.

Wealth.   The actual distribution of property in the United States is very difficult to determine because most very wealthy people have their money in assets that cannot be easily traced (foreign bank accounts, safe-deposit boxes, works of art, and the like). Nonetheless, several studies in the mid-1980s have provided valuable data on American wealth holders (Bureau of the Census, 1986; Joint Economic Committee, 1986; Federal Reserve Board, 1986).

In 1984 the Bureau of the Census conducted a special study of household wealth and asset ownership, the first such study since 1963. The percentages of American households at each level of **net worth** (assets minus debts) is shown in Table 6-2. As these data indicate, one-third of American households have net assets worth less than $10,000. Most of the remainder have some money in the bank, own a car, and are partial owners of their own home. But only 2 percent have assets greater than $500,000.

Asset ownership varies systematically by age, sex, race, education, occupational status, and yearly income. The largest difference is by race, with white households accumulating assets ten times those of African-American

Net worth consists of the value of all assets less all debts.

TABLE 6-1 The Prestige Ratings of Occupations in the United States

(Scale runs from 100 [highest] to 1 [lowest]; Score = average score for the sample)

Occupation	Score	Occupation	Score
Physician	82	Real estate agent	44
College professor	78	Fireman	44
Judge	76	Postal clerk	43
Lawyer	76	Advertising agent	42
Physicist	74	Mail carrier	42
Dentist	74	Railroad conductor	41
Banker	72	Typist	41
Aeronautical engineer	71	Plumber	41
Architect	71	Farmer	41
Psychologist	71	Telephone operator	40
Airline pilot	70	Carpenter	40
Chemist	69	Welder	40
Minister	69	Dancer	38
Civil engineer	68	Barber	38
Biologist	68	Jeweler	37
Geologist	67	Watchmaker	37
Sociologist	66	Bricklayer	36
Political scientist	66	Airline stewardess	36
Mathematician	65	Meter reader	36
High school teacher	63	Mechanic	35
Registered nurse	62	Baker	34
Pharmacist	61	Shoe repairman	33
Veterinarian	60	Bulldozer operator	33
Elementary school teacher	60	Bus driver	32
Accountant	57	Truck driver	32
Librarian	55	Cashier	31
Statistician	55	Sales clerk	29
Social worker	52	Meatcutter	28
Funeral director	52	Housekeeper	25
Computer specialist	51	Longshoreman	24
Stockbroker	51	Gas station attendant	22
Reporter	51	Cab driver	22
Office manager	50	Elevator operator	21
Bank teller	50	Bartender	20
Electrician	49	Waiter	20
Machinist	48	Farm laborer	18
Police officer	48	Maid/servant	18
Insurance agent	47	Garbage collector	17
Musician	46	Janitor	17
Secretary	46	Shoeshiner	9
Foreman	45		

Source: Davis and Smith, 1984.

TABLE 6-2   Household Net Worth

Net Worth in Dollars	Percent of U.S. Households
Negative or zero	11.0
$1–$4,999	15.3
$5,000–$9,999	6.4
$10,000–$24,999	12.4
$25,000–$49,999	14.4
$50,000–$99,999	19.2
$100,000–$249,999	15.3
$250,000–$499,999	4.0
$500,000 and over	2.0
	100.0

Source: U.S. Bureau of the Census, P-23, 1986, p. 10.

households. Married couples have more assets than the nonmarried; and households headed by people 55 and over are wealthier than those headed by younger persons. According to the Census Bureau data, the top 10 percent of wealth holders account for about 40 percent of total asset ownership in the United States.

Using a slightly different data set and covering more sources of wealth than the Bureau of the Census, the Federal Reserve Board, in 1983, found an even higher degree of concentration of wealth, with the top 10 percent of wealth holders having almost two-thirds of this nation's privately owned assets (Avery and Kennickel, 1989).

Figure 6-1 compares the 1983 data with comparable information from 1963 and shows that although the top one-half of 1 percent of households ("super rich") accounted for 25 percent of the total wealth of the United States in 1963, this proportion had grown to 35 percent in 1983. Given recent changes in our tax code that favor high-income earners, it is likely that the "super rich" own close to 40 percent of the total private wealth of the nation today.

Income.   The Bureau of the Census also collects yearly data on *earned income:* the amount of money received in a given year as reported by households, families, and individuals. This money comes from wages/salaries, dividends and capital gains, and other sources reported to the Internal Revenue Service. The distribution of income by families in 1988 is shown in Table 6-3.

As you can see, family income varies by race or ethnic origin, educational level, number of earners, region of the country, whether the family is headed by a couple or only one parent, and the sex of the householder. The median, remember, is the midpoint of the entire distribution with 50 percent above and 50 percent below. Thus, in 1988, families headed by a married couple earned more than twice the income of families headed by a woman alone;

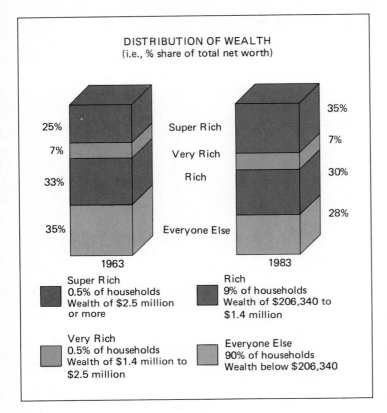

DISTRIBUTION OF WEALTH
(i.e., % share of total net worth)

1963

Super Rich — 25%
Very Rich — 7%
Rich — 33%
Everyone Else — 35%

1983

Super Rich — 35%
Very Rich — 7%
Rich — 30%
Everyone Else — 28%

Super Rich
0.5% of households
Wealth of $2.5 million
or more

Very Rich
0.5% of households
Wealth of $1.4 million to
$2.5 million

Rich
9% of households
Wealth of $206,340 to
$1.4 million

Everyone Else
90% of households
Wealth below $206,340

FIGURE 6-1   (Sources: Joint Economic Committee, U.S. Congress, 1986, p. 35; *Wall Street Journal,* August 15, 1986, p. 1.)

white families earned almost twice the income of African-American families (largely because a high proportion of the latter are headed by women).

What the data in Table 6-3 do *not* show is the difference between household and family income. Households often consist of only one person, usually a young person just entering the labor force or an older widow living on Social Security, and therefore tend to have median incomes lower than families'. Clearly, in terms of the income hierarchy, it is best to be married, to be white, and to have two adult wage earners (Danzinger et al., 1989).

The Disappearing Middle

During the 1960s and 1970s, the income gap between the richest and poorest earners narrowed, the proportion in poverty was sharply reduced, and most Americans considered themselves part of the comfortable middle. In the 1980s, however, it appears that the poor have gotten poorer; the rich, richer; and the middle is shrinking (Levy, 1988). Between 1978 and 1987, for example, the income of the lowest 20 percent of families declined by almost 10 percent, whereas that of the top fifth increased more than 15 percent (U.S. House of Representatives, 1989).

TABLE 6-3   Median Income of American Families in 1988

Family Characteristics	Median Income (Dollars)
All races	
All families	32,191
Married couples	36,389
Female householder, no husband present	15,346
White	
Married couples	36,840
Female householder, no husband present	17,672
Black	
Married couples	30,385
Female householder, no husband present	10,657
Hispanic[a]	
Married couples	25,667
Female householder, no husband present	10,687
Education[b]	
Less than 4 years of high school	14,142
High school: 4 years	27,842
College: 4 years or more	45,490
Number of earners	
No earner	13,729
One earner	23,872
Two earners	38,702
Three earners	48,977
Region	
Northeast	36,454
Midwest	32,887
South	28,951
West	33,082
Earnings of Year-Round, Full-Time Workers	
Male	26,656
Female	17,606
Per person income	13,123

[a] Persons of Hispanic origin can be of any race.
[b] For householders age 25 and over.

Source: Adapted from U.S. Bureau of the Census, P-20, No. 162, 1989, p. 3.

Among the factors most commonly cited to explain this reversal are the following:

- Changes in the composition of the labor force, as women and entry-level baby boomers earn relatively low wages.
- Lingering effects of high unemployment rates during the 1981–82 recession, and the failure of former auto- and steelworkers to find employment at the same wage level.
- Breakdown of union power to bargain for higher wages and benefits.
- Relocation of manufacturing overseas or to states with lower wages and few or no unions.
- Federal policies that cut assistance to the poor and reduced tax liability of the wealthy.
- Increased use of part-time employees who do not receive fringe benefits (e.g., health insurance, pension rights).
- Growth of jobs at lowest end of the occupational skills spectrum.

Together, these trends have lowered "real wages" (the difference between increases in wages and the cost of living) among low-income earners, thus increasing inequality in the United States (Harrison and Bluestone, 1988; Levy, 1987).

Socioeconomic Status

Social scientists have long looked for one simplified measure of social rank. The common usage today is to refer to **socioeconomic status (SES),** based on a combination of income, occupational prestige, and education. In most American studies, SES is used as a measure of another abstract concept: *social class.*

Socioeconomic status (SES) is a measure based on a combination of income, occupational prestige, and education.

Figure 6-2 shows the distribution of American adults on the basis of education, occupation, and income in 1987, from which a rough social class structure can be derived. Class is perhaps the most powerful variable in the social sciences because almost every other factor of interest to us is influenced by it, from how long we live to how happy we are in marriage.

SOCIAL CLASS IN AMERICA

Measuring Social Class

There are many ways of defining social class: by reputation in the community, by life-style, by one's own self-classification, as well as by the various SES indexes. But these methods are all based on characteristics of the individual and are therefore somewhat unsatisfying to many sociologists.

Class awareness refers to the recognition that differences in income, occupational prestige, and life-style are reflections of one's own class position.

Class Awareness and Self-Perception

How do Americans themselves make class distinctions? **Class awareness** refers to recognizing differences in income, occupational prestige, and social power, and accurately locating one's own position. Most researchers have

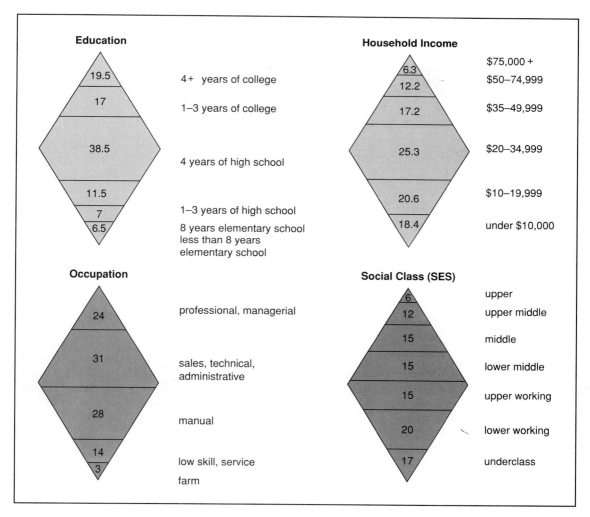

Education

19.5   4+ years of college

17   1–3 years of college

38.5   4 years of high school

11.5
7   1–3 years of high school
6.5   8 years elementary school
        less than 8 years
        elementary school

Household Income

6.3 $75,000 +
12.2 $50–74,999

17.2 $35–49,999

25.3 $20–34,999

20.6 $10–19,999

18.4   under $10,000

Occupation

24   professional, managerial

31   sales, technical,
        administrative

28   manual

14   low skill, service
3
        farm

Social Class (SES)

6   upper
12   upper middle

15   middle

15   lower middle

15   upper working

20   lower working

17   underclass

FIGURE 6-2   Dimensions of socioeconomic status (SES) in percentages in the United States: 1987. (Source: U.S. Bureau of the Census, 1988, pp. 125, 376–77, 1989, p. 27.)

found that Americans do indeed have a sharp awareness of class distinctions, have strong feelings about their own location in stratification systems, and tend to associate with people of equal rank (e.g., Jackman and Jackman, 1983; Vanneman and Cannon, 1987). These findings fit Weber's definition of classes as "status groups" originating in common economic interests and resulting in a shared sense of community.

In assigning a class position to themselves and others, survey respondents tend to use the standard objective variables of education, income, and occupational prestige, but also take into account the characteristics of the job:

workplace, authority, supervision, and self-employment. In the Vanneman and Cannon (1987) study, based on large-scale national survey data, the major line of division was between professional and managerial jobs (middle class) and manual and low-authority white-collar employment (working class). Although many respondents misclassified themselves (especially white men in nonsupervisory jobs who called themselves "middle class"), the majority clearly saw the importance of autonomy and control in the workplace (see also Vallas, 1987).

Class Consciousness

Class consciousness occurs when class awareness becomes the central organizing point of self-definition and political actions.

There is a crucial difference between *class awareness* and **class consciousness,** which occurs when awareness becomes central to a person's self-definition and political identification, and when people see their class interests in opposition to those of members of other classes. The apparent absence of class-based politics in the United States is often explained by reference to (1) the ideals of equality of the founders and lack of an inherited aristocracy; (2) the image of America as a nation of immigrants, for whom anything is possible; (3) the reality of upward movement in the stratification system as a result of three centuries of economic growth; (4) the failure of organized labor to create working-class solidarity in opposition to employers; and (5) the existence of ties and loyalties based, for example, on race, religion, and ethnicity, that cut across class lines.

Another explanation, from a conflict perspective, is offered by Vanneman and Cannon (1987): Both the weakness of unions and the lack of a working-class political party in the United States are the result of class-conscious actions by the upper strata, whose control over the economic and political systems has been almost absolute for the past 100 years. Rather than viewing class consciousness as an individual trait, and blaming workers for their own relative powerlessness, it would be more sociological for us to see shared identity based on class location as a *collective* reality, emerging from the experience of struggle (Fantasia, 1988). But there has been no class struggle in the United States because American labor has been thoroughly dominated by the combined powers of business and government.

Social Class and Social Order

As we have seen, social resources in American society are unequally distributed and awareness of these differences is widespread. Income inequality in the United States is, for example, ten times greater than in Sweden. Because inequality can produce discontent and reduce social cohesion, we must ask why our society has remained so stable.

In general, inequality itself does not necessarily produce disorder. As long as most citizens think that the rules are fair, inequality is tolerated. At some point, the have-nots may withdraw their support and take to the streets, but the monopoly of political force rests with the powerful, who typically crush the rebellion.

Ideological Supports for the American Class Systems.   In the United States, beliefs that justify inequality are deeply embedded. In view of the

Most of the unrest in Central and South America is due to extreme inequality in the distribution of wealth. The dramatic differences in living conditions are obvious in this picture of Mexico City.

concept of *ideological hegemony*, it seems logical to expect that the people who control the production of ideas and symbols have constructed a set of beliefs that justify, legitimate, and reinforce the existing distribution of societal resources (Feagin, 1986; Kluegel and Smith, 1986):

1. *The promise of equal opportunity.* Among the most enduring myths of our culture is the belief that with hard work and a bit of luck, anyone can rise from "rags to riches."
2. *Survival of the fittest,* or "social Darwinism," is based on the belief that society resembles a jungle in which the naturally superior will win out in the struggle for survival. Social inequality, therefore, reflects a law of nature and the inborn differences among people.
3. *Psychological determinism.* As part of our cultural emphasis on individualism, Americans prefer to believe that individual psychological traits—motivation, achievement needs, intelligence, and the like—are primarily responsible for success or failure in the workplace.
4. *The work ethic.* As described in Chapter 2, the American value system is built around the idea that work is a sacred task and that success in one's work can be seen as a sign of divine grace. Failure, therefore, must signify a lack of good qualities.
5. *The "culture of poverty."* Many people, including some social scientists (e.g., Lewis, 1959; L. Mead, 1986), suggest that a set of values and coping behaviors is transmitted from one generation to another, creating a distinct subculture that reinforces a cycle of poverty.

All these assumptions have shaped American beliefs about the causes of both wealth and poverty. As shown in Table 6-4, the general public believes that people are poor because they lack thrift, effort, ability, and morals. By the same reasoning, the wealthy are seen as possessing such positive charac-

187

EVERYDAY SOCIOLOGY

James R. Kluegel

James R. Kluegel received a B.A. and M.A. from the University of Minnesota, and his Ph.D. in 1975 from the University of Wisconsin at Madison. He is coauthor (with Eliot R. Smith) of Beliefs about Inequality: Americans' Views of What Is and What Ought to Be *and has published numerous articles in professional journals. He is professor of sociology at the University of Illinois at Urbana-Champaign, serving as head of the Department of Sociology for the past five years.*

I have long been intrigued by what might be called "everyday sociology"—how average Americans see and come to understand their social worlds. I can't trace my interest in this question to any single experience, but in general it stems from my years as a college student during the 1960s. The question, "How can someone believe that?" was everywhere. It was often asked of us by my generation's parents, as a part of the "generation gap" of that era. It also was often asked by my generation of their parents and of representatives of the established institutions of our society.

I was never poor as a child growing up in Minneapolis. My father and mother were, for the most part, steadily employed at relatively low-paying, white-collar jobs. Nevertheless, I came to find the level of hostility and often outright anger that most Americans directed toward poor people to be both puzzling and troubling. Americans have somewhat of a reputation for their generosity. When the media make the public aware of a personal tragedy, such as in the case of "Baby Jessica," the child trapped in a well a few years ago, offers of financial help and other types of help pour in. At the same time, letters to the editor of local newspapers commonly include bitter denunciations of the poor and their "welfare Cadillacs," and politicians continue to be elected by campaigning against the "welfare mess" and those who receive public aid. Why doesn't American generosity, in one of the richest nations of the world, extend to the poor?

As a college student, I was also puzzled and even more troubled about prevailing racial beliefs. This was the time of riots in our urban ghettos, of the murder of Martin Luther King, Jr., and of "white backlash" in both the North and South. The question of how people can be so hostile to other citizens is one that I, along with many social scientists, have tried to answer during the past several decades. Indeed, the modern-day field of social psychology has important historical roots in the effort to understand the causes of racial prejudice.

Thus, as I set out to answer my questions regarding popular beliefs about the poor and African-Americans, I was attracted to the field of social psychology. Because I wished to study the general public, I also acquired the skills necessary to conduct large-scale surveys and to analyze the data. I was fortunate to attend three major Midwestern universities that offered state-of-the-art training in social psychology and research methods—first as an undergraduate and graduate student at the University of Minnesota, then while completing my Ph.D. at the University of Wisconsin at Madison, and most recently as a faculty member of the University of Illinois.

As I have studied popular beliefs about the poor and African-Americans over the years, I have come to understand that there is an important link between these two categories in the public mind, beyond the fact that African-Americans are disproportionately poor. This link is *individualism*, a key element of American "everyday sociology." For the most part, individualist explanations of social events, and especially those in the economic realm, are deeply embedded in American culture. The image of the person as wholly responsible for her or his own fate is part of our literature, celebrated in the media, embedded in the work ethic and in the "American Dream." It is a central part of the common ideology of opportunity as well. The perception that America is the land of opportunity where people can make it on their own is pervasive. As Eliot Smith and I have shown in our research (1986), structural explanations—those that see contemporary social outcomes as the product of historical or institutional forces—are largely absent from the vocabulary of the amateur sociologist. Without structural explanations, many Americans come to see all economic inequality, whether between the rich and the poor or between African-Americans and whites, as the result of individual-level factors, such as personal weaknesses or failings. Although American individualism has a positive side in motivating hard work and resourcefulness, it also has the negative effect of making it politically difficult to implement solutions to racial or economic injustice.

Sociology, especially through the introductory course, has an important role to play in teaching that there are other explanations of our social world than the individualistic one. In my own teaching I strive to get students involved in structural thinking, to help them realize that there is another level of causation beyond what goes on inside the minds of individuals. In this way, and through my research, I am trying to move popular wisdom in a more sociological direction. It is often difficult to get people to abandon strictly individualistic thinking about American society. It is something most people learn very early in life. However, I believe the effort is necessary and worthwhile if we hope to live in a just society. I am enough of a democrat—in the sense of believing that solutions to social problems will be sought if the public demands them—to believe that one way to realize social and economic justice is to educate the public about the structural sources of our problems.

teristics as intelligence, a willingness to work hard, and the ability to defer gratification (Cummings and Taebel, 1978; Della Fave, 1980).

This ideology of individual responsibility operates at the social psychological level to reconcile people's belief in a "just world" with their own objective position in the stratification system. Americans tend to accept inequalities as legitimate when they can attribute success or failure to themselves (Shepelak, 1987). If we measure our own worth and that of others in terms of rewards, and if the distribution of rewards must be perceived as fair, then we must believe that the cause of differences is in individuals and not the social structure.

POVERTY IN AMERICA

Explaining Poverty

As Table 6-4 clearly shows, most Americans accept the individualistic view of the causes of poverty. And most Americans also believe that welfare benefits encourage the poor to remain impoverished (*New York Times,* August 23, 1989). This approach has been criticized by other social scientists as an example of "blaming the victim" (Ryan, 1972). Rather than focusing on individuals, conflict theorists look at societal-level or *structural* variables, such as items seven through ten in Table 6-4. From this perspective, poverty stems from a person's location in labor markets and from broad changes in the economic system itself that have reduced the availability of certain types of employment in the inner cities.

The poor are poor because they compete for jobs in sectors of the economy that offer little security and pay very low wages (Tienda and Lii,

TABLE 6-4   Percentages of Americans Who Felt the Following Reasons for Poverty Were Very Important, Somewhat Important, or Not at All Important, 1969–80

	1969			1980		
	Very	Somewhat	Not at All	Very	Somewhat	Not at All
1. Lack of thrift and proper money management	59	31	11	64	30	6
2. Lack of effort by the poor themselves	57	34	9	53	39	8
3. Lack of ability and talent	54	34	12	53	35	11
4. Failure of society to provide good schools for many Americans	38	26	36	46	29	26
5. Loose morals and drunkenness	50	32	18	44	30	27
6. Sickness and physical handicaps	46	39	14	43	41	15
7. Low wages in some businesses and industries	43	36	21	40	47	14
8. Failure of private industry to provide enough jobs	29	38	33	35	39	28
9. Prejudice and discrimination against blacks	34	39	27	31	44	25
10. Being taken advantage of by rich people	19	32	48	20	35	45
11. Just bad luck	8	28	63	12	32	56

Source: Kluegel, 1987, p. 88.

1987; Nelson and Lorence, 1988). Poverty is the involuntary outcome of political powerlessness combined with unemployment due to decisions made by business owners. Thus, the personality traits so often thought of as causes of poverty—lowered ambition, lack of thrift, enjoying what one can at the moment—may best be seen as logical responses to the reality of "living poorly in America" (Beeghley, 1983). And as long as the structural barriers to steady employment persist, so also will the life-styles called the "culture of poverty." But this set of attitudes and behaviors is not consciously transmitted from one generation to another; most poor parents are similar to their nonpoor counterparts in wanting their children to stay in school, work hard, and succeed.

Who Are the Poor?

During the Great Depression, one in three Americans lived in poverty. In the early 1960s, despite two decades of economic growth, 30 percent of our population remained impoverished. Figure 6-3 shows the dramatic decline in poverty rates during the "war on poverty" of the mid-1960s, due mostly to

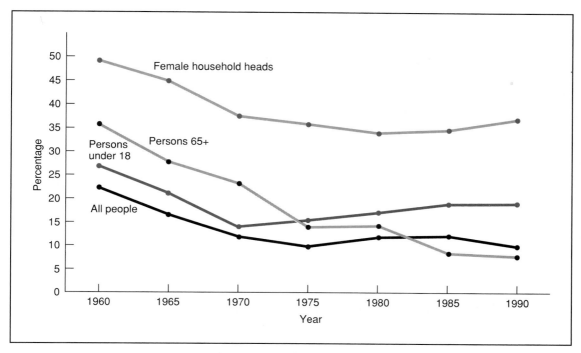

FIGURE 6-3   Poverty in the United States: 1960–90. (Source: U.S. Bureau of the Census, 1989. Data for 1990 extrapolated by the authors.)

programs targeted to the elderly and other "deserving" poor (Appalachian whites and unemployed fathers). In the 1980s, however, Reagan administration budget cuts combined with high unemployment and falling wages pushed the poverty rate upward.

In 1989, almost 32 million Americans, or close to 13 percent of our population, lived in households with incomes below the official **poverty level** (U.S. Bureau of the Census 1990). This threshold is a dollar amount set by the government as the minimum income needed to feed, house, and clothe household members. The formula for establishing the poverty level is based on a 1955 survey by the Department of Agriculture that discovered that families spent about one-third of their income on food. The Department determined the cost of a minimally nourishing basket of food, multiplied by three and came up with a number that has been adjusted yearly for changes in the cost of the food basket, but without considering that the cost of housing has been rising at a faster rate than that of food. The magic numbers for 1989 were slightly over $6,000 for a single person and about $10,000 for a family of three.

Another 10 million persons live in households with incomes that are 25 percent or less over the poverty threshold. If these "near poor" are added to the official poverty population, the total comes to more than 18 percent or about one in six Americans. It is also estimated that in 1988 an additional 15

The **poverty level** represents the minimum income needed to feed, house, and clothe household members.

million people were lifted just over the poverty line by Social Security benefits to widows, the disabled, and minor children of deceased workers (Pear, 1988).

Although poverty touches so many Americans, it is not evenly distributed across population categories. The great majority of poor people are white, but the poverty rate for whites in 1989 was 10 percent compared to 30.7 percent for African-Americans, and 26.2 percent for Latinos (U.S. Bureau of the Census, 1990).

And although 44 percent of poor families are two-parent households, the poverty rate for female-headed families is more than five times that for couples. In contrast to the pre-1970s poverty population dominated by elderly and married couples, today's poor are most likely to be children and their mothers. Children under age 18 composed more than 40 percent of the poor in 1989, an increase of more than one-third since 1979, a result largely of reductions in government assistance to poor pregnant women, infants, and children (Children's Defense Fund, 1989).

A large proportion of the poor are women and children. Why is this so in the wealthiest nation in the world?

The Feminization of Poverty. Most of today's poor are female, especially teenage mothers, single parents, divorced women of any age, and elderly widows. Even when they work full-time, and millions do, their wages are minimal and they are rarely covered by unemployment insurance (Pearce, 1985; Levitan and Shapiro, 1988).

Most of these women are not in the labor force because they are raising children, and they are poor because there is no wage earner in the family. For white women, poverty is typically the consequence of divorce or desertion by a husband (Arendell, 1987); for African-American women, the problem is a shortage of employed men to marry. And contrary to the claim of the political far-right, there is no strong evidence that women prefer to remain on welfare rather than work for wages that would put them over the poverty threshold (Ellwood, 1988). Nor do they have additional children in order to increase their welfare benefits. On the contrary, fertility rates for women on welfare are lower than for other poor women, and decrease steadily the longer they are on welfare (Rank, 1989).

The **feminization of poverty** refers to the fact that a majority of the adult poor are women.

Welfare Programs

Despite the growing numbers of the poor and near poor, most federal assistance programs were reduced or eliminated in the 1980s, especially housing subsidies, job training, school meals, and health/nutrition supplements for women and children. There are four major social welfare programs funded by the federal government:

- *Medicaid* repays physicians and hospitals for the health care expenses of the poor, but the reimbursement rate is so low that impoverished patients are often turned away.
- *Food stamps* are available to many below the poverty level, but fewer than one-third of the eligible households receive any stamps (Brown, 1988), in part because there has been only a limited effort to inform and assist possible participants. The average monthly value of the stamps, less than $100 for a family of three, has not been adjusted for the rise in the cost of food since 1980.
- *Supplemental Security Income (SSI)* covers aid to the blind, disabled, and elderly whose incomes remain well below the poverty threshold. Monthly payments average about $250, or half the poverty level. This program also reaches fewer than half of those eligible, largely because of regulations making it extremely difficult for recipients to claim benefits or to protest termination of coverage (Tolchin, 1989).
- *Aid to Families with Dependent Children (AFDC)* provides income to unemployed single parents, almost all of whom are women. The average monthly AFDC benefit in 1990 was under $400, rising only slightly in comparison to larger increases in the cost of living.

Welfare Facts. Despite low participation rates and minimal benefits, many Americans believe that vast numbers of ineligible people are "ripping off" the welfare system. In fact, very few able-bodied men receive federal welfare benefits, and some of these are single-parent fathers. The greatest number of recipients, by far, are children and their mothers, under AFDC (two-thirds of the total), and the blind, disabled, and elderly, under SSI (26 percent of the total). The small percentage who receive other forms of assistance do so on a temporary basis.

Only a small proportion of families remain on welfare for more than three to five years. Sixty percent of AFDC families, for example, receive benefits for less than three years, and only 8 percent have been on the welfare rolls for ten years or more. Most poor families drift in and out of poverty because of changes in health, marital status, or employment (Duncan et al., 1984; U.S. Bureau of the Census, 1989).

The poor are more likely than the nonpoor to be ill, to feel mental anguish, or to commit suicide; to be victims of crime and violence; to fail in marriage; and to see their children suffer from malnutrition, crippling diseases, or early death. The cause of inner-city poverty today is not welfare dependence but joblessness and low pay when employed (Wilson, 1987). In comparison to other modern societies, the United States spends proportionately less on social welfare programs. Most other industrial nations provide family allowances and old-age pensions as a right of citizenship, unrelated to need or to work history. Only 10.5 cents of your tax dollar goes to social welfare programs in contrast to 30 cents for military programs, 32 cents for Social Security, and 14 cents for interest on the national debt (Children's Defense Fund, 1988, p. 12).

SOCIAL POLICY ISSUE

Workfare programs are designed to prepare welfare parents for permanent positions in the labor force.

How Fair Is Workfare?

The most popular new idea for reducing both the cost and extent of welfare is to put recipients to work. Its advocates claim that **workfare** will accomplish many goals: (1) train single parents for paying jobs in the private sector, (2) restore a sense of self-worth to welfare recipients, and (3) lower the costs of the program as people move from welfare to employment, and as those who refuse to participate in workfare are eliminated from the welfare system (L. Mead, 1986). A welfare reform bill that embodies these principles was overwhelmingly passed by Congress in 1988.

The argument against these programs is based on two points: (1) workfare is not a revision but a subversion of the original intention of AFDC; and (2) workfare does not achieve its stated goals. The first argument is essentially that AFDC was designed, as part of the Social Security Act of 1935, as an income support program that would give poor women the same right to privacy as enjoyed by the nonpoor and the choice of whether or not to stay home and raise their children. In addition, because workfare mandates participation or else the mother loses benefits, it is actually "forced work." The goals are less to help the poor than to reduce government expenditures while also providing a pool of cheap labor for service industries (Abramovitz, 1988). The second argument rests on the fact that the kinds of jobs for which welfare clients are trained often pay wages so low that the family is not brought over the poverty threshold (Weinberg, 1988). For example, in 1989 a woman with two children, working full-time and year-round as a cleaning woman in a nursing home, would earn slightly more than a woman on welfare, but she would end up with less because of having to pay for child care and transportation to work. The working woman would also be without health insurance for herself and her children (*New York Times,* March 5, 1989, p. E6).

Because workfare programs are established and operated by the states, there are 50 possible versions. The plans with the best chance of success are those that offer extensive education and training, while providing child care and medical benefits until the mother can become independent of welfare. These programs are not inexpensive and therefore reduce anticipated tax savings to citizens. But not all states are able or willing to do more than minimal training, so that many women simply exchange taking care of their own households for cleaning other people's homes.

As currently structured, workfare programs have not had much impact on reducing poverty, but they have shifted the welfare burden from the federal government to the states and the families of the poor themselves (Morris and Williamson, 1987). Restructuring welfare and providing pathways out of poverty remain crucial and unrealized goals that *you* will have to deal with in the years ahead. Can workfare be both effective and respectful of the rights of the poor? How would you restructure the program? Would most Americans support such changes? ■

LIFE-STYLES OF THE RICH AND FAMOUS

At the other end of the stratification hierarchy, there are slightly more than 1 million Americans whose net assets are valued at $1 million or more. All but a very few are white males or widows of white males, and most are in their early sixties (*U.S. News and World Report,* January 13, 1986). (See the box, "The *Forbes* Four Hundred.") Although a number of sports and entertainment personalities are millionaires, at least for a few years, most of the people with *new* wealth fit the classic mold of the American Dream, having accumulated their assets through hard work, thrift, and risk taking in business. *Old* wealth, however, is inherited. The great founding fortunes of America have been preserved across generations through asset management, corporate investment, and tax avoidance (Allen, 1987; Maurer and Ratcliff, 1989; Rosenfeld, 1989).

In general, millionaires enjoy a relatively lavish life-style, even though a million dollars does not go as far as it used to. In fact, the cost of living for millionaires has risen at a rate twice that of the Consumer Price Index. A Rolls Royce Corniche convertible, for example, cost more than $205,000 in 1989, compared to $183,000 in 1988; and the cost of caviar, at $50 an ounce, is up more than 40 percent.

Millionaires are protected from extreme hardship by the tax system. Even though the 1987 income tax revisions removed many of the tax shelters enjoyed by the wealthy, the rate at which all types of income are taxed was greatly reduced, especially for the highest income earners. But many high-income taxpayers are still unwilling to pay. In 1989, New York State audited the tax records of millionaires working in New York but claiming to live outside the state and discovered that in the first batch of audits, every single claim was false (*New York Times,* February 2, 1989, p. 1). Similarly, the Internal Revenue Service found large numbers of the very wealthy paying federal taxes at a rate much lower than that of an average income earner (*New York Times,* October 22, 1989, p. 29).

The life-styles of the rich and famous provide endless fascination and entertainment for many Americans. The late Malcolm Forbes celebrated his 70th birthday in Morocco, by spending millions of dollars to fly several hundred of his closest friends to the party.

Wealth and Class

While wealth can buy luxuries, it is not an automatic entry card into the upper class. The American upper class is a very exclusive group, consisting of perhaps 60,000 families and individuals, and based as much on "blood" (family background) as on money (Baltzell, 1964; Ostrander, 1984; Allen, 1987). Until quite recently, our uppermost stratum was composed almost exclusively of white Anglo-Saxon Protestant families whose roots in America go back to the eighteenth century and whose fortunes were accumulated in the nineteenth century. The upper class is still all-white, but a few highly successful individuals from other religions and class origins have managed to win acceptance (Henry Kissinger and Lee Iacocca, for instance).

The upper class maintains its continuity over time through intermarriage and the socialization of its children in a series of social activities and private schools. The upper class is more than a collection of families; it also exists as a set of interrelated social institutions—"patterned ways of organizing the lives of its members from infancy to old age" (Domhoff, 1983). Private schools and clubs isolate and insulate members of the upper class, providing them with a distinct set of values and behaviors that set them apart from the rest of the stratification system and account for their high level of solidarity.

Despite the glaring differences between the life-styles of this one-half of one percent of our population, and the conditions of poverty or near-poverty that affect almost one-fifth of Americans, few people in the rest of the stratification system express a sense of outrage or even unfairness. On the contrary, public opinion data indicate that most respondents feel that the wealthy are entitled to their success, and that with a little luck or hard work, they or their children could someday join the ranks of the rich, if not the upper class itself (Kluegel and Smith, 1986). How realistic is this expectation?

Social mobility is the movement of persons and groups within the stratification system.

SOCIAL MOBILITY

The term **social mobility** refers to the movement of people and groups within the stratification system. The distinction between caste systems and class systems is the degree to which status lines can be crossed.

THE *FORBES* FOUR HUNDRED

Since 1982, *Forbes* magazine, a business publication, has identified the 400 richest people in America. In the 1990 edition, these 400 individuals had a total net worth (assets minus debts) of $272.5 billion. The minimum required to make the list was $260 million, and their average net worth was $681.9 million. Sixty men and six women have personal fortunes of at least one billion dollars (including David Rockefeller, Ted Turner, H. Ross Perot, and Harry Helmsley).

Forty percent of the top 400 inherited their wealth, another 6 percent built on relatively modest family resources, and 54 percent were essentially self-made. Few great American fortunes predate the Civil War, but this "old" money is the basis of an aristocracy of wealthy families such as the Rockefellers, the Du Ponts, and the Cabots. In contrast, the fortunes of the "new rich," accumulated since the 1940s, tend to be much larger only because there has been considerably less time for this wealth to be diluted through inheritance over several generations. Most of the new wealth has come from real estate, media ownership, and financial speculation (for example, that of Michael Milken).

Eighty-five percent of top wealth holders are men, and 15 percent are women, all but one of whom (Estée Lauder) inherited her wealth as daughter or widow of a very rich man. All are white, and the great majority are of Protestant Anglo-Saxon background. Non-Wasps, most notably Jewish men, predominate among the new rich, especially among the billionaires. Their average age was sixty-four, with only 13 under age forty. Most of the 400 live in major metropolitan areas—New York City, San Francisco, Los Angeles, Chicago, Dallas, or Washington, D.C. In terms of education, although fewer than one in five attended an elite university, most have four years of college, and a large number have graduate degrees, primarily in business or law. There are, however, a number of high school dropouts who have amassed enormous fortunes. The list also includes 19 immigrants, not all of whom entered the country penniless (for example, media magnate Rupert Murdoch).

Each year brings some new faces as familiar names—like Donald Trump in 1990—are dropped. Most of the 1990 newcomers entered through inheritance or sudden strokes of good fortune, such as a lucrative land deal or money awarded in a major lawsuit. Dropouts include those who have died and whose fortunes have been divided by heirs, those who have lost money, and still others whose fortunes have been surpassed by even wealthier people.

Source: *Forbes,* October 22, 1990.

Caste and Class

In a **caste system,** one's place in the social-stratification system is determined at birth. This *ascribed status* affects how much education people can have, what occupations they can enter, and whom they can marry. Thus, the hierarchy is preserved over time, with a few exceptions for particularly talented or lucky people. Although caste systems are usually associated with preliterate societies, caste remains an important feature of modern India and South Africa. In the South African case, a policy of segregation and political and economic

Caste systems are based on ascription, with minimal movement across stratum boundaries.

Apartheid refers specifically to the South African policy of segregation and political and economic discrimination against people of color within that country.

discrimination against people of color, called **apartheid,** separated the few whites from the many blacks, ensuring that whites hold the best land, run the government, and control the economy. Only in the 1990s has this system been seriously challenged.

The United States had similar laws until the 1960s. Elements of a caste system in our society can be seen in housing, schooling, and occupational structures where there are few, if any, African-Americans or Latinos. So it is possible to have features of both closed and open systems in the same society. Class systems are based on achieved (earned) as well as ascribed (given) traits. When the comparison is between the parents' status and that of their adult children, we speak of **intergenerational** (*inter* means "between") **mobility.** When the comparison is made between where one begins and where one ends up, it is called **intragenerational** (*intra* means "within"), or **career, mobility.** The American Dream is based on a belief in upward mobility through talent and hard work. Even those whose hard work has not made them millionaires believe *upward mobility* is possible for their children.

Intergenerational mobility involves status change between parents and their adult children.

Intragenerational mobility involves status changes during a person's own adulthood.

Downward mobility, that is, losing social rank, is portrayed as a disgrace to one's family and a denial of the meaning of our society (see the box "Falling from Grace: Downward Mobility in America Today"). Today many—perhaps most—Americans change jobs, move from one part of the country to another, divorce, and remarry. In all this movement, some people may experience only slight rank gains or losses, or *horizontal mobility.*

SOCIAL MOBILITY IN THE UNITED STATES

There is a truth to the dream of upward mobility, but it is not a uniquely American reality. All industrial societies with democratic political systems, low birthrates, and an ideology of equal opportunity had high rates of upward mobility between 1945 and 1965. In that period, there was a shift of about 30 percent from manual to nonmanual occupations in the United States, Great Britain, and other modern Western societies (Lenski, 1966). Most of this change was intergenerational—based on comparisons of fathers' and sons' jobs—rather than achieved during the son's lifetime.

The consistency of these findings across industrial societies strongly indicate that the structure of the economy determines mobility rates. Most movement in the occupational system can be explained in terms of societal-level variables rather than individual differences among workers.

Structural Mobility

Structural, or **demand, mobility** refers to societal-level factors affecting mobility rates.

The term **structural,** or **demand, mobility** refers to the societal-level factors that affect mobility rates. For example, the number and types of jobs available depend on economic system changes, whereas the number and types of people able and willing to fill the jobs depend on the birthrates of different generations. From such data, we can estimate the probabilities of upward or downward movement for various subgroups. As for who *exactly* moves up or down the stratification system, such personal traits as talent, motivation, and luck must be taken into account.

As can be seen in Figure 6-4 (p. 200), for example, the proportion of American workers engaged in farming has declined from more than 37 percent

FALLING FROM GRACE: DOWNWARD MOBILITY IN AMERICA TODAY

If success in life is a sign of God's grace, then failure to maintain social rank can be interpreted as a withdrawal of divine approval—a "falling from grace." This is the phrase that Katherine S. Newman has chosen for the title of her study of downward mobility in the United States today. Because of our cultural fascination with upward mobility, reverse movement in the stratification system has been a much neglected topic in sociology. Yet, over their lifetime, close to one-third of all Americans will experience either intergenerational (between generations) or intragenerational (within one's own worklife) status losses.

Three of the cases selected by Newman for intensive qualitative study involve intragenerational mobility from secure status in the middle class to much more problematic positions in the stratification hierarchy: (1) among a group of former high-level executives who were laid off and unable to find comparable employment; (2) among members of PATCO, the air traffic controller's union, who were fired as a group by President Reagan in 1981; and (3) among two generations of divorced wives of middle-class men. Because members of each category reached their current status through different processes, their responses were varied, but all had to deal with the self-perception of personal failure and the public image of being morally flawed.

Of these three subpopulations, the executives had the most difficulty reconciling their fate with their belief that individuals are responsible for their own destiny; they tended to blame themselves and to suffer from low self-esteem. The PATCO members remained unified, developing a sense of shared fate and maintaining relatively high morale; they could also claim that they were being unfairly punished for upholding the principle of employee rights. The divorced women had a double burden: adapting to downward mobility for themselves and their children and dealing with the stigma of failure in marriage.

In Newman's fourth case—blue-collar workers who lost their jobs because of a plant closing in a city with few other employment opportunities for skilled manual labor—the workers could reduce self-blame by directing their anger toward the company and other authorities. But the loss of self-esteem in having to accept lower-paying jobs in less prestigious occupations could not be totally avoided. This example illustrates the more general phenomenon of working-class families whose hopes of attaining some of the symbols of middle-class status (e.g., home ownership, a college education for their children) have been dashed by the stagnation of real income throughout the 1980s.

Sources: Newman, 1988; *New York Times,* October 3, 1989, p. B1.

in 1900 to less than 3 percent today. While farm employment declined, professional and managerial jobs more than doubled, and sales/clerical positions quadrupled over the century. These vast changes are typical of modern societies: from farm to factory in the early stages of industrialization, and then from factory to white-collar "service" jobs in the later stages. Today, nonmanual work accounts for more than half the jobs, compared to 17.5 percent in 1900.

What these structural shifts mean is that most intergenerational occupational mobility is simply forced by circumstances and that, in general, the

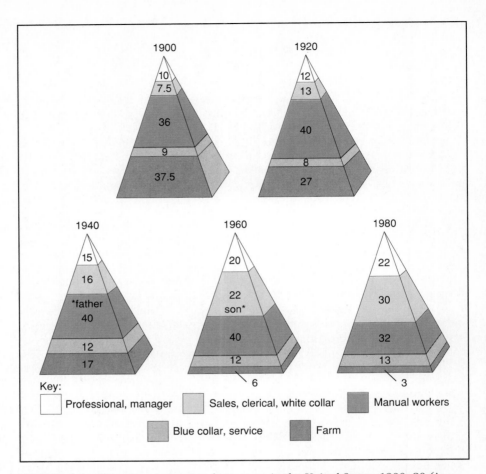

FIGURE 6-4 Changing occupational structure in the United States: 1900–80 (in percents). (Sources: U.S. Bureau of the Census, 1975, p. 139; *Statistical Abstract of the United States 1986,* p. 400.)

trend is toward jobs requiring increasingly higher levels of education and training. Such occupations tend to have higher wage scales than found in the manual and blue-collar sections *if* the jobs are filled by men. Whatever is defined as women's work, at any occupational level, is neither highly valued nor rewarded. In addition, mobility data are typically presented for men because the paths for women were thought to be very different, depending on marriage rather than occupation.

Occupational shifts are not the only structural factor accounting for the major spurt in upward mobility between 1945 and 1965. Equally important were the very low birthrates, especially within the middle class, during the Great Depression of the 1930s and early years of World War II. As a consequence, there was a relatively small pool of job applicants at the very time when the economy was expanding rapidly in the 1950s. White-collar managerial jobs were opening up at a faster rate than children of the middle class could fill them, creating a job vacuum into which young people from the working class could move.

In addition, if they were veterans of World War II, men (and a few women) from working-class backgrounds could take advantage of a program that provided a full four-year college education financed by a grateful nation. This option was taken advantage of primarily by whites, as few African-American youth could afford to stay out of the labor force for four years or find employment that permitted both supporting a family and attending college.

Absolute and Relative Mobility

As they surpassed their fathers in education, occupational prestige, and income, the sons enjoyed *absolute social mobility.* But because the entire occupational structure was being upgraded, their position *relative* to other workers might not be so different from their fathers'. If, for example, the father was a skilled carpenter (high-level manual worker) and the son an insurance underwriter (white-collar), the son's job and educational qualifications and life-style place him in a higher status rank than his father. Yet if most others in the son's generation also moved into white-collar employment, the positions of father and son compared to all other workers has not greatly changed, as also shown in Figure 6-4.

What are the prospects for your generation? Looking at both the structure of occupations and the size of the population born between 1967 and 1972, it is likely that upward mobility rates will be relatively low (Greenwald, 1989). The fastest growing occupations are not very well paid or prestigious (see Chapter 10). In addition, you follow 20 years of baby boomers who will clog avenues of job advancement for many years to come. Your best bet is to stay in school for as long as possible; the more you know, the fewer competitors you will have, and the more able you will be to change course and take advantage of new and unexpected opportunities.

STATUS ATTAINMENT

The Research Evidence

The assumption of continued social mobility in modern societies obscures the high level of **class immobility,** that is, the general tendency for social class rank to be reproduced from one generation to another. Most mobility—both between generations and during one's own career—is a matter of small steps rather than dramatic changes. Success in America, as in other modern societies, is profoundly influenced by the social status of one's family at birth (ascribed status). It also helps to be white, male, an only or firstborn child, and to be raised in a home that emphasizes **deferred gratification** (putting off immediate pleasure in order to achieve a future goal) and high achievement expectations (Coleman, 1988; Kerckhoff, 1989). As noted in Chapter 4, parents' occupation is associated with child-rearing techniques that affect self-control, creativity, intellectual flexibility, and interpersonal skills, which in

Class immobility occurs when social class rank is reproduced from one generation to another.

Deferred gratification is the postponing of current pleasure to achieve future goals.

turn prepare offspring for various types of jobs. Fathers whose jobs require high levels of self-direction tend to have sons who enter and remain in occupations characterized by on-the-job autonomy. It also helps to come from a small family and to have relatively old parents, especially an older father (Marz and Tzeng, 1989).

Status attainment research traces the paths by which people reach their ultimate position in the stratification system.

The Basic Model.   The dominant model of **status attainment**—based on extensive studies of men—is shown in Figure 6-5. The father's occupation (as indicator of family SES) and the son's education and first job are the primary determinants of eventual occupational status. Because family SES affects the quality and length of education, which, in turn, leads to that crucial first job, family background plays the key role. Families at different locations in the stratification system vary not only in wealth and social power but in social ties that open occupational doors and encourage the son to develop further social network resources (de Graaf and Flap, 1988; Marsden and Hurlbert, 1988).

To a great extent, the social rank of a married woman continues to be based on that of her husband, with her mobility measured by the difference between her father's and her husband's occupations or income. As more married women enter the labor force, however, their incomes increasingly raise the household's standard of living, and its ability to provide a college education for all their children (Danzinger et al., 1988).

Revisions of the Basic Model.   Although family background is the single most powerful predictor of social mobility, it is not all-determining. Men from similar backgrounds, indeed even from the same family, can vary widely in eventual occupational statuses. And under favorable circumstances working-class men can move sharply upward.

In addition, as educational differences are lessened, and half of high school graduates now enter college, the influence of family background should lessen. In the 1970s the link between rank of origin and destination did appear to have weakened, especially for African-Americans (Hout, 1984). This trend, however, has been reversed in the 1980s as the cost of a college education has increased at the same time as tuition aid programs have been sharply reduced (see Chapter 11).

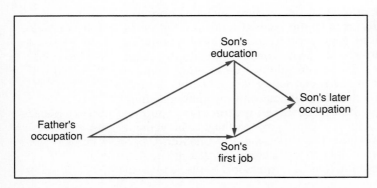

FIGURE 6-5   The status attainment model. (Source: Adapted from Blau and Duncan, 1967, p. 170.)

Criticism of the Status Attainment Model

The image of society that underlies the basic status attainment model is one of optimistic faith in meritocratic processes, in which equality of opportunity through the education system enhances upward mobility (Knottnerus, 1987). When the expected rewards do not materialize—as when a college degree brings less pay and occupational prestige to women or people of color than to white men—it is assumed that time and the logic of the marketplace will eventually even things out.

Yet despite the success of some individuals, the bulk of women, African-Americans, and working-class youth are channeled into occupations with limited chances for advancement, and their distribution in the stratification system has not greatly changed over the past 25 years (Hill et al., 1986). African-Americans also have other problems even when successful. For example, upwardly mobile African-American women have difficulty cutting themselves off from the family and community that were so supportive of their aspirations (Higginbotham and Cannon, 1986).

Although personal characteristics count, as long as ascribed traits such as gender, race, and social class at birth outweigh individual talent and intelligence in determining length of education and type of first job, conflict analysts claim that we really cannot speak of an open class system.

SOCIAL STATUS IN EVERYDAY LIFE

From the perspective of symbolic interaction, social statuses are examined at the level of face-to-face encounters. In the give and take of daily interaction, people transmit and receive information about themselves. In Chapter 4, we discussed Goffman's concept of *impression management*, which describes attempts to manipulate the image that we present to others in order to protect our self-image and to have our definition of self accepted (validated) by our role partners.

Status Symbols

Because people behave differently to those whom they perceive as social superiors, inferiors, or equals, it is important to be able to "locate" others in the prestige hierarchy. We are all rather skilled at picking up status information—speech patterns, dress, hairstyles, and the like. This information guides our conduct. Status superiors are addressed differently from inferiors or equals. These status considerations influence who speaks first or who ends the conversation, who can violate another's personal space, and countless other details of face-to-face encounters.

Status symbols are the outward signs of social rank by which people manage the impression they give. "Keeping up with the Joneses" describes the behavior of people who try to equal the status displays of their neighbors. Appearing to have less means instant loss of prestige just as appearing to have more confers esteem in our society. The advertising industry is largely devoted to stimulating people to ever higher levels of consumption so that they can achieve or maintain status in the eyes of others.

Status symbols are outward signs of social rank.

Status symbols are outward signs of social rank by which people manage the impression they give to others. What status symbols are being displayed here?

Status Consistency and Inconsistency

As individuals send and receive status information they adjust to one another and select the appropriate response, always protecting their self-image. This is a relatively easy task when role partners present clear and unambiguous cues, but in modern societies people are apt to have positions in several status hierarchies.

Status consistency occurs when a person occupies a similar rank across different hierarchies.

The term **status consistency** refers to the uniform placement of people across different hierarchies: the ascribed ones of gender, race, age, ethnic background, and family status at birth, as well as the achieved hierarchies of education, occupation, and income. A white male executive ranks high in wealth, prestige, and power. Similarly, a minority cleaning woman has a consistent position at the base of these hierarchies. Status consistency is greatest at both the top and the bottom of the stratification system, having all the features of a caste society.

Industrial societies, however, display relatively high levels of social mobility, particularly at the middle levels of stratification. Thus, the possibility of **status inconsistency**—occupying a different level or position across hierarchies—is characteristic of modern societies. For example, the head of a crime syndicate may have wealth and power but rank low in prestige. An athlete may have prestige and wealth but little social power.

Status inconsistency refers to occupying different ranks in different hierarchies.

Status inconsistency has important consequences in interpersonal relationships. The female lawyer or the African-American doctor, for instance, presents inconsistent cues: a combination of low-ascribed and high-achieved statuses. Some people respond by assuming that the woman or the person of color must be less qualified, thus creating consistency in their own minds. For the status-inconsistent person, the problem is trying to be accepted in the higher-status role (doctor, lawyer) while his or her role partners are responding to the lower status to maintain their own position. When the male colleague of a woman professional pulls out a chair for her at a board meeting, he is responding to her lower gender status rather than to her equal professional one. This may be the reason why, in attempting to emphasize their achieved characteristics, upwardly mobile women and people of color are often perceived as "pushy."

At the other extreme are people with high-ascribed but low-achieved statuses, such as a white Anglo-Saxon Protestant male who has dropped out of high school and who pumps gas for a living. Believing that their ascribed characteristics entitle them to a better fate than they have actually achieved, such men are likely to feel resentment at the achievements of people they consider their inferiors (Roebeck and Hickson, 1982). It is precisely among men of this type that organizations such as the Ku Klux Klan or American Nazi party find most of their recruits. This is a purely *structural* explanation of recruitment to the Klan or ANP; it is not prejudice that fuels resentment, but social locations that feed attitudes.

SUMMARY

1. Valued social resources—power, prestige, and property—are unequally divided among people and groups in all complex societies.

2. From a functional perspective, stratification is an inevitable and necessary outcome of individual differences.

3. From the conflict perspective, inequality is culturally structured and transmitted from one generation to another, reinforcing and maintaining the stratification system.

4. Weber's distinction among class, status groups, and parties is used to frame our discussion of power, prestige, and property as distinct, though interrelated, dimensions of stratification.

5. Socioeconomic status, based on a combination of occupational prestige, income, and education, is used by social scientists to place people and groups within a hierarchy of social classes. Other sociologists prefer to use control over one's work and that of others.

6. Contrary to the myth of "classlessness," researchers have found that most Americans are aware of class distinctions, hold strong beliefs about their place in stratification systems, and associate with others of equal rank.

7. Social inequality is not a threat to social order unless it is also perceived as unfair. In our society, there is little pressure for change.

8. Poverty remains a major social problem, primarily affecting women, children, and members of racial and ethnic minorities.

9. Social scientists locate the sources of poverty in structural rather than personality factors, interpreting the latter as responses to, rather than causes of, poverty.

10. Although the number of poor Americans has increased, most federal assistance programs were curtailed or eliminated in the 1980s.

11. In order to lower the cost of welfare programs, workfare programs, which put welfare recipients to work, have been introduced.

12. The wealthy enjoy an affluent life-style that combines conspicuous consumption with institutional arrangements that preserve their status.

13. In contrast to caste societies, most modern industrial societies are characterized by relatively high levels of upward mobility, both between generations and within a person's own work career.

14. Although absolute social mobility has occurred in the United States, the relative position of people and groups in the SES hierarchy is unchanged.

15. Studies of status attainment—the paths that lead from social placement at birth to adult occupational level—focus on individual-level variables, with family background and education the primary determinants of one's social status.

16. Conflict theorists explore structural barriers to mobility, such as hiring practices and differential wage scales between and within job categories.

17. Social rank influences everyday interaction. From a symbolic interaction perspective, status cues and status symbols are guides to behavior and structure impression management.

SUGGESTED READINGS

Gilbert, Dennis, and Joseph A. Kahl. *The American Class Structure: A New Synthesis.* 3d ed. Homewood, IL: Dorsey, 1987. A recent overview of the American class structure.

Halle, David. *America's Working Man: Work, Home, and Politics among Blue-Collar Property Owners.* Chicago: University of Chicago Press, 1984. An important study of the American working class.

Heller, Celia. *Structured Social Inequality.* 2d ed. New York: Macmillan, 1987. Various aspects of stratification in the United States and other societies.

Herlemann, Horst G. *The Quality of Life in the Soviet Union.* Boulder, CO: Westview Press, 1986. A critical view of Soviet life as a "classless" society.

Hout, Michael. *Following in Father's Footsteps: Social Mobility in Ireland.* Cambridge: Harvard University Press, 1989. Social mobility trends in Ireland during the 1960s.

Kluegel, James R., and Eliot R. Smith. *Beliefs about Inequality: Americans' Views of What Is and What Ought to Be.* Hawthorne, N.Y.: Aldine de Gruyter, 1986. An eye-opening account of how Americans evaluate social inequality.

Levy, Frank. *Dollars and Dreams: The Changing American Income Distribution.* New York: Russell Sage Foundation, 1987. Social structure and inequality; income distribution over the past 50 years.

Newman, Katherine. *Falling from Grace: The Experience of Downward Mobility in the American Middle Class.* New York: Macmillan, 1988. Millions of Americans whose dreams and beliefs have been negated.

Riemer, David R. *The Prisoners of Welfare: Liberating America's Poor from Unemployment and Low Wages.* New York: Praeger, 1988. The failures of American welfare policy and a program for its reform.

Sennett, Richard, and Jonathan Cobb. *The Hidden Injuries of Class.* New York: Random House (Vintage Books), 1973. A sensitive discussion of the subjective experience of social class.

Vanneman, Reeve, and Lynn Weber Cannon. *The American Perception of Class.* Philadelphia: Temple University Press, 1987. An examination of the class and status perceptions of Americans.

7

Sex and Gender

SEXUALITIES

- Although the mass media have proclaimed that fear of AIDS has brought an end to the "sexual revolution" in America, major change is reported only for some older unmarried women (McNally and Mosher, 1991).
- To the contrary, sexual behavior among unmarried women and men appears to have changed very little, whereas limited survey data indicate that rates of sexual intercourse among teenagers have risen steadily through the 1980s (Ku, 1990).
- In 1989, Congress eliminated funds for a large-scale survey of American sexual practices to be conducted by the Public Health Service (*New York Times,* July 26, 1989, p. B6).
- Throughout the 1980s, reports of sexual attacks and date rapes on college campuses have increased (Koss, 1988).
- Despite progressively more accepting attitudes toward homosexuality, lesbians and gay men remain targets of physical attacks and widespread discrimination in employment and housing (Levine, 1989).

These items reveal the many, often contradictory, aspects of sexuality in contemporary America. In general, sexual taboos have declined—just compare television programs from the early 1960s to what you can see on network TV today—and so have the traditional norms about sex before, during, and after marriage. Yet, although most Americans today accept the liberating and fulfilling potential of sexual expression, the level of sexual violence and exploitation also appears to have risen.

This dual image of human sexuality is not unique to modern society. But accepted behaviors and forbidden behaviors vary culturally and historically. The range of "normal" sexual conduct is as varied as the human imagination itself, and what is "natural" in one society may be deviant in another (Davis and Whitten, 1987). We have chosen to concentrate on the current American scene because of its obvious relevance to your personal life and because we feel that the sociological perspective can help you make sense of your experiences.

Sexual identity refers to seeing oneself as female or male *and* having the culturally shaped aspects of masculinity or femininity. Thus, we begin our discussion with one basic sociological assumption: Sexual identity and sexual behavior, like any other aspect of the self, are socially constructed and controlled. Sexuality is both public and private, personal and political, praised or punished—depending on who does what to whom and under what circumstances. Therefore, the norms that govern sexual expression are social products, subject to conflicting pressures and to change over time.

Sexual identity refers to seeing oneself as female or male and having the culturally shaped aspects of masculinity or femininity.

SOCIOLOGICAL MODELS OF SEXUALITY

The Functional Perspective

From the *functional* perspective, sexuality is viewed as a powerful drive, rooted in biology but not determined by it, that must be contained and channeled into socially productive directions. For example, restricting legitimate sexual activity to marriage partners serves to encourage family formation and high levels of marital fertility. Such norms are reinforced by defining deviations from marital heterosexuality as "sick" or "evil" or "disruptive of normal family life." This view dominated American society and sociology up to the 1960s, supported by the psychiatric establishment and social science authorities, as well as by political and religious leaders.

The Conflict Perspective

The *conflict* perspective retains the basic drive/socialization model, but interest shifts to the question of who defines the norms (Connell, 1987). In the United States, the regulation of public morality is largely left to the states, so that we actually have 50 different sets of laws that govern sexual behavior, with some being more "liberal" or "permissive" than others. Religious leaders are also important agents of social control, not only from the pulpit but also by influencing legislation.

Typically, men are allowed greater sexual freedom than women; many Americans believe that men who engage in extramarital sex are "doing what comes naturally," whereas women in similar circumstances are "depraved" (Lawson, 1988). With regard to race, laws forbidding marriage between whites and members of other racial categories remained on the books of several states into the 1960s.

Pressure on the legal system can also come from below, as people's behaviors and attitudes change. For example, it was only in 1965 that the Supreme Court recognized the right of nonmarried persons to receive birth control information and to purchase contraceptives without a physician's prescription. And it took until 1974 for the American Psychiatric Association to decide that homosexuality was not a serious mental illness.

The relevance of the conflict perspective can be seen today in the struggles over decisions as to what constitutes pornography and obscenity in works of art and entertainment; whether sex education should take place in public schools; and which reproductive choices will be made legally available to women.

The Symbolic Interaction Perspective

From the perspective of *symbolic interaction,* the focus shifts to a microsocial view, wherein sexuality is socially constructed—an assortment of meanings and behaviors, pieced together from the values, expectations, and images of the culture (Kimmel, 1989; Stein, 1989).

Sexual Scripts.   The concept of **sexual scripts** is an attempt to integrate macro- and microlevel phenomena (Simon and Gagnon, 1986). Scripts emerge as people interact in situations that provide broad cultural guidelines (scenarios) for behavior. The script allows us to organize perceptions and experiences into recognizable patterns, including our recognition of the self as a sexual being and/or the situation as one that is sexually charged. For example, the classroom is usually defined as nonsexual, but if the same people went from class to a singles' bar, the script would change and so would their behavior.

Sexual scripts allow individuals to organize their perceptions and experiences in order to behave appropriately in particular situations.

Out of the learning experiences of adolescence, most young people enter adulthood with a sexually conventional set of expectations and behaviors.

If sexual identity and sexual expression are not fully determined by hormones or early childhood experience, then sexuality is actually a flexible set of responses that changes from one situation to another and over the life course. From this point of view, children operate with very different scripts than do adolescents or adults (Gagnon and Simon, 1973). One task for children is to develop a sense of being female or male without linking these identities to sexual motives or meanings. It is in adolescence that these various elements—identity, motives, meanings, and behavior—come together to form the script for sexually aware and curious teenagers. Out of the learning experiences of adolescence, most young people enter adulthood with a conventional set of expectations and behaviors. Sexual activity peaks during ages 18 to 29 (Bachrach and Horne, 1988), and then gradually declines with marriage, parenthood, work commitments, and community involvement (Greenblat, 1989). Long-term intimate relationships are based increasingly on nonsexual factors such as familiarity, companionship, and mutual support.

In addition to differences among societies and over the life course, scripts will often vary from one subculture to another within a society. These scripts can also change over time. In our society, for example, the script for adult female sexuality has been dramatically transformed over the past three decades, from one organized around being a passive object of male desire (which may still affect young daters) to one in which women can become active seekers of pleasure. This shift is the result of trends in the broader society, such as (1) advances in contraception that effectively separate sexual intercourse from reproduction; (2) the movement for gender equality; and (3) easier access to information on sex and sexuality (Schneider and Gould, 1987).

SEXUALITY IN AMERICA

Historical Perspective

In their sweeping review of sexual norms and behaviors, D'Emilio and Freedman (1988) identify three distinct periods up to the 1970s. In the early period, from the 1600s to the mid-1800s, sexuality was closely tied to reproduction, and norms of fidelity were supervised by all members of the community.

As the nation moved from an agricultural to an industrial base, and as a white middle-class emerged in the cities, the emphasis shifted to a more "romantic" and privatized conception of sexuality in marriage. This shift was followed by a dramatic drop in white birthrates, from more than seven children per married couple at the beginning of the nineteenth century to slightly more than four by the century's close. At the same time, the large numbers of young single people flocking to the cities led to a loosening of norms regarding premarital sex and same-sex intimacy.

City life, industrialism, and the American business ethic, as they transformed the nation, also contributed to changing ideas of sexuality. Sexuality became commercialized, more "out in the open"; at the same time women won the right to vote and greater independence outside marriage. The ideal of romantic love and sexual fulfillment within marriage began to filter down from the educated, upper middle class to other strata. Finally, the 1970s brought strong challenges to the last vestiges of sexual traditionalism: gender inequality and the taboo on homosexuality. In this context, the New Feminist Movement and the Gay Liberation Movement represent the logical extension of trends throughout this century toward defining sexuality in terms of privacy and the pursuit of personal fulfillment as a positive value.

Sexual Norms and Behaviors Today

What people say and what they do are not necessarily the same, particularly in the area of sexuality. For example, many Americans strongly disapprove of **extramarital sex** (Klassen et al., 1989), but increasing proportions of married women as well as men report such relationships (Atwater, 1982; Lawson, 1988; Wyatt et al., 1988). Most of these recent studies, however, are based on small and nonrepresentative samples. The earliest effort to collect statistical

Extramarital sex refers to sexual relationships outside of marriage.

data on sexual practices was conducted by Dr. Alfred Kinsey and his associates in the late 1940s with a large but unscientific sample of American men and women (Kinsey et al., 1949, 1953). Their findings were considered quite shocking, with large proportions of respondents having behaved in ways that most people at that time defined as deviant. Although subsequent studies have used larger but nonrepresentative samples (e.g., surveys conducted by *Playboy* and *Redbook* magazines), we lack national survey data of the type that would permit strong generalizations on American sexual habits. Even though such information would be important to programs designed to prevent the spread of AIDS and other sexually transmitted diseases, Congress refused in 1989—on the grounds that it would intrude on personal privacy—to authorize the 10 to 15 million dollars needed for a proposed broad-based study.

The data on actual behaviors described in this chapter, then, are based on somewhat limited studies, but they are far more representative than the material Kinsey and his associates gathered from volunteers. Regarding the sexual habits of women, for example, comparison of the Kinsey data with information from a small sample of California women (N = 122) in 1985 found that present-day respondents began intercourse at an earlier age and not necessarily with a fiancé or husband as first partner. The women also reported a higher number of partners, as well as participation in a broader range of behaviors (Wyatt et al., 1988). Most disturbing to the researchers was that *almost half* the respondents reported having been sexually assaulted in childhood by an older male. That this figure is almost double that found by Kinsey at al. probably reflects women's greater awareness of the issue and their willingness to disclose the information.

For men, differences between the Kinsey and current findings are less dramatic, if only because the men in the earlier study already reported much higher rates of all forms of sexual activity than did the women. In general, as for women, the age of first intercourse is increasingly earlier, the number of partners higher, and the range of sexual acts wider. It seems fair to say that a major change in sexual habits for both women and men has taken place in America over the past three decades. These changes in adult behaviors are generally recognized as part of the trend toward the privatization of sexuality. Some idea of the level of tolerance for extramarital sex can be gleaned from the survey results shown in Table 7-1, which indicate that voters are much

TABLE 7-1   Factors Affecting Voting for a Candidate

Percentages answering yes to the following question: "Would any of the following disclosures prompt you personally to vote against a public official, regardless of other factors?" The candidate:

Accepted money from special interest groups pressuring for votes in their favor	77
Once failed to pay income taxes	64
Had a drinking problem	63
Was homosexual	45
Had extramarital affairs	36

Source: Gallup Organization for *Newsweek*, September 25, 1989, p. 19.

more worried about candidates who drink or fail to pay taxes than about those who engage in extramarital affairs.

Adolescent Sexuality

All the information available on sexual experience during adolescence, including data from national and specialized surveys between 1970 and 1988, indicates that teenagers are indeed becoming sexually active at earlier ages (Hofferth et al., 1987; Forest and Singh, 1990), with large increases for boys and girls under age 16, as shown in Table 7-2. In one recent study of junior high school students in Indianapolis, 55 percent had already had sexual intercourse—more than half the boys by age 13, and half the girls by age 15 (Orr, 1989; also National Center for Health Statistics, 1990). Among the boys, self-esteem was unrelated to sexual experience, but for the girls, being sexually active was associated with low self-esteem, which could be a cause rather than a consequence of early sexual experience.

Although there is evidence that hormone levels at puberty are associated with an early age of sexual intercourse for some adolescent males (Udry and Billy, 1987), the social and cultural context of the teenagers' lives also has a powerful effect (Furstenberg, 1987). Even though the rate at which teenagers become sexually active appears to have leveled off, a reversal of the trend is highly unlikely, given all the sexual cues and incentives to which a young person is exposed, such as the normalizing and glorification of sex on daytime and prime-time television, in movies with teenage appeal, and in popular music (Westhoff, 1988).

Faced with these realities, researchers on adolescent sexuality are in strong agreement over the need for extended sex education in the schools, beginning long before junior high. Public opinion polls show high levels of support for such programs: up to 85 percent in favor in 1988, with smaller majorities approving information on birth control, abortion, and homosexuality, even for 12-year-olds (Kenny et al., 1989). In part, support for sex

TABLE 7-2 Percentage of U.S. Metropolitan Teenage Women Who Had Ever Had Premarital Sexual Intercourse, by Age; 1971, 1976, and 1979 National Surveys of Young Women (NSYW) and 1982 National Survey of Family Growth (NSFG)

Age	Survey Year			
	1971	1976	1979	1982
TOTAL	(N = 2,739)	(N = 1,452)	(N = 1,717)	(N = 1,157)
15–19	**30.4**	**43.4**	**49.8**	**44.9**
15	14.8	18.9	22.8	17.0
16	21.8	30.0	39.5	29.0
17	28.2	46.0	50.1	41.0
18	42.6	56.7	63.0	58.6
19	48.2	64.1	71.4	72.0

Source: Hofferth et al., 1987, p. 47.

education in the schools reflects increasing alarm over the spread of AIDS and the rise in adolescent pregnancies.

Adolescent Pregnancy

Between the late 1950s and today, the teenage pregnancy rate has increased, even though the birthrate for adolescent females has actually declined, along with birthrates for most other age groups. These statistics reflect a number of trends: (1) earlier start of sexual activity, (2) relatively low use of contraception among young teenagers, and (3) the fact that fewer than one-half of teenage pregnancies are carried to term. Teenage birthrates might not be considered a social problem today if, as in the past, the mothers were married (Trussell, 1988; Farber, 1990).

It is not easy to gather data on pregnancies; they are not officially recorded, and an unknown number are ended by miscarriage, perhaps even without the knowledge of the woman. Statistics on voluntary termination **(abortion)** are also incomplete, as they reflect only medically recorded procedures. Nonetheless, from all the data available it appears that throughout

Abortion is the voluntary termination of a pregnancy.

It's like being grounded for eighteen years.

Having a baby when you're a teenager can do more than just take away your freedom, it can take away your dreams.

The Children's Defense Fund.

The Children's Defense Fund is one of the organizations trying to educate teenagers about the consequences of pregnancy. Do you think poster campaigns such as this one are reaching the right people? How can teenagers be reached?

the 1980s, 1 million teenagers became pregnant each year; of these pregnancies, 45 percent resulted in a live birth, 15 percent were ended by miscarriage or stillbirth, and 40 percent were voluntarily terminated (Henshaw and Van Vort, 1989). Adolescent birthrates are highest in the South and West, where abortion services are least available, especially for those who cannot pay private physicians. These states also have the least-developed sex education programs.

In general, African-American youth are more likely than their white age-peers to be sexually active and less likely to have contraceptive information or aecess to family planning services (Moore et al., 1986). They are also more likely than nonminority youth to receive peer encouragement for early sexual activity (Furstenberg et al., 1987). For young people of any race, the higher the educational and income level of one's family, the less likely one is to become an adolescent parent.

Yet despite relatively high income and educational levels in the United States, compared to other modern industrial societies our teenagers have the highest rates of unintended pregnancies, abortions, and births (Jones et al., 1987), as shown in Figure 7-1. The difference is almost entirely a result of American youth's lack of knowledge about birth control and limited access to low-cost family planning services. These findings have been confirmed in the few American cities with school-based pregnancy prevention clinics, where students seeking clinic help were more likely·than nonseekers to delay sexual activity and/or avoid pregnancy (Zabin et al., 1988). Despite this

FIGURE 7-1   Pregnancy rates among women ages 15–19 in Western countries: 1985. (Source: Based on data presented in Westoff, 1988, pp. 254–61.)

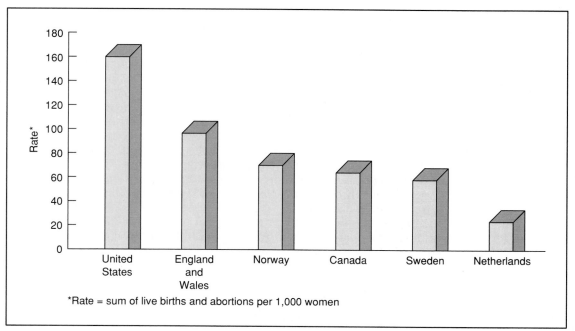

*Rate = sum of live births and abortions per 1,000 women

evidence, opponents of school-based family planning clinics have been successful in limiting federal and state funding for such programs.

There are a number of reasons why American teenagers engage in sex and why they fail to protect themselves against conception (Zelnick and Kantner, 1979; Winter, 1988). They are steeped in a general culture in which sexuality has been commercialized through every medium; many simply do not know the real risks involved; others are unable to resist peer pressure; and still others use sexuality to elevate their self-esteem. Contraception use is poorest among younger teenagers and most consistent among older teenagers, those in fairly long-term relationships, and women with positive feelings about their sexuality (Winter, 1988). Because contraception use requires some foresight and planning, many young women feel it would make them look promiscuous or scheming and would violate the sexual script that calls for being swept away by the passion of the moment.

The probability of medical problems connected to childbirth is higher for teenagers than for any other age group except women in their late 40s. Poor nutrition and health habits, a relatively immature reproductive system, lack of prenatal care, and emotional stress are quite common, leading to high rates of maternal death, miscarriage, and stillbirths. In contrast to children of older mothers, infants of teenage mothers are often underweight, experience breathing difficulties, and are more likely to have birth defects, as well as delayed physical development.

The consequences of early childbearing are largely negative, including dropping out of school, low lifetime earnings, unstable marriages, welfare dependency, and low levels of self-esteem. It is not surprising, therefore, that four out of ten pregnant teenagers elect to terminate the pregnancy, although the decision is not an easy one.

SOCIAL POLICY ISSUE

Abortion—Whose Body? Whose Baby?

Throughout most of this century, state laws made it illegal for a woman to terminate a pregnancy voluntarily. As a result, an unknown number of women risked their life and health at the hands of "back alley" abortionists, whereas middle- and upper-class women had the knowledge and means to secure illegal but safe abortions (Davis, 1989). But in 1973, in the case of *Roe v Wade*, the Supreme Court interpreted the U.S. Constitution as providing a right to privacy that covered a woman's decision, in consultation with her physician, to end a pregnancy (Faux, 1988). This right, however, must be weighed against the government's "compelling interest" in preserving the health and life of mother and child. Accordingly, the Court ruled that (1) during the first three months (trimester) of pregnancy, the states could not interfere, but (2) during the second trimester, states could enact rules designed to ensure medical safety, and (3) during the final trimester, when the fetus might be able to live outside the womb, the interest of the state could supersede the wishes of the mother. The sociological importance of this decision lies in making the abortion issue a medical one, thus denying women an absolute right to reproductive choice.

Following *Roe v Wade*, the number of legal abortions rose steadily from 1973 to 1980 but leveled off at about 1.5 million per year between 1981 and 1987. This translates into a yearly rate of 3 out of every 100 American women ages 15 to 44.

NOT the Church
NOT the State
WOMEN must decide their FATE

Abortion is an important political issue in the United States. This group of Americans is demonstrating in support of the Supreme Court decision that it is a woman's right, in consultation with her physician, to end a pregnancy.

These numbers are extremely disturbing to many religious conservatives in the United States, and *Roe v. Wade* activated a powerful backlash, spearheaded by the Roman Catholic clergy. The pro-life forces have been increasingly successful in persuading state legislatures to establish a range of conditions designed to limit access to abortion. Such limiting conditions include laws that forbid using Medicaid funds to pay for abortions of women on welfare, rules requiring teenagers to receive permission from both parents, and statutes setting such strict medical standards that the procedure can be performed only in a hospital, which is many times more expensive than in a private clinic. In addition, pressure from politicians and religious leaders have led many physicians and hospitals to discontinue performing abortions, especially in the South and in the Rocky Mountain states—even though the health risks of legal abortion are much lower than those of childbirth, particularly for teenagers (Imber, 1986).

Abortion also emerged as an important political issue. During his eight years in office, Ronald Reagan, an outspoken foe of reproductive choice, appointed three Supreme Court justices, selected in large part for their willingness to review *Roe v. Wade.* In July 1989, in the case of *Webster v. Reproductive Health Services,* the Court severely limited the scope of the 1973 decision. In essence, the compelling interests of the states were given priority over an implied right to privacy. Thus, the issue moved to state legislatures and to the political pressures that both sides can apply. Most affected will be women who are very poor, very young, unmarried, and who live in the South or the Rocky Mountain states. Over the next several years you will be asked to vote for politicians who will determine the availability of abortions in your local community and state. You will have to decide who has choice and who does not. ▪

Reproduction, Sexuality, and the Law

In vitro fertilization is a new procedure in which an egg is fertilized outside the mother's body and then replanted in the womb.

Still deeper legal and sociological issues arise from the development of new technologies that in effect separate sexuality from reproduction: artificial insemination, *in vitro* (laboratory) fertilization, surrogate motherhood, and embryo transfers (Rothman, 1987). What, for example, is the legal status of ova (eggs) fertilized in the laboratory but not yet implanted in a woman's womb—are they "pre-born" children, as the pro-life forces claim, or simply potential life with no legal rights? Furthermore, if reproduction and sexuality are no longer necessarily related to one another, what rationale is left for laws that control sexual acts among consenting adults?

HOMOSEXUALITIES: THE LESBIAN AND GAY MALE EXPERIENCE

Cross-Cultural and Historical Perspectives

Homosexuality refers to a preference for sexual partners of the same sex.

Throughout human history, in the great majority of societies, some small proportion of the population has preferred sexual partners of the same sex. Whether **homosexuality** is encouraged, ignored, or punished is a sociocultural variable, as are the meanings attached to such behavior. In some societies, same-sex relationships, at least among men, are considered superior to those with members of the opposite sex. In other societies, such as most of the Spanish-speaking world today, the term *homosexual* is used only to describe the passive partner in a same-sex relationship, and reflects contempt for women in general as much as for **gay** men (Davis and Whitten, 1987).

The term **gay** refers to homosexual males.

It has been argued that "homosexuality" is a category that has meaning only in societies where maleness and femaleness are assumed to be inborn and opposite traits and where only two sexes are recognized (Devor, 1987; Williams, 1987). Take, for example, the *berdaches* of Native American tribes, who are relatively passive males, not quite manly but not altogether womanly, enjoying same-sex lovers, yet who are also highly honored. The *berdaches* were in essence a third sex, thought to have supernatural powers and treated as guardians of the culture (Williams, 1986). Native American cultures were also receptive to the "manly-hearted woman" who shared male activities and often lived with another woman (Blackwood, 1984).

The *berdaches* of Native American tribes function as a third sex, neither fully male nor female.

In modern America we have not reached the point of recognizing more than two genders, and the range of toleration of homosexual relationships widens and narrows from one era to another. Gay men and **lesbians** have

Lesbians are homosexual females.

Some 500,000 citizens demonstrated in Washington, D.C., urging greater federal commitment to gay and lesbian rights and issues, particularly greater allocation of resources for AIDS patients and research.

been able to create a social space hidden from the broader society, especially in large cities, where an emergent **homosexual subculture,** centered in bars and other places of entertainment, offers protection and support. But most gays and lesbians have led double lives, fearful of publicly acknowledging their sexual identity lest they lose jobs, housing, and standing in the community (Adam, 1987; Duberman et al. 1989). The American culture is characterized by a strong streak of **homophobia** (actually, homophilophobia), an intense dislike of homosexuals and a fear of doing or saying anything that might suggest homosexuality to others.

Homosexual subcultures offer protection and support for gay males and lesbians.

Homophobia refers to intense fear of homosexuality or homosexuals.

Organizing for Gay Rights

Because of the stigma attached to homosexuality and the very real harm that could result to those openly declaring their sexual preference, early organizations of and for homosexuals were concerned with helping members adapt to the larger society. What small progress had been made in this direction was reversed during the 1950s, when a wave of antigay sentiment, supported by the medical and religious establishments, led to increased legal constraints.

But the societal mood shifted in the 1960s. In the wake of organized efforts to extend full rights of citizenship to students, African-Americans, and women, the idea of a **Gay Rights Movement** no longer seemed impossible. Gay rights activists had learned organizational skills and political savvy from their participation in these other attempts at social change and in the anti-Vietnam War movement. In addition, the aura of sexual liberation that characterized the 1960s helped normalize homosexuality in the minds of many Americans, particularly the more educated. Many gay men and lesbians were encouraged to **"come out"** (publicly acknowledge their sexual identity) and join umbrella organizations such as the National Gay Task Force, as well as a variety of local groups. Gay caucuses were formed on college campuses and in many professional organizations.

Along with other civil rights movements, the **Gay Rights Movement** emerged in the 1960s; it attempted to extend full rights of citizenship to all homosexuals.

"Coming out" refers to the public acknowledgment of one's homosexual identity.

Political pressure from organized homosexuals resulted in many striking gains in the 1970s: some communities passed laws forbidding discrimination in employment and housing; public opinion polls indicated increasing levels of tolerance; and the homosexual subculture gained a degree of legitimacy, especially in cities such as San Francisco and New York (Schneider and Lewis,

219

1984; Gallup, 1982, 1989; see Table 7-3). These gains, however, were stalled by the association of gay men with the outbreak of the AIDS epidemic in the 1980s, which coincided with a general conservative trend in the society. In this climate, AIDS was defined by some on the political right as the "gay plague," and homophobic attacks as well as barriers to employment and housing increased (Levine, 1989). In 1986, in a ruling on Georgia state laws forbidding certain sexual practices relatively common among both heterosexuals and homosexuals and deeming them "crimes against nature," the United States Supreme Court found no constitutional guarantee of sexual privacy among consenting adults. Consequently, each state can continue to define "normal" sexual behavior and enforce related laws.

Discrimination.   Gay men and lesbians are confronted daily with both open and subtle discrimination in the job and housing markets (Levine, 1989). Gay men are most tolerated when they hold "female jobs," for example, as artists, dancers, hairdressers, and florists, which is one reason why so many find employment in these fields. Gays who seek more "masculine" jobs tend to hide their sexual identity. The American military, despite recommendations of a Pentagon research center, maintains its opposition to homosexuals in the services (Sciolino, 1989).

Roots of Homosexuality

Americans tend to look for direct, single-cause answers to questions about nonnormative behavior: genes, hormones, weak fathers, and domineering mothers are the most common. But none of these alone is sufficient to explain sexual orientation. There is some evidence that gender nonconformity in childhood may predict a homosexual outcome for men, but there is little agreement on the causes of the original nonconformity (Green, 1987).

TABLE 7-3   Attitudes toward Homosexuality and Politics

Q: Should being a homosexual keep anyone from holding these public positions?

	Percent saying "should not"
President	50
Clergy	48
Teacher	50
Cabinet member	57
Judge	59
Member of Congress	60
City official	60
Police officer	61

Source: Gallup Organization for *Newsweek*, September 25, 1989, p. 19.

The sociological view is to see homosexuality as learned in the same way as heterosexuality: through experiences, labeling, and the internalization of self-definitions, which, in turn, make one type of sexual expression more comfortable than another. In this view, homosexuality is socially constructed through a long chain of events and multiple contributing factors that together make heterosexuality uncertain and homosexual activity relatively attractive. The power of the heterosexual script and rewards for conformity, however, ensure that the great majority of boys and girls emerge from adolescence as heterosexually oriented adults, however uncomfortable this may be for some. Indeed, a large proportion of both lesbians and gay men have at one time been in a heterosexual relationship (Kitzinger, 1988; Fay et al., 1989). Thus, rather than seeking any single causal factor, recent research focuses on the totality of a person's experience, on all the contexts in which sexual identity is continually being constructed.

NATURE AND NURTURE AND SEXUAL IDENTITY

A person's biological sex is determined by whether or not the mother's X chromosome is linked to either an X or Y chromosome from the father: XX for a female; XY for a male. The chromosomes carry messages that affect the production of hormones during pregnancy. These hormones determine the development of either male and female genitals and may also have some influence on the organization of the brain. In the vast majority of conceptions, this process plays itself out without problems.

But what happens when the hormones do not function normally? John Money, a noted researcher on the biology of sex, has studied a variety of medical conditions under which hormonal accidents produce, at birth, an infant that is chromosomally of one sex and has the outward characteristics of the other. What sexual identity do they develop? Quite simply, these children become the gender in which they are raised by their parents, provided that the parents are consistent and clear, and especially if appropriate corrective hormonal treatment or sur-

gery is applied. Most such persons will achieve a clear sense of sexual identity. Although the probability of becoming homosexual is relatively high, over half the females and two-thirds of the males lead normal heterosexual lives. The prenatal (before birth) effects of hormones on genital sex and brain organization must be supported by postnatal (after birth) influences; where these influences diverge, the postnatal ones appear to be stronger. Money further suggests that there is a "critical period" for sexual orientation, namely between the ages of five and eight.

Similarly, Money (1986) believes that various forms of deviant sexual practices among heterosexuals or homosexuals—for example, exhibitionism, fetishes, or child molestation—are the product of early childhood experience in which "normal" links between love and sex are upset by particularly traumatic events at the critical period of identity formation.

Source: John Money, 1986; 1987, p. 64.

The major problem with this constructionist approach is that it assumes that homosexuality is to a large degree chosen, whereas many gay men and lesbians see their sexual identity as something that was clear and fixed at an early age, that could not and cannot be otherwise (Whitam and Mathy, 1986). Politically, this is a position that allows lesbians and gay men to resist the suggestion that if they were sufficiently motivated they could change their sexual preferences. Quite possibly, some gay men and lesbians are inherently predisposed toward homosexuality, and others find their way to the same orientation along a variety of paths. Once committed to that identity, however, both find themselves labeled deviant and subjected to negative sanctions.

Prevalence of Homosexuality

How widespread is homosexuality? The generally accepted estimate is that in the United States between five to ten percent of men, and a smaller percentage of women, are attracted to persons of the same sex (Konner, 1989). There are, however, major difficulties in defining what constitutes homosexuality: many people are attracted but do not act on the impulse; some may have a few same-sex encounters in an otherwise heterosexual life; others are equally capable of both types of sexual relationship **(bisexuality).**

Bisexuality involves the ability to enjoy sexual relations with both males and females.

A 1988 national survey, for example, found that one in five American men had had at least one homosexual experience, but that less than three percent could be classified as "exclusively homosexual" (Fay et al., 1989). A considerably higher percentage of both women and men are bisexual rather than exclusively homosexual (Blumstein and Schwartz, 1983). In this category, women outnumber men. Although this option may seem a solution to problems of sexual identity for some, bisexuality may be so emotionally costly that the person is usually pushed into an exclusively heterosexual or homosexual life-style (Troiden, 1988).

Gay Life-Styles: Pair Relationships within the Homosexual Subculture

Contrary to common belief, gay men and lesbians do *not* typically recreate the gender-role differences found in the broader society of dominant males and passive females. To the contrary, relationships between homosexual partners are most likely to be egalitarian (Harry, 1984; Kitzinger, 1987).

Although there is evidence that gay men engage in a greater variety of sexual experiences, and with more partners, than do lesbians (McWhirter and Mattison, 1984), this difference has been greatly exaggerated (Schneider and Gould, 1987). The great majority of homosexuals, male and female, seek intimacy in a stable relationship, but given the limited pool of eligibles, success is more problematic than for heterosexuals. Recently, many of the extreme aspects of the homosexual subculture have been muted as a result of the AIDS epidemic and a renewed emphasis on "safe sex" (Siegel et al., 1988; Connell et al., 1989).

Research indicates that lesbians are more similar to heterosexual women than they are to men, gay or not, in terms of their emotional investment in intimate relationships (Luria et al., 1987). In addition, the limited data indicate that homosexual parents are as successful as other parents in raising emotionally stable children whose sexual identity is firmly fixed and whose sexual orientation is clearly heterosexual (Bozett, 1987).

Recognizing that gay and lesbian couples today are likely to be living together under the same circumstances as legally married pairs—sharing and caring through sickness and health—the cities of San Francisco and New York recently passed ordinances that extend some legal rights to "**domestic partners**" (*New York Times,* May 24, 1989; p. A20). These are cities with large concentrations of gay men and lesbians, as well as nonmarried heterosexual couples; one doubts that similar statutes will be passed in many other places, or that employers will soon embrace the idea of extending pension rights or health insurance coverage to domestic partners. Nonetheless, legal recognition of homosexual unions has become a major goal of the Gay Rights Movement.

Domestic partners include homosexual and nonmarried heterosexual couples who in some U.S. cities enjoy some of the same legal rights as married couples.

SEXUAL VIOLENCE

As traditional social controls have loosened, opening up previously forbidden areas of sexual pleasure, opportunities for the acting-out of harmful sexual impulses have also increased. The sociological study of sexual violence is relatively new. Few solid data exist for earlier years. Therefore we cannot make any strong statements about whether or not acts such as child molestation or rape have increased or simply appear that way because people are now willing to report them. In addition, some behaviors have only recently been given a name and defined as unacceptable, for example, sexual harassment.

In studying acts of molesters, rapists, users of violent pornography, or those who make obscene phone calls, sociologists ask: What are the common features of various forms of **sexual violence** and what does this tell us about our society and culture? The most obvious generalization is that this type of violence, like most others, is directed at the relatively powerless, namely women and children.

Sexual violence is typically directed against the relatively powerless.

A corollary observation is that violence against women and children, especially when it took place within the family, remained unnoticed, unrecorded, and unstudied until quite recently. Seemingly private matters become public issues when large numbers of people are involved, when incidents are well publicized, and when the definition of the situation changes so that the public responds with anger rather than indifference.

Child Molesting

In the case of child molestation outside the family, a number of trends converge to raise it to a public issue: publicity about runaway children and their involvement in prostitution and drugs, several incidents of torture and mass murders of boys, and reports of sexual abuse in child care facilities. These stories fit into a general climate of fear among American parents about losing control over their children (Best, 1987). Although most child molestation involves sexual abuse of girls by older men, the actions of homosexual child molesters often reinforce other broadly held fears and add to antigay sentiment. Abuses in child care centers can be seen as just punishment for women who abandon domestic duties. Yet, while worry over some children has increased, attempts to establish a "Child's Bill of Rights," including freedom from coercion and mistreatment, have been rejected on the grounds of interference with parental responsibilities.

Violence against Women

Redefining violence against women has been a central goal of the New Feminist Movement (Ferree and Hess, 1985). In the broadest sense, feminists see sexual violence as a means of reinforcing male power, from the wolf calls that make ordinary movement uncomfortable to acts of gang rape (Russell, 1984; Sheffield, 1987). From the men's point of view, sexual violence is often perceived as a necessary display of "real masculinity" in a society where only a wimp would let a woman get "out of control" (Kimmel, 1989, 1990). Most studies of convicted rapists have found that their primary motives were anger against women and a need to assert their superiority; furthermore, many of these men had themselves been victims of violence in their own childhood homes (Griffin, 1980; Ewing, 1989).

Date rape is sexual intercourse without consent in the dating relationship.

The likelihood of a woman's being a victim of sexual assault is quite high—estimates range from at least one out of four to close to 45 percent of women across their lifetime (Russell, 1984; U.S. Bureau of Justice Statistics, 1989). Many are assaulted in childhood by relatives or friends of the family. In adulthood, also, rapes and near-rapes are often committed by acquaintances. The incidence of **"date rape"** (sexual intercourse without consent in the dating relationship) on college campuses is a matter of increasing concern to women (Yegidis, 1986; Martin and Hummer, 1989). In general, it is very difficult for a woman who has agreed to date someone to claim that subsequent events were against her will.

Pornography

Pornography refers to sexually detailed pictures and stories.

Pornography (from the Greek *porne*, the lowest form of sexual slave, and *graphein*, to write about) refers to sexually detailed pictures and stories. Such pictures and stories are not easy to classify, and the Supreme Court has had its difficulties in establishing a universal standard to define obscenity. At the moment, it is left to state and local lawmakers to decide what offends community standards and is without any redeeming social value. Thus, a book that may be banned in Muncie, Indiana, could be a best-seller in San Francisco. Enforcement of the statutes is also uneven.

What appears to many men to be a harmless world of fantasy and unattainable freedom (Kimmel, 1989) is experienced by many women as a world where men receive encouragement to violence (Bart, Freeman, and Kimball, 1985; Sheffield, 1987). Yet pornography in America today is a multibillion-dollar industry. Although it is difficult to prove that sexually explicit material directly incites attacks against women, experimental evidence shows that pornography that links sex to violence increases men's tolerance of sexual aggression (Malamuth and Donnerstein, 1984; Donnerstein et al., 1987). Curiously, it is the sexual component in pornography and not the violent element that provokes calls for censorship from political and religious conservatives (Schwartz, 1987). At the moment, the goal of protecting women through

Research has shown that fraternities create a sociocultural context in which the use of coercion in sexual relations with women is common and in which there is little control to keep such behavior in check. At least one national fraternity has decided to educate their brothers, seeking to change their behavior.

regulation of violent pornography conflicts with the equally valued goal of upholding the First Amendment's guarantee of free speech.

Sexual Harassment

Most people would agree that when a student or worker is pressured for sexual favors by someone with power to award grades and promotions, saying no could have a negative effect on one's career. Yet what about a wolf call, a professor's comment in class, a supervisor's invitation to have a drink, or a pat on the behind? Perhaps these are relatively harmless gestures, but such expressions have increasingly been given a new name: sexual harassment.

Sexual harassment
involves deliberate and unwelcome comments, gestures, and acts of a sexual nature.

Sexual harassment is defined as "any deliberate, repeated, or unwelcome verbal comments, gestures, or physical contacts of a sexual nature" (Sheffield, 1987, p. 180). The emphasis is on "deliberate" and "unwelcome," that is, intended to place the other in an embarrassing situation and not desired by the recipient. Both men and women are potential targets of harassment. But because sexual pressures are typically initiated by those in superior positions against the less powerful, women are more likely than men to be the objects of unwanted attention, especially in the workplace (Gutek, 1985).

Many men are surprised to learn that their sexual advances have not been appreciated, whereas many women will misinterpret otherwise friendly overtures. This confusion and ambiguity occurs, in part, because men and women continue to see one another in sexual terms rather than as co-workers or students or faculty members, sex unspecified.

The solution, and the goal of antiharassment laws and policies, is to reinforce the definition of the workplace as devoted to work-related tasks, schoolrooms as settings for the pursuit of intellectual goals, and stores and streets as places where everyone can feel comfortable. A 1986 landmark Supreme Court ruling stipulating that sexual harassment violates federal laws against discrimination leaves it to employers to institute procedures for reporting, verifying, and appealing complaints. American colleges and universities have also established antiharassment policies and implemented investigation and appeals procedures. However, antiharassment policies, especially on college campuses, can be interpreted as violations of the First Amendment guarantee of freedom of speech. You might find it interesting to examine the wording of your school's policy and the various steps taken to ensure privacy and fairness.

THE FLIP SIDE OF THE SEXUAL REVOLUTION

Despite the problems and ambiguities resulting from changes in sexual attitudes and behaviors of the past three decades, we doubt that most Americans would want to return to the 1950s. The "good old days" were not really that good for individuals, although social order was maintained and the authority of men and family elders reinforced.

The sexual revolution and other liberalizing currents of the late twentieth century have shifted the focus of attention from the group to the individual and from duty to choice. Love, once considered the responsibility of women, is now more often seen as something that should be shared (Cancian, 1987). Although the self-centered pursuit of happiness has led many critics to condemn the selfishness of the "me" generation (Lasch, 1977), equality between men and women can only enhance personal well-being; through mutual dependence, whereby neither sex dominates the other's existence, and both can realize their full potential for love and work. This is the goal of the women and men who are part of the contemporary feminist movement throughout the world. In sociology, their work has produced the subfield of gender studies, based on the concept of sex and gender stratification systems.

GENDER STRATIFICATION

- In South Korea, four sisters attempted suicide by eating rat poison so that their parents could devote all of the family's meager resources to the education of their only brother (*New York Times,* March 7, 1988, p. 1).
- In Bombay, India, of 8,000 pregnancies voluntarily terminated after sex determination tests, 7,997 involved a female fetus (Hrdy, 1988).
- At the Wailing Wall in Jerusalem, several dozen Jewish women conducting holy services were attacked by extremely religious Jewish men whose faith forbids women to lead prayers or carry the sacred texts, "A woman carrying the Scriptures is like a pig at the Wailing Wall," declared the men's rabbi (*New York Times,* December 2, 1988, p. A10).
- For Pope John Paul II, femininity involves "the self-offering totality of love; the strength that is capable of bearing the greatest sorrows . . . limitless fidelity and tireless devotion." (*New York Times,* March 28, 1988, p. A12).
- In Saudi Arabia in 1990, 50 women, still veiled according to law, defied custom and law by driving automobiles for a short distance. The women were arrested.

These items illustrate **gender stratification**—the differential evaluation of people's social worth on the basis of biological sex, a view leading to the unequal distribution of power, prestige, and property. The result is a nearly universal gender hierarchy in which men have higher status than women. Gender stratification is a characteristic of the entire social system, linking family structure, the educational system, the economy, and the organization of work and is embedded in every aspect of culture (Brinton, 1988).

Gender stratification is the result of the differential evaluation of societal worth on the basis of biological sex.

SEX AND GENDER

The terms **male** and **female** describe a person's biological sex. **Feminine** and **masculine** are socially constructed genders. Once this distinction between biological and social—between sex and gender—is clear, we can refer to maleness and femaleness as *ascribed* traits, and to femininity and masculinity as *achieved* characteristics that are highly variable from one culture to another and in any society over time.

Male and **female** define biological sex. **Feminine** and **masculine** are social constructs.

But gender is more than a set of behavioral norms. We behave and think and have certain life chances because our language and social structures divide us, on the basis of sex, into distinct categories whose members are assumed to share particular abilities and personality traits. In other words, gender is a structural feature of society, in the same way as is social class.

As with other power relationships, gender is continually redefined and negotiated; men and women can and do rebel and resist (Gerson and Peiss, 1985; Kimmel and Messner, 1989). Precisely because gender is socially constructed, it can never be taken for granted, which is the reason why gender socialization is so intense and why gender deviance is so harshly sanctioned. Depending on the culture, gendered activities can overlap or be so different that women and men have difficulty understanding one another's experiences.

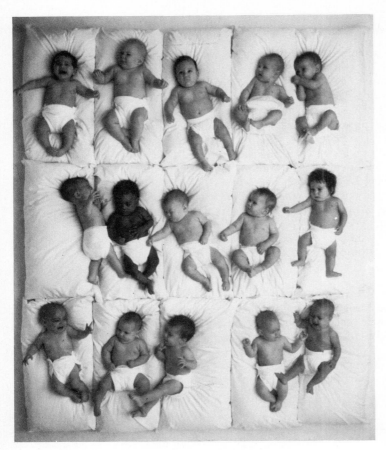

We are born male or female, but without socialization our gender might only be as evident as it is for the infants in this photo.

THE NATURE OF SEX DIFFERENCES

Biological Perspectives

Most of the biological arguments that were once put forward to explain gender stratification have not stood the test of careful scientific examination (Keller, 1985; Fausto-Sterling, 1986; Epstein, 1988). The critics raise five important points:

1. Biological theories and research on sex differences have been profoundly biased by assumptions of male superiority.
2. The data on sex differences are not very convincing or consistent. Take, for example, the claim that greater body strength and aggressiveness stemming from male hormones account for male superiority. This reasoning cannot explain variations over time and cross-culturally.
3. Similarities are far more important and common than differences but are

rarely reported. Although much has been written about sex differences in the organization of the brain, the similarities in cognitive abilities are massive compared to the slight differences (Kimura, 1985).

4. It is impossible to isolate the effects of genes and hormones because they involve only tendencies that work themselves out within social environments.

5. As for the evolutionary argument that humans carry forward the behavior patterns of their primate cousins, detailed studies of chimpanzees, the apes closest to humans, indicate that aggression in males and submissiveness in females are *less* common than among other primates.

A Sociological View of Sex Difference

From a sociological perspective, it is most useful to examine how sex differences in behavior are rooted in the social experiences of females and males rather than as being fixed in our genes or hormones or evolutionary history. For example, because women nurture infants and raise children, they develop a sense of connectedness to other people (Chodorow, 1978; Gilligan, 1982). By contrast, males, because they must separate themselves from their mother in order to become masculine (defined as nonfemale), come to see themselves as isolated individuals and to think in terms of hierarchy.

Although there is some controversy over the extent to which these differences are rooted in nature (biology) or nurture (society), most scholars agree that the two aspects are intertwined, and that each is influenced by the other (Rossi, 1985). Furthermore, there is increasing agreement that individual and societal well-being depend on the ability to combine the virtues of both individuality and connectedness.

The Distribution of Sex Differences

Even where sex-linked traits are found, it must be kept in mind that the data reported are for *group* or *collective differences.* That is, when large numbers of males and females are tested, their measurements will vary *on the average* for the entire sample. For example, if a researcher is studying acts of nurturance among boys and girls, it is very likely that the total score for girls will be higher than for boys. Let us say that 100 girls produced 600 acts of nurturance in the period under study, whereas 100 boys produced 400. This result does not mean that each girl produced two more nurturant acts than each boy. Rather, when each child's score is arranged along a continuum, the pattern illustrated in Figure 7-2 emerges.

Note that some boys outscored the average girl and that some girls scored below the average boy. Most of both sexes have scores clustering around 5. Moreover, the difference between the highest- and lowest-scoring girls or boys (0–10) is greater than the difference between the group averages (2). Thus, more variation exists within each sex category than between the two sexes. An observer guessing which child would be more nurturant than another on the basis of sex only would be correct in six of ten guesses. By chance alone, an observer would be correct five of ten times. The added advantage of the sex-linked guess is often only slightly greater than if one picked names from a hat.

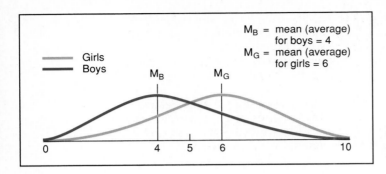

FIGURE 7-2   Comparison of girls' and boys' scores on acts of nurturance.

A SOCIOLOGICAL MODEL OF GENDER STRATIFICATION

Patriarchy refers to male dominance.

Although all gender stratification systems generally favor men, there are varying degrees of male dominance, or **patriarchy**, from one culture to another and from one time period to another. At one extreme are societies in which women's power is minimal and limited to a few domestic matters (e.g., Saudi Arabia). At the other end of the continuum of patriarchy are relatively *egalitarian* societies in which power differentials are narrowed and women have important roles in nonfamily institutional spheres (e.g., Norway and Sweden). There is only scattered evidence of historical societies in which women as a category have had greater social power than men or held it for long periods (Gimbutas, 1989).

How can we explain the universality of male dominance? If there are no "natural" or innate abilities that should lead to gender stratification, the causes must be located in social arrangements. Most scholars today point to the division of labor built on the single, crucial biological distinction between the sexes—only women bear and nurse children. Weakened by pregnancy and childbirth, and limited in movement by the need to breast-feed, it is logical that women assume tasks centered on the household and child care. In contrast, men are assigned the more risky jobs, those that require being away from the base camp over long periods, that bring them in contact with other groups, and that lead to control over space, weapons, tools, and certain types of knowledge.

Thus, as long as high birthrates are required for the survival of the group, it is important for women to be socialized to nurturing and men to risk-taking. And for almost all of human history, infant death rates have been extremely high and the lives of women very short, so that adult women would spend the greater part of their lives either pregnant or nursing infants. However, if the group is small, with plentiful food supply and little need to accumulate resources or defend against enemies, any type of stratification will be minimal (Hope and Stover, 1987), as in the case of gathering bands.

Once hunting becomes a highly specialized activity, the division of labor sharpens; men and women spend their time differently and develop separate skills and bodies of knowledge. Such divisions within a society increase as the mode of subsistence becomes more complex. This is the origin of all social stratification: the unequal distribution of power, prestige, and property within any collectivity. Some men become more important than others, but all men become more important than women.

Male dominance, along with other forms of stratification, tends to increase with the amount of private property held by the family—whether it be hunting rights, cattle, land, or wives and children. Where possessions can be directly passed from father to son, patriarchy and control over women reach a high point, most notably in herding and plow-agricultural societies (Collier, 1988). The link between the group's economic base and the degree of male dominance is illustrated in Figure 7-3.

Although the general pattern in modern societies is toward egalitarianism, the trend is uneven. It is important to distinguish between formal (declared, official) equality and the actual distribution of prestige, power, and property. In the Soviet Union, for example, official ideology supports gender equality, but women are still assigned primary responsibility for home and children, while taking on poorly paid full-time jobs (Mamonova, 1989).

Functional and Conflict Perspectives

From a *functional perspective,* gender inequality reflects the distribution by sex of traits required for group survival—toughness for men, nurturance for women. Because these characteristics are thought to follow from differences in reproductive biology and/or organization of the brain, they are often assumed to be both natural and necessary (Gilder, 1987).

From the *conflict perspective,* however, this division of labor and the inequality that flows from it are primarily socially constructed and not the result of nature. Sexual stratification has the same basis as any form of ine-

FIGURE 7-3 Degree of gender stratification by mode of subsistence. (Sources: Adapted from Chafetz, 1984; Huber, 1986.)

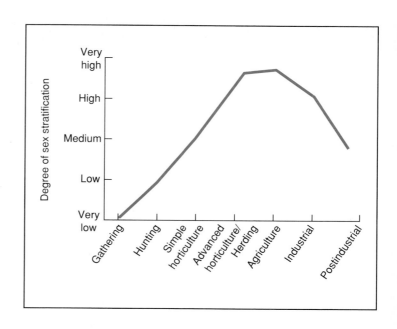

The stereotype of women as physically weaker is contradicted by many activities pursued by women, including service in the armed forces. In Israel, for example, all able men and women are required to serve in the military.

quality: differential access to the means of production (tools, land, knowledge) *and* the products themselves (goods and services).

In general, women's social and personal power is related to (1) their economic contribution to the society or family, (2) their ability to retain control over what they produce or earn, and (3) their ability to inherit property. That is why, as shown in Figure 7-3, male dominance is lowest in societies where women provide a major share of the food and decide how to distribute it and highest where land and its products are firmly controlled by men (Ward, 1984; Blumberg, 1988; Hendrix and Hossein, 1988). Thus, whatever the original basis of inequality, once a system of gender stratification is established, it is reinforced by powerful mechanisms of control—physical, psychological, and social (including force or the threat of force) (Connell, 1987).

Of all the systems of control, however, none is stronger than women's responsibility for bearing and rearing children. So long as women are solely responsible for child care, and so long as they cannot choose the spacing and number of their children, they cannot participate fully in other institutional spheres. If gender stratification is ultimately based on who has control over women's bodies, then giving women reproductive freedom is a profound challenge to patriarchy.

SOCIALIZATION TO GENDERED IDENTITIES

Gender stereotyping begins with expectations for an infant before its actual birth. These expectations become social reality when parents respond to the baby's appearance and gestures (as seen in the box). From birth on, children receive very clear gender-typed messages about what boys and girls are supposed to want and do. The end product is typically a person who fits the cultural definition of feminine or masculine, whatever these traits are in that society. Evidence also exists showing that, at a very early age, the child becomes an active agent in its own socialization, developing the motivation as well as specific skills for sex-appropriate behavior.

Socialization also affects **cognitive structures,** that is, how the mind processes information. According to Rose Laub Coser (1986), the often observed difference between boys and girls in mathematics skills can be accounted for by differential socialization to anticipated family roles. Girls are encouraged to remain close to home, to limit their exploration of physical space, and to have few but intense friendships. As a consequence, they do not have the same experiences of expanding control over physical space, of dealing with abstract ideas rather than practical details, and of weaving complex social networks. The result is that boys develop the cognitive abilities associated with mastery in mathematics and science, while girls become rooted in everyday concerns and relatively simple role systems. Coser notes that recent changes in the socialization of girls have resulted in improved performance on tests of math skills, suggesting that sex differences in this cognitive area may be narrowing (see also Eccles and Jacobs, 1986; Baker and Entwisle, 1987; and Kolata, 1989). But differential socialization, because it is so deeply ingrained in everyday activities, will be extremely difficult to change.

> **Cognitive structures** shape how the mind processes information.

Gendered Self-Images

As you learned in Chapter 4, socialization includes the formation of a self-image as well as internalization of the norms. One of the most consistent findings in social psychology is the lower self-esteem and greater self-hatred of females compared to males (Hoelter, 1983). Women as well as men tend

THE EYE OF THE BEHOLDER

A research team interviewed the parents of firstborn sons and daughters as soon as possible following birth. The fathers had seen the infant through the windows in the hospital nursery; the mothers had held and fed the child. The parents were asked to "describe your baby as you would to a close friend or relative" and also to fill out a short questionnaire containing descriptive terms: firm/soft, fussy/easygoing, hardy-delicate, cuddly/not cuddly, and the like.

The parents of sons were more likely than the parents of daughters to rate the infant as firm, large-featured, well coordinated, alert, strong, and hardy. The parents of female infants tended to describe their daughters as small, cute, delicate, and cuddly. Fathers gave more extreme ratings to the child than did the mother.

These findings are especially significant in view of the fact that the infants themselves *did not differ significantly* by sex on measures of weight, length, skin color, muscle tone, reflexes, heartbeat, or respiratory rate. In other words, the parents saw in their newborns the characteristics associated with adults of the same sex as the baby.

Source: Rubin, Provenzano, and Luria, 1979, pp. 134–141.

to disparage (think less of) women's accomplishments, imputing them to manipulation or luck rather than to skill. For example, when a scholarly article carried the name of a male author, students of both sexes found it more informative and better written than the identical article with a woman's name as author (Goldberg, 1968; Paludi and Strayer, 1985).

Lowered self-esteem is a logical outcome of enacting social roles of little power or social worth (Miller, 1987). Even motherhood, while lavishly praised, offers few societal rewards, such as money or political power, while adding to a woman's dependence on men (Sorensen and McLanahan, 1987). Note also that when others are hired to assist in household tasks, they are typically the lowest paid, least trained workers. Whatever power and prestige are to be gained from the role of wife and mother must come through one's children, a situation that often leads to overprotecting, especially of sons. But in many traditional societies, once a woman has completed her major tasks of bearing and rearing children, her status in the society improves. Middle age often brings personal freedoms and enhanced social power (Brown and Kerns, 1985).

SYSTEMS OF GENDER INEQUALITY

The umbrella term *status of women* hides as much as it reveals. In most societies there is no simple status of women, but variations depending on the dimension of stratification—power, prestige, control over property—and the institutional sphere—family, politics, religion, economic system. Furthermore, there are great differences *within* the population of women, on the basis of social class, race, and ethnic background (*Signs,* 1989). Even though all women may be subordinate to men in the society, women of the higher classes enjoy advantages denied to other women, and in racially stratified societies such as South Africa, white women of any social rank share reflected power over women of color. The term **gender inequality** is used today to describe differences between the sexes in the distribution of societal resources (Mason, 1986).

Gender inequality refers to the differences between men and women in the distribution of societal resources of power, prestige, and property.

The Power Dimension

All but a very few positions of power in America—in politics, business, the military, religious and educational institutions—are occupied by white males. This situation is often justified by the belief that women do not project images of leadership; that they are not socialized to be comfortable with power; and that, in any event, they do not have the same driving ambition to reach the top as men do. These beliefs take male achievement as the norm, against which women are seen to fall short because of their own failures or basic nature.

In contrast to these views, most recent research on power inequality in politics and business has examined social-structural variables such as informal networks, the sex ratio of the workplace, information channels, support from senior officials, availability of child care, and flexible work schedules (Austen, 1988; Blum and Smith, 1988; Moore, 1988; Zimmer, 1988). From this perspective, the barriers are in the situations rather than in the individuals. Most obviously, as long as women must assume major responsibility for raising children, they cannot compete on equal grounds with men for positions that are thought to require extraordinary investments of time and energy. Despite structural obstacles, however, the numbers of women seeking high positions in politics and business has risen dramatically in the past decade. An equally strong shift has also taken place in public attitudes toward women in these fields.

In Politics. As late as 1990 there were very few women holding national office: two senators, four governors, roughly 5 percent of members of Congress, and one or two cabinet-rank officers, even though a growing number of women had worked their way up the political party structure, winning nomination for Congress and governorships. Least accepting of women candidates are older people, Southerners, rural and small-town residents, and blue-collar workers (National Women's Political Caucus, 1989), and the higher the office, the less support for a woman, from both women and men (Foderaro, 1989).

Although the number of women in elected and appointed office is about four times higher than in 1975, most of the gains have been made at the lower levels: school boards and municipal and county offices (see Table 7-4). At the level of state legislature and cabinet posts, women have also increased their representation, but not in leadership roles. At the federal level, although more women than ever ran for Congress in 1990, very few were successful. The situation is even more limited for African-American women, who compose 6 percent of the total population but hold less than one-half of one percent of all elected offices. In 1990 there was one Asian-American woman in the House of Representatives (from Hawaii) and only one African-American woman (from Illinois), in contrast to more than two dozen men of color. Throughout the industrialized world, however, and even in some developing nations, woman are slowly moving into national politics, although the path has not been smooth or swift.

In Business. In the world of business, women now fill almost 40 percent of all management posts (compared to 19 percent in 1972), but very few reach the top: only 3 percent of the highest-ranking corporate officers are women, and only one of the Fortune 500 chief executive officers in 1989 was a woman (*New York Times,* August 31, 1989). Nonetheless, women are flocking to graduate schools of business administration, where they now compose

TABLE 7-4   Percentages of Women in Selected Elective Offices: United States

U.S. Senate	2	1989
U.S. House	6	1989
State Legislature	17	1989
Statewide Elective Office	14	1989
County Governing Boards	9	1988
Mayors of Cities with Populations over 30,000	13	1989

Source: The National Information Bank on Women in Public Office (NIB), a service of the Center for the American Woman and Politics, Eagleton Institute of Politics, Rutgers University, 1989.

As women rapidly move into the world of big business, many have to decide how to meet the competing demands of career and family life. Are men also concerned about balancing the needs of work and family?

40 percent of the student body, compared to 15 percent in 1976. The number of women with MBAs has quadrupled since the mid-1970s (U.S. Department of Education, 1989).

Because the world of business is not only stratified by gender but by race as well, the proportion of women of color in business schools and executive positions is exceedingly small. Indeed, a 1987 survey of the nation's 1,000 largest companies found only four African-American senior executives, all men (*New York Times,* May 22, 1987, p. D4). Against such odds, few African-American or Latina women are willing to invest their time and money in executive training. Successful women of color are typically in self-owned businesses or in the fields of cosmetics and fashion.

Although women are rapidly moving into the world of big business, their career paths are very different from those of men (Powell, 1988). Within corporations, women executives tend to be located in human resources, public relations, and other "people-oriented" departments and not in production, sales, and financial management—the royal roads to corporate power. In terms of economic sectors, women executives are especially prominent in book publishing, retailing, fashion and cosmetics, and public relations. But real economic clout lies in oil and chemicals, transportation, real estate, financial services, and investment banking, where ownership and top management remain almost totally male and white. In terms of directorships or corporate boards, women now occupy less than 5 percent of director chairs in the Fortune 1,000 leading companies in America, typically only one per board. This is a form of **tokenism,** the appointment or promotion of one or two "outsiders" (women or persons of color) to high positions for display but typically without great power in the organization.

Tokenism refers to the appointment or promotion of one or two "outsiders" to high positions.

Female executives soon reach a "glass ceiling" on their way to the top, a mixture of corporate tradition, gender stereotypes, and the fact that men still feel uncomfortable dealing with women on an equal level in business (*Wall Street Journal,* March 24, 1986). Success in the corporate world also depends on access to information and on informal relationships that men establish in the dining rooms, golf courses, and locker rooms of private clubs that do not have women members (or Jewish or African-American members, for that matter). Under these circumstances recent court cases have challenged the tax deductibility of club membership as a business expense. Many clubs will be forced either to admit women or to lose members who can no longer afford to join as private persons.

"Fast Tracks" and "Mommy Tracks."   The primary problem for many executive women, however, is the difficulty of combining family and work responsibilities (reviewed in Galinsky and Stein, 1990). The corporate "fast track" is very demanding—60-hour work weeks, weekend meetings, constant travel, unpredictable crises—all of which conflict with the requirements of stable child care. Because large companies have not yet made the changes that would be necessary to retain women managers, such as on-site day care centers, parental leave without loss of benefits or seniority, and flexible work schedules, American women are faced with difficult choices (Gini and Sullivan, 1988; Hayghe, 1988). Overall, the presence of women in positions of great political and economic power is only slightly greater than it was two decades ago. A determined few, who are also wives and mothers, will reach the upper levels with the assistance of supportive husbands, expensive child care, and household help. It is women in middle management or at the start of a political career who are most likely to have to make compromises.

Some will decide to stay on the fast track and delay childbearing or forgo motherhood altogether. Others will opt for the "mommy track," giving up hope of reaching the top in order to bring work and family life into balance. Others will leave the corporate world to establish their own business, with greater control over working conditions. Today, almost 30 percent of small business firms in the United States are owned by women (mostly retail shops and women-oriented services such as beauty salons).

Prestige

If prestige is measured by occupational rank—the value to society of the job and the standard of living it permits—very few women enjoy high prestige as a function of their employment. In fact, when respondents are asked to rank particular women and men according to the prestige of their occupation, there is much less agreement on scores for women than for men. This means that women are less penalized than men for having low status jobs but also less rewarded with prestige points for high-ranked jobs.

Even though they are less encouraged and less rewarded for striving for high occupational status, women have entered the professions in greater numbers than ever since the beginning of the New Feminist Movement in the mid-1960s. For example, women today comprise one-third of medical school graduates compared to 5 percent in 1960; more than 21 percent of graduating dentists compared to less than 1 percent in 1960; more than 40 percent of law graduates, up from 2.5 percent three decades ago; and 12.5 percent of recipients of graduate degrees in engineering, up from four-tenths of 1 percent in 1960 (*Statistical Abstract,* 1988, p. 151).

Today, almost the same proportions of male and female college students enter premedical undergraduate programs and receive roughly the same grades; but when it comes time to apply to medical school, males outnumber women almost two to one. Data from 1929 to 1984 indicate that female and male applicants to medical schools are equally likely to be accepted but that until recently very few women applied (Cole, 1986).

Women physicians and lawyers tend to be clustered in what are considered the low prestige ends of their professions: pediatrics rather than surgery, for example, family law rather than corporate mergers (Morello, 1986; Zimmerman, 1987), or in the public rather than the private sector (Wharton, 1989).

A similar pattern is found in higher education, with women concentrated in the lower ranks of faculty and in nontenured positions. In 1988, for example, only 11 percent of tenured full professors at both 2- and 4-year colleges were women (National Women's Studies Association, 1988), with approximately 14 percent in the field of sociology (Miller et al., 1988). These numbers are expected to improve as senior people retire and junior faculty move up and also as employers increasingly offer day care and other family-oriented benefits.

In science and engineering the number of women remains small. In addition to the usual barriers to professional careers, girls and women are less likely to be encouraged to develop the required science and mathematics skills in high school or college (Wilson and Boldizar, 1990). The field of computer sciences has also become the special property of males. Even though millions of women routinely work with computers, mostly as word processors, it is boys and men who spend endless hours playing and probing their mysteries (Markoff, 1989). The more the field becomes associated with maleness, the less inviting it becomes to females, even though, as a new field, computer sciences have no long history of sex segregation.

In general, the higher the prestige rank of the occupation, the fewer the number of women (Jacobs, 1989). Conversely, when an occupation is dominated by women, it is considered relatively low in prestige. When women move into a previously male field, the men often move out and the occupation is redefined. Bank telling, for example, used to be the first step in a banking career for young men, but after 1945, when other occupations looked more attractive for men, banks hired women as tellers, which then became a relatively dead-end job (Cohn, 1985).

Labor Force Participation

Most women, like most men in the labor force, have not "careers" but "jobs"— fairly routine, closely supervised, and with limited potential for promotion. However, to the degree that their employment provides money of their own, an opportunity to be out of the home, and personal friendship networks, labor force participation typically reduces dependency on husbands or fathers (Voydanoff, 1987). When we discuss labor force participation of women, we tend to see this as a recent phenomenon and to forget that most women, especially African-Americans, have always worked for a living—if not in the paid labor force, then by taking in boarders, tending shops, and producing goods and services within the home.

Full-time motherhood has always been a luxury reserved for the well-off. Only after World War II, when many families moved from cities to the new suburbs, were large numbers of women cut off from the stream of community life, becoming totally absorbed in homemaking and child care. The period 1945 to 1965 saw birthrates soar, and the economy flourished on the production of goods and services for the home. But not all women left the labor force following World War II, although they were often shifted to lower-paying jobs. In 1940, before the war, 27 percent of American women worked outside the home, a figure that rose to 35 percent at the height of the war effort. Yet in 1955, at the peak of the baby boom, one-third of American women were employed outside the home, a percentage not much lower than in 1943 and that has risen each year since. Today, 67 percent of American women are in the labor force, including 81 percent of college graduates, and four out of five are full-time, year-round employees (Shank, 1988; *Statistical Abstract, 1990*, p. 379).

In addition to these rising numbers, there has been a major change in the *composition* of the female labor force, from one composed largely of single women, through 1940, to one increasingly dominated by married women. In addition, the labor force participation of women with small children has risen dramatically since 1970, as seen in Figure 7-4.

FIGURE 7-4   Married women in the labor force: 1950–88. More married women, husband present, with children have been joining the labor force in recent years, and a higher share of women with children than those without children are working or looking for work. (Source: U.S. Bureau of Labor Statistics, 1988.)

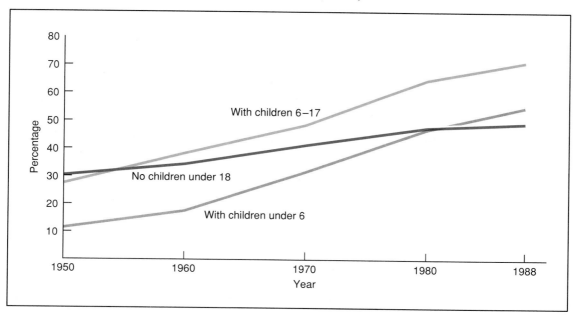

Women enter the work force and stay there for several reasons. Those without husbands must earn their own living. Those who are married can enjoy the benefits of a two-paycheck income—one-third higher than the median for families in which the husband is the only wage earner. But the challenge of the job and social contacts with other workers are also very important aspects of women's attachment to paid work (Fox and Hesse-Biber, 1985). Interestingly, during the same period that women's labor force participation rates have risen so dramatically, those for men have slowly but steadily *declined,* largely because older men are choosing early retirement. If these trends continue, by the year 2000 women will compose almost half of the American labor force, as shown in Figure 7-5. Most women who are not in the labor force are also working, though not for pay. They provide a range of needed services for other household members—shopping, food preparation, laundry, transportation—that do not then have to be purchased from outsiders.

The Wage Gap

For every woman who enters the labor force in a nontraditional or high-paying position, several others enter at the lower levels. Furthermore, most employed women in the future will continue to work in low-pay, dead-end

FIGURE 7-5 The increase of women in the work force. (Sources: Stanford Kay/ Paragraphics *Ms.* magazine and U.S. Bureau of Labor Statistics, 1988.)

pink-collar jobs (Reskin and Hartmann, 1986). The overall effect has been to maintain a **gender wage gap** in earnings that has changed very little since the 1950s. On average, among full-time workers in the United States, women earn between 65 to 72 cents for every dollar earned by men, one of the lowest ratios in the industrial world. Some of the earnings difference can be traced to women's household responsibilities, which reduce their labor time and limit their ability to change employment (Shelton and Firestone, 1989; Burkhauser and Duncan, 1989). The gap is narrowest among new workers, especially college-educated women, and could close even further if they remain in the labor force and work full-time throughout adulthood (Smith and Ward, 1985).

The **gender wage gap** refers to the discrepancy between average earnings of women and men.

An emphasis on the qualities brought to the labor market by individuals, however, cannot account for continued sex differentials in pay for people with similar qualifications in the same occupation. Nor can personal characteristics explain the continued existence of occupations dominated by one sex when there is nothing in the work itself that logically favors one over the other.

The key factor appears to be **sex segregation** in the workplace, both by occupations and by specific job categories within a given occupation, as well as within particular work organizations (Harkess, 1985; Bielby and Baron, 1986; Reskin and Hartmann, 1986; Berheide et al., 1987; Tienda et al., 1987). Although the degree of sex segregation in jobs and the workplace has declined slightly in the past 15 years, most workers are in occupations dominated by members of their own sex. Because occupations are sex segregated, different pay scales and fringe benefits can be justified by employers (Perman and Stevens, 1989) even in the public sector (Bridges and Nelson, 1989). For example, in 1984 at Yale University, administrative assistants with graduate degrees and reading knowledge of foreign languages, all of whom were women, received annual salaries of $13,000 to $13,600, compared to $18,000 per year for the university's truck drivers, all of whom were male.

Sex segregation occurs when women or men are concentrated in a given occupation or in particular jobs within an organization.

Comparable Worth

In order to reduce the gender gap in wages caused by job segregation, women's rights groups are currently promoting the concept of *comparable worth,* or *pay equity* (Blum, 1987; Steinberg, 1987; Acker, 1989; England, 1989). What this means is that people who occupy jobs that require similar levels of skill, training, and supervisory responsibility, and that are carried out in similar conditions of safety and comfort, should receive similar wages. Pay equity would, for example, suggest that the Yale administrative assistants should be paid at least as much if not more than the truck drivers, on the basis of their training and job responsibilities.

Although hailed by feminists as "the issue of the 1980s," the concept of comparable worth has been vigorously opposed by both the Reagan and the Bush administrations, and business organizations such as the Chamber of Commerce. They claim that revising wage scales in the *public* sector (government employment) would require either raising taxes or lowering men's pay, neither of which would be politically popular. A second argument is that if women want higher pay, they should move into jobs that offer it. A third and related point is the belief that women select themselves for low-pay, low-benefit, sex-segregated employment, because that type of work either suits their temperament or allows them to move in and out of the labor market according to obligations to home and family.

In contrast, pay scales in the *private* (business) sector are matters of negotiation between employers and employees. In cases of overt and widespread discrimination, an employee or group of workers could sue under the Civil Rights Act with a 50–50 chance of success (Burstein, 1989). But a series of decisions by the Supreme Court in 1989 have shifted the burden of proof from employer to employee and made it extraordinarily difficult for workers to pursue an extended legal battle against employers, who are often major corporations.

As with so many of the issues that become public policy debates, the solution to this one is probably political. The side that can bring out the most voters will be able to influence legislators to pass pay equity laws.

Education

As seen in Chapter 6, education is a central component of socioeconomic status, not only through its link to occupational chances but also because education affects life-style choices: where one lives, how one spends leisure time, attitudes and opinions on politics and social change. Education is gendered in many ways: in the school setting itself; in differential expectations by teachers; and in the probabilities of attending college and graduate school.

Elementary and high schools are basically "feminine" settings in that most teachers are women, and students are expected to sit still, speak when called on, be neat, and show other virtues associated with female role behavior. In general, girls outperform boys in elementary school, and continue to do so through high school in subjects requiring verbal skills. By high school, however, the boys outperform the girls in mathematics and many sciences. Overall, the more feminine the characteristics of both girls and boys, the better their school performance (Burke, 1989).

When it comes time to apply to college, however, the picture changes: men do better than women on the SATs, win more academic as well as athletic scholarships, and are more likely to apply to college regardless of school grades. Some of these gender differences may be a result of bias in the testing process, that is, having questions deal with material more recognizable by males than females (American Association of University Women, 1988); but when it comes to actually attending college the key variable is the parents' resources. Even today these are distributed along gender lines: Sons are more likely than daughters to be encouraged to attend college and to receive financial support for doing so (Stage and Hossler, 1988).

Marriage and parenthood are also major barriers to entering or completing college, more so for women than for men (Teachman and Polonko, 1988). Nonetheless, in the 1980s, female high school graduates entered college in the same proportion as males. Once in college, female students perform at a level the same as or higher than that of males, although their educational credentials have a lower payoff in the job market.

WINDS OF CHANGE

As a result of increased labor-force participation, expanded educational opportunities, and declining fertility rates, many American women have gained a sense of independence. And their continued experience with the gender-stratification system has led some to organize and challenge gender inequality in the family and society (Ferree and Hess, 1985). Not surprisingly, the far-ranging goals of contemporary feminism have unleashed a powerful backlash from individual women and men who perceive many losses and few gains from any change in the gender-stratification system. From a sociological viewpoint, however, vast and probably irreversible changes have taken place and are likely to continue.

Changes in Men's Lives

Despite the major changes in women's lives, the socialization of boys at home, at school, and within the peer group has changed little over the past two decades. Furthermore, the successes of the women's movement in challenging male dominance have been viewed by many Americans, women as well as men, as very threatening. The late 1980s, for example, featured many movies and television programs that revolved around men only—even portraying them raising children by themselves. Depicting women as "airheads" and "bimbos" was also back in style.

As Kimmel (1986) notes, traditional definitions of masculinity have been threatened (by economic changes as much as by women's rights activism)

Some American corporations, such as Stride-Rite, offer on-site child care so that fathers or mothers can spend some time with their children during the work day.

THE SOCIOLOGY OF MASCULINITY

Michael S. Kimmel

Michael S. Kimmel is assistant professor of sociology at the State University of New York at Stony Brook. Among his books are Against the Tide: Pro-Feminist Men in America, 1775–1990 *(Beacon, forthcoming);* Men's Lives, *edited with Michael Messner (Macmillan, 1989);* Changing Men: New Directions in Research on Men and Masculinity *(Sage, 1987); and* Men Confront Pornography *(Crown, 1990). He is currently writing a book about the relationship between gender and sexuality.*

When I first mentioned that I was preparing to teach a course on "the sociology of the male experience" my friends and colleagues were intrigued. "Why do you need a separate course on men?" many asked. "Aren't all courses that don't have the word 'woman' in the title implicitly 'about men'?" some wondered. "Isn't this just a way for men to jump on the sex-role bandwagon and, in effect, steal the area away from women?" remarked others.

Each of these statements is partially true. That's the reason why I decided to develop this new course and to educate myself about the sociology of the male experience. It's true that courses not specifically about women are about men, but they are about men only by default. We study men as historical actors—statesmen, soldiers, presidents—or as writers, as psychological "personalities," as members of revolutionary mobs, as classes or status groups, as economic producers or consumers, or filling occupational roles. Rarely, if ever, are men discussed *as men;* rarely is the experience of being a man seen as analytically interesting.

But the core insight of women's studies, it seemed to me, was that gender, like race or class, was a "master status," one of the central organizing principles of social life. Inspired by this, I decided to look at men's lives as gendered lives, as lives in which masculinity was no longer taken for granted but became the prism through which the life was viewed.

It was like putting on a new pair of glasses. I was seeing the world—a world I thought I knew—in a completely different way. (This is what I understand to be the essential experience of the sociological imagination.) I remembered how architect Louis Sullivan described his ambition as creating "masculine" forms: strong, solid, commanding respect, and how composer Charles Ives criticized a contemporary rival as scoring weak-willed, even "feminine," symphonies that lacked vigor and power. I recalled how President Theodore Roosevelt was praised for his "hard-muscled frame" and his "crackling voice," as a "masculine sort of person with extremely masculine virtues and palpably masculine faults." Or how Ernest Thompson Seton, an organizer of the Boy Scouts of America, described its founding in 1910 as the antidote to a culture that had "turned robust, manly, self-reliant boyhood into a lot of flat chested cigarette smokers with shaky nerves and doubtful vitality." And I also remembered how President Lyndon Johnson, when informed that a liberal senator was going to oppose his policies, made a remark suggesting that the senator's anatomy was decidedly not male! I realized that the idea of masculinity had formed a core around which men's experience had revolved; it had become the metaphor by which they understood their experiences. Perhaps its centrality, and the fact that it has been, for so long, the normative gender, has made masculinity so invisible.

With this realization, themes of masculinity were suddenly everywhere I looked, especially in the late 1980s and early 1990s, when men appear so confused about what it means to be a "real" man that scores of books and articles advise us on the subject. My male students were echoing this theme, confessing that they didn't know whether they were expected to be Rambo or Tootsie, Phil Donahue or Clint Eastwood, Ashley Wilkes or Rhett Butler, Alan Alda or Sylvester Stallone.

As a historical sociologist, my impulse is to understand a contemporary phenomenon by examining its historical antecedents. And I soon discovered that the 1980s was not the first historical era in which such confusion about the meaning of masculinity was evident. The issue surfaced in the pivotal decades of the late nineteenth century, when changes in the organization of work following the late-century rapid industrialization, the closing of the frontier, and the perceived "feminization" of American culture (as socialization—home, school, and Sunday School—became increasingly the domain of women) dislodged the definition of masculinity from its traditional moorings. Between 1880 and 1920, advice manuals mushroomed, and the Boy Scouts and Young Men's Christian Association (YMCA) were founded in England and transported as deliberate attempts to reverse the enervating trends in American society.

To discover another era of "crisis" of masculinity was intellectually puzzling but the parallels between then and today are instructive. Today, the rise of multinational corporations and the shift to a service economy, themselves phenomena of the globalization of production and the "deindustrialization" of advanced countries, have reshaped both the American economy and the ways in which individuals relate to their work. We also experience the closing of a frontier, as movements of national liberation and decolonization in the Third World seek independence from American influence. And there is renewed concern about the "feminization" of America, a nation grown slothful and indolent, in which the gains of the women's movement (and not coincidentally the rise of a visible

gay culture) are seen as sapping the masculine strength of the nation.

Not all men are reacting against the new definitions of femininity being developed by women in the workplace and the home. And my continuing research project has been to chronicle the history of "profeminist" men in American history, those men who actively supported women's claims for equal opportunity, equal education, political participation (suffrage, ERA), sexual autonomy (birth control, abortion), family reforms (divorce, child custody), and against male violence. Here my own experiences came into play, informing my research and my teaching, helping to frame my questions.

My interest in men who supported feminism has its origins in my college years, when I was one of the first male students at Vassar College in 1968–71. I stumbled upon, or more accurately, was pushed against the wall by feminist women, whose analysis seemed accurate, even if it did make me uncomfortable. I heard about earlier "Men of Vassar," men like Matthew Vassar himself, who was dedicated to providing an education for women that would be every bit as good as the one men received at Yale or Harvard. And, there was the turn-of-the-century president of the college who organized campus suffrage demonstrations.

I also became involved in the National Organization for Changing Men, a group that supports feminist women and gays and lesbians, and applauds "the insights and positive social changes that feminism has stimulated for both women and men." The organization serves as a national network of men who are active in areas such as counsel-

ing men who batter women, enlarging men's options as friends, lovers, husbands, and fathers, and fighting discrimination against gay men and lesbians. I serve as the organization's national spokesperson.

These experiences have also been decisive in my preparation for my course, Sociology of the Male Experience. The class explores what it means to be a man in contemporary American society, what we mean by masculinity—not as a fixed and static role, but as a socially constructed and historically variable set of attitudes and behaviors. I wanted to look at how the meaning of masculinity changes across cultures, in any one culture over time, and over the course of an individual man's life. Like a photograph album, we pause at various pivotal moments—childhood socialization, education, peer relations, sports, the military, sexuality, relationships with women and men, marriage, fatherhood, and aging—to observe how social scientists, historians, and writers and poets had understood those issues. The variations in men's experience—by race, age, class, and sexual orientation—has become one of the course's most significant subtexts.

In fact, these variations in men's experience make it impossible to speak about masculinity as a singular entity. It's more appropriate, I think, to speak of *masculinities* to reflect the large variation in men's lives by race, class, ethnicity, age, sexual orientation. The singular masculinity to which we often refer is actually very specific: It is white, middle class, middle aged, and heterosexual. This becomes the model by which all masculinities are judged, and those that deviate from this standard are seen as problematic. It is through this sleight of hand that the "normative," that which is enforced by power relations, becomes perceived as "normal." But it's central to understanding gender in America that we see that "hegemonic" masculinity is built both on men's power over women and the power of some men over other men.

Mine is only one of a growing number of courses in "Men's Studies," which tap an interest in gender issues generally, and in men's experiences in particular. Perhaps courses like this will become part of the regular curriculum in many colleges and universities, courses in which masculinity is "deconstructed," examined sociologically, and perhaps "reconstructed" within a vision of sexual equality and gender justice.

during other historical periods, with the same predictable reactions: an anti-feminist backlash, a reassertion of masculine dominance, and the emergence of a small but important group of men who grasp the possibility of far-reaching change in gender relations. And, indeed, today a small but academically influential "men's movement" seeks to reduce gender inequality (Brod, 1987; Franklin, 1988; Kimmel and Messner, 1989). The "new man" is one who rises above traditional role expectations and power plays, who is capable of sensitivity, intimacy, and commitment, and who is very supportive of the "new woman." Although the number remains small, a growing proportion of men are committed to the goal of gender equality—often in response to the experiences of their wives and daughters (Astrachan, 1986).

The area in which current changes in men's roles is expected to have greatest impact is that of child care. Although there is some evidence that paternal involvement in childbirth and infant care has a positive effect on the quality of the marriage and the parent-child relationship, it is not easy for men to invest time and energy in fathering (Pleck, 1989). And not many employers look kindly on men taking leave to attend to family matters. In the rare cases where men are raising children as single parents, they tend to develop attitudes and behaviors similar to those of mothers—further evidence that it is the role and not any "natural" ability to nurture that determines how human beings think and act (Risman, 1987). In addition, cross-culturally, fathers' participation in child rearing is associated with a lessening of male dominance. However, even if employers encouraged parental leave, and even if men received cultural and social support for doing "woman's work," the fact is that men today and in the future will spend a *smaller* proportion of their lifetime in families with children than did men in previous generations (Eggebeen and Uhlenberg, 1985). This is so because of the later ages at which people marry today, the fewer children each couple has, the greater incidence of divorce, and the earlier age at which children become independent of parents.

Changing Attitudes

The impact of the New Feminist Movement can also be seen in a general shift in public opinion toward greater support for improving the status of women (*Time,* December 4, 1989). Two recent analyses of survey data from 1977 to

1985 detail these attitude changes (Mason, 1988; Losh-Hesselbart, 1988). In general, support for feminist positions increased among all subgroups and both sexes, with the measured change in women's attitudes twice that of men.

For all the changes in gender relations of the past two decades, most Americans feel that there is more to be done before gender equality is a reality, as seen in Table 7-5. Two-thirds of the female respondents and slightly

TABLE 7-5   Assessing the Women's Movement

Percentage of adults who agreed with this statement:

	The United States continues to need a strong women's movement to push for changes that benefit women.	
	Women	Men
Total	**67%**	**51%**
Race		
White	64	49
Black	85	63
Hispanic	76	47
Age		
18–29 years	71	56
30–44 years	72	54
45–64 years	62	35
65 years or older	57	36
Family income		
Under $12,500	67	44
$12,500–$24,999	66	55
$25,000–$34,999	71	47
$35,000–$50,000	67	53
Over $50,000	67	50
Marital status		
Married now	64	47
Married previously	73	48
Never married	70	62
Employment		
Employed full time	72	48
Employed part time	68	54
Not employed	60	57
Employed with child under 18	73	50

Source: *New York Times*, August 22, 1989, p. A18.

more than half of the male respondents feel that our society continues to need a strong women's movement (similar findings are reported by *Time,* December 4, 1989). Women of color, younger women, single people, and women in the labor force are most likely to support the women's movement; whites, younger men, married people, and women who are not employed have the lowest levels of support. Interestingly, men feel that they and the society have changed to a greater extent than women perceive such changes.

The Impact of Feminist Scholarship

In one field of study after another, feminist scholars, both male and female, have challenged gender biases built into theory, research methods, and analysis of data. As a consequence, the content of all academic disciplines has been revised and expanded, more so in some fields than others (Stacey and Thorne, 1985). These changes have not come without resistance, even in sociology (Hess, 1990), but if you were to compare this textbook with one published a decade ago, you would see differences in every chapter.

In history, for example, rather than focus only on the lives of "great men" (generals, politicians, and diplomats) and on wars and treaties, why not ask what the "little people" (peasants, townsfolk, women in general) were doing? Looking from the bottom up rather than the top down gives an entirely different picture of history. What was good for the elite was not necessarily so for the masses, and historical periods long thought to represent great advances in human freedom often were beneficial only for men. For quite some time no one had bothered to note that the rank of women actually declined during the Golden Age of Greece or the Italian Renaissance (Kelly, 1984).

The spirit of the new feminism, embodied in a generation of scholars who are just now moving into the higher academic ranks, will continue to affect what is defined as "truth." In the interactions of daily life as well as in the legal system, equality is never given but must be continually constructed.

SUMMARY

1. Sexual identity and sexual behavior are socially constructed and socially controlled. Sexual experience is learned, like any other behavior, through socialization.

2. From a functional perspective, sexuality is seen as a powerful drive rooted in biology. The conflict perspective focuses on the question of who determines sexual norms and who regulates public morality.

3. The symbolic interaction perspective focuses on the concept of flexible sexual scripts, which help organize perceptions, experiences, and situations.

4. Studies of sexual norms and behavior in the United States indicate important changes but also the persistence of traditional norms.

5. Research evidence indicates that American adolescents are becoming sexually active at earlier ages. Compared to other industrial societies, American teenagers have less knowledge about birth control and lack access to low-cost family planning services.

6. The results of childbearing at a young age include low lifetime earnings, dropping out of school, unstable marriages, dependency on welfare, and lower levels of self-esteem.

7. The social policy implications of changes in abortion laws and of reproductive technology include the issues of privacy and the consequences of state interference in acts between consenting adults.

8. In most societies some proportion of the population has preferred sexual partners of the same sex. The sociological view is that homosexuality is socially constructed through many events that eventually make gay identity more attractive and rewarding than heterosexuality.

9. Sexual violence is directed at the powerless, mostly women and children. Pornography is also based on the exploitation of women, and sometimes children, through a multibillion-dollar industry.

10. Increased attention has been focused on various forms of sexual harassment, defined as unwelcome, deliberate, and repeated comments, gestures, or physical contact of a sexual nature.

11. Gender stratification focuses on the differential evaluation of people's social worth on the basis of biological sex, which in turn leads to the unequal distribution of power, prestige, and property.

12. Most of the biological arguments used to explain gender inequality have been criticized because they are biased by assumptions of male superiority; the data on sex differences are not consistent.

13. The sociological perspective focuses on how sex differences are rooted in the social experiences of males and females. The universality of male dominance is explained by the division of labor based on the fact that only women can bear children.

14. From a functional perspective, gender inequality merely reflects the way traits needed for group survival are distributed among men and women. The conflict perspective focuses on power inequalities, male dominance, and female subordination.

15. Socialization to gendered identities begins early and continues over the life course. Gender inequality refers to the disadvantages experienced by women in terms of power, prestige, and property.

16. To reduce the gender gap in wages caused by job segregation, women's rights groups have advanced the concept of comparable worth, or pay equity.

17. Education is gendered in many ways: in the school setting itself, in differential expectations by teachers, and in the probabilities of attending college and graduate school.

18. To date, changes in women's lives have been greater than those for men, who have more to lose under conditions of gender equality. The impact of movements for change is reflected in the general shift in public attitudes toward greater support for improving the satus of women.

SUGGESTED READINGS

Abramowitz, Mimi. *Regulating the Lives of Women: Social Welfare Policy from Colonial Times to the Present.* Boston: South End Press, 1989. The way women's lives have been controlled by the social welfare system.

Acker, Joan. *Doing Comparable Worth: Gender, Class, and Pay Equity.* Philadelphia, PA: Temple University Press, 1989. A study of equal pay for work of equal value—a project by the state of Oregon to evaluate 35,000 jobs.

Andersen, Margaret. *Thinking about Women: Sociological Perspectives on Sex and Gender. 2d ed.* New York: Macmillan, 1988. Sexism, culture biology, socialization, work, family life, health, religion, crime and deviance, and social change in women's lives.

Baca Zinn, Maxine, and Bonnie Thornton Dill, eds. *Women of Color in American Society.* Philadelphia: Temple University Press, 1991. New scholarship on issues of race and gender.

Bozett, Frederick W., ed. *Gay and Lesbian Parents.* New York: Praeger, 1987. The experiences of lesbian mothers, gay fathers, and their children.

Cancian, Francesca M. *Love in America: Gender and Self-Development.* Cambridge: Cambridge University Press, 1987. The meaning of love, sex, and marriage in the United States in the nineteenth and twentieth centuries.

D'Emilio, John, and Estelle B. Freedman. *Intimate Matters: A History of Sexuality in America.* New York: Harper & Row, 1988. A history of sexuality in America, focusing on race, gender, social class, and commercial exploitation.

Franklin, Clyde W. *Men and Society.* Chicago: Nelson-Hall, 1988. Men's changing roles in American society.

Hess, Beth B., and Myra Marx Ferree, eds. *Analyzing Gender: A Handbook of Social Science Perspectives.* Newbury Park, CA: Sage, 1987. Dimensions of gender stratification.

Jones, Elise F. et al. *Teenage Pregnancy in Industrialized Countries: A Study.* New Haven: Yale University Press, 1987. A comparison of the relatively high teenage pregnancy rates of the United States and lower rates in other developed countries.

Kimmel, Michael S., and Michael A. Messner, eds. *Men's Lives.* New York: Macmillan, 1989. Men's socialization experiences, sports and war, work, sexuality, health, family life, and relationships.

Risman, Barbara J., and Pepper Schwartz, eds. *Gender in Intimate Relationships: A Microstructural Approach.* Belmont, CA: Wadsworth, 1989. The social context of intimate relations and intimacy as experienced by women and men.

Troiden, Richard R. *Gay and Lesbian Identity: A Sociological Analysis.* Dix Hills, NY: General Hall, 1988. A blend of theoretical perspectives and empirical research on homosexual identities.

8

Racial, Ethnic, and Religious Minorities

- In 1989, Moldavian, a language almost identical to Romanian, was reestablished as the official language of the Soviet Republic of Moldavia. Moldavia joined Estonia, Latvia, Lithuania, and Tadzhikistan as Soviet republics that have reintroduced their native non-Russian language, each in a move to assert their own ethnic heritage.
- An Israeli tax collector was killed by Palestinians, and three other Jews were wounded as they drove through a West Bank town. The same day, an Arab Palestinian teenager died after a beating by Israeli soldiers.
- In a primarily white, upper-middle-class, New England suburb, a ten-year-old Korean boy, adopted by white parents, was harassed daily on the school bus by classmates who called him Slanty Eyes and Oriental Mental.
- In an Italian-American section of Brooklyn, an African-American teenager was murdered when he and three friends came to the neighborhood to look at a used car. The whites had been lying in wait for an African-American male whom they believed was coming to visit a former girlfriend of one of the assailants. The African-Americans were surrounded, and, according to witnesses, one of the whites said, "Let's club the "[expletive] nigger"; another said, "No, let's not club. Let's shoot one" (*New York Times,* September 23, 1989).

These disparate incidents reflect the importance of personal characteristics such as skin color, ethnicity, or religion as social categories that influence social placement in any society. Societies vary greatly in the degree to which their members comprise different ethnic and religious groups. Some nations, such as Denmark, Sweden, and Norway, are relatively **culturally homogeneous:** that is, the members of the society are similar in language, religious observance, and country of origin. Such societies do not experience the difficulties of absorbing many people whose norms and cultures differ. Nonetheless, even such countries as Sweden have been shaken by attacks on "guest workers," imported as unskilled or semiskilled labor from southern Europe or North Africa.

Cultural homogeneity results from similarity in race, religion, and national origin.

Other societies are **culturally heterogeneous:** that is, their citizens differ greatly in color and appearance, in beliefs and values, and in language and culture. The Soviet Union has over two hundred such nationality groups within its borders, and varying numbers exist in Yugoslavia, Australia, New Zealand, South Africa, Israel, Canada, and the United States. In such societies, social order depends on (1) how the various groups are brought into contact with one another (intergroup relations) and (2) how scarce resources are allocated. The basic themes of this chapter are (1) the extent to which the statuses of race, religion, and ethnicity influence placement in the major stratification hierarchies and (2) the experiences of minority groups in the United States.

Cultural heterogeneity occurs when members of a society differ greatly in color and appearance, in beliefs and values, and in language and culture.

Minority groups are defined in contrast to the **dominant group** of the population. The dominant group is not necessarily numerically larger. Dominance refers to *control* over central sectors of social life, including the power to define standards of beauty and worth. Thus, although WASPs are a numerical minority of the American population, their influence on our culture, language, ideology, and law has shaped the nation more than the influence of any other group. In contrast to the WASP ideal, those who are not white, northern European, or Protestant have characteristics that not only set them apart but

Dominant groups exercise control over societal resources.

The cultural heterogeneity of American society is illustrated in this naturalization ceremony in Miami's Orange Bowl, during which 10,000 people, from a number of foreign countries, were sworn in as U.S. citizens.

become cues for different, typically unequal treatment. There are four elements necessary to defining **minority group status:**

1. *Visible ascribed traits,* by which some minority group members can be recognized.
2. *Differential treatment* on the basis of possessing these traits.
3. The *organization of self-image* around this identity.
4. An *awareness of shared identity* with others in the same group.

Members of such groups can be thought of as belonging to *subsocieties.* Participation in a subsociety fills three functions for its members: (1) it provides the in-group identity needed for self-definition, (2) it maintains patterns of primary group relations *(Gemeinschaft),* and (3) it interprets the broader national society through the particular filter of minority group traditions (Gordon, 1978). Thus, minority group members can construct a subculture that protects and nurtures those who remain within its network of primary and secondary ties. Belonging to a minority group, however, often makes it difficult to enter mainstream society.

Minority group status involves visible traits, differential treatment, self-image, and shared identity.

ETHNICITY, RACE, AND RELIGION

Ethnicity refers to national background or cultural identity. People and groups vary in how much they retain the physical appearances, customs, language, and surnames of their country of origin.

Ethnicity refers to cultural identity.

Religion is a set of beliefs and rituals associated with the sacred.

Race is a social construction; there are no "pure" racial types.

Religion is a set of beliefs and rituals associated with the sacred. People of the same religion recognize each other through shared worship.

Race is much more difficult to define. Although most of us speak of race as if we were sure of its meaning, it is almost impossible to define the term scientifically. From a biological perspective, as a result of extensive intermarriage over the centuries, it is difficult to say that different races exist today; there are no "pure" racial types based either on physical appearance (phenotype) or on genetic makeup (genotype).

The various levels of economic, social, and political power of groups determine the importance of racial categories and the meaning of race within a society (Stone, 1985; Omi and Winant, 1987). It is the *definition of the situation* that is most significant in defining race. That is, people act on the belief that Jews, African-Americans, Latinos, WASPs, Asians, and so forth comprise a distinct racial category even though members of these groups vary tremendously in genotype, phenotype, and cultural backgrounds. Race, even though a social construct, becomes a central axis for social relations.

Social class, unlike ascribed traits such as race or ethnicity, is considered an *achieved* status in modern industrial societies. However, by definition, access to positions of power, prestige, and property is controlled by the rules and actions of the dominant group within a society. Members of racial, religious, or ethnic minorities find higher or lower barriers to achievement depending on several factors, including (1) how closely they resemble the dominant culture in appearance and customs, (2) the skills and talents (including education) they bring to the society, and (3) the state of the economy. This means that the historical experiences of different minority groups in America have varied greatly, so that generalizations are somewhat difficult to make. For example, despite similarities in their treatment within our dominant institutions, African-Americans, because of their greater visibility in white society, are much more likely than Jews to experience barriers to social mobility.

In the United States, ascribed statuses often serve as *caste* boundaries, limiting entry into mainstream positions of prestige and power. Whereas race remains an extremely difficult social boundary to overcome, over time both religion and ethnicity have become less powerful barriers to achievement. Al Smith, a Catholic, could not be elected president in 1928, but John Kennedy, also a Catholic, was elected in 1960. Henry A. Kissinger, born in Germany of Jewish parents, was a recent U.S. secretary of state, and Zbigniew Brzezinski, born in Poland, was a recent head of the National Security Council. Jews and Italian-Americans now manage major corporations. In terms of the ability to achieve high positions in a society, however, some subgroups are more privileged than others.

MODELS FOR THE INTEGRATION OF MINORITY GROUPS

How can a varied population be welded into a unified whole? To maintain social stability, a common set of values and norms has to be forged so that the members of different ethnic, racial, and religious groups can interact in an orderly fashion. Several models for the integration of minority groups have been proposed, among which are the *melting pot* and *cultural pluralism.*

The Melting Pot

The model of the **melting pot** (a concept referring to the melting down of differences) is based on the belief that immigrants could and should, through exposure to the mass media and a common educational system, gradually lose their differences and come to share a common language and culture, enjoying equal opportunities for success in the New World. In time, it was thought, all newcomers would conform to American norms and beliefs, producing a distinct American population.

The **melting pot model** of integration assumes that immigrants will lose their cultural uniqueness and become part of the dominant American culture.

Despite a strong national belief in the melting pot, and despite the success of the public-school system in teaching a common language and culture to millions of immigrants, ethnic minorities have in many ways remained "unmeltable." Not only was the melting-pot ideology founded on an overly simple theory of human nature, its supporters overlooked the crucial importance of race, religion, and ethnicity as sources of identity, self-respect, and community. They also assumed that WASP norms, values, and life-styles were superior ideals that others must follow.

To ease their way on the path to upward mobility early in this century, many people changed their names to disguise their religious and ethnic background. Elite universities were known to have quotas for Jews and those whose names "ended in vowels." Few minority-group members thought it possible to run for political office, and even fewer were accepted into the management of banks, corporations, or stock exchange firms.

By 1950 recent immigrants and their children composed a relatively small percentage of the United States population, and many differences that had once marked ethnic communities were disappearing. The foreign born and their children moved to other parts of the city or to the suburbs. It seemed as if the melting pot had indeed melted down many of the distinctive aspects of ethnicity. But other divisions were still evident. Religious affiliation rather than ethnicity began to emerge as the crucial trait by which white Americans identified themselves (Archdeacon, 1983). For example, by 1950, British, German, and Scandinavian Protestants frequently intermarried, as did Irish, Italian, and Polish Catholics. Yet while people crossed ethnic lines to choose mates, relatively few crossed Protestant, Catholic, or Jewish lines. It seemed that ethnic differences were being melted down in America, but into three pots rather than one (Archdeacon, 1983).

This **triple melting pot** model of intergroup relationships was, however, relatively short-lived. The persistence of ethnicity, race, and religion both as important aspects of personal identity and as barriers to acceptance and achievement led to a reexamination of the ways in which groups were absorbed in the social structure of the United States. *Cultural pluralism* became the new ideal.

The **triple melting pot** suggested that ethnic differences were melting but religious differences, between Catholics, Protestants, and Jews, were not.

Cultural pluralism emphasizes the special contributions of various immigrant cultures to the diversity of American society.

Cultural Pluralism

The **cultural pluralism** model emphasized the special contributions of various immigrant cultures to the diversity and vitality of American cultural life—as in a salad, in which every ingredient remains distinct yet contributes to the whole. Cultural pluralism implies an acceptance of differences in relatively personal matters such as family, religious rituals, and community associations. Members of different ethnicities, racial groups, and religions thus live the most intimate parts of their lives within their own traditions. Cultural pluralism, however, does not mean a number of multiple cultures, in the proper sense of the word *culture.* The United States could not survive in its present form if there were compartmentalized, parallel power systems and a loss of concern for the common good of the nation as a whole.

It was once thought that as a result of urban industrial life and the realization of equal opportunity, later-generation minority-group members would gradually become *less* identified with their ethnic, racial, or religious backgrounds, so that only surface differences would remain. In the 1960s this belief was challenged, as African-Americans, Latinos, and Native Americans protested against continued inequality of opportunity. A new ethnic consciousness was sparked and the discovery and celebration of one's past roots served to mobilize these minority groups for political action. For example, the slogan "black is beautiful" strengthened the identity of African-Americans with each other. Formation of such action groups as the Mexican-American La Raza (literally, "the race"), the American Indian Movement (AIM), and the Congress of Racial Equality (CORE) created bonds of mutual support among people who otherwise felt isolated. Such groups also provided an avenue through which political pressure could be brought to bear on the power structure of American society. These organizations also provided a model for other, more advantaged immigrant groups to develop and express an appreciation of their own roots.

PROCESSES IN THE INTEGRATION OF MINORITY GROUPS

Minority groups are linked to the larger society in several ways, together forming a *continuum* from near isolation (segregation) to a blending into the dominant culture (amalgamation). This continuum is depicted in Figure 8-1.

Segregation

The term **segregation** refers to attempts to isolate minority groups.

De jure segregation is supported by law. **De facto** segregation is the result of custom and personal choices.

Segregation describes efforts to isolate minorities and may be of two types: **de facto** and **de jure**. *De jure* means "supported by law." *De facto* means "in fact," but not necessarily supported by law. An example of *de jure* segregation is the *apartheid* ("apartness") policy of the Republic of South Africa up to the early 1990s, where a small minority of whites dominated the country, and the majority—blacks, persons of mixed race, and Asians—had limited freedom of movement, confined to rural reservations or specific urban areas. Until very recently, separate school systems, transportation, and public facilities were established by law for the different races, with the quality of nonwhite education, jobs, and housing distinctly inferior. Such an arrangement is similar to the legally sanctioned separate facilities provided for African-Americans in the South up to the mid-1960s. Following a series of U.S. Supreme Court decisions, *de jure* segregation in the United States is now prohibited. *De facto* segrega-

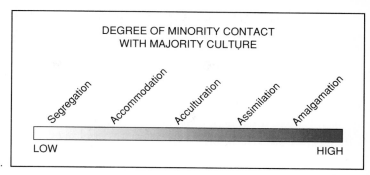

FIGURE 8-1 Processes of integration.

tion, however, remains, as individual families choose where to live and in many cases what schools their children attend.

Accommodation

Accommodation is the phase in which the members of a minority become aware of the norms and values of the dominant culture but do not necessarily change their own norms and values. They adapt to the dominant culture without fully participating in it. For example, established Cuban residents of Miami have developed businesses and industries within the Cuban community that allow them to remain culturally and linguistically distinct from the English-speaking community. Yet they have learned to deal effectively with the mainstream social institutions, such as the schools and the political economy (Rumbaut, 1986).

> **Accommodation** occurs when the members of a minority group are aware of dominant norms and values without having internalized them.

Acculturation

Acculturation, sometimes called *cultural assimilation,* occurs when the people in a minority group adopt the norms, values, and behavior patterns of the dominant society but are still not admitted to more intimate social groups. For example, even Jews who are directors of corporations are rarely invited to become members of elite clubs to which WASP business leaders belong (Zweigenhaft, 1982).

> **Acculturation** takes place when minority group members adopt the dominant values and norms but are not admitted to intimate groupings.

Assimilation

Assimilation is sometimes called *structural assimilation* to distinguish it from acculturation or cultural assimilation. *Assimilation* describes the entry into the dominant society through friendships and other close associations (see Chapter 3). The rate of assimilation of different minority groups varies both by the degree of their physical differences, such as skin color, and by the degree to which their cultural traits depart from the dominant ideal. It has been easier for light-skinned English-speaking people to become assimilated in the United States than for darker people or those who do not speak English.

> **Assimilation** occurs when people from minority groups are accepted in major social institutions and more personal groupings.

Amalgamation

Amalgamation is the mixing of minority and dominant groups through intermarriage.

The final process, **amalgamation,** is most closely associated with the melting pot. Amalgamation occurs when cultures or races mix to form new cultural and racial types, primarily through intermarriage. Although the rates of ethnic and religious intermarriage have increased dramatically within the last few decades, *interracial* marriages remain rare, accounting for less than 3 percent of all marriages. Indeed, even interracial friendship choices among high school students are uncommon, reflecting both personal choice and institutional-level tracking within a school, whereby African-American and white students are resegregated. They are thus denied the opportunity to recognize their similarities and to develop friendships that would foster positive interracial sentiments (Hallinan and Williams, 1989).

BARRIERS TO INTEGRATION

The three major barriers to the integration of minority groups are *prejudice, discrimination,* and *institutional racism.* Prejudice and discrimination involve individual responses; institutional racism is a widespread structural arrangement.

Prejudice

Prejudice involves prejudging members of ethnic, religious, and racial groups.

Stereotypical thinking occurs when a set of characteristics is attributed to all members of a social group.

Prejudice literally means "prejudging" without knowledge. Thus, ethnic, racial, religious, or other social categories are **stereotyped.** A *stereotype* is an image in which a single set of characteristics, favorable or unfavorable, is attributed to an entire group. Students today will probably recognize some of the stereotypes subscribed to by college students of more than half a century ago:

> Jews: shrewd, money-grabbing
> Blacks: lazy, happy-go-lucky
> Italians: impulsive, passionate
> Irish: quick-tempered, witty, stupid
> (Katz and Braly, 1933)

Why do such stereotypes persist? Many people, although flexible and knowledgeable in many ways, are closed minded and unbending in others. Holding stereotypes provides mental shortcuts, but prevents us from viewing other people as individuals. The roots are complex but, like other attitudes and behaviors, prejudice is learned, most often within a primary group, and tends to conform to the norms of the community. Prejudice is thus generally an *institutionalized pattern* rather than a personal quirk.

Scapegoating refers to finding someone else to blame for one's misfortune.

Scapegoating.   Prejudice is also reinforced by **scapegoating,** or finding someone else to blame for one's misfortune. The term *scapegoating* refers to the biblical practice of sacrificing a goat to appease God for human sins. Scapegoating consists of blaming a particular group for social ills. In Nazi Germany, for example, Jews were blamed for the massive economic problems

Jewish concentration camp prisoners at Buchenwald peer out at Allied liberators at the end of World War II. In Nazi Germany, scapegoating and genocide went hand in hand.

of the nation. In the United States, at approximately the same time, people who were dissatisfied with economic and political conditions were also likely to express anti-Semitic attitudes (Campbell, 1947). Today, whites who are unhappy with their own opportunities for economic advancement frequently resent affirmative action policies and blame African-Americans for their own lack of advancement. These are all examples of scapegoating.

Discrimination

Whereas prejudice is a set of attitudes, **discrimination** is the *practice* of treating people unequally. The two are closely related. That is, prejudice often leads to discrimination. Discrimination, in turn, reinforces prejudice, in a vicious circle that limits opportunity and produces a self-fulfilling prophecy. This vicious circle is shown graphically in Figure 8-2. Note that a visible difference in race, sex, ethnicity, or religion can start off the cycle and lead to either discrimination or prejudice, or both. Many years ago, for example, when Irish-Americans were poorly educated, they were denied opportunities for training in skills. Therefore, when a job opening presented itself they did not have the requisite qualifications. In turn, the belief that the "Irish are stupid" was "confirmed."

Yet prejudice and discrimination are two *separate* dimensions. For example, a person who fears Jews might nevertheless vote to admit them to his fraternity if other members are strongly in favor. Conversely, real-estate agents with no personal hostility toward African-Americans may nonetheless steer

Discrimination is the practice of unequal treatment.

259

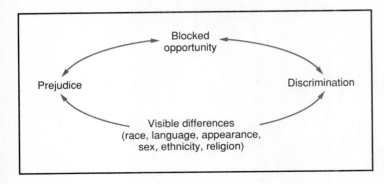

FIGURE 8-2   The vicious circle of prejudice and discrimination.

darker-skinned buyers away from houses located in white neighborhoods because of a belief that the norms of the community require such discrimination. In short, people's behavior is usually designed to try to ensure approval and validation from others in the groups to which they belong. As Table 8-1 indicates, discrimination can be diminished *without* attitude change by encouraging group norms that define such behavior as unacceptable.

Impact of Discrimination

Prejudice and discrimination can destroy life, health, and property. They also affect the self. The victims of prejudice and discrimination often internalize negative self-images, leading to low self-esteem. There are also costs to the majority. In *de jure* segregation, duplicate or parallel facilities, such as separate school systems and restrooms, must be provided. The majority group wastes resources in trying to maintain its dominant position, and dominance easily shades into arrogance and abuse of power.

Fear of Displacement.   Prejudice and discrimination are most likely to be displayed by those who are the most threatened by the success of minority

TABLE 8-1   An Illustration of the Relationship between Attitudes and Behavior

		Attitude	
		Prejudiced	*Accepting*
Behavior	*Discriminatory*	Not only hates having strangers next door but actively attempts to prevent having them (e.g., by cross burning and retaining exclusionary zoning laws).	Does not care who lives where but will not fight institutional racism/inequality.
	Nondiscriminatory	Does not want strangers next door but will not do anything to prevent their moving in or their continued residence.	Does not object to and may even welcome strangers' moving into neighborhood.

group members. They fear that they may lose status when others gain it. For example, the hostility toward immigrants in the nineteenth and twentieth centuries was most marked among members of the working class, who felt that the entry of new groups into the labor market would threaten their ability to improve their own working conditions. Business owners also benefit from prejudice and discrimination because such attitudes and behaviors thwart the possibility of African-American and white workers organizing together on the basis of their common interests.

Today, many disadvantaged whites maintain self-esteem through hatred of minority groups; whatever their failures, they can claim that they are not African-American or Latino or Asian, and so forth. Whites in direct competition with minorities for low-paying, low-skilled jobs claim that affirmative action policies prevent them from getting jobs or promotions (MacLeod, 1987).

Institutionalized Discrimination/Racism

In many areas of social life, discrimination is built into the entire structure of norms and behavior and reinforced by both formal and informal agents of social control; this is called **institutional discrimination,** or institutional racism. For example, segregated housing patterns are often maintained by the practice of **redlining,** through which banks and other lending institutions refuse to make mortgage money available for housing in racially mixed neigh-

Institutionalized discrimination occurs when discrimination is built into normative structures and reinforced by formal and informal agents of social control.

Redlining is the practice of banks and other lending institutions of refusing to make mortgage money available for housing in certain neighborhoods.

Institutionalized racism was practiced in many communities throughout much of American history and was enforced by formal agents of social control. The photo shows the reaction of Birmingham, Alabama, police to attempts, in 1963, by African-Americans to register voters.

borhoods. Few areas of social life are free of institutionalized patterns of discrimination in routine business conduct.

Genocide.   The most extreme result of prejudice and discrimination is **genocide,** that is, the deliberate attempt to murder an entire category of people. The most well-known attempted genocide was the Holocaust, in which millions of European Jews were sent to death camps by the Nazis during World War II. Today, genocidal attacks occur in parts of Asia, Africa, and the Middle East, committed by friends as well as by enemies of our government, and at times by a people against its own people, as happened in Cambodia in the 1970s.

Genocide is the deliberate attempt to murder an entire category of people.

The Persistence of Prejudice and Discrimination

From a functionalist perspective, prejudice and discrimination have both positive and negative consequences for a society. Despite their negative impact on minority individuals, prejudice and discrimination help build social solidarity and reaffirm the values of the dominant group. Moreover, prejudice and discrimination may actually aid the economy by providing a pool of low-skill, low-wage employees for the "dirty work" of society. Few people would choose a career as a street cleaner, ditch digger, or migrant farm worker if other options were readily available. But prejudice and discrimination are also highly dysfunctional in that millions of people are denied the opportunity to contribute fully to society.

Can prejudice and discrimination be eliminated? Racial, ethnic, and religious prejudice and discrimination are deeply embedded in our society. But so, also, are the values of fairness and achievement. These two conflicting themes in American culture create a strain that, as Myrdal (1945) suggested more than 40 years ago, make social change inevitable. Indeed, the Civil Rights Movement of the 1960s forced many Americans to confront the basic conflict between discrimination and equality.

The range of access to economic and social power gives rise to racial and religious conflict. As may be seen in Table 8-2, in a study in which racial and religious conflicts spanning the period from 1965 to 1985 were identified, African-Americans were the most frequent target of attacks, 92 percent of which were initiated by whites, whose religious origin was not identified. Whites (ethnicity or religion not specified) ranked as the second most likely to be targeted, and Jews ranked third. The remaining conflicts were initiated against the growing proportions of Southeast Asians and Latinos. Violence predominated regardless of the target or initiator (Olzak and West, 1989).

IMMIGRATION TO THE UNITED STATES

The population of the United States is composed of immigrants. The estimated 5 million (Thornton, 1987) Native Americans residing in the continental United States in 1492 were themselves descended from immigrants who probably came across a land bridge between Siberia and Alaska. Today, both

TABLE 8-2 Conflict Events by Characteristics of Target and Initiating Group

Target of Conflict	Initiators of Incident			
	Total	White[a]	Black	Other[b]
Black	136	125	0	11
White	99	0	69	30
Jewish	55	11	5	39
Hispanic	5	0	2	3
Asian	4	2	1	1

[a] "White" denotes no specific ethnic or religious groups identified as target or initiator.
[b] "Other" includes a combination of minorities, including Hispanics, Italians, Gypsies, and Jews.
Source: Adapted from Olzak and West, 1989.

legal and illegal immigration continue to account for population growth in our society.

By the time of the revolutionary war, America's population was already culturally, racially, religiously, and ethnically diverse. Until the mid-nineteenth century most immigrants were from northern Europe. By the 1880s, however, the major streams of immigration came from southern and eastern Europe. Between 1875 and 1926, about 9 million Italians immigrated to the United States, along with millions of Russians, and hundreds of thousands of Poles, Hungarians, Slovaks, Czechs, Romanians, and Jews. The newcomers were not only resented for their differences in language, religion, and values, but also because they were willing to work for lower wages than were native-born workers. Laws passed in the 1920s established a quota system limiting immigration from southeastern Europe and Asia. By this time, also, the demand for workers had declined as the nation headed into the Great Depression.

By 1965, however, the quota system established 40 years before was viewed as outmoded, and a new set of immigration laws was enacted. In recent years, as shown in Figure 8-3, immigration is higher than it has been since the 1920s. In fact, immigration has replaced births as the major factor in population growth. There has also been a dramatic shift in the origin of America's immigrants within the last 20 years, as may be seen in Figure 8-4. Somewhat more than 80 percent of legal immigrants admitted to the United States from 1980 to 1985 were from Latin America and Asia: up 21 percent from the period 1921 to 1960. At their current rate of growth, people of Latino origin will increase from about 8 percent of the population today to close to 20 percent by 2080, but it is far more likely that over several generations, Latinos will adopt the same low fertility patterns of other immigrant groups (Kahn, 1988). Over the same period, Asian-Americans are expected to increase their representation in the population from 2 percent to 12 percent (Davis, 1982). There are indications that many of today's new immigrants experience some degree of rejection, with certain groups considered more "desirable" than others.

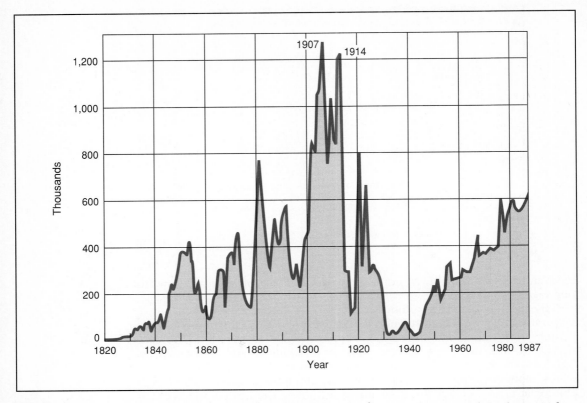

FIGURE 8-3 Legal immigration to the United States: 1820–1987. (Sources: Bouvier and Gardner, 1986, p. 10; *Statistical Abstract of the United States 1989,* p. 12.)

RACIAL MINORITIES

Native Americans

Estimates of the size of the Native American population prior to the invasion of Europeans in North America vary; a conservative estimate is 5 million when Columbus discovered America. Because Europeans viewed their own cultures as superior, the physical characteristics of Native Americans were taken as evidence of biological inferiority. The widely varying cultures of the so-called "Indians" were destroyed in the cause of promoting Christianity and civilization. Native American populations were further reduced by European-brought diseases such as smallpox and measles.

Because Native Americans were not considered to be entitled to equal status with whites, treaties with the "Indian Tribes" were ignored, and whole Native American nations were resettled forcibly into reservations distant from centers of population and business. The complex interaction of relocation, war, forced culture change, and disease reduced the Native American popu-

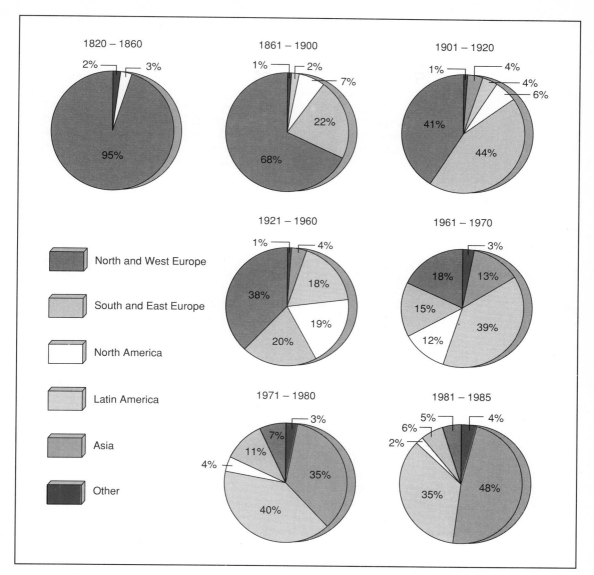

FIGURE 8-4 Places of origin of legal immigrants to the United States. (Sources: Data from Population Reference Bureau, graph from *New York Times,* April 10, 1988, p. C5.)

lation to its low point of roughly 250,000 in 1900 (Thornton, 1987). By the early 1980s, about 53 million acres, or 2.4 percent, of United States land was managed in trust by the Bureau of Indian Affairs. These reservations became notorious for their lack of economic opportunities, so that Native Americans remain the poorest and the most disadvantaged of all racial or ethnic groups in the United States. However, only slightly more than half of all Native Americans live on reservations. Many live in metropolitan areas in the West and the Great Lakes area; others are farmers and migrant laborers in the Southwest and north central regions; and many live in New York State and New England. Better education and jobs bring the earnings of urban Native Americans significantly above those in rural areas and on reservations (Snipp and Sandefur, 1988).

For those few Native American nations whose reservations contain natural resources such as mineral and energy reserves, the social cost of partial economic self-sufficiency has been high. In the Navaho nation in Arizona, where uranium mines have been operated since the 1950s, a high frequency of birth defects, miscarriages, and stillbirths have occurred among both children and livestock. Uninformed about radiation danger, many Navaho used radioactive rocks to build their homes, and cannot afford to build new ones.

Self-determination and economic self-sufficiency cannot be achieved easily when the most basic needs, such as adequate education, housing, and health care, have not yet been met. Death rates from a range of diseases are greater than among the U.S. population as a whole. Deaths from alcohol-related causes among Native Americans remains about 22 times higher than the national average, and the suicide rate is twice the national average. Housing is substandard, and nearly half the hospitals built by the Indian Health Service were built before 1940 and are both understaffed and in need of repairs.

Far from being on the verge of extinction, however, the Native American population is growing faster than the U.S. population as a whole. According to government statistics, there are around 1.5 million Native Americans, most heavily concentrated in the Southwest. It is difficult, however, to know the precise size of the current Native American population, as the federal government uses a variety of criteria to count "Indians."

Demonstrations and lawsuits have called attention to the treaties broken by the U.S. government and the unmet needs of Native Americans. Several lawsuits have resulted in a return of native lands and/or multimillion-dollar reparation payments. But despite the rising tide of political activity illustrated by the American Indian Movement (AIM), the great variety among Native Americans has made it difficult to create a unified political front.

African-Americans in America

African-Americans and Stratification Hierarchies.   In 1989, 30 million African-Americans accounted for almost 13 percent of the total population of the United States. To what extent have African-Americans moved into and up the stratification system?

Power.   Although all legal barriers to voting have been removed, African-Americans are less likely to vote than whites, primarily as a result of lower income and less education, which, in turn, are associated with lower voter turnout in general. Also, feelings of powerlessness and alienation reduce the motivation to vote ("What good would it do?").

The number of African-American state legislators rose from about 168 in 1970 to over 400 today, as has the proportion of other elected officials. But the rate of increase declined through the 1980s, and is only about one-third of what it was from 1970 to 1976. At the moment, elected African-American officials represent considerably fewer constituents than would reflect their almost 13 percent portion of the American population.

Historically, better-educated minority members have found more job opportunities and higher pay in federal, state, and local government jobs than in the private sector. However, salaries in upper-level city government positions for racial minorities and women have continued to lag behind those of white males (Moss, 1988). Recent Supreme Court interpretations and laxer enforcement of affirmative action policies during the Reagan and Bush administrations have combined with job cutbacks to lessen opportunities for mobility through government jobs.

Socioeconomic Status.   In the arenas of employment, occupation, income, and wealth, African-Americans remain disadvantaged compared to whites. As we noted in Chapter 6, the median income for white families is 60 percent higher than for African-American families. Furthermore, the income gap between African-Americans and white men has not narrowed since 1948 (Farley and Allen, 1987). About one African-American in three lives below the poverty line today compared to about one in ten whites, and the rate of unemployment for young African-American men is three times that of young white men, a

Although increasing numbers of African-American families are enjoying middle-class status, research indicates that they work harder for equal rewards.

THE CHANGING BLACK CLASS STRUCTURE

Bart Landry

After receiving his Ph.D. in sociology from Columbia University, Bart Landry taught briefly at Purdue University. He is now an associate professor of sociology at the University of Maryland, College Park, where he has taught for many years. His book, The New Black Middle Class, *was published by the University of California Press in 1987. At present he is completing a companion book on the black middle-class family.*

My professional interest in class differences among blacks developed by chance. As a graduate student at Columbia University in the late 1960s, it was the study of development or "modernization"—as it was then called—that fascinated me. However, a proposed dissertation on "Landlords and Peasants in Turkey" did not materialize because of a worsening political situation in that country. My first teaching position at Purdue University offered scant opportunity beyond an interdisciplinary faculty seminar to pursue my interest in modernization. It was at this point that my research interest began to shift toward the black experience in the United States.

Although the study of modernization had been my focus in graduate school, a variety of experiences at that time had prepared me for this new emphasis. My entry into graduate school had come shortly after the Civil Rights Movement and coincided with the War on Poverty, the development of the student movement, the antiwar movement, the emergence of the Black Panther party, and the women's movement. I still remember that period as a tremendously exciting time that had a profound impact on my intellectual growth. In a sense, these events were not very far removed from my interest in development. All were somehow concerned with change.

At Purdue, I began writing sociological papers on black politics. I also became involved with local black politics and attended the first National Black Political Convention held in Gary, Indiana, in 1972. When in 1973 I was asked to write a chapter on "The Economic Position of Black Americans" for the edited work *American Minorities and Economic Opportunity,* the stage was set for a shift in interest to class differences. As the research for this chapter progressed, it became clear that blacks were still economically far behind whites. So I began wondering about the outcome of the War on Poverty. Had it succeeded in moving some blacks into the economic success column? At that time, I

was still thinking in terms of income differences rather than class. As the idea germinated, my thinking began to shift imperceptibly from a focus on income differences to a focus on class. The new question became: How many blacks have been able to achieve the American Dream of the middle class?

The notion of class was still hazy in my mind, however. Sociology in the United States was not, at that time, noted for a preoccupation with class. As I began reading for clues to the meaning of class and middle class, I found no consensus in either the sociological or popular literature. And it was quite some time before I arrived at what I considered sociologically sound definitions, based on Max Weber's approach to class. Although Karl Marx's name is the most closely associated with the concept, it was Weber who developed the more usable definition for comparing groups in the same society. Thus, for Weber, classes, except for the upper class, were viewed as groups of workers with similar positions in the market. Over time, consensus developed among followers of Weber, identifying white-collar workers as middle class and blue-collar workers as working class.

By this time I had moved from Purdue to the University of Maryland in College Park, where I was successful in securing a large grant to collect a national sample of middle-class blacks and whites to answer the question posed above. What I discovered was both encouraging and un-nerving. I found that tremendous change had occurred in the class structure of blacks in the 100 years preceding my survey in 1976. From a largely undifferen-tiated mass of poverty-stricken sharecroppers and urban laborers in the late nineteenth and early twentieth centuries, there had developed a class of black pro-fessionals and entrepreneurs around the turn of the century. They included teachers, minis-ters, doctors, lawyers, and, later, newspaper publishers, undertak-ers, and owners of small busi-nesses. A few managed to accu-mulate small fortunes.

On the negative side, I found that this class was re-stricted to those occupations serving the black community, and—just as important—its members lived in a segregated world where they could not spend their money as they wished. This situation might have continued indefinitely had it not been for the Civil Rights Move-ment. Laws passed in 1964 not only ended formal segregation in public accommodations, they also opened the doors to the whole range of middle-class oc-cupations. Black college students eagerly sought careers as engi-neers, accountants, scientists, and university professors. The black middle class doubled in size dur-ing the 1960s and has continued to grow.

However, the 1970s and 1980s have not been as helpful to economic progress among blacks as were the 1960s. The pace of middle-class growth has perceptibly slowed, along with all other indicators of progress. Still, the 1960s proved to be a watershed in the black experi-ence. Along with a persistent high rate of poverty, a growing black underclass, and a working class, there is now a significant black middle class. The black class structure is definitely diver-sified. It took the Civil Rights Movement and prosperity in the 1960s to accomplish this. I be-lieve that only a renewed com-mitment to equal opportunity and affirmative action will permit this trend to continue during a prolonged period of economic slowdown such as we have been experiencing.

disparity that has actually increased over the past three decades. Among young, central-city African-American men, unemployment rates (excluding "discouraged workers") are as high as 50 percent (Farley and Allen, 1987). In 1980, more than a century after the abolition of slavery, there were still more African-American women employed as domestics than there were Afri-can-American women professionals (Farley and Allen, 1987).

In nonmetropolitan areas, two in every five African-Americans of either sex are without jobs, cannot find a full-time job, or cannot earn enough to raise themselves significantly above the poverty level. Less than half of all African-American households own their own homes, compared to two-thirds of all white households. African-Americans are also less likely to receive mortgages enabling them to buy homes, even when all conditions are taken into account (Bradbury, Case, and Dunham, 1989).

High unemployment, poverty, and economic tension have taken their toll. African-Americans suffer from higher rates of almost all cancers and are 33 percent more likely to develop diabetes. Higher rates of heart disease and stroke among African-American women account for nearly half of the five-year black-white difference in female life expectancy; cancer, homicide, and strokes account for 50 percent of the six-year difference between African-American and white men (Farley and Allen, 1987). Nearly 40 percent of all African-American mothers receive no prenatal care in the first trimester of pregnancy. One in eight African-American infants is born at a low birth weight, and the infant mortality rate is twice that of white infants. African-American children are more likely to drop out of elementary or high school and less likely to attend college.

Much has been written about the increasing numbers of African-American families that have moved into the middle-class (Wilson, 1980, 1981), but they still work harder for equal rewards (Landry, 1987). At corresponding levels of education and occupation, for whites and African-Americans, the latter's wages still are lower.

Prestige.   Clearly, many sources of personal and social prestige are systematically denied to African-Americans. In one area of rapid gains, education, advancement may be more apparent than real, as may be seen in Figure 8-5.

African-Americans have made occupational gains since 1960, but ones not as significant as those of whites, particularly white males. In the world of sports, for example, although 57 percent of total members of the National Football League were African-American by 1987, they held only 6.5 percent of the administrative posts. Even African-Americans in positions that pay well and sound prestigious have complained that they have been placed in high-visibility, dead-end jobs (Jones, 1986).

Caste or Class?   Although much evidence supports the caste model of racial stratification in the United States today, debates over the relative importance of class and race continue. Some analysts (Wilson, 1980, 1986) claim that race itself is less important than the overwhelming effects of poverty. Others cite continuing racism as a major factor in perpetuating the cycle of poverty. For generations, despite their familiarity with American customs and language, African-Americans were systematically denied the right to vote, to be on juries, and even to be promoted in the military (Lieberson, 1981).

Comparative studies of African-American and white ethnic immigrants indicate that the greater success of whites in achieving middle-class status has been aided by "a set of bootstraps that must be government issued . . . a system of protection that takes the civil rights of groups to acquire property and to pursue a wide range of economic opportunities" (Smith, 1987, p. 168). African-Americans have not been issued the "bootstraps" that enable collective entry into the middle class. Table 8-3 summarizes recent estimates of how long it will take African-Americans to achieve parity (equality) with whites, given their present options for power, prestige, and occupational opportunity.

SOCIAL POLICY ISSUE

Is Racism on the Increase?

Despite the gains of the Civil Rights Movement of the 1960s, or perhaps because of them, racism appears to be once again on the rise. A former Ku Klux Klan official was elected to the Louisiana legislature in 1989 and almost succeeded in being nominated for governor. The growth of the American skinhead movement, with groups adopting names such as Kicker Boys, Immoral Discipline, and the Youth Defense League, is, according to some reports, the fastest growing violent movement of people devoted to white power. Although not all skinheads espouse prejudice as a uniting force, growing proportions have joined forces with such groups as the Ku Klux Klan, Aryan Nation, and neo-Nazi groups in such states as New York, Florida, California, and Oregon.

Overtly racist popular music, reflecting white power and a belief in violence disguised as "Americanism," includes such songs as "Race and Nation"

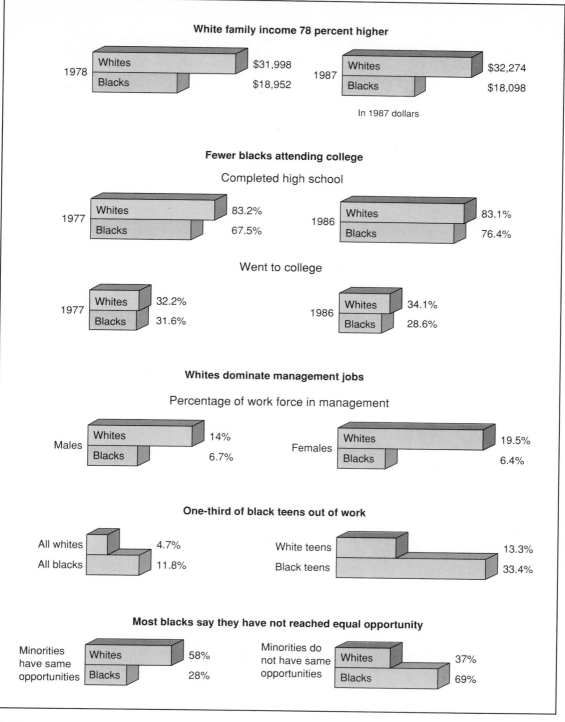

White family income 78 percent higher

1978 — Whites $31,998 / Blacks $18,952

1987 — Whites $32,274 / Blacks $18,098

In 1987 dollars

Fewer blacks attending college

Completed high school

1977 — Whites 83.2% / Blacks 67.5%

1986 — Whites 83.1% / Blacks 76.4%

Went to college

1977 — Whites 32.2% / Blacks 31.6%

1986 — Whites 34.1% / Blacks 28.6%

Whites dominate management jobs

Percentage of work force in management

Males — Whites 14% / Blacks 6.7%

Females — Whites 19.5% / Blacks 6.4%

One-third of black teens out of work

All whites 4.7% / All blacks 11.8%

White teens 13.3% / Black teens 33.4%

Most blacks say they have not reached equal opportunity

Minorities have same opportunities — Whites 58% / Blacks 28%

Minorities do not have same opportunities — Whites 37% / Blacks 69%

FIGURE 8-5 Economic disparity between blacks and whites. (Source: Adapted from *USA Today,* January 25, 1989, p. 6A.)

TABLE 8-3 Some Projections of the Relative Progress of African-Americans: In What Year Will They Reach Parity with Whites?

Achievement	Year Parity Expected
High school completion	2005
Female life expectancy	2021
Overall life expectancy	2029
Male life expectancy	2042
Managerial and professional occupations	2043
College enrollment	2044
Poverty rates (individuals)	2148
Poverty rates (families)	2158
Home ownership	3152

Source: Adapted from National Urban League, 1989.

and "White Power." The growing popularity of such music signals the increased acceptability of ethnic and racist stereotyping (Pareles, 1989). An alarming increase in racist taunts is occurring on college campuses as widespread as Smith, the University of Wisconsin, Dartmouth, and Stanford. Numerous colleges and universities have attempted to counter such activities with racial awareness programs. What is the situation on your campus? How would you explain the resurgence of open racism, and how would you deal with the issue? ■

Asians in the United States

Like European-Americans, Asian-Americans come from many different cultures and religious backgrounds and speak various languages. Yet a tendency to classify all Asians together has dominated both immigration policy and popular attitudes.

The Asian-American population increased by 142 percent between 1970 and 1980. Despite their growing importance, the decennial census performed by the Federal Bureau of the Census is the only source of detailed information about Asians currently available. Unlike Latinos, on whom data are collected through Census sample surveys each year, Asians are still too small a category to be so described. Not until the results of the 1990 Census are published will we have more recent counts. The diversity of people described by the Bureau of the Census as Asian may be seen in Table 8-4. The only other source of national data on Asians comes from the Immigration and Naturalization Service, indicating that the three largest groups of Asian immigrants during the past few years have been Chinese, Filipino, and Korean, comprising more than 20 percent of the total number of legal immigrants.

Chinese.   In the mid-nineteenth century, young Chinese males were imported to work on the transcontinental railroad. Unable to bring a wife with them or to send for a woman to marry, those who remained in the United States formed an almost exclusively male community, concentrated in a few

Table 8-4 Asian-American Ethnic Groups, 1980

Group	Number In Population	Percent Foreign Born	Percent Below Poverty
Chinese	812	63.3	10.5
Filipino	782	64.7	6.2
Japanese	716	28.4	4.2
Asian Indian	387	70.4	7.4
Korean	357	81.9	13.1
Vietnamese	245	9.5	35.1

Source: *Statistical Abstract of the United States 1989*, p. 39.

occupations (Siu, 1987). Chinese men were victims of extreme prejudice, discrimination, and open violence until the outbreak of World War II, when suddenly they became the "good" Asians compared to the "evil" Japanese. Restrictive immigration laws ended in the 1960s, and, as may be seen in Table 8-4, 63.3 percent of Chinese-Americans in 1980 were foreign born.

The majority of Chinese live in seven states, with California having the highest concentration (40 percent), followed by New York, Hawaii, Illinois, Texas, Massachusetts, and New Jersey. As barriers to discrimination were lifted, Chinese-Americans entered colleges and universities in growing numbers (see the box "The Asian Success Story"). Figure 8-6 also shows the high proportion of both American- and foreign-born Chinese in high-status occupations in 1980, and this percentage is growing. Although residential discrimination still exists in some areas, it has been less difficult for Chinese than for African-Americans to assimilate culturally or to amalgamate.

Japanese. According to one social scientist (Kitano, 1976), Japanese immigrants "came to the wrong country and the wrong state (California) at the wrong time (immediately after the Chinese) with the wrong race and skin color, with the wrong religion, and from the wrong country" (p. 31). After the outbreak of World War II, the Japanese in North America were forcibly moved from their homes and "relocated." More than 100,000 West Coast Japanese-Americans were placed in detention camps, with guard towers and barbed-wire fences. Their property was confiscated, sold, or stolen. Among the long-term effects of relocation were a reduction in the relative power of men over women in the family, a weakening of control over offspring, and reinforcement of a sense of ethnic identity.

In the history of U.S. race relations, few nonwhite minorities have established as secure an economic position as whites. The Japanese-Americans in California are a notable exception and have been upwardly mobile in part because of their economic ethnic hegemony. *Ethnic hegemony* refers to the power exerted by one ethnic group over another. Japanese-Americans achieved economic control over produce agriculture, thereby dominating an important economic area that permitted them to interact from a position of power with the majority culture (Jiobu, 1988).

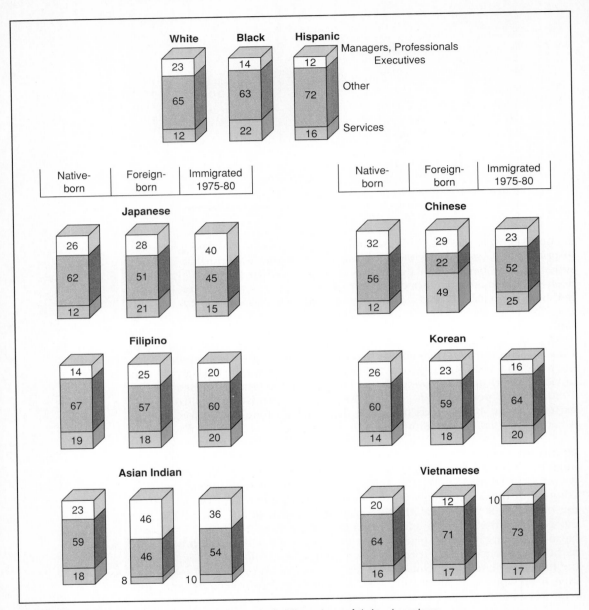

FIGURE 8-6 Occupational status of white, black, Hispanic, and Asian-American native-born and immigrant workers: 1980 (number = percent). (Source: Population Reference Bureau, 1985.)

Greater mobility, in turn, has been associated with a shift from jobs in the ethnic community to employment in the corporate economy, and, consequently, to greater assimilation (Bonacich and Modell, 1980). For example, third-generation Japanese-Americans have a higher percentage of non-Japanese friends than do first- or second-generation Japanese-Americans. They are also more likely to have non-Japanese spouses, to live in a non-Japanese neighborhood, and to profess non-Japanese religious beliefs (Montero, 1981). In short, as occupational and financial mobility has occurred, greater cultural, structural, and marital assimilation has taken place. The most highly educated and most successful Japanese-Americans have become the most cut off from their ethnic background. The irony of this trend toward amalgamation is that Japanese-Americans may lose their roots in the very tradition that gave rise to their upward mobility.

Southeast Asians.   Southeast Asians include Vietnamese, Cambodians, Thais, and Laotians. In 1960 a total of only 59 immigrants were admitted to the United States from Vietnam, Laos, and Cambodia combined; all but three of these came from Vietnam. However, in the decade following the end of the Vietnam War, about 842,000 Southeast Asian immigrants, primarily refugees, arrived in the United States. In 1988 alone, more than 53,000 Southeast Asians immigrated to the United States and now represent more than one in five Asian-Americans.

Within the Southeast Asian population, there are marked cultural and linguistic variations. Only about one-sixth came as part of the largely elite first wave of South Vietnamese, who brought with them money and skills. In contrast, recent arrivals have been both more numerous and more diverse: Vietnamese "boat people," lowland Laotians, almost all of the Hmong or Laotian hill tribes, and Cambodians. Many of these people came from rural backgrounds, had little education or transferable occupational skills, no knowl-

The decade following the Vietnam War brought some 840,000 immigrants to the United States from Indochina, mostly refugees. Many came from rural areas with little education and no knowledge of English but with a supportive network of kin. The difference between their desperate arrival on boats in 1973 and their situation by the late 1980s is quite dramatic.

edge of English, and had spent long periods in refugee camps prior to coming to the United States. Moreover, their arrival coincided with inflation, recession, and growing fears of displacement among the native-born population (Rumbaut, 1986). Despite government policies that attempted to settle these new refugees throughout the United States, about 40 percent of Southeast Asian immigrants live in California, and 8 percent in Texas. Laotians can be found in such states as Minnesota, Rhode Island, and Oregon, with a large concentration of Hmong in agricultural central California.

THE ASIAN SUCCESS STORY

For the last few years, the top ten winners in the Westinghouse Science Talent Search, conducted among high school students, have been disproportionately Asian-American. Although Asian-Americans make up less than 2 percent of the American population, in 1985 they comprised 8 percent of undergraduates at Harvard, 19 percent at MIT, and 25 percent at the University of California, Berkeley, and their representation in the most prestigious colleges and universities is growing. Asian-Americans' typically score about 30 points higher than whites on the math section of the college admissions Scholastic Aptitude Test. Regardless of their parents' level of education or socioeconomic status—two common predictors of academic achievement—Asian-Americans consistently get better grades than other students. Paradoxically, the more English that was spoken in the students' homes, the less well Asian-Americans did in school.

These results seem to indicate, in part, that Asian-Americans work harder. For example, a 1982 U.S. Department of Education study showed that 46 percent of Asian-Pacific students spent five or more hours on homework compared to 29 percent of whites, 25 percent of the African-Americans, and 16 percent of Latinos. And foreign-born and first-generation Asian-American students spend more time on homework on the average than do their second, third, and fourth generation Asian American peers.

Some sociologists have suggested that the Confucian ethic is a dynamic factor in Asian achievement. Confucius was a Chinese philosopher who lived in the fifth century, whose ideas spread throughout Asia. According to the Confucian ethic, people can always improve themselves by proper effort and instruction. People are encouraged to work for the honor of the family, not only for oneself.

But there are signs that growing numbers of Asian-American students have, ironically, been hampered by the success of previous students, which has been said to have led to the use of hidden "Asian quotas" by college admissions offices. Once admitted, Asian-American students have also complained that while special counseling and language help is available to African-American and Latino students, similar services are not provided for them.

The pressure of high expectations placed on Asian-American students by their families was expressed by one who was elected 1989 student body president at the University of California, Berkeley: "The stereotype is imposed on you that you're supposed to make the grade, and when you can't, it's very difficult."

Sources: Butterfield, 1986, pp. 18–23; Browne, 1986; Bernstein, 1988, p. L–16.

Other Asians.   In 1980 there were about 1.7 million people of other Asian nationalities in the United States. Filipinos accounted for 45 percent, followed by Asian Indians and Koreans. Koreans showed the most remarkable growth, increasing from 69,999 in 1970 to 357,000 by 1980. The reception given to the arrival of Asian-Americans, like that of most new immigrants who are not of northern European origin, has been mixed. However, Asians, whether from Korea, India, or elsewhere, may be the achievers of the future. An incredible 52 percent of adult Asian Indians and more than one-third of Filipinos are college graduates, although it is important to note that most Asian Indians admitted to this country came with higher levels of education.

ETHNIC MINORITIES

The great variety of nationalities is a defining characteristic of American society. To illustrate general themes in the immigrant experience as well as to introduce you to the fastest-growing ethnic minorities in the United States, our discussion will focus on two recent entrants: Latinos and Middle Easterners.

Latinos

Latino is a category made up of many separate cultural and racial subgroups bound together by a common language, Spanish (although language patterns do vary by country of origin). In 1989 about 21 million Spanish-speaking people were officially recorded as residing in the United States, and several million others are believed to have entered without official documents. Because of their generally younger ages and high birthrates, it is likely that Spanish-speaking Americans will soon outnumber African-Americans as the single largest minority group in the United States.

In 1989 the four major ethnic subdivisions within the Spanish-speaking population were Mexican-Americans; Puerto Ricans; people from Central and South American countries, particularly the Dominican Republic, Colombia, and El Salvador; and Cubans (see Figure 8-7). The remainder were from other Spanish-speaking nations. As Table 8-5 indicates, differences within the Spanish-speaking minority are striking, especially in terms of education and income. Each ethnic group has its own immigration history, cultural patterns, and its own internal diversity. Race and ethnicity combine to determine the relative status of Spanish-speaking Americans, both within the stratification system of the wider society and within the hierarchy of the Latino subculture. These divisions reduce the likelihood of the development of shared interests necessary to build a unified Latino power base.

Mexican-Americans.   When the United States conquered its territories in the Southwest, these areas had already been settled by Mexicans. A gradual pattern of economic and social subordination of the Mexicans, as well as Native Americans, developed as white Americans ("Anglos") migrated west (Moore and Parker, 1985).

Like many other ethnic groups that have not been accepted by the majority group, Mexican-Americans tend not only to live in particular geographic areas, such as Southern California, South Texas, and New Mexico, but to live in distinctly Mexican neighborhoods, or *barrios*. However, depending

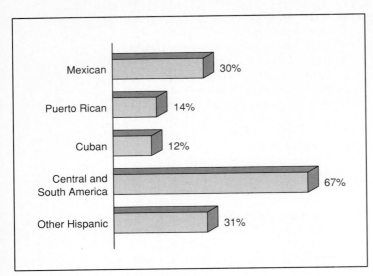

FIGURE 8-7 Percent change in Hispanic population: March 1982–89. (Total increase = 4.7 million.) (Source: U.S. Bureau of the Census, *The Hispanic Population of the United States,* March, 1989.)

on the community in which they live, residential conditions range from highly segregated to almost completely nonsegregated living patterns.

Although the stereotype of the Mexican farm laborer persists, in contrast to the employment pattern of their parents, relatively few Mexican-Americans today work on farms. This change reflects the increasing industrialization of agriculture rather than gains in job status or income. The present generation has moved from farm labor mainly into other unskilled jobs, such as work in canning factories. Many undocumented workers from Mexico have been employed in low-wage service and manufacturing jobs to keep labor costs low and to prevent unionization.

On various measures of social mobility, Mexican-Americans rank below the average for the population as a whole. In general they have less education

TABLE 8-5 Selected Social Characteristics of People of Hispanic Origin, 1987

	Country of Origin				
	Mexico	Puerto Rico	Cuba	Central/South America	Other
Characteristic					
Median age (in years)	23.5	24.3	35.8	27.3	30.9
Median years of school completed	10.8	12.1	12.4	12.3	12.4
Percent of married couple families	74.8	53.0	77.6	66.8	72.0
Percent of families below poverty level	24.9	38.1	13.3	18.7	19.4
Median family income in 1986 dollars	$19,326	14,584	26,770	22,246	24,240
Average family size	4	3.5	3.2	3.7	3.5

Source: U.S. Bureau of the Census, 1989.

The discovery and celebration of one's cultural roots can serve to strengthen the identity of an ethnic group.

than do non-Latinos or African-Americans. The traditional Mexican family is an extended one, with the kinship group being both the main focus of obligation and the source of emotional and social support. Birthrates are relatively high, especially among first-generation and poorly educated women (Bear and Swicegood, 1985). Within the family, gender roles are well defined. Both mothers and daughters are expected to be protected and submissive and to dedicate themselves to caring for the males of the family. For the Mexican male, *machismo,* or the demonstration of physical and sexual prowess, is basic to self-respect.

These traditional patterns protect Mexican-Americans against the effects of prejudice and discrimination, but they also reinforce isolation from the majority culture. An upwardly mobile Mexican-American must often choose between remaining locked into a semi-isolated ethnic world or becoming alienated from family, friends, and ethnic roots (Arce, 1981).

Puerto Ricans. Citizens of the United States since 1898, Puerto Ricans began to arrive on the mainland in large numbers in the 1950s because of the collapse of the sugar industry on their island. One-third of all Puerto Ricans now reside in the mainland United States. Of the 2.3 million mainland Puerto Ricans, 80 percent live in six states: New York, New Jersey, Connecticut, Illinois, Pennsylvania, and Massachusetts. Although almost two-fifths of the Puerto Ricans in the continental United States have incomes below the poverty level, their expectations of success are higher than the expectations of those who have remained in Puerto Rico.

Although Puerto Ricans are often grouped with Mexican-Americans, the

279

two populations are very different in history, culture, and racial composition. Puerto Rico's culture is a blend of African and Spanish influences, with a heavy dose of American patterns. In Mexico, both Spanish and Native American elements combine. The Puerto Rican experience on the mainland has included a continuing struggle for stability and achievement in education, politics, the arts, and community control. Puerto Ricans have been elected to the U.S. Congress, to state legislatures, and to city councils. Growing numbers of Puerto Ricans have moved from the inner city to middle-income, homeowner suburbs, and young Puerto Ricans are entering the fields of law, business, medicine, and teaching (Rogler and Cooney, 1986). Yet, others continue to have difficulty on standardized English and math tests, to drop out of school, and to face unemployment. About 43 percent of Puerto Rican families are likely to be headed by a woman with no husband present.

Cubans.   Cuban immigration to the United States began in large numbers when Fidel Castro came to power in the mid-1950s. Between 1954 and 1978, more than 325,000 Cubans were admitted as permanent residents in the United States, especially in the Miami, Florida, area. In early 1980 an additional 115,000 refugees entered the country in a sudden, somewhat chaotic exodus from Cuba. Although it is too early to determine how these new Cuban immigrants will fare in the United States, it is noteworthy that many earlier immigrants have achieved success operating businesses within Cuban communities (Rumbaut, 1986), and that a Cuban-American woman from Florida was elected to Congress.

Of all Spanish-speaking subgroups, the Cubans are older and better educated; are more likely to live in metropolitan areas, though not the central city; and have the highest median income. Much of their success, however, can be attributed to the educational and occupational characteristics of the first wave of Cuban immigrants to America. Theirs was an upper- and middle-class emigration in contrast to that of the Cuban newcomers of 1980, who were, on the average, younger, less educated, and less skilled. Recent Cuban immigrants have also been received with greater hostility and fear, and they are experiencing barriers to mobility within the established Cuban communities as well as outside of them.

Middle Easterners

In recent years, a new group of immigrants from the Middle East has begun to emerge as a visible urban minority. The number of immigrants from Middle Eastern countries has averaged more than 18,000 annually since 1970. Yet little is known about them. One study of the "Arab community" in New Jersey (Parrillo, 1983) found substantial diversity among the new immigrants. They came from a number of different countries such as Egypt, Syria, Lebanon, Iran, and Jordan, and they speak a number of languages. Their religious affiliations include Muslim, Coptic Christian, and Melkite Catholic, and they bring with them diverse cultural norms. Many would not describe themselves as "Arabs"; they do not speak Arabic or identify with Arabic history and culture. The one common denominator of these different ethnic groups is their Middle Eastern origin. The socioeconomic position of the various ethnic groups also varies: the Lebanese, the Syrians, and the Iranians are primarily middle class, other groups are mostly working class.

Some observers claim that the most recent wave of arrivals from the Middle East has not assimilated as readily as earlier immigrants, perhaps because many came as refugees who hope to return to their native countries when political conditions become calmer. In the Detroit area, which now has the largest concentration of Arabic-speaking people outside the Middle East— more than 200,000 Lebanese, Palestinians, Yemenis, and Iraqi-Chaldeans— there has been conflict between Middle Easterners and other ethnic groups. From the limited information available (Parrillo, 1985), however, there seems to be little racial tension, juvenile delinquency, or crime within Middle Eastern immigrant communities. Recent tensions stem from changing habits—drinking and dating—and language, as younger people become acculturated to the norms of the dominant society and reject traditional values and behavior.

RELIGIOUS STRATIFICATION

Religion, like ethnicity and race, has affected self-identification as well as access to the good life in America.

Protestants

The United States is predominantly a Protestant nation, both numerically and ideologically. Although the framers of the U.S. Constitution refused to establish a state religion, until very recently being Protestant was an accepted require- ment for economic and political leadership.

Because Protestantism includes Episcopalian Wall Street brokers as well as African Methodist sharecroppers, it is difficult to make general statements about social class among Protestants. The various denominations (see Chapter 11) can be roughly ranked in terms of the wealth of their members, their levels of education, and their occupational attainment. In this hierarchy, white Episcopalians are usually at the top. Presbyterians are next, followed by Methodists, Lutherans, and Baptists. A rule of thumb is that the hierarchy of prestige within American Protestantism runs from the most formal to the least formal (in terms of ritual), from the whitest to the darkest members, and from high to low socioeconomic status of congregants. Data on religion such as that found in Table 8-6 is not routinely collected by the census and is thus drawn from sample surveys that summarize differences in family income and education for socioreligious groups. Although intermarriage among various Protestant subgroups is high, marriage with Catholics or Jews remains low. According to sample surveys, at least up to 1980, 83 percent of those who come from Protestant backgrounds have married other Protestants (Archdea- con, 1983).

Catholics

Although individual Catholics in U.S. history have enjoyed high prestige, such as John Carroll, who signed the Declaration of Independence, Catholics as a group were long regarded with suspicion by the dominant Protestant popu- lation. In addition, there is a stratification hierarchy within American Cathol- icism that reflects time of immigration and racial and ethnic factors. The internal status system is headed by the Irish and other northern Europeans,

TABLE 8-6   Percentage of Whites with Four or More Years of
College Education and with Incomes of $25,000 or More,
1977–80 Dollars, by Religion

Religion	4+ Years of College	Income $25,000 or More
Protestant, all	14	6
Episcopalian	46	12
Presbyterian	22	11
Methodist	18	8
Lutheran	11	6
Other Protestant	15	10
Baptist	8	6
Catholic, all	13	8
Irish	23	11
Polish	16	7
Italian	12	7
Mexican	5	0
Jews	42	26

Source: Archdeacon, 1983.

followed by southern and eastern Europeans, with Latinos at the bottom. The proportion of Catholics in the United States has risen dramatically over this century, from about 10 percent of the total population in 1900 to about 25 percent today, as a result of both immigration and relatively high birthrates.

At one time, because of the different social-class positions of the ethnic groups, it was a source of great agony to both families if an Irish Catholic sought to marry an Italian Catholic. As anti-Catholic sentiment has waned in the society as a whole, so also have many internal divisions within Catholicism, as well as many differences between non-Latino Catholics and Protestants in family size, education, occupation, and income.

Discrimination today is more related to race and ethnicity than to religious preference. It had once been thought that the emphasis on community fostered by the parish church would reduce the motivation for individual achievement among Catholics. And for some decades, the closeness of the religious and ethnic group, along with discrimination against Catholics, limited their upward mobility. These barriers now appear to have been overcome, and Catholics are increasingly well represented in politics, business, and higher education.

At the same time, the Catholic church provides a basis for identity and for the development of primary-group relationships. Despite considerable intermarriage, most Catholics still marry within their faith, and many continue to send their children to parochial schools.

Jews

Among Jews, as with so many other minority groups, an internal stratification system exists, based on time of immigration, ethnic origin, and social-class background. In general, Jews have enjoyed great success in the educational and economic spheres in the United States. They are overrepresented among college graduates and high-income earners. Jews are, however, less likely to climb up the corporate ladder, the most common route to business success for non-Jews. Although part of the corporate elite today, Jews typically enter through investment banking or law or by starting their own corporations (Domhoff and Zweigenhaft, 1983). They are also unlikely to belong to elite corporate social clubs.

Jews have a lower divorce rate than non-Jews and have fewer children (Cohen, 1984). Although intermarriage has eroded the Jewish community (see Chapter 9), most Jews still live in areas of at least medium Jewish concentration. Jewish organizations range from religiously Orthodox to secular but converge on belief of separation between church and state. American Jews increasingly express their identity through Jewish friendship and identification rather than by means of religious rituals (Goldscheider, 1986).

EMERGING THEMES IN GROUP RELATIONS

In this brief overview of racial, ethnic, and religious minority groups in the United States, several themes are clear: Minorities meet resistance to achieving high status in the stratification system. They are subject to various levels of prejudice and discrimination. There is a tendency to create status hierarchies even within the minority community, although there are varying degrees of success in transferring these rankings to the stratification system of the society as a whole. Members often rely on the support of the minority community. Their ethnic roots are important in giving identity to members of minority groups in our modern industrial society. Between the first and third generations of immigrants, great changes have occurred in all minority groups in the direction of approximating the patterns of dominant group norms and behavior. Slowly, the effects of religious and ethnic distinctions have been lessened, but these are more surface differences than are those of race or sex.

If minority groups have similar experiences of discrimination and low status in the United States, why do the most disadvantaged not unite to challenge the control of the dominant groups? One of the rallying cries of the 1960s was the need for a "coalition of the oppressed": women, African-Americans, Latinos, homosexuals, and the idealistic young whites who joined forces with them. By the 1970s these elements of a coalition had failed to stick together. In the 1980s, not only did each group tend to go its own way, but it often found itself in conflict with one or more of the other groups. Coalitions among minority groups or between dominant and minority groups remain relatively rare. In 1989, two noteworthy elections of African-Americans to political office occurred: Virginia elected the first African-American governor in the United States, and New York City elected an African-American mayor. Such events were noteworthy precisely because they were unanticipated; many people had expected that there would be a "white backlash" among voters, as commonly occurs when the economy is not growing. In a *zero-sum* situation, where one group's gain must be at the expense of another, each will be concerned only with its own goals (Thurow, 1980). However, no group alone can muster enough strength to influence the dominant elites;

thus, the final result of a splintering of minority groups is to weaken the possibility of major change in the structure of the American stratification system.

SUMMARY

1. Race, religion, and ethnicity are ascribed characteristics that influence the placement of groups and individuals in the stratification system.

2. Dominant groups control societal resources and shape the experiences of minority-group members.

3. Minority-group status is defined in terms of visible ascribed traits, differential treatment, a self-image based on the traits, and a shared identity with others in the same group.

4. There are many ethnic, religious, and racial minorities in the United States.

5. Two of the explanations for the integration of minority groups are the melting pot and cultural pluralism models.

6. Minority groups occupy a continuum ranging from near isolation to a near complete blending into the dominant culture.

7. Barriers to integration include individual responses of prejudice and discrimination, as well as institutional patterns of racism built into the norms and structure of society.

8. Prejudice and discrimination have strongly negative effects on people's lives, health, employment opportunities, housing, income, and self-images.

9. The population of the United States is comprised of immigrants. Today, both legal and illegal immigration continue to account for population growth in our society.

10. The roots of racism on the part of white settlers date back to the destruction of tribal cultures and the seizure of land and resources belonging to Native Americans.

11. Although African-Americans have made important gains in political power, economic status, and prestige, especially since 1965, the gaps between African-Americans and whites persist.

12. Like Europeans, Asian-Americans come from various cultural and religious backgrounds and speak various languages.

13. Currently, the fastest growing ethnic minority are Latinos, who represent several distinct cultural and ethnic groups sharing a common language.

14. Religion is another form of differentiation affecting access to power, prestige, and property and influencing identity and self-image. There are differences in stratification within Protestantism and among Catholics and Jews.

15. Although religious and ethnic distinctions have weakened, institutional patterns of racism, along with personal prejudice and discrimination, still reinforce social inequality in America.

SUGGESTED READINGS

Baltzell, E. Digby. *The Protestant Establishment: Aristocracy and Caste in America.* New York: Vintage, 1964. The position of WASPs in American society and their reaction to increasing social diversity.

Bean, Frank D., and Marta Tienda. *The Hispanic Population of the United States.* New York: Russell Sage Foundation, 1988. A study based on Census data from 1960, 1970, and 1980. Mexican, Puerto Rican, Cuban, Central South American, and other Latino populations, having relatively little in common save for a common language and some shared cultural themes.

Blauner, Bob. *Black Lives, White Lives: Three Decades of Race Relations in America.* Berkeley: University of California Press, 1989. Changes in race relations from 1968 to 1986.

Caplan, Nathan, John K. Whitmore, and Marcella H. Choy. *The Boat People and Achievement in America: A Study of Family Life, Hard Work, and Cultural Values.* Ann Arbor: University of Michigan Press, 1989. Educational and economic achievements of the Southeast Asian boat people, who came to the United States after 1978.

Cohen, Steven M. *American Assimilation or Jewish Revival?* Bloomington: Indiana University Press, 1988. The question of whether or not Jews will remain a distinct entity or be totally absorbed into the larger society.

Farley, Reynolds, and Walter R. Allen. *The Color Line and the Quality of Life in America.* New York: Russell Sage Foundation, 1987. The status of African-Americans relative to whites from 1900 to the present based on the 1980 Census data.

Lieberson, Stanley, and Mary C. Waters. *From Many Strands: Ethnic and Racial Groups in Contemporary America.* New York: Russell Sage Foundation, 1988. Sixteen major European ethnic groups, African-Americans, and Latinos, based on the 1980 Census.

Parrillo, Vincent. *Strangers to These Shores: Race and Ethnic Relations in the United States.* 3d. ed. New York: Macmillan, 1990. Experiences of the major racial and ethnic groups in the United States.

Rieder, Jonathan. *Canarsie: The Jews and Italians of Brooklyn Against Liberalism.* Cambridge: Harvard University Press, 1985. A powerful ethnography of a white community.

Rodriguez, Clara. *Puerto Ricans: Born in the U.S.A.* Winchester, MA: Unwin Hyman, 1989. A portrait of Puerto Ricans living in the United States.

Sandefur, Gary D., and Marta Tienda, eds. *Divided Opportunities: Minorities, Poverty, and Social Policy.* New York and London: Plenum, 1988. Incidence, causes, and consequences of poverty among minority groups and the kind of social policies needed.

Schuman, Howard, Charlotte Steeh, and Lawrence Bobo. *Racial Attitudes in America: Trends and Interpretations.* Cambridge: Harvard University Press, 1988. Racial attitudes in America.

Snipp, C. Matthew. *American Indians: The First of This Land.* New York: Russell Sage Foundation, 1989. Status of American Indians including their social, economic, and political situation.

B

Health Care and an Aging Population

PATTERNS OF HEALTH AND ILLNESS

Epidemiology is the study of the patterns of occurrence of illness in a population.

One of the most important indicators of the quality of life in any society is the health status of the population. Health is closely linked not only to the level of industrial development of a country but also to the age and sex composition of its people and to the distribution of wealth, power, and prestige. The study of the patterns of the occurrence of specific diseases, disabilities, and defects within a population is known as **epidemiology.** Social epidemiologists focus on how life-styles relate to the occurrence of diseases,

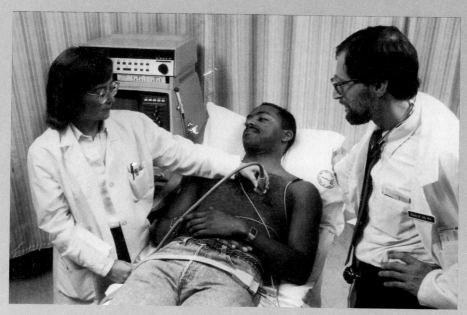

Social epidemiology studies the occurrence of specific diseases, disabilities, and defects within a population. Epidemiological patterns are determined by accumulating data from a great number of individual cases.

analyzing the relationships among a specific disease agent, the individual, and the social and physical environment.

The number of new cases of a disease that occur within a specific population during a stated time period is the *incidence rate*. Incidence measures give us a picture of how new cases are distributed in the population, and they provide a basis for studying the origins of a disease. The total of known cases of a disease in a particular population within a specified time, regardless of when the disease began, is the *prevalence rate*. The four basic factors in social epidemiologic research are age, sex, race or ethnicity, and social-class membership. Each of these is related to differences among people in health, illness, and death rates among subgroups.

Age. Life expectancy at birth is the average number of years that a person can expect to live. A great increase in life expectancy has occurred during this century in the United States and other industrialized nations. Until recently, death was very much a part of everyday life. When life expectancy was short, death was likely to occur at any age, and people were drafted into roles such as worker or parent far earlier than today. As late as 1900 the average number of years that an American could expect to live was 47; by 1989 this number had risen to 75. This increase is attributable to significant improvements in living and work conditions, in diet and sanitation, and, to a lesser degree, improved medical technology, such as antibiotics and new surgical techniques. It has been accompanied by a great increase in the proportion of people who will survive into old age.

Surprisingly, although the United States currently spends more of its domestic gross national product (GNP) on health than any other industrialized nation, because of problems in the U.S. health care system Americans do not have as long an average life expectancy at birth as do people in other industrialized nations.

Sex.   The life expectancy of females in industrialized societies is much higher than that of males—about seven years in the United States today. The percentage of males dying at any age is greater than the percentage of females, for all causes except diabetes. The gap between male and female life expectancy is widening, suggesting that women have greater biological resistance to infectious and chronic diseases.

Race and Ethnicity.   One reflection of social inequality in the United States is the difference in health among various racial and ethnic groups. African-Americans, Mexican-Americans, Puerto Ricans, and Native Americans continue to have lower life expectancies than other Americans. Their poorer health is a result of a complex set of factors, including generally lower income, overcrowded housing, fewer sanitary facilities, limited access to health facilities, as well as prejudice and discrimination.

Social Class.   Social-class differences in life expectancy and illness have been observed for centuries. Poverty, overcrowding, exposure to toxic substances, and limited access to medical care all play a part in disease and death rates for those in the lower social strata. In old age, the feminization of poverty and related medical risk is especially evident.

Other factors throughout the life course are also important in the study of epidemiology. The occurrence of such stressful events as unemployment, the death of a spouse or child, and divorce are associated with the onset of illness; but these effects can be cushioned by social supports.

SOCIAL CHARACTERISTICS OF AN EPIDEMIC: THE CASE OF AIDS

Between 1979, when acquired immune deficiency syndrome (AIDS) was first recognized as a disease, and 1981, only 83 cases were reported. From 1982 to 1983, the number of AIDS cases increased 215 percent. Since then, the incidence has slowed although the number of AIDS victims has increased. By March 1990, almost 168,000 Americans had died of the disease according to government estimates. The actual number of cases of AIDS in the United States is much higher than the death rate reflects, for there is no cure for the disease at the present time. Even if infections associated with AIDS were treated successfully, the resistance of AIDS victims is so poor that other illnesses usually follow, until one occurs that cannot be treated, and death results.

In the few years since AIDS has been recognized, researchers have discovered the virus that causes it, developed a test for identifying antibodies, and found drugs that seem to control some symptoms. But finding a *cure* may be more difficult, for the AIDS virus targets the entire immune system, thus making it basically unlike other conditions. Any cure must not only destroy viruses but also increase immunity.

Who is most likely to develop AIDS? Almost 90 percent of the known victims in 1990 were members of one or more of three main risk groups: homosexuals, bisexuals, and intravenous drug users. AIDS, which is transmitted by an exchange of body fluids, can be transmitted through conventional heterosexual sex, receipt of blood transfusions or tissue, and passed by a pregnant woman to her unborn child.

As of this writing there is *no* evidence that AIDS can be acquired from touching a person with AIDS, from kissing with exchange of saliva, from the cough or sneeze of a person with AIDS, from a bus or toilet seat, or from food served in a restaurant. Nonetheless, AIDS victims have lost their jobs (although a 1987 Supreme Court decision ruled that workers could not be fired on the basis of infectious disease).

Despite the widespread public concern about AIDS, its victims do not receive widespread sympathy. AIDS victims have been denied treatment at nursing homes and had their homes burned, and children with AIDS have been excluded from schools and day care. Why are AIDS victims dreaded, despite evidence that the disease cannot be spread by casual social contact?

The answer lies in the social characteristics of the majority of known victims of the illness. The disease was first diagnosed in a socially devalued group—homosexual men with previous histories of multiple partners and sexually transmitted diseases. Its incidence among homosexual men led it to be initially called GRID (Gay Related Immunodeficiency Disease). This also provoked conservative religious critics of homosexual life-styles to view it as just retribution for deviance—"God's way of spanking." Some homosexuals in turn regarded the AIDS controversy as a deliberate attack on the emergent gay liberation movement. Many victims of AIDS have been understandably hesitant to indicate they had the disease. It was not, for example, until after the death of film star Rock Hudson that it was known that he had AIDS or that he was homosexual. Similarly, the cause of death for the pianist/entertainer, Liberace, was not reported as AIDS until after a compulsory autopsy. Such is the power of social stigma.

As long as AIDS was considered the "gay plague," requests for research funds were generally ignored. AIDS, however, is not exclusively a disease of homosexual men. Indeed, shortly after the discovery of numerous cases of AIDS among homosexual men, two other socially devalued groups were observed to have the disease: drug users and Haitians. Drug users, primarily heroin addicts, contracted the disease through contaminated needles, and Haitians, the majority of whom were neither homosexual nor drug users, were believed to transmit the virus through blood rites associated with voodoo; a belief later challenged when scientists realized the disease could be transmitted through heterosexual intercourse (Altman, 1986). Because of the low social value accorded these AIDS victims, funds for their disability benefits or medical care were not initially available, despite the average patient's inability to work and huge expenses. It was not until 1983—four years after the AIDS

AIDS has become an epidemic in the United States. As of March 1991, about 168,000 people had already died of the disease and it is estimated that more than 1.5 million have been exposed to the AIDS virus. This memorial quilt carries the names of AIDS victims nationwide.

epidemic began—that its victims were granted almost automatic disability benefits under federal programs. Prior to that time, many waited up to two years to become eligible, by which time most of them had died.

Recent increases in research funds and medical benefits reflect in part the discovery that AIDS occurs not only among people with hemophilia (an inherited blood disease requiring frequent transfusions), but also among people of all ages who have received blood transfusions or tissue for any medical reason, among married heterosexual couples, and among children. The long latency period of up to ten years between infection and symptoms of AIDS suggests that many young adults contracted the disease during adolescence. By 1989, when the first national survey of AIDS virus infection among college students was released, 2 of every 1,000 students showed signs of being infected with the virus. Although the survey did not use random sampling and looked only at blood samples collected at college health centers for other reasons, the evidence suggests that the infection rate on campuses is similar to that found in other low-risk groups. Nonetheless, if the infection rate found in the study is typical of the more than 12 million American college students, about 25,000 may already be infected with the virus. If present trends continue, AIDS will soon rank as the number-five killer of Americans from birth to their 24th birthday. For many students and young and middle-aged adults, AIDS may change the rules of the dating game. Fear of AIDS has already altered sexual behavior among unmarried heterosexuals and within the homosexual community (Fox, 1987). In addition total sales of condoms doubled in dollar sales between 1980 and 1986, and special brands have been designed to appeal to female consumers. The effect of AIDS on dating behavior is thus an ongoing illustration of the impact that a disease may have, not only on health but on other aspects of life as well.

AIDS is also an international problem. According to conservative estimates by the World Health Organization, by 1986 there were 100,000 people with AIDs worldwide, 300,000 to 500,000 with ARC (AIDS related complex, now no longer used as a separate diagnosis in the United States), and between 5 million and 10 million symptom-free carriers, many of whom will ultimately die. Known in some African nations as "the slim disease" because of the weight loss associated with it, AIDS is spread in central, eastern, and southern Africa and the Caribbean primarily through heterosexual rather than homosexual contact. An almost equal number of males and females who are neither homosexual, bisexual, nor IV drug users have AIDS, and infants are frequently born with the virus. The discovery that AIDS may be neither associated with homosexuality, multiple sex partners, drug use, or deviant religious beliefs has begun to alter both attitudes and funding for research.

Yet a number of questions remain unanswered. Is there a cure for AIDS within the foreseeable future? How will the costs of medical and nursing care for AIDS victims be met and by whom? Will new drugs be affordable? How successful will public education campaigns for "safe sex" and against intravenous needle use be? For these questions to be answered, careful scientific research and social planning rather than an attitude of blaming AIDS victims for their condition are needed.

HEALTH AND ILLNESS AS SOCIAL IDENTITIES

In American society, health is highly valued and is essential to a wide variety of social roles characteristic of industrialized societies. As Kalish (1976) pointed out, if it can be said that there is a common religion in the United States, it is health, and its high priests are physicians. Yet **health** and **illness** are *concepts* used to describe a process of adaptation to the changing demands of everyday life and the meanings we give to living (Mechanic, 1978). Definitions of health and illness are constantly being redefined as new knowledge and technology are introduced, as the relative power of social institutions fluctuates, and as mechanisms of social control change. Diseases such as tuberculosis, smallpox, and malaria are easy to identify and are treated by the institution of medicine. In contrast, conditions such as alcoholism, drug abuse, depression, and bed-wetting tend to be more controversial; they are physical or behavioral deviations from the norm that pose personal or social problems for the individual and/or for the community.

Health and illness are concepts that describe adaptations to everyday life and the meanings that we give to living.

CLINICAL MODELS OF ILLNESS AND DISEASE

Although most sociologists define health or illness from a nonclinical, social-system viewpoint, other scientists use clinical models to identify abnormalities in a way that will direct diagnosis and treatment (Mercer, 1972).

The **pathological model** focuses on biological symptoms and abnormal functioning in an organism.

The **statistical model** defines health or illness in terms of the average of a population.

The **pathological model,** most commonly used in medicine today, describes diseases by the physical symptoms that accompany them and focuses on defining the nature of "abnormal" functioning. This model emphasizes biological explanations, single, specific causes, and what is wrong with a person rather than what is right. The **statistical model** defines health or illness in terms of the average of a population, assigning the term "normal" or "average" to the arithmetical average of the population being studied. People who deviate most from the majority are "abnormal." Both the statistical and pathological models of illness are important because each of them affects the society in which it prevails. In general, the broader the definition of illness and the more conditions or acts there are that are viewed as symptoms of disease, the more powerful are health institutions.

THE GROWTH OF AMERICAN MEDICINE

The American health care system as we know it evolved primarily within the past 100 years in response to changes in technology, pressures of competing interest groups, and felt social needs. Hospitals in the late nineteenth century began to provide care to large numbers of people, yet antiseptic procedures were almost unheard of. Relatively few medical practitioners had formal science instruction or medical training.

By the middle of the twentieth century, physicians were prosperous, unified professionals, in control of the market for health care. Since 1950 physicians' fees have increased 75 percent faster per year than prices for other goods and services. The frequency and types of services physicians provide have also expanded dramatically, while hospitals have become the central institution in delivery of health services (Rosenberg, 1988). As a result, expenditures for health care have also risen.

The Rise of Medical Dominance

The development of modern health care as an industry was initially stimulated by work in social epidemiology and the rise of the public health movement aided by scientific discoveries such as the germ theory of disease, anesthetics, and immunizations. By 1910 a landmark study, *The Flexner Report,* which called for closely supervised education and training of physicians, set in motion the reorganization of medical training and dominance of physicians. Medical diploma mills were driven out of business by new medical universities, and the general quality of American medicine improved (Starr, 1982).

These reforms set the stage for an increased demand for health care, and for the governing of supply. The practice of medicine was restricted by both training and licensing requirements established by professional organizations such as the American Medical Association. Women, African-Americans, Jews, and other ethnic minorities were systematically excluded (Ehrenreich and English, 1980)—a pattern that continued until the 1970s, when antidiscrimination legislation was enforced and admission policies were revised.

The New Medical Industrial Complex

There are signs today of a major power shift in the delivery of health care, as the solo practitioner or small group practice is gradually being replaced by profit-making companies that own chains of hospitals, nursing homes, medical office centers, and walk-in clinics. In response, some physicians have formed their own companies and health care clinics. These trends suggest considerable conflict within the medical establishment, which, along with a rising number of physicians, will result in more health care choices for consumers. A potential problem, however, is the development of one health care system for the affluent and another for the poor.

Nursing: A Profession in Flux.   Nurses compose the largest group of health professionals in the United States today. From 1854—when Florence Nightingale organized a group of affluent English women to care for the wounded and sick soldiers of the Crimean war—through the 1920s, nursing provided women with one of the few options for a responsible profession. Since then, nursing has become a less attractive option because of physicians' and hospital administrators' demands for cheap and easily controlled labor (Rosenberg, 1988).

Nurses have increasingly striven to be recognized as professionals rather than as helpers to physicians. Training has been upgraded, qualifications for nursing degrees have risen, and nurses today are less willing to perform many unskilled or semiskilled tasks.

The women's movement, too, has encouraged nurses to press for higher pay and more recognition, and the rise in costs of health care plus the increasing specialization within the medical profession have encouraged the development of new types of expertise. The **nurse administrator** and the **nurse practitioner** are two new career directions that require training beyond the bachelor's level. But as professional opportunities in other fields have increased for women (who make up 97 percent of American nurses), enrollments in nursing schools have declined, even as the demand for nurses continues to increase.

> The **nurse administrator** and the **nurse practitioner**, new career paths, require training beyond the bachelor's level.

Physician Assistants.   The term **physician assistant** (PA) covers health workers who perform a wide range of tasks usually performed by physicians. There are now over sixty PA programs accredited by the American Medical Association and enrollment remains predominantly male. Many physician assistants are absorbed into private medical practices by physicians, mainly to increase profits. Large numbers of physician assistants, like nurse practitioners, have established their own independent practices, although it is highly unlikely that either will ever achieve the power, prestige, or wealth of a physician.

> **Physician assistants** are personnel who perform a wide range of duties usually performed by physicians.

Marginal Health Practitioners.   Health professions not in the mainstream of the American health care system include chiropractors, osteopaths, and midwives. Although their approaches to the treatment of illness vary, these professions traditionally share a distaste for the medical doctor's use of drugs.

THE GROWTH OF HOSPITALS

Paralleling the physician's dominance of medical practice has been the growth of hospitals as major health care centers. In the early part of this century, as medicine became increasingly recognized as a healing art, more people who could afford it sought medical care. To meet the growing need, nonprofit community hospitals, supported by patients' payments, were founded to provide acute and surgical care. Physicians gained critical power, for only they could order the admissions that filled the beds.

Today's hospitals can be divided into three categories of ownership: (1) for-profit (or proprietary) private, (2) nonprofit private, and (3) public. Proprietary chains are rapidly growing for-profit hospital networks that, in addition to purchasing and constructing facilities, hold contracts to manage an increasing number of nonprofit hospitals. Although there seems to be little difference in quality of care between profit-making and nonprofit facilities, the for-profits do not provide the same amount of care to the poor as the community-based nonprofits. Most uninsured or low income patients are sent ("dumped," according to critics) into public hospitals, resulting in one type of medical care for those with insurance and money, and another for the uninsured.

HEALTH AND ILLNESS IN OLD AGE

It has become a truism to say that health care needs and costs increase with age. Yet utilization of health care throughout our lives is influenced not only by actual illness but by socioeconomic characteristics, sex, race and ethnicity, individual preferences, and broader social-structural factors, including the organization of the health care system (Dutton, 1986; Estes, 1989; Rice and La Plante, 1988). In old age, the low-income elderly are more likely to be disabled and to have poorer health than those of higher socioeconomic status. The very poor elderly make fewer physician visits than their age peers above the poverty level, and African-American elderly make significantly fewer visits than whites (Villiers Foundation, 1987).

Financial barriers to hospitalization of poor and minority elderly were lowered in 1965 with the enactment of Medicare and Medicaid. The elderly tend to be hospitalized twice as often as the general population and to stay in the hospital approximately 50 percent longer. Because hospital costs have risen more rapidly than other medical expenditures, Congress enacted a system of hospital prospective payment in 1983. Under this law, Medicare pays hospitals fixed amounts based on the average cost for a specific diagnosis. Prospective payment is based on 473 diagnosis-related groups (DRGs), which correspond to specific flat (or "average") payments rather than the amount or type of service delivered to each individual patient. If a hospital can treat a patient for less than the average payment, it may keep the difference; but if treatment costs exceed the average, the hospital must absorb the loss.

Medicare, a Federal program for those 65 and over, covers only about 49 percent of all personal health care expenditures of the elderly. Other public programs, including Medicaid, which covers poor of all ages, account for 19 percent. The remaining 32 percent is paid by the elderly themselves or by private health insurance. Not only are the poorest old least likely to have supplements to the basic Medicare provisions, but lack of a regular health care provider and difficulties in transportation are additional barriers. The upshot is that in old age, as throughout their lives, the rich receive more—and perhaps better—services than the poor, who are more likely to be disabled.

Medicare and Medicaid have had a large impact on the use of nursing homes. Before 1965, many old people in institutions were in mental hospitals, especially geriatric wards. Today, however, few are in mental hospitals and many more are in nursing homes, partly as a result of greater numbers of older people in the general population, and also as a result of the closing of public facilities along with increased financing for nursing home construction (Vladeck, 1985).

For every person 65 or older in a nursing home, almost four times as many who require long-term care live in the community and rely exclusively on unpaid sources of care, most often from a relative. Medicare still does *not* cover the cost of the great majority of nursing home care. At an average annual cost of $25,000 (GAO, 1988), nursing home expenses are prohibitive; an estimated one-third of all elderly households would be financially ruined if the family were to pay the costs of only 13 weeks in a nursing home (U.S. Senate, 1988).

The rapidly rising cost of health care for the elderly is a critical policy issue. At present, no single system exists for the financing and delivery of long-term care. Options for people who wish to purchase private insurance against the risk of long-term care expenses are limited and remain too expensive for those at greatest risk. An estimated 37 million Americans of all ages have no health insurance. If these people are unable to afford care now, the likelihood of their being sick in old age increases. A growing proportion of old people are expected to rely in the future on nursing home and formal home health care services, and long-term care costs are also expected to rise as the population ages.

Among Western industrialized nations, only the United States and South Africa lack a national health program that makes health care a right for all people of every age and social status. Supporters of the belief that health care *is* a right argue that without national health insurance and governmental regulation the regional and class differences in health services that now exist in the U.S. cannot be overcome. Those who oppose such increased government intervention argue that it would lower the quality of care and that people are not willing to pay the higher taxes that would be required to afford a national health program. Clearly, how to provide appropriate and equitable health services, including long-term care, for all citizens remains a crucial and unanswered challenge.

SUMMARY

1. Health and illness are socially defined. Definitions vary historically and from one society to another. Health and illness are linked to the level of economic development and technology of a country, its norms and values, and its population characteristics.

2. Epidemiology is the study of the patterns of occurrence of illness in a particular population. Age, sex, race and ethnicity, and social class are important factors in epidemiologic studies.

3. The pathological and the statistical models of health are used in today's medicine. Each leads to a different diagnosis and treatment.

4. The current American health care system is dominated by physicians, who are able to control the market for health care.

5. The dominance of hospitals as centers for the delivery of health services has paralleled the development of medicine.

6. Nurses, the largest group of health workers, are members of a profession striving for greater recognition and higher pay.

7. The United States spends more on health care than several other countries but with poor results, as demonstrated by life-expectancy data. Controversy about the organizing and financing of health care in the United States continues.

8. For the elderly with limited financial resources, available health care options—outpatient, hospitals, nursing home, and family support—are often inadequate.

SUGGESTED READINGS

Adams, Rebecca G., and Rosemary Blieszner, eds. *Older Adult Friendship*. Newbury Park, CA: Sage, 1989. The crucial importance of friendships in later life.

Berkowitz, Edward D., and Wendy Wolff. *Group Health Association: A Portrait of a Health Maintenance Organization*. Philadelphia: Temple University Press, 1988. The development of a Health Maintenance Organization.

Brubaker, Timothy H., ed. *Family Relationships in Later Life*. Newbury Park, CA: Sage, 1990. Information, drawn from research, about issues facing older families.

Chudacoff, Howard P. *How Old Are You? Age Consciousness in American Culture*. Princeton: Princeton University Press, 1989. Aspects of age-appropriate behavior and roles most Americans take for granted.

Conrad, Peter, and Rochelle Kern, eds. *The Sociology of Health and Illness: Critical Perspectives*. 3d ed. New York: St. Martin's Press, 1990. The social production of disease and illness, medical care organization, and health care alternatives.

Elder, Glen H. *Children of the Great Depression*. Chicago: University of Chicago Press, 1974. A classic study of the depression years cohorts and the impact of social-historical events on their lives.

Flood, Ann Barry, and W. Richard Scott. *Hospital Structure and Performance*. Baltimore: Johns Hopkins University Press, 1987. A study of differences in "postsurgical mortality rates" among hospitals with different organizational structures.

Gevitz, Norma, ed. *Other Healers: Unorthodox Medicine in America*. Baltimore: Johns Hopkins University Press, 1988. Historical accounts of healers in America and perceptions of them as a threat to the emerging institution of organized medicine.

Halpern, Sydney. *American Pediatrics: The Social Dynamics of Professionalism, 1880–1980*. Berkeley: University of California Press, 1988. The development of pediatrics and how physicians established new areas of medical practice.

Hess, Beth B., and Elizabeth W. Markson, eds. *Growing Old in America*, 4th ed. New Brunswick, NJ: Transaction Books, 1990. A collection of original essays and recent reprints at the cutting edge of social gerontology.

Hill, Carole. *Community Health Systems in the Rural American South.* Boulder: Westview Press, 1988. A demonstration of the importance of class and race in the provision of adequate health care, based on research in rural Georgia.

Kammerman, Jack B. *Death in the Middle of Life: Social and Cultural Influences on Death, Grief, and Mourning.* Englewood Cliffs, NJ: Prentice-Hall, 1988. The changing meaning of death and dying in contemporary America.

Shilts, Randy. *And the Band Played On: Politics, People, and the AIDS Epidemic.* New York: St. Martin's Press, 1987. The book traces the rise of AIDS from the 1970s to the late 1980s through poignant narratives, and it powerfully describes the apathy of medical and political institutions despite the dramatic increase of AIDS victims.

Turner, Charles F., Heather G. Miller, and Lincoln E. Moses. *AIDS: Sexual Behavior and Intravenous Drug Use.* Washington: National Academy Press, 1989. An important summary of social and behavioral scientific knowledge about sexual behavior, IV drug use, and changing health behaviors including 54 public policy recommendations. The three major questions addressed include the following: How many Americans are infected with HIV, and what are their characteristics? How can transmission of HIV be stopped? And how do we know that public health interventions are working?

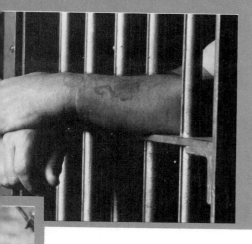

INSTITUTIONAL SPHERES

The next three chapters examine the major areas of socially constructed norms and behaviors essential to the survival of individuals and societies. These are the *institutional spheres,* which encompass family life, economic activity, politics, education, and religious systems. Over the course of human history, as cultures and social structures have grown increasingly complex, each of these spheres of activity has become separated from the others and from their common embeddedness in kinship relations. In modern societies, a large part of our activities are conducted in places apart from the home and in relationships other than those based on family ties. The statuses people have in these various institutional spheres are generally independent of their ascribed positions through birth or marriage. This process is called *structural differentiation.*

9

Courtship, Marriage, and the Family

- The Tiwi of northern Australia place great importance on the mother-in-law/son-in-law relationship. A young woman is introduced to a man who becomes the husband of any daughters she may subsequently bear by any of the men she chooses as a lover. This son-in-law remains her servant for life.
- In contemporary India, where daughters are an economic drain on a family's resources, prospective grooms are offered as much money and goods as a bride's family can afford. A very high rate of "accidental deaths" of young wives leaves the husbands free to contract a new marriage and receive more gifts.
- Conversely, in Egypt today, the growing concern is the number of husbands killed by their wives. Under Islamic law, husbands can divorce simply by declaring their intention, and the wife cannot object. Although Egyptian women had enjoyed increasing rights under the revolution that began in the 1950s, recent shifts toward a more traditional patriarchal system have left them angry and frustrated. As a result, some women have resorted to murdering their husbands rather than allowing them to walk away from a long-term marriage (*New York Times,* September 23, 1989, p. 4).

These three items are a small sample of the enormous cross-cultural variety of customs that regulate courtship, marriage, and family interaction. The way in which we, as Americans today, select our marriage partners and conduct family life is relatively unique to industrial societies and very different from the patterns followed by our own grandparents.

Despite all that you may have read about the "breakdown," "decline," or even "death" of the modern family, young people continue to marry, although at later ages; to have children, although fewer than in the 1950s; and to expect their family relationships to provide emotional security, although with a higher risk of failure.

From a sociological perspective, the family system must be analyzed in the same way as any institutional sphere: *as a set of socially constructed norms and behaviors essential to the survival of individuals and societies.* In functionalist terms, every society must solve certain basic problems: the control of sexuality, maintaining order within the household, pairing people off for reproduction, and meeting needs for intimacy and care. The solutions to these problems are as varied as human culture itself, with each society developing its own peculiar norms, values, beliefs, and practices, all of which may undergo change over time. The rules that govern courtship, mate selection, and marriage relationships serve to adapt sexual impulses to the needs of the collectivity. Family life, therefore, is not biologically given but socially constructed.

BASES OF THE FAMILY

The human family differs from the loose bands of other primates because of the unique qualities of culture mentioned in Chapter 2: language, foresight, self-control, the ability to construct norms to govern behavior, and the capacity to plan collectively. Families based on relatively permanent relationships between adult females and males are possible only when more than sexual attraction is involved and when the needs of the group as well as those of individuals are taken into account (McLaren, 1984). It seems likely, therefore, that the first and most powerful set of cultural norms are those that limit and direct sexuality into socially productive channels.

Functional Explanations

The **incest taboo** forbids sexual relations between certain family members.

Incest Taboos.   The social control of sexual impulses is accomplished through rules that specify (1) who can legitimately have sexual intercourse with whom and (2) who can marry whom. Some relationships are approved and others are forbidden. As a cultural universal, the **incest taboo** refers to the prohibition of sexual relationships among people defined as relatives, typically between parents and their children and between brothers and sisters. Just who else is included in the taboo varies widely, from only a few close blood relatives to everyone remotely related (Arens, 1986).

Many social scientists also consider incest rules to be the foundation of group survival. By forbidding sexual relations within a given unit, the taboos force sons and daughters to marry *outside* their immediate family. Thus, alliances are made between one family and another. Marrying outside the

Marriage and family systems represent a set of socially constructed norms and behaviors essential to the survival of individuals and groups. Here is a traditional Korean wedding.

family also reduces the likelihood of mental and physical birth defects by bringing a new gene pool into the breeding group, although this benefit was unknown until the last century. It also reduces in-group conflict caused by competition for sex partners.

Exchange Factors. Levi-Strauss (1969) and others have suggested that the exchange of brides and grooms is the original *social* relationship, serving as an example of all exchanges that bind individuals and families together in enduring social systems. Underlying all social relations is the concept of **reciprocity:** A gift obligates the receiver to return something of equivalent value later. And in nearly all societies, many types of exchange accompany a marriage: between one family and another and between guests and hosts.

Reciprocity obligates the receiver of a gift to return something of equivalent value.

The Principle of Legitimacy. A third basis for marriage and family is described by Malinowski (1929/1962) as the "principle of legitimacy," by which he meant that the function of marriage is to identify one man as being responsible for the protection of a woman and her children and for their placement in the social system. By ascription, the status of the father typically determines the social position of children. Note that the "father" who accepts responsibility is a **social father,** but does not have to be the biological parent.

Conflict Explanations

When a conflict theorist asks who benefits from marriage arrangements, the answer is clearly the kinship groups, heads of families, and men in general (Smart, 1987). *Incest taboos* and the rules regulating who can marry whom are often used to keep property within a given kinship line. For example, what appear as violations of the taboo, such as brother–sister marriages in the ruling families of ancient Egypt, prevented the dividing up of the family's estates. Even today, in many societies, especially in Muslim countries, the most desirable marriage choices, for the same reason, are among cousins.

The *exchange of marriage partners* among kinship groups is part of a society's power system. Family rank is advanced or maintained through marriages, and the power of males—as fathers or brothers—is shown in their "giving away" the women of their family. Similarly, the concept of *social fatherhood* reinforces the superior position of men in most societies. High rates of illegitimacy are tolerated in societies or social classes where fathers cannot transmit resources or place their offspring in the ongoing social system, such as among the poor in modern societies.

The principle of legitimacy, or **social fatherhood,** identifies one man as responsible for the protection of a woman and her children and for the children's placement in the social system.

KINSHIP IN CROSS-CULTURAL PERSPECTIVE

Kinship systems vary both from one society to another and over time. In general, five variables describe kinship systems: how many marriage partners (spouses) are permitted at one time, who can marry whom, how descent and transmission of property are determined, where a couple lives, and what the power relations are within the family. The many differences between traditional and modern patterns are shown in Table 9-1.

TABLE 9-1   Kinship in Cross-Cultural Perspective

	Traditional Societies	Modern Societies
Number of spouses at one time	One (**monogamy**) or Plural (**polygamy**) **Polygyny**—two or more wives **Polyandry**—two or more husbands	One (**monogamy**)
Choice of spouse	Choices made by parents to enhance family power	Relatively free choice
Line of descent	From males (**patrilineal**) From females (**matrilineal**)	Both equally (**bilateral kinship**)
Couple's home	With groom's family (**patrilocal**) With bride's family (**matrilocal**)	Place of one's own (**neolocal**)
Power relationships	Various degrees of male dominance (**patriarchy**)	Greater equality (**egalitarian**)
Functions of family	All-embracing, to protect the kinship group as a whole	Specialized, to provide a stable environment for child rearing and emotional support
Structure	Extended	Nuclear
Focus of obligation	Blood relationships	Marriage tie and children

Cultural Universals and Variations

The five characteristics of kinship systems determine the family structure of a society. Elaborated over time, along with other rules governing courtship, child rearing, divorce, and widowhood, these family systems present a fascinating picture of human variability and adaptability. The one common thread in patterns of mate selection and marriage in preindustrial societies is the protection of the interests of kinship groups.

Marriage rituals are also universal because the society as a whole has a stake in orderly reproduction. The ceremony symbolizes the union of separate families through the exchange of gifts, and the public nature of the marriage signifies the couple's responsibilities to their society. For most people throughout human history, marriage has been less a personal than a familial and societal affair. Many of you may have grandparents whose marriages were arranged by family elders, and this custom is still preferred throughout most of the world.

THE FAMILY IN HISTORICAL CONTEXT

Extended-Family Systems

The **extended family** is a relatively large unit composed of several related households, most often involving three or more generations.

Throughout human history and in most of the world today, the needs and interests of family groups outweigh the needs or interests of individuals. The kinship, or descent, group is often referred to as an **extended family,** that is, a relatively large unit composed of several related households, either a father

The nuclear family has both advantages and disadvantages when compared to the extended family. If you could live in either family system, which one would you choose? Why?

and his sons and their families, or a mother, her brother, her daughters and their families. Another type of extended family, in societies that practice **polygamy,** is composed of a man or a woman with more than one marriage partner at the same time.

Extended families have many advantages: shared wealth and power, protection, and a supply of potential grooms and brides for alliances with other families. Horticulture and agriculture, you will remember, are based on human labor and the ownership of land, so that over the thousands of years that farming was the major mode of adaptation to the environment, the extended family was central to survival. Before the rise of the modern nation-state, with public provision for the care of the young and the old, for protection of property rights, and for education of the young, these tasks fell to the kinship group. Without centralized governments to keep public order, each extended family guarded its own land and protected its members.

Polygamy creates extended households composed of a woman or man with more than one marriage partner at the same time.

Nuclear Families

Each nuclear family is a unit composed of a married pair and their dependent children living together. In any society this **nuclear family** is more or less closely linked to other nuclear families in the kinship group. In other words, the major distinction is not nuclear *versus* extended but the degree to which nuclear units in the same kinship line share residence, resources, work, and responsibilities for blood relatives.

The **nuclear family** is a unit composed of a married couple and their dependent children.

In general, extended-family systems are typical of nonindustrial societies and the rural sectors of modern societies. In this sense, extended-family systems are *traditional,* whereas the nuclear family as a relatively independent unit is *modern.*

Historical evidence indicates that nuclear families actually predate the Industrial Revolution in many parts of Europe, but also that extended kinship groups proved functional in easing the adaptation of family members to the demands of industrial work (Hareven, 1987; Kertzer and Hogan, 1988). The existence of extended households also fluctuates with the number of people available to join them, such as unmarried relatives or widowed parents (Ruggles, 1987), and with the economic capacity of family members to support separate households.

305

The Family in American History

As helpful as the extended-kinship group may have been in the early decades of industrialism, it has never been the dominant family form in our society. The typical household consisted of a husband and wife and their young children, perhaps joined for a few years by a widowed grandparent but rarely containing other adult relatives (Mintz and Kellogg, 1988).

. There is no strong evidence that past generations of parents and adult children wished to live together any more than they do today. For two centuries and more, young people went "west," leaving their kin behind. Most immigrants from Europe were young, single people who established families only after arriving in America. Many of these families eventually became extended, as adult children remained with the parental couple, more because they could not yet afford their own home than because of traditions brought from the "old country." In other words, most extended-family households in America have been temporary adjustments. This is still true today, particularly among the poor (Wilson, 1988).

From Traditional to Modern

Eventually, people who live in industrial societies come to share certain "modern" attitudes about individual rights and family obligations, and the balance between the two. What makes a family modern is not its structural isolation but its shift of sentiment inward, to the nuclear unit and away from the bloodline of extended kin.

This shift in sentiment to the nuclear family tends to appear in societies as they become industrialized, which is accompanied by moving from villages to cities, higher levels of formal education, lower birthrates, and greater freedom of young people. These economic and social changes lead to greater support for individual rights against the power of the larger kinship group.

THE MODERN FAMILY

The transition from traditional to modern family forms has often been described in terms of losses of function for the extended kin group. The nuclear family in a modern society is much less powerful and versatile than was the traditional extended family. Tasks once assumed by extended kin are now performed by outside agencies. In the *economic* sphere, for example, the family is, as a rule, no longer self-sufficient; it is dependent on wages earned outside the home. The Industrial Revolution dramatically changed the relationship between home and workplace, which became physically separated and came to evoke different emotional commitments. As a consequence, women and children lost their economic value and became dependent on the earnings of the husband.

The modern family is now primarily a *consuming* unit, highly dependent on the economic system beyond the home. In the *political* sphere, armies, police forces, and courts replace armed relatives. The public-school system has been created to *educate* people for work in an industrial economy. *Religious* needs are also increasingly met by specialists outside the family setting.

As the extended family becomes less and less important as a source of goods and services, the young are freed from the control of their elders. At the same time, the challenges of modern life create needs for affection and emotional support that cannot easily be met by family members with whom one has relationships of unequal power or rivalry. The modern nuclear family is specialized to gratify expressive needs rather than to perform the instrumental functions of extended families. Expressive needs are best met by intimacy with a few people. Hence the importance of mate selection, not for the kinship-based needs of the past but for emotional compatibility. The **romantic love syndrome** (Goode, 1959) becomes the modern basis for choosing a husband or a wife.

> The **romantic love syndrome** involves the selection of a mate on the basis of love rather than kinship-based needs.

Mate Selection in Modern Societies

If romantic love is the only legitimate reason for choosing a marriage partner, then people must be free to make their own choices. Parents can no longer arrange marriages for their children, although they can influence such choices directly (by signs of approval or disapproval) and indirectly (by moving to a certain part of town or joining a particular church). But in a modern society the burden of choice rests with the young people themselves, and each generation of youth has elaborated a set of norms and behaviors—dating rituals—to help them select a mate (Bailey, 1988).

Although dating rituals change over time in response to other changes in the society, the general pattern begins with a form of group dating where sets of boys and girls, for example, go skating, to the movies, or just hang out. Gradually, the numbers involved become smaller: perhaps three or four couples together, for comfort and protection; then, by high school, double or single dating. As in simple societies, gifts are exchanged: bracelets, pins, rings. The difference is that the gifts are exchanged by the dating couple and not by their families.

Then follows a period of semiengagement prior to the formal wedding announcement. Up to this time, either young person can be released from the relationship, not without pain, but with relative ease. Once the public announcement is made, families and friends and the world at large are witnesses to the intention to marry; larger and more expensive gifts are exchanged. These customs reinforce the process—followed in most societies—of progressively bringing the weight of the community to bear on mate selection. Marriage is still too important to families and societies to be left entirely to the engaged couple.

In contrast to marriage arranged by kinfolk, this pattern of mate selection can be described as relatively "free," but there are many ways in which such choices are channeled by parents and peers. Thus, although theoretically you could choose any one of hundreds of millions of persons of the opposite sex, you are confined to a rather limited subset: the people you actually meet and those whom you can confidently bring home to dinner. These factors alone automatically exclude all but a small "pool of eligibles"—people likely to be very similar to you in terms of social background characteristics.

The tendency to select a mate of the same race, religion, social class, ethnic group, educational level, and age as oneself is called **homogamy** (*homo* = "like"; *gamy* = "marriage"). People similar to oneself are easy to

> **Homogamy** is the practice of selecting a mate with similar social background characteristics.

be with for a number of reasons. First of all, there is a foundation of shared values and attitudes as a result of similar socialization, which reduces the likelihood of disagreement and misunderstanding. Second, people who agree with us are very rewarding to be with because they reinforce our own sense of rightness. Third, we avoid negative reactions from family and friends.

But modern societies provide widened opportunities for meeting people from different geographic areas and social backgrounds—at college, in the armed forces, at the workplace, in singles bars, and even through personal advertisements or video dating services. Women, in particular, have greater freedom than in the past to meet and date a variety of men. Thus, increasing numbers of American marriages are **heterogamous** (*hetero* = "different") in terms of race, religion, and ethnicity (Rytina et al., 1988). Heterogamy has its benefits in exposing marriage partners to other ways of thinking and doing, thereby adding an element of variety and challenge to the relationship.

Heterogamy is the practice of selecting a mate with different social background characteristics.

It has been generally assumed that homogamous marriages are somewhat more stable than heterogamous unions, and that cross-racial marriages are especially vulnerable, as are those that encompass wide differences in age, education, and social class. The data, however, are not altogether clear. In general, as barriers to heterogamy fall, couples are able to adjust and adapt more easily than when such unions were rare and subject to strong parental and peer disapproval.

The Marriage Market.   The mate selection process in contemporary America has many features of a marketplace, and people must make the best bargains they can. Each person's value in this market is determined by the possession of qualities desired by others. A woman's beauty and youth are the traits most often valued by men. In contrast, women often look for occupational potential in males. This means that, over time, a woman's value on the marriage market tends to decline, whereas a man's is likely to increase.

Social class, race, and ethnicity are also important. Although most people marry within the same stratum, men can "marry down" because it is their accomplishments that usually determine the couple's place in the status system. A woman is urged to marry at a level the same as or higher than her father's (Schoen et al., 1989). This pattern may change as women achieve occupational status in their own right and as a family's socioeconomic status (SES) is determined by both parents' achievements.

Sociologists have compared the mate selection process in the United States to that of a marketplace where people make the best bargains they can. How does this apply to the experiences of single men and women?

From a functional perspective, the marriage market has traditionally represented a mutually beneficial exchange: Women receive protection, economic support, and social rank; in return, they provide emotional and sexual sustenance, maintain the home, and produce offspring. When one partner feels that the exchange is no longer fair, she or he may try to strike a better bargain with another partner.

But as long as men and women have different levels of social power and resources, the exchanges cannot be entirely fair. From the conflict perspective, then, mate selection takes place under conditions that generally favor men: They have a wider range of choice, they do not lose their market value with age, and they retain their independence in the world outside the home. These conditions rarely exist for women, who must often remain in an unsatisfying relationship rather than risk reentry into an unfavorable mate market (England and Kilbourne, 1988).

Nonetheless, the relative power of women in the mate selection process has increased in recent years largely because of their ability to remain economically independent. As a result, the median age at first marriage has risen dramatically: for women, from 20.8 years in 1970 to almost 24 years today, and for men, from 23.2 in 1970 to 26 in 1989. Looked at another way, in 1970 almost 66 percent of American women were married by age 24; today, only 40 percent are. This delay, a stunning reversal of the pattern for women before 1970, as shown in Figure 9-1, reflects a desire to complete a college education and to establish oneself in an occupation before marriage and parenthood. Most women expect and wish to be married but are taking longer to search for a husband, even at the risk of remaining single. And it seems likely that a higher proportion of women may never marry than was the case in the recent past. But we should remember that marriage rates between 1947 and 1967 were at an all-time high: close to 95 percent of all Americans.

Although women's newly found independence is often cited as a major cause of family "breakdown," there is much evidence that today it is men who are most interested in self-fulfillment and least tolerant of the restraints of marriage and parenthood (Mintz and Kellogg, 1988). It appears that both men and women today can find emotional and economic security outside of marriage, and although married people still report higher levels of happiness and life satisfaction than the nonmarried, the difference between the two groups has become smaller over the past decade (Glenn and Weaver, 1988).

Egalitarianism

In general, intimate relationships, within or outside marriage, are increasingly characterized by reduced power differentials between partners and between parents and children. This trend, called **egalitarianism,** has its modern ideological roots in the Western ideal of individual rights, which has only recently been extended to women and children. In practice, egalitarianism is realized only when people have similar resources. As we discussed in Chapter 7, inequality between men and women is lowest in gathering bands, where food and tasks are shared, and is greatest in societies where ownership of land is held exclusively by the kinship line of males and where women and children are bargaining chips in the family power game.

Women's power in marriage is highest in societies where property passes

Egalitarianism refers to reduced power differences between husbands and wives and between parents and children.

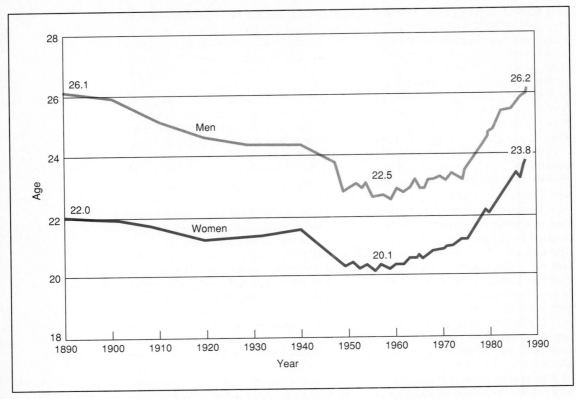

FIGURE 9-1   Median age at first marriage, 1890–1990, by sex. (Source: U.S. Bureau of the Census, P-20, No. 445, 1990, p. 1.)

through the female line and where nuclear families predominate (Warner et al., 1986). In modern industrial societies, the nuclear family functions primarily as a source of affection and emotional support—feelings that are more likely to flow from mutual respect among equals than from inferiors' fear of or obligation to superiors (see Mirowsky, 1985).

Parents and Children.   Relationships between parents and children in modern societies are also characterized by less inequality than in the past. The reasons for this change are both material and ideological. The material conditions include the dramatic drop in infant death rates in modernizing societies, in addition to the marked decline in fertility in industrialized societies where children under age 14 are forbidden to enter the paid labor force. These trends mean that each family will have fewer children than in the past, but the great majority of offspring will survive to adulthood. Thus, parents can now invest more time and emotional energy in each child. The child becomes important in its own right rather than as an economic asset or potential marriage pawn.

Tracing this changing definition of the child in our society, Zelizer (1985) sees the period between 1870 and 1930 as one in which the economically valuable child of preindustrial society is gradually replaced by the "economically worthless but emotionally priceless child." For example, in the nineteenth century, foster parents preferred older boys for their labor value; in the twentieth century, the pattern shifts toward legal adoption, with infants, particularly baby girls, preferred for their sentimental value.

In industrial societies, young people are less dependent on parents for occupational and marital placement, and intergenerational affection can no longer be demanded; it must be earned. This requires a more egalitarian relationship than was possible or necessary in the past.

The Family Cycle

Modernization has also brought changes in the timing of family events across the life course. Comparing the typical pattern of American families formed in 1900 with that of a couple marrying today, we can see how extensive these changes are. The 1900 marriage would have followed a rather long courtship period while the husband-to-be established himself economically; despite the long wait, both would enter marriage with limited sexual experience. The couple would probably have four children, the last being born when the mother was in her mid-thirties. By the time the youngest child was ready to leave home, it was likely that one parent had died. The widowed spouse would survive for a half-decade or more, often living with an unmarried child.

In contrast, couples today enter marriage after a short courtship and relatively long history of sexual experience. The childbearing phase of the family cycle will consist of two offspring, closely spaced, and be completed by the time the mother is age thirty. When the children are in school full-time, if not before, the mother will reenter the labor force. The children will be out of the house—in college or living on their own—when the parents are in their early fifties (Teachman et al., 1987; Rindfuss et al., 1988). Given the great increase in life expectancy during this century, the parents will now enjoy at least *two decades* of being alone together again. This is a dramatic change, a phase of the life cycle—the **empty nest stage**—that did not exist for most couples in the past (Glick, 1989). The empty nest is typically followed by five to ten years of widowhood, as wives survive their husbands.

The combined effects of later marriage, increased divorce rates, and older women living alone can be seen in Table 9-2. The proportion of households occupied by a married couple has declined, while the proportions of single-person and single-parent households have risen.

The **empty nest stage** of the family cycle occurs when all the children are out of the house and the parents are alone together again.

Parenthood

Delayed age at first marriage, extended education, women's labor force participation, the high costs of raising children, legalization of contraception, and the spread of modern norms of child rearing—all combine to reduce the number of children per family in industrialized societies. Overall, birthrates for American women increased between 1947 and 1967 (the baby boom years) and then declined steadily. Today, on average, American women expect to bear two children, which has been the case for the past two decades. The only age group that shows a significant increase in births are women in their

THE PARENTAL NEST: WHEN TO FLY AWAY AND WHEN TO RETURN

Before the Second World War, most young adults (people ages 20 to 29) did not leave home to attend college, nor did they have the economic resources for independent living. Young women left when they were married, and young men when they could afford to do so. In the 1950s, however, postwar economic growth and the expansion of higher education, coupled with the new cultural emphasis on individualism, led to the expectation that young adults would and *should* leave home as soon as possible, even if not fully economically independent. Between 1954 and 1974 the proportion of young adults living with their parents dropped sharply, especially in the middle class, where personal independence was valued. The norm of independent living is particularly strong for males and for children whose families have substantial resources and lowest among offspring in families with strong ethnic and religious involvement. (Goldscheider and Goldscheider, 1987).

The resulting "empty nest" has been hailed as a triumph of modern child rearing, the successful launching of an independent young person and an opportunity for new forms of personal fulfillment on the part of the parents. But the nest may not stay empty for long. Over the past 15 years, the proportions of young adults living at home has *increased,* so that today, the percentage for 20- to 24-year-olds is as high as in 1954, and almost as high among 25- to 29-year-olds (Schnaiberg and Goldenberg, 1989).

Those who stay at home longer or who return home are primarily males, and the majority are from middle-class families (Riche, 1987). This return to the nest may be caused by psychological factors (lack of maturity, inability to break with one's parents) and practical factors (parents continue to provide food and laundry service, especially for sons, but would expect daughters to assist in housework). Some adult children will return for a brief period between jobs or marriages, others remain until they are fully established in a career, and still others stay until pushed out.

Sources: Riche, 1987, pp. 36–38; Goldscheider and Goldscheider, 1987, pp. 278–285; Schnaiberg and Goldenberg, 1989, pp. 251–269.

---

early thirties (from 3 percent of all *first* births in 1970 to 12.5 percent in 1988), but 25 percent of women in this age group are childless (U.S. Bureau of the Census, Series P-20, No. 436, 1989). What these data suggest is that most American families will be relatively small, concentrating emotional and financial resources on one or two children. Although the small family has many benefits for both parents and children—in terms of achievement orientation, mobility, and life satisfaction—it also results in fewer sources of social support for the parents in old age (see Chapter 12).

These small families reflect the dominant ideology of individualism and self-fulfillment, as well as economic conditions in the wider society. Historically, when jobs are plentiful and incomes rise, so do marriage and fertility rates. Today, however, improved economic chances for women have meant the delay of both marriage and parenthood (Teachman and Schollaert, 1989). Slightly more than half of all women giving birth in 1988 were in the paid

TABLE 9-2   Household Composition, United States, 1970–2000[a] (in percents)

	1970	1990	2000
Family Households	81.2	70.8	68.2
Married couples	70.5	56.2	53.0
Male heads	1.9	2.7	3.0
Female heads	8.7	11.8	12.0
Nonfamily Households	18.8	29.2	31.8
Men alone	5.6	9.7	10.4
Women alone	11.5	15.0	16.4
Other	1.7	4.5	5.0

[a] Estimate by U.S. Bureau of the Census, on basis of middle-range projections of marriage, divorce, and death rates.

Source: U.S. Bureau of the Census, P-20, No. 437, 1989, p. 45.

labor force: as high as 60 percent for women with four or more years of education, compared to 34 percent for women who did not graduate from high school. Women with fewer years of education also tend to be more traditional in gender expectations, to marry earlier, and to enter parenthood at younger ages compared to their age peers with less traditional expectations (Morgan and Waite, 1987; Rindfuss et al., 1988). Not all parenthood occurs under conditions of marriage. Indeed, between 1985 and 1988, four out of ten first births to women ages 15 to 29 were out-of-wedlock or conceived before the woman's first marriage (see Chapter 7).

Modern Marriage: Doing It Less and Enjoying It More?

Many strains are unique to contemporary marriages. If one chooses one's own mate, marries for love and love alone, and is expected to provide emotional support in a relationship that could last for more than five decades in the privacy of a nuclear household, can there be any wonder that many couples find the challenge more than they can handle? The current high divorce rate largely reflects the very high marriage rates in our society since World War II—when almost everyone gets married, it is unlikely that everyone chooses wisely.

Yet, social surveys consistently record very high levels of satisfaction in marriage, largely because the people who are not happy have ended the relationship through divorce, desertion, or separation. Also, many people find any marriage preferable to not being married.

Benefits of Marriage.   From the functional perspective, it has long been assumed that "the family" is a unit of shared interests, in which wives provide services in return for economic security, where husbands are motivated to earn adequate incomes, and where children are well socialized. From the conflict perspective, however, such basic harmony of interests can no longer be assumed (Curtis, 1986).

Not only do family members have individual interests to protect, often at cross-purposes, but the family unit itself is not necessarily well suited to the modern industrial system. Increasingly, American husbands and wives are sharing economic responsibilities outside the home without any major change in the division of labor within the household and without the range of public programs available in other industrial societies (e.g., parental leave, day care, home health services, housing subsidies). Within the family, conflicts must be handled without the help of other kin or the community at large. In many respects, therefore, the nuclear household is an emotional hothouse, with all emotions focused on its very few members.

Under these circumstances, family roles are subject to *negotiation,* never fixed and continually redefined. An idealized emphasis on romantic love has diverted attention from the very real contests for control and self-definition that take place in the household. But marriage partners bring very different levels of power into their struggle to define the relationship (Blumberg and Coleman, 1989). In general, men are thought to be less dependent on marriage than women for their well-being, and women, who have more at stake in remaining married, are thought to have less power in the relationship.

Durkheim noted a century ago that marriage is beneficial for both men and women. In contrast to the nonmarried, married people tend to live longer, report higher levels of personal happiness, and to be in better physical and mental health (Doherty and Campbell, 1988). Yet there is some controversy among sociologists regarding the relative benefits of marriage for men and for women. Some research shows that marriage is more important to the physical and mental well-being of men (reviewed in Bernard, 1982), whereas other data indicate an advantage for women (Thoits, 1986).

But when married women are compared to married men, the women's rates of mental distress are higher. For many wives, employment offers an alternative source of esteem, and their mental and physical health is superior to women who are exclusively homemakers (Verbrugge and Madans, 1985). For others, the combination of homemaking, employment, and child care is a source of role conflict and overload, with negative effects on emotional well-being (Bolger et al., 1989).

Violence in the Family

The emotional closeness of modern family life has its darker side; people who are intensely dependent upon one another are also very vulnerable. Estimates of the extent of family violence vary widely. The best guess is that between 10 and 20 percent of American households are arenas of interpersonal violence. Similarly, with respect to violence against children, the overall incidence remains high; almost two-thirds of households reported some acts of physical punishment (mostly slapping and spanking); but the percentage reporting severe violence (beating, kicking, threatening with gun or knife) declined from 14 percent in 1975 to about 11 percent in 1985 (Gelles and Straus, 1988). However, not all violence is reported.

Although some domestic violence is directed against husbands and parents, the most common victims are wives and children (Stark and Flitcraft, 1988). Historically, the physical punishment of children has had widespread support in America. The basic issue in domestic violence is the pattern and structure of family authority and not, as commonly assumed, a personality problem of either abuser or victim (Shupe et al., 1987; Swartz, 1988a).

Roots of Family Violence.   Reviews of the growing body of research on child abuse and wife battering suggest that family violence is a complex response to societal-level factors as well as to the internal dynamics of the family (e.g., Steinmetz, 1987).

- At the cultural level, the United States is a society in which violence is not only accepted as a legitimate means of settling disputes but positively exalted and associated with true masculinity.
- At the institutional level, the contemporary nuclear household is protected by a veil of privacy against interference by the neighbors, the community, or the state.
- Structurally, our society is characterized by widespread inequality: in socioeconomic status, by gender, and by age. Inequality is a prime breeding ground for the use of excessive force by the powerful and for resentment among the less powerful.

Under these circumstances it is not difficult to imagine how failure and frustration experienced outside the home can be vented in the relative "safety" of the household. Thus, despite claims that family violence touches all social classes, it is strongly associated with low educational and occupational status, early marriage, and unplanned pregnancy (Fergusson et al., 1986; Gelles and Straus, 1988). It is also more characteristic of families associated with institutions that demand absolute obedience, such as the military and the deeply religious (Shupe et al., 1987).

There is some research and much speculation on the intergenerational transmission of violence. A link appears to exist between observing fighting between one's parents and subsequent violence in one's own marriage, either as victim or abuser (Seltzer and Kalmuss, 1988). In addition, one large-scale study of teenagers' violence toward parents indicates that this behavior is learned in families where parents used severe physical punishments against their children (Peek et al., 1985).

Women are often the targets of physical abuse in families with violent behavior patterns. What can women do to protect themselves?

Dealing with Abuse. In-depth interviews with battered women indicate that they react to their victimization either by constructing rationalizations that permit them to remain in abusive relationships, or by ultimately redefining their situation as intolerable (Ferraro and Johnson, 1983). Battering takes place in an emotional and social field that rarely permits any simple solution; one has to admit having made crucial mistakes, then decide to change the entire course of one's life. It is often easier to find excuses, blame oneself, and look at only the better moments. Often, too, the victim fails to perceive any alternatives. Nonetheless, as Schwartz (1986) points out, most women are not helpless victims; they can and do take charge of their life.

The police have also become sensitized to the complexities of family violence. Under pressure from advocates for protection of battered women, many states and communities now require officers to make arrests rather than to ignore the criminal dimensions of domestic violence. Although there is evidence that wife battering has declined in jurisdictions where the new laws are strictly enforced, research also demonstrates the difficulties in enforcement (Ferraro, 1989).

Divorce and Remarriage

The proportion of marriages that end in divorce has risen steadily over the past two decades but appears now to have reached a plateau, as seen in Figure 9-2. An unknown number of marriages are also dissolved through desertion

FIGURE 9-2 Marriage and divorce rates in the United States: 1930–88. (Source: National Center for Health Statistics, 1989.)

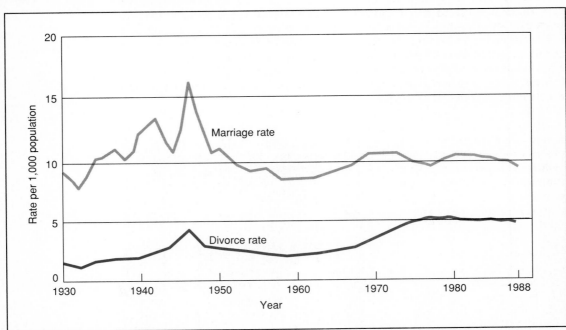

and separation. Current estimates are that fewer than half of all marriages contracted today will remain intact for 30 years or more (Weed, 1989). But we must also remember that a large percentage of marriages in the past were ended by the early death of one spouse, so that a child's risk of family disruption has remained relatively stable (Sweetser, 1985). The effects of divorce on children's emotional well-being, however, appear to be stronger than those of parental death (Glenn and Kramer, 1985).

Why Are Divorce Rates So High?   Divorce is the other side of the coin of romantic love. Any marriage system based on expressive needs rather than instrumental goals must provide a way out of unsatisfying unions. Thus, in all but a few modern industrial societies, divorce laws have been liberalized.

Among the many changes in modern societies that increase the likelihood of divorce are the value attached to self-fulfillment, geographic and social mobility, and alternative sources of financial and emotional well-being for women, most notably labor force participation. Furthermore, as divorce becomes more common, it also becomes more acceptable, although not necessarily less stigmatizing as a sign of failure on the part of those involved (Gerstel, 1987).

Risk Factors.   In general, the probability of divorce is associated with youthful marriage, unplanned and premarital pregnancy, limited education, low income, husband's unemployment, and residential moves. Controlling for other variables, employed wives are more likely than nonemployed wives to leave an unsatisfying marriage (e.g., South and Spitze, 1986; Raschke, 1987).

Conversely, factors that tend to preserve a marriage include participation at religious services, shared decision making, planned pregnancies, adequate income, and emotional maturity. Once a couple is married, the most powerful predictor of continued stability is, quite simply, the length of the marriage itself: the longer it lasts, the lower the likelihood of divorce. As seen in Table 9-3, the great bulk of divorces occur in the first five years of marriage. Contrary to popular belief, there is no "second peak" once a couple reaches midlife (Weed, 1989). Rather, with each added year, the marriage gains in strength as the couple jointly copes with life's challenges.

The total number of children involved is quite high, with perhaps as many as half of all American children spending some years in a single-parent family (McLanahan and Bumpass, 1988). To the extent that having children serves to keep a couple together, it appears that having sons reduces the risk of divorce in contrast to having daughters. The reason for this is that fathers are more involved with raising sons than daughters and therefore less likely to allow the marriage to collapse (Morgan et al., 1988). Thus, more daughters than sons will experience parental divorce and live in a single-parent household.

Consequences of Marital Disruption.   Although it may be a solution to some problems, the end of a marriage has many negative consequences, especially for children and for the women who become single parents. The effects on children will vary by sex and age, and many children of divorce will continue to be troubled by their parent's unhappiness for a decade or more (Wallerstein and Blakeslee, 1989). The data suggest that the effects will

TABLE 9-3   The Life of a Marriage

Over half of new marriages today end in divorce. The odds of divorce fall to 30 percent by the tenth anniversary.

		(Duration of marriage for all marriages, U.S., 1985)	
Years of Marriage	Percent Ended by Divorce in This and Later Years	Years of Marriage	Percent Ended by Divorce in This and Later Years
0	51.6	13	24.6
1	50.9	14	22.6
2	49.1	15–19	21.0
3	46.7	20–24	13.8
4	44.0	25–29	7.8
5	41.9	30–34	3.8
6	39.0	35–39	1.9
7	36.5	40–44	0.9
8	34.1	45–49	0.4
9	32.2	50–54	0.2
10	30.0	55–59	0.1
11	28.0	60 +	0.1
12	26.2		

Source: Weed, 1989.

be stronger for girls than boys; women who spent part of their childhood in a single-parent family were themselves more likely than other women their age to marry early, bear children early, give birth before marriage, and experience divorce (McLanahan and Bumpass, 1988).

These negative effects have a number of causes: the poor example set by parents, the lack of supervision in a one-parent household, drastically lowered standard of living when the male wage earner is gone, role overload experienced by an employed single parent, and a child's feelings of personal failure and of responsibility for the parents' divorce. Nor does it seem to make much difference to a child's well-being whether or not the divorced father remains in contact, although his financial support helps reduce problem behavior (Furstenberg et al., 1987).

But living in an intact family where the parents are continually fighting does little to enhance a child's mental and physical health. One recent longitudinal community study found that high levels of family conflict were associated with anxiety, depression, and symptoms of physical stress among teenagers (Mechanic and Hansell, 1989). In the same sample, parental divorce was not associated with change in health status, nor did these outcomes vary by age or sex.

Remarriage.   The great majority of divorced people remarry, although this rate has declined since 1970. Those who divorce at younger ages tend to remarry in higher proportions and sooner than do older divorced persons. Remarriage rates among women were highest for young mothers and for

THE REVOLUTION THAT FAILED

In the 1970s divorce laws throughout the United States were revised to reflect the belief that many negative effects of divorce could be minimized if conflict and hostility were removed from the divorce process. The concept of "no-fault" divorce allowed the courts to dissolve a marriage without having to attach blame to one partner or the other. Judges were also directed to divide marital property between the ex-spouses.

But research in the 1970s found that the new law worked against the interests of women, especially those who had been exclusive homemakers during their marriage (Weitzman, 1985). When the marital assets were split, ex-wives were often forced to sell the family home and take half the profits. Judges failed to take into account any special advantages the husband had gained in business training and experience during the marriage. Women who had remained out of the labor force for a decade or more in order to help their husband's careers were given enough money for job training and then expected to fend for themselves. As a consequence, the ex-husband's standard of living rose by 42 percent after divorce, while the ex-wife's dropped a full 73 percent. This income effect persists for many years following divorce. In addition, divorced wives are often barred from claims on their ex-husband's pension rights and typically lose medical insurance coverage.

The vast majority of divorced women do not receive *alimony* (personal support payments) from their ex-spouse. In 1985–86 (the most recent year for which data are available), alimony was awarded in less than 15 percent of all divorces, and only 73 percent of those awards were even partially honored. The average alimony payment was under $4,000 per year, well below the poverty level for one person.

Child-support payments were awarded to fewer than half the divorced women with children under age 21 in 1985. Of these, less than half received the full amount, and 26 percent received exactly nothing. But as the average yearly payment was about $2,200, divorced mothers would not receive much protection from poverty (U.S. Bureau of the Census, 1989).

The bottom line is that divorce is an economic disaster for millions of women. Solutions to this personal problem and public issue include making divorce more difficult, beefing up enforcement of child-support decrees by attaching the ex-spouse's wages, and encouraging judges to include "career assets"—the advantages built up in business training and experience during the marriage—as part of the family property.

Sources: U.S. Bureau of the Census, 1989; Weitzman, 1985.

women who had not graduated from high school. In contrast, women without children and those with a college education were less likely to remarry. Men's remarriage rates are higher than those for women at all ages. Not only do men have a larger pool of eligibles from which to select, but marriage provides greater protection against ill health and early death than is the case for women. The probability of divorce in remarriage is somewhat higher than that for a first marriage (National Center for Health Statistics, 1989) as a result of choices determined by the relatively small pool from which to select a mate the second time around.

Blended families consist of a husband and wife, children of previous marriages, and any children from the new marital union.

Another source of instability arises from the fact that remarriage today often creates a family that combines children from previous marriages as well as any from the remarriage. Such **blended families** magnify all the stresses of family life in general and have some unique characteristics. Sibling rivalry can be exaggerated by anger at one's own parent, and all types of hostility can be directed at stepparents, the "evil ones" of fiction and fantasy (Spanier and Furstenberg, 1987).

VARIETIES OF AMERICAN FAMILIES

When Americans think about the family they have an image based on ideals of the dominant culture: a nuclear unit composed of a married couple and their minor children, with the husband/father employed outside the home and the wife/mother devoted to child care and homemaking. This is the image of the modern American family enshrined in sociologist Talcott Parsons's functional analysis (noted in Chapter 1).

In actuality, today there is no "American family" but rather a range of household structures that meet people's needs at various points in their life or that are forced on them by circumstances (see Table 9-4). In this section we will explore the causes and consequences of these variations.

Minority Families

In contrast to the ideal pattern, ethnic and racial minorities are often characterized by extended households. Although frequently interpreted as a reflection of cultural differences, such households are primarily a response to economic conditions. Poor families of all ethnic and racial groups depend on kinship ties and shared resources for their survival (Wilkinson, 1987). In most cases of immigrant families, however, the nuclear type is dominant by the third generation, as acculturation and assimilation take their course.

Latino Families in the United States.   Largely as the result of racial and ethnic prejudice and discrimination, the majority of Latino families—across the many different Spanish-speaking groups (see Chapter 8)—have not been fully integrated into mainstream institutions. As a consequence of their relative

TABLE 9-4   United States Households: 1970 and 1988

Type	Percent of All Households	
	1970	1988
Married couple, children under 18, husband-only earner	70.6	9.5
Married couple, children under 18, dual-earners		17.0
Married couple, no children under 18		30.0
One-parent household	10.6	15.0
One-person household	17.1	24.0
Two or more unrelated individuals	1.7	4.5

Source: U.S. Bureau of the Census, P-20, No. 437, 1989, p. 45.

isolation, some traditional patterns have been retained. For example, fertility rates for Latina women are higher than for all American women. Within the family, the authority structure remains more male dominated than is the norm in our society, and Latina women are discouraged from assuming roles outside the household. This type of closeness, with its traditionalism and patriarchal control over women, is called **familism.**

Familism, patriarchy, and a sense of fatalism (not being in charge of one's fate) are often thought to be deeply rooted and dysfunctional cultural characteristics that served as barriers to social and economic mobility (e.g., Staples and Mirande, 1980). It was also thought that with further acculturation, these traditional patterns would be replaced by more modern family structures and relationships.

> **Familism** refers to family closeness, traditionalism, and male dominance.

These earlier assumptions, however, failed to appreciate the full effects of continued economic segregation (Bridenthal, 1981/87). Rather than being a static institution, the Latino family, as any other, is deeply influenced by the economic system. And as long as minority workers are channeled into low-paying employment, often in the nonindustrialized sector (agriculture, food service, janitorial), upward mobility would be highly unlikely regardless of family structure. Thus, it is most fruitful to look at Latino family patterns as a means of coping with a harsh and oppressive environment (Baca Zinn and Eitzen, 1987).

African-American Families. The effects of exclusion from mainstream institutions are clearly seen in data on African-American families. Compared to other ethnic/racial groups, African-Americans are more likely to postpone marriage or never to marry; to experience divorce, desertion, and separation; and to forgo remarriage (McAdoo, 1988). As a result, only 51 percent of African-American families contain a married couple, compared to 79 percent for whites. Forty-three percent are headed by a woman with no husband present, in contrast to 13 percent of white families (U.S. Bureau of the Census, 1989).

The very low marriage rate for African-Americans is due in part to difficulties faced by many men in their role as family provider and in part to the fact that there are many more adult females than males (Bennett et al., 1989). The family goals and ideology of African-Americans are no different from those of whites. But social-structural conditions make realizing these goals impossible for large numbers of poorly educated, low-skilled minority males (French, 1987). Among the inner-city poor, employed fathers are twice as likely as unemployed men to marry the mother of their first child. Contrary to the assumptions of some conservative critics, it is not the possibility of receiving welfare that depresses marriage rates among the poor but lack of employment (Testa, 1989).

The Inner-City African-American Family: Matriarchal or Matrifocal? Many scholars object to the word *matriarchal* ("female dominated") to describe the poor, inner-city African-American family. A more accurate term is **matrifocal,** meaning "centered on the woman," a term describing 43 percent of African-American families in 1988. This matrifocal system is held together by the extended line of female kin: mother, daughters, and their children sharing a household and pooling resources. If the women have power within this family group, it is by default, and whenever men join

> **Matrifocal** refers to families centered on the woman.

A major reason for egalitarian relationships among many middle-class African-American couples is the greater likelihood of the partners having similar educational and occupational achievements.

the household, they are typically accorded the status given other males in our society.

Research on the matrifocal family system has taken two directions. One points to the strengths of the matrifocal pattern in maintaining generational continuity, providing services to kin in general, and resisting the negative impact of pressures outside the family. The second details these outside pressures: unemployment, low pay, assignment to demeaning tasks, residential segregation, and other institutionalized patterns of discrimination. In both views, the matrifocal family is a *response* to the conditions of poverty rather than the cause.

The Stable Middle-Class African-American Family. In contrast to the situation among the poor, two-thirds of high-income African-American men are in strong and stable marriages. And an increasing proportion of African-American families do have incomes over the national median—up from 10 percent in 1950 to more than 30 percent today.

These middle-class families differ somewhat from their white counterparts. Most are composed of *two* adult wage earners, often both professionals, whose joint income still falls short of that earned by one white professional. Only among couples under age 35 do two wage earners reach an income comparable to that of a white couple. In the dual income family, the relationships between husband and wife are typically more egalitarian than in either dual-earner white families or single-earner African-American families (Wilkinson, 1987; McAdoo, 1988). One reason is that the husband and wife, unlike their white counterparts, are likely to have equivalent education and jobs.

ALTERNATIVE LIFE-STYLES

Other variations on the ideal American family reflect the increasing array of options that have been legitimated over the past several decades: living alone, living as a nonmarried couple, voluntary childlessness, single parenting, and dual-earner couples.

Living Alone

As shown in Table 9-4 on p. 320, almost one in four American households consists of one person living alone. This is a significant increase from 13 percent in 1960. Live-alones are not necessarily more socially isolated than their married age peers, nor do there appear to be negative psychological consequences, provided that this is their chosen life-style (Alwin, 1984). The live-alone population consists of three distinct subgroups that differ in age, marriage expectations, and financial resources.

The Never or Not Yet Married.   Over the past two decades, the number of young people who have been postponing marriage has increased dramatically, as can be seen in Figure 9-1, p. 310, and in Table 9-5.

These data are best understood as reflecting changing values and behavior on the part of young people. Today, marriage is not the only option for young women upon graduation from high school. Alternatives may include completing a college education, establishing oneself in the work force, living independently, and taking one's time in selecting a mate (Goldscheider and Waite, 1986). In addition, the widespread availability of effective contraception permits an active sex life without marriage. There have also been supportive changes in public attitudes toward singlehood and sex relations before marriage (Virginia Slims, 1986), even among American Catholics (Smith, 1985). However, the glamorous singles scene portrayed in the media is far from the norm for most nonmarried people, who lead lives little different from their married friends (Shostak, 1987; Stein, 1989).

Most of the never married will eventually marry, although it is estimated that as many as 15 percent may remain single, a significant increase from the 7 to 10 percent who never married in earlier cohorts. To some extent, the experience of living alone itself erodes traditional family expectations, at least among young women (Waite et al., 1986).

Divorced.   Divorced people account for one-fifth of the live-alone population and tend to be somewhat older than the never marrieds. Remarriage rates differ by age and sex, with more women than men remaining unmarried and establishing single-person households, especially at older ages.

TABLE 9-5   Percentage of Men and Women Remaining Single in the United States, 1960–88

	1960	1970	1980	1988
Women				
20–24	28.4	35.8	50.2	61.1
25–29	10.5	10.5	20.8	29.5
Men				
20–24	53.1	54.7	68.6	77.7
25–29	20.8	19.1	32.4	43.3

Source: U.S. Bureau of the Census, P-20, No. 410, 1986, pp. 16–18; P-23, No, 162, 1989.

Widowed.   The third category of live-alones, and the fastest growing sub-group, are elderly widows and widowers, who overwhelmingly prefer independent residence as long as health and income permit. A major problem for very old women, however, is that their health care needs increase as their resources decline. There is also a current shortage of suitable and affordable housing as federal subsidy programs have been eliminated and as single-room occupancy hotels and boarding houses are being converted to condominiums that most widows cannot afford.

Cohabitation.

Not all single people live alone. In 1988 about 4.5 percent of American households were composed of a nonmarried couple. This pattern is called **cohabitation** (living together) and over half are defined by the Census Bureau as "persons of the opposite sex sharing living quarters"—POSSLQs. The Census does not ask details of the relationship, so that it is possible that some fraction are not also sexual partners. Most cohabitors today are between ages 25 to 44, in contrast to the years before 1970 when the majority of cohabitors were age 45 and over (U.S. Bureau of the Census, 1986, pp. 14–15). Although the public image of cohabitation is of young college people, living together as an unmarried couple has always been most common among the less educated (Bumpass and Cherlin, 1988).

On all sociological variables but one—religiosity—there do not appear to be any major differences between cohabitors and their noncohabitating age peers (Macklin, 1987). Nor, until recently, was there strong evidence that cohabitation had any effect on subsequent marital stability, but careful analysis of long-term data in both Sweden and the United States indicate that people who cohabit before marriage have significantly higher rates of divorce than do noncohabitors (Bennett et al., 1988; Bumpass and Sweet, 1989). These findings do not necessarily mean that cohabitation ruins a marriage; rather, it could be that the type of people who cohabit are less likely than others to remain in an unsatisfactory marriage. It is also possible that they are less committed to marriage in general and are under less religious pressure to stay married.

Although households composed of nonmarried couples represent only a small fraction of all American households at any given time, cohabitation before marriage has become widespread. Data from a 1987–88 national survey of 13,000 Americans found that among those in their mid-thirties, more than 40 percent have lived with someone to whom they were not married (Bumpass and Sweet, 1989). Similar findings among marriage license applicants in Oregon between 1970 and 1980 have led one researcher to speak of the "institutionalization of premarital cohabitation" (Gwartney-Gibbs, 1986).

Childlessness

Involuntary Childlessness.   Although there have always been married couples without children (10 to 15 percent in modern societies), this has usually been the result of inability to conceive—**involuntary childlessness.** Despite the long-term decline in birthrates, bearing at least one child remains a normative expectation of married couples in our society (Rindfuss et al.,

---

Cohabitation occurs when unmarried people share living quarters.

Involuntary childlessness refers to the inability to conceive.

1988). Therefore, not to bear children is a form of deviance, and childless couples feel stigmatized (Miall, 1986). Some will choose to experiment with the many new reproductive technologies such as *in vitro* (in the laboratory) fertilization, artificial insemination, or the use of a surrogate mother. Others will adopt. Most, however, will gradually adapt to remaining childless.

Members of this last group use a number of protective strategies to manage their stigmatized identities, for example, selective disclosure of medical problems, willingness to admit deviance, and various means of hiding or manipulating information. These techniques are used most actively by women married to infertile men, in an effort to shield their husbands (Miall, 1986).

Voluntarily Child-Free Couples.   Several trends have increased the proportion of couples who choose to be child free. Women planning professional careers may postpone both marriage and childbearing until the odds of a safe pregnancy turn against them; some will find that other spheres of activity provide greater rewards than those thought to come from child rearing. Upwardly mobile couples may feel that parenthood would be inappropriate to their life-style; others will be inhibited by the emotional and financial costs (Houseknecht, 1987).

Voluntary childlessness refers to the decision to remain child free.

Estimates of the proportion of women who will remain child free in the future range as high as 29 percent, but this includes never-married women (Thornton and Freedman, 1983). For married women, the figure could, however, be considerably higher than in the past—perhaps one in five (U.S. Bureau of the Census, 1989a). The disruptions of divorce and remarriage also contribute to increased childlessness.

Single-Parent Households

We have already noted the dramatic increase in single-parent households as a result of divorce and nonmarital childbearing, the great majority of which will be headed by a woman. Of all American families with children, *close to one in four is headed by a single mother.* It is estimated that more than 40 percent of white children and more than 85 percent of African-American children will spend some years being raised by only one parent (Rawlings, 1989). Roughly one-third of these children will never see the absent parent, another 25 percent will have contact less than once a month, and only 10 to 12 percent will have very frequent contact (Bianchi and Seltzer, 1986).

When compared with two-parent families, those headed by one person experience a number of problems, the most severe being low income (Stirling, 1989). More than half of children who live with their mothers are poor, compared to 10 percent of children living with two parents. The single parent is also under stress in having to handle the role obligations of mother and father. Because single parents tend to have lower educational, occupational, and health statuses than do parents in intact families, even employment does not fully solve financial problems. Also, being employed adds to difficulties in allocating time for necessary child care activities (Sanick and Mauldin, 1986). In terms of psychological well-being, long-term single parenting is a long-term (chronic) source of distress (Thompson and Ensminger, 1989).

The children in single-parent families also experience special difficulties. They must adjust to a changed household structure as well as to more difficult

CHILD CARE AS A PUBLIC POLICY IN THE UNITED STATES AND SWEDEN

Phyllis Moen

Phyllis Moen has a joint appointment in the Department of Human Development and Family Studies and in the Sociology Department at Cornell University. In 1988 and 1989, she served as director of the sociology program at the National Science Foundation. She is the author of **Working Parents: Transformations in Gender Roles and Public Policies in Sweden** *(Madison: University of Wisconsin Press, 1989) and* **Women's Two Roles: A Contemporary Dilemma** *(forthcoming).*

What attracted me to the field of sociology, though I probably could not express it at the time, was C. Wright Mills's view of the relationship between private troubles and public issues. Individuals and their families confront a myriad of problems and challenges. But these seemingly personal difficulties must be placed against the backdrop of social and economic conditions within the larger society. To me, this proposition lies at the bedrock of sociology. It also provides a useful perspective on women's lives generally and my own life in particular.

A continual challenge for me has been to reconcile my educational and career aspirations with my family responsibilities. Like most women who grew up in the 1950s and early 1960s, I thought that to be a good wife and mother was to be a full-time homemaker, at least while my children were young. But I also aspired to be a college professor. As a consequence, the path to my educational and career goals was inevitably marked by interruptions and delays. As a sociologist studying the family, I came to regard these problems as much more than my own private troubles, particularly as unprecedented numbers of American women began to combine mothering with employment. Thus, the dilemmas that parents, especially mothers, of young children faced in balancing work and family obligations emerged as a public issue, and the lack of attention to the needs of working parents became increasingly evident.

I had been taught by my graduate mentor, Rueben Hill, that only by comparing and contrasting different societies or social groups can we hope to understand stability and change in the human condition. Following this advice, in the early 1980s, I looked for a society where public policies and attitudes kept pace with changes in gender relationships, where supports were provided to help parents combine employment with the raising of children. What I found was Sweden.

What makes the Swedish case especially instructive is the concerted effort made by government, organized labor, and other institutions to distribute the burden of parenting between men and women, and to facilitate the employment of all adults, including those caring for infants and children. Sweden offers a natural "laboratory" in which to examine the issues that are coming to the fore in the United States in the 1990s.

The 1970s were a decade of major changes in Sweden; the proportion of mothers of pre-schoolers in the labor force rose from 36 percent to almost 80 percent, and policies providing vital supports for working parents were adopted, expanded, or strengthened. These policies included paid parental leaves for both mothers and fathers and the option of a reduced work week, without loss of benefits, for parents of young children.

There are two competing views in sociology regarding the psychological consequences of maternal employment. One holds that women who perform both work and family roles will experience increased role strain. The other emphasizes the positive consequences of employment for mothers' well-being, resulting from their reduced social isolation. I suggest the need for a third approach, the life course perspective, which highlights the context of lives. Whether maternal employment has positive or negative effects depends on the *context* in which it occurs. It is also important to locate individual lives within a historical time frame. Swedish mothers and fathers in 1968 raised their children in quite different social and cultural circumstances than did parents in 1981. The policies adopted in the 1970s to support working parents by reducing the costs and promoting the benefits of employment for mothers of young children have allowed mothers in Sweden to spend more time with their children than can mothers in the United States, where to be employed often means working full-time with little or no leave available following the birth of a child. The options available to working parents in Sweden are used primarily by working mothers, although such options are available to fathers also. The generous paid parental leave and part-time work options (with benefits and the option to moving back to full-time hours) allow mothers to maintain an attachment to the labor force while devoting time to their children, thus reducing the strains of combining mothering with employment.

I see the lessons from Sweden as providing not a grand blueprint for the United States—there are too many differences between the two countries—but a promising new perspective and concrete examples of ways to deal with critical issues of gender, work, and family. Sweden's experience illustrates potential limits in achieving gender equality; women continue to be the principal caretakers of children. However, the Swedish example also shows that legislation can facilitate the balancing of work and family responsibilities. For example, a significant percentage of Swedish fathers take parental leaves, an option that is rarely available to American fathers. We in the United States can no longer cling to an outdated vision of the American family and of American society. By framing issues of employment policy with specific reference to the needs of working parents, the United States can begin to address today's (and tomorrow's) realities, public issues of growing urgency.

economic circumstances. One long-term study has found that the longer children are in a one-parent family, the less schooling they receive, especially white males (Krein and Beller, 1988). In cases where family income is comfortable and assured, where the custodial parent has satisfying employment, and where social supports—friends, relatives, day care facilities—are adequate, children from single-parent families do quite well. But these are not the typical conditions.

The limited data on single-parent fathers indicate that they feel comfortable and perform competently in the role (Risman, 1986). Compared to single-parent mothers, however, fathers do enjoy higher incomes and occupational prestige; they can more easily hire household help and will remarry sooner. But they also develop warm and intimate relationships with their child, particularly if they fought to have custody.

Dual-Earner Families

Dual-earner families have become the new norm. Almost 60 percent of married women are now in the labor force, including more than 73 percent of those with school-age children and 57 percent of those with preschoolers (*Statistical Abstract, 1990,* p. 385). Families with two earners have significantly higher median incomes than do those with one earner. Employed wives tend to be in better emotional and physical health than nonemployed wives (although some of this difference may be due to the fact that healthier women will enter the labor force). At the same time, there are conflicting data on the effects of wives' employment on their husband's sense of well-being—some men will feel relief at sharing financial responsibility and enjoying a higher

Dual-earner refers to families or couples with both partners in the labor force.

standard of living; others will find it difficult to give up traditional role expectations.

As for the effects of a wife's employment on the marriage relationship, dual-earner marriages do tend to be less stable than those with one earner (Raschke, 1987). But these data are difficult to interpret. Wives in less satisfying marriages may be most likely to seek employment; or, being employed and having financial security makes it possible for a woman to leave an unhappy marriage. A wife's labor-force participation does require adjustment as the power balance shifts, and there are problems of meshing work and leisure schedules with the demands of homemaking. One problem is finding time to spend together; the more time spent in joint activity, the more satisfying is the marital relationship of dual-earner couples (Kingston and Nock, 1987). Finding time to spend with children is another concern, typically solved by a working mother's reducing time spent on marginal child care activities, such as clothes shopping and housekeeping, rather than increased time spent by fathers (Nock and Kingston, 1988).

The wife's gains in mental health and sense of control are partially offset by *role overload,* as most employed women also take full responsibility for household and child care tasks. The typical employed wife spends a total of 70 to 80 hours a week on work inside and outside the home. In this situation, a great deal of role negotiation must take place, as family members come to accept her employment and eventually to take it seriously (Hood, 1983). Couples that cannot negotiate a satisfactory adaptation will be under stress. If the wife leaves the labor force, she may become resentful; if she stays, other family members will feel neglected. Authentic role-sharing marriages are extremely difficult to achieve (Smith and Reid, 1986).

For many critics of the contemporary family, the major obstacle to the goal of gender equality is that women continue to perform the great majority of household and child care tasks, regardless of the time they spend in the paid labor force (Berk, 1985; Brannon and Wilson, 1987). Although there is some evidence that men are now spending more time doing housework and women less, these changes have taken place for *both* employed and nonemployed women (Kiker, 1988; Pleck, 1989). Gender differences in child care are equally persistent. Despite agreement with the ideal of shared child care, or at least of increased paternal involvement, relatively few men put it into action, even if they are willing (Hochschild and Machung, 1989).

However, there are signs of change. Traditional sex role attitudes are related to age and birth cohort, with new cohorts of young adults increasingly approving of shared roles, especially those in dual-earner families (Harris, 1987). As a consequence, many young couples will begin marriage with flexible role expectations. But attitudes also change in response to actual situations, so that couples who start out in traditional roles find themselves adopting different behaviors and beliefs during their marriage, depending on their work experience, whereas others who had expected greater sharing find themselves drifting into traditional patterns.

Although the change in women's roles has been gradual but constant over the past two decades, there is also evidence of important changes taking place for men, particularly younger men (Stein, 1984; Pleck, 1989). For example, one study shows that, compared to their fathers, young men held a more "nurturing" view of fatherhood, with less emphasis on the "provider" role (Pruett, 1987; Entwisle and Doering, 1988).

For children, their mother's employment has no strong or consistent negative effects (Piotrkowski et al., 1987; Gottfried and Gottfried, 1988). If the mother is working because she wishes to, if there is support from her husband and others, and if there are adequate child-care arrangements, the children's social and intellectual development is no different from that of children raised by full-time homemakers. However, questions about availability, adequacy, and affordability have elevated the issue of day care from a personal problem to a public issue (Galinsky and Stein, 1990).

Who's Minding the Children?

Almost 60 percent of all mothers of children under the age of six are in the labor force; half are full-time workers; and the great majority are either the sole support of their children or have a husband earning less than $20,000 per year. Who cares for their children?

The most recent data from the Bureau of the Census (1988) is shown in Figure 9-3. As you can see, fewer than one in four children is in an organized child care facility. Slightly less than one-third are cared for in their own home, often by a father while the mother works off-hour shifts. Close to 40 percent are cared for in the home of another person, often a relative, but most likely a paid but unlicensed day care worker.

The United States is one of the few modern industrial societies without a comprehensive system of child and family assistance; little federal aid is available. However, some states have passed parental leave legislation. For example, Minnesota recently became the first state to require employers of 21 employees or more to offer up to six weeks of unpaid leave to both mother and father of a newborn. This type of legislation is fiercely opposed by

FIGURE 9-3 Primary child care arrangements used by working mothers for their children under five years old. Figures from winter 1984–85 have been rounded. (Source: U.S. Bureau of the Census, P-70, No. 9, 1987.)

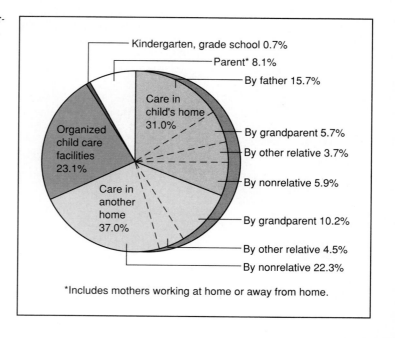

Kindergarten, grade school 0.7%
Parent* 8.1%
By father 15.7%
Care in child's home 31.0%
By grandparent 5.7%
By other relative 3.7%
Organized child care facilities 23.1%
By nonrelative 5.9%
Care in another home 37.0%
By grandparent 10.2%
By other relative 4.5%
By nonrelative 22.3%

*Includes mothers working at home or away from home.

Chambers of Commerce and other business groups, who claim that it would be a major expense for business in lost productivity, training new workers, and carrying health insurance costs. Nonetheless, a few major corporations have realized workers' needs for child care and have developed supportive policies (Auerbach, 1988).

Much resistance also comes from political and social conservatives who feel that child care is solely a parental responsibility and who fear the government's intrusion into the privacy of the family. Critics also worry about the long-term effects of any child care that is not provided by parents or grandparents.

On the other side, political liberals argue that worker morale would be strengthened and the rate of turnover reduced if child care were publicly funded and regulated; that day care centers are not necessarily inferior to a child's home, especially for the poor (Burchinal, 1987); and that families might actually be strengthened by government programs that encourage parental leave, as appears to be the case in Sweden (Moen, 1989).

Because the number of young mothers in the labor force is expected to continue to rise, and because many of you plan to combine work and child rearing, this is an issue you will be dealing with in the years and decades ahead. What child care policies would you prefer, and why? ■

Dual-Career Families

Dual-career families or couples are ones in which both husband and wife have a career.

A variation on the dual-earner family is the **dual-career family** (Hertz, 1986; Scarf, 1987). Hertz interviewed well-to-do families whose joint incomes allowed them to buy the various support services that enabled both husband

"New fathers" share child care and housework with their wives not only because they want to but because they can. However, few employers offer benefits that would lower the conflict between work and family responsibilities for parents.

and wife to advance their careers and to have a comfortable life-style. Because careers are demanding, some stress still existed; couples had to work out a new set of expectations with regard to work and family obligations. Feminists, especially, find themselves in a dilemma because this new class of highly paid businesswomen depends on maintaining a large pool of lower-income women who work as domestics and child care givers.

Given the probably irreversible trend toward wives' employment, it is safe to predict increasingly egalitarian marriages, with a division of labor, both within and outside the home, more flexible than in our recent past. Among the new family life-styles that could become more common in the future are (1) the family organized around the wife's career—the "WASP" or "*Wife as Senior Partner*" pattern (Atkinson and Boles, 1984)—in which a husband's job permits greater flexibility, the wife has a high-status position, and there are no young children in the household; and (2) the **"commuter marriage,"** in which both partners are equally committed to their careers as well as to their marriage, but work in different cities (Gerstel and Gross, 1984). The commuter marriage usually involves two separate households with the partners alternating weekend visits. Both these variations on the dual-career model are extreme departures from normative expectations of the wife's role and have a number of built-in stresses. However, researchers have found that they also have compensations, including great flexibility in negotiating marital roles.

Commuter marriages occur when husband and wife work in different cities and typically maintain separate households.

Men in Families

Traditionally, even in the sociology of the family, mention of husbands and fathers is usually confined to their role as major breadwinner. Only recently has a research literature emerged on such aspects of men's family roles as causes, correlates, and consequences of increased participation in parenting and homemaking (Lamb, 1986; Lewis and Salt, 1986; Chafetz, 1987; Franklin, 1988; Kimmel and Messner, 1989; Pleck, 1985, 1989).

The great majority of men will get married at least once, most will also become fathers, and a higher proportion of men than women, at all ages, will be married and living with a spouse. Clearly, family life continues to provide many comforts and benefits to men and may bring even more satisfaction to the men who participate most fully (Lewis, 1986).

The New Father.   As part of the "natural childbirth" movement, increasing numbers of young husbands have joined their wives in birthing courses and taken part in the actual delivery. Although it is doubtful whether this experience alone creates a father-child bond of special strength, the men who choose this experience are likely to be different from those who do not in terms of attitudes and values related to child care.

A small proportion of new fathers will also assume a major role in caring for the infant (Risman, 1987; Kimmel and Messner, 1989). These men tend to be highly educated, married to women in high-status jobs, and to have flexible time schedules and an ideological commitment to gender equality (Russell, 1983). As much as many men might wish to take a more active role in child care, they are inhibited by the demands of outside employment. Employers could, if they valued the loyalty of employees (both men and women), lessen the conflict between work and family responsibilities by providing flexible work schedules, parental leave without loss of benefits, and educational programs at the workplace (Thorne, 1987).

The New Husband.   As few employers offer such supports, and as time spent on family tasks brings lower rewards to men than to women, there has *not* been a major shift in the division of household labor over the past two decades, except, perhaps, in the "fun" parts of child care (Pleck, 1985; 1989).

The day of the "househusband" remains very distant. But if there are few men who are full-time child care givers or homemakers, there is no question that the division of household labor is becoming increasingly varied. The process of role negotiation will lead to many different outcomes, which can be seen as a strength rather than a weakness of our family system. In all its variety, the American family system has adapted to the conditions of postindustrial society. According to recent survey data, for most Americans intimacy and sharing are the goals of relationships, and family life continues to be the leading source of satisfaction; the vast majority of young people expect to marry and raise children.

SUMMARY

1. As with any other institution, the family can be understood as a set of socially constructed norms and behaviors clustered around the essential activities of reproduction, socialization, protection, care, and intimacy.

2. The functionalist explanation of the bases of the family focuses on the incest taboo, reciprocity between families, and the principle of legitimacy.

3. The conflict explanation of the bases of the family focuses on who and what groups benefit from given family arrangements.

4. Though kinship systems vary from one society to another, they can be described in terms of how many spouses are permitted at one time, who can marry whom, how lines of descent and the flow of resources are determined, where the new couple lives, and what power relations exist within the marriage and the family.

5. The major historical change has been from extended family systems to the nuclear family. The modern family has become a unit specializing in emotional support and the early socialization of children.

6. From a functional perspective, the marriage market has traditionally represented a mutually beneficial exchange. From a conflict perspective, mate selection takes place under conditions that generally favor men.

7. The modern family is characterized by reduced power differences between husbands and wives and between parents and children.

8. Modernization has also changed the timing of family events, including age at first marriage, premarital sexual experiences, the timing and number of children, mothers reentering the labor force, the empty nest stage, and probable widowhood.

9. Marriage and parenthood continue to be almost universal among Americans. Despite high levels of satisfaction among married, there is evidence that conflict is also a feature of family life. Most violence is directed at wives and children, and the economic impact of divorce is especially hard on them.

10. The variety of American families includes minority families (both Latino and African-American), singles living alone, cohabitors, childless couples, single-parent households, and dual-earner and dual-career families.

11. There is conflicting evidence as to how much change is occurring in men's participation in child care and housework.

12. Evidence suggests acceptance, especially among younger Americans, of flexible family roles, sharing of child care and housekeeping tasks, and of greater support for each other's work and careers.

SUGGESTED READINGS

Blumstein, Philip, and Pepper Schwartz. *American Couples.* New York: Morrow, 1983. Couples—married, gay, lesbian, and living together—and the importance of money, work, and sex in their lives.

Chilman, Catherine, Elam Nunnally, and Fred Cox, eds. *Variant Family Forms.* Newbury Park, CA: Sage, 1988. Family forms, including single parents, cohabitors, gay and lesbian families, widows and widowers, adoptive families, remarriage, and related public policies.

Demos, John. *Past, Present, and Personal: The Family and the Life Course in American History.* New York: Oxford, 1986. The social history of the family.

Henslin, James M., ed. *Marriage and Family in a Changing Society.* 3d ed. New York: Macmillan, 1989. Aspects of marriage and family life.

Hochschild, Arlie, with Anne Machung. *The Second Shift: Working Parents and the Revolution at Home.* New York: Viking, 1989. A study of working couples indicating that women do most of the work; and why many men are unwilling to share housework and child care.

McAdoo, Harriette Pipes, ed. *Black Families.* 2d ed. Newbury Park, CA: Sage, 1988. The history of African-American families; economic, educational, and demographic patterns; male-female relationships; and socialization processes.

Mintz, Steven, and Susan Kellogg. *Domestic Revolutions: A Social History of American Family Life.* New York: Free Press, 1988. An analysis of the history of families, from colonial days to the present.

Moen, Phyllis. *Working Parents: Transformations in Gender Roles and Public Policies in Sweden.* Madison: University of Wisconsin Press, 1989. The changing patterns of work-family relations in Sweden.

Price, Sharon J., and Patrick C. McKenry. *Divorce.* Newbury Park, CA: Sage, 1988. The processes involved in divorce: economic issues, the impact on wives, husbands, and children, and the adjustment process.

Voydanoff, Patricia. *Work and Family Life.* Newbury Park, CA: Sage, 1987. An interesting examination of the many facets of work and family life.

10

Economic and Political Systems

- In hunting-and-gathering bands such as the !Kung of Central Africa or the Semai of Southeast Asia, women typically gather foodstuffs for distribution within the family, while the meat from the men's hunting is carefully divided among all the families in the society (Lee, 1984).
- The Kwakiutl of the American Northwest and British Columbia mark important occasions with a *potlatch*—a huge public feast in which the host showers guests with gifts, engages in boasting contests with other "big men," and even destroys some of his family's property. Guests remain status inferiors until they can return more than they have received. Several social functions are served: goods are redistributed from the successful to the less favored, people are attracted to prosperous villages, and high productivity is encouraged among all families (Rohner and Rohner, 1970).

These are only two of the many ways in which human societies have solved the problem of producing, distributing, and consuming goods and services. Economic systems in all societies have a symbolic dimension and are linked to the other institutional spheres of the society—political structure, patterns of marriage and family, socialization practices, and belief system.

ORIGINS AND HISTORY OF ECONOMIC SYSTEMS

Economic systems originate in the trial-and-error attempts of human groups to survive in specific locations. Collectivities that fail to produce necessary resources or to motivate members to contribute to the well-being of all will quickly disappear.

The term **mode of subsistence** refers to how the group adapts to its environment in order to secure sufficient food and protection for individual and collective survival. We assume that for most of human history, small bands subsisted on what could be gathered immediately. Relatively late in human history, other economic systems evolved, each progressively more complex in knowledge and technology: hunting, fishing, herding, horticulture, agriculture, and industrialism (see Chapter 2, Figure 2-1). Over time, many societies undergo change in their mode of subsistence; others remain much as they were centuries ago.

> **Mode of subsistence** refers to how the group adapts to its environment in order to survive.

The long-term trend, however, has been toward increased division of labor, specialization of tasks, more efficient use of energy, and linkage to the economic systems of other societies. Once a mode of subsistence is established, the original patterns (folkways) are invested with a sense of sacredness (mores) and ultimately supported by a set of impersonal rules and sanctions (laws) (see Chapter 2). This is the process of **institutionalization,** whereby a given adaptation becomes a way of life and affects all other areas of activity.

> **Institutionalization** is the process whereby a given adaptation becomes an established pattern.

COMPONENTS OF ECONOMIC SYSTEMS

The **economic system** of any society consists of norms and patterned activities regulating (a) *production* of goods and services, (b) their *distribution,* and (c) their *consumption.*

> **Economic systems** encompass the production, distribution, and consumption of goods and services.

Production

Primary production consists of taking directly from the earth and using without much processing, as in hunting, gathering, farming, and mining. *Secondary* production involves making something from raw materials, such as pottery, baskets, bows and arrows, automobiles, or nuclear weapons. Modern societies are further characterized by the dominance of a third level of production: providing a service. *Tertiary* production or **service work** involves providing assistance and information and covers activities from baby-sitting, to international banking, to sports and entertainment.

Service work refers to providing assistance and/or information.

As seen in Figure 10-1, the United States is rapidly becoming a "service society," as the proportion of jobs in manufacturing declines relative to those in the service sector. According to the U.S. Bureau of Labor Statistics (1987), between now and the year 2000 the fastest growing occupations will be the following:

- Paralegal personnel
- Medical assistants and technologists
- Physical and occupational therapists
- Data processing equipment repairers
- Computer programmers and analysts
- Dental hygienists and assistants
- Physician assistants

Notice that this is a list solely of support personnel. For every new high-tech/high-status service sector job, many more will be created at the low-tech/low-status end of the service spectrum. (see Table 10-1).

Not only is the service sector expanding, but most of these jobs will be at the lowest-paying end of the wage scale, while relatively high-paying jobs

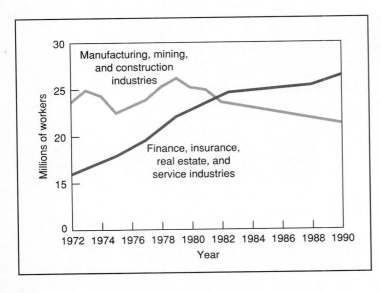

FIGURE 10-1 Number of workers in manufacturing or service employment, 1972–90. (Source: U.S. Bureau of Labor Statistics, 1989).

TABLE 10-1 Where the New Jobs Will Be: 1986–2000

Industry	New Jobs (in thousands)
Eating and drinking places	2,471
Offices of health practitioners	1,375
New and repair construction	890
Nursing and personal care facilities	852
Personnel supply services	832
State and local government, education	784
Machinery and equipment wholesalers	614
Computer and data processing services	613
Grocery stores	598
Hotels and other lodging places	574
Outpatient facilities and health services*	547
State and local general government*	546
Research, management, and consulting services*	531
Legal services	522
Credit agencies and investment offices	499
Credit reporting and business services*	497
Hospitals, private	481
Department stores	386
Real estate	353
Services to dwelling and other buildings	341

* Not elsewhere classified.

Source: Silvestri and Lukasiewicz, 1987, p. 46.

in the manufacturing sector, as in the steel and automotive industries, will disappear overseas (Morehouse and Dembo, 1987; Tigges, 1987; Harrison, 1987). High-prestige and high-income occupations require the ability to think abstractly, to express oneself articulately, and to view phenomena in context— precisely the capacities developed through higher education.

Distribution

Once the goods and services have been produced, each society must develop rules for the distribution of its resources. Whenever resources cannot be allocated equally, the distribution rules become the basis of social stratification (see Chapter 6).

Hunting-and-gathering societies typically share the day's yield of food among all members of the band. In more complex economic systems, there will be surplus goods or services to exchange within the collectivity or between societies. The simplest means of distributing surplus is by direct exchange, or *barter,* of goods and services judged to be of equivalent value by the traders. The means of exchange could be indirect, as in the potlatch,

The **rule of reciprocity** holds that giving gifts obligates the recipient to return something of similar value.

which also illustrates a very common distributive principle: the **rule of reciprocity,** whereby the giving of gifts obligates the receiver to return something of similar value at some later date.

Once a society has reached the degree of complexity that requires a centralized government, its rulers can collect taxes and demand payments from weaker neighbors. The rulers then decide how to *redistribute* this wealth in order to maintain their own power and keep most citizens content. Although some redistribution takes place in modern societies through social-welfare programs, the major method of distribution in industrial societies is the **free market system,** in which the worth of any item depends on how much others are willing to pay for it, which, in turn, depends on how many other buyers and sellers there are in the marketplace.

In a **free market system,** the value of goods and services is determined by supply and demand factors.

Consumption

Literally, *consume* means "to eat up." How members of a society use and consume goods and services is an important aspect of culture. In most societies throughout human history, the household has been both a unit of production and consumption. The unique feature of industrialism, however, is the separation of workplace and household. Production takes place outside the household—in factories and offices—and is performed by one or more adult members of the family. The household then becomes primarily a consuming unit, and its nonemployed members become economically dependent on the wage workers. Figure 10-2 illustrates the typical consumption patterns of American households in 1987.

In a market economy system, the value of any item depends on how much others are willing to pay for it.

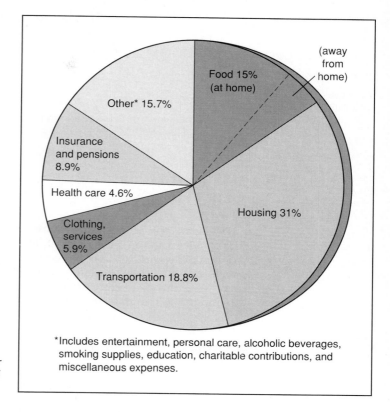

FIGURE 10-2 Household expenditures, 1987. (Source: U.S. Bureau of Labor Statistics, 1989, p. 2.)

Patterns of consumption reflect and reinforce locations in the stratification system. The symbolic significance of consumer goods and activities is constantly reinforced in our culture through advertising. An advanced capitalist economy depends on consumers being convinced that they "need" newer, bigger, better, and just more of anything and everything. Specific consumer choices are further influenced by cultural and subcultural values concerning beauty or quality.

CONTEMPORARY ECONOMIC SYSTEMS

Modern economic systems can be arranged along a continuum representing the degree to which economic activity is regulated by **public agencies** representing the society as a whole (e.g., government bureaus) or is left to the **private interests** of those individuals, families, or corporations that control the means of production. This continuum is represented in Figure 10-3. At one extreme is **free-enterprise capitalism,** with minimal public ownership or control. At the other extreme is a fully **socialist economic system,** characterized by central planning of production and distribution by the government.

These terms refer to economic systems and are not necessarily linked to

Public agencies represent the society as a whole.
Private interests are held by individuals, families, or corporations.
Free-enterprise capitalism involves minimal public ownership or controls.
Socialist economies involve public control of production and distribution.

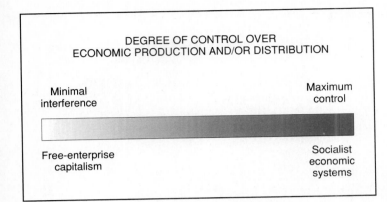

DEGREE OF CONTROL OVER
ECONOMIC PRODUCTION AND/OR DISTRIBUTION

Minimal
interference

Maximum
control

Free-enterprise
capitalism

Socialist
economic
systems

FIGURE 10-3   A continuum of economic systems.

any particular type of government: capitalist economies are found in demo-cratic countries (the United States), in dictatorships (some of Central and South America), and in caste societies (South Africa). Conversely, socialist elements are found in both democracies (Sweden) and in dictatorships (Cuba). Note also that Figure 10-3 represents a *continuum* and not an either/ or situation. The two extremes are theoretical ideals that are rarely found in any one society over an extended period of time.

Capitalism

In a capitalist economy, the means of production (land, factories, knowledge, corporations) are privately owned and operated for the profit of the owners. In theory, the free play of supply and demand and competition among pro-ducers will drive out the less efficient firms, lead to lower prices, and enhance the well-being of the society and its members. Both owners and workers are motivated by the promise of keeping the fruits of their labors.

In practice, capitalism has been remarkably successful in unleashing pro-ductive power and raising standards of living over the long run. But although capitalism generates prosperity, it is often associated with high levels of ine-quality, as seen in Chapter 6. When the ability to pay is the only way to receive goods and services, some individuals will be able to control more of the collective resources than others, regardless of need. To reduce the polit-ically destabilizing effects of inequality, capitalist societies, especially those with democratic governments, have moved progressively away from a pure market system of distribution to incorporate welfare programs, health insur-ance, old-age pensions, and so forth.

In the economic arena, an emphasis on private profit and short-term gain encourages speculation in place of investment. This almost brought about the collapse of the entire free market system in the 1920s and 1930s, an event that led to political controls over banking, stock markets, business practices, and the supply of money.

Thus, the economic system of the United States and other industrial nations is best described as **welfare,** or **state, capitalism**—essentially free markets within limits designed to ensure social stability. By distributing aid to both the wealthy and the poor, a certain level of social justice can be achieved without greatly reducing the efficiency of the economy (Barr, 1987).

Welfare, or **state, capitalism** refers to free markets existing within limits designed to ensure social sta-bility.

Nonetheless, it remains an economic system controlled by private interests and largely paid for by the working classes (Dickinson and Russell, 1987).

Despite its great successes, capitalist economic behavior has a number of built-in aspects that could lead to problems in the future. One is the movement of jobs overseas, which maximizes immediate profits but drastically reduces wage growth and buying power for American workers (Harrison and Bluestone, 1988). At the same time, an advanced capitalist economy depends on ever-increasing levels of demand for goods and services, so that consumer debt rises and capital is directed toward filling these needs rather than investment in improving plants and machinery.

Trends toward Concentrations of Power.   Another built-in problem for free enterprise is the reduction of competition through concentration of wealth and economic power in fewer and fewer hands. First is the tendency for larger companies to acquire competitors in the same line of business. For example, dozens of independent book publishers in the United States have recently been bought by a few large companies such as Paramount Communications. This trend toward **monopolization,** or exclusive control of a commodity or service in a particular market, can also be seen in newspaper publishing. The free play of the market is also distorted by the growth of **conglomerates,** in which one holding company owns controlling interests in other companies in a variety of commercial areas.

Along the same lines, **interlocking corporate directorships,** whereby the same individuals sit on the boards of directors of a number of different companies, lead to increasing concentration of power in the hands of a small group of executives (Mintz and Schwartz, 1987). The interlocks also serve in the long run to decrease competition and increase corporate profits. With the contemporary trend toward mergers, buyouts, and takeovers—for short-term gains to stockholders, lawyers, brokers, and speculators—fewer and fewer companies and corporate officers dominate the private sector.

The accountability of major American business firms is further eroded by their increasing involvement in *multinational* economic enterprises (Bornschier and Chase-Dunn, 1985; Moran, 1985; Vernon, 1987). Many American firms have branches or manufacturing plants in other countries, just as foreign firms and individuals have increasingly bought into American enterprises. The resulting growth of **multinational corporations** presents problems in loyalty and control. Many multinationals do not fall under the supervision of any one government. Decisions are based solely on corporate goals rather than on the well-being of any one nation.

In these many ways, the nature of advanced capitalism differs greatly from the original ideal of small firms competing in a perfect market in which only economic criteria influence decision making. Despite flaws in the system, capitalist influences have recently spread to the economies of its two most prominent opponents: the Soviet Union and the People's Republic of China.

Socialism

Socialism is an economic system in which the means of production are collectively owned and in which the distribution of goods and services is guided by public needs. Socialist goals include the reduction of inequality based on inherited wealth or status and the widest possible distribution of

Monopolization refers to the tendency for a company to acquire exclusive control of a commodity or service in a particular market.

Conglomerates exist when one company owns controlling shares in other companies in a variety of commercial areas.

Interlocking corporate directorships involve members of one board of directors sitting on the boards of other companies.

Multinational corporations are firms with branches and factories in many countries and whose ownership is not linked to one nation.

Socialism is an economic system in which the means of production are collectively owned and the distribution of goods and services is guided by public needs.

such basic resources as education, health care, and housing (Harrington, 1989). But just as the promise of general prosperity under capitalism remains unfulfilled, so also do the egalitarian ideals of socialism. Economic systems cannot be understood in isolation from other institutional spheres.

Contemporary socialist theory owes much to Karl Marx's critique of capitalism (see, e.g., Clegg et al., 1986; Dickenson and Russell, 1987). From this perspective, "forces of production"—modes of subsistence and their relevant skills and knowledge—are best realized under certain political arrangements, belief systems, and family structures. For example, because industrialism needs a disciplined labor force, a religion based on work as a calling and households dependent on a male wage earner are both highly functional. And allowing workers to vote helps to siphon off discontent, provided that the party of the working class remains less than a majority (Przeworski and Sprague, 1986).

The ultimate step in the replacement of capitalism by socialism comes when the workers themselves own or at least control the means of production, eliminating the basic source of social conflict. However, the socialist utopia remains unrealized in the real world and, like all visions of a perfect order, may never be fully realized (Horowitz, 1989).

Contemporary Socialism.   Socialism has many contemporary forms. At one extreme, in the Soviet Union and pre-1990 Eastern Europe, centralized controls have had a negative impact on economic growth and worker motivation. Indeed, recent changes in these societies, as well as in the People's Republic of China, have encouraged steps toward private enterprise and greater freedom for local managers (Szelenyi, 1988).

More limited and flexible forms of economic planning, however, are found in almost all Western democracies, especially in Sweden and Denmark, where

Many consumer goods have been in short supply in the Eastern European countries and in the Soviet Union for some time now. The supply of goods has not yet improved under *glasnost* and *perestroika,* as is evident by this rather long line outside a household appliance store in Moscow.

production remains largely in private hands but the distribution of many goods and services is centrally controlled. This system is often called **democratic, or welfare, socialism.** Paying for welfare socialism involves relatively high rates of taxation—for example, in Sweden over half the value of the total goods and services produced, compared to roughly one-third of that in the United States. Yet if we add up what American families pay out-of-pocket for medical insurance and health-related expenses, college costs, and care of elderly relatives, the total financial burden is at least as high as that paid in taxes by Swedes. The major difference is that the burden of cost and the benefits of the services are spread more equally among Swedish citizens than in our country.

Under **democratic, or welfare, socialism,** goods and services may be privately produced, but the distribution of essential services is centrally controlled.

In general, the democratic socialist nations of Western Europe have succeeded in avoiding economic crises and in combining low unemployment and inflation with high levels of government spending that have reduced educational and income inequality (Goldthorpe, 1985; Barkan, 1989). In the Soviet Union and Eastern Europe, however, socialism did not bring the same level of benefits; inequality remained high, not only in the political sector, but in education, housing, and a wide range of consumer goods. Inefficiency in production led to shortages that raised prices and increased the gap between the politically favored and others.

A final criticism of socialism points out the deadening effects of large and deeply entrenched bureaucracies (see Chapter 3). The expanding number of jobs in government is functional in providing employment for college graduates and the upwardly mobile, but it can be dysfunctional when speed and risky decisions are required. The process of *goal displacement* often leads to a greater emphasis on protecting one's job than on enhancing efficiency and productivity (Shlapentokh, 1987).

WORK ORGANIZATION AND COMMITMENT

Division of Labor

Industrial economies, whether capitalist or socialist, are characterized by extreme specialization, or **division of labor,** which is the separation of work into distinct parts, each of which is performed by an individual or a group of people. In the United States, for example, the Department of Labor publishes a *Dictionary of Occupational Titles* with more than 12,000 entries. But when each worker does only one small task and participates in the culture in a limited way, it is difficult to generate a sense of shared values and common fate among all citizens.

Division of labor refers to the separation of work into distinct parts, each of which is performed by an individual or a group of people.

Durkheim worried about the lack of intermediate groups between the individual worker and the impersonal forces of government and business. Weber spoke of "disenchantment" and "demystification" as modern life becomes increasingly subject to technological controls. And Marx saw it all as leading to **alienation**—feelings of powerlessness, normlessness, and of being cut off from the product of one's labor, from other people, and ultimately from oneself (Blauner, 1964; Seeman, 1972).

Alienation is the feeling of powerlessness, normlessness, and being cut off from the product of one's labor, from other people, and from oneself.

The central social structure of industrialism is the factory. Factories bring workers out of their homes to one central location where machines and labor power can be used most efficiently and where management can exercise direct control over the work force (Burawoy, 1985; Gartman, 1986). The perfect embodiment of the rationalization of work is the assembly line, with each step in the production process separated from other steps and given to one worker. The relationship of the assembly-line worker to the finished product is rendered all but invisible. Compare, for example, the worker in a shoe factory with a shoemaker. The shoemaker makes an entire shoe and enjoys a feeling of creative accomplishment in the result, whereas the worker in a shoe factory might only attach a heel to each shoe as it passes down the line, with little sense of personal creativity.

This process has been described as "deskilling" (Braverman, 1974), in contrast to the accumulation of artistic skills required of craftspeople in the past. Deskilling is not confined to the factory floor; much white-collar work has been similarly routinized (Feldberg and Glenn, 1982). This is especially the case where machines increasingly deskill the work and even take over tasks previously performed by human workers (Thompson, 1984). Conversely, many changes in occupational technology involve a redefinition of status and potential upgrading (Diprete, 1988), as when typists learn the intricacies of word processing programs.

Automation

Automation is the replacing of workers with machines.

The ultimate in impersonal production is **automation,** replacing workers with machines. Although initial costs may be high, in the long run machines are cheaper than people—and easier for management to supervise. Machines do not take lunch breaks or join unions. But for many tasks they are not any more efficient than human workers (Howard, 1985). In addition, the highly experienced blue-collar workers who actually operate automated machines often keep their special knowledge of quirks and shortcuts to themselves in

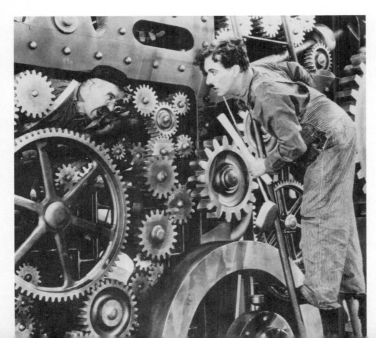

The film *Modern Times,* with Charlie Chaplin, satirizes the effects of machinery and assembly lines on workers. Have you ever felt like a cog in a machine on your job?

order to maintain control of the work process as well as to expand their own free time on the job (Halle, 1984).

But management also has ways to protect its interests. Workers who continue to insist on wage increases and improved benefits can be threatened with loss of their jobs by the introduction of computers and robots. In addition, automation can improve management's ability to control and supervise employees (Erickson, 1986; G. Marx, 1986). Video-camera surveillance, drug testing, wiretaps, computer monitoring, and beepers are all commonly used today to keep track of employees and their activities in the workplace.

Worker Satisfaction

Despite the objectively negative characteristics of most employment, the great majority of American workers express satisfaction with their jobs, although younger workers tend to be less content than older employees (*Society,* 1989). Many people lower their expectations to fit reality and to avoid a sense of failure. Others find compensating sources of satisfaction in their workplace friendships and the nonwork pleasures that can be purchased with earnings. And many workers accept the conditions of their jobs when they believe their employer is acting legitimately (Halaby, 1986; Fuller and Dornbusch, 1988).

Worker satisfaction is highest in jobs where an employee has some control over the work process and is not closely supervised. Such **job autonomy** involves making decisions about the timing and sequence of tasks, exercising one's own judgment, and having a distinct impact on the outcome—all of which contribute to a sense of self-esteem, intellectual flexibility, and low levels of job stress (Kohn et al., 1989; Whiddon and Martin, 1989; Mortimer and Lorence, 1989). In general, high-autonomy jobs are in the better-paying occupations. Conversely, dissatisfaction is highest where employees are kept to a tight schedule, closely monitored, where the tasks are repetitive and routinized yet require complex skills, and where the worker feels under pressure.

Job autonomy involves making decisions about the timing and sequence of tasks, exercising judgment, and having an impact on the outcome.

What Is a Good Job? Researchers (Jencks et al., 1988) trying to devise an Index of Job Desirability surveyed a large sample of workers on the objective characteristics of their work, such as wages, fringe benefits, hours, promotion opportunities, autonomy, and authority over others. Respondents were also asked how "good" they thought their jobs were in comparison with the "average." Although income was the single most important factor in determining the desirability of a job, taken together, 13 of the nonearning aspects of the job—for example, vacations, on-the-job training, job security, variety, autonomy, and not getting dirty on the job—were twice as important as pay.

The New Industrial Contract

Because satisfied workers are also more productive, many employers are experimenting with techniques for enhancing employee morale, increasing their participation in decision making, and offering family-oriented benefit packages (Kamerman and Kahn, 1987; Galinsky and Friedman, 1990).

Innovations in the workplace include the following:

1. *Flextime* refers to variations on the standard nine-to-five workday five days a week. This is especially helpful for dual-earner parents.
2. With *job sharing,* two part-time workers perform a job ordinarilly held by one full-time employee and also share fringe benefits.
3. *Quality circle* (QC) involves teams of employees and managers who typically meet for an hour a week to discuss how to improve their work performance. Still, even though ordinary workers get to call the bosses by their first names in the QC, most of the workweek is characterized by the basic relationship of industrial production: extreme inequality between employers and employees (Grenier, 1988).
4. *Team production system* involves groups of workers and a "group leader," who control the entire production process, and who therefore feel responsible for the quality of their product.
5. *Workplace democracy* exists where employees become the owners (Rothschild and Russell, 1986; Gartman, 1986). Worker-owned firms, still rare in the United States, are more common in Europe and Israel. The argument for workplace democracy emphasizes the possibility of greater efficiency when people work for themselves rather than for impersonal management. It is also thought that relationships of cooperation and sharing will be encouraged, as power inequality among workers is lessened. Although some of these positive effects have been found in European experiments (e.g., Whyte and Whyte, 1988; Cornforth et al., 1988; Taylor et al., 1987), the limited American experience has shown less success, with workers taking on the same attitudes of management that led to dissatisfaction in the first place (Greenberg, 1986).
6. Short of full workplace democracy, some companies have agreed to *employee stock ownership plans* (ESOPs), whereby owners contribute shares in the company as part of the workers' benefit package. Receipt of the stock and voting rights are usually deferred until one leaves or retires (Adam and Ellerman, 1989).

Throughout Western Europe, the economic interests of the working class have been represented by a "labor," or "social democratic," political party in a system of class-based parties. In the United States, although there is a tendency for capitalists to vote Republican and for manual workers to vote Democratic, the two parties embrace voters and issues across class and status lines. The interests of American workers have been largely represented by self-governing unions rather than by a nationwide, centrally organized political institution (Marks, 1989).

THE AMERICAN LABOR MOVEMENT

Among industrial democracies, Japan and the United States are unique in the tameness of their labor organizations, which have been largely coopted by management and contained by government. From the very beginning, the American labor movement was fiercely resisted by employers and all levels of government, to the point of extreme violence. In 1886, for example, Chicago police opened fire on a rally of workers supporting the radical idea of an eight-hour workday.

The resistance of capitalists in business and government delayed the growth of a broad-based union movement; when the unions were finally granted the right to organize in 1935, they were first cleansed of all radical elements (Montgomery, 1987; Griffen et al., 1986; Goldfield, 1987). The result was a labor movement more opposed to "foreigners," women workers, and nonwhites than to the class-based interests of the owners. Within the movement there was a constant tension between trade unions of skilled craft workers (American Federation of Labor) and the broad-based industrial unions (Congress of Industrial Organizations). Only in 1955 did the two groups join ranks to form the AFL-CIO. But by then, the union movement had already crested.

From a high point of 35 percent in 1945, the proportion of unionized workers in the labor force has fallen to approximately 16 percent today. This decline in membership can be traced to a number of broader economic trends: (1) the loss of jobs in highly unionized "smokestack" industries such as automobile manufacture and steel milling; (2) lack of interest, until recently, in organizing service industries with large numbers of women and minority employees; (3) the success of employer-sponsored welfare plans in blunting unionization (Cornfield, 1986); and (4) the actuality and threat of relocating to states and countries without strong labor organizations (Jaffe, 1986).

Always under attack from management and conservative politicians, the union movement has also been criticized from the left for its failure to become a class-based political force in opposition to capitalist control of the society. Critics claim that not only have union leaders "sold out" the movement in order to achieve respectability (as advisers to American presidents, for example), but that the workers who have profited most from the union movement—highly skilled white males—have turned their backs on other workers and on the original goals of organized labor: to improve the status of all

In a display of union solidarity, pilots and flight attendants joined these machinists in striking Eastern Airlines and its antiunion president, Frank Lorenzo.

workers, reduce inequality in the society, and bring democracy to the workplace.

As the history of American labor shows, unionization was often accompanied by verbal and physical attacks on immigrants and African-Americans (Olzak, 1989). Early labor leaders were openly racist and sexist and, although often themselves immigrants, not very hospitable to more recent arrivals. Minority workers gained access to craft unions only in the late 1960s and only after considerable legal pressure (Schutt, 1987). An additional basis of criticism is that many local units and national unions have been taken over by corrupt or criminal interests.

The strength of organized labor depends on unions being willing to support one another by engaging in sympathy strikes or refusing to cross a picket line. But American labor has generally failed to create "worker solidarity" across different types of unions. In 1981, for example, pilots and flight attendants did not support the striking air traffic controllers (Shostak and Skocik, 1986), and although both unions did join machinists in striking Eastern Airlines in 1989, the pilots soon left the picket lines and settled with management.

One final criticism of the union movement today involves the concept of goal displacement. Union leadership has itself become a set of entrenched bureaucracies in which the goal of maintaining the organization and one's own job becomes at least as important as the goal of serving the members.

Yet for all their faults, the unions have had a powerful, positive effect on the status of all American workers (Freeman and Medoff, 1984; Shostak, 1990) and can take credit for the eight-hour day and five-day workweek, health and pension benefits, sick leave and unemployment insurance, the minimum wage, and safer and more sanitary workplaces. The unions were—and perhaps still are—the only large organized force for economic democracy in our society (Nyden, 1984).

Yet if the union movement is to hold its own and possibly expand, its leaders must find a way to reach previously nonunionized populations: both high- and low-skill service workers, managers, professionals, part-timers, and female service employees. It must also adapt to a labor force that is younger, more educated, less likely to be married, and far more likely to be female than only a decade ago.

LABOR SEGMENTATION

The **core sector** consists of major industries, large investments in plants and equipment, unionized labor, monopolies, and high profits.

The **periphery** consists of smaller, competitive low-profit firms employing low-pay, nonunion manual workers.

Although organized labor has been successful in raising the status of some workers, it has generally failed to reduce inequality within the working class (Form, 1985). A major source of *intra*class inequality is the stratification of the economy itself; there are broad differences between "core" and "peripheral" industries. The **core sector** consists of major industries (e.g., heavy manufacturing, chemicals) characterized by large investments in plants and equipment, unionized labor force, monopolies, and high profits. The **periphery,** in contrast, is composed of smaller, relatively competitive low-profit firms (e.g., fast-food shops, clothing manufacture), with a heavy investment in low-pay manual workers (typically nonunion). In general, owners and workers in the core sector enjoy greater political power than those at the periphery (Apostle et al., 1985).

This **dual economy** is complemented by a **split,** or **segmented, labor market,** differentiated by race and gender. Core workers are disproportionately drawn from a labor pool of white men, while peripheral employers draw heavily on women and low-status minority populations. People with similar years of education and training will receive very different wage returns depending on where they are employed (Tolbert et al., 1980; Kaufman, 1986). Thus, the gender and race wage gaps noted in Chapter 6 are most often a product of labor-force location rather than individual work-related traits.

The dual economy/segmented labor market model is very helpful in isolating firms at the two extremes, but is far less useful for explaining wage and promotion differences among workers in the great majority of firms that have mixed characteristics (Hodson, 1984). Firms also vary in terms of job-related benefits: health insurance coverage, parental leave, paid vacations, and, most important, pension plans (Pearce, 1987; Perman and Stevens, 1989). These inequalities within the labor force accumulate over the worklife and continue into retirement (O'Rand and MacLean, 1986).

Dual economy refers to the existence of two separate types of employing firms: core and peripheral.

The **split,** or **segmented, labor market** is differentiated by race and gender, core workers being primarily white males and peripheral workers being primarily women and minorities.

Employment and Unemployment

As you might expect, employment and unemployment rates reflect the dual economy as well as the overall state of the economy (Aston, 1986). Employment and unemployment are measured by the U.S. Bureau of the Census each month. Almost 60,000 sample households are asked whether or not family members were employed, even for only a few hours, during the previous month; any paid work is classified as "employment." If a person was not employed but actively seeking a job, he or she is officially classified as "unemployed." This definition, then, understates the amount of *joblessness* on the part of people who have become so discouraged with their job search that they have given up looking, as well as *underemployment* of all those forced to settle for part-time work or work below the level of their skills and educational achievement.

During the recession of 1982–83, unemployment in the United States rose to a postdepression high of more than 10 percent, fell gradually to 5.3 percent by 1989, and rose to 7 percent in 1991. Unemployment among African-Americans, however, remains twice that of all workers especially among young males.

As noted earlier in this chapter, most new jobs are in the low-pay service sector rather than in high-wage manufacturing or even the relatively low-wage clothing and textile industry. The jobs lost through plant closings and layoffs in the core sector during the recession had been largely filled by unionized white men. Some were still unemployed three years later, but most had found new employment by 1988. However, half of the new jobs paid less than the old ones (*New York Times,* December 14, 1988, p. B12). The jobs in clothing and textiles, while also unionized, had been filled by blue-collar women, but even these pay scales were far higher than manufacturers need to pay overseas. As a consequence, many owners have closed down their United States factories.

Nonworkers

In addition to the millions of homemakers, students, and retired persons who remain out of the labor force voluntarily, another 10 to 20 million are involuntary nonworkers. This category includes discouraged job seekers, single mothers for whom employment means a lowered standard of living because of the cost of child care and loss of medical benefits, and the 15 percent of the labor force classified as "employed" yet who work less than six months a year for incomes barely above the poverty level.

Some nonworkers simply cannot afford to work; others may refuse to accept menial jobs; and still others are judged to be physically or mentally unfit for employment. Many nonworkers are actually part of the informal "underground" economy (Sassen-Koob and Grover, 1986). Included here are people who do odd jobs and get paid in cash "off the books," so that neither their employment nor their income is officially recorded. Many will be engaged in activity that is altogether illegal (such as drug dealing) but which pays far more than regular employment and may also bring greater status rewards.

Youth Unemployment

For youth who do not attend college, steady employment is the socially legitimate way to achieve adult status. Unfortunately, unemployment rates among young people are two to three times higher than for adults age 25 and over, and the gap between white and African-American rates has continued to widen. As a result, for young African-American men, the likelihood of establishing stable marriages and long-term commitment to the labor force is particularly problematic.

Nonetheless, many of these young men have continued to fight the odds and to find work that promises some advancement. These youngsters are more likely than the unemployed to come from families in which parents are employed, who do not live in public-housing projects, and who also attend church once a week or more (see also Williams and Kornblum, 1985). The long-term solution to minority teenage unemployment involves interventions in many institutional spheres: stable families, decent housing, adequate schooling, strong community organizations, control of street crime, and containment of the drug culture.

CORPORATE LIFE

Corporate Power

The sociology of economic systems also embraces the study of corporations as social structures in their own right (Bidwell and Kasarda, 1985), as well as the life-styles of business elites (see also Chapter 6). While the American public may always have been somewhat mistrustful of big business, at no time has corporate power been seriously challenged, even during the reform period of the 1930s, following the collapse of the stock market and banking system. Corporations often seek to soften their public image by making charitable contributions and supporting local causes, but these gifts amount, on average, to less than 1 percent of income before taxes (*Statistical Abstract,* 1988, p. 516). In a 1986 poll, before the "insider trading" scandals, only 24 percent of respondents thought that moral and ethical standards were higher in big corporations than in the federal government (Clymer, 1986; Schneider, 1987). In the same poll, most people felt that corporations had failed to help local communities, protect the environment, or see to it that their executives behave legally. Nevertheless, a majority (higher among men and whites) also thought that it was still possible for anyone to work hard in business and become rich and that personal ability was the key to success.

Corporations have a structure that can be analyzed in the same way as any other social system; so, too, can their corporate cultures. Culture, remember, consists of beliefs, values, and norms that define the boundaries and meaning of the collectivity, encourage conformity, and generate solidarity (Kilman et al., 1985). Corporate symbols (the logo and all the emotions it arouses) and rituals (the annual executive fishing trip or company picnic) perform the same functions as a totem pole or rain dance. Fine distinctions of power are marked not by facial paint or headdresses but by the size and location of an office and whether or not it has carpeting and a window.

Corporations have shown a remarkable ability to adapt to broad changes in the economic system. Although specific firms have risen or fallen as the economy moved through the phases of early, mature, and advanced capitalism, the strength of the business sector as a whole has not diminished. Business elites have been able to find new opportunities for profit, using the money and power already accumulated. Indeed, what at first might appear to be a major threat to company executives—a "hostile takeover" by outside investors—has typically been turned into an opportunity to make an enormous personal profit—the "golden parachute" that cushions their fall (Hirsch, 1986; *Business Week,* May 1, 1989).

Corporations and the Community

With the growth of conglomerates and multinationals, and the emphasis today on short-term profits through mergers and takeovers, the links between a large national corporation and the local communities in which its plants and offices are located have become very thin. The owners do not live in the community and may never even have seen it; the plant or office building is simply a piece of property on the company's books to be kept or sold in order to enhance the value of the corporation's stock, as happened in the U.S. automobile industry throughout the 1980s. In addition, the threat of closing or relocating can be used to get workers to agree to give back previously won raises and benefits.

Corporate Structure

The American labor force is spread over close to 15 million business firms, two-thirds of which have only one owner and typically employ fewer than 20 people. More than 1.6 million are owned by two or more partners. But it is the 3 million *corporations* that employ the bulk of the labor force and control the business assets of the society. The 100 largest industrial corporations in the United States today account for more than 70 percent of all

Corporations are formal organizations that are legal actors in their own right.

industrial assets in our economy, and the 200 largest account for more than 85 percent (*Statistical Abstract, 1989*).

A **corporation** is a formal organization that can enter into contracts, accumulate assets, go into debt, or go bankrupt without its members (owners, managers, or employees) being held personally responsible. Ownership in corporations is widely held: 43 million people own shares in one or more American corporations. Although these data suggest that income from corporate profit is spread across the stratification system, the great majority of stockholders are in the upper portion of the SES hierarchy. Most shares, however, are held by other corporations, banks, and pension funds.

Although one of the defining features of the corporation in a capitalist economy is the separation of ownership (stockholders) from management (the executives who run the corporations), this line has become increasingly blurred as executives are rewarded with corporate stock while they engineer or resist takeovers, mergers, and buyouts. The bottom line for boards of directors who award the bonuses has been the profit margin of the firm, which today does not necessarily depend on producing and selling a product but on selling and buying corporations or divisions of conglomerates.

This shift in how profits are made—away from an emphasis on products and the marketplace to the current trend toward increasing profits through acquisitions, mergers, buyouts, and takeovers—is reflected in historical changes in how top leadership in American corporations is selected. As traced by Fligstein (1987), until World War II corporation presidents were most likely to be the individuals who founded the company or who came from the manufacturing division. In the middle decades of the century, the top slots were occupied by people from the sales and marketing departments; most recently, financial experts have risen to the highest positions.

SOCIAL
POLICY
ISSUE

How Much Is Too Much or Too Little?

Is a CEO really worth more than $2,000,000 a year? (This is the average yearly compensation package, including salary, bonus, and stock options.) If the executive enhances the value of the corporation by hundreds of millions of dollars, the percentage paid in salary appears very small indeed and well worth the cost to shareholders. But what about the other end of the spectrum, at which 8 million Americans work for the minimum wage?

In reaction to the devastation of the Great Depression, Congress enacted legislation establishing a minimum wage of 25 cents per hour. Because of extremely high unemployment rates and the absence of social welfare programs to support the families of unemployed workers, employers had been able to hire people to work 50 hours or more for less than $10 a week. Yet, during the 50 years between 1938 and 1988, attempts to raise the minimum wage met with fierce opposition from employer groups and those on the political right who feel that government has no right to dictate business practices.

Nonetheless, by 1981 the minimum wage was up to $3.35, where it remained until 1989, when Congress tried to raise the floor to $4.55 an hour. This was several dimes higher than what the White House was willing to accept, and President Bush vetoed the legislation. The veto was sustained when a vote in the House of Representatives fell short of the two-thirds needed to override. Five months later, Congress and the Bush Administration compromised on an increase to $3.80 an hour in 1990 and $4.25 in 1991, plus a *sub*minimum wage of $3.35 for 16- to 19-year-olds in their first job (Rosenbaum, 1989).

Yet even at $5 an hour, a person working full-time every week of the year would earn about $10,400 *before* taxes and work-related expenses such as child care, transportation, clothing, and lunch. Once these expenses are taken into account, the worker's income would fall well below the poverty level for a parent and two children. Furthermore, when adjusted for inflation, the new minimum wage is actually 30 percent *lower* than 1970s minimum wage.

Who are the 7 percent of the labor force who work for a minimum wage? Contrary to common belief, almost 85 percent are 18 years of age and older; 80 percent are non-Latino whites; 60 percent are women; and more than 85 percent are in service occupations (*New York Times,* August 21, 1988). They work at nonunionized jobs, such as on a cleaning staff or in fast-food restaurants. One argument against raising the minimum wage is quite simply that because such workers are typically in businesses that have a low profit margin, any additional cost to the employer would lead to cutting the jobs altogether.

In addition to the 8 million estimated by the Department of Labor, there are probably tens of thousands more whose minimum wages are unreported and unrecorded—recent immigrants, for example, who work in illegal garment factories (sweatshops). Because even the minimum wage is higher than many workers could earn in their country of origin, and also because many do not have proper immigration papers, the employees do not report their working conditions.

The minimum-wage battle reflects two very different political philosophies as well as economic concerns. Should the state be neutral in its effects on individuals? Should it assist only the most needy? Or should it favor the wealthy and successful in the expectation that they will use their wealth to create more jobs and raise productivity? Even though the conflict takes place in an economic context, it will be solved in the political arena by individual voters like you. How would you vote now, and how do you think you will vote ten years from now? This is only one example of the close link between economic and political concerns in any society. ■

THE POLITICAL SYSTEM: POWER, POLITICS, AND MILITARISM

In the opening days of 1990, the following events took place:

- Douglas Wilder became governor of Virginia, and David Dinkins was sworn in as mayor of New York. Both men are the first African-Americans to hold these positions.
- Bulgarians who had just forced their Communist leaders to make democratic political changes took part in mass demonstrations against extending civil rights to the Turkish minority in that country.
- As the threat of Soviet power in Europe diminished, the United States Defense Department argued that other ongoing missions—the "war on

drugs" and protecting American interests in Latin America and the Middle East—would require maintenance of its budget.

- The government of the People's Republic of China ended military control of its capital city, Beijing, where martial law had been imposed seven months earlier to crush student-led prodemocracy demonstrations.

These news items reflect major strands in the study of political systems: relationships of power, processes of government, and the growing militarization of the modern world.

POWER

Max Weber defined power as the probability of realizing one's goals regardless of the will of others. Because power is a resource that is distributed unequally among members of a collectivity or among groups within a society, it is a major dimension of stratification systems (see Chapter 6). Power is also a *social relationship,* implying followers as well as leaders who affect each other (Lawlor and Bacharach, 1987). Power is an aspect of all interactions, from the dating dyad to the declaration of war.

Authority is power that is exercised through legitimate and institutionalized channels.

Weber also distinguished **authority**—the exercise of control through legitimated and institutionalized channels—from *influence*—the exercise of informal persuasion. In this chapter, our focus will be on authority, most of which flows from the status occupied by the individual. Of particular interest to sociologists is the institutional sphere in which the dynamics of power are the central subject matter: the political system itself.

AUTHORITY

Max Weber (1922/1958) distinguished three distinct bases of legitimated power: traditional, charismatic, and legal-rational.

Traditional authority is based on habit and acceptance of the group's customs.

Traditional authority is based on force of habit and customs. Weber singled out patriarchy—the rule of men as fathers, husbands, lords, monarchs, and religious leaders—as the ideal form of traditional authority. As there are few restraints on traditional leaders, Weber regarded this type of power as basically irrational because it was not grounded in any special talent for the task.

Charismatic authority is based on some extraordinary quality of the leader or the leader's ideas.

Charismatic authority is based on some extraordinary quality of the leader or the leader's ideas (*charisma* means "gift"). Followers believe in the leader's superhuman characteristics and are willing to follow commands without question (Willner, 1984). Historical figures with charismatic qualities are such founders of world religions as Jesus and Muhammad. This century has seen several leaders with a charismatic appeal, such as Vladimir Lenin, Franklin Roosevelt, Adolf Hitler, Winston Churchill, Fidel Castro, Charles de Gaulle, and John Kennedy; as well as religious figures such as, Mahatma Gandhi, Martin Luther King, Jr., and the Ayatollah Khomeini. With a few exceptions—the faith healer Aimee Semple McPherson and Argentina's Eva Perón, for example—women are rarely perceived as charismatic leaders.

Because charismatic authority is based on a unique gift and because followers act out of blind faith, by Weber's definition it, too, is irrational. **Legal-rational,** or **bureaucratic, authority,** according to Weber, is the most rational form of power because it is based on an impersonal bond between ruler and the ruled. Power is limited by laws that apply to all officeholders, regardless of personal quality or social status. This form of authority, Weber claims, offers the greatest protection against arbitrary use of force.

Legal-rational, or **bureaucratic, authority** is based on laws that limit the power of officeholders.

Origins of Political Systems

From a functional perspective, political systems serve some basic survival need, namely the need for internal order and defense against external enemies. Thus, some members of the collectivity are granted power to define and enforce the norms. In the most simple of gathering bands, all adults could join in this task. But the more complex the society, the harder it is to have decisions made by the collectivity as a whole. Different degrees of power become linked to different statuses (Glassman, 1986). At the very least, in all but the most simple societies, age and sex become minimal bases for power differences: elders can give orders to juniors, and men to women.

The more complex the society, the greater the need to coordinate the activities of many specialists and to settle disputes among kinship groups or other social units. At some point, loyalty to the society as a whole must supersede family and local allegiances. A governing group becomes the focus of such loyalty, with the power to make rules and enforce them. Such groups range from the tribal councils of preliterate societies to the Congress of the United States. Leaders can be witch doctors, queens, emperors, military dictators, or presidents.

Loyalty to this larger entity and its leader is created and reinforced through *ritual* and other unifying symbols (Kertzer, 1988; Cerulo, 1989). When ceremonies and sacred objects fail to generate solidarity, the collectivity disintegrates into hostile factions. While the ruling elites are especially eager to use rituals to legitimize their rule, opposition groups also need unifying symbols. Thus, in the United States during the protests against the Vietnam War in the late 1960s and early 1970s, supporters of the war waved American flags and protesters carried images of the peace symbol. Most recently, in the case of the Persian Gulf War, yellow ribbons and the American flag appeared everywhere, completely overwhelming any alternative symbols.

As the concept of *cultural,* or *ideological, hegemony* (Chapters 2 and 6) suggests, those already in power have a profound advantage in creating and manipulating rituals and their meanings, from the circuses of ancient Rome to the massive demonstrations staged by the Nazis in Germany in the 1930s to the week-long celebration of the 200th anniversary of the French Revolution in Paris in 1989. In modern societies, the effect is magnified with the assistance of the mass media.

Political Institutions in Complex Societies

The political organization of a complex society is called the **nation-state.** States are organized sets of institutions that govern and defend a given territory. As simple as this definition may seem, there is much debate today on the nature of the state as a sociological entity (e.g., Skocpol and Amenta,

The **nation-state** is the political organization of a complex society.

1986; Block, 1987). Until the 1970s, discussions of political sociology were dominated by two oversimplified visions: (1) the functionalist view that industrialization eventually leads to certain social policies in all modern societies, producing a similar form of "welfare state" regardless of other differences; or (2) the Marxist view that the state is the political arm of capitalism, engaged in policies that reproduce the stratification system. Today, however, the historical evidence suggests a more complicated picture in which the state operates as a relatively autonomous (self-directing) institutional sphere, with its own history and logic, while also linked to the other institutions, especially the economic system.

The Political Economy of the Welfare State. Modern industrial societies are characterized by varying degrees of public (government) intervention in the workings of the economic system. Over the past century, the *welfare state* has expanded its range, beginning with education and old-age pensions and gradually extending the rights of citizens to other resources, such as housing, unemployment insurance, and family supports. The role of state agencies and political leaders in initiating or expanding these programs is the central focus of much political sociology today (Friedmann et al., 1987; Ringen, 1987; Amenta and Carruthers, 1988; Thomas and Lauderdale, 1988; Korpi, 1989; Quadagno and Meyer, 1989). Researchers also note the effects of national values and the power of business elites and labor movements to determine the scope of the welfare state.

A Continuum of Political Systems

In this chapter, we distinguish political systems along a continuum from totalitarian to democratic, based on the degree to which the right to express opposition to the state is protected, as shown in Figure 10-4.

In **totalitarian regimes**, the government attempts to exercise total control over society and its members.

Totalitarian Government. As the name implies, **totalitarian regimes** attempt to regulate all aspects of the society and its members, including beliefs and private lives. Leaders of totalitarian societies have absolute power and are often called dictators. They can be civilians (as in the Soviet Union) or military figures (as in many parts of South America and Africa) or religious authorities (as in Iran). Fascist dictators claim to rule in the name of racial or religious elites; communist dictators do so in the name of the masses. In either case, one small group has exclusive control over the political process. Totalitarianism is most common in societies lacking preconditions of democracy: wide-

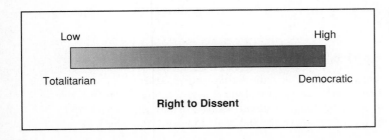

FIGURE 10-4 The right to dissent in political systems.

Public executions are used by totalitarian governments to destroy dissent. Here, prodemocracy demonstrators are about to be executed by a firing squad in Shanghai. These 1989 executions were shown on prime-time television in the People's Republic of China.

spread literacy, economic stability, and an egalitarian ideology. But even industrialized democratic states are vulnerable to the appeal of dictators when economic problems become overwhelming, as when a Hitler or a Mussolini comes to power. In other cases, fear of communism leads people to accept equally totalitarian noncommunist leaders, such as the late Ferdinand Marcos, former president of the Philippines.

An important aspect of totalitarianism is control over cultural products. The media, schools, and theaters are carefully supervised; only certain kinds of art and music are considered appropriate. Public meetings are closely watched for any hint of opposition. Books are burned and the people who wrote them are sent to prison. In the 1980s this was as true in capitalist South Africa as in the socialist People's Republic of China.

Democratic States.   What distinguishes a **democratic society,** then, is not how many people vote—dictatorships tend to have very high voter turnouts—but whether or not there is a legitimate opposition. In the United States, some basic guarantees of democracy are contained in the First Amendment to the Constitution:

> Congress shall make no law respecting an establishment of religion, or prohibiting the free exercise thereof; or abridging the freedom of speech, or of the press; or the right of the people peaceably to assemble, and to petition the Government for a redress of grievances.

These rights are called **civil liberties.** The Bill of Rights—the first ten amendments to the Constitution—is designed to protect citizens against abuse of power by the government.

However, freedom of the press, of speech, and of assembly are always under attack by people who claim to be acting on behalf of American de-

Democratic societies protect the right to dissent.

*The rights to speak, publish, and assemble are **civil liberties**.*

mocracy. Defenders of the First Amendment, by contrast, claim that the freedoms are hollow unless extended to those whose ideas we most fear and hate. In 1989 a Supreme Court decision interpreted an act of flag burning as "symbolic speech" that falls within the protections of the First Amendment. This so aroused politicians and the public that attempts were made, with the encouragement of the President and the Attorney General, to exempt flag-burning from the protections of the First Amendment. Arguments for the exemption focused on the fact that flag burning was a universally condemned, specific action that destroyed something of great symbolic value; if burning a building is arson, why cannot burning the flag also be considered a crime? The counterargument held that the flag is a symbol of precisely those rights that permit burning the flag as a form of protest. It is quite likely that you will have to judge political candidates, in part, on their position on this issue in the coming years.

Manipulating Public Opinion

Both totalitarian and democratic governments depend on influencing public attitudes in order to reinforce their claim to legitimacy. The flow of information from leaders to citizens is subject to manipulation through propaganda, censorship, and repression, and among citizens through the chilling of dissent. Even in a democratic society, people with little political knowledge are highly vulnerable to manipulation by political leaders.

Propaganda involves the selective release of information favorable to those in power, designed to generate high levels of solidarity.

Propaganda. **Propaganda** refers to the selective release of information thought to be favorable to those in power and designed to generate high levels of support and solidarity. To boost morale in wartime, civilian populations are continually told how well their side is doing. In peacetime, governments release reports that put a positive light on the regime's accomplishments. Sometimes propaganda is designed to frighten citizens into supporting government goals, as when misleading reports of an enemy's military strength are used to gain public approval for increased defense budgets.

Censorship involves the selective withholding of information.

Censorship. In contrast to propaganda, **censorship** involves the selective withholding of information (Jansen, 1988). In totalitarian societies, newspapers often appear with blank columns where the government censors have forbidden publication. In democracies, it is far more difficult to censor news, but governments often try to do so on the basis of protecting national security.

In the United States, in recent years, the government has stopped publication of books by former members of the Central Intelligence Agency (CIA) about events that took place decades earlier. For a brief period in 1979 the government was able to stop publication of the *Progressive,* a small-circulation, left-wing periodical that carried an article on how to build a nuclear weapon, based solely on material that the reporter was able to find in a public library. More recently, in 1989 the White House admitted that it had censored testimony by government scientists on the effects of global warming as a result of pollution from industry that ran counter to the administration's position (*New York Times,* May 9, 1989, p. C1).

In a recent example of censorship, the Corcoran Gallery in Washington, D.C., canceled a retrospective of Robert Mapplethorpe's work, fearing that his explicit photos would upset federal grant givers. Supporters of Mapplethorpe projected an image of the artist, who died of AIDS, on the museum wall.

Chilling Dissent. There are a number of ways in which governments can make people think twice about what they say and with whom they associate. These "chilling" tactics include wiretapping, opening mail, and direct surveillance. Although such techniques are part of everyday life in dictatorships, they have also been used in the United States: against suspected Socialists in the 1920s and 1930s; suspected communists targeted by Senator Joseph McCarthy in the 1950s; antiwar activists in the 1960s; and today, against religious groups helping refugees from South and Central American dictatorships.

Although catching potential spies can be considered necessary to preserving democracy, an essential tension exists between the First Amendment and the methods of the CIA and FBI. Because these agencies work in secrecy, it is difficult even for government authorities to check their excesses and correct their mistakes (Jeffreys-Jones, 1989).

FBI and local law enforcement files of 1985 were shown by Laudon (1986) to include a minimum of 12,000 mistaken warrants and reports issued each day. If current plans to establish a nationwide computerized information system are approved, each of us would have a file in which all kinds of information from medical records to credit card purchases and false arrest forms were freely available to police, creditors, employers, and health insurance companies (Congress of the United States, 1988).

Coercion, Repression, and Genocide. The ultimate in social control is the use of force, or *coercion* (see Chapter 3), to ensure obedience. The threat of force is also highly effective, so that a well-publicized case, such as a treason trial, will be enough to keep most other people quiet. A public execution of "troublemakers" is a familiar tactic in totalitarian regimes, as seen in 1989 in the People's Republic of China, where several prodemocracy demonstrators were put before a firing squad on prime-time television.

Repression involves such open restraints on opposition as house arrest, imprisonment, curfews (forbidding people to be on the streets at certain hours), and the forcible breakup of protests. The most extreme step in reducing opposition is to do away with dissenters altogether through *genocide* (see Chapter 8).

Repression involves the forceful denial of civil liberties.

359

POLITICAL CONSEQUENCES OF INEQUALITY

In societies marked by extreme differences in economic and social power between the few who rule and the many who are controlled, social order is maintained by increasingly repressive measures. These acts create further hostility among citizens, which, in turn, often leads to political violence (Muller, 1985). In the past decade, popular revolutions in Iran and the Philippines have toppled absolute rulers and, most recently, overturned totalitarian systems throughout Eastern Europe.

According to the British historian Lord Acton's famous maxim, "Power tends to corrupt; absolute power corrupts absolutely." No matter how "good" the original intentions of power holders, all too often they cannot resist using their power for personal gain (Kipnis, 1976).

The Iron Law of Oligarchy

Even in organizations that represent "the masses," the leaders, including those who are democratically elected, tend to become cut off from their followers. **Oligarchy** means "rule by a few," and the "iron law" proposed by Robert Michels (1911/1962) states that because decision makers have a crucial interest in being proven correct, they tend to manipulate information and individuals in order to gain support.

Oligarchy is the rule of the many by the few.

Regardless of the personalities of rulers, exercising power leads to arrogance—feelings of superiority coupled with contempt for others. If the followers are able to create a revolution and overturn their rulers, the iron law suggests that the new rulers will also be drawn to limiting dissent and using propaganda and censorship to influence public opinion. Although this may not always happen, critics of President Corazon Aquino of the Philippines say she has taken steps to reduce opposition; the religious leaders who succeeded the Shah of Iran have become every bit as totalitarian as the Shah.

The beauty of democracy is that every two, four, or six years, our rulers must appear before us and justify their actions, in competition with other candidates. Citizens in a democracy can periodically replace one set of leaders with another, so that even if government remains in the hands of the elite and the iron law cannot be repealed, no one can stay in office long enough to become fully corrupted by power (Etzioni-Halevy, 1983).

Yet examples of the iron law at work can be seen in the recent history of the United States. Lyndon Johnson pursued an increasingly unpopular war, fed false information to the press, was shielded from bad news by his subordinates, and, until the last moment, had no idea of the reality of his situation. Richard Nixon was engaged in an active cover-up of a crime, lied to the public, and resigned only as he was about to be impeached. Advisers to Ronald Reagan thought that they could conduct a secret foreign policy in direct contradiction to the will of Congress.

POLITICAL PARTICIPATION

Political participation in the United States takes place in several ways: running for office, contributing money to candidates, working on campaigns, or voting.

Office Holding

As we saw in Chapters 7 and 8, despite recent gains few women, African-Americans, and Latinos hold public office, elected or appointed. The higher the office, the less likely it is to find people occupying it who are not white men. In part, this is because people without economic and interpersonal power are not perceived as strong candidates. But there are also structural explanations. One path to becoming a candidate is to have worked your way up the political party organization, helping others until you have earned a chance to run for office yourself. At this time, very few African-Americans and Latinos have this background experience, and women are only now emerging from the political pipeline. The other route to candidacy involves having enough money to mount an effective campaign, an advantage not common among most women, African-Americans, and Latinos.

Campaign Activity

Only a small proportion of citizens take an active role in political campaigns as contributors or volunteer workers. Although there are now limits on the amount of money an individual can contribute to a particular organization, there is no limit on the number of organizations to which one can contribute. As a consequence, an increasing number of organizations, especially **political action committees** (PACs), have been created. PACs can use their funds to support causes and candidates, especially incumbent members of Congress who sit on committees that oversee particular areas of activity.

Political action committees (PACs) are special organizations that use funds to support causes and candidates.

Apart from ideology, there are practical reasons for supporting candidates who are likely to endorse tax and regulatory policies favorable to one's personal and business interests (Burris, 1987; Eismeier and Pollock, 1988).

As seen in Table 10-2, most PAC money comes from unions and trade associations and is typically funnelled to members of Congressional committees who serve on the committees that oversee the PAC's area of interest. These funds are a significant reason why those already in office (incumbents)

TABLE 10-2 Who Gave the Most . . . (in millions)

Top political action committee contributors to federal candidates in 1988 elections.

1. National Association of Realtors	$3.0
2. International Brotherhood of Teamsters	2.9
3. American Medical Association	2.3
4. National Education Association	2.1
5. National Association of Retired Federal Employees	2.0
6. United Auto Workers	1.9
7. Association of Trial Lawyers of America	1.9
8. National Association of Letter Carriers	1.7
9. American Federation of State, County & Municipal Employees	1.6
10. International Association of Machinists and Aerospace Workers	1.5

Source: *New York Times*, June 5, 1989, p. 15

have an advantage over challengers. In 1990 all but one sitting senator and only a few representatives failed to win reelection.

Volunteer workers, however, do not have to be wealthy or even motivated by personal or ideological considerations. Most campaign workers become active when drawn in by friends. The low political involvement of working-class and poor people may reflect not only powerlessness and lack of education but relative isolation from social networks (Zipp and Smith, 1982).

Voting

The fundamental act of political involvement is voting. As can be seen in Table 10-3 and Table 10-4, not all eligible Americans are registered to vote, and not all who are registered exercise the right to vote. Indeed, the trend over the past two decades in registration and voting has been downward.

These rates are roughly half of those of other Western democracies. In part, this difference reflects the fact that elections in other nations are held on weekends rather than on workdays, so that hourly-wage earners find it easier to participate (Beeghley, 1986). Voting in the United States is also made relatively difficult by the registration process and rules of eligibility, which vary from one state to another.

Who Votes and Who Doesn't

Registration and voting vary by gender, race, ethnicity, and age. In addition, as seen in Table 10-4, the probability of voting is associated with such indicators of social class as education, occupation, and income. As these data are no secret, politicians are well aware of the relatively small numbers of African-

---

TABLE 10-3 Voting in Presidential Elections, United States: 1968 and 1988 (percentage of eligible voters)

| | Percentage Voting | |
	1968	1988
Total	**67.8**	**57.4**
White	69.1	59.1
Black	57.6	51.5
Spanish origin	—	28.8
Male	69.8	56.4
Female	66.0	58.3
18–20	33.3	33.2
21–24	51.1	38.3
25–44	66.6	54.0
45–64	74.9	67.9
65+	65.8	68.8

Source: U.S. Bureau of the Census, P-20, No. 440, 1989.

TABLE 10-4   Percentage of Voting-Age Population Voting in the Election of 1988, by Education, Employment, and Income

	Voting
Years of School Completed	
Elementary	36.7
High school: 1–3 years	41.3
High school: 4 years	54.7
College: 1–3 years	64.5
College: 4 years or more	77.6
Labor Force Status	
Unemployed	38.6
Agriculture	53.0
Private wage and salary	54.6
Self-employed	63.3
Government worker	75.2
Not in labor force	57.3
Family Income	
Under $5,000	34.7
5,000–9,999	41.3
10,000–14,999	47.7
15,000–19,999	53.5
20,000–24,999	57.8
25,000–34,999	64.0
35,000–49,999	70.3
50,000 and over	75.6

Source: U.S. Bureau of the Census, P-29, No. 440, 1989, p. 4.

Americans, Latinos, and people 18 to 24 who exercise this right with frequency. As a result, party platforms are not constructed around the interests of these groups. And policy changes are unlikely to come until *after* underrepresented groups show up in the voting booth.

Thus, people who might have the most to gain from government intervention are actually the least likely to vote: victims of discrimination, the young, the poor, the less educated. The subgroup with the lowest voting rates is people 18 to 24, many of whom may not have lived in one community long enough to qualify and who are also likely to be in the midst of many status changes. But later, when these young adults settle down to family, work, and community roles, when they have a mortgage to pay off and children in the school system, they are more likely to vote and to enjoy the benefits of public policies. However, because so many Americans do *not* vote, the few who do can exert influence far beyond their numbers (see Figure 10-5).

Nonvoting may also be seen as another symptom of the withdrawal of the powerless from a system that does not recognize their needs. This effect is strongest among both inner-city African-Americans and white rural poor. Despite much talk about the need to register all possible voters, neither major political party appears sufficiently interested in empowering the most deprived among us. Some activists believe that if the poor could be registered

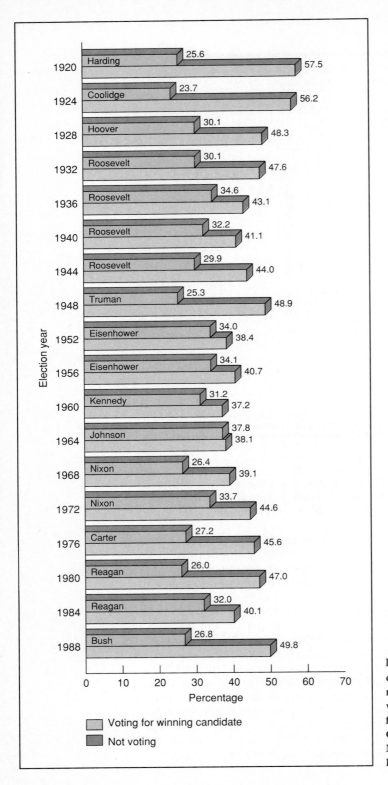

FIGURE 10-5 Nonvoting Americans. Percentage voting for the winning candidate and percentage not voting: 1920–88 (after universal suffrage). (Sources: U.S. Bureau of the Census, P-23, No. 102, 1980; P-20, No. 405, 1986; *New York Times,* December 18, 1988, p. 36.)

as they wait on line in welfare offices or on unemployment lines, they might emerge as a major force in local politics (Piven and Cloward, 1987).

In 1989, Congress finally agreed to legislation that requires states to provide voter registration forms along with applications for driver's licenses and to permit mail registration. Yet most Americans appear quite comfortable with restricted voting; a 1987 public opinion poll found little support for making it easier to register and vote (*New York Times,* May 31, 1987, p. E4). The dominant feeling was that if people did not care enough to make an effort to register, they probably should not be allowed to vote.

The Gender Gap

The one voting pattern with the greatest long-term political significance involves women. In 1980, for the first time since gaining the right to vote in 1920, women's voting rate exceeded that of men, and it has diverged even more with each succeeding election. This trend is doubly important because women also outnumber men at all adult ages, so that the electorate is now largely female and will become more so as the population itself ages.

Voting patterns for white women differed significantly from those of white men. In contrast to their male counterparts, white women were more likely to vote Democratic, support women candidates, and to hold different opinions on a range of topics (Center for the American Woman and Politics, 1989). These sex differences did not appear among African-Americans, largely because both women and men concentrated on issues of race rather than gender (Welch and Sigelman, 1989).

In the presidential election of 1988, women split their votes almost evenly between George Bush and Michael Dukakis, whereas men favored Bush by 15 percentage points. When it came to other offices, the women's preferences made the difference in at least ten races, to the advantage of the Democratic candidate. Clearly, politicians will have to pay greater attention to what have become defined as "women's issues": child welfare, health care, environmental concerns, workplace equity, and world peace. This gap will probably persist, if not widen, because of structural changes in the society: increased labor force participation of women, the feminization of poverty and impoverishment of children, and the group consciousness produced by the women's movement (Brackman and Erie, 1986). The politicization of women is also evident in a growing number of grass-roots organizations headed by women and concerned with education, health, and safety in the workplace and neighborhood (Bookman and Morgan, 1988; Garland, 1988).

When women are elected to high office, do they govern differently than do men? The examples of Indira Gandhi, Corazon Aquino, Margaret Thatcher, and others might suggest not. But the experience of Norway offers evidence of the particular slant women can bring to governing. The prime minister and almost half the cabinet are women, as are 40 percent of the ruling party members in parliament. As a result, child care subsidies and paid parental leave have been expanded without destroying the economy. Similarly, in the United States, as the proportion of women in the state legislature of Arizona increased, so did the number of proposals centered on "women's issues" (Saint-Germain, 1989).

POLITICAL SOCIALIZATION AND VALUE ORIENTATIONS

Political socialization includes the influences and experiences that determine one's political orientation.

The term **political socialization** refers to the influences and experiences that lead people to define their political orientation as either conservative or liberal. As Figure 10-6 illustrates, the process of political socialization combines elements of both early and later influences. There is a direct link between political attitudes formed by the time one enters college and those held in later adulthood, but intervening experiences also have an effect. In many cases, occupational roles will reinforce earlier attitudes—for example, a conservative student who pursues a business career, or a liberal student who pursues a social work career.

Although it is often assumed that social class should have a profound effect on political orientations, empirical findings are not that clear-cut. It is important to distinguish (1) attitudes toward "economic" issues such as private ownership, taxation, and budget priorities from (2) attitudes on "social" issues such as women's rights, school prayer, and racial integration. In general, the upper-middle class is most liberal on social issues and the working class the least. On economic matters, the class positions are reversed. These differences, however, appear to be more related to *educational level* than to income or occupation (Zipp, 1986). Salaried professionals such as academics and other "knowledge workers," tend to be the most liberal of all occupation/ education groups (Macy, 1989).

Yuppie stands for young upwardly mobile professional.

The difference between social and economic attitudes is especially visible in data on young upwardly mobile professionals—**yuppies.** One longitudinal study of 1965 high school graduates found that by age 40, only 15 percent met the yuppie criteria: a four-year college education, professional or managerial employment, and relatively high household income (Jennings and Markus, 1986). Compared to their nonyuppie age peers, their attitudes were deeply influenced by the antiwar and other social movements of the 1960s, and they remained very liberal on social issues but turned extremely conservative on economic matters. Because yuppies have very high rates of political participation, they will have an effect on social policy far greater than their numbers.

THE STRUCTURE OF POWER IN AMERICA

A recurring theme in political sociology is the debate over who rules America: a small homogeneous class (the *power-elite* model) or many and competing bases of power (the *pluralist model*).

The **power-elite model** assumes that decision making is concentrated in the hands of a few similarly socialized people.

The Power-Elite Model

In 1956 sociologist C. Wright Mills published a book entitled *The Power Elite* in which he traced the social-class backgrounds of leaders in business, government, and other major spheres of influence and authority. As products of similar class locations and socialization experiences, these leaders will think

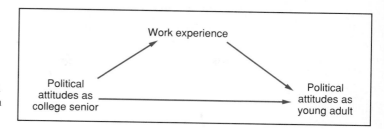

FIGURE 10-6   A model of political socialization. (Source: Adapted from Lorence and Mortimer, 1979.)

alike, share a vision of what is fair and good, and act in ways that maintain the existing stratification system. These relationships are shown in Figure 10-7.

The empirical tests of Mill's thesis have centered on identifying a "national upper class" whose members own most of the nation's wealth, manage its corporations and banks, run the universities and foundations, control the mass media, and staff the highest levels of government and the courts (Schwartz, 1987). It is worth noting in this regard that contrary to the "log cabin" myth, all but five of our presidents were from the upper or upper-middle classes, including Abraham Lincoln (Pessen, 1984; Baltzell and Schneiderman, 1988).

In recent research the emphasis has been less on the content of socialization than on the structural links among the members of this elite: from schools and clubs to marriages and jobs. These are interlocks that extend beyond the world of business to involve politics, education, and control over information. This phenomenon is most obvious in presidential appointments (Riddlesberger and King, 1989) and in the actual movement of people from one sphere to another, as when corporate officers become cabinet members.

Other studies have examined the flow of campaign contributions from wealthy individuals (Allen and Broyles, 1989) and major business groups to political campaigns. One study of corporate political contributions between 1974 and 1980 found that more than 80 percent of the total from these sources went to Republican candidates (Kouzi and Ratcliffe, 1983). Similarly, corporate contributors to the 1980 elections displayed a high degree of unity

FIGURE 10-7   The power elite is composed of members of the upper classes who have achieved the highest possible positions in each of these centers of power.

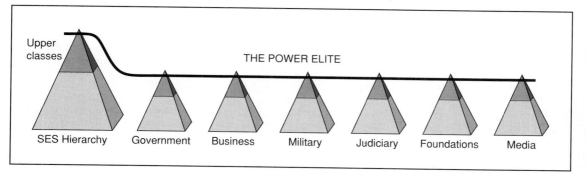

CORPORATE POLITICAL BEHAVIOR

Mark S. Mizruchi

Mark S. Mizruchi is associate professor of sociology at Columbia University. He received his Ph.D. from the State University of New York at Stony Brook in 1980. Before moving to Columbia in 1987, he was an assistant professor and statistical consultant at the Albert Einstein College of Medicine. He is the author of The American Corporate Network, 1904–1974 *(Sage, 1982), coeditor (with Michael Schwartz) of* Intercorporate Relations *(Cambridge University Press, 1987), and author of numerous articles on these and other topics. His current research includes an examination of corporate political behavior and a longitudinal study of organizational responses to capital dependence. He is completing a manuscript entitled* The Structure of Corporate Political Action: Interfirm Relations and their Consequences.

My interest in corporate power dates from my undergraduate days at Washington University in St. Louis, Missouri. As a canvasser for George McGovern's 1972 presidential campaign, I went door-to-door trying to convince registered Democrats in white working-class neighborhoods to support their party's nominee. Much to my disappointment, the vast majority of my respondents either supported Richard Nixon or were neutral. It made no sense to me that people who were struggling economically would reject a candidate who promised to redistribute income from the wealthy and end U.S. participation in a war whose main casualties were working-class men. My respondents had more hostility toward students and people of color than they did toward corporations and the wealthy! I decided to major in sociology to find out why.

American sociology in the early 1970s was divided between proponents of the "order" and the "conflict" perspectives. The order perspective suggested that workers' conservatism was a reflection of their acceptance of the American value system, which they saw as threatened by student protests and African-American militance. The conflict perspective suggested that the dominant values of a society are those of its most powerful class. To the extent that workers accepted these ideas, they were the victims of "false consciousness," the internalization of attitudes directly contrary to their own interests. But how could this occur in a democratic society?

This question led me to the study of political sociology, in which a parallel debate was taking place between pluralists, those who viewed American society as basically democratic, and elite theorists and Marxists, who viewed American society as dominated by elites who pursued their own interests with little regard for the general public. The key issue separating participants in this debate was the extent to which these elites were unified. Pluralists argued that conflict among elites provided the conditions for democracy, since the group that was out of power could always appeal to the electorate. Elite theorists and Marxists argued that elites, especially business elites, were basically unified, which gave them the power to pursue their collective interests.

During my second year in graduate school at the State University of New York at Stony Brook, I took a seminar with Michael Schwartz, who was studying interlocking directorates among large American corporations (an interlock occurs when a member of a firm's board sits on the board of another firm). Schwartz and his students had found that large corporations were extensively interlocked through their boards of directors, a finding that suggested a high degree of unity among corporate elites. Because their work focused on only one point in time, however, it was difficult to know if the extent of business unity had declined over time, as pluralists argued.

My dissertation, a historical study of interlocks among large

American firms at seven time points between 1904 and 1974, was designed to test this pluralist argument. I found that the cohesiveness of the network declined between 1912 and 1935 but then rose slightly thereafter. Contrary to the arguments of many pluralist theorists, this finding suggested the continued existence of a cohesive corporate elite. But a problem remained. Critics of this research raised the question, So what? "What is the political meaning of these interlocks?" they asked. "What are the behavioral consequences? What difference does it make that corporations share directors?" Interlock researchers, including myself, had implied that the demonstration of a tightly connected network of firms was evidence of corporate political unity. But we had no evidence to demonstrate this conjecture.

One response to this question was the case study method, a detailed examination of a particular issue or a few issues. J. Allen Whitt's *Urban Elites and Mass Transportation* is an excellent example of this approach. Unfortunately, although Whitt's study suggested the existence of business unity, other studies, such as Bauer, Pool, and Dexter's *American Business and Public Policy*, suggested the absence of business unity. This led me to two conclusions. First, quantitative analyses of a large number

of cases would be necessary to make large-scale generalizations. Second, business unity is not an either/or phenomenon. Rather, sometimes business is unified and at other times it is divided. The task is to identify the *conditions* under which business unity occurs. The presence of interlocks, I hypothesized, provided one such condition.

My search for an answer to the So what? question led me to an examination of two forms of business political behavior: the campaign contributions of corporate political action committees (PACs) and the content of business testimony before Congress. Using an approach called "network analysis," I studied whether firms with director interlocks were more likely than firms without interlocks to contribute to the same congressional candidates and to express similar opinions at congressional hearings. In the case of both political campaign contributions and testimony before Congress, firms that share directors are more likely to behave similarly, even when the firms operate in different industries and are headquartered in different states. These findings suggest that interlocking directorates facilitate political unity among corporations.

But the hypothesis that a unified group is more politically effective remains to be tested. One approach is to examine the

relation between political unity within an industry and the industry's success in securing favorable legislation (or preventing unfavorable legislation). In addition, a group's effectiveness is likely to be affected by the strength and unity of its opposition. This suggests the need to study the political conflicts between business and its opponents, including labor, consumer, and environmental groups. I am currently doing research in both of these areas that should shed further light on the nature and extent of corporate political power.

References

Bauer, Raymond A., Ithiel de Sola Pool, and Lewis Anthony Dexter. *American Business and Public Policy: The Politics of Foreign Trade.* New York: Atherton Press, 1968.

Mizruchi, Mark S. *The American Corporate Network, 1904–1974.* Beverly Hills, CA: Sage, 1982.

———. "Similarity of Political Behavior Among Large American Corporations." *American Journal of Sociology* 95(1989):401–24.

Whitt, J. Allen. *Urban Elites and Mass Transportation.* Princeton, NJ: Princeton University Press, 1982.

in their shared conservative beliefs (Mizruchi, 1989; Clawson and Neustadl, 1989).

Since the 1980 elections, business leaders have been crucial to the rise of the New Right, a coalition of interest groups with extremely conservative agendas: the anti-gun-control lobby, antiabortion groups, free-market economists, anticommunists, supporters of school prayer, proponents of military strength, and fundamentalist Protestants.

Another source of support for the power-elite vision of the world lies in the vast resources of the major American foundations—tax-exempt organizations built on endowments from very wealthy families. Funds from the interest on the endowments are used to finance various educational and charitable causes chosen by the trustees and managers of the foundations. As members of the elite strata, foundation heads are not likely support to people or organizations whose goal is to overthrow the existing system or to challenge American interests abroad.

The Pluralist Model

The **pluralist model** assumes that there are many different and competing bases of power, with no one group dominating another.

Critics of the power-elite model suggest that it oversimplifies reality, assumes a greater uniformity among leaders than actually exists, and underestimates the sources of conflict within the ruling class.

Pluralists contend that business interests are very diverse, and policies that benefit core industries may be disastrous for peripheral firms. Furthermore, the various power sectors are usually in competition for scarce resources, as when the military competes with consumer industries for electronics experts, or when the government competes with private enterprise in providing health care. In the political sphere itself, pluralists point out that power is widely diffused across the three layers of government: local, state, and federal.

The basic assumption of pluralism is that the diversity of interests in mass society ensures that no one group can control decision making throughout the system (Riesman, 1950). As shown in Figure 10-8, each power sector serves as a potential buffer against uncontrolled expansion of any other.

Although the two models are often presented as mutually exclusive, they are best seen as alternative explanations depending on the system under analysis. The power structure of a small town would probably resemble the elite model, with local leaders in frequent contact and making decisions that are mutually beneficial. The power structure of a college or university, however, might come close to the pluralist ideal, with administration, faculty, staff, and students competing for scarce resources and serving to limit the concentration of power in any one group.

THE MILITARY

A primary characteristic of the state is its monopoly over the legitimate use of force. Governments—whether tribal councils, absolute monarchies, or modern democracies—are expected to settle disputes within the collectivity and to defend the society from outside enemies. To serve these functions in complex societies, two types of specialists emerge: a *police force* for internal order (see Chapter 6); and a *military* for external defense (Giddens, 1985).

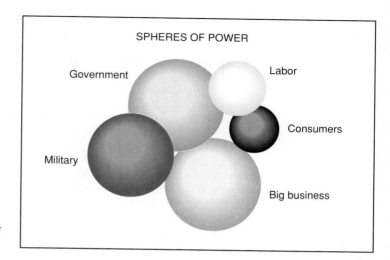

FIGURE 10-8   Model of counter-vailing forces—competing power sectors may form coalitions to prevent the uncontrolled expansion of another sector.

The American Military

Until recently the United States was unique among modern societies in not having a large professional military. Rather, the ideal was the "citizen-soldier," a civilian who could be called on to join a local military unit only when the need arose and who would return to civilian life when the emergency was over (Moskos, 1988; Segal, 1989). Examples include the militias of the revolutionary war and the state National Guard units of this century. But when volunteers were lacking, citizens could be forced—conscripted—into the military, as was the case during the Civil War, both World Wars, and the Vietnam War (Jacobs, 1986). From 1945 to 1973, conscription (the draft) continued through periods of peace as well as war.

The All-Volunteer Force.   In 1973 the draft was ended and the citizen–soldier ideal was replaced by the "economic man" model of military service (Moskos, 1988). Military service would no longer be seen as an obligation of citizenship but as a job, like any other, to which recruits could be attracted by relatively high pay, the chance to travel, educational opportunities, and other special benefits. It was thought that an **all-volunteer force** (AVF) would be smaller and more professional than the citizen army, and that because recruits would make a career of military service the higher pay scales would be offset by lower turnover rates (White, 1989). The contemporary AVF is a military establishment very different from its predecessors. The expected reduction in active-duty armed forces has taken place—from an average of 15 per 1,000 population in the 1960s to about 9 per 1,000 today. The AVF has also had dramatic effects on the race and gender composition of the American military. In addition, a majority of active-duty personnel today are married, many with their spouse and children living on base.

The **all-volunteer force** is composed of people who enter the military as a full-time career.

Racial Factors.   The AVF has a higher proportion of minority personnel—African-American and Latino, particularly—than did the conscripted armed forces. Minority men and women compose 27 percent of the enlisted (non-officer) personnel, somewhat higher than their representation in the total population. In fact, the U.S. Army is the most integrated institution in our society—but only at the lower ranks. Among officers, only 5 percent are African-American. Although many civil rights leaders hail the AVF as an important employment/education opportunity for inner-city youth, others question why a disproportionate number of people of color might die in defense of the society (Halloran, 1986).

From the point of view of minority enlisted personnel, the armed forces appear to offer greater equality of opportunity for training and advancement than does the civilian labor force. Contrary to the public image, recruits of any race are *not* low achievers or from marginal subgroups; rather, most are drawn from upwardly mobile middle and lower-middle class families (Berryman, 1988). As a consequence, reenlistment rates have increased sharply (Halloran, 1988). Although military service removes large numbers of African-American males from the marriage pool in their home communities, it also allows many to afford marriage and to establish a family.

Interracial relations in the military reflect those of the wider society. When blacks and whites are on duty together, segregation is minimal and relationships relatively smooth. Once off duty, or off the post, however, the members of different racial groups tend to go their own ways (Moskos, quoted in Halloran, 1986).

Women in the Military. Although there have been women in the American military since the early 1940s, the AVF, under considerable outside pressure, has actively recruited women to its ranks. In general, the educational standards for women enlistees is higher than those for their male counterparts. Today, more than one in ten members of the armed forces—almost 220,000—is a

Today, one in ten members of the armed forces is a woman, and some women have gradually worked their way into the officer corps. Despite these changes, the military remains a man's world. How do you think women's experiences in the military differ from those of men?

woman: 12.5 percent of the air force, 10.5 percent of the army, 9 percent of the navy, and 5 percent of the Marine Corps. These percentages are all much higher than for any Western European country. Gradually, some of these women have worked their way into the officer corps, where they command men as well as women. And, gradually, they have come to be accepted as colleagues (Halloran, 1988). In fact, although women compose 12 percent of enlisted personnel, they also account for 13 to 16 percent of all junior officers (below the rank of major or lieutenant commander).

Originally, the job categories open to women recruits were limited to the clerical and medical areas. In 1986 the air force approved all-women crews for the Minuteman 2 nuclear missile, and the navy now permits women aboard support ships that could be called into combat. After a lengthy review, the army in 1988 opened up 11,000 new positions to allow women entry and opportunity for advancement. As seen in the Persian Gulf war, the line between combat and noncombat roles has been eroding, with military women working and dying alongside their male peers.

Militarism and Militarization

Militarism refers to a societal emphasis on military ideals and virtues and a glorification of war and warriors. Militarism is associated with heavy expenditures on weapons and training, as well as an aggressive foreign policy. **Militarization** refers to the mobilization of entire societies around militaristic goals. Until recently, the United States was able to avoid the militarism of other modern nation-states by its physical and ideological isolation from the rest of the world. Today, however, the United States ranks among the most militarized of modern societies. In part, militarism is an inevitable correlate of the centralized state and the international system of trade, where wars are fought for economic as well as political goals. The rise of militarism in America is also related to our assuming, at the end of World War II, the role of "leader of the free world," followed in the 1950s by the developing cold war between the United States and the Soviet Union, which has only recently thawed. It remains to be seen whether there will be a "peace dividend" and decline in the power of the military, or whether the overwhelming success of the campaign against Iraq in 1991 will enhance the stature of the armed forces and increase support for further military actions.

Militarism invades the culture: movies, television, and children's toys and cartoon programs all glorify combat as a solution to political and social problems. Nor are civilian adults immune from the excitement of military things: camouflage suits, shooting galleries, video war games, soft air guns, training camps for would-be mercenaries, magazines such as *Soldier of Fortune*, and mail order catalogs for destructive weapons all enjoy great popularity. And despite the presence of military women, militarism also reinforces beliefs in the superiority of men and masculinity (Jeffords, 1989). The greatest impact of militarism, however, will be felt in the area of domestic policy and priorities for federal spending.

The Military-Industrial State.   In his Farewell Address to the Nation in January 1961, President Dwight D. Eisenhower, a military leader of World War II, warned the country about a new threat to democratic government and the

> **Militarism** refers to a societal emphasis on military ideals and a glorification of war.

> **Militarization** occurs when an entire society is mobilized around militaristic goals.

The **military-industrial complex** consists of a large, permanent military establishment combined with an immense armament industry.

pursuit of world peace: the combination of a large, permanent military establishment and an immense arms industry (1961/1985). This **military-industrial complex** could, he believed, become an independent power in setting priorities in both our domestic and foreign relations. Supporting such a vast apparatus would take funds from civilian projects; once in place, the complex would have a vested interest in world conflict rather than peace.

Thirty years later, out of a total proposed budget of more than 1 trillion dollars, 25 percent (or $303,300,000,000) is earmarked for military expenses. In comparison, roughly 11 percent of the 1991 total was budgeted for education, transportation, and health services (Office of Management and Budget, January, 1990). Most of the current and future American military budget is devoted to complex weapons systems such as the MX missile, Trident submarines, Stealth bombers, and the Strategic Defense Initiative ("Star Wars").

Throughout the world, military spending has escalated since the 1960s; today the international trade in armaments is greater than that in food. In Third World countries, military expenses absorb the money needed to improve agriculture or build industries. In Ethiopia, for example, where famine is widespread, 42 percent of the government budget went to the military in one year (Worldwatch, 1986). The leading arms merchant in the world today is the United States, where weaponry is a multibillion dollar industry.

Warfare Welfare. The military-industrial complex, as Eisenhower foresaw, has great power to persuade Congress and the public that our military needs are paramount. Members of Congress compete to win defense contracts for their districts; defense contractors spend a great deal of money on political candidates; retired Pentagon officers take jobs in defense industries. A vast system of "weapons welfarism" has emerged, that is, public subsidies for war industries, with little supervision by civilian authorities (Feagin, 1986). As a consequence, vast cost overruns are the norm. Although a large proportion of defense companies are under criminal investigation for fraud, little has been done to insulate defense contracts from political pressure.

As increased numbers of people depend on the military budget for their livelihood, it becomes more difficult to change priorities. Once the complex weapons systems are in place, the temptation to use them grows, while the sheer number and variety of offensive weapons in every part of the world today raises the possibility of accidental war (Evans and Hilgartner, 1987).

Nuclear War. Today's nuclear weapons are faster, more accurate, and far more powerful than imagined only a decade ago. Although only a few nations admit to having produced nuclear weapons, another two dozen could be well on their way. Nuclear power reactors and research facilities are a global phenomenon. Compared to the total power of munitions used in World War II, the combined power of the world's *known* stockpile of nuclear weapons is 5,000 times greater, as seen in Figure 10-9, where you can see the vast amount of firepower available today compared to what was used in three previous wars.

Because the dangers of radioactivity have been played down and the positive aspects of the nuclear age emphasized, nuclear policy was not fully debated in its formative stages, but left in the hands of "experts" with their own agendas.

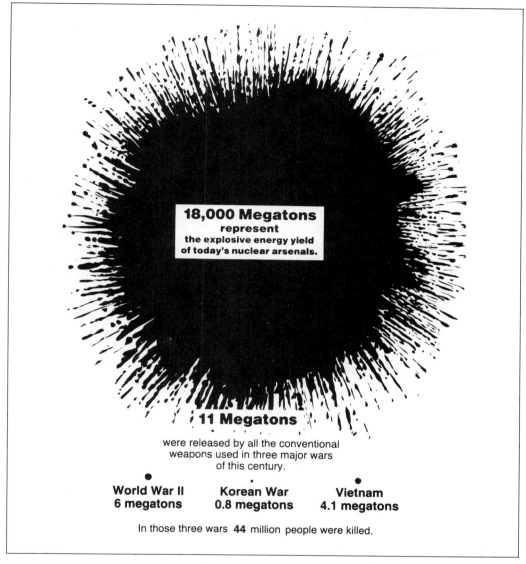

FIGURE 10-9 The world's stockpile of nuclear weapons. (Source: Sivard, 1989, p. 14.)

The threat of nuclear extinction has served to focus attention on these issues, and as a result, the sociology of peace and war is now a recognized speciality within the American Sociological Association. Research topics include the power of the military-industrial complex, the manipulation of public opinion, military personnel as social actors, masculinity and militarism, the dynamics of international cooperation and competition, and the consequences of the arms race.

The threat of nuclear war in the late 1980s underwent dramatic change when Mikhail Gorbachev of the Soviet Union and American leaders agreed on reductions in the stockpiling of nuclear weapons. But the sheer numbers of such weaponry and the increasing number of nations with nuclear capability continue to feed fears of an accidental holocaust.

SUMMARY

1. The origins and historical development of economic systems are closely linked to the human group's adaptations to their environment.

2. Economic activities involve the production, distribution, and consumption of goods and services. Modern societies are increasingly characterized by the growth of the service sector.

3. Contemporary economic systems can be arrayed along a continuum representing the degree to which economic activities are under public or private control.

4. The trend under capitalism has been toward greater concentration of power through the monopolization of commodities and services and through the growth of conglomerates.

5. Industrial economies are typified by a complex division of labor that may lead to alienation, powerlessness, and the deskilling of work. Yet worker satisfaction remains high. Firms are increasingly experimenting with ways to improve morale and productivity.

6. The American labor movement, unlike its European counterparts, has not become an oppositional force to capitalism. Unions remain the only organized force for economic democracy in the United States, yet they represent fewer than one-fifth of those in the work force.

7. The future of unions depends on attracting high- and low-skill service workers, managers, professionals, and especially women.

8. A major source of inequality among workers is their location in the economy itself, whether in core or peripheral industries. This dual economy is reinforced by a segmented labor market, differentiated by race and gender.

9. The probability of being employed or unemployed is also related to the dual economy, as well as to the overall state of the economy. Although unemployment rates have declined from their high in 1982–83, the gap between white and African-American rates has increased.

10. American workers are employed by more than 15 million business firms, but it is the 3 million *corporations* that employ most workers and control most of the business assets.

11. Corporations, like any systems, have a culture consisting of beliefs, values, and norms. Corporate power is concentrated through interlocking directorates.

12. The study of political systems begins with an analysis of power, a resource unevenly available to members of a society and an important dimension of social stratification.

13. The type of power called authority—traditional, charismatic, or legal-rational—refers to the exercise of control through legitimated and institutionalized structures.

14. As social systems become more complex, the political organization becomes the nation-state.

15. In all societies, the political system, although relatively autonomous, is linked to other institutional spheres, particularly the economy.

16. Political systems can be ranged on a continuum from totalitarian to democratic, based on the degree to which citizens have rights against the state and can freely express dissent.

17. Governments can manipulate public opinion through propaganda and censorship and chill dissent through surveillance. The iron law of oligarchy states that all power holders are tempted to manipulate their citizens.

18. In a democracy, citizens participate in the political process by running for office, working on campaigns, and voting. The major change in U.S. voting patterns over the past 20 years involves women's high voter turnout.

19. Political socialization involves the influences and experiences that lead people to define themselves as either politically conservative or liberal.

20. Sociologists have developed two models for analyzing power in the United States—the power-elite model and the pluralist model.

21. The state has a monopoly over the use of legitimate force—the police for internal order and the military for external defense. Historically, the American military has been guided by the ideal of the civilian-soldier, but since 1973 it has been composed of volunteers.

22. The military-industrial complex is a dominant feature of our economy and of our foreign trade.

23. Although the threat of nuclear war has receded somewhat recently, the absolute number of weapons available to the United States and the Soviet Union continues to feed fears of an accidental outbreak of war.

SUGGESTED READINGS

Acheson, James M. *The Lobster Gangs of Maine.* Hanover, NH: University Press of New England, 1988. The importance of a balance between cooperation and competition, mutual aid and sharing, and self-interest in the lobster industry.

Ashton, David N. *Employment under Capitalism: The Sociology of British and American Labor Markets.* Westport, CT: Greenwood, 1986. Differences in the locations of England and the United States in the international division of labor that produce different patterns of employment and unemployment.

Block, Fred. *Revising State Theory: Essays in Politics and Postindustrialism.* Philadelphia: Temple University Press, 1987. The political economy of postindustrialism, its new productive forces, and the existing relations of control.

Bose, Christine, Roslyn Feldberg, and Natalie Sokoloff, eds. *Hidden Aspects of Women's Work.* New York: Praeger, 1987. Recent research on labor and gender, focusing on issues of race, class, and ethnicity.

Brown, Michael K. ed. *Remaking the Welfare State: Retrenchment and Social Policy in America and Europe.* Philadelphia: Temple University Press, 1988. How the welfare state has come apart during the Reagan years in the United States and in Europe.

Dye, Thomas R. *Who's Running America.* 5th ed. Englewood Cliffs, NJ: Prentice-Hall, 1990. An overview of the networks among America's power elite.

Harrington, Michael. *Socialism: Past and Future.* New York: Arcade, 1989. The successes and failures of socialism in the United States and around the world.

Hill, David B., and Mary M. Ken. *Election Demographics.* Washington, DC: Population Reference Bureau, 1988. The major factors involved in campaigns, voting, forecasting results, and the impact of demographics on elections.

Jackall, Robert. *Moral Mazes: The World of Corporate Managers.* New York: Oxford, University Press, 1988. Based on hundreds of interviews: how managers survive.

Kallberg, Arne L., and Ivar Berg. *Work and Industry: Structures, Markets, and Processes.* New York: Plenum, 1987. A set of matrices for examining the structures of work and markets.

Laudon, Kenneth C. *Dossier Society: Value Choices in the Design of National Information Systems.* New York: Columbia University Press, 1986. Threats to democracy posed by computing and telecommunication systems that enable government to control the lives of American citizens.

Portes, Alejandro, and John Walton. *Labor, Class, and the International System.* New York: Academic Press, 1988. Analysis of empirical research dealing with migration, modes of production, and social class structure in periphery and core countries.

Rothschild, Joyce, and J. Allen Whitt. *The Cooperative Workplace: Potentials and Dilemmas of Organizational Democracy and Participation.* New York: Cambridge University Press, 1986. Small alternative organizations committed to collective and democratic decision making.

Zuboff, Shoshana. *In the Age of the Machine: The Future of Work and Power.* New York: Basic, 1988. A study of the computerized workplace.

Zurcher, Louis, Milton L. Boykin, and Hardy L. Merritt, eds. *Citizen-Sailors in a Changing Society: Policy Issues for Manning the United States Naval Reserve.* Westport, CT: Greenwood, 1986. The changing role of the citizen-sailor in an era of an all-volunteer force.

11

Educational and Religious Systems

EDUCATION

In 1925 a public school teacher in Dayton, Tennessee, named John Scopes, was arrested for teaching Darwin's theory of evolution in violation of state law. After a famous trial, Scopes was found guilty and fined $100. The Tennessee Supreme Court later overturned the conviction on the grounds that the fine was too high but left the law standing. Sixty-one years later, in 1987, the Supreme Court of the United States ruled that states could not be required to teach the biblical story of creation along with material on evolution. Yet attempts are still being made at the state level for "equal time" for the creation view (Mydans, 1989).

Throughout our history the schools have been a battleground of competing interests. In the 1960s and 1970s, civil rights and feminist groups criticized textbooks for racist and sexist biases. In 1987 close to two-thirds of all U.S. schools reported receiving objections from community groups over teaching materials (People for the American Way, 1987). Particular targets were sex education courses in general, certain school plays, literary works such as *The Grapes of Wrath* and *Death of a Salesman*, and sociology textbooks. In most cases, the parents claimed that their religious freedom was being infringed by having their children exposed to "unchristian" concepts, especially the idea that values can be relative rather than absolute standards of good or evil (Hechinger, 1986).

As a major institutional sphere of any society, education is linked to other structures—the family, the economy, the polity, and the belief system—so that the schools often reflect the tensions generated in other parts of the society (Reese, 1986).

FUNCTIONS OF EDUCATION

Education extends the socialization process that starts in the family. Because family members often cannot teach all that a child needs to know, other agents of the society take over the task of presenting specialized knowledge. In simple gathering bands, both boys and girls learn very similar skills by watching and imitating older children or adults. In more complex societies with specialized occupations, family members may be able to retain control over certain skills, as in apprenticeship programs. Still other jobs require long periods of special training. The earliest schools were developed for such tasks: for scribes in Egypt and China, philosophers in Greece, and priests in Judea. In modern industrial societies, all children are expected to spend most of their youth in formal educational institutions.

Educational systems in complex societies are also charged with the societal goal of promoting unity within the collectivity. The assumption is that if all children learn the same basics—language, values, and beliefs—there will be fundamental agreement on societal goals ("value consensus"). Many of the functions of education are **manifest**, that is, stated and intended goals such as transmitting the culture to newcomers (whether children or immigrants), training people for adult roles, developing skills, and creating new knowledge.

Schools also serve **latent** functions, that is, there are consequences of

Manifest functions of education are its stated and intended goals.

Latent functions are consequences of the educational process that are not part of its stated and intended goals.

the educational process that are not part of its stated or intended goals. For example, extending the years of schooling and mandating attendance provides a massive societal baby-sitting service and controls the flow of young people into the job market.

Manifest Functions

Transmitting the Culture.   Because of the great diversity of our society, it is not easy to define American culture as a single entity (see Chapter 2). Finding common ground is made even more difficult by our educational system, which is based on local control by school boards in more than 16,000 separate districts representing diverse populations. As a consequence, the task of presenting a standard version of school material has fallen to the writers and publishers of textbooks.

The economics of textbook publishing also play a part. Publishers are eager to produce books that will sell in all parts of the country, and to do so involves offending the fewest number of school board members and parents. One solution is simply to omit discussions of controversial issues, such as world hunger, the women's movement, and, of course, evolution.

Thus, the culture that is transmitted is typically colorless and weighted toward the *status quo* (things as they are), downplaying conflict and dissent and defining inequality as a personal problem. The books reflect the world of those who have done well, a world from which many students are excluded and to which many are made to feel inferior (Bourdieu and Passeron, 1977; Friere, 1985).

Schools function to prepare children for adult roles in the community, family, and workplace, whether in India or the United States. What might these children be learning in this classroom in India?

Acculturation of Immigrants.   During the great waves of European immigration between 1880 and 1920, it was the city school systems that were to be the "melting pots" in which diverse ethnics or their children would learn English, lose their uniqueness, and pick up the skills needed for industrial employment. Because these were decades of enormous economic growth, with the job market absorbing millions of entry-level workers, the schools were relatively successful as avenues of mobility. But not all children entered the public schools or stayed for long. Today, however, the schools must accept almost all students, keep them longer, and send them into a changed job market.

Training for Adult Statuses.   The schools also function to prepare children to accept their eventual roles in community, family, and the workplace. From the first day in school to the last, students receive instruction in conformity, good work habits, and respect for status superiors. Young people are also presented with direct and indirect training in traditional family roles. Although schoolbooks have moved away from idealized images of suburban family life, they are far from portraying modern realities.

Socialization to work roles is both general (obedience, punctuality, discipline) and particular (by dividing students into college preparatory and vocational categories). *Vocational education* is still largely sex segregated and targeted to children from the working class, whereas middle-class youth are typically placed in the college-preparatory courses. Similar patterns are found in many modern societies characterized by racial/ethnic stratification (Shavit, 1990).

Latent Functions

The **hidden curriculum** refers to what is learned, such as ethnocentrism and respect for authority, but is not part of the official curriculum.

Each manifest function also has unacknowledged, if not necessarily unintended, consequences. The term **hidden curriculum** refers to the unannounced lessons that a student learns such as ethnocentrism and respect for authority. In American schools, children may also learn lessons in anticommunism, homophobia, competitiveness, and a belief in the superiority of nonmanual labor. Many critics charge that these latent functions are actually the heart of schooling. Learning to know one's place, to obey superiors, to believe that the system is fair, are lessons that last a lifetime. Thus, the educational system is a channel of social placement, gatekeeper to the occupational system, sorting students into "winners" and "losers" at an early age.

FUNCTIONAL AND CONFLICT PERSPECTIVES ON EDUCATION AND STRATIFICATION

Meritocracy is a hierarchy of talent, in which rewards are based on one's abilities and credentials.

A central element of the American value system is the belief that the schools offer an equal opportunity for individual talent to be identified and nurtured. By offering each child a "free" (publicly funded) education, the schools will become an impartial link between ability and mobility. From the functional view, then, schools encourage competition in order to separate the best students from the less able, thus creating a hierarchy of intelligence, or a **meritocracy,** based primarily on an individual's innate talent. The underlying assumptions are that (1) school personnel can accurately identify bright and dull students, (2) standardized tests are an objective means for achieving this goal, and (3) differences in test scores reflect innate differences in intellectual functioning. The basic premise is that given an equal opportunity to learn, unequal outcomes are the result of personal qualities.

Both functional and conflict theorists see the educational system as a "filtering process" that channels students into particular programs and academic careers. However, from the conflict perspective, with its focus on the hidden curriculum, analyses suggest that

- Schools sort students into winners and losers on the basis of *nonacademic* variables such as race, gender, and social class (Apple, 1986).
- The educational system is designed to reproduce inequality, in support of the existing economic system (Bowles and Gintis, 1977; Freire, 1986).
- A belief in meritocratic selection leads people who do not succeed to blame themselves for their failure.
- The approved "culture" as reflected in curriculum and textbooks works to *delegitimize* other ways of perceiving (Bourdieu, 1984).
- Middle-class parents are able to secure privileges for their children in contrast to the relative powerlessness of lower-strata parents with children in the same schools (Sieber, 1981).

The Evidence

Most evidence suggests that the United States has a long way to go before the claim of a meritocracy can be supported (Krauze and Slomcyznski, 1985). In general, for example, children from the middle and upper social strata score higher on standardized tests and are likely to remain in school longer, regardless of their test scores, than do other children.

In addition to the direct benefits that family wealth can provide for upper- and middle-class students, there are a number of indirect mechanisms through which social class is translated into academic advantage: tracking, accumulated cultural capital, parental expectations, and structural features of the family such as size and composition.

Tracking. Today's students are assigned to **tracks,** or "ability groups," and are exposed to programs of varying content and pacing at increasingly earlier ages. A single school class will therefore be divided into several levels that often coincide with social-class background. This track placement, in turn, affects the quality and length of education received by the student (Gamoran and Mare, 1989; Natriello et al., 1989).

Tracks are programs of varying content and pacing, to which students are assigned.

Tracking appears to be deeply entrenched even though evidence suggests that methods such as peer tutoring are more effective (Fiske, 1990; Carnegie Corporation, 1989). In part, the popularity of ability grouping reflects the widespread belief in the existence of "intelligence" within an individual, rather than human potentials generated and expressed through interaction.

Cultural Capital. Quite apart from their financial resources, which can be used to purchase tutoring or private schooling, wealthier parents also transmit

Cultural capital refers to a style of talking and thinking as well as knowledge of music, art, and literature that prepares individuals for membership in the dominant strata.

cultural capital (Bourdieu, 1984; Dimaggio, 1982). Cultural capital refers to a style of talking and thinking, as well as knowledge of music, art, and literature that allows a person to feel comfortable in intellectual settings and to understand the world defined by dominant elites. The cultural and educational resources of the family determine how long a student stays in the school system, as well as how successfully she or he performs (Teachman, 1987; Lamb, 1989). Family influence on children's work habits has an important influence on a teacher's perception of the student's ability, which then affects the pupil's grades (Farkas et al., 1990).

Achievement Expectations.   As we noted in Chapter 4, the use of "psychological" rather than physical disciplining techniques by middle-class parents leads to internalized guilt and high-achievement motivation in their children (Looker and Pineo, 1983). Because middle-class parents have more control over their environment, they can make "deferred gratification" pay off; their offspring know this, in contrast to children from low-income families who accurately perceive their parents' relative lack of social power.

Family Size.   Middle-class students also benefit from having fewer siblings than is typical for working-class families. Since children develop verbal and cognitive skills through interaction with parents, those from small families spend more time with parents than with peers and siblings (Zajonc, 1986; but see Ernst and Angst, 1983).

Family size often outweighs the effect of social class, as seen in the achievement of working-class youth from small families (Alwin and Thornton, 1984; Blake, 1985). If this is so, then the general societal trend toward small families should weaken the advantages currently enjoyed by middle-class students.

Household Composition.   In addition to its size, the composition of a household has an effect on school grades. In general, children from households with two parents do better on cognitive tests than do children from households headed by a single parent. In large part, these differences are more related to low income and its problems rather than to living with one parent. Yet teacher's perceptions of a child's ability and the grades given for classroom performance are typically lower for children in single-parent families and higher for those from intact families (Thompson et al., 1988). Research indicates that two *adults,* not necessarily marriage partners, are able to provide a child with more supervision and educational experiences than is one parent, and consequently to convey higher achievement expectations. These expectations are translated into higher school grades. And because of the link between social class and household composition, middle-class youngsters receive an additional advantage.

For all these reasons, then, regardless of ability, youth from the higher social strata compared to other students, do better in school, stay there longer, and are ultimately prepared to move into higher-status occupations. Educational attainment has long-term positive effects on earnings and cognitive development, and the longer one stays in school, the greater the benefits (Natriello et al., 1989; Cutler, 1989).

THE STRUCTURE OF THE AMERICAN EDUCATIONAL SYSTEM

In all modern industrial societies, education has become increasingly *differentiated* and *specialized,* moving from the one-room schoolhouse to today's elementary, intermediate, junior high, and high schools. Knowledge is similarly separated into categories, to be taught by specialists. Eventually, students are expected to choose one distinct package of information (their "major") that will prepare them for the world of work. This career specialization is most marked at the **postsecondary** (after high school) level.

Postsecondary education takes place after high school.

Inclusiveness

The American education system is **inclusive,** so that almost all children ages 5 to 16 are currently enrolled. The American high school provides a general ("comprehensive") education, although within the schools students are often channeled into college-preparatory and vocational tracks.

The American education system is **inclusive***, or open, to almost all children of given ages.*

Before Kindergarten.   *Pre*kindergarten schooling is on the increase, for children of both the poor and the wealthy (Fiske, 1986). For disadvantaged children, Head Start and similar programs are designed to remedy the lack of cultural capital in their homes and neighborhoods. For offspring of the well-to-do, early childhood education is seen as a means of encouraging cognitive development. Many schools now run half- and even full-day programs for three and four-year-olds, which is a great help to both dual-earner parents and single parents.

As one might expect, Head Start programs for disadvantaged children differ in many ways from preschools for children of the middle class, with the former stressing cooperation and group activities and the latter greater individualism and relationships to adults (Lubeck, 1985). Educational experts are almost unanimous in praising Head Start and similar efforts. But they are much less enthusiastic about preschool experiences designed to speed up the cognitive growth of middle-class children, which accelerate peer competition and parental pressures along the way.

After Graduation.   Education does not stop at high-school or college graduation. Millions of Americans are enrolled in adult education classes, both academic and vocational, and thousands more are part-time college students. In all, one in four Americans today is enrolled in school.

Educational Attainment.   As a result of the trend toward inclusiveness, the percent of young adults (ages 25 to 29) who completed high school has risen dramatically since 1940: from 11.5 percent to 86 percent in 1988. In the same period, the proportion completing four or more years of college rose from 10.2 percent to 23.6 percent (*Statistical Abstract,* 1989, pp. 130–131).

Indeed, the proportion of Americans age 25 and over who have had any college education—about 40 percent—is the highest in the world. Over the past two decades, differences in educational attainment by race, sex, and age have decreased, but income differences among people with different levels of education have increased.

Each year, some students will drop out for one reason or another. Consider the collective career of pupils entering kindergarten in 1975. For every 100 who entered fifth grade in 1980, close to 90 entered high school. Over the next four years, another 10 left because of academic failure, employment opportunities, pregnancy, and/or marriage. Approximately 80 of the original 100 graduated from high school, and almost 40 percent of these entered college, but only half will complete their studies by 1991. Although half of the college dropouts will eventually return and earn degrees, this means that only 1 in 4 of the original 100 will become a college graduate. Nonetheless, these figures are an impressive improvement from 50 years ago, when only one-third of the class would graduate from high school.

IQ, Test Scores, and Race

Some social scientists (for example, Jensen, 1981) believe that the abilities measured by standardized tests of intelligence are largely inherited. Therefore, they claim, consistent differences in test scores between white and African-American children can be used as evidence of a basic inherited difference in intellectual capacity. Most scientists, however, argue that there are few, if any, inborn, biologically based differences by race (or religion or ethnic background), even though each person is different from any other. Intelligence is not a single trait but a bundle of capacities that people have in different combinations and strengths at various ages. Moreover, reported IQ differences refer to *group* averages and not individual differences. Conclusions about the intellectual abilities of any racial or ethnic group are probably more *political* than scientific. Nonetheless, IQ tests have increasingly come to be regarded as scientific measures of intelligence, and they are used to identify and separate children of varying abilities. Yet, one careful review of existing theories and data concluded that inherited differences may account for some variation among American whites in average or better-than-average homes, but that cognitive differences by race are largely the result of cultural and life-style factors. Other research has shown that early intervention can dramatically affect the subsequent development of intellectual skills, as seen in the long-term gains registered by some Head Start children in the United States (Carmody, 1988).

A review of national education tests between 1969 and 1980 found strong gains in the performance of African-American students, which were attributed to a belief that schooling would lead to career options that simply were not available before (Burton and Jones, 1982). From 1980 to 1988, test scores for African-American and Latino students rose more sharply than those for white students at all ages (Daniels, 1990). Other educators agree that federal and state assistance (including hot meals) to low-income school districts and needy children have had a measurable positive effect on school grades and test scores. Nonetheless, federal and state funding for these programs has been greatly reduced in recent years, an early victim of cost-cutting and anti-tax sentiments.

Public and Private Systems

Another structural feature of American education is the existence of two separate school systems: one supported by public taxes and open to all, the other paid for by private fees and selective in admissions. Today, approximately 15 percent of elementary and secondary school students attend private schools.

Parochial Schools.   By far the largest number of private schools are church related, or **parochial** (meaning confined to the parish). The most extensive parochial school system in the United States is operated by the Roman Catholic Church, encompassing about 9,000 elementary and high schools, with an enrollment of 2.5 million students. As large as these figures may seem, they are one-third smaller than the size of the Catholic school system only two decades ago. This decline is largely the result of the movement of Catholics out of central cities and the rising costs of school operation.

> **Parochial schools** are private schools operated by religious organizations.

The fastest-growing sector in parochial education today is the American Christian school system, operated by Protestant churches; its enrollment doubled between 1970 and 1980 and is still increasing (National Center for Education Statistics, 1989).

Preparatory Schools.   The latent functions of private education are especially important in a majority of the 20 percent of nonpublic schools that are not church related. Such schools offer expensive and academically rigorous educations, usually away from home, in preparation for entry into elite colleges and occupations (hence the term **preparatory**).

> **Preparatory schools** are private schools developed to prepare children of well-off parents for entry into elite colleges.

This socialization experience prepares primarily upper-strata students for assuming positions of power in the society—through the curriculum, which builds on and extends the cultural capital of upper-status individuals; the sports programs, which emphasize both competitiveness and teamwork; the role models provided by the teachers, themselves often well-educated members of the upper-middle class; and, above all, formal and informal rituals that reinforce a sense of superiority and service as members of a privileged class (Cookson and Persell, 1985). These elements compose what the researchers call a "moral education," through which students develop high levels of self-esteem and confidence, and learn to justify their positions of power.

Public Schools.   The other 85 percent of American schoolchildren attend one of 86,000 elementary and secondary schools financed out of local taxes. The history of public education in America illustrates the interplay of values, economic interests, and educational opportunity.

In the nineteenth century, many public schools were selective in their admissions (Labarree, 1984); at the same time large numbers of young people simply failed to attend, mostly because their labor was needed for the family's economic survival (Walters and O'Connell, 1988). Between 1870 and 1940, however, a major effort was made to upgrade the qualifications of teachers, to remove administrative jobs from political influence, and to expand enrollments—reforms that were more successful in the major cities, than in small towns. Eventually, however, the public school system was reformed and today is characterized by compulsory attendance, acceptance of all but a few severely disabled children, professionalized teaching staff, and democratically elected school boards.

Educational Quality.   Are there major differences in the quality of education offered by public and private schools? One influential study (Coleman et al., 1982) has reported higher achievement-test scores for private school students compared with those in the public system, but these findings have been criticized by other sociologists on various grounds (e.g., Crain and Howley, 1982; Heyns, 1986). It is unclear whether the test-score differences reflect the fact that private schools can screen out difficult students, or are the product of what is taught and how. Public schools, even those in low-income areas, often operate as effectively as private schools.

INSIDE THE SCHOOLS

The functions and structure of the educational system are macrolevel topics. But schooling actually takes place at the microlevel—in face-to-face interaction among students and teachers in specific classrooms and institutions. These interactions compose the social system of the classroom. Yet this system cannot be understood without reference to the enduring values of our culture: success, achievement, competition, individualism. From the beginning, children learn that their own success depends on the failure of others. Because there can be few best pupils, students compete with one another; thus, the recognition of hierarchy and stratification is built into the school experience. Typical teaching styles reinforce dependence on authority, straight-line thinking, hands-off learning, and passivity (Goodlad, 1983; McNeil, 1986). To some analysts (Sedlak et al., 1986), it appears that a bargain has been struck whereby many students agree to behave reasonably well in return for not being greatly challenged.

Suburban Schools

Schools in middle-class suburbs have been very successful in encouraging self-discipline, conformity, and a taste for competition. Their graduates enter and complete college at relatively high rates. Yet for some the suburban high school is a place where boredom rules and where the student body is fragmented into subcultures of jocks, nerds, rah-rahs, skins, deadheads, and others too bored even to form a subculture (Larkin, 1979). This fragmentation of the students works to the advantage of administrators in maintaining order; meanwhile, it prepares students for a lifetime of political apathy and obedience, concentrating their energies on personal relationships.

Urban Schools

The relatively motivated students, concerned parents, and favorable financial conditions of suburbia are less likely to be present in today's inner-city schools. Unlike the past, city schools today must absorb more children of the

In 1981, wealthy businessman Eugene Lang encouraged a group of sixth graders to stay in school by promising to finance their college educations if they graduated from high school. Eight years later, the school that previously had a drop out rate of 75 percent, now graduated most students from high school with close to one-half of such graduates in college. Lang is pictured with two of the students who benefited from his offer.

very poor, keep them in school longer, and send them into declining blue-collar labor markets. The buildings have continued to deteriorate, experienced teachers have chosen to work in other districts, and the neighborhoods are made hazardous by gangs of unemployed youth. Powerless parents have difficulty in imparting a sense of high expectations to their children.

Despite such obstacles, urban education can work when the following conditions are present: (1) strong administrative leadership, (2) a climate of expectation in which no child would be allowed to fall behind, (3) an orderly but not oppressive atmosphere, (4) small size, (5) fair and effective disciplining—precisely the characteristics that give a scholastic advantage to students from private schools (Carnegie Corporation, 1986; Lee and Bryk, 1989).

Dropping Out. Approximately 10 percent of high school students do not complete the full four years; the drop-out volume is especially high in inner-city schools, where one-third to one-half the students leave or are pushed out by school authorities. On the one hand, this process clears the schools of the "difficult cases" who are hard to teach and discipline, which should improve the educational chances of remaining students. On the other hand, it leaves the youngsters most in need of remedial academic services with no help at all.

The drop-out rate among Latino students is exceptionally high, particularly for older pupils and for females (Velez, 1989). For example, in 1987, 40 percent of Latinos ages 25 to 29 had stopped their education at less than four years of high school, compared to 14 percent for all Americans in that age category (*Statistical Abstract*, 1989, p. 131). One consequence is a much lower literacy rate for Latino young adults and related long-term economic disadvantage (Olneck and Kim, 1989).

Teachers' Expectations

The self-fulfilling prophecy has long been assumed to exist: the way in which teachers react to students will influence the pupils' scholastic achievement. The research evidence, however, is not altogether consistent on the strength of this effect or how it is achieved. There is, however, ample evidence that teachers often react to a student on the basis of such ascribed characteristics as race, religion, ethnicity, social class, and gender (Wilkinson and Marrett, 1985). For example, teachers tend to treat girls and boys quite differently—to the detriment of both (Marland, 1984). In the early grades, school personnel reward girls for their ability to sit quietly and for their verbal skills, thus making life very uncomfortable for the boys, who squirm more and are less articulate. At the higher grades, however, particularly in working- and lower-middle-class districts, the system rewards boys in terms of career interests and encouragement to explore their environment, leaving the girls ignored and relatively powerless.

With respect to class and race, the crucial variable appears to be the fit between social class status of students and teachers (Alexander et al., 1987). High-status teachers, regardless of race, tend to perceive lower-income and minority pupils as relatively immature, to expect low performance from them, and to grade accordingly. African-American children are most affected by this process, becoming caught in a spiral of failure, low expectation, and more failure.

In addition, African-American adolescents are singled out for punishment much more frequently than their white classmates at the same level of self-reported deviance (McCarthy and Hoge, 1987). The key variable was teachers' perceptions based on students' past records. Once a student is differentially sanctioned, the stigma persists throughout the school career, and the academic disadvantages accumulate over time.

Can Schools and Classrooms Learn?

Cooperative learning occurs when students pool talents and help one another.

Children learn under specific circumstances, and manipulating the structure of the school and classroom will produce clear results. Research findings are striking and consistent, and very different from the philosophy that has traditionally governed American education: **Cooperative learning** is more effective than competition or ability grouping in raising student performance. When pupils pool talents and help one another to learn, students at *all* ability levels show improved test scores (Metz, 1986). This also frees the teacher to introduce increasingly sophisticated material to classrooms with large numbers of disadvantaged students (Cohen et al., 1989). In this same vein, the Carnegie Corporation (1989) report on early adolescent education proposed the following changes:

- Make schools smaller. If the district cannot redesign the existing system, then minischools of 200 to 300 pupils should be established within larger schools.
- Assign each student to an adult who has the time to talk with the youngster.
- Encourage small groups of students to work together to solve problems.
- Organize teachers into teams with authority to revise schedules and curriculum.
- Support student volunteer work in the community.
- Abolish tracking in favor of peer tutoring.
- Involve parents in their children's schooling.

ILLITERACY

A large number of Americans are unable to read or write adequately to function in a modern industrial society. Just how many people are *illiterate* is a matter of some debate. The most recent Bureau of the Census report (1986) places the illiteracy rate at 13 percent of American adults, or roughly 26 million persons age 14 and over.

Other researchers put the figure even higher. One critic of the American educational system (Kozol, 1986), uses the figure of 60 million, or one-third of all adults, as being incapable of handling such important tasks as reading the labels on aspirin bottles, the want ads in newspapers, or even instructions for public transportation.

According to a recent report from the Department of Education, most Americans age 21 to 25 are able to read as well as the average fourth grader, which is the technical measure of literacy. Beyond that, however, there is widespread "functional illiteracy," with four-fifths of the sample—and these are our most recently educated adults—unable to handle a bus schedule and nine-tenths incapable of correctly filling out a mail-order form (Kirsch and Jungeblut, 1986).

Regardless of which numbers turn out to be accurate, the level of illiteracy in our society is shockingly high. The cost—in illness, crime, unemployment, poor workmanship, wasted talent—is not easy to calculate. The federal government response, in terms of money spent on the problem, has been minimal—up to $160 million in 1989, or roughly $6.00 for each person requiring literacy training. The states will spend an additional $200 million, or $7.70 per person.

A larger role is now being played by American industry worried about the skills of its workers, as well as by private charitable agencies and programs such as Operation Read and Literacy Volunteers of America (Daniels, 1988).

Sources: Kozol, 1986; Rohter, 1986; U.S. Bureau of the Census, 1986; Kirsch and Jungeblut, 1986; Daniels, 1988.

HIGHER EDUCATION

Functions and Structure

The primary manifest functions of higher education are (1) transmission of existing knowledge, (2) production of new information, and (3) preparation of the next generation of scholars. As a consequence of the increasing **specialization of knowledge,** universities are organized into relatively discrete units—departments, programs, schools, divisions—on the basis of particular "bundles" of knowledge (B. Clark, 1983). These units enjoy a wide degree of autonomy (self-direction), as only peers can judge another's work. Yet the entire institution must be able to operate as a unified whole, which is the job of the administration. This dilemma leads to some tension between the faculty's need for academic freedom and the administration's concern with institutional survival.

The administration does not, however, operate in a vacuum. Although *private* colleges and universities are relatively independent—financed pri-

The increasing **specialization of knowledge** in universities and colleges leads to relatively discrete units of organization.

marily by student fees, alumni gifts, and an accumulated endowment fund—they are under nominal control of a board of trustees and are bound by some government guidelines if they receive any federal aid. Even private schools must adapt to the community in which they are located.

Public institutions—state colleges and universities, and the community colleges—in contrast, are largely funded by tax dollars allocated by state and county legislatures and so are more vulnerable to political pressures than are the private schools. Thus, many public colleges and universities have invested heavily in programs of special concern to state and local industries or have avoided offending business interests, as when the university of a tobacco-growing state rescinded a campus no-smoking plan after state legislators threatened to cut funding (*New York Times,* November 25, 1988, p. A25). Public colleges also benefit by having nationally ranked athletic teams (Hochfield, 1986).

For both private and public universities, the need to find revenues from sources other than government or rising tuition fees has led to an increased emphasis on research. Universities are contracting with private business for the commercial marketing of technology developed in the university laboratories (Ehrenfield et al., 1987; Rule, 1988; Daniels, 1989; Etzkowitz, 1988; Weiner, 1989). This trend raises two issues: (1) ought not the results of publicly funded research be publicly owned? and (2) the essence of the scientific method is full disclosure, but information is held secret when patents are owned by private companies.

Stratification within Higher Education.   Institutions of higher education in the United States form a ranked hierarchy. At the top are a handful of private universities (e.g., Harvard, Princeton, Yale), followed by elite private colleges (e.g., Amherst, Vassar, Dartmouth), state universities, state colleges, and, at the base, the community colleges. The more highly ranked the institution, the higher are both its fees and standards of admission. As might be expected, the proportion of students or faculty who are female, minority, or of working-class origins is higher as institutional prestige declines.

The Faculty

The faculty is also stratified on the basis of *academic rank:* distinguished professor, full professor, associate professor, assistant professor, instructor. Promotions and tenure (job security) depend on years of service and quantity and quality of publications. Except in community colleges, teaching skills are rarely a major factor; indeed, the higher the academic rank, the *fewer* hours spent in classroom teaching.

Faculties also reflect the *race* and *gender* stratification systems of the larger society. There are very few Latinos and African-Americans—perhaps 1 percent of the faculty in predominantly white institutions, with only a handful at the highest ranks. These figures are actually *down* from a peak in the late 1970s and will not rise soon because the number of African-Americans in graduate schools has also declined. As long as median salaries for professors remain in the $40,000–$49,000 range, college teaching will not be an extremely attractive choice for talented, upwardly mobile minority youth.

The question of why there are so few faculty women has been hotly debated. On one hand are those who contend that the absence of women in high ranks reflects their lower level of scholarly productivity, probably because of competition from their family obligations (e.g., Cole, 1979). On the other hand, a growing body of research finds little difference in either the quantity or quality of women's and men's publications, once you take into account the fact that male professors are more likely to have been at their jobs for a longer period of time and to be at institutions that demand and support scholarly research.

But even if all else were equal, the merit system does not operate impartially (Persell, 1984; Theodore, 1986; Richardson and Kaufman, 1982). It is easier for male graduate students to find a mentor and to be recommended for posts at high-ranked institutions. Despite dramatic gains over the past 20 years in the numbers of women faculty and in their proportion at the higher ranks, women graduate students continue to have difficulty finding senior sponsors (Solomon, 1986) or doing so without being subjected to sexual harassment (Glaser and Thorpe, 1986). In addition, women are no more likely to hold administrative positions today than they were in the early 1900s (Shakeshaft, 1987).

The Graying of the Faculty.   Because relatively few full-time faculty have been hired over the past decade, the average age of the teaching staff has been rising. In order to open up more opportunities for junior faculty and to cut salary costs, a number of schools are offering inducements for senior faculty to take early retirement.

Even so, most faculties are top-heavy with older tenured teachers, leading to a possible *shortage* of highly qualified full-time faculty in the next decade (Fiske 1989; Hill, 1989). Thus, it is possible that college teaching will once more become an attractive option for young intellectuals.

The Student Body

In 1990 approximately 12.8 million men and women were enrolled in one of more than 3,000 degree-granting institutions of higher education in the United States. While this represents an increase of 40 percent since 1970, the number of college students may decline slightly in the future as a reflection of lowered fertility since the late 1960s. Some of the new collegians are high school graduates taking advantage of affordable higher education in community colleges; others are having difficulty finding jobs with adequate pay and mobility prospects without a college degree; and a large number are returning to complete interrupted educational careers.

These trends have created greater diversity within the student body than in the past, specifically an increase in older students, women, and people of color. In terms of age, approximately 40 percent of college students today are age 25 or older, raising the median age of students to over 21, the age at which many had graduated in the past.

Racial Diversity.   The presence of people of color in the student body has increased from 10 to 18 percent of the total since 1985. But while Asian enrollments continued to rise in the 1980s, those for African-Americans increased modestly for women but dropped sharply for men, as Figure 11-1 shows (American Council on Education, 1989).

African-American enrollments are not evenly distributed across the academic spectrum; large numbers attend two-year rather than four-year institutions, and about one-third have chosen predominantly minority schools in the South (Center for Education Statistics, 1989). In general, African-American men perform best in colleges where they are the majority, while women of color are more successful in predominantly white, co-ed schools (Fleming, 1984).

The decline in both African-American male and Latino enrollments can be traced to severe cutbacks in financial aid programs during the Reagan years, coupled with rising costs. Because these trends reduce the overall supply of minority students, the most highly qualified will be heavily recruited by elite institutions.

But many high-ranking institutions will have great difficulty recruiting minority students because of outbreaks of racism both in the past and present. Some white students born after the civil rights drama of the 1960s resent what they consider preferential treatment for African-American students, while the latter are angered over what they perceive as insensitivity on the part of nonminority students, faculty, and administrators.

Gender. As noted in Chapter 7, the 1980s witnessed a major shift in the gender composition of the campus, with women enrolling in greater numbers than men. Despite their generally lower SAT scores, women college students' academic performance equals and often surpasses that of their male classmates, even though their education will bring fewer rewards in income and occupational status (Mickelson, 1989).

Once welcome only at "women's colleges," female students today are everywhere, even on traditionally elite male campuses. Although women who attend predominantly women's colleges are more likely than graduates of other schools to enjoy high career accomplishment (Rice and Hemmings,

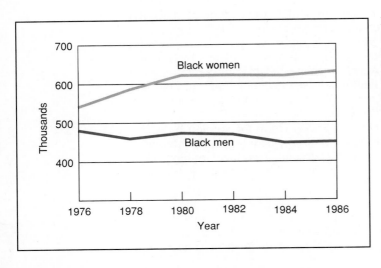

FIGURE 11-1 The number of black men and women in colleges and universities each year, 1976–86. (Sources: American Council on Education, Office of Minority Concerns, graph in the *New York Times*, February 5, 1989.)

1988), it is not clear whether the effect is related to campus characteristics (less competition from men, same-sex role models, lower probability of sexual harassment, and the opportunity to receive leadership training) or some selection factor, whereby high achievers apply to these schools.

Social Class. The enrollment gains of women and minority students since 1965 can be traced to pressures on the schools from civil rights organizations. Thus far, no similar groups have pushed for increased admission of working-class youth in general (Karen and McClelland, 1983). Indeed, the trend since the early 1980s has been in the opposite direction, as federal financial aid has dropped and costs have soared.

As you can see from Table 11-1, fees at some elite institutions equal *half* the median income of all American households. Tuition costs at state universities are considerably lower, especially for residents, and lower still at the state and community college level. This means that, regardless of ability, children from large families and those at the low- or moderate-income levels will be enrolled in the less prestigious institutions, although they will not necessarily receive a lower-quality education.

Even given these very high fees for private colleges the investment in education is worthwhile: employers see a diploma as a sign of ambition and self-discipline, and the degree from a private institution carries that much more clout. In other words, the longer you stay in college, the higher the income return throughout your worklife.

Higher education is a primary factor in the maintenance of the social-stratification system of any modern society (Useem and Karabal, 1986). In both the United States and England, graduates of preparatory schools and selective private colleges and universities are disproportionately represented in the ranks of religious, economic, political, and social leaders. Until the late 1940s high-ranked universities such as Harvard and Yale systematically excluded Jews and Catholics from their faculty and carefully controlled the proportions of these groups admitted as undergraduates (Oren, 1985; Synnott, 1979), thereby serving as gatekeepers to the power elite.

In other European countries and in Japan, a few public universities with rigorous admissions standards serve the same screening function (e.g., Mihiyara, 1988). The process of educational stratification also characterizes Communist countries, where entry into the leading institutions of higher education is tilted toward the offspring of highly placed officials and Communist party members (Taubman, 1986). In the United States attending *any* college has

TABLE 11-1   Fees for Tuition, Room, and Board, 1989–90, in Selected Private Colleges and Universities

Brandeis	$20,101
Bennington	19,975
New York University	19,630
Barnard	19,413
Dartmouth	19,335
Yale	19,310
Harvard/Radcliffe	18,380

historically been more strongly associated with family income than with high school grades, and the overall trend from 1980 on has been toward strengthening the link between family income and length of schooling.

The increased diversity of the student body and faculty has spurred heightened concern for broadening the curriculum to reflect the experience of previously excluded populations. This trend has led to a public debate among faculty members over what should be taught as "core curriculum." Many professors of philosophy and English literature believe that there is a basic set, or "canon," of books that represent the accumulated wisdom of Western civilization and that must not be neglected in the effort to include works from other traditions (e.g., Bloom, 1988). Most anthropologists and sociologists, however, believe that the goal of education is to open students' minds to a variety of cultures and worldviews, so that inclusiveness rather than exclusiveness will characterize the courses offered to undergraduates.

Community Colleges

Two-year public colleges were originally designed in the 1960s to fill two distinct goals: (1) to relieve some of the pressures of the expected baby-boom enrollments on the state university system and (2) to provide local industries with a reliable source of trained workers (Pincus, 1989). Responding to both needs, community colleges became the academic growth industry of the 1970s. Today there are more than 1,000 two-year public colleges, enrolling about 5 million students.

Some community colleges in cities and industrial areas, are primarily institutions of "higher voc ed" (Pincus, 1980), in which low-income students are prepared, at taxpayers' expense, for entry-level jobs in local industry (Dougherty, 1988). Other community colleges, in suburbs and wealthier areas, have maintained their college-transfer programs, but primarily for their white middle-class students. Even there, most students today are enrolled in the "career" courses: secretarial, computer science, business and accounting, me-

For millions of Americans, education continues throughout adulthood through evening and weekend college classes as well as nondegree adult education classes. The fastest growing segment of the educational market is adult education.

chanical technology, nursing, and the like. Critics claim that the schools actually *limit* rather than expand students' opportunities, "cooling out" the losers by giving the impression that they have had a chance to better themselves (Pincus, 1983; Weiss, 1985).

Nonetheless, community colleges have many advantages—low tuition, convenient locations, part-time programs, evening and weekend courses, and a student body far more varied in terms of race, ethnicity, age, and social class than found in a typical four-year college. But large numbers of students need remedial help in order to handle college-level material, which also benefits local businesses as well as enhancing individual competency.

CONTEMPORARY CONTROVERSY

Quality and Inequality

A major controversy in contemporary education centers on the perceived conflict betwen (1) educational *quality,* or what some people call the "pursuit of excellence" in individuals, and (2) *equality,* using the schools to promote social justice. These two goals need not be mutually exclusive, but they have come into conflict because of the limited resources available to the schools and because many Americans seem to believe that individual talents are not evenly distributed across racial and ethnic groups (see Kingston, 1986). In addition, the courts in many states have ruled that the property tax to fund local schools is unconstitutional because it denies equality in education guaranteed by state constitutions.

Schooling and Racial Equality.   The issue of racial equality illustrates the enduring tension between two aspects of the American value system: recognition of individual merit on the one hand, and social justice on the other. Can there ever be equal opportunity in education without major changes in neighborhood and family structures? Controversy over racial integration of the schools has revived political conflict between broad national goals and the tradition of local control of schools (J. L. Hochschild, 1984).

School Desegregation and Integration.   Before 1954 school systems throughout the country systematically denied equal educational opportunity to African-American students and teachers by drawing district lines that kept the races apart and then investing three to four times more money on white schools (Ravitch, 1983). In response to a legal challenge, the Supreme Court in 1954 declared that a racially segregated school system created by local authorities was, in and of itself, a violation of the constitutional guarantee of equal treatment under the law and that such systems must be dismantled "with all deliberate speed" *(Brown v. Board of Education of Topeka, Kansas).*

More than 35 years later, after much deliberation at a very slow pace, the record on desegregation is mixed. Southern school districts have gradually changed, but in the meantime thousands of white children have been taken out of the public school system and placed in private schools. In the North, where segregation had not been legally imposed, the schools were also becoming racially separated as white families moved from city to suburb. Thus, racial segregation of the schools has generally *increased* in many areas since 1970.

EDUCATION AS A PROCESS OF CHANGE

Margaret L. Andersen

Margaret L. Andersen is professor of sociology at the University of Delaware. She is the author of Thinking about Women: Sociological and Feminist Issues, *2d ed. (New York: Macmillan, 1988) and* Social Problems *(New York: Harper and Row, 1989), coauthored with Frank R. Scarpitti. She teaches courses on race, class, and gender and has won the University of Delaware's Excellence-in-Teaching Award. She is codirector of the American Sociological Association MOST (Minority Opportunity Summer Training) Program.*

My interests as a teacher are primarily in the areas of race relations and the sociology of sex and gender. I want students to understand how race, gender, and class shape all our experiences, not just the experiences of those who are the victims of inequality. My education has been critical to realizing the significance of these social categories, though it is the connection between my education and my personal experience that has helped me see their sociological importance.

I grew up the oldest child in a white, upwardly mobile middle-class family with working-class origins. I was one of the first in my family to go to college and the first to earn a Ph.D. My parents' and grandparents' aspirations for their children were the basis for much of my educational achievement. In 1958, my family moved from the urban neighborhood in Oakland, California, where I was born, to the small town of Rome in northwest Georgia. I was ten years old at the time and thought of this as a big adventure.

Moving to the South with little awareness of race relations was a profound experience for me—one that in many ways shaped my later path as a sociologist. I do not remember witnessing overt discrimination as a child in Oakland or being consciously aware of prejudice, but I am certain both were present, directed not only at African-Americans but also at Asian-Americans. Moving into the pre-1960s South, seeing separate water fountains and rest rooms for whites and "coloreds," and attending a completely segregated school system were shocking to me.

As a newcomer in the South, I was an outsider, labeled a Yankee by my white peers. I felt different, excluded, and uncomfortable but was very anxious to be accepted. I quickly learned that becoming accepted meant learning the racist ways of those around me. I tried to assimilate but was teased by my peers for "talking funny." I concentrated on doing well at school and tried to make friends. Now I realize how profoundly my race shaped those years, how my desire to fit in isolated me from the growing political consciousness of African-Americans and a few whites who were active in the Civil Rights Movement. A few years later, when I was in junior high school, my family moved again—this time to Boston, and though I was excited about going to a new part of the country, I once more worried about being accepted. I was still an outsider among my peers—only this time because I was perceived as a southerner. Teased again for the way I talked, I was nicknamed "Dixie," an identity I always found odd since I had never thought of myself as southern. The Boston public schools were not formally segregated—at least not in the way of the Georgia schools. But there was only one African-American student in my class—astonishing in a school of more than 2,000 students.

A few years later, my family returned to Georgia, where I finished my last two years of high school. It was during my senior year that the city schools were desegregated—that is, if you call the placement of 3 African-American students in a senior class of 164 students desegregation. Some of my white friends abruptly changed schools, moving to newly opened private schools. Other friends dropped out of class contests—afraid that they might be paired with one of the African-American students. I was learning the sociological lessons of the impact of racism on both African-Americans and whites.

Thus, throughout my education, I was surrounded by evidence of racial stratification in America. I think that my frequent moves—an outsider in both the North and the South—were the basis for much of my sociological imagination. But, it is also a feature of my white privilege that I acquired my conscious awareness of racism in an academic setting. As a college senior, I enrolled in an introductory sociology course—a group requirement chosen because "I liked people." That course encouraged me to think about the relevance of race, gender, and class in my life and in the society around me. I was lucky to have a teacher who taught us the lessons of C. Wright Mills—that the task of sociology is understanding the connection between history and biography.

It was in this introductory sociology course that my political and sociological imagination was born. Leaders from the Black Power and emerging feminist movements were guest speakers. I remember agreeing with what they said, despite the intense criticism of other students. Sociology was radical stuff to me, especially if you consider the historical context. Women were not allowed to wear pants to class; the dean of women daily roamed the halls with a measuring stick to make sure one's hemline was not too high above the knee! Sitting in that class was a sequence of awakenings. I began to see the structural origins of the connections between race and gender. I was fascinated by the prospect that sociologists could be paid to study what interested me about human life. When I learned that the salary of a graduate assistant was as much as I was earning as a full-time departmental secretary, I decided to begin graduate school.

I have learned that education can and should be a process of change—both within individuals and in society. I believe that education should provide the personal, intellectual, and material resources for people to live with and create change. Of course, change through education is often unrealized, since educational systems typically reinforce existing patterns of inequality. But, if education teaches us to understand the effects of race, class, and gender in our individual and collective experiences, then it can also work as a catalyst for liberating social changes.

Photo by R. Rosenfeld.

Local opposition to school desegregation, especially when accompanied by busing, remains very strong, especially in "defended neighborhoods," defined by Buell (1982) as areas within the city where community tradition and ethnic *Gemeinschaft* are still quite powerful. It is typically poor, working-class areas that are targeted for integration.

Yet there are a number of cities in which school districts have been successfully integrated, thanks to the cooperation of many community groups, local political leaders, and the business community (Willie and Greenblatt, 1981; Orfield, 1988). But even in integrated school districts, tracking and other ways of dividing the student body can render minority students invisible (Oakes, 1985; Pressman and Gartner, 1986).

Solutions. Under threat of court order, school systems have undertaken various approaches to reducing segregation and to stemming white flight. One way to keep white youngsters in inner-city schools is to offer **magnet schools,** which attempt to attract students with special interests to a particular program offered only in that school, such as music and art, science, athletics, or specific teaching techniques that many parents will consider worth the bus trip for their children. However, some magnet schools have also managed to deny entry to minority pupils (*New York Times,* August 3, 1989).

Magnet schools are designed to attract students by offering specialized educational programs.

Grade differentiation divides a district's students into separate schools for given grade levels.

Another way to divide children into desegregated units is through **grade differentiation**—specific schools for different grades. That is, School X is for all students in the district in kindergarten through second grade; School Y is for the third through the sixth grades; and School Z is the intermediate school. Thus, all children will have some years in their neighborhood school and other years away.

For areas where whites are in the suburbs and minority children in the cities, one integration method is the *merging of school districts,* so that both sets of students are in the same district, with busing to create racial balance among all the schools in the new district. Politically, this is not a popular solution, but it might be ordered by the courts.

If integration cannot be achieved, then an *enrichment of the inner-city schools* can at least provide equal, if separate, education. This course of action requires the willingness of all citizens to support extra taxes for the benefit of nonwhite children, another politically unpopular course.

Programs for the Disabled.   How fair is an educational system that teaches only those who can come to school and meet the expectations of classroom teachers? What are school districts to do about their physically and developmentally disabled youngsters? In 1975, Congress passed legislation requiring school districts to provide an "appropriate education" for all those who "need or require special education." It took another federal court order, in 1989, to require that schools provide suitable education to *all* children, a decision that has been upheld by the U.S. Supreme Court (*New York Times,* November 11, 1989, p. B10).

Without pressure from the courts, the cost of special education and shortage of trained personnel have effectively limited the numbers of children served. Of the 8 million disabled young people in the United States today, roughly half are actually receiving any educational assistance. Of the 10 percent of all students who are enrolled in special education programs, only one in five is in school full-time, with the majority receiving fewer than 10 hours of instruction per week (*Statistical Abstract,* 1987, p. 124). The largest category—47.0 percent—are classified as "learning disabled," and another 23 percent are "speech impaired." Fifteen percent are labeled "mentally retarded" and 9 percent "emotionally disturbed" (*Statistical Abstract,* 1990, p. 146).

But several recent studies (Carrier, 1986; Coles, 1987) cast doubt on the scientific validity of the concept of "learning disabilities" or the "minimal

Mainstreaming makes the school experience different for both the disabled and the nondisabled by breaking the pattern of isolation that often exists between these groups. Mainstreaming is particularly helpful in providing less restrictive educational experiences for those who are disabled.

brain damage" presumed to underlie the pupils' inability to conform to the discipline of the classroom. Clearly, the concept serves to reinforce the naturalness/normality of middle-class performance standards, while providing employment to learning disabilities evaluators and teachers. Even though it also stigmatizes and isolates their children, parents appear to prefer the label "disabled" rather than "mentally retarded" or "emotionally disturbed" (Carrier, 1986). But this view takes responsibility for school failure away from the schools and places it on the children.

The negative effects of labeling and isolation can be partially minimized by integrating disabled children into the regular school program, or **mainstreaming.** Although hard to implement, this method normalizes the experience of the handicapped and lets other students interact with those who differ from them.

Mainstreaming involves integrating handicapped students into the regular school program.

A REPORT CARD FOR THE EDUCATIONAL SYSTEM

The American educational system has received both high marks and failing grades.

Successes

- The establishment of a universal and comprehensive school system in a nation of students from many backgrounds and with varied needs.
- Basic assimilation tasks performed by the elementary schools in the first half of the twentieth century.
- A postsecondary educational system with a wide range of options, potentially available to most high school graduates.

Failures

- Inequality is still built into the dual and parallel school systems. Even as the educational level of all groups has risen, the relative position of racial and ethnic subgroups has remained unchanged.
- In the United States since the mid-1960s, there has been a *general* decline in the scores of high-school students on standardized achievement tests, although the downward trend appears to have leveled off and been reversed for many categories of youths.
- Millions of Americans cannot write or read well enough to address a letter correctly or to understand a bus schedule.

A PLURALISTIC FUTURE

The trend for the remainder of this century is likely to be toward *pluralism*— greater diversity among schools. Some schools will feature innovative classrooms, others a more traditional structure. Some will appeal to artistic students, others to budding scientists, and so forth. It is expected that most will be public schools, although a considerable number will be private, profit-making businesses.

One sign of the trend toward pluralism and private ownership is the revival of the **voucher** concept. In a voucher plan, school-tax monies in a given district are redistributed to families as certificates ("vouchers") worth a particular sum of money that can be used for tuition in a school of the parents' choice. This approach encourages the establishment of a variety of educational facilities so that, theoretically, each child can be placed appropriately.

The **voucher system** would allow families to spend a given sum of tax money for any type of schooling available.

At this writing, the Bush administration is strongly behind "parental choice" proposals, at least for the public schools. The arguments in favor are that parents will be empowered; schools will be forced to compete to attract students (an incentive for quality); and rules can be enacted to preserve racial balance. The arguments against the proposal center on the potential for elitism, and, if parochial schools are included, the violation of separation of church and state.

SOCIAL POLICY ISSUE

Disentangling Church and State in the Classroom

One of the underlying themes of this textbook has been the interdependence of various institutional spheres in modern societies—how politics, religion, economic activities, and family patterns are linked in feedback loops of mutual influence, even as each sphere becomes physically separated from the others. We have also emphasized the importance of the First Amendment to the U.S. Constitution in protecting citizens from the unchecked power of government. Both of these themes are central to understanding several current issues in the relationship among church, state, and schools.

The first clause of the First Amendment (see p. 357) states that Congress shall make no law respecting the establishment of religion, or prohibiting the free exercise thereof, and the Fourteenth Amendment forbids the states from abridging the privileges of citizenship. Notice that there are two different rights protected: the right to be free of government-sponsored religious observances, and the right to practice the rituals of your chosen faith. That these rights can be in conflict is illustrated in the issue of prayer in the schools. On the one hand, because public schools are under control of local governing boards, mandated prayers are a violation of the First Amendment's ban on establishing religious practice. On the other hand, to forbid children to pray could be considered an attempt to abridge freedom of religious expression. Yet no students who wish to pray can be forbidden from doing so silently at any time they wish.

If, as recent court cases indicate, prayers with a clearly religious content violate the First Amendment, what about a moment of silence before the school day? Is this a way to allow some student to pray without coercing the others, or is it smuggling something close to religion back into the classroom?

School prayer is only one area in which the line between church, state, and the schools is continually being tested. For example, should school classrooms be open to community religious groups for evening meetings, especially if other local organizations are permitted use of the rooms? Or, is it constitutional to use public school funds to provide busing to parochial schools? If the parents of such students are also taxpayers, are they not entitled to some services in return? And what about the school Christmas display; does it become acceptable if symbols of the Jewish midwinter holy days are also included? Can school authorities refuse to enroll students whose religion is based on faith healing and who, therefore, have not been vaccinated? Can the state force such children to be vaccinated against the wishes of their parents, or does this violate both religious freedom and family privacy?

These are only a few of the many possible First Amendment dilemmas with which you will have to deal as a parent and a citizen of this democracy. It is not too early to ask yourself how you would vote on such issues. ■

BELIEF SYSTEMS: RELIGIONS AND SECULAR IDEOLOGIES

- Members of the Hagan tribe of Papua New Guinea believe that a girl child's upper teeth develop first because they grow downward, pointing to the earth to which Hagan women become rooted. Boys tend to cut their lower teeth first, symbolizing eventual growth upward toward the sky and manliness (Strathern, 1980, p. 206).
- The Aztecs of Mexico had 5,000 priests in their capital city whose goal was to delay the end of the world. To please the gods, the priests had to offer up at least one beating heart every day of the year. It is estimated that 15,000 persons a year were ritually sacrificed, their hearts removed, and the remainder of their bodies eaten by members of the society, possibly to compensate for the loss of other animal protein as a result of rapid population growth (Harner, 1977; Harris, 1985).
- In Hinduism, the male god represents the passive aspect of eternity, while the female goddess symbolizes the active dynamism of earthly time. Together, they signify the oneness and unity of the divine essence (Nanda, 1988).
- In the United States today, a large proportion of the Fortune 500 corporations send their executives to training sessions where they are taught how to meditate and visualize positive images that will change their behavior and influence others. Other programs for business leaders specialize in walking on coals, staring at crystals, laying on hands to restore health, and reaching upward to touch one's higher self (Bordewich, 1988).

These are only a few of the many thousands of different belief systems through which humans give meaning to their life. In this section of the chapter we examine the essential characteristics of systems of beliefs and rituals, their functions and forms, with special emphasis on recent trends in the United States.

THE SOCIOLOGICAL STUDY OF BELIEF SYSTEMS

At the beginning of Chapter 2, you were asked to imagine the development of culture and social structure on a deserted island to which your sociology class had been miraculously transported during a nuclear attack. At some point, members of the group would begin to retell the story of their amazing

A **belief system** is a set of shared ideas about the meaning of life.

Religion is a belief system based on the concept of a divine force guiding destiny and directed toward the supernatural.

Secular ideologies are belief systems based on worldly rather than super-natural forces.

good fortune, find explanations for their miraculous survival, praise themselves for the rules they have created, and decide that they have a great mission to perform. In essence, the group would produce a **belief system**—ideas about the meaning of life that are shared among members of a collectivity. If members had also agreed that some divine force was guiding their destiny, we would call this particular kind of belief system a **religion.** Belief systems anchored in this world and centered on human rather than divine agency are called **secular ideologies.**

Sociologists have studied belief systems from the very beginning: Auguste Comte, Emile Durkheim, Karl Marx, and Max Weber each had a unique view on the subject of religion.

Durkheim

Durkheim saw belief systems as a celebration of society itself. In his classic study, *The Elementary Forms of the Religious Life* (1912), he proposed that ideas about the ultimate meaning of life and the ceremonies expressing these beliefs arise out of the collective experience of the group (Chang, 1989). First, beliefs, like language or any other symbol system, depend upon *agreement among minds* for their meaning. Second, the content of belief systems—the ideas expressed, objects worshiped, ceremonies enacted, and values held sacred—all express the *shared fate* of believers. For Durkheim (1912/1961), *all* systems of belief were true, regardless of specific form or content: "there are no religions that are false. All are true in their own fashion; all answer, though in different ways, to the given conditions of human existence" (p. 15).

Durkheim's (1912) definition of religion remains the starting point for the sociological study of belief systems:

> A religion is a unified system of beliefs and practices relative to sacred things, that is to say, things set apart and forbidden—beliefs and practices which unite into one single moral community . . . all those who adhere to them. (p. 62)

Weber

Weber's concern was the relationship between ideas and actions. In *The Social Psychology of the World Religions* (1922–23), Weber examined the central ideas of Islam, Buddhism, Hinduism, Confucianism, Christianity, and Judaism to see how each provided a psychological and practical context for economic activity.

In *The Protestant Ethic and the Spirit of Capitalism* (1904–1905), Weber demonstrates how the religious emphasis on personal responsibility for one's state of grace generated anxieties about salvation that proved very compatible with the hard work and clean living essential for accumulating capital for investment. In contrast, Hinduism and Buddhism turn away from this world, while Confucianism emphasizes ascribed statuses and an unchanging order of obedience and obligation. Sociologists do not question the truth of any belief system, but ask "What happens because people believe it?" This is an empirical question; it can be answered by systematic observation of the *manifestations* and the *consequences* of belief.

Defining Belief Systems

A belief system exists wherever the human need for meaning is expressed in beliefs and rituals that characterize a community of believers. Precise content is irrelevant as long as the ideas and ceremonies reduce individual anxiety and produce social cohesion.

There are universal aspects of all belief systems, whether religious or secular. According to Yinger (1969), religion is found (1) where people are aware of the continuing problems of daily life, (2) where explanations and rituals have been developed around this awareness, and (3) where specific role incumbents are assigned the task of maintaining the awareness and the ceremonies. This formulation links all three levels of sociological analysis: individual, collective, and cultural.

FUNCTIONS OF BELIEF SYSTEMS

Systems of belief and ritual fill both individual and group needs. They are systematic ways of interpreting a broad range of earthly (and otherworldly) phenomena. People turn to worship at times of great personal misery or happiness, times when collective unity is under strain.

Many religions also serve a "cooling-out" function by softening anger at injustice. The poor, especially, need to feel that something better awaits them—if not in this world, at least in the next one. And it clearly serves the interest of the ruling classes to have the less fortunate direct their sense of injustice elsewhere and not threaten social order. This is the context of Karl Marx's statement that religion serves as the "opiate" (pain killer) of the masses.

This boy's Bar Mitzvah, celebrated at the Wailing Wall in Jerusalem, Israel, helps bridge a life transition to adulthood. It also reinforces Judaic religion and tradition for his kin and community.

Manifest and Latent Functions

Beliefs and rituals have both manifest (expressed, intended) and latent (unacknowledged, often unanticipated) functions. Ceremonies such as holy communion, bar/bat mitzvah, rain dances, witch hunts, and even human sacrifice, for example, are openly intended to help people and groups deal with the unknown or threatening aspects of life—the future of the young person, natural disasters, evil within and enemies without.

Yet these rituals also have the latent functions of reinforcing tradition and of giving people an immediate experience of group unity. Thus, while the rain dance may not produce a thunderstorm, it temporarily relieves the personal and social stresses caused by prolonged drought. In American history, periodic "witch hunts" for subversives may not turn up many enemies of the people, but they have served to unite the people in support of capitalism against the "red menace" of socialism.

Dysfunctions of Belief Systems

Most belief systems assume that one and only one set of ideas reflects the truth. But if each belief system is *The Word*, then others must be false. Moreover, those who possess the one and only truth often feel obligated to spread it. Thus, there is always potential conflict among those who hold different beliefs. World history is filled with religious wars and persecution, forced conversion, and wholesale slaughter, even though most faiths proclaim mercy and brotherhood, at least among believers.

Sectarian conflict refers to interreligious strife.

Within a given society, the presence of more than one faith is often associated with conflict. The United States has avoided major **sectarian conflict** (interreligious strife) by making tolerance of religious differences a legal and moral principle. However, the First Amendment has not always checked anti-Catholic and anti-Jewish passions. The Ku Klux Klan, for example, was organized to save the nation from the "foreign" influence of Catholics and Jews as well as African-Americans (Parillo, 1985).

These examples illustrate a major sociological principle: The same social pattern can be both adaptive (functional) and maladaptive (dysfunctional), depending on the context and the specific collectivities involved.

STRUCTURE OF BELIEF SYSTEMS

Every religon or ideology has three essential components based on these personal and societal needs:

An **origin myth** is the story of how a particular group began.

1. An **origin myth** (the word *myth* indicates that the events being described cannot be verified) is a tale of how a group began, such as the biblical story of the Creation or the Tiwi belief that they originated in the waters.
2. *Rules of conduct* to be followed: proscriptions (prohibitions) and prescriptions (recipes for the good life) to guide the individual. These codes

of conduct reinforce social order, as, for example, the Ten Commandments or most of the Koran, the holy book of Islam.

3. A vision of the future: a mission such as spreading the good word or
   leading the revolution. A sense of destiny unifies all true believers and
   gives meaning to both individual existence and human history.

Marxism as a Secular Ideology

The writings of Karl Marx, along with those of the Soviet leader Lenin (1870–
1924), form the basis of a secular ideology called *Marxism*, which gives its
believers the same certainty that Christianity or Judaism brings to others. As
the official ideology of the Soviet Union, the People's Republic of China, Cuba,
and elsewhere, Marxism contains all the elements of any belief system: an
explanation of history, a guide for behavior in the present, and a vision of the
ultimate triumph of justice, but all without reference to divine powers.

In Communist countries, as in all societies, myths and rituals reinforce
the existing order, support authority, and motivate citizens to sacrifice for the
good of the collectivity. In the Soviet Union, attempts were made to replace
traditional religious ceremonies with secular ones, especially at important
moments in the life course: birth, marriage, and death. Special rituals also
mark the entry into and the exit from youth groups, school, the military, and
the workplace (Lane, 1981). Important events in Marxist-Leninist history are
celebrated as holidays in which the society as a whole is honored.

VARIETIES OF THE RELIGIOUS EXPERIENCE
ACROSS TIME AND PLACE

An explanation of belief systems as rooted in social structure and the material
world does not always satisfy those who seek a more spiritual and personal
(rather than social) basis for this universal phenomenon. Through the years,
philosophers and social scientists have suggested a number of other factors,
such as awe at the power of nature, fear of death, the need to interpret
dreams, guilt over the wish to kill one's parents, and original sin. Some
sociologists speak of a human need for **transcendence,** to escape the limits
of one's own senses and to feel that one's life has significance beyond daily
experience (Berger, 1965).

But the endless variety of belief systems and their changes over time
depend on a society's particular culture and social structure. Anthropologist
Marvin Harris (1985) suggests that the kinds of gods people worship reflect
the social relationships within the society. In simple hunting and gathering
bands, the gods, like the people they guide, are basically an egalitarian bunch,
with little distinction between male and female. In agricultural societies,
especially those with centralized states and well-defined social classes, the
gods themselves are seen as highly stratified and insistent on strict obedience
to standards of conduct and morality.

It is also probable that divine beings were once thought of in feminine
terms (Gimbutas, 1989). The link between the fertility of nature and of
humans could logically lead to the worship of female forces; indeed, among

> **Transcendence**
> refers to the need to
> go beyond the limits
> of one's own senses
> and feel that life has
> meaning beyond one's
> daily experiences.

the earliest objects of a clearly religious nature are tiny statues of females in an advanced stage of pregnancy.

There is also evidence that important ritual functions were once per- formed by women such as the vestal virgins in ancient Europe, Druid pries- tesses in Britain, and members of women's cults in early Roman history (Pace, 1985). Statues of a mother goddess from ancient Crete and wall paintings from Stone Age Turkey (Barstow, 1978) suggest an even more central role for women, not only in religious ritual but in the society as a whole. Indeed, there is evidence of widespread mother worship throughout the world, from prehistoric to contemporary societies (Preston, 1983).

Yet the major world religions are strikingly dominated by male imagery: a supreme father figure, ruling through spiritual sons. The leaders of biblical Hebrews were called *patriarchs;* Christianity is thoroughly masculine in its doctrine, symbols, and power structure; and Islam is almost exclusively male oriented, forbidding women to enter the main body of the mosque. Although the major Eastern religions—Buddhism, Hinduism, and Shintoism—are less openly masculine, women's role in ritual is very limited. These regularities in belief and practice, originating in *agricultural* societies of the Near and Far East, still reflect the male-dominated social systems of the time and place of their emergence.

Sacred and Profane

Sacred behaviors and objects are invested with holy, divine, mys- tical, or supernatural force.

Profane behaviors and objects are not holy but rather earthly and understandable.

Religious roles in- volve supervision of sacred objects and ceremonies.

As Durkheim noted, in all societies there are two very different sets of behav- iors and objects. One set is considered **sacred** and is thus invested with holy, divine, mystical, or supernatural force. The other realm is the **profane,** which is earthly and understandable in its own terms. Just which behaviors and objects go into which category is a matter of wide variation among all the world's religions and ideologies. Sacredness is not built into any object; it is a characteristic imposed by the group. Thus, sacred burial places of the Plains Indians are just so much good pastureland for Midwest farmers.

In all societies, certain people—shamans, witch doctors, priests and pries- tesses, ministers, rabbis, and mullahs—are placed in charge of the sacred items and places. Indeed, **religious roles** are among the earliest to emerge in human history ("the second oldest profession")

Magic

Magic refers to be- havior designed to manipulate unseen forces.

People throughout the world also attempt to control the supernatural. **Magic** refers to behaviors designed to manipulate unseen forces, whereas religion involves coming to terms with a superior power. Magical formulas, words, and gestures are used to reduce uncertainty. Among the Trobriand Islanders of the South Pacific, for example, fishing in the calm waters of a lagoon requires little in the way of ceremony, as success depends only on skill; but when the same men and boats venture into the ocean beyond the lagoon, where high winds can make fishing hazardous, the departure of the vessels is marked by solemn rituals (Malinowski, 1925/1955).

Magic is used whenever an outcome cannot be predicted by rational, "scientific" knowledge. Yet even we "moderns," when faced with the unpredictable, cross ourselves, stroke a rabbit's foot, or make bargains with unseen forces.

BELIEF SYSTEMS AND SOCIAL CHANGE

Because belief systems deal with the eternal (either truth is everlasting or it is not truth), most religions tend to be conservative and supportive of the *status quo,* if not openly reinforcing existing political and economic inequality. Yet religions and secular ideologies can also be agents of social change (Ackerman, 1985; Lincoln, 1985). New movements are continually being formed within established belief systems, even in simple societies. Typically, a charismatic leader introduces changes in the traditional practices that, over time, become the basis for a new religion. Both Jesus and Muhammad were such leaders.

Religious traditions have also been used to justify resistance to authority, as in Communist Poland, where the Catholic Church, having lost its control over secular life, became a symbol of challenge to the Communist regime. When, however, a new breed of Catholic clergy developed a "liberation theology" on behalf of oppressed peasants in Central and South America, where the church remains a powerful ally of secular authorities, traditional religious leaders denounced them for being too secular (Brooker, 1989).

Priests and Prophets

The dual nature of belief systems—as support for the *status quo* or as an agent of change—is captured in Max Weber's distinction between the *priestly* and the *prophetic.* In general, **priestly** functions involve the specific tradition of the faith in which the priest is a trained and ordained leader. In religious terms, the priest is a conservator, a protector of sacred places and objects, and, in political terms, often supports the existing structure of power. The **prophet,** on the other hand, is a charismatic figure, often from the ranks of untrained laypersons, and is a witness to a revelation calling for a new order. As the definer of this new order, the prophet is by definition at odds with established authorities.

Weber spoke of the **routinization of charisma,** whereby the prophet's beliefs are institutionalized and the spiritual mission is transformed into a worldly organization. The resulting bureaucracy of priests often becomes the deadening structure described by Marx. Thus, many religions begin as forces of social and political change but eventually become the new establishment, and create the conditions for the emergence of a new prophet.

A basic tension exists between religion and its emphasis on the holy, and the world as it is, full of imperfection and temptations. Religious leaders must continually warn and threaten the less faithful. Some religions, claimed Weber, survive because the members form religious communities separate from the rest of society (for instance, the Hutterites and the Amish of modern America). Or, as Confucians and Orthodox Jews do, believers create two spheres of activity with different rules for each. Orthodox Jews, for example, can be

Priestly functions deal with specific traditions of the faith, supporting the existing structure of power.

The **prophet** is a charismatic figure, witnessing a revelation calling for a new order.

The **routinization of charisma** occurs when the prophet's beliefs are institutionalized and transformed into a worldly organization.

devoted to secular business concerns for part of the day but, in the rest of their activities, follow a purely religious way of life.

RELIGIONS OF THE EAST

In contrast to religions originating in the Near East—Judaism, Christianity, and Islam, with their emphasis on one god (*monotheism*) and their relatively this-world orientation—the major belief systems of Southeast Asia and the Far East are more focused on nature and the afterlife, and are polytheistic (accepting many gods). The questions posed by such religions as Buddhism, Hinduism, Shintoism, and Confucianism are these: What is my place in the universe? Which path shall I take to happiness? What is the way of harmony? What is life? The element of searching and seeking in these questions is very different from the insistence on received doctrine of Islam, Judaism, or Christianity.

Three elements of Eastern religion that appeal to young people in the United States today are (1) the emphasis on self-discipline (not unlike early Calvinism); (2) a belief in the unity of all life, that is, humans with nature, past with present, and one person with another, all linked together in one chain of life; and (3) the higher value placed on experience than on intellect, whereby knowledge comes from an opening of the mind to feeling and intuitive understanding.

Hinduism, Buddhism, Confucianism, and Shintoism, however, have distinct histories and doctrines: The great theme of *Hinduism* is that of an everlasting cycle of life in which all things are reincarnated (born over and over again); the grand goal of human existence is to transcend this endless cycle through meditation, which brings perfect peace from earthly desires.

Buddhist monks regard materialism as a barrier to spiritual development. Here, the monks collect a bowl of rice for lunch at a monastery in Mandalay.

Buddhism is based on a knowledge of correct conduct through suffering and contemplation, with the goal of *nirvana,* a complete emptying of the self so that Buddha's insights can enter and free the person from the cycle of reincarnation.

Confucianism is founded on a reverence for the past and is full of rules of behavior, much as are Western religions. The key concept is *piety* (respect and righteousness), first expressed in the family as the worship of one's ancestors and obedience to one's parents, and then extended to the state.

Shintoism, the native religion of Japan, combines the worship of nature and ancestors. People prayed to the spirits in the natural world for good crops and fishing. The emperor was thought to be the descendant of the sun goddess and to rule by divine right.

MODERNIZATION

Today, the most powerful source of social change is **modernization:** the spread of industrialization and urbanization in a society that is becoming more internally differentiated and complex and in which science and technology guide change. Kin-based production is replaced by cash-crop agriculture or the assembly line; traditional authority is challenged at all levels; family members migrate to where they can find jobs; and tribes and clans are expected to be loyal to an arbitrarily imposed nation-state. Few societies can absorb all these changes without a great deal of personal stress and social strain.

> **Modernization** refers to the spread of industrialization and urbanization in a society that is becoming more internally differentiated and complex and in which science and technology guide change.

The destabilizing effects of such rapid and thoroughgoing change have led to several revivals of highly traditional religious patterns, most notably the rise of Islamic fundamentalism in Iran, under the late Ayatollah Khomeini.

And as we discuss later in this chapter, the recent surge of Christian revivalism in the United States also reflects widespread feelings of powerlessness in the face of profound economic and social changes that have transformed small-town life and threatened the taken-for-granted structures of control in the family and community.

Secularization

The transition from traditional to modern societies has also been marked by **secularization,** with its focus on this world and on reason, science, and technology to solve problems, as opposed to unquestioned faith and a focus on the next world.

> **Secularization** is the shift in focus from the next world and unquestioned faith to this world and reason, science, and technology.

Science need not, however, be viewed as being in opposition to faith. No matter how much we know scientifically, there are always questions that science cannot answer (Hammond, 1985). Nonetheless, the areas of life in which technical mastery has replaced faith are ever widening. And although religious observance may be important for individuals in time of stress, most members of modern societies base their daily personal decisions on a rational calculation of costs and benefits rather than relying on the commands of spiritual leaders.

It is this modern way of thinking (the *secular mind*) that most conflicts with religion. The belief that human beings themselves can change the conditions of their lives, without reliance on divine intervention, is the greatest challenge to traditional faith. The secular spirit, moreover, is marked by an emphasis on *consumption* (enjoyment of the good life on earth rather than in the hereafter) and a focus on the *individual* rather than the community of believers. These characteristics reflect the thrust of the Protestant work ethic, but they disturb the new prophets of Protestant revivalism, who have defined "secular humanism" as the great enemy because it denies the power of God.

The essence of *secular humanism* is a belief in the perfectibility of human beings through their own effort, as can be seen in this selection from the *Humanist Manifesto,* which was published in 1933 by a group of American intellectuals, including the educational reformer John Dewey:

1. A faith in human intelligence and abilities.
2. A commitment to democracy and civil liberties.
3. A belief in the importance, if not the divine origin, of the Ten Commandments and of the ideals of social equality, the community of humankind, and world peace.
4. Opposition to all theories of predestination, divine determination, and fatalism.
5. Compassionate concern for all human beings.

So vigorous is conservative Christian opposition to these beliefs that Congress passed a clause in the Education Act of 1985 prohibiting federal magnet school money from being used for "any course of instruction the substance of which is secular humanism." As this example illustrates, the triumph of science in everyday matters has not diminished the fervor of true believers. Religious beliefs and practices are alive and well in most modern societies.

Religious Organizations

Social scientists (Weber, 1922–23; Troeltsch, 1931; Yinger, 1969; Roof and McKinney, 1987; Johnstone, 1988) distinguish among various forms of religious organization, all of which testify to the high degree of religious pluralism in modern societies. These forms include:

Denomination, or *church.*   The formal organization of a religion, with a set of structured roles and places of worship.

Mainstream, or *mainline, churches.*   Religious organizations that represent the central values of the culture; the generally recognized legitimate faiths of the society.

Ecclesia.   An "official" church, automatically embracing all members of the society, and where the church hierarchy and political leadership are mutually protective of each other's interests.

Sect.   Often the result of denominational schism over matters of faith or ritual, sects tend to be less tolerant of doctrinal differences, more exclusive in membership, and less supportive of political authority than the denominations from which they split.

Cult. This term covers many types of organizations and movements, some of which have a religious orientation, some that are defiantly secular, and some that combine elements of both. But all operate outside the mainstream religious traditions.

ORGANIZED RELIGION AND RELIGIOUS BEHAVIOR IN AMERICA

Religious Affiliation

About six in ten Americans are formally linked to (affiliated with) a religious congregation. These figures are somewhat misleading, however, since some churches count children and others count only adults. Roman Catholics comprise the single largest body of believers, with approximately 55 million members or one-fourth of all Americans. All Protestant denominatons combined, however, account for 80 million individuals, well over half of all church members in the United States. In 1990 there were an estimated 6 million members of Jewish congregations (three percent of the total), 4 million members of the Eastern Church, 1 million other types of Catholics, and about 100,000 Buddhists (Jacquet, 1990).

These figures represent a slight rise from the previous year and continue a trend of very slow growth in church membership in the 1980s, at the same rate as the population as a whole (Jacquet, 1990). However, the Roman Catholic church and the major established Protestant denominations have experienced slow declines, while new smaller sects have gained.

Importance of Religion

National survey data continue to show that about 60 percent of Americans say that religion is "very important" in their lives. This is significantly lower than the high of 75 percent in 1952. Protestants were slightly more likely than Catholics or Jews to say religion is "very important." Women, nonwhites, older people, residents of small towns, and those in the lower educational and income strata are most likely to endorse the importance of religion in their lives (Gallup Poll, 1987; Greeley, 1989). More than 90 percent of all Americans say that they believe in God, 85 percent claim personally to embrace the Ten Commandments, and 75 percent say that they pray every day (Briggs, 1984).

Attendance

Despite such strong expressions of faith, actual attendance at religious services has declined by 20 percent since 1955 and remained at a plateau of about 40 percent in the 1980s (Jacquet, 1990). Many who do not attend services will, however, listen to religious programming on radio or television.

Participation in organized prayer is highest among women, the elderly, people who live in cities (Fincke and Stark, 1988), and the religiously conservative (Hertel and Hughes, 1987). Aging remains associated with increasing rates of religious observance but each incoming cohort does so at a lower level than the one before.

Religious commitment takes place in a social network in which personal relationships are more important than ideology or specific doctrines (Stark and Bainbridge, 1980). Because young people today are more likely than those of the past to attend college, to travel, and to meet people from different backgrounds, it should not be surprising that ties to traditional faith are weakened.

Civil Religion

Our society is unusual in the variety of religions it embraces and is unique in the range of religious expression protected by custom and law. But how, under conditions of denominational pluralism, can the need for establishing a unifying system of beliefs at the societal level be met? Sociologist Robert Bellah (1970, 1975) found the functional equivalent of a common faith in the **American civil religion,** by which our nation and its institutions are seen as divinely blessed, with a moral mission in the world, and guided by ethical standards derived from the Puritan emphasis on good citizenship. This "universal religion of the nation" has served the essential functions of any belief system: to legitimize and sanctify (make sacred) the social order and to integrate its members, despite differences of faith. The intermix of nationalism and religion is visible both when we make secular holidays sacred, as on the Fourth of July, and when we transform sacred holy days into commercial orgies, as at Christmas.

American civil religion is a set of unifying beliefs that sees America as divinely blessed, with a moral mission and guided by ethical standards.

One criticism of the "civil religion" is the potential loss of authentic spiritual commitment in a vague sea of secular piety, where simply having a religious affiliation was more important than fully living one particular set of beliefs (Herberg, 1960). Other critics fear that religious symbolism has been coopted by political and economic leaders in order to justify controversial policies. The civil religion may be in place, but the social unity beneath it has already crumbled as Americans remain deeply divided on the basis of race and wealth (Demerath and Williams, 1985, 1989).

Politics is not the only sphere in which the line between church and state has been obscured. Business leaders today often conduct "prayer breakfasts" before going to work and making decisions based on their firm's need to show a short-term profit. In professional athletics, members of the Sports World Ministry conduct locker room services to ask God's support for their efforts. It is difficult to tell whether this blurring of institutional boundaries signifies a diluting of the religious sphere or its revitalization as an active influence in everyday life.

African-American Churches

Religion has always been a major spiritual resource for the oppressed, but the African-American churches are of special importance as the only major institution in the members' world that was not under white control. The great majority of African-Americans are Protestant and denominationally Baptist, but embrace diverse elements of African and Southern United States culture

(Steinfels, 1989). Services typically involve a high level of participation by members, with great emphasis on music as an integral part of the religious experience.

A small percentage of African-Americans are Roman Catholic, and a growing number are affiliated with Muslim mosques. Indeed, African-Americans account for almost 90 percent of recent American converts to Islam (Goldman, 1989), which provides a clean break with what many African-Americans perceive as a failed past. Islam, while incorporating almost the entire Hebrew and Christian Bibles, is a much more demanding and disciplined religion than mainstream Protestantism: no choirs, only chanting; strict dietary laws; prayers five times a day; no alcohol, gambling, or nightclubs.

African-American religious life, even today, can be understood only within the context of the pervasive racism of the larger society. The churches do more than offer hope to the deprived; they are places where a sense of pride is nurtured and where people can organize for social change and provide help to one another (Smith, 1982; Mukenge, 1983; Baer, 1984; Gilkes, 1985). All but a few of the leaders of the civil rights movement in the 1960s came from the ranks of clergy.

The leadership role of the churches was made possible, first, by their almost total segregation from outside control and, second, by the fact that the church was often the only avenue of upward mobility for those talented and ambitious young people who were systematically excluded from high-prestige occupations in the larger society. (However, now that gifted men and women of color can have careers in law, medicine, business, and academics, proportionately fewer enter religious studies.)

African-American churches have also been characterized by a relative openness of leadership roles to women (Gilkes, 1985; Briggs, 1987). To the extent that the church has been the historical center of the community, the bearer of a distinct tradition, and the catalyst of collective action, women have been important figures, even though men retained nominal (in name) authority.

As long as most African-Americans continue to experience barriers to achievement in mainstream institutions, the church has a vital mission, and there seems to be little lessening of its central role in the local community. Indeed, as outside sources of support continue to be reduced, the church may once again have to function as an all-purpose social welfare agency (Carnegie Corporation, 1987–88).

CONTEMPORARY TRENDS

Secularization and the Mainstream Religions

The great paradox of contemporary American religion is this: amid widespread religiosity, in which the nation itself is rendered sacred, the *mainstream churches* have experienced declines in membership and influence. According to sociologist Robert Wuthnow (1988), religious divisions in our society today are not as in the past between churches or among denominations, but between religious liberals and conservatives *within* each church (Hertel and Hughes, 1987). These opposing camps, furthermore, are linked to clear-cut differences in social background and therefore to different locations in the social structure as well as different reactions to the broad currents of political and economic change (Roof and McKinney, 1987). In general, compared to religious liberals, the conservatives are older, from small towns in the Midwest or South, upper-working or lower-middle class, and likely to have been disclocated by shifts in the economy.

In order to attract or maintain the commitment of their liberal members, mainstream churches have tried to become "more relevant," particularly to the interests of younger congregants. But such changes as the use of English in place of Latin or Hebrew, replacing hymns with folksongs, and calling the pastor by his or her first name have done little to attract younger people and much to alienate older worshipers who derive comfort from traditional usage. As a consequence, the more liberal Protestant and Jewish denominations recently have moved toward a more traditional position on both the form of worship and on social issues (Steinfels, 1989). These observations lend weight to Peter Berger's (1969) claim that people seek a profoundly moving experience from their religious devotions, and the more routinized one's everyday experience, the greater the need for transcendence through faith.

Another explanation for high levels of piety amidst the pleasures of modern life was offered by the French visitor Alexis de Tocqueville (1830) more than 160 years ago. Even then, he was struck by the American combination of religious fervor and materialism. Appreciating the value of religious pluralism and separation of church and state, de Tocqueville also noted that people require some type of moral restraint on selfishness. Because civil government lacks this kind of authority in a democratic society, citizens will cling to religion to set limits on their behavior (Caplow et al., 1983).

Special Concerns of the American Catholic Church.   The Roman Catholic church shares many of the problems of mainstream religion in general but also some peculiar to its hierarchical and patriarchal organization. The Roman Catholic population in the United States will continue to grow at a faster rate than that of Protestants or Jews, largely because of immigration of young adult Latinos, with their relatively high birthrates. As these new migrants become acculturated, however, they will most likely follow the pattern of previous Catholic ethnic groups whose fertility rates have declined to the same level as the Protestant majority. In the process, many Catholic couples practice birth control in ways still forbidden by the church (Gallup and Castelli, 1987; *New York Times*/CBS Poll, 1987). The normative conflict between church teaching and personal conduct has caused large numbers of young couples to stop attending mass, although most remain "communal Catholics," deeply aware of their religious identity and fully expecting to rejoin the church at a later date (Hout and Greeley, 1987). Although a majority of Catholics disagree with much of the official doctrine, eight in ten feel that one can disagree with the Pope and remain a good Catholic (D'Antonio et al., 1989).

A far more serious problem for the Roman Catholic church is the steep decline in persons entering holy orders and the consequent graying of the clergy. Between 1966 and 1986, for example, the number of Catholic nuns dropped by 37 percent, with very few new recruits. Half of American nuns today are over age 62. The situation among parish priests is even more serious.

In 1970, 37,000 active parish priests served America's 50 million Catholics; today, fewer than 25,000 minister to 55 million parishioners. Nor are there sufficient new recruits in the seminaries. To the contrary, as many as 20,000 former priests, nuns, and brothers have left holy orders over the past three decades, either to marry or to fulfill their vows of service in a secular capacity (Waite, 1989).

All American faiths have been affected by decline in candidates for religious careers (Steinfels, 1989). The potential shortage of clergy has led to modern-style recruitment drives and also to a reassessment of the role of laypersons and of women in the conduct of religious rituals and congregational affairs.

Women in the Church

Another new direction that has brought some turmoil into church affairs is the increasing participation of women in all aspects of religious life, including ordination to the clergy (Lehman, 1985; Briggs, 1987). Despite long and strong resistance, over half of all Protestant denominations now have women in the ministry, as do the Reform and Conservative branches of Judaism. Greatest resistance has come from the Orthodox branch of Judaism and the Catholic church.

Today, women account for at least one-fourth of all students at theological seminaries, where they tend to be academically superior to the male students, owing largely to greater motivation and fewer competing avenues for achievement (Austin, 1983). When women were first ordained, they had difficulty

Despite a lengthy resistance, the mainstream Protestant Churches, as well as reform and conservative branches of Judaism, have decided to ordain women. Pictured is Barbara Harris, the first woman Bishop of the Episcopal Church.

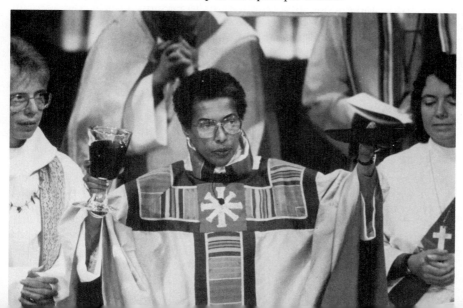

finding pulpits of their own, but a majority of newly ordained women have been accepted as leaders of their own congregations.

In a related development, women who have received theological training are rethinking their religious traditions, reinterpreting sacred documents to include women's experience, and reconstructing rituals (Daly, 1984; Ruether, 1985; Fiorenza, 1985; Plaskow and Christ, 1989). Although this effort has stirred controversy, particularly among those who believe in the literal wording of scripture, it has also spurred a reexamination of texts and practices by mainstream scholars, both male and female. Other feminists, giving up on the possibility of changing the established religions, have rediscovered prepatriarchal beliefs and rituals and woven them into a "women's spirituality movement" (Walker, 1985; Starhawk, 1989).

Mainstream Churches and Social Activism

Throughout our history, the line between church and state has wavered and blurred, as religious authorities have felt called upon to influence public morality and as political leaders have manipulated religious impulses in support of secular policies, including wars (Johnson and Tamney, 1986). In the 1960s the challenge of the Civil Rights Movement brought large numbers of clergy out of their pulpits and into the streets, where they were conspicuous in the front ranks of antisegregation demonstrators. Many of these religious activists also joined in the antiwar movement at the end of the decade.

Their parishioners, however, were less than thrilled about these decisions and by the early 1970s, contributions and membership in mainstream Protestantism had dropped dramatically. Forced to choose between commitment to the general goals of justice and peace and their responsibility to congregants, most clergy redefined their mission as one of serving local needs. For those clergy still dedicated to social activism and "liberal" causes, the 1980s have brought new and less controversial crusades: saving the environment; avoiding nuclear war; reducing world starvation; ending racial segregation in South Africa; and encouraging corporations to be more ethical.

However, the more conservative denominations also have their causes: anticommunism, antiabortion, and antisecularism, among others. The Catholic church has supported issues on both ends of the liberal-conservative continuum; it is in the forefront of the antiabortion movement and was instrumental in defeating the Equal Rights Amendment, but it has also advocated the reduction of economic inequality, abolition of the death penalty, and nuclear disarmament.

Fundamentalism represents a back-to-basics approach to religion, resisting modernity and seeking to restore an original faith.

Fundamentalist Protestantism

The most fascinating development on the current American religious scene is the revival of Protestant **fundamentalism.** Fundamentalists believe that every word of the Bible must be taken literally, that a true believer must spread the good word and live a clean life, that Satan is alive in the world, that a fearful destruction will precede the return of the Messiah, and that there is a clear structure of authority from God to His chosen ministers and then to the husband as head of the family (Barnhart, 1987). By drawing a firm line between themselves as "true believers" and all others, fundamentalists create close-knit communities in which intensive interaction reinforces faith (Ammerman, 1987).

Because these traditional beliefs did not fit the image of "modern" mainstream Protestantism in the middle of the twentieth century, the more extreme fundamentalist sects were gradually pushed to the fringe of the Protestant establishment, where they organized independently of the major denominations. Yet, in the past twenty years, as participation in mainstream Protestant denominations declined, membership in independent fundamentalist sects has risen sharply.

There has also been a fundamentalist revival within American Catholicism in the "charismatic prayer group." And in American Judaism, the highly observant, emotional and joyful Hasidic branches have attracted many converts from the more liberal Jewish congregations (Danzger, 1989). It would appear that many people are seeking an expressive religious experience in which they can feel a closeness to a holy spirit that directly enters their lives.

Another explanation for the revival of religious fundamentalism emphasizes its functions for people who believe that they are losing control over their way of life (Page and Clelland, 1978). Such *status anxiety* is easily transformed into the type of moral outrage that is at the heart of Protestant fundamentalism (Lipset and Raab, 1981). This interpretation is supported by data on the sociodemographic characteristics of people attracted to Protestant fundamentalism—southerners and midwesterners who grew up in small towns; women; the elderly; and persons with relatively low educational and occupational statuses (Hunter, 1983; Cardwell, 1984). These are subgroups whose sense of mastery has been eroded by secularization and by the shift from local to national economic and political decision making.

Explaining social movements in terms of individual feelings of alienation or loss of certainty is, however, not completely satisfying to sociologists. Another explanation for today's fundamentalism is that the movement's leaders took advantage of public distress over the manifest failures of modernism. For fundamentalists, the 1960s and 1970s offered one example after another of the breakdown of social order—student protest, antiwar demonstrations, riots, assassinations, the women's movement, gay rights marches, and Supreme Court decisions on civil rights, school prayer, and abortion. The only aspect of life not out of control was faith in the old-time religion.

The New Christian Right

Because of their vulnerable position as unaffiliated sects, Protestant fundamentalist churches had historically been strong supporters of the separation of church and state. It was a major shift, therefore, when, only two decades ago, fundamentalist leaders joined forces with far-right political action groups to form the **New Christian Right** (Liebman and Wuthnow, 1983). By combining their mailing lists, media know-how, and funding sources, organizations that had previously been considered "too extremist" to have much effect on

The **New Christian Right** is composed of fundamentalist religious organizations and far-right political groups.

public policy suddenly became a powerful force in electoral politics (Miller, 1986; Lechner, 1989).

The New Christian Right gained legitimacy in the 1980 election, when the candidates it supported won the White House and a dozen seats in the U.S. Senate. Once the line between church and state had been blurred, NCR leaders were quick to define the "Christian" position on a range of issues, not all of which appear directly religious, including women's and gay rights (against), nuclear power (for), sex education (against), defense spending (for), antipoverty programs (against), aid to the Nicaraguan rebels (for), and gun control (against).

Thus, the rise of the New Christian Right can best be explained in terms of "resource mobilization"—the ability to raise money, to activate existing networks of churchgoers and local activists, and to forge alliances with a large number of single-interest groups, rather than in terms of any great change in people's religious and political ideologies. Support for the fundamentalist moral/political agenda is not confined to people with status fears. Large contributions have come from such wealthy families and corporations as the DuPonts, the Hunt brothers of Texas, Pepsico, Mobil Oil, and the founders of the Coors beer company (Koenig and Boyce, 1985; Magrass, 1986).

But there are also signs that the NCR is not as powerful or monolithic as the media and movement leaders suggest (Lechner, 1989). With so many special interests at stake—both political and religious—some conflict is inevitable, and rivalry among leaders can be expected.

Prime-Time Preachers.   Although technology has brought us "the electronic ministry" there is no technical reason why the religious airwaves should today be dominated by fundamentalist ministers. Again, resource factors are important: the ability to raise money, to purchase television time, and to construct an independent media network. The fundamentalist preachers understand the value of showmanship and of a single clear message in language that most viewers can immediately grasp, and in the earthy accents of the South and Midwest.

The trends that distress so many people and cause them to turn to electronic ministries are distant and complex—changing labor markets, the shift to a service economy, the decline of American influence abroad, falling birthrates, and the rise of modern feminism. It is comforting to believe that what ails society can be cured by religious prescriptions offered via the electronic media (Frankl, 1987). However, following the sex and money scandals that tarnished the images of leading prime-time preachers Jimmy Swaggart and Jim and Tammy Faye Bakker, television ratings have fallen for all TV ministries, although millions continue to watch and contribute (Shipp, 1991).

Evangelicalism

Evangelical refers to an emphasis on the personal witnessing of God's presence.

Although the term **evangelical** is often used interchangeably with "fundamentalist," it is useful to distinguish the two forms of Protestantism. Evangelicals stress the personal witnessing of God's presence coupled with an obligation to spread "the word." The concept of being **born again** is central to the Protestant evangelical doctrine; it means having an experience that changes one's life through acceptance of the Lord.

The enthusiasm of their witnessing and the relatively lower social status of members have historically set American evangelical churches apart from the more liberal mainstream Protestant denominations, but not quite so distant as the fundamentalist sects. There are many evangelicals who do not insist upon a literal interpretation of the Bible, who oppose the arms race, support women's rights, and are involved in social activism on behalf of the poor (Warner, 1988).

Hunter (1987) concludes that American evangelicalism has both resisted and adapted to the modern world, largely as a result of higher education. Unlike an earlier generation of evangelical leaders, who rose from relatively humble social and educational origins (Jimmy Swaggart, for example, was a high school dropout), the leaders of tomorrow are college educated, having been exposed to all the secularizing influences of academe. For the time being, however, the older, more conservative leadership dominates the evangelical scene.

Cults and the New Religious Movements (NRMs)

Another source of competition with mainstream religion is the variety of cults attracting both young and older adults. Although numerically and politically less important than the fundamentalist movement, the cults have attracted a great deal of attention because of the sometimes unusual behavior of believers and because of the fear generated among parents of young converts (Robbins, 1988). Some of the modern cults are offshoots of fundamentalism; others derive from Eastern religions; still others center on the supernatural or, at the opposite extreme, one's own self. In addition, several expressly political cults have emerged among relatively powerless minorities. Among the NRMs that have received media attention are those based on non-Western belief systems, such as Zen Buddhism, Yoga, ISKCON (the organization of Hare Krishnas), and dozens of smaller groups centered on total obedience to a *guru,* or "wise one."

Other frequently studied NRMs are the Church of Scientology (a self-improvement cult with a spiritual overlay) and Children of God (from the Protestant fundamentalist tradition). However, the cult that has drawn the most publicity and the sharpest reaction from the general public and that has stimulated the most academic debate is the Unification Church of the Reverend Sun Myung Moon, whose followers are popularly known as Moonies.

The Unification Church claims a membership of more than 40,000 in the United States, primarily young adults, one-third of whom are engaged in full-time work for the church (Petranek, 1988; Beckford, 1985). The church's doctrines combine elements of Christianity with strong support for capitalism and the American military; its practices emphasize hard work, self-discipline, and communal living. Where Unification theology departs from standard Christianity is in the belief that because Jesus failed to bring the millennium, a

Born again means having an experience that changes one's life through the acceptance of the Lord.

Cults and **new religious movements** develop outside mainstream religious groupings.

second Messiah, born in Korea—the birthplace of Reverend Moon—is about to fulfill the Biblical phrophecy. The Unification Church maintains close ties with elements of the New Christian Right, and the church-owned newspaper, the *Washington Times*, is considered a major conservative voice in the nation's capital.

Parents of Unification recruits have difficulty understanding their children's irrational behavior, which they attribute to brainwashing and being held against their will. Some parents feel that it is perfectly legitimate to try to kidnap their offspring and "deprogram" them. In actuality, most recruits join willingly and leave just as quickly. Most vulnerable to recruitment are young people without many close ties—single, only partially committed to work or schooling, recently moved. The longer one stays in the cult, however, the harder it becomes to leave and to admit that one has made a major mistake. Conversion to a cult follows the same pattern as conversion to any belief system.

Self-Awareness Cults. The fastest-growing type of cult in our society today is one that attracts older adults and is devoted in the cultivation of the self, to developing one's capacities for making money and being successful in work and love. This collection of groups has been called the **New Age movement** (Lindsey, 1986) and embraces believers in many kinds of occult (supernatural) forces, such as psychic healing, reincarnation (rebirth to another body), and talking to the dead through mediums.

> The **New Age movement** refers to a number of groups centered on the supernatural and on psychic healing, reincarnation, and similar mystical experiences.

Another branch of the New Age movement has its origins in the human-potential movement of the 1950s. The combination of mysticism and self-improvement in organizations such as Scientology, National Training Institutes, Silva Mind Control, and Lifespring have attracted a largely middle-class and increasingly middle-aged following. Indeed, many large corporations now pay for their managers to take seminars on expanding consciousness, altered states of mind, meditation, hypnosis, even fire walking, in the hopes that the executives will become more productive.

The variety of belief systems available to Americans today is truly impressive—and we have not even mentioned witchcraft cults (Luhrmann, 1989) or the organizations for people who believe in UFOs, lost continents, and space aliens that once populated the earth (Harrold and Eve, 1988). There are so many choices and so few certain guides. Is it any wonder, then, that many Americans have become "spiritual junkies," moving from one religious experience to another? But perhaps we have more to fear from those who would limit the range of "true religion" than from those who seek to expand the boundaries of belief.

SUMMARY

1. Educational institutions are formal extensions of socialization, designed to transmit the culture, train people for adult statuses, develop talent, and generate new knowledge.

2. Functionalists view the educational system as a meritocracy. Conflict theorists view schools as mechanisms for reproducing the existing system of stratification.

3. In all industrialized societies, education has become increasingly differentiated and specialized.

4. The American educational system is inclusive, providing a general education, although within schools students are tracked for college-preparatory or vocational slots.

5. About 85 percent of American children are enrolled in public schools. Private schools include parochial and preparatory institutions.

6. Although all schools prepare students for adult roles, there are significant differences between suburban and urban school systems. Drop-out rates are especially high in urban schools.

7. Sociologists focus on what actually goes on inside schools and classrooms between teachers and students and among students. Research indicates that cooperative learning is more effective than competition or ability groupings.

8. The major functions of high education include the transmission of existing information, the production of new knowledge, and the education of future generations of scholars.

9. Higher education reinforces existing divisions of wealth and power and is itself a stratified system of two-year colleges, four-year colleges, and universities. Within colleges, faculties are stratified by academic rank, gender, and race, and the system.

10. The educational system has been criticized for failure to meet the needs of disabled students, teaching only those who can come to school and meet the expectation of classroom teachers.

11. Shared ideas about the meaning of life constitute a belief system. Religion is a belief system based on the concept of a divine being guiding people's destiny.

12. All belief systems have certain elements in common: ideas about the meaning of life; the use of rituals; a community of believers; an origin myth; rules of conduct, and a vision of the future. Marxism, the official ideology of many countries, can be understood as a belief system.

13. According to sociologists, the specific beliefs of any group emerge from its culture and social structure. Distinctions are made between the sacred and the profane, and rituals help people deal with major transitions and times of danger.

14. Belief systems are conservative and support the status quo, but they also serve as agents of social change. Modernization and secularization have had profound effects on contemporary religious practices and organizations, yet religious beliefs and affiliation remain important to the majority of Americans.

15. African-American churches represent the only major institution in the members' world that is not under white control.

16. Religious divisions within our society are no longer between churches but between religious liberals and conservatives within each church.

17. The participation of women has increased in all aspects of religious life. Today, women account for one-fourth of all students at theological seminaries.

18. Over the past four decades, dramatic changes have occurred in the involvement in secular matters by church leaders.

19. Much spiritual renewal is taking place outside mainstream churches through the rise of Protestant fundamentalism and the emergence of various cults.

SUGGESTED READINGS

Apple, Michael W. *Teachers and Texts: A Political Economy of Class and Gender Relations in Education.* New York: Routledge and Kegan Paul, 1986. How current trends are standardizing the practice of public education and taking away the teacher's autonomy and individual teaching approaches.

Baltzell, E. Digby. *Puritan Boston and Quaker Philadelphia.* New York: Free Press, 1979. A classic comparative study of the role of elites in Boston and Philadelphia.

Bromley, David G., ed. *Falling from the Faith: Causes and Consequences of Religious Apostasy.* Newbury Park, CA: Sage, 1988. The process of disaffiliation from both mainstream churches and alternate religious groups.

Bromley, David G., and Phillip E. Hammond, eds. *The Future of New Religious Movements.* Macon, GA: Mercer University Press, 1987. Interesting papers focusing on a number of recent religious movements.

Chalfant, H. Paul, Robert E. Beckley, and C. Eddie Palmer. *Religion in Contemporary Society.* 2d ed. Palo Alto, CA: Mayfield, 1987. Current religious trends, organizational changes, leadership, and membership.

Clark, Burton, ed. *The Academic Profession: National, Disciplinary, and Institutional Settings.* Berkeley: University of California Press, 1987. A comparison of universities, professional schools, and academic professionals in the United States, England, France, and West Germany.

Grant, Gerald. *The World We Created at Hamilton High.* Cambridge: Harvard University Press, 1988. Three decades of successes, tensions, failures, and new successes in one urban high school.

Greeley, Andrew M. *Religious Change in America.* Cambridge: Harvard University Press, 1989. Social surveys that indicate constant rates of church membership, church attendance, prayer, church activity, and belief in life after death.

Lawless, Elaine J. *God's Peculiar People: Women's Voices and Folk Tradition in a Pentecostal Church.* Lexington: University Press of Kentucky, 1988. Women's roles in a Pentecostal church, focusing on the oral, traditional, and informal elements.

McGuire, Meredith B. *Religion: The Social Context.* 2d ed. Belmont, CA: Wadsworth, 1987. An overview of the sociological study of religion.

Useem, Michael. *Liberal Education and the Corporation: The Hiring and Advancement of College Graduates.* Hawthorne, NY: Aldine, 1989. Corporate career paths of college graduates and comparative advantages of liberal arts, business, and engineering degrees.

Warner, R. Stephen. *New Wine in Old Wineskins: Evangelicals and Liberals in a Small-Town Church.* Berkeley: University of California Press, 1988. Changes in one Presbyterian church in California, reflecting changes in American Protestantism between 1950 and the 1980s.

Weikart, David P. *Quality Preschool Programs: A Long-Term Social Investment.* New York: Ford Foundation, 1989. The importance of preschool education particularly for poor children.

Weis, Lois, ed. *Class, Race, and Gender in American Education.* Albany: State University of New York Press, 1988. Essays showing how class, race, and gender affect students' school experiences.

Wexler, Philip. *Social Analysis of Education: After the New Sociology.* New York: Routledge and Kegan Paul, 1987. An analysis of American education focusing on systematic reproduction of social class inequalities.

MODERNIZATION: SOCIAL MOVEMENTS AND SOCIAL CHANGE

The final chapter deals explicitly with the mechanisms and consequences of cultural and social change. No set of social arrangements or beliefs remains forever the same, although the rate of change will vary greatly. Because social systems are collective creations, and because humans are capable of developing new patterns of social behavior, society is an ever-changing collection of values, norms, and relationships. This chapter reviews the broad currents of cultural and social change across time, focusing on *modernization* as a master process through which recent history has unfolded. The chapter also explores collective behavior and social movements—noninstitutionalized responses to flux and change.

Throughout this text, by showing you how culture and society are constructed, we have also given you the intellectual tools for deconstructing and reconstituting social systems. It is our hope that your introduction to sociology will encourage you to examine critically the values, beliefs, and institutions of contemporary America and to work toward a society that embodies your highest ideals of fairness and justice.

12

Social Change: Modernization and Social Movements

MODERNIZATION, TECHNOLOGY, AND SOCIAL CHANGE

For many generations, a hunting-and-gathering tribe called the Teuso lived in the mountains of east-central Africa. Nomadic bands of Teuso tracked big game in a yearly cycle that led them past food-gathering and watering sites and back to their main grounds. The Teuso were careful never to take more from the land than necessary, and to maintain a balance between population and resources. Moreover, when first visited by anthropologist Colin Turnbull, the Teuso were an open and friendly people. Their society, like most hunting-and-gathering cultures, was characterized by a high level of cooperation and informal, open social relationships. Women made important contributions to economic security and were recognized accordingly.

The peaceful world of the Teuso was drastically disrupted after World War II, when new countries were formed in central Africa. The leaders of these emerging nations sought to unify the vastly different cultural, social, and linguistic tribal societies within their new geographic boundaries. As part of this process, the Teuso, now called the Ik, found that the newly established government had turned their traditional hunting grounds into a national park, forbidding the Ik to pursue the game that had once been their source of food. Instead, government officials disastrously attempted to convert the Ik into farmers on rocky land with little rainfall.

Indeed, when Turnbull revisited the tribe in the 1960s, he found that the Ik had become an unfriendly, uncharitable, inhospitable, and generally mean people (Turnbull, 1972). All ties of affection and pity had disappeared. Threatened with starvation, each member of the society acted in terms of immediate self-interest, even grabbing bits of food from a child or an ill person. Thus we see how major changes in the mode of subsistence can destroy a culture and affect every other aspect of life, *including personality.*

Yet even if all the members of a society were to resist any change from within and insist that everything be done as it always had been done, there would still be forces beyond their control that would produce change. No culture, not even that of simple societies, is exactly the same today as it was 500 or even five years ago. **Social change** is the process through which values, norms, institutions, social relationships, and stratification systems are altered over time.

> **Social change** is the process through which values, norms, institutions, stratification systems, and social relationships alter over time.

SOURCES OF CHANGE

Social change comes about through processes and events that are either internal or external to a society. Some common ways in which such changes occur include (1) environmental events, (2) invasion and war, (3) cultural contact and diffusion, (4) innovation, and (5) population shifts.

Environmental changes include both (1) natural events, such as earthquakes, disease, and climate shifts and (2) situations produced by people, such as pollution or overuse and overkill of natural resources. Any one of these environmental factors could produce changes in the economic base and social ties of a group. When a flood occurred in Buffalo Creek, as you recall

> **Environmental changes** include both natural and socially produced events.

The recent war in the Gulf region of the Middle East wreaked havoc among the people of the region and their environment. A Kuwaiti oil field worker kneels for midday prayers near a burning oil field in Kuwait, a grim reminder of the changes caused by war.

from Chapter 4, not only were homes destroyed but the entire social structure of the community was altered (Erikson, 1976).

Invasion occurs when one group's or nation's territory is overrun and controlled by another's.

Invasion of one group's territory by other tribes, colonial powers, or economic interests is another major source of social change, as is war. Either may require adaptation to new customs and beliefs, or result in geographic relocation of a group, with changes in the mode of subsistence. For example, when European settlers colonized South Africa, they not only displaced the native residents but altered their economies and created a stratification system based on color. Similar experiences have faced native populations in South America, Southeast Asia, and the United States.

Culture contact involves learning from people from other societies.

Culture contact with people from other societies, in which one group learns how the other has coped with the tasks of survival, is a frequent source of change.

Diffusion describes the process by which new ideas, actions, technology, and beliefs of a culture spread from one person, group, or society to another.

Diffusion refers to the process by which new ideas, actions, technology, beliefs, and other items of culture spread from person to person, group to group, and society to society. A few vital innovations in culture were probably necessary for survival of the species. Fire, animal traps, and ways of keeping track of the seasons, for example, were discovered in only one or two places and then diffused by culture contact throughout the inhabited world. A common example of diffusion today is that of consumer goods, such as Coca-Cola and McDonald's hamburgers.

Innovation refers to both the discovery and invention of something new.

Innovation describes both discovery and invention of something new. A discovery involves the awareness of some aspect of nature that already exists but had not been recognized before, such as the laws of relativity or the infection theory of disease. Inventions involve the combination of existing parts of culture in a new way, such as in the design of a personal computer.

Population shifts are changes in the size and composition of the population.

Population shifts, or changes in the size and composition of the population, are another source of change. If the group outgrows its resource base, some members will be forced to migrate, as the potato famine in the nineteenth century prompted large numbers of the Irish to move to the United States.

Not all cultural items that are diffused are equally likely to be accepted, however. Technology is generally most easily diffused, for it is relatively simple to determine whether a new technique is more efficient than an old one. For example, it is not too difficult to demonstrate that a gun is more effective than a spear in hunting game. In contrast, nonmaterial items of culture, such as beliefs and values, are much less readily adopted, as the Chinese have discovered since their takeover of Tibet. Although monasteries there have been closed or neglected, the Tibetans have persisted in a Buddhist rather than Marxist belief system.

In many cases, even enhancing a group's standard of living might not be welcome if the new technique is believed to involve radical changes in other aspects of culture. People often fear both the immediate and long range impact of social change. During the early days of the French factory system, for example, new equipment was literally sabotaged by workers who threw *sabots* (the French word for wooden shoes) into the machinery. Although in the long run more jobs have been created than destroyed, the new jobs often fail to emerge until after a period of profound dislocation and transition.

Acceleration of Change

Once innovations are diffused and accepted, a group increases its cultural base; that knowledge, in turn, encourages further discoveries and inventions. The more culture items there are to work with, the greater the probability of recombining elements into something else. This is why the **rate of change** is higher in complex than in simple societies. Inventiveness is not related to differences in intelligence among the peoples of the world. Rather, it is associated with the accumulated knowledge of the group. This is the reason that, over the broad course of human history, social change has occurred at an increasingly accelerated pace.

The term **cultural lag** (Ogburn, 1922) describes the tendency for the parts of a culture to change and adapt at different rates after the introduction

The **rate of change** is directly related to the size of the culture base; the greater the base, the greater the chances of further change.

Cultural lag refers to the tendency for the parts of a culture to change and adapt at different rates after the introduction of a new technology.

The rate of change is faster in complex societies due to accumulated knowledge. Robots have increasingly replaced humans on the production line. Robot virtues include the fact that they do not complain, take coffee breaks, join unions, come to work late, or have interpersonal problems.

Through **adoption** people substitute a new technology for an older one.

Through **accommodation**, one institutional sphere makes internal changes to use the new technology better.

of a new technology (see Chapter 2). For example, the effects of the introduction of the mass-produced automobile in the United States in the 1920s are still being felt in other parts of American society. The distribution of the population between city and suburb, patterns of work and leisure, and even dating behaviors have been dramatically changed by the ability of most people to own cars. The physical environment has also been altered, as superhighways, drive-in theaters, and shopping malls sprawl across the land. Moreover, the full effects of pollution from fuel emissions may not be felt for many decades. Even relatively minor technological innovations, such as the development of the VCR, have had far-reaching effects, changing not only the recreational habits of millions of Americans but creating new industries.

One model, designed to explain the various aspects of cultural lag between the introduction of a new technology and the many other adaptations that follow in every area of social life is the technology diffusion model (Coates, 1983), which is shown in Figure 12-1. As you can see, the first result of technological change is that of **adoption,** where people substitute the new, more efficient, technology for an old one. The second step is **accommodation,** in which one institutional sphere undergoes internal changes in order

FIGURE 12-1   The technology-diffusion model: how an institution responds to a new technology. (Source: Coates, 1983, p. 80.)

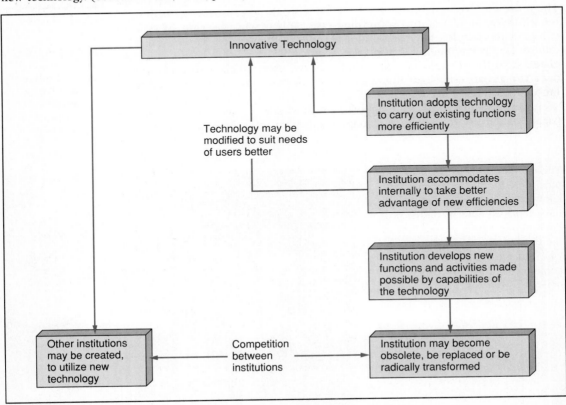

to make more efficient use of the new technology. In the third step, other areas of social life develop new functions and internal organizational changes in response to the technology. New institutions could also be created at this time. In stage four, an institution may become obsolete, be replaced, or change radically. Thus, the introduction of a major new element of culture leads to changes throughout the social system.

Using Figure 12-1, can you plot the many institutional transformations that have followed the introduction of the personal computer (PC) in millions of American households, offices, and schools. Before the PC, large and expensive computer systems had been gradually taking over data processing functions for government, corporations, research institutions, and libraries. But the PC brought such systems within the reach of individuals, schools, and small businesses. Many workers had to learn the new technology to keep their jobs, amid widespread fears of "being replaced by a machine." New industries emerged: for creating programs, instructing users, servicing the equipment, and thinking up even more sophisticated functions for existing computer systems. Electronic mail and bulletin boards bring instantaneous communication, bypassing such traditional gatekeepers as librarians. Today, anyone who can learn the program and pay for computer time can have immediate access to vast information banks.

TRENDS IN SOCIAL CHANGE

General and Specific Change

Although the course of social change in any society depends on specific historical events, sociologists have long sought to discover the overall direction of social change, to find some basic principle or law that has operated over the many thousands of years of human history. The basic model we have used in this book assumes that there has been **cumulative social change,** that is, a general development from simple to more complex societies, from small bands of gatherers, with their limited material culture, to the social and technological complexities of modern industrial society. Many types of societies may exist at the same time, however. For example, China had a highly differentiated social structure when much of Europe was inhabited by small bands of hunters and gatherers. Even in the United States today there are many different ways of life, ranging from the industrial cities and suburbs of the Northeast to the relatively simple rural farming communities of the Mennonites. Yet when the history of all known societies is added together, there is a general cumulative trend. Certain technologies and types of knowledge do not develop without a set of prior conditions. It is impossible that the automobile as we know it would have been invented without some notion of a combustion engine, or that open-heart surgery would succeed without a knowledge of sterile procedures.

Not all social institutions become more complex as societies become more intricate, however. For example, family and belief systems are more complex in simple societies than in modern ones, where both institutions have been considerably reduced in scope. When kinship ties and religious authorities no longer control everyday behavior, other social institutions de-

Cumulative social change is the gradual development from simple to more complex societies.

velop or change to handle these tasks. In our society today, the government, the educational institutions, and the nuclear family carry out socialization and social-control tasks that once were managed by kinship networks and religious organizations.

The Rise of the Nation-State

The *nation-state,* as a separate political unit of a complex society, is relatively new. For most societies throughout human history, nationality meant little. Rather, tribal loyalties, kinship, and ascribed status were the bases for social cohesion. **Nationalism** is a belief shared by many people that they have something in common (such as territory, beliefs, language, history, or a common enemy) powerful enough to make them seek political unity. It has become a major means of unifying peoples in one geographic area only within the last 400 years or so.

Although the existence of strong, relatively stable monarchies promoted the rise of nationalism in Europe, at least two other factors favored the concept of the nation-state as a basis for political authority and self-identity: (1) *capitalism* and (2) *colonialism.* Indeed, for many countries, the growth of capitalism coincided with the emergence of nationalism. As capitalistic economies developed, there was a search for wider markets and for raw materials to be exploited, especially by England, France, Germany, the Netherlands, and Spain.

With the discovery of the New World, traders and settlers from Europe entered territories whose peoples had little sense of national identity. The lack of national identity among the native populations promoted greater nationalistic feeling within those European countries that claimed and colonized other continents. Thus, the stage was set for the development of a nationalism that went beyond allegiance to the local community, region, or clan.

This has not been the pattern among Third World societies, however. Because of economic and political control of much of Africa and Asia by four nations—the United Kingdom, the United States, Germany, and France—a sense of nationhood was slow to develop. In the early 1950s, however, a new wave of nationalism developed in precisely those countries dominated by European and American economic and political power only a few years before. As a new, native middle class formed in Third World nations, its members learned not only the general rules and uses of colonial nationalism but the bitter fact that their own career aspirations were limited by it. For the Third World, nationalism became a liberation movement in which the common element was not language, culture, shared social institutions, or economic expansion, but anticolonialism.

By encouraging the breakup of old stratification and authority patterns, the new nationalism has stimulated diversified, independent economic growth. Yet because of the internal variation and the old tribal loyalties of many Third World nations, nationalism has various meanings among social classes and cultural groups within the same country. Although the established middle classes tend to favor independence without radical change, the old elites often want a return to an idealized past, whereas intellectuals and workers press

Nationalism is a consciousness of shared identity among the members of a politically distinct territory.

for radical social change. All of this has led to the instability of governments in Africa, Asia, and Central and South America today.

More recently there has been a resurgence of nationalism among the 15 republics of the Soviet Union, spreading from the Polish border to the Sea of Japan. Contrary to what many Americans believe, the Soviet Union is ethnically very diverse, and its 289 million people include not only Russians (51 percent), but more than 100 other ethnic and religious groups united by tenuous economic ties (see Table 12-1). Although Marx and Lenin predicted that

TABLE 12-1 The Two Major Ethnic Groups in Each of the Fifteen Republics of the Soviet Union

Republic	Ethnic Group	Percentage
Armenia	Armenians	90
	Azerbaijanis	5
Azerbaijan	Azerbaijanis	78
	Armenians	8
Byelorussia	Byelorussians	79
	Russians	12
Estonia	Estonians	65
	Russians	28
Georgia	Georgians	69
	Armenians	9
Kazakhstan	Russians	41
	Kazakhs	36
Kirghizia	Kirghiz	48
	Russians	26
Latvia	Latvians	54
	Russians	33
Lithuania	Lithuanians	80
	Russians	9
Moldavia	Moldavians	64
	Ukrainians	14
Russian S.F.S.R.	Russians	83
	Tatars	4
Tadzhikistan	Tadzhiks	59
	Uzbeks	23
Turkmenistan	Turkmen	68
	Russians	13
Ukraine	Ukrainians	74
	Russians	21
Uzbekistan	Uzbeks	69
	Russians	11

ethnic and religious differences would disappear as people developed a common sense of identity in the socialist state, linguistic, religious, and ethnic identities have remained strong, often as a form of resistance to the Soviet government.

Variations in Change

Although nationalism has been a recent, powerful factor in social and cultural change, it does not determine the history of any particular society. Some societies undergo rapid social change, whereas others remain relatively untouched. Throughout the world, societies that have survived for thousands of years are faced with the prospect of adapting to new circumstances, including nationalism.

In the Near East, previously isolated herding and farming societies are in the process of rapid and sudden growth, modernization, and nationalism. Saudi Arabia is one example. The rate of change may be more than the existing culture can support, so that a countermovement (Islamic fundamentalism), seeking a return to traditional ways, has developed, as in Iran in the early 1980s.

Within a given culture, not all change is toward increased complexity. Some societies emerge from prehistory to become sophisticated nation-states before undergoing a long period of decline and returning to a more simple structure. For example, ancient China had a highly specialized and differentiated social structure; yet for many centuries thereafter it existed as an unorganized, basically agricultural territory, parts of which were controlled by a succession of other nations. However, as in the case of China, some of these societies have experienced a rebirth as modernizing nations. No two societies are alike in all respects, and the probabilities of further growth are not predetermined but are subject to historical and technological forces.

From Pre- to Postindustrial Society

Modernization is a process through which a society becomes more internally differentiated and complex and in which science and technology guide change.

Mobilization involves the weakening of previous patterns of social, economic, and psychological commitments making people receptive for socialization to new patterns.

Social differentiation involves a shift from diffuse to specialized roles.

What do such different countries as the Soviet Union and the United States have in common that can shed light on social change and trends in contemporary societies? Both are examples of the modern society built on the notions of rationality and the bureaucratization of authority. **Modernization** is a social process through which a society becomes more internally differentiated and complex and in which science and technology guide change. As societies become modernized, they tend to converge, that is, to become more alike with respect to social structures, status hierarchies, and power and authority relationships. Nonetheless, each society retains its unique historical and cultural features.

The sociocultural change associated with modernization has two important aspects: (1) **mobilization,** in which old patterns of social, economic, and psychological commitments are weakened and people become available for socialization to new patterns; and (2) **social differentiation,** that is, a shift from diffuse to specialized roles (Eisenstadt, 1966).

Modernization is linked to three other trends discussed in earlier chapters: urbanization, industrialization, and secularization. Modern societies are composed of large numbers of workers and consumers, engaged in the production and the distribution of specialized goods and services and guided by rational-legal norms. Max Weber used the term **rationality** to refer to a type of social action in which the traditional and emotional bases for behavior are replaced by belief in a logical relationship between means and ends. Rationality has led to new technologies in the economic system, including the replacement of physical labor by machines.

Yet legal-rational power is a relatively new idea, whose development parallels the rise of European industrial society and of the nation-state. To understand how the sociocultural changes associated with modernization occur, recall some of the contrasts between *preindustrial* and *industrial* societies (see Chapter 2). Preindustrial societies have economies based on primary production (hunting, gathering, herding, and farming). Industrial societies have an economic and social organization based on machine technology and large-scale systems of production and distribution. The development of capitalist economies in the sixteenth century, coupled with technological, cultural, and political systems that encouraged profit, gave Western countries great advantages in economic development.

Investment and risk taking spread Western financial power throughout the world. As a result, a few industrialized nations dominate the rest of the world economically and politically. These dominant Western nations are now beginning to enter a new phase of economic development—postindustrialism. In postindustrial societies, science and technology are emphasized more heavily than manufacturing and productive capacity (Bell, 1973).

The driving force behind **postindustrial society** is the rapid development of information technology. Development of microchips, for example, has permitted one tiny piece of silicon costing a few dollars to contain circuits that, prior to miniaturization, would have required about ten years work by a worker soldering separate parts onto a board. Newer technologies are constantly being introduced; photonics, for example, transmits large amounts of information through laser or optical fibers and has the capacity to transmit the entire contents of the 30 volumes of the *Encyclopedia Britannica* in a few seconds.

To what extent does technology change society and with what risks? A major problem for postindustrial societies is not economic growth but efficient organization and codification of knowledge. A premium is placed on technical skill, knowledge, and managerial abilities as bases of power. Ascribed statuses (see Chapter 3) become less important for access to power or wealth than in the past. Instead, education and special skills provide ready routes to wealth, power, and prestige (although ascribed status and informal social networks based on stratification remain important factors).

Sociologists such as Daniel Bell (1989) have proposed that the information revolution is shaping a new interdependent international economy. For example, you may drive a Japanese car, buy shoes made in Brazil, watch a VCR manufactured in Korea, and wear clothes made in Sri Lanka. However, individual Western nations are increasingly unable to deal effectively with the implications of such an economy.

From a conflict perspective, technology has extended the capitalist "robber baron" philosophy, in which indifference to the human condition and

Rationality replaces traditional and emotional bases for behavior with the belief in a logical connection between means and ends.

The driving force behind **postindustrial society** is the rapid development of information technology.

worker alienation are commonplace. The computer is only one of a long series of technological innovations that management has used to take knowledge away from workers and exert control over them (Braverman, 1974).

<table>
<tr><td>

SOCIAL POLICY ISSUE

</td></tr>
</table>

Risks of Postindustrial Technology

With increased segmentation of tasks, workers are "deskilled"; that is, they neither understand the complexity of the organization within which they work nor have the skills to be easily promoted (see Chapter 10). For example, fast-food chains use tiny microprocessors to regulate both food production and customer service; because cash registers have buttons marked "med coke," "hamburger," and so on, cashiers do not even need to know the price of items they are selling or how to add up a check. Even relatively well paid professionals may be deskilled, turning the office into an "electronic sweatshop." Airline reservation personnel no longer need to know all the fares, routes, and policies, as that information is computerized. Salaries for reservation agents have accordingly declined, and computers track agents' productivity, giving management a powerful monitoring tool. Another consequence of the information revolution may be boredom. Klapp (1987) has suggested two escape routes: meaningful variety, requiring new learning and adaptation; and continuity of important customs to give texture to the culture.

As you think about the changes that technology is making in the types of employment available, the organization of work, and the ways in which the "information revolution" is changing your life and that of your family and friends, what do you think are the major social issues associated with present technological change? On what sociological concepts are your ideas based? ■

Safety and Postindustrial Technology

As technology increases, so do the risks associated with its use. Even the simplest equipment or product can be accidentally misused or have unanticipated consequences. Focusing on internal organizational characteristics as well as those of the industrial system itself, Perrow (1986) identified four characteristics of the internal system of an organization affecting safety behavior: (1) rate of growth (gradual or rapid); (2) length of experience with the technology needed to understand its hazards; (3) centralized or decentralized organizational structure; and (4) ability of the organization to conduct crisis training and drills. Industry characteristics, such as the amount of information in the unit, how it is shared, separation of supervision and sponsorship, and independent inspection also affect safety.

For example, industrial and medical *biotechnology* (e.g., genetic engineering) has several system characteristics that increase the likelihood of accidents. First, biotechnology has increased rapidly with little past experience to draw on. Trials cannot be gradual. Competition among laboratories is keen. Regulation or inspection by outside agencies is minimal or nonexistent and, at best, confused. Information flow is often restricted because of the desire to make a profit and to put out a product before the competition.

As technology advances, so do the risks associated with its use. Each year more than 2,000 cases of cancer in the United States are estimated to be caused by the billions of pounds of toxic chemicals released into the air each year.

Moreover, there are few strong groups outside the industry advocating safety regulation (Perrow, 1986).

Once an accident occurs, how is the catastrophe handled? Accidents that have already occurred in our oil and chemical industries, the space program, and nuclear power facilities suggest that the built-in risks of technological systems have been underestimated, concealed whenever possible, or initially explained as errors of human operators, rather than as system failures. In addition, several independent investigations have disclosed a pattern of mismanagement associated with risk taking, as well as a history of prior near-catastrophes. When such mistakes are uncovered, formal penalties are usually mild, and any changes that are introduced are relatively minor and do not prevent future occurrences (Perrow, 1986). The nuclear accident at Chernobyl in the Soviet Union in 1986 is one example. Nuclear power plants, like many other significant new technologies, are indeed "risky business" (Perrow, 1986). The full extent of risk may be unknown precisely because the technology is new and investment in its development is substantial.

Risk taking is inherent in the development of new technologies. But many managers may have lost contact with the technologies they are supposed to be managing. For example, compared to the rest of the postindustrial world, American managers are less likely to have a technical background than those in Europe or Japan, while engineers and scientists may believe so strongly in

untried technologies that they plunge ahead without assessing the nontech-
nological consequences (Thurow, 1987).

How can the balance between innovative technology and its potential
risks be reduced? Responsible decision making, in both the public and private
sector, and constant vigilance are required. Prompt, correct, and decisive
human intervention is needed to prevent catastrophe. Breadth of knowledge,
diagnostic ability, team cooperation, and ability to intervene quickly are human traits that cannot yet be equaled by systems controlled primarily by
computer programs or "fail-safe" systems (Hirshhorn, 1984). Without this
human intervention, unanticipated and catastrophic social change will continue to occur as a side effect of technological innovation.

THE SELF AND SOCIAL CHANGE

What happens to the self when social change occurs? Among the Ik described
at the beginning of this chapter, changes in the mode of subsistence were also
associated with drastic changes in personality and sense of self. Change in a
society thus consists not only of structural, economic, and cultural shifts but
of psychological changes. Our very selves and our positions in the social
structure are mutually reinforcing. For example, from a conflict perspective,
the mode of production shapes the self. The alienation that results from a
worker's relationship to the modes of production under industrialism is part
of his or her very being, so that people in supervised work have different
personality profiles than those in more self-directed jobs.

As described in Chapter 4, much of the self is molded by the actions and
the reactions of others toward us. The variety—and sometimes the unpre-
dictability—of others' reactions to us is far greater in modern, urban societies
than in the relative stability of isolated simple communities. Complex societies
also provide a greater range of roles than are available in tradition-based or
developing nations. This can be a mixed blessing, permitting more personal
freedom and allowing us to live in a variety of social worlds, yet requiring
that each of us must constantly read, process, and select among the cues given
us by others.

Modern urban societies, according to sociologist Georg Simmel (1918–
1950), promote a different kind of consciousness, a "blasé attitude," or indifference to many of the people and the events around us. This indifference is
a type of survival mechanism, developed to screen out the constant stimulation of other people, sights, smells, noises, and activities that are part of
modern life.

The effect of social structure on personality has been described in a
classic study by David Riesman (1950). Contrasting three different ideal types,
each associated with a particular level of industrial development, Riesman
identified the **tradition-directed** person, whose behavior is governed by
customs; the **inner-directed** person, whose behavior is governed by an
internal mechanism not upset by external forces and who is the prototype of
the capitalist or the worker in industrial society; and the **other-directed**
person, characteristic of postindustrial society, who is equipped with a psychological radar that scans the environment for appropriate messages to guide
behavior.

The **tradition-directed** person's behavior is governed by customs.

The **inner-directed** person's behavior is governed by an internal mechanism typical of industrial society.

The **other-directed** person, typical of the postindustrial society, constantly reacts and adapts to the expectations of others.

This reactive-adaptive (other-directed) self is another mixed blessing. The ability to adapt ourselves to a variety of situations allows us to anticipate and prepare for changing roles. Yet it may also result in anxiety and a crisis of the self. In sum, personality is mobilized as a resource in modern society, and the self is rationalized. Success, achievement, conscious control, and self-improvement are primary goals. The self, as the "me" orientation that dominated the United States in recent years illustrates, becomes treasured above all else as an object to be used to achieve desired ends.

ACCEPTING CHANGE

As we have noted, not all change is immediately accepted. Nor are diffused traits, however superior they may appear to be, universally welcomed. The new item must be compatible with the existing culture of the receiving society. Innovations must be seen as meeting a need or as conferring a benefit that outweighs the cost of changing behavior. Moreover, in any society, there are people with a vested interest in maintaining the status quo, that is, who derive power, prestige, or wealth from the existing arrangements, and who typically are people with great influence in the group. No African witch doctor could have resisted medical missionaries any more thoroughly than members of the American Medical Association fought against Medicare for the elderly between 1945 and 1965.

Change is promoted or resisted by people who occupy statuses in social systems. Some statuses are more influential than others, so that the people who occupy them are more likely to be **agents of change.** If the tribal chief or shaman (wise person) adopts an innovation, others in the tribe are likely to follow. In any society, there are *trendsetters* and *gatekeepers* who can influence the direction of change.

Agents of change occupy statuses through which they can influence the direction of change.

Although in modern societies the media play a significant part in the introduction of new items, formal and informal interpersonal channels of communication remain as important for Americans as for Australian aborigines. *Social networks* carry the message from one person to another. For example, an early study of the diffusion of innovation in medicine (Coleman et al., 1957) found that a new drug was more readily adopted by physicians who were profession-oriented and integrated into a network of local physicians than by those who were patient-oriented and relatively isolated from their medical peers.

The acceptance of specific social changes thus depends on many factors, including (1) the extent to which the new trait or idea is consistent with what already exists in the culture; (2) the perceived costs of adopting the new item or giving up old ways of thinking and behaving; (3) resistance by those with a vested interest in the status quo; (4) a general fear of the long-term effects of change; and (5) the influence of events producing change.

Indeed, not all agents of change are appreciated. Many are labeled as troublemakers or heretics and are subjected to social control and negative sanctions, including ridicule as well as imprisonment, assassination, and execution. When such forces of social control are brought into play, broad currents of change are temporarily slowed. The effectiveness of agents of change depends largely on the context in which they act rather than the importance of their ideas. For example, in 1987 the Czechoslovak government placed five organizers of a music group, the Jazz Section, on trial. Their offenses were the introduction of non-Socialist modern music, namely, American jazz. Ironically, in 1990, after the old Communist elite had been deposed by a more democratic government, American rock musician Frank Zappa was appointed by the new government as cultural affairs liaison to the West.

TYPES OF CHANGE

There are also important variations in the *pace* and the *extent* of change required by the introduction of new elements into an ongoing social system.

Gradual, or Incremental, Change

Gradual, or incremental, change is a long process in which one modification is followed by another.

Some changes are part of a broad trend whose final impact is unknown. **Gradual,** or **incremental, change** may long go unnoticed until a major transformation has occurred. For example, the agricultural revolution of prehistory was not a sudden, dramatic shift in the mode of subsistence but a long, gradual process affecting all institutional spheres. The same can be said of the Industrial Revolution, some elements of which were evolving in Europe long before the introduction of factories. The cumulative outcome, however, is a radical departure from the past. A silent revolution is occurring today as computers grow in sophistication and power, prompting widespread effects in the United States and elsewhere.

In general, the trends in modern society have been toward increased political participation, civil liberties and civil rights, sexual privacy, and educational attainment. But these results of incremental change are not as inevitable as was once thought. Modern industrial states can also be marked by political repression and a reduction in personal choice and freedom. In the United States, long-term changes in the status of women, increased tolerance of religious and other minorities, and greater family privacy appear to be firmly established, although subject to temporary setbacks.

The movement of birth cohorts and their flow through the social system are also important sources of unplanned change, particularly in modern societies, where the social system itself undergoes rapid alterations. Thus, even if cohort characteristics did not change greatly, cohort members would be moving through a different set of structures than did those who preceded them or who will follow. In fact, the causes and the effects of changes are interactive; that is, the cohort modifies the social system and the culture, while also being influenced and shaped by the existing structures.

Another type of gradual unplanned change occurs in belief systems. The members of a society at any one historical moment see the world through the lens of a particular model of reality (Kuhn, 1962). This world view organizes reality as, for example, the concept of an unchanging natural universe did in medieval thought. Gradually, however, bits and pieces of information accumulated that did not conform to this model, and a new view of the natural universe emerged, one that introduced the concept of evolution through natural selection. This new interpretation of reality was developed by several different observers at the same time because the evidence was so compelling. Similarly, the theory of relativity marked a major shift in scientific world view.

Revolutionary Change

Revolutionary change involves a "sudden, basic transformation of a society's political and socioeconomic (including class) structure" (Skocpol, 1979, p. 5). But revolutions do not simply happen. They arise from revolutionary situations.

The most influential modern theory of revolution has been that of Karl Marx. As described by Skocpol (1979), Marx's theory has three main elements: First, each revolution is historically grounded in a certain type of society; therefore, there can be no general theory of revolution. Second, organized movements for social change can succeed only where a revolutionary situation exists because of irreconcilable class conflict within the society. Third, because class conflict defines the revolutionary situation, the revolution is completed only when the power of the dominant class(es) is destroyed.

Skocpol (1979) modified Marx's model in light of actual events. Modern revolutions have occurred not, as Marx predicted, in industrial capitalist countries but in agricultural societies under pressure from outside forces. Moreover, the internal problems that make revolution possible have been political (competing power blocs) rather than economic (defined in Marxist terms as class conflict). Although the revolutionary mass has historically been composed of peasants rather than an urban working class, it has been not the oppressed workers, or even the peasants, but members of the educated elite who have assumed leadership and established the new state organizations. Finally, it is not the class system that changes as much as the political structure. These alterations in the distribution and functions of the state organization may, in turn, lead to dramatic changes in the social-class and economic systems.

From her study of the French, Russian, and Chinese revolutions, Skocpol (1979) concluded that the state structure—the political system—should be viewed as more than merely the governing arm of the economic ruling class. Furthermore, if we are to understand modern revolutions, we must take into account the international military rivalry among the industrial states and between the industrialized and the developing nations within a capitalist world economy. That is, the specific society undergoing change is itself embedded in larger systems of interacting states.

> **Revolutionary change** brings basic alterations in the political and socioeconomic structure of a society.

Social Changes and World Systems.   The term **world system** refers to the economic and political relationships among societies, particularly between the industrial states and the less-developed nations (Wallerstein, 1974). Modern industrial societies can be considered the economic "core" of the world system, and the less-developed nations the "periphery," providing raw materials for the core countries and then becoming a market for their manufactured goods. This was the logic of colonialism, but in a postcolonial world raw materials must now be paid for rather than taken, and markets must be won in competition with other exporters.

Third World countries possessing essential raw materials are now in a position of unaccustomed strength in their dealings with industrial societies.

> The **world system** consists of the economic and political relations among industrial and less-developed nations.

The late 1980s saw the mass mobilization of Eastern Europeans whose demands for change brought down their communist governments without bloodshed. Demonstrations such as this one in Prague, Czechoslovakia, were a weekly and often daily sight throughout Eastern Europe.

The oil-producing nations are a good example. Their monopoly over a scarce resource has permitted them to raise prices on the world market. These raised prices have led to a heavy outflow of money from the core nations, as well as to major changes in life-styles and industrial growth within both the core and the oil-exporting societies—changes that are politically destabilizing.

However, most peripheral societies lack a needed raw material. Most are extremely poor, overpopulated, and politically unstable. The poor nations grow poorer and the wealthy ones wealthier. This process is a major source of political instability in the underdeveloped nations of Asia, Africa, and Central America, the potential trouble spots of the globe.

From this perspective, revolutions need not be elaborately planned; rather, they will arise from strains in the social structure, as when a totalitarian regime is no longer able to suppress public revolts (e.g., the Philippines, Eastern Europe). But each specific revolt will have its own history within this general pattern. The outcome, however, is likely to be the same everywhere: increased centralization of power and bureaucratization when the new order is stabilized, as well as mobilization of the masses to support the revolution.

Revolutionary Events, Situations, and Outcomes. Revolutionary situations are different from revolutionary outcomes. According to Tilly (1978, 1986), a *revolutionary outcome* occurs when one set of power holders is displaced by another. A **revolutionary situation** exists when (1) two or more political units claim control over the state; (2) these interests cannot be reconciled; and (3) the opposition party receives support (money, loyalty, soldiers) from a sizable segment of the population. Such is the case in Northern Ireland today. The revolution ends when only one claimant remains. Tilly identified a range of *revolutionary events,* from a *coup,* in which one segment

A **revolutionary situation** occurs when two or more political units claim control over the state, these interests cannot be reconciled, and the opposition party receives support from a sizable segment of the population.

of the elite displaces another, to a *silent revolution,* in which a revolutionary outcome takes place with very little overt hostility, to the *great revolution* (for example, the American or French or Russian revolutions).

As for the long-term effects of the revolutionary event, these also vary by time and place. Tilly noted that there are very few examples of moral rebirth as a result of the revolutionary experience; people soon return to their usual round of activities. Such short-term gains may even be erased over the long run (for example, women's rights in the early days of the Russian Revolution), whereas short-term setbacks (such as the Reign of Terror at the beginning of the French Revolution) are ultimately followed by broad-scale transformation. In general, outcomes have positive and negative elements, and the costs may be very high indeed. As the iron law of oligarchy (see Chapter 10) suggests, unless vigilance is extended beyond the revolutionary moment, power holders tend to become more concerned with maintaining their control than with fulfilling the goals of the revolution.

THEORIES OF CHANGE

Does change take place along a single path (*unidirectional*), leading to some predestined goal—the Kingdom of Heaven, for example? Or has the direction been a progressive decline from some golden age? Or does change occur in a circular fashion as civilizations rise and fall? You have probably heard popular versions of each of these theories of social change.

Evolutionary Theories of Change

In late-nineteenth-century England, **unidirectional theories of evolutionary progress** were very popular. The path upward ran from savagery, represented by the simple societies discovered by British colonizers, to high civilization, represented, of course, by Victorian England (Spencer, 1860/1896). Some Americans might make the same claim for the United States today as a nation chosen by God to lead the free world against its enemies. The belief that one's social system is superior to that of other people provides a basis for the economic exploitation of less-developed societies.

> **Unidirectional theories of evolutionary progress** assume that social change occurs in one direction only.

Cyclical Theories of Change

The notion that cultures are like organisms, developing from birth to ultimate decline, fit into the intellectual currents of early-twentieth-century Western culture, in which many disciplines emphasized biological functioning and in which there was a feeling that European civilization was decadent and corrupt. But European civilization has proved far sturdier than predicted. Cultures do flourish and decline over long periods, but there is little evidence that **cyclical theories of social change** have much predictive value.

A more sociological theory of cyclical change was proposed by Sorokin (1941), who suggested that world history has alternated between periods of rationality and order, on the one hand, and emotionality and letting go on the other.

The two theories of social change that stimulate most interest among

> **Cyclical theories of social change** are based on the view that society resembles a living organism, going through phases of growth and decline.

contemporary social scientists, however, are related to the two macrosocial perspectives of functionalism and conflict. A coming together of these two positions has been a connecting thread throughout this volume, and nowhere is the blending of these two approaches more apparent than in the analysis of change.

Classical Models

Many of sociology's classical theories have proposed two-part schemes to describe the cumulative direction of social structural change. Durkheim, for example, contrasted *mechanical solidarity* in simple societies, where every member was interchangeable with others, to the *organic solidarity* of modern societies brought on by an increasing division of labor, so that members play complementary roles and are bound together by ties of interdependence.

Tönnies's concepts of *Gemeinschaft* and *Gesellschaft* reflect a similar model of change: a trend from close primary relationships as the basis of social life to the more varied, fragmented, temporary, and role-specific mode of modern life (see Chapter 3). The same general process was described by the anthropologist Redfield (1941) as a drift from *folk communities* toward *urban society*. In all these schemes, structural complexity is associated with population density and the specialization of tasks.

Neoevolutionary theory traces changes in cultural and societal complexity without making value judgments about the superiority of one society over another.

The *neoevolutionary model* that we have used in this text is a more sophisticated version of these developmental schemes. **Neoevolutionary theory** is based on four simple propositions: (1) growth of the population depends on the mode of subsistence; (2) changes in technology lead to new adaptations that typically support larger populations; (3) increased density leads to the specialization and coordination of tasks; and (4) the need to create order among different kinds of workers leads to more complex organizations and the emergence of distinct institutional spheres (see Figure 12-2).

Critics of the neoevolutionary model do not object to its assumptions of cumulative change and increasing structural complexity. But they question the additional assumption made by functional theorists that institutional arrangements tend toward balance and internal adjustment. In other words, functional theory minimizes the possibility that strain may arise from *within* the system, generated precisely from existing institutional arrangements.

The Conflict Model

The **conflict view of social change** stresses the recurrent and enduring sources of strain among the groups within society.

The **conflict view of social change** focuses on the recurrent and lasting sources of tension and struggle among individuals and groups within any society (see Part II). At any given moment, social systems consist of competing interest groups, so that conflict is built into social organization. It seems to us that the conflict perspective completes the model of social and cultural change that we have developed from functional and neoevolutionary sources because it specifies the sources and the processes of change in the social system. Only by looking at the specific circumstances that give rise to discontent and change in any society can we understand why some social systems last and others decay and why some undergo gradual and relatively peaceful change, whereas others experience violent revolution.

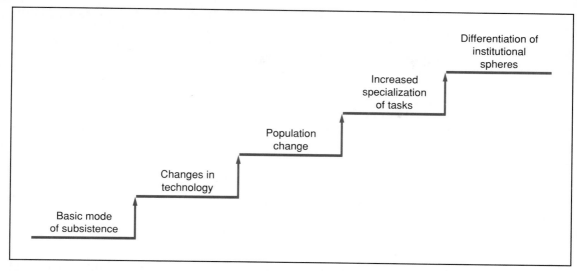

FIGURE 12-2   Steps in the structural differentiation of society.

For Karl Marx, the competing groups within industrial society were the social classes and their relationship to the means of production, namely, the owners and those who sold their labor. Marx thought that the conditions of modern work would eventually be so alienating that the workers would revolt against the owners of capital. Yet, as we have seen, the working classes of the world have not become revolutionary—quite the opposite, in fact. Ronald Reagan, a candidate closely linked to capitalist interests, received almost half of all working-class votes in the United States in 1984. Ironically, perhaps, the workers of Communist Poland were more militantly class-conscious than those in the United States, successfully pressing their interests against the controller of the means of production, which happened to be, until 1989, the Communist party.

But Marx's theory of social change does not rely on the necessity of violent revolution. Viewing human history in its totality, Marx described a **dialectical model of social change.** At any given moment, the social system of interconnected parts makes up a *status quo,* or **thesis,** out of which competing or warring elements emerge to challenge the given order of things. These forces of opposition are called the **antithesis.** Out of the conflict between thesis and antithesis—the power of vested interest and the forces of protest—comes a new social order: **synthesis.**

In the **dialectical model of social change, thesis** is represented by the status quo, **antithesis** is the force of opposition. **Synthesis** emerges from the conflict between those two.

A Unified Model of Change

To synthesize the neoevolutionary and the conflict models, we propose that general change can be best explained in terms of changes in the economic base of society. Collectivities that do not experience shifts in modes of subsistence are not likely to undergo changes in other institutional spheres—unless, of course, they are invaded. But where subsistence modes do undergo change, other social patterns are ultimately affected. Some changes, as in the case of the Ik, are disastrous. Other societies are more fortunate and adapt to the new conditions at a more complex level of organization. Such has been the pattern of history.

Change *within* a given society, however, can be analyzed in terms of class-based interests. The outcome of any conflict depends on the power of those with vested interests to subvert, coopt, or suppress movements for change. Because ruling elites are typically stronger than protesters, rapid and radical change is generally resisted successfully. However, gradual, almost unnoticed changes within a society may occur, so that over a long period of time different patterns in the social and cultural fabric of a group become obvious. The gains of the women's movement, for example, although slow and incremental, have ultimately brought major institutional changes to our society, despite powerful backlash pressures.

THE FUTURE: WHAT NEXT?

What can we expect in the future? Both social change and the problems of the future will be, in part, results of and reactions to current technology and institutionalized patterns of social relationships. In the past, the United States and other major industrialized nations have relied on cheap raw materials from preindustrial nations. As a result, industrialized society has developed social and economic institutions based largely on waste and the depletion of the world's resources. Americans in particular are used to the idea of disposables—from cars to cups—and repairing items is for many people a lost art.

Yet there is growing evidence that scarcity can be anticipated in a number of areas—scarcity caused by the demands of technology and by the widespread modification of the environment. For example, there are limits to the supply of water and fossil fuels that may have far-reaching implications for

As you sail into the future, we hope you will make good use of the sociological perspective. Because social systems are developed by humans, they can be changed and reconstructed.

almost every economic system. We could delay these potential shortages by reducing our use of water and fossil fuels, by manufacturing longer-lasting goods, and by planned recycling. But this solution, too, has its costs. Longer-lasting goods lead to increased unemployment. After all, fewer workers would be required to turn out fewer but more durable products. Many social analysts claim that there is no single, one-time solution to problems that we can expect to face in the foreseeable future.

Various visions of the future have been proposed, all of which emphasize the importance of technological change. For example, the rise of computer technology has led some futurists to predict a society in which technology will become too complex for the average person to understand. Others, such as Naisbitt (1982), foresee a multiple-option society, in which the range of personal choices is expanded by "high tech/high touch" developments — technological innovations accompanied by compensatory human responses. Whatever the future holds, a sociological perspective—that is, an awareness of how you are shaped by and shape the world in which you live—is essential to informed participation in the design of the future.

COLLECTIVE BEHAVIOR AND SOCIAL MOVEMENTS

In 1989 many middle-aged Americans celebrated the 20th anniversary of one of the most astounding instances of collective behavior in American history: the Woodstock Music and Art Fair of the weekend of August 15, 1969. At least 400,000 young people from all parts of the Northeast had experienced three days of music-making and art exhibits during which it rained, the food ran out, sanitary facilities stopped working, and roads in and out were impassable. Yet they stayed for the entire weekend, celebrating their youth, their affection for one another, and their commitment to peace (Makower, 1989).

Woodstock represented the flowering of the "hippie" counterculture of the 1960s; it was an event that marked a special moment in the lives of the participants and in the cultural transition from the conventional ethic of the 1950s to the self-centered, laid-back expressiveness of the 1970s. Less than a year later, National Guard troops fired at students at antiwar protests at Kent State and Jackson State Universities, and the 1960s came to both a spiritual and chronological end.

Woodstock and the legends that surround it; long hair, love beads, and psychedelic drugs; other large gatherings of the 1960s; the riots and protests, demonstrations and sit-ins—all are forms of what sociologists call **collective behavior.**

Collective behavior refers to noninstitutionalized responses to flux and change.

TYPES OF COLLECTIVE BEHAVIOR

One way to make sense of the diversity of collective behaviors is to arrange types of activity along such dimensions as (1) spontaneous versus structured forms, (2) short-term versus long-term commitments, (3) expressive versus instrumental goals, and (4) unconscious versus conscious motives. For example, a continuum of spontaneity might look like the one in Figure 12-3.

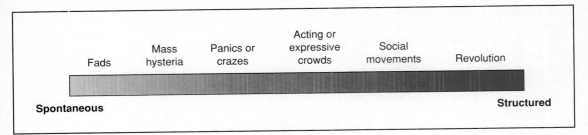

FIGURE 12-3 A continuum of collective behavior.

Relatively Spontaneous Forms of Collective Behavior

In general, events that are relatively spontaneous are also short-lived, expressive, and lacking in clear-cut goals. Such widespread phenomena as fads, panics, and mass hysteria appear to be so unpredictable that they are also assumed to be irrational. But collective behavior, even the most unstructured, is rarely random.

Mass hysteria involves uncontrollable emotional reactions to anxiety within a group; but these, too, are grounded in social processes and realities. For example, the seventeenth-century New England schoolgirls who claimed to be possessed by witches were no doubt suffering from a combination of boredom and puberty in a sexually repressive society (Boyer and Nussbaum, 1974). Accused witches were usually relatively isolated, older, unmarried women in marginal social statuses who were feared for their nonconformity. Today, outbreaks of mass hysteria typically involve schoolchildren and women whose jobs involve simple, repetitive tasks at a fast pace (Golden, 1990)— both groups being relatively powerless, engaged in extremely boring work, and given cultural permission to act "irrationally."

Panics are typically grounded in perceived threats and fears, as illustrated in the famous *War of the Worlds* radio broadcast of 1938, which millions of listeners took to be an actual account of martians landing on earth. Similar fears surface today in periodic "sightings" of unidentified flying objects (UFOs), none of which has yet been shown to be of extraterrestrial origin. The essence of panic behavior is an overwhelming need to escape danger. Panics also occur on Wall Street when brokers, fearing losses, sell off securities, creating a massive drop in values that leads to more selling.

Crazes, on the other hand, involve an intense desire to have something that everyone else appears to be enjoying—for example, Nintendo games or all-terrain vehicles.

Fads are very short-lived but widely copied outbursts of unexpected and often playful behavior. Colleges and universities are prime sites for fads, such as swallowing goldfish, eating Pop Tarts, dying one's hair green, or "streaking" (running naked across campus). For a brief period in the spring of 1974, more than 1,000 cases of streaking were reported. A careful analysis of these events shows that they were far from random; the likelihood of a streaking incident

Mass hysteria in-volves uncontrollable emotional reactions to anxiety within a group.

Panics are actions caused by a sudden overwhelming need to escape danger.

Crazes involve a desire to have something that everyone else appears to be enjoying.

A fad is a short-lived but widely copied outburst of unexpected and often playful behavior.

was associated with the prestige of neighboring schools where streaking occurred, the composition of the student body, the risks involved, media coverage, and interpersonal networks (Aguirre et al., 1988).

Fashions are more enduring, widespread, and socially significant than either crazes or fads. Trendsetters define what is "in" and networks of influence carry the message. The direction of influence can be from the top down, as with "designer" clothes being copied in less expensive versions, or from the masses up, as with blue jeans or punk style.

Dress and body adornment carry important information about a person's social status, in modern as well as preliterate societies (Rubinstein, 1985). In a society without a hereditary aristocracy, it may be necessary for the higher strata to be distinguished from the lower in some very visible way. Conversely, it could be argued that mass production in our society permits a democratization of dress that obscures the reality of social-class differences. In an authentic classless society, fashion could be subversive—thus, in the People's Republic of China, until recently all citizens were encouraged to wear the same type of simple, functional clothing. In a caste society, however, fashion would be unnecessary, as status distinctions are very clear without variations in adornment (Blumer, 1974).

Rumors are unverified items of information, usually from anonymous sources, that pass quickly from one person to another. A rumor is a group product that may or may not be correct; it exists only at the level of interaction. Although some rumors may be intentionally planted, many are unconscious distortions of normal communication that reinforce existing anxieties and prejudices.

Fashions are more enduring, widespread, and socially important than fads.

Rumors are unconfirmed information, which may or may not be correct.

The fears and fantasies that become the making of urban legends are often exploited in the headlines of the more sensationalist press.

Urban legends are items of modern folk-lore involving rumors that resonate to deeply held fears and anxieties regarding aspects of modern life beyond personal control.

You have probably heard rumors or **urban legends** such as the one about the baby in the microwave, the missing women sold into sexual slavery, and products that carry Satanic symbols (Brunvand, 1988; Wachs, 1988). Or how about the "Halloween sadist" who passes out apples with hidden razor blades (Best, 1985)? Not one of these stories has ever been verified. It appears that the stories not only resonate to deeply held fears, but also relieve anxieties by explaining things that seem beyond personal control.

In a social-psychological perspective, the life of a rumor resembles the children's game of "pass it on," where with each telling some details are exaggerated and others forgotten. In one famous experiment, white students were shown a picture of a white man threatening a black man on a subway train; as one student described the picture to the next, the situation was soon reversed, with the black threatening the white, because this version was more compatible with their preexisting world view (Allport and Postman, 1947).

From a purely sociological perspective, however, it is more important to note that rumors typically originate among persons of low prestige or who are relatively isolated, and then spread through the most convenient networks (Koenig, 1985). Rumors are a way of striking back and of becoming noticed. Identifying an "enemy" often enhances the solidarity of the group.

In some cases, stories with some verifiable elements are intentionally elaborated. For example, the "missing children" problem is based on highly inflated estimates of the number of children who might actually be kidnapped by a stranger. Although law enforcement agencies estimate that the number of stranger abductions is about 100 to 200 children each year, missing child organizations have used figures in the tens of thousands.

In reality, the vast majority of missing children are adolescents who have voluntarily run away from home for a very short period. Another large number of missing children, estimated to number 100,000 annually, have been taken by a noncustodial parent. But as long as the higher estimates are accepted, organizations devoted to finding kidnapped children will receive publicity and funding.

A **public**, or **mass audience**, consists of people who are not in the same place at the same time but who relate similarly to particular issues.

Publics.   Unlike the other collective behaviors discussed in this chapter, a **public,** or **mass audience,** is composed of people who are not in the same place at the same time but who relate similarly to particular issues. For example, Richard Nixon's concept of the *silent majority* referred to an assumed public that strongly supported the Vietnam War but that did not take to the streets to demonstrate its approval of his policies.

All advertising is designed to create a public for a product, whether it is a bar of soap or a politician. Other publics consist of people who have some preexisting common interest—the environment, gun control, abortion, or civil rights, for example—and whose opinions may be formed individually but whose commitment can be activated by events reported in the media.

An **interest group** develops when members of a public seek others with similar feelings about an issue.

An unorganized public can become an **interest group** when people on one side of an issue feel strongly enough to move beyond letter writing and to seek out others with similar feelings. Until recently, it was very difficult, if not impossible, to reach all the members of the society simultaneously; today, it can be done in a moment by radio and television.

Crowds

A **crowd** is a temporary gathering of people that is brought together by some common concern or activity, and in which there is an awareness of the presence of others. Yet a crowd is not a group in the sense of having structure, such as a division of labor with patterned roles. Under some circumstances, an individual can literally as well as figuratively become "lost in the crowd" and therefore be released from the norms that typically regulate behavior.

A **crowd** is a temporary gathering of people brought together by some common concern or activity.

Types of Crowds.   There are many kinds of temporary collections, or *aggregates,* of people, from shoppers in a supermarket to a lynch mob.

A **casual crowd** is an accidental gathering of people who are following individual goals in the same place at the same time (e.g., shoppers, travelers, strollers) and who then share a common focus—as witnesses to an accident, for example—that makes them aware of one another. At the other extreme, a **conventional crowd** is composed of people who have intentionally gathered together at events governed by established norms, such as religious services, sports events, or theater performances. Here, behavior is highly patterned and therefore highly predictable.

A **casual crowd** is an accidental gathering of people.

A **conventional crowd** is composed of people who are gathered as spectators, audiences, or participants at events governed by established norms.

Both casual and conventional crowds can be transformed into expressive and acting crowds (Blumer, 1951). An **expressive crowd** emerges when participants are gripped by feelings that overwhelm customary normative controls. Sports fans have been known to tear up the turf on a playing field; people have been trampled at religious rallies. In contrast, the **acting crowd** has a goal beyond the mere expression of emotion. Fueled by the belief that only action outside the norms can accomplish desired changes, the acting crowd could easily become a *mob.*

An **expressive crowd** shows strong feelings with outbursts of emotion.

Acting crowds have some goals beyond expression of emotion; they desire to take action.

A **mob** is a cohesive, emotionally aroused acting crowd, often engaged in violent or disruptive acts. The Boston Tea Party was a mob action that has become a hallowed event in American history, much as the storming of the Bastille in 1789 is glorified by the French.

A **mob** is a cohesive, emotionally aroused crowd, often engaged in violent or disruptive acts.

Riots are another type of violent acting crowd. Somewhat less spontaneous than mob actions, riots typically embrace larger numbers of people over longer periods of time. Race and ethnicity have been focal points of riot behavior throughout our history. Gangs of whites burned and looted African- and Asian-American neighborhoods in the 1940s and 1960s. In the late 1960s minority ghetto residents destroyed white-owned properties in a number of northern cities.

Riots are usually less spontaneous than mob actions and tend to involve more people over longer periods of time.

The definition and evaluation of acting crowds depends on who is involved. Students, prisoners, and nonwhites are usually described in the media as "rioters." In contrast, National Guard troops out of control, strikers, and desegregation protesters are rarely labeled that way even though identical behaviors are being observed. For example, in Cincinnati, Ohio, in 1979, a crush of primarily young people arriving for a concert by the Who ended in the death of 11 people. The incident was immediately reported in the media as a "stampede" of young "barbarians," high on dope and drink. In actuality, as careful research by Norris Johnson (1987) shows, the young people were trying to escape the crush of the crowd, and no one intentionally stomped on anyone else.

Demonstrations are temporary but highly organized acting crowds with a clearly defined goal.

Demonstrations are acting crowds with a clearly defined goal, either to protest or support a particular public policy. Demonstrations, while usually short-lived, are often highly organized. An effective demonstration requires considerable planning and preparation: permits, publicity, transportation, portable toilets, entertainment, and speakers. The purpose of a demonstration is twofold: (1) to generate publicity about the cause and show widespread support and (2) to bring "true believers" together so that they can be reinforced in their shared commitment.

Organizers announce a massive rally at a symbolic location—a nuclear power plant, the steps of the Supreme Court, or a store selling fur coats—and then must ensure that enough people take part to influence politicians and sway public opinion. The size of the crowd becomes crucial; if fewer people than expected show up, the cause is described as losing steam; if more people than anticipated arrive, the cause is perceived as gaining adherents. For example, the 1989 March for Women's Equality and Women's Lives was announced and planned three months in advance. The organizers played it safe by estimating that 250,000 would come, and when the crowds clearly exceeded that number, the organizers then claimed 600,000 participants. Government authorities, the targets of the protest, spoke of "about 300,000," and veteran demonstration watchers pegged the actual count at between 350,000 and 400,000.

Common Elements of Crowd Behavior.   Although there are many ways in which crowds can vary—in size, duration, cohesion, and goals—Turner and Killian (1972) list the following characteristics as those found to some degree in most crowds:

- Lack of certainty about what should be done.
- A feeling that something should be done.
- The spread of this feeling among participants.
- Creation of a particular *mood* based on this uncertainty.
- Openness to suggestions about what to do.
- Relaxation of customary restraints on behavior.

Because crowd behavior is relatively unstructured and variable, outcomes are less predictable than for other social interactions.

MODELS OF COLLECTIVE BEHAVIOR

What turns an otherwise ordinary collection of people into a group of hysterical twitchers or a destructive mob? Early theories of collective behavior were framed primarily in a social-psychological perspective, with an emphasis on individual motivations and perceptions.

The **emotional contagion model** focuses on how the intensity of crowds develops.

The Contagion Model

In Blumer's (1951) **emotional contagion model,** an initial stage of aimless milling around is followed by a focusing of attention on a single theme or leader. This emerging definition of the situation is reinforced as members of the crowd interact. Thus, the crowd is primed for action, often sparked by a rumor.

From a more sociological perspective, the crowd is seen as a field for evolving relationships and norms. That is, through their interaction, participants gradually develop a set of meanings—an "emergent construction of reality" (Wright, 1978)—that makes sense of their actions.

The Value Added Model

In a more systematic formulation, the **value added model,** proposed by Neil Smelser (1968), lists six conditions as necessary *and* sufficient to produce some form of collective behavior:

1. *Structural conduciveness.* Social institutions are organized to encourage or discourage collective behavior.
2. *Structural strain.* Tension is introduced into the situation because of inequalities that are seen as unfair and as the result of social structural conditions.
3. *Growth and spread of a generalized belief* occurs as people seek explanations for their intolerable situation.
4. *Precipitating factors* are dramatic events that support the generalized belief. The events need not have actually occurred; a rumor will spark crowd reaction if the rumored event fits the generalized belief.
5. *Mobilization for action* comes when a leader emerges to give a sense of direction to willing crowd participants.
6. *Social control factors* are the responses of the authorities. Crowds can be encouraged or discouraged from a given course of action by the way in which a situation is handled by politicians, police, the courts, and the media.

The **value added model** specifies six conditions that are necessary and sufficient to produce collective behavior.

Sociologists ask: Why does a particular social protest emerge when it does? What accounts for its success and failure? Theories of individual motivation cannot answer these questions.

Resource Mobilization

Over the past 15 years, a basically organizational approach to collective behavior has emerged: the **resource mobilization** model. In this view, protest activities and organized efforts to produce or resist change (social movements) are not abnormal events that attract alienated or marginal followers, but part of the ongoing process whereby social goods are distributed (Tilly, 1978; Zald and McCarthy, 1987).

The resource mobilization perspective on collective behavior emphasizes (1) the financial, political, and recruitment resources that can be activated ("mobilized") by protesters and (2) the strength of agents of social control to resist change. Neither shared grievances nor generalized beliefs—both essentially social-psychological variables—are sufficient to explain the emergence of protest activity; nor are participants necessarily the most alienated members of society. For example, it was not the most deprived African-

The **resource mobilization model** stresses the supports available to protesters, as well as the tactics used by social control agents.

Americans who forged the civil rights protests, nor was it the most powerless women who founded the feminist movement.

Success therefore depends on securing a variety of resources from the environment: leaders, administrative skills, communication networks, members and potential recruits, and a certain degree of legitimacy in the eyes of the public and political leaders (Wuthnow, 1987). Not only money and people, but *symbolic* resources are important. Resource mobilization theorists assume that in modern industrial societies there will always be grounds for protest, and that participants are rational decision makers who have decided that the goals of the protest are worth the time and effort required to fight for them (e.g., Olson, 1965; Rule, 1989).

Modifications of the Resource Mobilization Model. Over the past decade, sociologists have expanded the model to include variables such as ideology and legitimacy (Zald and McCarthy, 1987; Walker et al., 1987); the goals of collective action are seen as important in activating support.

In addition, social-psychological variables, such as the type and level of felt discontent or *grievance* and the perception that goals can be accomplished, have been introduced into the model. Two recent studies of antinuclear activism in the United States (Cable et al., 1988) and Western Europe (Opp, 1988), for example, found that preexisting dissatisfaction was an important element in recruiting members after accidents at nuclear energy plants.

These modifications of resource mobilization theories have brought the individual back into the study of collective behavior, but always in relation to the characteristics of the groups and organizational contexts through which protest is channeled.

Why Join? What do people receive in return for spending their time and money on collective action and possibly risking their health or job or standing in the community? There are three broad types of personal reward: (1) emotional satisfaction and a sense of group solidarity, (2) material items such as goods and services, and (3) a feeling of efficacy, that one can make things happen and that goals can be achieved (Olson, 1965).

In one study of the effect of different types of incentive on member involvement in a collective-action organization, the American Association of Retired Persons (AARP), the researcher found that material benefits were not powerful motivators of participation (Knoke, 1988). It was, rather, the members concerned with realizing the principles and enhancing the prestige of AARP who contributed the most time and money to the organization.

Who Joins? Recruitment to collective activity, as you are well aware by now, is conducted largely through interpersonal contacts. We join because we are urged by friends or coworkers.

For example, examining recruitment to a very high-risk program, the 1964 Freedom Summer Project in which white college students went to Mississippi to engage in voter registration drives and other civil rights activity, McAdam (1988) found that the major variables that distinguished the students who actually participated from those who had applied but failed to come were the following: (1) a larger number of organization memberships, (2) higher levels of previous civil rights activity, and (3) stronger and wider ties with other students taking part in the project.

Network pressure can also operate despite a person's attitudes. A study of physicians' participation in an antiabortion campaign found that their motivation was based largely on a fear of being isolated from other doctors and potential patients (Eckberg, 1988). In fact, few of the physicians agreed fully with the philosophy or goals of the Right to Life movement, but they were willing to join rather than risk their livelihood or standing in the community.

The Mobilization Process.   From the foregoing research, a model of mobilization and participation can be described. Successful mobilization depends on (1) creating a potential base of support in the population, (2) forming recruitment networks to tap potential members, (3) arousing motivation among targeted individuals, and (4) removing barriers to participation (Klandermans and Oegma, 1987). People who do not participate in collective action may not do so for reasons such as the following: they do not approve of the goals, they have not been personally approached; their motivation has not been aroused; or there are too many costs involved.

In the case of the Iranian revolution of 1978–79, for example, collective action against the absolute ruler, the Shah, was fueled less by ideology than by the negative effects of state policies on the economic positions of bazaar merchants, skilled industrial workers, and the white-collar middle class (Parsa, 1988). Once the bazaar merchants mobilized their resources, small protests turned into larger ones as more and more aggrieved subgroups joined the revolution. The Ayatollah Khomeini, who had come to symbolize resistance to the government, was then able to unify the opposition forces and bring down the monarchy.

SOCIAL MOVEMENTS: BELIEFS AND ACTIONS

Social movements involve large numbers of people mobilized to promote or resist social and cultural change. McCarthy and Zald (1977), however, felt it important to distinguish the sentiments that make collective action possible from the formal structures created to achieve these goals. They defined a **social movement** as a "set of opinions and beliefs" within the population in favor of change in the institutional spheres and stratification system—as, for example, the Women's Movement or the Civil Rights Movement. A **countermovement** is a set of opinions and beliefs within the population that is opposed to the goals of a social movement—for example, the profamily movement or the white-power movement.

Social movement organizations are specific formal associations such as the National Organization for Women (NOW), Stop-ERA, the National Urban League, or the Knights of the Ku Klux Klan (KKK). When several organizations are formed around the same goal, or when organizations representing different movements join their efforts, a *social movement industry* is forged.

A **social movement** is a set of opinions and beliefs in favor of institutional change.

A **countermovement** is a set of opinions and beliefs within the population that is opposed to the goals of a social movement.

Social movement organizations are specific formal organizations that channel discontent into concrete actions.

Classifying Social Movements

Social movements can be classified in a number of ways, one of which is *duration.* Blumer (1974) distinguished *general* or long-term gradual (secular) changes from *specific* social movements that are limited in time and place. For example, although the secular trend in America has been in the direction of full inclusion of African-Americans, specific movements within this broad current (abolition in the 1860s, civil rights in the 1960s) pushed for particular goals. In turn, specific countermovements periodically thwart and even reverse movement gains.

The three variables most often used to describe specific movements are (1) the *depth of change* in the social order being advocated, (2) whether the *goal state* is a return to some earlier social order or looks forward to a new type of society, and (3) whether the *tactics* involve engagement with the existing structures or separation and the development of parallel institutions. Combining these three elements allows us to identify four major types of social movements:

Reform movements seek fundamental changes in norms and institutions.

Revolutionary movements call for radical structural and value change in the society.

- **Reform movements** call for changes within the existing system. For example, extending the Fourteenth Amendment's guarantee of equal protection to homosexuals or the disabled involves relatively simple legislative or judicial actions.
- **Revolutionary movements,** in contrast, aim for fundamental changes in values and institutions. Such a radical goal justifies extraordinary tactics, designed to attract public attention and to spread fear and uncertainty. Some movements may engage in acts of violence and terrorism: in

Revolutionary movements generally lack any resources other than violence or threat of violence to gain their ends. The publicity achieved through these actions brings their cause to the attention of the general public, which would otherwise ignore them. However, the results of such actions often harm or kill innocent bystanders, as did this bombing in Paris, France.

the Near East, especially, but also in Ireland, Western Europe, and South and Central America.

- **Resistance movements** are designed to stop change and to restore what are referred to as "traditional" values and norms. Examples include such contemporary countermovements as the New Christian Right (see Chapter 11), the antiabortion movement, and various white supremacy groups.
- **Utopian movements** seek an ideal society for a select group of true believers with the hope that their example will be a guide to change in the broader social system. Ironically, the word *utopia* means "no place," and of the many attempts to create such a community, few have been successful over time.

Phases in the Development of Social Movements

A number of models have described the "natural history" or life course of social movements (Hopper, 1950; Zald and Ash, 1969; Bumer, 1974). Although different terms are used, all these models distinguish four major phases, characterized by (1) personal discontent and vague unrest in the society, (2) a focusing of concern and the emergence of information networks, (3) development of formal organizations, and (4) acceptance of the movement's goals or its gradual decline through membership loss. The four phases are summarized in Table 12-2.

In *phase one,* widespread unrest is usually linked to some condition in the wider society: economic crises, war, migration, technological change, and so forth. Some social movements—nativistic revivals, for example (see Chapter 11)—emerge when a traditional way of life is threatened. Other movements arise when conditions actually appear to be improving. The gap between expected benefits and actual gains creates a **revolution of rising expectations.**

At such times, people's feelings of being deprived may be absolute or relative. **Absolute deprivation** is a lack of basic necessities, which often leads to feelings of powerlessness. **Relative deprivation** occurs when people compare their condition unfavorably to that of others thought to be like themselves. The type of leader likely to emerge at this period is the *prophet* (to believers) or the *agitator* (to agents of social control).

Phase two involves the realization that many others share one's feelings of anger or injustice. But to transform personal problems into public issues requires an *ideology* that explains the societal sources of discontent, provides an alternative view of reality, and offers a plan of action. At this stage information networks are crucial to linking individuals, and the media have a major role in legitimating the claims of charismatic movement leaders.

In *phase three,* movement participants are able to **mobilize** the resources required to sustain formal organizations: money, mass membership, and social tolerance (or at least the absence of open repression). The transformation to a social movement organization also involves reinforcing charismatic leadership with managers and administrators.

No matter how high the level of discontent or how righteous the cause,

Resistance movements are designed to stop change and to restore traditional values and norms.

Utopian movements seek an ideal society for true believers.

The **revolution of rising expectations** refers to the gap between expected benefits and actual gains.

Absolute deprivation is a lack of the basic necessities of survival.

Relative deprivation occurs when people feel unfairly treated in comparison to others thought to be their equals.

The **mobilization** stage of a social movement occurs when members gain the resources required to create an organization, active participation, and social tolerance for its existence.

TABLE 12-2   Model of Social Movement Development: Four Phases

Phase	1 Preliminary	2 Focusing of Concern (Crystallization)
Characteristics	Widespread but isolated feelings of discontent and deprivation	Recognition that others share feelings
Challenges	Media access Grass-roots organizing	Ideological development Communications network
Structure	Informal	Local units (cells)
Leadership	Prophet or agitator	Charismatic leader

Phase	3 Organization (Mobilization)	4 Institutionalization
Characteristics	Centralization of power Mass membership	Public recognition and acceptance of ideas
Challenges	Organization survival Avoiding internal conflicts Maintaining members' commitment	Organizational legitimation Benefiting members Resisting cooptation
Structure	National organizations Alliances with other groups	Bureaucracy
Leadership	Managers (statespersons)	Bureaucrats (priests)

a social movement will succeed only to the extent that it can make alliances with other groups, avoid conflict within its own ranks, and maintain the commitment of members over the long haul (Staggenborg, 1988). To accomplish these goals, movement organizations tend to become bureaucratized with power centralized in a small group of leaders (Gamson, 1975). It also helps if opposition groups are disorganized or vulnerable to accidents, as in the case of nuclear energy plants (Walsh, 1986).

The fate of the movement is decided at *phase four.* Success takes the form of **institutionalization,** when the movement's beliefs become part of the taken-for-granted world and its goals are embodied in stable organizations. The other possible outcome for a social movement is defeat. Early successes often provoke powerful countermovements. For example, the Women's Christian Temperance Union (WCTU) enjoyed victory with the Prohibition Amendment, only to experience total defeat with its repeal—less than 14 years later (Blocker, 1985).

In other cases, only some movement goals are realized. Partial success creates problems in maintaining member commitment. Leaders must continually emphasize the unmet goals while opponents claim nothing more needs to be done. Manipulation of public opinion is a crucial factor at this point. Today, for example, both the civil rights and the women's movements are fighting the public belief that their major goals have already been accomplished and may even have gone too far in correcting past discrimination.

Institutionalization of a social movement occurs when its beliefs are accepted and its goals are embodied in stable organizations.

Substantive successes are often hazardous to the health of a social movement. The coalition formed to press for women's suffrage in the United States could not survive the ratification of the Nineteenth Amendment in 1920. The struggle to gain the vote was the only issue holding the coalition together, and it was not until four decades later that a new broad-based feminist movement emerged.

There are other dangers in becoming successful organizationally, most notably **goal displacement,** whereby maintaining the formal structure of the movement organization replaces the original goals of the social movement. As leadership passes from cause-oriented charismatic leaders (prophets) to bureaucrats (priests) whose loyalty is to the organization, the threat of a new ruling elite is raised (see Chapter 10 on the iron law of oligarchy). Power struggles among successors can divert attention from the common goal (Ryan, 1989).

Goal displacement occurs when movement goals are displaced by the goal of maintaining formal structures.

Societal Reactions to Social Movements

The success or failure of a social movement also depends on outside variables. Groups in power frequently support a movement's goals, convinced of the movement's legitimacy or power. More often, authorities see social movements as threats to social order. Agents of social control can use two basic strategies: *repression*—such as jailing, deportation, and harassment (see Chapter 10), and *cooptation*—the process of bringing opponents of the system into the established leadership structure. A civil rights leader who becomes a presidential adviser or a feminist appointed to a judgeship becomes part of the power elite against which she or he had previously fought.

CONTEMPORARY SOCIAL MOVEMENTS

Social movements typically appear in clusters. The underlying conditions that make protest both necessary and possible usually fuel more than one social movement. Ideas and strategies flow from one group to another.

A Decade of Protest: 1963–1973

One period in recent American history in which a variety of social movements flourished simultaneously was the span from the early 1960s to the early 1970s. The period's undercurrent of unusual activism among college students began with the Free Speech movement on the Berkeley campus of the University of California and the rise of the New Left, and ended less than a decade later with National Guard troops firing at students protesting the Vietnam War.

At the same time, a massive civil rights movement, forged within African-American communities at the local level, came to national attention (Blumberg, 1984; Morris, 1984). By the mid-1960s, a new feminist movement was also emerging, partly sustained by women who had first been mobilized by the New Left and the civil rights movements (Ferree and Hess, 1985; Katzenstein and Mueller, 1987). Members of all these movements were soon joined by other students, religious leaders, politicians, and large numbers of previ-

THE CIVIL RIGHTS MOVEMENT: PERSONAL COMMITMENTS AND ACCOUNTS

Aldon Morris

Aldon Morris is an associate professor of sociology and a research associate at the Center for Urban Affairs and Policy Research at Northwestern University. His book The Origins of the Civil Rights Movement *was co-winner of the 1986 American Sociological Association Award for best book in sociology. Currently, he is conducting research, with Dr. Shirley Harchett, on the black-power phase of the Civil Rights Movement. He is also a coeditor with Dr. Carol Mueller of a forthcoming book on social movement theory. He is past president of the Association of Black Sociologists and a consultant for the television documentary "Eyes on the Prize."*

Human societies and human interactions have always fascinated me. I seldom take social reality for granted. The fact of cultural variability is nothing less than amazing. The ways in which societies survive, change, engage in conflict, build structures of inequality, generate culture and great human liberation movements are complex and dif-

ficult to understand. On the interpersonal level, individuals interact with each other and even their own consciousness. As individuals interact they have social experiences that make them laugh, cry, or be angry, reflective, and even embarrassed.

The wonderful task of the sociologist is to study and generate knowledge concerning the human drama at both the societal and interpersonal levels. Which aspect of the human drama a sociologist studies and writes about is heavily conditioned by that person's own life experiences. It is no accident that I study social movements in general and the United States Civil Rights Movement in particular. My decision to study social movements is directly linked to the fact that I grew up as a member of an oppressed and exploited racial group. As a young African-American I quickly came to realize that racial discrimination and inequality were, in fact, real and had devastating consequences for members of the African-American community. This was a problem that perplexed and worried me for it was difficult to conceive of ways to change this wretched situation.

Then, as if by magic, the Civil Rights Movement exploded on the American scene. All of a sudden African-Americans, along with some whites, were marching for racial justice by the thousands and being cursed, beaten,

jailed, and even killed for their dignified protest against racial injustice.

The Civil Rights Movement caught my interest immediately. I saw it as a force capable of transforming race relations in America. Even as the attack dogs were lunging at demonstrators throughout the South during the 1960s, I wondered about the origins, development, and personalities of this ground-breaking movement. While completing my graduate studies in sociology I decided that my first research objective was to produce a major study of the Civil Rights Movement.

My research provided answers to a number of significant sociological questions. First, I discovered that the Civil Rights Movement did not occur suddenly or spontaneously. To the contrary, I found that there had always been a black movement for change in this country and that these historic protest streams converged in the 1960s, producing a dynamic and more powerful movement for change. Sociologically, then, movements appear to be part of ongoing struggles rather than spontaneous occurrences. Second, I found that ordinary grass-roots people working through mass-based community organizations constituted the real power behind the movement. This finding suggests that during certain historical periods the actions of ordinary people can bring about important societal change. Third, my research demonstrated how social movements actually function as vehicles of social change. Fourth, my research challenged the common view that the white community, especially northern liberals, financed the modern Civil Rights Movement. In response to the question, From where did the money come? I found that the overwhelming majority of local struggles that constituted what we call the Civil Rights Movement were actually financed by the African-American community itself. Local people dug deep into their pockets to finance their own efforts of liberation. It is as if they clearly understood the words of the black abolitionist Frederick Douglass, who declared, "He who would be free must himself strike the first blow." Thus, oppressed people can act to free themselves.

Fifth, my research makes it clear that African-American women were also crucial to the rise and success of the Civil Rights Movement. They assumed both leadership and behind-the-scene roles. This should not be surprising, because African-American women have always been in the forefront of the black liberation struggle. The nature of the brutal oppression of African-Americans has always prevented women from being exclusively relegated to the domestic sphere. Throughout the history of African-Americans, women have had to assume work roles outside the home and household, as well as in the church and community. Building on their rich tradition of activism, African-American women played those pivotal roles that made the movement strong and focused.

The Civil Rights Movement was able to overthrow legally enforced racial segregation and it was successful in its quest for voting rights in the South. Moreover, this movement changed American politics forever. It provided a model for all oppressed groups to follow. Thus, the modern women's, students', farm-workers', Native Americans', and the physically challenged movements all drew their inspiration from the Civil Rights Movement, using many of its tactics in their respective strategies. In addition, the Civil Rights Movement served as a training ground for many of the activists who organized other social change movements. The Civil Rights Movement has also influenced democratic movements abroad including those in South Africa, the Near East, and China.

Nevertheless, this powerful and important movement was not successful in its goal of eliminating economic inequality between the races. Reducing inequality in employment and wages may well be the task of the next great social movement in America.

Meanwhile, the human drama continues to unfold in all of its magnificence. Sociologists will never find themselves without opportunities to exercise the sociological imagination.

---

ously inactive citizens in protesting the conduct of the war in Vietnam. Also taking root during these years were the gay rights movement (see Chapter 7), the children's rights movement (Thorne, 1987), and the movements against both nuclear power and nuclear war (Price, 1982).

Perhaps because many participants in those events are now, two decades later, professors of sociology, the 1960s decade of protest has been the subject of much research, including ten books published in 1988 (see review by Kimmel, 1989) and a number of follow-up reports on student activists (Fendrich and Lovey, 1988; Marwell et al., 1989; Dunham and Bengtson, 1989). In general, men and women who participated in protest as college students are more likely than their nonactivist peers to have remained politically involved and to have less conventional family or work lives.

Countermovement Activism

As each movement involved profound challenges to established values and authorities, each was also met by organized resistance. Student protest was the easiest to control because of constant turnover in personnel; the fact that students are together only part of the year; their vulnerability to parental pressure; and the willingness of authorities to use force. Countermovement violence was also directed at civil rights demonstrators—in the form of police dogs, cattle prods, hoses, tear-gas canisters, stays in southern jails, and, most severely, lynching or assassination.

Gay rights activists and antiwar demonstrators have been physically attacked by the police and by "hard hats" carrying the American flag. Women's movement advocates, however, are most frequently ridiculed or trivialized, whereas antinuclear groups must compete against the political and financial power of major business interests. In general, violence by countermovement, or "backlash," activists has been less effective than their manipulation of the law and the media (McAdam, 1983; Barkan, 1984).

Despite the great strength of countermovement forces, however, the major social movements of the 1960s and early 1970s were able to mobilize sufficient resources to achieve important goals. As noted elsewhere in this book, the structure of *de jure* segregation has been dismantled; public support for homosexual civil rights remains relatively high even in the face of great fear over AIDS; and women's rights have been partially secured.

Out of the interplay of movement and countermovement come some gains, some failures, and much unfinished business. For example, let us examine briefly the Civil Rights Movement and the countermovement by the various white supremacy groups that have gained prominence in the 1980s.

The Civil Rights Movement

Understanding the African-American Civil Rights Movement (CRM) of the 1960s is not always easy for today's college students, most of whom were born after the major events of that era, and who have grown up in a society substantially altered by the CRM's legal and social legacy. Yet it was only a generation ago that it was against the law in many parts of this country for whites and people of color to use the same schools, restaurants, beaches, or other public facilities. Interracial marriage was forbidden, and voting by African-Americans was made extremely difficult through a series of taxes, tests, and outright threats. Most residential areas were completely segregated, and public services such as electricity and water were often denied to minority householders.

Emergence of the CRM: 1955–1965. As degrading as conditions were, the legal, political, and economic climate for African-Americans had actually improved between the end of World War II and the mid-1950s. Expanding opportunities, especially in the industrialized cities of the North, led to a **cognitive liberation** in which the idea of collective protest could be seriously considered (McAdam, 1982). Some communities had accumulated the resources necessary to support civil rights activism: leadership (largely through the church), a small middle class, and networks of students in primarily minority colleges in the South (Morris, 1984). By the mid-1950s, then, most of the preconditions for mobilization were present. In addition, the power of the traditional land-based, southern white elite was being eroded by a new business class less resistant to change (Bloom, 1987).

The legal groundwork for the CRM was laid in 1954 when the Supreme

Cognitive liberation occurs when the idea of collective protest can be seriously considered.

Court struck down the "separate but equal" doctrine that had been used for a century to legitimate segregation. The Court ruled that the "equal protection" clause of the Fourteenth Amendment meant "same" and not "separate." Nonetheless, this legal breakthrough had minimal effect then (or now, in many cases) on the actions of local and state officials. The decision did, however, add to the moral legitimacy of the CRM and the organized protests that began in the South.

The first protest activities were not spontaneous outbreaks of the most deprived, but carefully rehearsed challenges to southern custom and law. Rosa Parks acted intentionally when, in 1955, she refused to move to the back of the bus in Montgomery, Alabama, and the conductor obliged her by calling in the police. The arrests of Parks and the civil rights leaders who came to her defense led to a well-organized boycott of Montgomery buses and white-owned businesses that ended only when the courts ruled that segregated buses were unconstitutional. Similarly, the students who defied the law and sat down at a "whites only" lunch counter at a Woolworth's store in Greensboro, North Carolina, in 1960, were part of a network of student activists trained by local civil rights units.

In 1957, President Eisenhower sent troops to Little Rock, Arkansas, and U.S. marshals elsewhere to enforce school desegregation, and Congress passed a largely symbolic Civil Rights Act. The political situation became more favorable with the Kennedy election in 1960, but it was not until the presidency of Lyndon Johnson that comprehensive civil rights legislation was enacted in the mid-1960s (Blumberg, 1984).

By this time, movement leaders had forged a national coalition able to

In March 1965, Dr. Martin Luther King, Jr., (shown in the center with his wife, Coretta Scott King) led thousands of civil rights demonstrators on a 50-mile march from Selma to Montgomery, Alabama.

mobilize the mass of African-American citizens as well as white sympathizers, with resources such as funding and donated professional legal and organizational services.

Goals and Tactics.   From the very beginning, the goal of the movement was clear and simple, and reformist: to extend the protections of the Constitution to all Americans. Having preempted the moral high ground, movement leaders chose to adopt the strategy of nonviolent "civil disobedience." **Civil disobedience,** as perfected by Mahatma Gandhi in India, involves a peaceful refusal to obey "unjust" laws in the name of a higher morality. Large rallies and marches drew reporters and TV cameras, especially if there was also the threat of danger. Mass demonstrations sent a message to politicians and when demonstrations also triggered a violent response, federal authorities were forced to intervene in support of the protesters (McAdam, 1983). The most massive—and peaceful—civil rights march took place in Washington in 1963 and is best known today as the occasion for Reverend Martin Luther King, Jr.'s "I Have a Dream" speech. It is important to remember, however, that this high point of the movement came after one full decade of organizing.

Organizational Dilemmas.   Despite major gains in the late 1960s, three decades of civil rights activism have not achieved the total elimination of discrimination in jobs, housing, and education, nor has the equal protection of the laws become a full reality. Episodes of violence by urban African-Americans in the late 1960s provided a rationalization for the withdrawal of ideological and material support from many civil rights organizations, although the most moderate groups remained well funded (Haines, 1984; Marger, 1984).

The movement was greatly weakened in 1968 by the assassination of Dr. King, who had served as a charismatic focus for various groups within the movement as well as for white sympathizers. In addition, once the civil rights laws were passed, the focus shifted to enforcement by the courts and government agencies, both of which are subject to political pressure heavily weighted toward the white majority. The burden of protecting minority civil rights has fallen on the courts, but almost all new appointments to the federal judiciary since 1980 have been conservatives known for their lack of sympathy for civil rights initiatives. Recently, as limited gains of the Civil Rights Movement have brought minorities into direct competition with whites for jobs and homes, racism has resurfaced across the country.

Without a unified national leadership, lacking the commitment of the federal government, and about to lose support in the federal courts, the Civil Rights Movement today is facing its greatest challenge since the 1930s. In addition, public opinion has also shifted sharply, with most Americans today believing that African-Americans have only themselves to blame for not taking advantage of the opportunity to succeed. To revive the movement, civil rights leaders are attempting to rebuild the community structures that gave birth to the movement in the 1950s, namely church and neighborhood organizations. Another direction is to strengthen and consolidate African-American political influence—through voter registration drives and running candidates for state and national office.

Civil disobedience involves peaceful refusal to obey unjust laws in the name of a higher morality.

The New Supremacists

Minority gains have combined with declining mobility opportunities for many working-class and lower-middle-class whites to produce a sense of relative deprivation—the strong feeling that one is not receiving the rewards to which one is entitled. Specifically, some people voice the belief that (1) property values will decline when neighborhoods become integrated; (2) less qualified minority students are getting a free ride into colleges that are beyond the reach of one's own children; (3) affirmative action discriminates against men and whites; (4) welfare costs have led to higher taxes; (5) the criminal justice system is too soft on violent criminals, the overwhelming majority of whom are minority males; and (6) America is in danger of being overrun by nonwhite immigrants.

This list was taken from brochures distributed in northern New Jersey in 1990 by the Invisible Empire Knights of the Ku Klux Klan. Similar material is found in publications of the American Nazi party and in magazines associated with young people who call themselves skinheads. These groups are classified as being on the extreme right wing of American politics—the polar opposite of the Marxists who occupy the far left wing. Although it appears that membership in any of these far-right organizations is quite small, most observers believe that the numbers are growing (Anti-Defamation League, 1988).

Such extremist organizations have certainly increased their visibility, especially with coverage by the mass media (e.g., *Newsweek,* September 7, 1987; *McLean's,* January 23, 1989; *The New Republic,* April 3, 1989). Renewed interest in the extreme right-wing followed the election of a former Klan leader to a seat in the Louisiana State legislature, as well as other successful appeals to racial fears in the 1988 presidential election.

The sentiments expressed by members of the Klan and American Nazi party are not really new in our culture. There is a strong streak of grass-roots **populism** in American history that has periodically surfaced as a curious mixture of antibusiness sentiment, a focus on the "little people," and fierce hatred of those who are not white or Christian (Dobratz and Shanks-Meile, 1988; McNall, 1988; Schwartz, 1988; Flynn and Gerhardt, 1989). The populist label is another legitimating symbol for the extreme right. Thus it is not surprising that several of these organizations joined in 1988 to create the Populist Party of America, with the motto "America First."

People who define themselves as utterly respectable have little difficulty expressing their fear and hatred, as seen recently in various sections of New York City where interracial hostility has erupted in fatal violence. These incidents have occurred largely in "defended neighborhoods," traditionally white, ethnic enclaves undergoing pressure from surrounding communities of nonwhites.

Civil rights is only one area in which a powerful social movement from the 1960s has generated a backlash countermovement. But understanding sociology enables one to analyze and assess the possibilities of further social and cultural change. Throughout life, individuals have opportunities to participate in the change process and to join movements that embody personal values and ideals. Just as collective efforts have shaped the past, you can be part of creating the future.

Populism refers to grass-roots social movements in America that combine antibusiness sentiment with intolerance of racial, religious, and ethnic minorities.

SUMMARY

1. Social change is a fundamental process that alters values, norms, institutions, stratification systems, and social relationships.

2. The sources of social change in a society may be internal or external. Diffusion is perhaps the most important of all processes of social change.

3. Generally there has been a trend from simple to more complex societies. Rates of change vary and are higher in complex than in simple societies.

4. Cultural lag refers to the tendency for parts of society to change at different rates.

5. The nation-state is a relatively new form of social organization providing a source of group identity and shared beliefs and values.

6. As they become modernized, societies tend to become more alike with regard to social structure. Industrial society is characterized by machine technology and large-scale systems of production.

7. Postindustrial society is characterized by greater emphasis on science and technology and its capacity to transmit information.

8. Social change also involves psychological changes as modern societies promote and reward personality characteristics that are different from those rewarded in traditional societies.

9. Changes are accepted or rejected depending on several factors, including people's vested interest in maintaining the status quo.

10. Social changes may be gradual and incremental or revolutionary. Changes in any one society cannot be considered without taking into account the broader trends in the world system.

11. Collective behavior refers to noninstitutionalized responses to change. The diversity of collective behavior is illustrated by the variation of its structures, commitments, goals, and motives.

12. Hysteria, panics, crazes, fads, and rumors lack clear goals and are generally short-lived and expressive.

13. Publics, or mass audiences, are composed of people who react similarly to common events.

14. Crowds illustrate a more closely linked collective behavior. They are usually greater in number and more conscious of their commonality.

15. The value added model of collective behavior posits six conditions that are necessary and sufficient to produce collective behavior.

16. The resource mobilization model emphasizes available resources and the response of agents of social control. Recent modifications include less materialistic concerns as well as social-psychological variables.

17. Social movements are organized efforts to bring about social change, ranging from reform of existing institutions to a revolutionary overhaul of the entire system.

18. Social movements develop through four phases: general unrest and personal discontent, crystallization of concern and building of networks, emergence of organizations to promote change, and adoption of movement goals or the collapse of the movement.

19. Resistance to change is often channeled into countermovements, which face similar problems of resource mobilization.

20. The dialectical interplay between movement and countermovement is illustrated by the history of the Civil Rights Movement.

SUGGESTED READINGS

Adam, Barry D. *The Rise of a Gay and Lesbian Movement.* Boston: Twayne, 1987. One of the least studied social movements of the 1960s and 1970s, with special attention to the role of political culture.

Blumberg, Rhoda Lois. *Civil Rights: The 1960's Freedom Struggle.* 2d ed. Boston: Twayne, 1991. Sit-ins, freedom rides, and voter registration drives of the 1960s; urban riots and the rise of the black power movement.

Chirot, Daniel. *Social Change in the Twentieth Century.* 2d ed. New York: Harcourt Brace Jovanovich, 1986. A world-systems approach to understanding core and periphery relations among nations.

Connor, Walter D. *Socialism's Dilemmas: State and Society in the Soviet Bloc.* New York: Columbia University Press, 1988. Issues in the Soviet Union and Eastern Europe such as stratification and social and political transformations.

Foss, Daniel A., and Ralph Larkin. *Beyond Revolution: A New Theory of Social Movements.* South Hadley, MA: Bergin & Garvey, 1986. The "developing" aspect of collective action; instances of social change and the influence of social movements in the 1960s.

House, Ernest R. *Jesse Jackson and the Politics of Charisma: The Rise and Fall of the PUSH/Excel Program.* Boulder: Westview Press, 1988. Jackson's efforts to implement changes in urban high schools to serve African-American youths.

Klandermans, Bert, Hanspeter Kriese, and Sidney Tarrow, eds. *International Social Movement Research, Vol. I: From Structure to Action: Comparing Social Movement Research across Cultures.* Greenwich: JAI Press, 1988. Social movements in Italy, West Germany, the Netherlands, and the United States: women's, student, peace, and environmental movements.

Kurtz, Lester R., Robert D. Benford, and Jennifer E. Turpin. *The Nuclear Cage: A Sociology of the Arms Race.* Englewood Cliffs, NJ: Prentice-Hall, 1988. Causes and consequences of the proliferation of nuclear weapons.

Lofland, John. *Protest: Studies of Collective Behavior and Social Movements.* New Brunswick, NJ: Transaction, 1985. The experience and organization of protest, from the symbolic-interactionist perspective.

McCrea, Francis B., and Gerald E. Markle. *Minutes to Midnight: Nuclear Weapons Protest in America.* Newbury Park, CT: Sage, 1989. The movements of antinuclear weapons campaigns in America.

McNall, Scott G. *The Road to Rebellion: Class Formation and Kansas Populism, 1860–1900.* Chicago: University of Chicago Press, 1988. A history of Kansas populism informed by social movement theories.

Oliner, Samuel P., and Pearl M. Oliner. *The Altruistic Personality: Rescuers of Jews in Nazi Europe.* New York: Free Press, 1988. The basis for moral development, differentiating "rescuers from the nonrescuers."

Reitzes, Donald C., and Dietrich C. Reitzes. *The Alinsky Legacy: Alive and Kicking.* Greenwich: JAI Press, 1987. The lingering influence of the work of organizer Saul Alinsky.

Rochon, Thomas R. *Mobilizing for Peace: The Antinuclear Movements in Western Europe.* Princeton: Princeton University Press, 1988. Peace movements in Great Britain, the Netherlands, West Germany, and France.

Rubenstein, Richard E. *Alchemist of Revolution: Terrorism in the Modern World.* New York: Basic Books, 1987. Revolutionary violence and factors that generate terrorism.

Taylor, Michael, ed. *Rationality and Revolution.* Cambridge: Cambridge University Press, 1988. Reasons behind mass participation during revolution.

Tilly, Charles. *From Mobilization to Revolution.* Reading, MA: Addison-Wesley, 1978. The classic analysis of revolution.

Waller, Altina L. *Feud: Hatfields, McCoys, and Social Change in Appalachia, 1860–1900.* Chapel Hill: University of North Carolina Press, 1988. The infamous Hatfield and McCoy feud; modernizers and precapitalist dwellers.

Wallerstein, Immanuel. *The Politics of the World-Economy: The States, the Movements, and the Civilizations.* Cambridge: Cambridge University Press, 1984. Influential essays by one of the most important theorists of world-systems.

West, Guida, and Rhoda L. Blumberg, eds. *Women and Social Protest.* New York: Oxford University Press, 1990. Women's participation and leadership in social movements including those in the United States, China, South America, and Europe.

Zald, Mayer, and John D. McCarthy, eds. *Social Movements in an Organizational Society: Collected Essays.* New Brunswick, NJ: Transaction Books, 1987. An influential study of social movements, based on organizational theory and economics.

GLOSSARY

Note: Numbers in parentheses following each glossary term definition indicate the chapter in which the term appears.

Abortion is the voluntary termination of a pregnancy. (7)

Absolute deprivation is a lack of the basic necessities of survival. (12)

In the process of integration, **accommodation** occurs when the members of a minority group know the dominant norms and values of a society but have not internalized them. (8)

In the acceptance of technological change, **accommodation**, denotes the process by which one institutional sphere makes internal changes to use the new technology better. (12)

Acculturation takes place when minority group members adopt the dominant values and norms but are not admitted to intimate groupings. (8)

Achieved statuses are positions occupied as a result of choice, merit, or effort. (3)

Acting crowds have some goals beyond expression of emotion; they desire to take action. (12)

Through **adoption,** people substitute a new technology for an older one. (12)

Affective factors refer to feelings and emotions. (4)

Agents of change occupy statuses through which they can influence the direction of change. (12)

Agents of socialization are people and organizations responsible for teaching rules and roles. (4)

Alienation is the feeling of powerlessness, normlessness, and being cut off from the product of one's labor, from other people, and from oneself. (10)

The **all-volunteer force** is composed of people who enter the military as a full-time career. (10)

Amalgamation is the mixing of minority and dominant groups through intermarriage. (8)

American civil religion is a set of unifying beliefs that sees America as divinely blessed, having a moral mission, and being guided by ethical standards. (11)

The **American ethos** is a set of core values guiding the beliefs and behaviors of Americans. (2)

Anomie refers to situations in which norms are absent, unclear, or confusing. (3)

Anticipatory socialization involves rehearsing prior to assuming a role. (4)

Apartheid refers specifically to the South African policy of segregation and political and economic discrimination against people of color within that country. (6)

Artifacts or material culture, consist of tools and other human-made objects. (2)

Ascribed statuses are based on characteristics over which a person has little or no control, such as sex, age, race, and ethnicity. (3)

Assimilation occurs when people from minority groups are accepted in major social institutions and more personal groupings. (8)

Authority is power that is exercised through legitimated and institutionalized channels. (6, 10)

Automation is the replacing of workers with machines. (10)

Backstage interaction is free of public performance constraints. (3)

Behaviorism concentrates on the study of observable activity as opposed to reported or inferred mental and emotional processes. (4)

A **belief system** is a set of shared ideas about the meaning of life. (11)

The **berdaches** of Native American tribes function as a third sex, neither fully male nor female. (7)

Biological determinism is based on the belief that genetic factors explain differences in human behavior. (1)

Bisexuality involves the ability to enjoy sexual relations with both males and females. (7)

Blended families consist of a husband and wife, children of previous marriages, and any children from the new marital union. (9)

Born again means having an experience that changes one's life through the acceptance of the Lord. (11)

Boundary setting occurs when shared norms and values set the limits of acceptable behavior. (5)

The **bureaucracy** is a formal organization characterized by rationality and efficiency. (3)

Capital punishment is another term for the death penalty. (5)

Career contingencies involve a series of social factors that determine outcomes for people by opening up or closing off certain options. (5)

Caste systems are based on ascription, with minimal movement across stratum boundaries.

A **casual crowd** is an accidental gathering of people. (12)

Censorship involves the selective withholding of information. (10)

Charismatic authority is based on some extraordinary quality of the leader or the leader's ideas. (10)

A **circuit of agents** includes both informal networks and formal agents. (5)

Civil disobedience involves peaceful refusal to obey unjust laws in the name of a higher morality. (12)

Civil law provides sanctions against violations of the interests of private people. (5)

The rights to speak, publish, and assemble are **civil liberties.** (10)

Class awareness refers to the recognition that differences in income, occupational prestige, and life-style are reflections of one's own class position. (6)

Class consciousness occurs when class awareness becomes the central organizing point of self-definition and political actions. (6)

Class immobility occurs when social class rank is reproduced from one generation to another. (6)

Coercion is the use of force to induce compliance. (3)

Cognitive factors refer to how people think and process information. (4)

Cognitive development refers to changes over time in how we think. (4)

Cognitive liberation occurs when the idea of collective protest can be seriously considered. (12)

Cognitive structures shape how the mind processes information. (7)

Cohabitation occurs when unmarried people share living quarters. (9)

Collective behavior refers to noninstitutionalized responses to flux and change. (12)

A **collectivity** is a set of people that can be as unconnected as an aggregate or as closely linked as a group. (1)

"Coming out" refers to the public acknowledgment of one's homosexual identity. (7)

Commuter marriages occur when husband and wife work in different cities and typically maintain separate households. (9)

Competition results when situations are defined as ones in which scarce resources are unequally distributed. (3)

Compromise involves giving up extreme demands to achieve limited goals. (3)

Conflict occurs when parties try to destroy or disable their opponents. (3)

Conflict models assume that laws serve the interests of the dominant class. (5)

Conflict theory examines disagreement, hostility, and struggles over power and resources in a group. (1)

The **conflict view of social change** stresses

the recurrent and enduring sources of strain among the groups within society. (12)

Confrontations test the limits of acceptable behavior. (5)

Conglomerates exist when one company owns controlling shares in other companies in a variety of commercial areas. (10)

The **consensus model** is a structural/functional model based on the idea that norms become laws because they reflect customs and general agreement about appropriate behavior. (5)

Conspicuous consumption is the open display of wastefulness designed to impress others. (2)

Constants are characteristics that do not change from one person or time to another. (1)

A **conventional crowd** is composed of people who are gathered as spectators, audiences, or participants at events governed by established norms. (12)

Cooperation is the sharing of resources in order to achieve a common goal. (3)

Cooperative learning occurs when students pool talents and help one another. (11)

Cooptation occurs when members of a dissenting group are absorbed by a dominant group. (3)

The **core sector** consists of major industries, large investments in plants and equipment, unionized labor, monopolies, and high profits. (10)

Corporations are formal organizations that are legal actors in their own right. (10)

Correlation refers to how change in one variable is associated with change in another variable. (1)

Countercultures represent oppositional lifestyles for those not conforming to the dominant norms. (2)

A **countermovement** is a set of opinions and beliefs within the population that is opposed to the goals of a social movement. (12)

Crazes involve a desire to have something that everyone else appears to be enjoying. (12)

Crimes without victims violate moral standards, but those involved are willing participants. (5)

Criminal law provides sanctions against conduct believed to be against the interests of the society or the state. (5)

Cross-cultural comparisons examine relationships among variables in different societies. (1)

A **crowd** is a temporary gathering of people brought together by some common concern or activity. (12)

Cults and **new religious movements** develop outside mainstream religious groupings. (11)

Cultural capital refers to a style of talking and thinking as well as to knowledge of music, art, and literature that prepares individuals for membership in the dominant strata. (11)

Cultural, or **ideological, hegemony** refers to control over the production of values and norms by those in power. (2)

Cultural heterogeneity occurs when members of a society differ greatly in color and appearance, in beliefs and values, and in language and culture. (2)

Cultural homogeneity results from similarity in race, religion, and national origin. (8)

Cultural lag refers to the tendency for the parts of a culture to change and adapt at different rates after the introduction of a new technology. (12)

Cultural pluralism emphasizes the special contributions of various immigrant cultures to the diversity of American society. (8)

Cultural relativism involves an effort to understand the world as seen by members of other societies. (2)

Cultural universals are basic elements found in all cultures. (2)

Cultural variability reflects the variety of customs, beliefs, and artifacts devised by humans to meet universal needs. (2)

Culture is the map for living of a group whose members share a territory and language, feel responsible for one another, and recognize their shared identity. (2)

The **culture conflict model** stresses value differences and a belief that the laws reflect the values of the most powerful groups. (5)

Culture contact involves learning from people from other societies. (12)

Cumulative social change is the gradual development from simple to more complex societies. (12)

Cyclical theories of social change are based on the view that society resembles a living organism, going through phases of growth and decline. (12)

Date rape is sexual intercourse without consent in the dating relationship. (7)

Deferred gratification is the postponing of current pleasure to achieve future goals. (6)

Definition of the situation is the process by which people interpret and evaluate the social context to select appropriate attitudes and behaviors. (3)

Deindividualization is the process of removing a person's civilian identity. (4)

Deinstitutionalization involves the release of mental patients into the community. (5)

De jure segregation is supported by law. *De facto* segregation is the result of custom and personal choices. (8)

Delinquent and **criminal subcultures** originate in the differences between aspirations and blocked opportunity structures. (5)

Under **democratic, or welfare. socialism,** goods and services may be privately produced, but the distribution of essential services is centrally controlled. (10)

Democratic societies protect the right to dissent. (10)

Demonstrations are temporary but highly organized acting crowds with a clearly defined goal. (12)

Dependent variables are influenced by independent variables. (1)

Desocialization is learning to give up a role. (4)

Deviant behavior violates generally held norms. (5)

Deviant subcultures are supportive peer groups and networks for deviants. (5)

In the **dialectical model of social change,** **thesis** is represented by the status quo, **antithesis** is the force of opposition. **Synthesis** emerges from the conflict between those two. (12)

The theory of **differential association** states that deviant behavior is learned in primary groups and involves the same learning processes as nondeviant behavior. (5)

Diffusion describes the process by which new ideas, actions, technology, and beliefs of a culture spread from one person, group, or society to another. (12)

Discrimination is the practice of unequal treatment. (8)

Division of labor refers to the separation of work into distinct parts, each of which is performed by an individual or a group of people. (10)

Domestic partners include homosexual and nonmarried heterosexual couples who in some U.S. cities enjoy some of the same legal rights as married couples. (7)

Dominant groups exercise control over societal resources. (8)

The **dramaturgical view** sees social interaction as a series of mini-dramas—all role partners are actors performing roles in a social setting or on a stage. (1, 3)

Dual-career families or couples are ones in which both husband and wife have a career. (9)

Dual-earner refers to families or couples with both partners in the labor force. (9)

Dual economy refers to the existence of two separate types of employing firms: core and peripheral. (10)

The **dyad,** or two-person group, is intimate, has a high exchange of information, and presents great possibilities for total involvement and conflict. (3)

Dysfunctional patterns reduce the capacity of a system to adapt and survive. (1)

Eccentric behavior is not viewed as disruptive or threatening to the social order. (5)

An **economic system** consists of the norms and activities regulating the production, distribution, and consumption of goods and services. (10)

Egalitarianism refers to reduced power differences between husbands and wives and between parents and children. (9)

Ego defenses protect the self-image. (4)

Ego development involves the possibility of change and growth across the life course. (4)

Ego identity refers to a sense of continuity and sameness in the self-concept across time and situations. (4)

The **emotional contagion model** focuses on how the intensity of crowds develops. (12)

Empirical referents are items that can be measured and counted. (1)

The **empty nest stage** of the family cycle occurs when all the children are out of the house and the parents are alone together again. (9)

Environmental changes include both natural and socially produced events. (12)

Epidemiology is the study of the patterns of occurrence of illness in a population. (essay 2)

Ethnicity refers to cultural identity. (8)

Ethnocentrism is the belief that one's own culture is the best and therefore the standard by which other cultures are consequently judged. (2)

Ethnomethodology involves probing beneath the "taken-for-granted" reality. (1)

Evangelical refers to an emphasis on the personal witnessing of God's presence. (11)

Exchange and **rational-choice models** adopt an essential economic model of cost and benefi᠁ ᠁xplain people's behaviors. (1)

Experiments come closest to the scientific ideal of control over variables. (1)

Expressive behavior is valued in its own right. (3)

An **expressive crowd** shows strong feelings with outbursts of emotion. (12)

Expressive roles are oriented toward the expression and release of group tension. (3)

The **extended family** is a relatively large unit composed of several related households, most often involving three or more generations. (9)

Extramarital sex refers to sexual relationships outside of marriage. (7)

A **fad** is a short-lived but widely copied outburst of unexpected and often playful behavior. (12)

Familism refers to family closeness, traditionalism, and male dominance. (9)

Fashions are more enduring, widespread, and socially important than fads. (12)

Feeling rules shape how, when, with whom, and where emotion is expressed. (3)

The **feminization of poverty** refers to the fact that a majority of the adult poor are women. (6)

Field experiments are conducted in the real world. (1)

Folkways are approved standards of behavior passed on from one generation to the next. (2)

Foraging involves picking readily available foods for immediate consumption. (2)

Formal agents of social control are people in social roles specifically devoted to norm enforcement. (5)

Formal organizations are social structures characterized by formality, ranked positions, large size, relative complexity, and long duration. (3)

Free-enterprise capitalism is an economic system with minimal public ownership or controls. (10)

Frontstage interaction occurs in full view of the public. (3)

Functional analysis examines the relationship between the parts and the whole of a social system. (1)

Fundamentalism represents a back-to-basics approach to religion, resisting modernity and seeking to restore an original faith. (11)

Games are characterized by rules and structure. (4)

Gathering involves transporting, storing, and preserving readily available foods. (2)

The term **gay** refers to homosexual males. (7)

Along with other civil rights movements, the **Gay Rights Movement** emerged in the 1960s; it attempted to extend full rights of citizenship to all homosexuals. (7)

Gemeinschaft refers to small, traditional communities, characterized by primary-group relationships and intergenerational stability. (3)

Gender inequality refers to the differences between men and women in the distribution of societal resources of power, prestige, and property. (7)

Gender stratification is the result of the differential evaluation of societal worth on the basis of biological sex. (7)

The **gender wage gap** refers to the discrepancy between average earnings of women and men. (7)

The **generalized other** reflects societal standards of acceptable behavior in the role. (4)

Genocide is the deliberate attempt to murder an entire category of people. (8)

Gesellschaft refers to contractual relationships, wherein social bonds are voluntary, based on rational self-interest, and characterized by instrumental behavior. (3)

A **gesture** is a symbol whose meaning is shared by group members. (4)

Goal displacement occurs when movement goals are displaced by the goal of maintaining formal structures. (12)

Grade differentiation divides a district's students into separate schools for given grade levels. (11)

Gradual, or **incremental, change** is a long process in which one modification is followed by another. (12)

A **group** is characterized by a distinctive set of relationships, interdependence, a feeling that members' behavior is relevant, and a sense of membership. (3)

Health and **illness** are concepts that describe adaptations to everyday life and the meanings that we give to living. (essay 2)

Heterogamy is the practice of selecting a mate with different social background characteristics. (9)

The **hidden curriculum** refers to what is learned, such as ethnocentrism and respect for authority, but is not part of the official curriculum. (11)

Historical societies have left written records. (2)

Homogamy is the practice of selecting a mate with similar social background characteristics. (9)

Homophobia refers to intense fear of homosexuality or homosexuals. (7)

Homosexual subcultures offer protection and support for gay males and lesbians. (7)

Homosexuality refers to a preference for sexual partners of the same sex. (7)

Hypotheses are specific statements derived from a theory about relationships among variables. (1)

The **"I"** is the creative spontaneous part of the self, whereas the **"me"** consists of the internalized attitudes of others. (4)

Ideal culture reflects the highest virtues and standards of a society. (2)

Ownership of means of production by the ruling class extends to **ideas** as well as things. (1)

The **incest taboo** forbids sexual relations between certain group members. (9)

The American education system is **inclusive,** or open, to almost all children of given ages. (11)

Independent variables have the greatest impact, come first in the chain of events, are relatively fixed, and/or affect dependent variables. (1)

Index crimes include murder, forcible rape, robbery, and aggravated assault. (5)

Influence is the ability to persuade others to follow one's will. (6)

Informal primary groups develop within bureaucracies to meet personal needs. (3)

In-groups are the primary or secondary groups to which a person belongs. **Out-groups** are ones to which a person does not belong. (3)

The **inner-directed person's** behavior is governed by an internal mechanism typical of industrial society. (12)

Innovation refers to both the discovery and invention of something new. (12)

Institutional spheres are major areas of social activity. (1)

Institutionalization is the process whereby a given adaptation becomes an established pattern. (10)

Institutionalization of a social movement

occurs when its beliefs are accepted and its goals are embodied in stable organizations. (12)

Institutionalized discrimination occurs when discrimination is built into normative structures and reinforced by formal and informal agents of social control. (8)

Institutionalized evasion of norms occurs within organizations as a permanent official part of the system and may be tolerated because it helps get the job done. (5)

Instrumental behavior is a means to some other goal. (3)

Interaction processes refer to the ways in which partners agree on their goals, negotiate behaviors, and distribute resources. (4)

An **interest group** develops when members of a public seek others with similar feelings about an issue. (12)

Intergenerational mobility involves status change between parents and their adult children. (6)

Interlocking corporate directorships involve members of one board of directors sitting on the boards of other companies. (10)

Interpretive sociology focuses on processes by which people make sense of daily life. (1)

Intragenerational mobility involves status changes during a person's own adulthood. (6)

Invasion occurs when one group's or nation's territory is overrun and controlled by another's. (12)

In vitro fertilization is a new procedure in which an egg is fertilized outside the mother's body and then replanted in the womb. (7)

Involuntary childlessness refers to the inability to conceive. (9)

Jargons are special languages of subgroups/subcultures. (2)

Job autonomy involves making decisions about the timing and sequence of tasks, exercising judgment, and having an impact on the outcome. (10)

The **juvenile court system** is separate from the adult system and was designed to protect children and adolescents from the stresses of labeling and severe punishment. (5)

Juveniles come to the attention of law officials because they have committed a crime or status offense or have been neglected or abused. (5)

Kinesics is the study of nonverbal communication. (2)

Labeling theory emphasizes the process of defining a person's behavior as deviant. (5)

Latent functions are unexpected and unintended consequences. (1)

Laws are norms that govern behavior considered essential to group survival. (2)

Legal-rational, or **bureaucratic, authority** is based on laws that limit the power of officeholders. (10)

Lesbians are homosexual females. (7)

Longitudinal studies follow a group of respondents over time. (1)

The **looking-glass self** suggests that we see ourselves reflected back in the reactions of others. (4)

Macrosociology focuses on society as a whole and on social systems at a high level of abstraction. (1)

Magic refers to behavior designed to manipulate unseen forces. (11)

Magnet schools are designed to attract students by offering specialized educational programs. (11)

Mainstreaming involves integrating handicapped students into the regular school program. (11)

Male and **female** define biological sex. **Feminine** and **masculine** are social constructs. (7)

Manifest functions are open, stated, and intended goals. (1)

In a **market system**, the value of goods and services is determined by supply-and-demand factors. (10)

Mass culture refers to elements of popular culture that are produced and distributed through the mass media. (essay 1)

Mass hysteria involves uncontrollable emotional reactions to anxiety within a group. (12)

Master status is the most important status occupied and one that affects almost every aspect of a person's life. (3)

Matrifocal refers to families centered on the woman. (9)

The **mean** is an average. (1)

The **means of production** refers to the tools, land, factories, information, and wealth that form the basis of a society. (1)

Measures of central tendency are single numbers that summarize an entire set of data. (1)

The **median** is the midpoint of an entire set of cases. (1)

Mediation refers to the use of a third party to resolve issues. (3)

The **melting pot model** of integration assumes that immigrants will lose their cultural uniqueness and become part of the dominant American culture. (8)

Mentors are teachers who act as guides and sponsors. (4)

Meritocracy is a hierarchy of talent, in which rewards are based on one's abilities and credentials. (6, 11)

Microsociology focuses on smaller units of social systems, such as face-to-face interactions. (1)

The **military-industrial complex** consists of a large permanent military establishment combined with an immense armament industry. (10)

Minority-group status involves visible traits, differential treatment, self-image, and shared identity. (8)

A **mob** is a cohesive, emotionally aroused crowd, often engaged in violent or disruptive acts. (12)

Mobilization involves the weakening of previous patterns of social, economic, and psychological commitments making people receptive for socialization to new patterns. (12)

The **mobilization stage of a social movement** occurs when members gain the resources required to create an organization, achieve active participation in it, and obtain social tolerance for its existence. (12)

The **mode** is the single most common category of cases. (1)

Mode of subsistence refers to the way in which a group adapts to its environment through the production of goods and services. (2, 10)

Modeling is the copying of characteristics of admired people. (4)

Modernization is a process through which a society becomes more internally differentiated and complex and in which science and technology guide change. (11, 12)

Monopolization refers to the tendency for a company to acquire exclusive control of a commodity or service in a particular market. (10)

Moral reasoning involves the application of standards of fairness and justice. (4)

Mores are norms that cover moral and ethical behavior. (2)

Multinational corporations are firms with branches and factories in many countries and whose ownership is not linked to one nation. (10)

The **nation-state** is the political organization of a complex society. (10)

The **National Crime Survey** is based on samples of U.S. households and businesses. (5)

Nationalism is a consciousness of shared identity among the members of a politically distinct territory. (12)

Natural experiments involve measuring the same population before and after a natural event that is assumed to change the situation. (1)

Negative sanctions convey disapproval of role performance. (4)

Neoevolutionary theory traces changes in cultural and societal complexity without making value judgments about the superiority of one society over another. (12)

Net worth consists of the value of all assets less all debts. (6)

The **New Age movement** refers to a number of groups centered on the supernatural and on psychic healing, reincarnation, and similar mystic experiences. (11)

The **New Christian Right** is composed of fundamentalist religious organizations and far-right political groups. (11)

Norms are rules of behavior that define acceptable conduct. (3)

The **nuclear family** is a unit composed of a married couple and their dependent children. (9)

The **nurse administrator** and the **nurse practitioner,** new career paths, require training beyond the bachelor's level. (essay 2)

Oligarchy is the rule of the many by the few. (10)

Organizational crimes are carried out in one's role as employee to achieve corporate goals. (5)

Organized crime is committed by members of formally structured groups operating outside the law. (5)

An **origin myth** is the story of how a particular group began. (11)

The **other-directed person,** typical of the postindustrial society, constantly reacts and adapts to the expectations of others. (12)

Panics are actions caused by a sudden overwhelming need to escape danger. (12)

Parochial schools are private schools operated by religious organizations. (11)

In **participant observation,** the researcher becomes part of the interaction under study. (1)

The **particularistic fallacy** occurs when a correlation at the collective level is applied to individuals. (1)

The **pathological model** focuses on biological symptoms and abnormal functioning in an organism. (essay 2)

Patriarchy refers to male dominance. (7)

Peers are equals and an important source of information and socialization. (4)

A **percentage** indicates how many of a given item there are in every one hundred. (1)

The **periphery** consists of smaller, competitive, low-profit firms employing low-pay, nonunion manual workers. (10)

Personal troubles are private matters, limited to aspects of daily life of which a person is directly aware. (1)

Petty violations of norms are trivial and minor violations of rules. (5)

Physician assistants are personnel who perform a wide range of duties usually performed by physicians. (essay 2)

Play expands a child's ability to take the role of another. (4)

Plea bargaining is negotiation between the prosecution and the accused to reduce the charges if the defendant pleads guilty. (5)

The **pluralist model** assumes that there are many different and competing bases of power, with no one group dominating the others. (10)

The **police** in every society have the right to use coercive force to control behavior. (5)

Political action committees (PACs) are special organizations that use funds to support causes and candidates. (10)

Political socialization includes the influences and experiences that determine one's political orientation. (10)

Polygamy creates extended households composed of a woman or man with more than one marriage partner at the same time. (9)

Popular culture consists of what people do in their leisure time and the products designed for mass consumption. (essay 1)

Population shifts are changes in the size and composition of the population. (12)

Populism refers to grass-roots social movements in America that combine antibusiness sentiment with intolerance of racial, religious, and ethnic minorities. (12)

Pornography refers to sexually detailed pictures and stories. (7)

Positive sanctions indicate approval of role performance. (4)

Positivism is based on the idea that science can be value free and objective. (1)

The driving force behind **postindustrial society** is the rapid development of information technology. (12)

Postsecondary education takes place after high school. (11)

The **poverty level** represents the minimum income needed to feed, house, and clothe household members. (6)

Power is the ability to impose one's will on others. (6)

The **power-elite model** assumes that decision making is concentrated in the hands of a few similarly socialized people. (10)

The **predispositional view** assumes that there is a tendency among certain people to act in certain ways. (5)

Prejudice involves prejudging members of ethnic, religious, and racial groups. (8)

Preliterate societies do not have a written language. (2)

Preparatory schools are private schools developed to prepare children of well-off parents for entry into elite colleges. (11)

Prescriptive norms dictate what is expected. (5)

Prestige refers to respect given by others. (6)

Priestly functions deal with specific traditions of the faith, supporting the existing structure of power. (11)

Primary deviance is behavior that violates a norm. (5)

A **primary group** is a small group in which members have warm, intimate, personal ties with one another. (3)

Principled challenges are deliberate attempts to confront the norm setters. (3)

Principles of exchange govern relationships among people as they bargain for desired goods and services. (3)

Private interests refer to property held by individuals, families, or corporations. (10)

Probability refers to the statistical likelihood of a given event. (1)

Control over the production of popular culture is a major concern for sociologists in the conflict tradition. (essay 1)

Profane behaviors and objects are not holy but rather earthly and understandable. (11)

Propaganda involves the selective release of information favorable to those in power and is designed to generate high levels of solidarity. (10)

Property refers to wealth owned. (6)

Property crimes, such as burglaries, larceny, and theft, are much more prevalent than crimes against people. (5)

The **prophet** is a charismatic figure, witnessing a revelation calling for a new order. (11)

Proscriptive norms govern forbidden conduct. (5)

Public agencies are institutions, such as governments, that represent the society as a whole. (10)

A **public**, or **mass audience**, consists of people who are not in the same place at the same time but who relate similarly to particular issues. (12)

Public issues are factors outside one's personal control and are caused by crises in the larger system. (1)

Qualitative research relies primarily on interpretive description rather than statistics. (1)

Quantitative research utilizes the features of scientific objectivity, including complex statistical techniques. (1)

Race is a social construction; there are no "pure" racial types. (8)

Random sampling occurs when all possible respondents have an equal chance of being chosen. (1)

The **rate of change** is directly related to the size of the culture base; the greater the base, the greater the chances of further change. (12)

Rates are the number of times a given event occurs in a population, on a base other than 100. (1)

A **ratio** compares one subpopulation to another. (1)

Rationality replaces traditional and emotional bases for behavior with the belief in a logical connection between means and ends. (12)

Real culture refers to actual behavior. (2)

Through **reciprocal socialization** children modify their parents' view of the world. (4)

Reciprocity obligates the receiver of a gift to return something of equivalent value. (9)

Redlining is the practice by banks and other lending institutions of refusing to make mortgage money available for housing in certain neighborhoods. (8)

Reductionism involves reducing social life to individual behavior or biology. (1)

A **reference group** exerts a strong influence on one's identity, norms, and values, whether or not one actually belongs to that group. (3)

Reform movements seek fundamental changes in norms and institutions. (12)

Rehabilitation means restoration to a former state. (5)

Reification is the logical fallacy of treating an abstract concept as a concrete object. (1)

Relative deprivation occurs when people feel unfairly treated in comparison to others thought to be their equals. (12) .

Reliability refers to whether the measuring instrument yields the same results on repeated trials. (1)

Religion is a belief system based on the concept of a divine force guiding destiny and directed toward the supernatural. (11)

Religious roles involve supervision of sacred objects and ceremonies. (11)

Replication involves repeating a specific study, often with different types of respondents in various settings and at other times. (1)

Political **repression** involves the forceful denial of civil liberties. (10)

Psychological **repression** involves the placing of unacceptable impulses below the level of consciousness. (4)

Repressive control systems use extensive power to restrain many behaviors. **Restrained** control systems involve less intense use of power and control over fewer behaviors. (5)

Mental illness is **residual deviance** that is less easily identified than more obvious norm violations. (5)

Resistance movements are designed to stop change and to restore traditional values and norms. (12)

Resocialization is learning important new norms and values. (4)

The **resource mobilization model** stresses the supports available to protesters, as well as the tactics used by social control agents. (12)

The **revolution of rising expectations** refers to the gap between expected benefits and actual gains. (12)

Revolutionary change brings basic alterations in the political and socioeconomic structure of a society. (12)

Revolutionary movements call for radical structural and value change in the society. (12)

A **revolutionary situation** occurs when two or more political units claim control over the state, these interests cannot be reconciled, and the opposition party receives support from a sizable segment of the population. (12)

Riots are usually less spontaneous than mob actions and tend to involve more people over longer periods of time. (12)

Rites of passage are the ceremonies marking important changes in a person's position in the group. (2)

Ritualized release of hostility occurs when hostility is expressed under controlled situations. (3)

Rituals are culturally patterned ways of expressing central values and recurring concerns. (2)

Role is the expected behavior associated with a particular status. (3)

Role conflict occurs when two or more of a person's statuses have incompatible demands and expectations. (3)

Role distance is the space placed between the self and the self-in-the-role. (4)

Role prescriptions are norms for permissible and desirable behavior of the occupant of a status. (3)

Role strain results from contradictory demands and expectations built into one status. (3)

The **romantic love syndrome** involves the selection of a mate on the basis of love rather than kinship-based needs. (9)

The **routinization of charisma** occurs when the prophet's beliefs are institutionalized and transformed into a worldly organization. (11)

The **rule of reciprocity** holds that giving gifts obligates the recipient to return something of similar value. (10)

Rumors are unconfirmed information, which may or may not be correct. (12)

Sacred behaviors and objects are invested with holy, divine, mystical, or supernatural force. (11)

Some deviance serves as a **safety valve** for disruptive tendencies. (5)

A **sample** is a selection from the entire population of interest. (1)

Sanctions refer to reactions that convey approval or disapproval of behavior. (2)

Scapegoating refers to finding someone else to blame for one's misfortune. (8)

The **scientific method** consists of objective observations, precise measurement, and full disclosure of results. (1)

Secondary analysis involves the use of data collected by others. (1)

Secondary deviance results from the social responses to primary deviance. (5)

Secondary groups are characterized by few emotional ties and by limited interaction. (3)

Sectarian conflict refers to interreligious strife. (11)

Secular ideologies are belief systems based on worldly rather than supernatural forces. (11)

Secularization is the shift in focus from the next world and unquestioned faith to this world and reason, science, and technology. (11)

The term **segregation** refers to attempts to isolate minority groups. (8)

Self-identity is an organization of perceptions about who and what kind of person one is. (4)

Service work refers to providing assistance and/or information. (10)

Sex segregation occurs when women or men are concentrated in a given occupation or in particular jobs within an occupation or work organization. (7)

Sexual harassment involves deliberate and unwelcome comments, gestures, and acts of a sexual nature. (7)

Sexual identity refers to seeing oneself as female or male and having the culturally shaped aspects of masculinity or femininity. (7)

Sexual scripts allow individuals to organize their perceptions and experiences in order to behave appropriately in particular situations. (7)

Sexual violence is typically directed against the relatively powerless. (7)

Significant others are persons whose affection and approval are particularly desired. (4)

The **situational view** assumes that the social situation and statuses and roles assigned to people produce certain kinds of behavior. (5)

The **Skinner box** is a completely controlled environment. (4)

Social change is the process through which values, norms, institutions, stratification systems, and social relationships alter over time. (12)

Social controls are techniques for getting people to conform. (5)

Social differentiation involves a shift from diffuse to specialized roles. (12)

Social facts are patterned regularities that describe the collectivity. (1)

The principle of legitimacy, or **social fatherhood**, identifies one man as responsible for the protection of a woman and her children and for the children's placement in the social system. (9)

A **social hierarchy** is a set of ranked statuses. (6)

The **social injury model** sees laws as a means of protecting members of the society. (5)

A **social institution** is a cluster of systems, values, norms, statuses, and roles that develop in response to basic needs. (3)

Social integration refers to the degree to which a person is part of a larger group. (1)

Social learning theory states that both deviant and conforming behaviors are learned through reinforcement. (5)

Social mobility is the movement of persons and groups within the stratification system. (6)

A **social movement** is a set of opinions and beliefs in favor of change in the institutional spheres and stratification system. (12)

Social movement organizations are specific formal organizations that channel discontent into concrete actions. (12)

A **social network** comprises the sum total of one's group memberships and relationships. (3)

Social norms are rules of behavior. (2)

Social statistics refer to official records and systematic observations from which social facts can be deduced. (1)

Social stratification refers to hierarchies of statuses based on unequal distribution of power, prestige, and property. (6)

Social structure comprises the patterns of social relationships within which behavior is carried out. (3)

A **social system** represents an arrangement of statuses and roles that exist apart from the people occupying them. (1, 3)

Socialism is an economic system in which the means of production are collectively owned and the distribution of goods and services is guided by public needs. (10)

A **socialist economic system** is marked by central planning of production and distribution by the government. (10)

Socialization is the lifelong process whereby one internalizes culture and develops a sense of self. (4)

Sociobiology is the study of the inheritance of genetically determined behaviors. (1)

Socioeconomic status (SES) is a measure based on a combination of income, occupational prestige, and education (6)

A **sociogram** identifies interaction patterns in studying group structure. (3)

The **sociological perspective** focuses on the totality of social life, the context of social interaction, the individual as part of a collectivity, and interaction among individuals as collectivities. (1)

Sociology is the study of human behavior as shaped by collective life. (1)

The **sociology of emotions** demonstrates that emotions are socially constructed, exchanged, and maintained. (3)

The **sociology of knowledge** is the study of the way in which the production of knowledge is shaped by the social context of thinkers. (1)

The increasing **specialization of knowledge** in universities and colleges leads to relatively discrete units of organization. (11)

The **split, or segmented, labor market** is differentiated by race and gender, core workers being primarily white males and peripheral workers being primarily women and minorities. (10)

The **statistical model** defines health or illness in terms of the average of a population. (essay 2)

Statistics are numerical techniques for the classification and analysis of data. (1)

Status is a position in a social system and is characterized by certain rights and duties. (3)

Status attainment research traces the paths by which people reach their ultimate position in the stratification system. (6)

Status consistency occurs when a person occupies a similar rank across different hierarchies. (6)

Status inconsistency refers to occupying different ranks in different hierarchies. (6)

A **status offense** is an act that would not be considered a violation if committed by an adult. (5)

A **status set** consists of all the statuses occupied by a person. (3)

Status symbols are outward signs of social rank. (6)

Stereotypical thinking occurs when a set of characteristics is attributed to all members of a social group. (8)

A **stigma** is a morally undesirable label that tends to be generalized to other undesirable characteristics as well. (5)

Stratification systems rank some individuals as more deserving than others. (6)

Street crimes are actions that directly threaten people or property. (5)

Structural, or demand, mobility refers to societal-level factors affecting mobility rates. (6)

Subcultures consist of variations in values, beliefs, norms, and behavior among societal subgroups. (2)

Subjective knowledge derives from an individual's own frame of reference. (1)

Subjective reality is developed through social interaction and refers to the ideas and feelings we have about ourselves and the world. (1)

Surveys or **polls** yield information from a large group of respondents. (1)

A **symbol** is a sound, object, or event that is given meaning by members of a group. (2)

Symbolic interaction views social systems as

products of interaction and the meanings that people give to their situations. (1)

Tables consist of rows and columns of figures arranged to clarify relationships among variables. (1)

Task, or **instrumental, roles** are oriented toward specific goals. (3)

A **theory** is a set of logically related statements that explain an entire class of events. (1)

Tokenism refers to the appointment or promotion of one or two "outsiders" to high positions. (7)

Total institutions, such as prisons and jails, control and monitor all aspects of inmates' lives. (5)

In **totalitarian regimes,** the government attempts to exercise total control over society and its members. (10)

Tracks are programs of varying content and pacing, to which students are assigned. (11)

The **tradition-directed person's** behavior is governed by customs. (12)

Traditional authority is based on habit and acceptance of the group's customs. (10)

Transcendence refers to the need to go beyond the limits of one's own senses and feel that life has meaning beyond one's daily experiences. (11)

The **triad,** or three-person group, is more stable than the dyad, with a greater division of labor. (3)

The **triple melting pot** suggested that ethnic differences were melting but religious differences, between Catholics, Protestants, and Jews, were not. (8)

Unidirectional theories of evolutionary progress assume that social change occurs in one direction only. (12)

Uniform Crime Reports are compiled by the FBI from city, state, and county police information. (5)

Urban legends are items of modern folklore involving rumors that resonate to deeply held fears and anxieties regarding aspects of modern life beyond personal control. (12)

Utopian movements seek an ideal society for true believers. (12)

Validation of self requires assurance that one is who one claims to be. (4)

Validity refers to whether the measuring instrument is really measuring what it was designed to. (1)

The **value added model** specifies six conditions that are necessary and sufficient to produce collective behavior. (12)

Values are the central beliefs of a culture that provide a standard by which norms are judged. (2)

Variables are factors that differ from one person or collectivity to another or that change over time. (1)

Verstehen is the ability to see the world as it might be experienced by others. (1)

A **virtual self** awaits us in each role we perform. (4)

Voluntary childlessness refers to the decision to remain child free. (9)

The **voucher system** would allow families to spend a given sum of tax money for any type of schooling available. (11)

Welfare, or **state, capitalism** refers to free markets existing within limits designed to ensure social stability. (10)

White-collar crimes are illegal activities committed by individuals of high status, usually by nonviolent means, in the course of their employment, for their own benefit. (5)

The **work ethic** refers to a set of beliefs that emerged in Western Europe in the sixteenth century and that are associated with the rise of modern capitalism. (2)

Workfare programs are designed to prepare welfare parents for permanent positions in the labor force. (6)

The **world system** consists of the economic and political relations among industrial and less-developed nations. (12)

Yuppie stands for young upwardly mobile professional. (10)

BIBLIOGRAPHY

Abramovitz, Mimi. "Why Welfare Reform Is a Sham." *The Nation.* September 26, 1988, pp. 1ff.

Acker, Joan. *Doing Comparable Worth: Gender, Class, and Pay Equity.* Philadelphia: Temple University Press, 1988b.

Ackermann, Robert John. *Religion as Critique.* Amherst: University of Massachusetts Press, 1985.

Adam, Barry D. *The Rise of a Gay and Lesbian Movement.* Boston: Twayne, 1987.

Adams, Frank, and David Ellerman. "The Many Roads to Worker Ownership in America." *Social Policy,* Winter 1989, pp. 12–18.

Aguirre, B. E., E. L. Quarantelli, and Jorge L. Mendoza. "The Collective Behavior of Fads: The Characteristics, Effects, and Career of Streaking," *American Sociological Review* 53 (1988): 569–584.

Akers, Ronald L. *Deviant Behavior: A Social Learning Approach* 2nd ed. Belmont, CA: Wadsworth, 1977.

Alba, Richard D. *Ethnicity and Race in the USA: Toward the Twenty-first Century.* New York: Routledge & Kegan Paul, 1985.

Alexander, Jeffrey C., ed. *Neofunctionalism.* Beverly Hills, CA: Sage 1985.

Alexander, Karl L., Doris R. Entwisle, and Maxine S. Thompson. "School Performance, Status Relations, and the Structure of Sentiment: Bringing the Teacher Back In." *American Sociological Review* 52 (1987): 665–682.

Allen, Michael Patrick. *The Founding Fortunes: A New Anatomy of the Super-Rich Families in America.* New York: E. P. Dutton, 1987.

Allen, Michael Patrick, and Philip Broyles. "Class Hegemony and Political Finance: Presidential Campaign Contributions of Wealthy Capitalist Families." *American Sociological Review* 54 (1989): 275–287.

Allport, Gordon, and L. Postman. *The Psychology of Rumor.* New York: Henry Holt, 1947.

Alonso, William, and Paul Starr, eds. *The Politics of Numbers.* New York: Russell Sage Foundation, 1987.

Altman, Dennis. *AIDS in the Mind of America: The Social, Political, and Psychological Impact of a New Epidemic.* Garden City, NY: Anchor, 1986.

Alwin, Duane F., and Arland Thornton. "Family Origins and the Schooling Process: Early versus Late Influence of Parental Characteristics." *American Sociological Review* 49(6) (1984): 784–802.

Amenta, Edwin, and Bruce G. Carruthers. "The Formative Years of U.S. Social Spending Policies: Theories of the Welfare State and the American States During the Great Depression." *American Sociological Review* 53 (1987): 661–678.

American Association of University Women. "College Admissions Tests: Opportunities or Roadblocks?" Washington: AAUW; June 1988.

American Psychiatric Association. *Diagnostic and Statistical Manual III-R.* Washington: American Psychiatric Association 1987.

Ammerman, Nancy Tatom. *Bible Believers: Fundamentalists in the Modern World.* New Brunswick, NJ: Transaction Press, 1987.

Andersen, Margaret L. *Thinking About Women: Sociological and Feminist Perspectives* (2nd ed.). New York: Macmillan, 1988.

Anti-Defamation League of B'nai Brith. *Young and Violent: The Growing Menace of America's Neo-Nazi Skinheads.* New York: Anti-Defamation League of B'Nai Brith, 1988.

Apostle, Richard, Don Clairmont, and Lars Osberg, "Economic Segmentation and Politics." *American Journal of Sociology* 91 (1985): 905–931.

Apple, Michael W. *Teachers and Texts: A Political Economy of Class and Gender Relations in Education.* New York: Routledge & Kegan Paul, 1986.

Arce, Carlos. "A Reconsideration of Chicago Culture and Identity." *Daedalus* 110(2) (Spring 1981): 177–191.

Archdeacon, Thomas J. *Becoming American: An Ethnic History.* New York: Free Press, 1983.

Archer, Dane et al. "Homicide and the Death Penalty: A Cross National Test of a Deterrence Hypothesis." *Journal of Criminal Law and Criminology* 74 (Fall 1984): 991–1013.

Arendell, Terry J. "Women and the Economics of

Divorce in the Contemporary United States." *Signs* 13 (1987): 121–135.

Arens, W. *The Original Sin: Incest and Its Meaning.* New York: Oxford University Press, 1986.

Asch, Solomon. "Studies of Independence and Conformity: A Minority of One against a Unanimous Majority." *Psychological Monographs* 70 (1956): 1–70.

Ashe, Arthur R., Jr. *A Hard Road to Glory: A History of the African-American Athlete,* Vols. 1–3. New York: Warner, 1988.

Ashton, David N. *Unemployment Under Capitalism: The Sociology of British and American Labour Markets.* Westport, CT: Greenwood Press, 1986.

Astrachan, Anthony. *How Men Feel: Their Response to Women's Demands for Equality and Power.* New York: Anchor/Doubleday, 1986.

Atkinson, Maxine P., and Jacqueline Boles. "WASP (Wives as Senior Partners)." *Journal of Marriage and the Family* 46 (1984): 861–870.

Atwater, Lynn. *The Extramarital Connection: Sex, Intimacy, and Identity.* New York: Irvington, 1982.

Auerbach, Judith D. *In the Business of Child Care.* New York: Praeger, 1988.

Austin, Charles. "Women Ministers Are Feeling Dual Role." *The New York Times,* April 10, 1983, p. 30.

Avery, Robert B., and Arthur B. Kennickel. "Rich Rewards." *American Demographics,* June 1989; pp. 19–22.

Baca Zinn, Maxine. "Family, Feminism, and Race in America." *Gender & Society* 4 (1990): 68–82.

Baca Zinn, Maxine and D. Stanley Eitzen, *Diversity in American Families.* New York: Harper and Row Publishing Company, Inc. 1987.

Bachrach, Christine A., and Marjorie C. Horn, "Sexual Activity among US Women of Reproductive Age," *American Journal of Public Health* 78 (1988): 320–321.

Baer, Hans A. *The Black Spiritual Movement: A Religious Response to Racism.* Knoxville: University of Tennessee Press, 1984.

Bagdikian, Ben H. *The Media Monopoly* (2nd ed.); Boston: Beacon Press, 1988.

Bagley, Christopher. *Racial and Ethnic Composition.* New York: Bantam, 1985.

Bailey, William C. "Deterrence and the Severity of the Death Penalty: A Neglected Question in Deterrence Research." *Social Forces* 58(4) (June 1980): 1308–1332.

Baker, David P., and Doris Entwisle. "The Influence of Mothers on the Academic Expectations of Young Children: A Longitudinal Study of How Gender Differences Arise." *Social Forces* 65(3) (1987): 670–694.

Bales, Robert F. *Interaction Process Analysis.* Reading, MA: Addison-Welsey, 1950.

Baltzell, E. Digby. *Puritan Boston and Quaker Philadelphia.* New York: Free Press, 1979.

Baltzell, E. Digby. *The Protestant Establishment: Aristocracy and Caste in America.* New York: Random House, 1964.

Baltzell, E. Digby, and Howard G. Schneiderman. "Social Class in the Oval Office." *Society,* September/October 1988; pp. 42–49.

Barkan, Joanne. "Sweden: Not Yet Paradise, But. . . ." *Dissent,* Spring 1989; pp. 147–151.

Barkan, Steven E. "Strategic, Tactical and Organizational Dilemmas of the Protest Movement Against Nuclear Power." *Social Problems* 27(1) (October 1979): 19–37.

Barkan, Steven E. "Legal Control of the Southern Civil Rights Movement." *American Sociological Review* 49(4) (1984): 552–565.

Barr, Nicholas. *The Economics of the Welfare State.* Stanford, CA: Stanford University Press, 1987.

Barstow, Anne. "The Uses of Archeology for Women's History: James Mellaart's Work on the Neolithic Goddess at Catal Hüyük." *Feminist Studies* 4(3) (October 1978): 7–18.

Bart, Pauline B., Linda Freeman, and Peter Kimball. "The Different Worlds of Women and Men: Attitudes toward Pornography and Responses to "Not a Love Story"—A Film about Pornography." *Women's Studies International Forum* 8 (1985): 307–322.

Bean, Frank D., and Gary Swicegood. *Mexican-American Fertility Patterns.* Austin: University of Texas Press, 1985.

Becker, Howard S. *Outsiders: Studies in the Sociology of Deviance.* New York: Free Press, 1973.

Beckford, James A. *Cult Controversies: The Societal Responses to the New Religious Movements.* New York: Tavistock, 1985.

Bedau, Hugo Adam, and Michael L. Radelet. "Miscarriages of Justice in Potentially Capital Cases." *Stanford Law Review* 40(1987): 21–179.

Bee, Helen. *The Developing Child* (5th ed.). New York: Harper & Row, 1989.

Beeghley, Leonard. *Living Poorly in America.* New York: Praeger, 1983.

Beeghley, Leonard. "Social Class and Political Participation." *Sociological Forum* 1 (1986): 496–513.

Bell, Daniel. *The Coming of Post-Industrial Society.* New York: Basic Books, 1973.

Bell, Daniel. "The Third Technological Revolution

and Its Possible Socioeconomic Consequences." *Dissent,* Spring 1989; pp. 164–176.

Bellah, Robert N. "Civil Religion in America." In Robert N. Bellah, *Beyond Belief: Essays on Religion in a Post-Traditional World.* New York: Harper & Row, 1970.

Bellah Robert N. *The Broken Covenant: American Civil Religion in a Time Trial.* New York: Seabury Press, 1975.

Benedict, Ruth. *Patterns of Culture.* Boston: Houghton Mifflin, 1934.

Bennett, Neil G., Ann Klimas Blanc, and David E. Bloom. "Commitment and the Modern Union: Assessing the Link Between Premarital Cohabitation and Subsequent Marital Stability." *American Sociological Review* 53 (1988): 127–138.

Bennett, Neil G., David E. Bloom, and Patricia H. Craig. "The Divergence of Black and White Marriage Patterns." *American Journal of Sociology* 95 (1989): 692–722.

Berger, Peter L., and Thomas Luckmann. *The Social Construction of Reality.* Garden City, NY: Doubleday, 1966.

Berheide, Catherine White, Cynthia Chertos, Lois Haignere, and Ronnie Steinberg. "A Pay Equity Analysis of Female-Dominated and Disproportionately Minority New York State Job Titles." *Humanity and Society* 11 (1987): 465–485.

Berk, Sarah Fenstermaker. *The Gender Factory: The Apportionment of Work in American Households.* New York: Plenum, 1985.

Berkman, Lisa F. "The Relationship of Social Networks and Social Support to Morbidity and Mortality." in S. Cohen and Leonard Syme (eds.), *Social Support and Health.* Orlando, FL: Academic Press, 1985.

Bernard, Jessie. *The Future of Marriage.* New Haven, CT: Yale University Press, 1982.

Bernstein, Richard. "Asian Students Harmed by Precursors' Success." *The New York Times,* July 10, 1988, p. L16.

Berryman, Sue E. *Who Serves? The Persistent Myth of the Underclass Army.* Boulder, CO: Westview Press, 1988.

Best, Joel. "Rhetoric in Claims-Making: Constructing the Missing Children Problem." *Social Problems* 34 (1987): 101–121.

Best, Joel, and Gerry Horiuchi. "The Razor Blade in the Apple. The Social Construction of Urban Legends." *Social Problems* 32 (1985): 488–499.

Bianchi, Suzanne M., and Judith A. Seltzer. "Life Without Father." *American Demographics* 8 (1986): 43–47.

Bidwell, Charles, and John Kasarda. *The Organiza-* *tion and Its Ecosystem: A Theory of Structuring in Organization.* Greenwich, CT: JAI Press, 1985.

Bielby, William T., and James N. Baron. "Men and Women at Work: Sex Segregation and Statistical Discrimination." *American Journal of Sociology* 91 (1986): 759–799.

Biesty, Patrick. "If It's Fun, Is It Play? A Meadian Analysis." In Bernard Mergen (ed.), *Cultural Dimensions of Play, Games, and Sport,* pp. 61–72. Champaign, IL: Human Kinetics, 1986.

Birdwhistle, Ray. *Kinesics and Context.* Philadelphia: University of Pennsylvania Press, 1970.

Blackwood, E. "Sexuality and Gender in Certain Native American Tribes." *Signs* 10 (1984): 127–142.

Blake, Judith. "Number of Siblings and Educational Mobility." *American Sociological Review* 50(1) (1985): 84–94.

Blau, Judith R. "High Culture as Mass Culture." *Society,* May–June 1986, pp. 65–69.

Blau, Judith R., and Otis Dudley Duncan. *The American Occupational Structure.* New York: John Wiley, 1967.

Blauner, Robert. *Alienation and Freedom: The Factory Worker and His Industry.* Chicago: University of Chicago Press, 1964.

Block, Alan A., and William J. Chambliss. *Organizing Crime.* New York: Elsevier/North Holland, 1981.

Block, Fred. *Rethinking State Theory:* Philadelphia: Temple University Press, 1987.

Blocker, Jack S. "Separate Paths: Suffragists and the Women's Temperance Crusade." *Signs* 10(3) (1985): 460–476.

Bloom, Jack M. *Class, Race, and the Civil Rights Movement: The Changing Political Economy of Southern Racism,* Bloomington: Indiana University Press, 1987.

Blum, Linda M. "Possibilities and Limits of the Comparable Worth Movement." *Gender & Society* 1 (1987): 380–399.

Blum, Linda M., and Vicki Smith. "Women's Mobility in the Corporation: A Critique of the Politics of Optimism." *Signs* 13 (1988): 528–545.

Blumberg, Rae Lesser. *Women and the Wealth of Nations: Theory and Research on Gender and Global Development.* New York: Praeger, 1989.

Blumberg, Rae Lesser, and Marion Tolbert Colemen. "A Theoretical Look at the Gender Balance of Power in the American Couple." *Journal of Family Issues* 10 (1989): 225–250.

Blumberg, Rhoda Lois. *Civil Rights: The 1960 Freedom Struggle.* Boston: Twayne, 1984.

Blumer, Herbert. "Collective Behavior." In Alfred

McLung Lee (ed.), *New Outlines of the Principles of Sociology.* New York: Barnes & Noble, 1951.

Blumer, Herbert. "Social Movements." In R. Serge Denisoff (ed.), *The Sociology of Dissent,* pp. 74–90. New York: Harcourt Brace Jovanovich, 1974.

Blumstein, Philip, and Pepper Schwartz. *American Couples: Money, Work, Sex.* New York: Morrow, 1983.

Bohme, Gernot and Nico Stehr. *The Knowledge Society: The Growing Impact of Scientific Knowledge on Social Relations.* Dordrecht, Netherlands: Kluwer, 1986.

Bolger, Niall, Anita DeLongis, Ronald C. Kessler, and Elaine Wethington. "The Contagion of Stress Across Multiple Roles." *Journal of Marriage and the Family* 51 (1989): 175–183.

Bookman, Ann, and Sandra Morgen (eds.) *Women and the Politics of Empowerment.* Philadelphia: Temple University Press, 1988.

Bordewich, Fergus M. "Colorado's Thriving Cults." *The New York Times Magazine,* May 1, 1988; pp. 37ff.

Bornschier, Volker, and Christopher Chase-Dunn. *Transnational Corporations and Underdevelopment.* New York: Praeger, 1985.

Bose, Christine E. Roslyn Feldberg, and Natalie Sokoloff. *Hidden Aspects of Women's Work.* New York: Praeger, 1987.

Boserup, Ester. *Women's Role in Economic Development.* New York: St. Martin's Press, 1970.

Bourdieu, Pierre. *Distinction: A Social Critique of the Judgement of Taste.* Cambridge, MA: Harvard University Press, 1984.

Bourdieu, Pierre, and Jean-Claude Passeron. *Reproduction in Education, Society, and Culture.* Beverly Hills, CA: Sage, 1977.

Bouvier, Leon F., and Robert W. Gardner. "Immigration to the U.S.: The Unfinished Story." *Population Bulletin* 41(1) (November 1986): 10.

Bowles, Samuel, and Herbert Gintis. *Schooling in Capitalist America.* New York: Basic Books, 1976.

Bowers, William J., Glenn L. Pierce, and John F. McDevitt, *Legal Homicide: Death as Punishment in America, 1964–1982.* Boston: Northeastern University Press, 1984.

Boyer, Paul, and Stephen Nussenbaum. *Salem Possessed: The Social Origins of Witchcraft.* Cambridge, MA: Harvard University Press, 1974.

Bozett, Frederick W., ed. *Gay and Lesbian Parents.* New York: Praeger, 1987.

Brackman, Harold, and Steven P. Erie. "The Future of the Gender Gap." *Social Policy* Winter 1986, pp. 5–10.

Bradbury, Katherine L.; Karl E. Case, and Constance R. Dunham. *Geographic Patterns in Lending in Boston, 1982–1987.* Boston: Federal Bank of Boston, 1989.

Brannen, Julia, and Gail Wilson. *Give and Take in Families: Studies in Resource Distribution.* London: Allen & Unwin, 1987.

Braverman, Harry. *Labor and Monopoly Capital.* New York: Monthly Review Press, 1974.

Bridges, William P., and Robert L. Nelson. "Markets in Hierarchies: Organizational and Market Influences on Gender Inequality in a State Pay System," *American Journal of Sociology* 95 (1989): 616–658.

Briggs, Kenneth. "Religious Feeling Seen Strong in U.S." *The New York Times,* December 9, 1984, p. 30.

Briggs, Sheila. "Gender and Religion." In Beth B. Hess and Myra Marx Ferree (eds.), *Analyzing Gender: A Handbook of Social Science Research.* Newbury Park, CA: Sage, 1987, pp. 408–441.

Brinton, Mary C. "The Social-Institutional Bases of Gender Stratification: Japan as an Illustrative Case." *American Journal of Sociology* 94 (1988): 300–334.

Brod, Harry, ed. *The Making of Masculinities—The New Men's Studies.* Boston: Allen & Unwin, 1987.

Brodeur, Paul. *Outrageous Misconduct: The Asbestos Industry on Trial.* New York: Pantheon Books, 1985.

Brown, Gregory M. "End of Purchase Requirement Fails to Change Food Stamp Participation." *Monthly Labor Review,* July 1988: pp. 14–18.

Brown, Judith K., and Virginia Kerns. *In Her Prime: A New View of Middle-Aged Women.* South Hadley, MA: Bergin & Garvey, 1985.

Browne, Malcolm W. "A Look at Success of Young Asians." *The New York Times,* March 25, 1986.

Brunvand, Jan Harold. "Letter to the Editor," *The New York Times,* December 24, 1988.

Buell, Emmett H., Jr., and Richard A. Brisbin, Jr. *School Desegregation and Defended Neighborhoods.* Lexington, MA: Lexington Books, 1982.

Bumpass, Larry, and James Sweet, "Preliminary Evidence on Cohabitation," University of Wisconsin, Center for Demographic Ecology, Working Paper #2, 1988.

Bumpass, Larry, James Sweet, and Andrew Cherlin. "The Role of Cohabitation in the Declining Rate of Marriage," paper presented at the annual meeting of the Population Association of America, Baltimore, MD, March 1989.

Burawoy, Michael. *The Politics of Production: Fac-*

tory Regimes under Capitalism and Socialism. London: New Left Press, 1985.

Burgess, Robert L., and Ronald L. Akers. "A Differential Association—Reinforcement Theory of Criminal Behavior." *Social Problems* 14(2) (Fall 1968): 132–147.

Burke, Peter J. "Gender Identity, Sex, and School Performance." *Social Psychology Quarterly* 52 (1989): 159–169.

Burkhalter, S. Brian and Robert F. Murphy. 1989. Tappers and Sappers: Rubber, Gold and Money among the Mundurucu. *American Ethnologist* 16 (February 1989): pp. 100–116.

Burris, Val. "The Political Partisanship of American Business: A Study of Corporate Political Action Committees." *American Sociological Review* 52 (1987): 732–744.

Burstein, Paul. "Attacking Sex Discrimination in the Labor Market: A Study in Law and Politics." *Social Forces* 67 (1989): 641–665.

Burt, Martha R. and Barbara E. Cohen. *America's Homeless: Numbers, Characteristics, and Problems that Serve Them.* Washington, D.C.: Urban Institute Press, 1989.

Burton, N. J., and L. V. Jones. "Recent Trends in Achievement Levels of Black and White Youth." *Educational Researcher* 11(4) (1982): 10–14.

Business Week. "Is the Boss Getting Paid Too Much?" May 1, 1989, p. 46–52.

Butterfield, Fox. "Why Asians Are Going to the Head of the Class." *New York Times,* August 3, 1986, Sect. 12, pp. 18–23.

Cable, Sherry, Edward J. Walsh, and Rex H. Warland. "Differential Paths to Political Activism: Comparisons of Four Mobilization Processes After the Three-Mile Island Accident." *Social Forces* 66 (1988): 951–969.

Cancian, Francesca M. *Love In America: Gender and Self-Development.* New York: Cambridge University Press, 1987.

Caplow, Theodore, et al. *All Faithful People: Change and Continuity in Middletown's Religion.* Minneapolis: University of Minnesota Press, 1984.

Cardwell, Jerry D. *Mass Media Christianity: Televangelism and the Great Commission.* Lanham, MD: University Press of America, 1984.

Carnegie Corporation of New York: *A Nation Prepared: Teachers for the 21st Century.* New York: Carnegie Corporation, 1986.

Carnegie Corporation of New York. "Black Churches: Can They Strengthen the Black Family?" *Carnegie Quarterly,* Fall/Winter 1987–1988.

Carnegie Corporation of New York. *Turning Points: Preparing American Youth for the 21st Century.* New York: Carnegie Corporation, June 1989.

Carrier, James G. *Social Class and the Construction of Inequality in American Education.* New York: Greenwood, 1986.

Cerulo, Karen A. "Sociopolitical Control and the Structure of National Symbols." *Social Forces* 68 (1989): 76–99.

Chafetz, Janet Saltzman. *Sex and Advantage: A Comparative Macro-Structural Theory of Sex Stratification.* Totowa, NJ: Rowman & Allenheld, 1984.

Chang, Patricia Mei Yin. "Beyond the Clan: A Re-Analysis of the Empirical Evidence in Durkheim's *The Elementary Forms of the Religious Life.*" *Sociological Theory* 7 (1989): 64–69.

Children's Defense Fund. *A Children's Defense Budget FY 1989: An Analysis of Our Nation's Investment in Children.* Washington: CDF, 1988.

Chodorow, Nancy J. *The Reproduction of Mothering.* Berkeley: University of California Press, 1978.

Clark, Burton R. *The Higher Education System: Academic Organization in Cross-National Perspective.* Berkeley: University of California Press, 1983.

Clawson, Dan, and Alan Neustadtl. "Interlocks, PACs, and Corporate Conservatism." *American Journal of Sociology* 94 (1989): 749–773.

Clegg, Stewart, Paul Boreham, and Goeff Dow. *Class, Politics and the Economy.* London: Routledge & Kegan Paul, 1986.

Clinard, Marshall B., and Peter C. Yeager. *Corporate Crime,* New York: Free Press, 1980.

Clinard, Marshall, and Robert Meier. *Sociology of Deviant Behavior* 2nd ed. New York: Holt, 1985.

Cloward, Richard A., and Lloyd E. Ohlin. *Delinquency and Opportunity.* New York: Free Press, 1960.

Clymer, Adam. "How Americans Rate Big Business." *The New York Times Magazine,* June 8, 1986, p. 69.

Coates, Vary T. "The Potential Impact of Robotics." *The Futurist,* February 1983, pp. 28–32.

Cockburn, Alexander. "Some Radical Notions about Fighting Drugs." *Wall Street Journal,* September 11, 1986, p. 31.

Cockerham, William *Medical Sociology.* New York: Prentice-Hall, 1979.

Cohen, Elizabeth, Rachel A. Lotan, and Chaub Leechor. "Can Classrooms Learn?" *Sociology of Education* 62 (1989): 75–94.

Cohen, Steven M. "Jews, More or Less." *Moment,* September 1984.

Cohn, Samuel. *The Process of Occupational Sex-Typing: The Feminization of Clerical Work in*

Great Britain. Philadelphia: Temple University Press, 1985.

Cole, Stephen. "Sex Discrimination and Admission to Medical School 1929–1984." *American Journal of Sociology* 92 (1986): 549–568.

Cole, Stephen, Jonathan R. Cole, and Gary A. Simon. "Chance and Consensus in Peer Review." *Science* 214 (4523) (November 20, 1981): 881–886.

Coleman James S. "Recent Trends in School Integration." *Educational Researcher* 4 (1975): 3–12.

Coleman, James S., "Social Capital in the Creation of Human Capital," *American Journal of Sociology* 94 (1988): S95–S120.

Coleman, James S., Elihu Katz, and Herbert Menzel. "The Diffusion of Innovation Among Physicians." *Sociometry* 20 (1957): 253–269.

Coleman, James S., Thomas Hoffer, and Sally Kilgore. *High School Achievement: Public, Catholic, and Private Schools Compared.* New York: Basic Books, 1982.

Coleman, James William. "Law and Power: The Sherman Antitrust Act and Its Enforcement in the Petroleum Industry." *Social Problems* 32 (1985): 264–274.

Coleman, Lerita, and Toni Antonucci. "Women's Well-being at Midlife." *Institute for Social Research Newsletter,* Winter 1982.

Coles, Gerald. *The Learning Mystique: A Critical Look at "Learning Disabilities."* New York: Pantheon, 1987.

Collier, Jane Fishburne. *Marriage and Inequality in Classless Societies.* Stanford, CA: Stanford Univrsity Press, 1988.

Congress of the United States. *Science, Technology and the First Amendment,* Special Report. Washington, D.C.: U.S. Government Printing Office, Office of Technology Assessment, 1988.

Connell, R. W. *Gender and Power: Society, the Person, and Sexual Politics.* Stanford, CA: Stanford University Press, 1987.

Connell, R. W., June Crawford, Susan Kippax, G. W. Dowsett, Don Baxter, Lex Watson, and R. Berg, "Facing the Epidemic: Changes in the Sexual Lives of Gay and Bisexual Men in Australia and Their Implications for AIDS Prevention Strategies." *Social Problems* 36 (1989): 384–402.

Cookson, Peter W., Jr., and Caroline Hodges Persell. *Preparing for Power: America's Elite Boarding Schools.* New York: Basic Books, 1985.

Cooley, Charles Horton, *Social Organization: A Study of the Larger Mind.* New York: Scribners, 1909.

Cornforth, Chris, Alan Thomas, Jenny Lewis, and Roger Spear. *Developing Successful Worker Co-operatives.* London and Newbury Park, CA: Sage, 1988.

COSSA. *See* Consortium of Social Science Organizations.

Costa, Paul T., Jr., Alan B. Zonderman, Robert R. McGrae, Joan Cornoni-Huntley, Ben Z. Locke, and Helen E. Barbano. "Longitudinal Analysis of Psychological Well-Being in a National Sample: Stability of Mean Levels." *Journal of Gerontology* 42 (1987): 50–55.

Crain, Robert L., and Willis D. Hawley. "Standards of Research." *Society,* January–February 1982; pp. 14–21.

Cullingford, Cedric. *Children and Television.* New York: St. Martin's, 1984.

Cummings, Scott, and Del Taebel. "The Economic Socialization of Children: a Neo Marxist Analysis." *Social Problems* 26(2) (December 1978): 198–210.

Cundy, Donald T. "Televised Political Editorials and the Low-Involvement Viewer." *Social Science Quarterly* 70 (1989): 911–922.

Currie, Elliott P. "Crimes Without Criminals: Witchcraft and Its Control in Renaissance Europe." *Law and Society Review* 3(1) (August 1968): 7–32.

Curtis, Richard F. "Household and Family in Theory on Inequality." *American Sociological Review* 51 (1986): 168–183.

Curtiss, S. *Genie: A Psycholinguistic Study of a Modern World "Wild Child."* New York: Academic Press, 1977.

Cutler, Blayne. "Up the Down Staircase." *American Demographics,* April 1989a, pp. 32–41.

Daly, Mary. *Pure Lust: Elemental Feminist Philosophy.* Boston: Beacon Press, 1984.

Daniels, Lee A. "Illiteracy Seen As a Threat to U.S. Economic Edge." *The New York Times,* September 7, 1988, p. B8.

Daniels, Lee A. "Some Top Universities in Squeeze Between Research and Academics." *The New York Times,* May 10, 1989, pp. 1ff.

Daniels, Lee A. "Tests Show Reading and Writing Lag Continues." *The New York Times,* January 10, 1990; p. B8.

Danzger, M. Herbert. *Returning to Tradition: The Contemporary Revival of Orthodox Judaism.* New Haven, CT: Yale University Press, 1989.

Danziger, Sheldon, Peter Gottschalk, and Eugene Smolensky. "How the Rich have Fared, 1973–87." *American Economic Review* 79 (1989): 310–314.

Davis, Cary. "The Future Racial Composition of the United States." *Intercom,* September–October 1982, pp. 8–10.

Davis, D. L., and R. G. Whitten. "The Cross-Cultural Study of Human Sexuality." *Annual Review of Anthropology* 16 (1987): 69–98.

Davis, Nanette J. *From Crime to Choice: The Transformation of Abortion in America.* Westport, CT: Greenwood Press, 1985.

de Certeau, Michel. *The Practice of Everyday Life* (Steven F. Randall, trans.). Berkeley and Los Angeles: University of California Press, 1984.

Deegan, Mary Jo. *American Ritual Dramas: Social Rules and Cultural Meanings.* New York: Greenwood, 1989.

de Graaf, Nan Dirk, and Hendrick Derk Flap. " 'With a Little Help from My Friends': Social Resources as an Explanation of Occupational Status and Income in West Germany, The Netherlands, and the United States." *Social Forces* 67 (1988): 452–472.

Della Fave, L. Richard. "The Meek Shall Not Inherit the Earth: Self-Evaluation and the Legitimacy of Stratification." *American Sociological Review* 45 (1980): 955–971.

Demerath, J. N., III, and Rhys H. Williams. "Civil Religion in an Uncivil Society." *Annals of the American Academy of Political and Social Science* 480 (1985): 154–166.

Demerath, J.N., III, and Rhys H. Williams. "Religion and Power in the American Experience." *Society,* January/February 1989, pp. 29–38.

D'Emilio, John, and Estelle B. Freedman. *Intimate Matters: A History of Sexuality in America.* New York: Harper & Row, 1988.

Denisoff, R. Serge. *Tarnished Gold: The Record Industry Revisited.* New Brunswick, NJ: Transaction Press, 1986.

Denisoff, R. Serge. *Inside MTV.* New Brunswick, NJ: Transaction Press, 1988.

Denisoff, R. Serge and Ralph Wahrman. *An Introduction to Sociology,* (3rd ed.). New York: Macmillan, 1983.

Denzin, Norman K. "Behaviorism and Beyond." *Contemporary Sociology* 15(4) (1986): 553–556.

Denzin, Norman K. *The Alcoholic Self.* Newbury Park, CA: Sage, 1987.

de Tocqueville, Alexis. *Democracy in America* (1830). New York: Mentor, 1956.

Devor, Holly. "Gender Blending Females: Women and Sometimes Men." *American Behavioral Scientist* 31 (1987): 12–40.

Dickinson, James, and Bob Russell, eds. *Family, Economy, and State: The Social Reproduction Process Under Capitalism* New York: St. Martin's Press, 1987.

DiMaggio, Paul. "Cultural Capital and School Success: The Impact of Status Culture Participation on the Grades of U.S. High School Students." *American Sociological Review* 47 (1982): 189–201.

Diprete, Thomas A. "The Upgrading and Downgrading of Occupations: Status Redefinition vs. Deskilling as Alternative Theories of Change." *Social Forces* 66 (1988): 725–746.

Dobratz, Betty A., and Stephanie Shanks-Meile. "The Contemporary Ku Klux Klan and the American Nazi Party: A Comparison to American Populism at the Turn of the Century." *Humanity & Society* 12 (1988): 20–50.

Domhoff, William G. *Who Rules America Now?: A View for the '80s.* Englewood Cliffs, NJ: Prentice-Hall, 1983.

Domhoff, William G., and Richard L. Zweigenhaft. "Jews in the Corporate Establishment." *New York Times,* April 24, 1983, Sect. 3, pp. 2ff.

Donnerstein, Edward, Daniel Linz, and Steven Penrod. *The Question of Pornography.* New York: Free Press, 1987.

Doob, Anthony N. "Deviance: Society's Side Show." *Psychology Today* 5 (October 1971): 47–51, 113.

Doolin, Joseph. "Planning for the Special Needs of the Homeless Elderly." *The Gerontologist* 25(3) (June 1986): 229–231.

Dougherty, Kevin. "Educational Policy-Making and the Relative Autonomy of the State: The Case of Occupational Education in the Community College." *Sociological Forum* 3 (1988): 400–432.

Douglas, Jack, and Frances Chaput Waksler. *The Sociology of Deviance: An Introduction.* Boston: Little, Brown. 1982.

Duberman, Martin Bauml, Martha Vicinus, and George Chauncey, Jr, eds. *Hidden from History: Reclaiming the Gay and Lesbian Past.* New York: New American Library, 1989.

Dunaway, David King. "Music as Political Communication in the United States." In James Lull (ed.), *Popular Music and Communication* pp. 36–52. Newbury Park CA: Sage, 1987.

Duncan, Greg J., with Richard D. Coe, Mary E. Corcoran, Martha S. Hill, Saul D. Hoffman, and James N. Morgan. *Years of Poverty, Years of Plenty: The Changing Economic Fortunes of American Workers and Families.* Ann Arbor, MI: Institute for Social Research, 1984.

Dunham, Charlotte Chorn, and Vern L. Bengtson. "Married with Children: Protest and the Timing of Family Life Course Events." Paper presented at the 84th annual meeting of the American Sociological Association, San Francisco, August 1989.

Durkheim, Emile. *The Division of Labor in Society* (1893). (New York: Free Press, 1984).

Durkheim, Emile. *Suicide* (1897). Translated by John A. Spaulding and George Simpson. Glencoe, IL: Free Press, 1966.

Durkheim, Emile. *The Elementary Forms of the Religious Life* (1912). New York: Collier Books, 1961.

Dutton, D. "Social Class, Health and Illness." In L. Aiken and D. Mechanic (eds.), *Applications of Social Science to Clinical Medicine and Health Policy.* New Brunswick, NJ: Rutgers University Press, 1986.

Eocles, Jaquelynne S., and Janis E. Jacobs. "Social Forces Shape Math Attitudes and Performance." *Signs* 11 (1986).

Eckberg, Douglas Lee. "The Physicians' Anti-Abortion Campaign and the Social Bases of Moral Reform Participation." *Social Forces* 67 (1988): 378–397.

Eggebeen, David, and Peter Uhlenberg. "Changes in the Organization of Men's Lives: 1960–1980." *Family Relations* 34 (1985): 251–257.

Ehrenfield, David, James Applegate, and Dominic Durkin. "Rutgers is Taking a Detour On the Road to 'Excellence.'" *The New York Times,* February 15, 1987; p. NJ 38.

Ehrenreich, Barbara, and Deirdre English. *For Her Own Good: 150 Years of the Experts' Advice to Women.* Garden City, NY: Anchor/Doubleday, 1980.

Eismeier, Theodore J., and Philip H. Pollack, III. *Business, Money, and the Rise of Corporate PACs in American Elections.* Westport, CT: Quorum Books, 1988.

Ellwood, David T. *Poor Support: Poverty in the American Family.* New York: Basic Books, 1988.

Ember, Carol R. "The Relative Decline in Women's Contribution to Agriculture with Intensification." *American Anthropologist* 85 (1983): 285–304.

England, Paula. *Comparable Worth: Theories and Evidence.* New York: Aldine de Gruyter, 1989.

England, Paula, and Barbara Stanek Kilbourne. "Markets, Marriages, and Other Mates: The Problem of Power." In Roger Friedland and Sandy Robertson (eds.), *Beyond the Marketplace: Rethinking Society and Economy.* New York: Aldine de Gruyter 1989.

Entwisle, Doris R., and Susan Doering. "The Emergent Father Roles." *Sex Roles* 18 (1988): 119–126.

Epstein, Cynthia Fuchs. *Deceptive Distinctions: Sex, Gender, and the Social Order.* New Haven, CT: Yale University Press, 1988.

Erikson, Erik H. *Childhood and Society* (rev. ed.). New York: W. W. Norton, 1964.

Erikson, Kai. *The Wayward Puritans.* New York: Wiley, 1966.

Erikson, Kai. *Everything in Its Path: Destruction of Community in the Buffalo Creek Flood.* New York: Simon & Schuster, 1976.

Erikson, Kai. "On Work and Alienation." *American Sociological Review* 51(1) (1986): 1–8.

Ernst, Cecile, and Jules Angst. *Birth Order: Its Influence on Personality.* New York: Springer-Verlag, 1983.

Eskenazi Gerald. "Arena of Big-Time Athletics Is Showcasing a Younger Act." *The New York Times,* March 5, 1989, pp. 1ff.

Estes, Carroll L. "Aging, Health, and Social Policy: Crisis and Crossroads." *Journal of Aging and Social Policy* 1 (1/2): (1989): 17–32.

Etzioni, Amitai. "Shady Corporate Practices." *The New York Times.* November 15, 1985, p. A35.

Etzioni-Halevy, Eva. *Bureaucracy and Democracy: A Political Dilemma.* Boston: Routledge & Kegan Paul, 1983.

Etzkowitz, Henry. "Entrepreneurial Science in the Academy: A Case of the Transformation of Norms." *Social Problems* 36 (1989): 14–29.

Evan, William M., and Stephen Hilgartner, eds. *The Arms Race and Nuclear War.* Englewood Cliffs, NJ: Prentice-Hall, 1987.

Ewing, Wayne. "The Clinical Advocacy of Violence." In Michael Kimmel and Michael Messner (eds.), *Men's Lives,* pp. 393–398. New York: Macmillan, 1989.

Fantasia, Rick. *Cultures of Solidarity.* Berkeley: University of California Press, 1988.

Farber, Naomi. "The Significance of Race and Class in Marital Decisions among Unmarried Adolescent Mothers." *Social Problems* 37 (1990): 51–63.

Farkas, George, Robert P. Grobe, Daniel Sheehan, and Yuan Shuan. "Cultural Resources and School Success: Gender, Ethnicity, and Poverty Groups Within an Urban School District." *American Sociological Review* 55 (1990): 127–142.

Farley, Reynolds and Walter R. Allen. *The Color Line and the Quality of Life in America.* New York: Russell Sage Foundation, 1987.

Fausto-Sterling, Anne. *Myths of Gender: Biological Theories about Men and Women.* New York: Basic Books, 1985.

Faux, Marian. *Roe vs. Wade: The Untold Story of the Landmark Supreme Court Decision That Made Abortion Legal.* New York: Macmillan, 1987.

Fay, Robert E., Charles F. Turner, Albert D. Klassen, and John H. Gagnon. "Prevalence and Patterns of Same-Gender Sexual Contact Among Men." *Science* 243 (1989): 338–343.

Feagin, Joe R. *Social Problems: A Critical Power-Conflict Perspective* (2nd ed.). Englewood Cliffs, NJ: Prentice-Hall, 1986.

Feldberg, Roslyn, and Evelyn Nakano Glenn. "Technology and Work Degradation: Effects of Office Automation on Women Clerical Workers." In Joan Rothschild (ed.), *Women, Technology and Innovation.* New York: Pergamon. 1982.

Fendrich, James Max, and Kenneth L. Lovoy. "Back to the Future: Adult Political Behavior of Former Student Activists." *American Sociological Review* 53 (1988): 780–784.

Fergusson, David M., L. John Horwood, Katheryn L. Kershaw, and Frederick T. Shannon. "Factors Associated with Reports of Wife Assault in New Zealand." *Journal of Marriage and the Family* 48 (1986): 407–412.

Ferraro, Kathleen J. "Policing Women Battering." *Social Problems* 36 (1989): 61–74.

Ferraro, Kathleen J., and John M. Johnson. "How Women Experience Battering: The Process of Victimization." *Social Problems* 30 (1983): 325–339.

Ferree, Myra Marx, and Beth B. Hess. *Controversy and Coalition: The New Feminist Movement.* Boston: Twayne, 1985.

Fine, Gary Alan. *With the Boys: Little League Baseball and Preadolescent Culture.* Chicago: University of Chicago Press, 1987.

Finke, Roger, and Rodney Stark. "Religious Economies and Sacred Canopies: Religious Mobilization in American Cities, 1906." *American Sociological Review* 53 (1988): 41–49.

Fiorenza, Elisabeth Schussler. *Bread Not Stone: The Challenge of Feminist Biblical Interpretation.* Boston: Beacon Press, 1985.

Firth, Simon. "The Industrialization of Popular Music." In James Lull (ed.), *Popular Music and Communication,* Newbury Park, CA: Sage, 1987. pp. 53–77.

Fiske, Edward B. "Shortages Predicted for 90's in Professors of Humanities." *New York Times,* September 13, 1989c, pp. 1ff.

Fiske, Edward B. "More and More Educators Agree that Grouping Students by Ability is Misguided." *The New York Times,* January 3, 1990; p. B6.

Fleming, Jacqueline. *Blacks in College: A Comparative Study of Students' Success in Black and White Institutions.* San Francisco: Jossey-Bass, 1984.

Fligstein, Neil. "The Intraorganizational Power Struggle: Rise of Finance Personnel to Top Leadership in Large Corporations, 1919–1979." *American Sociological Review* 52 (1987): 44–58.

Flynn, Kevin, and Gary Gerhardt. *The Silent Brotherhood: Inside America's Racist Underground.* New York: Free Press, 1989.

Foderaro, Lisa W. "Women Winning Locally, but Higher Office Is Elusive." *The New York Times,* April 1, 1989, p. 29.

Forbes. "The Forbes Four-Hundred." October 27, 1986.

Forbes. "The Forbes Four-Hundred." October 23, 1989.

Form, William. *Divided We Stand: Working Class Stratification in America.* Urbana: University of Illinois Press, 1985.

Fox, Mary Frank, and Sharlene Hesse-Biber. *American Women at Work.* Palo Alto, CA: Mayfield, 1985.

Fox, Robin. "Report to International AIDS Conference." Washington, June 5, 1987.

Frankl, Razelle. *Televangelism: The Marketing of Popular Religion.* Carbondale: Southern Illinois University Press, 1987.

Franklin, Benjamin. *Poor Richard's Almanac* (1784). New York: David McKay, 1970.

Franklin, C. W. *Men and Society.* Chicago: Nelson-Hall, 1988.

Freeman, Richard B., and James L. Medoff. *What Do Unions Do?* New York: Basic Books, 1984.

Freire, Paulo. *The Politics of Education: Culture, Power, and Liberation.* Translated by Donald Macedo. South Hadley, MA: Bergin & Garvey, 1985.

French, Howard W. "Report Cites Fewer Men in Black Neighborhoods." *The New York Times,* March 7, 1987, p. 31.

Freud, Sigmund. *Civilization and Its Discontents* (1930). Translated by James Strachey. New York: W. W. Norton, 1962.

Friedmann, Robert R., Neil Gilbert, and Moshe Sherer, eds. *Modern Welfare States: A Comparative View of Trends and Prospects.* New York: New York University Press, 1987.

Friedrichs, J., ed. *Affordable Housing and the Homeless.* New York: de Gruyter, 1988.

Fuller, Bruce, and Sanford M. Dornbusch. "Organizational Construction of Intrinsic Motivation." *Sociological Forum* 3 (1988): 1–24

Furstenberg, Frank F., Jr., S. Philip Morgan, Kristin A. Moore, and James L. Peteron. "Race Differences in the Timing of Adolescent Intercourse." *American Sociological Review* 52 (1987a): 511–518.

Furstenberg, Frank F., Jr., S. Philip Morgan, and Paul D. Allison. "Paternal Participation and Childrens' Well-Being After Marital Dissolution." *American Sociological Review* 52 (1987b): 695–701.

Gagnon, John, and William Simon. *Sexual Conduct:*

The Social Sources of Human Sexuality. Chicago: Aldine, 1973.

Galinsky, Ellen and Dana Friedman. *Corporate Reference Guide.* New York: Families and Work Institute, 1991.

Gallup, George, Jr., and Jim Castelli. *The American Catholic People: Their Beliefs, Practices, and Values.* Garden City, NY: Doubleday, 1987.

Gallup Organization. Reported in *Newsweek,* September 25, 1989, p. 19.

GALLUP POLL on Worker Satisfaction. Reported in *Society* 27 (November/December 1989): 2.

Gamoran, Adam, and Robert D. Mare. "Secondary School Tracking and Educational Inequality: Compensation, Reinforcement, or Neutrality?" *American Journal of Sociology* 94 (1989): 1146–1183.

Gamson, William A. *The Strategy of Social Protest.* Homewood, IL: Dorsey, 1975.

GAO. *See* U.S. General Accounting Office.

Garfinkel, Harold. *Studies in Ethnomethodology.* Englewood Cliffs, NJ: Prentice-Hall, 1967.

Garland, Anne Witte. *Women Activists: Challenging the Abuse of Power.* New York: Feminist Press, 1988.

Gartman, David. *Auto Slavery: The Labor Process in the American Automobile Industry, 1937–1950.* New Brunswick, NJ: Rutgers University Press, 1986.

Geertz, Clifford. *The Interpretation of Cultures.* New York: Basic Books, 1973.

Gelles, Richard J., and Murray A. Straus. *Intimate Violence.* New York: Simon & Schuster, 1988.

Gerson, Judith M., and Kathy Peiss. "Boundaries, Negotiation, Consciousness: Reconceptualizing Gender Relations." *Social Problems* 32(4) (1985): 317–331.

Gerstel, Naomi. "Divorce and Stigma." *Social Problems* 34 (1987): 172–186.

Gerstel, Naomi, and Harriet Gross. *Commuter Marriage: A Study of Work and Family.* New York: Guilford Press, 1984.

Gerth, Hans H., and C. Wright Mills (eds.), *From Max Weber: Essays in Sociology,* pp. 196–244. New York: Oxford University Press, 1946.

Giddens, Anthony. *The Nation State and Violence.* Vol. 2. *Contemporary Critique of Historical Materialism.* Berkeley: University of California Press, 1985.

Gilder, George. "Sexual Suicide" (1973). Republished as *Men and Marriage.* Gretna, LA: Pelican, 1987.

Gilkes, Cheryl Townsend. "'Together and in Harness': Women's Traditions in the Sanctified Church." *Signs* 10(4) (1985): 678–699.

Gilligan, Carol. *In a Different Voice: Psychological Theory and Women's Development.* Cambridge, MA: Harvard University Press, 1982.

Gilligan, Carol, Janice Victoria Ward, and Jill McLean Taylor. *Mapping the Moral Domain: A Contribution of Women's Thinking to Psychological Theory and Education.* Cambridge, MA: Harvard University Press, 1989.

Gimbutas, Marija. *The Language of the Goddess.* San Francisco: Harper & Row, 1989.

Glass, Jennifer, Vern L. Bengtson, and Charlotte Chorn Dunham. "Attitude Similarity in Three-Generation Families: Socialization, Status Inheritance, or Reciprocal Influence?" *American Sociological Review* 51 (1986): 685–698.

Glassman, Ronald M. *Democracy and Despotism in Primitive Society.* Port Washington, NY: Kennicott Press, 1986.

Glassman, Ronald M., William H. Swatos, Jr., and Paul L. Rosen. *Bureaucracy against Democracy and Socialism.* Westport, CT: Greenwood Press, 1987.

Glenn, Norval D., and Kathryn B. Kramer. "The Psychological Well-Being of Adult Children of Divorce." *Journal of Marriage and the Family* 47 (1985): 905–912.

Glenn, Norville and Charles N. Weaver. "Marital Roles." *Journal of Marriage and Family* 50(2) (May 1988).

Glick, Paul C. "The Family Life Cycle and Social Change." *Family Relations* 38 (1989): 123–129.

Goffman, Erving. *The Presentation of Self in Everyday Life.* Garden City, NY: Doubleday, 1959.

Goffman, Erving. *Asylums.* Garden City, NY: Doubleday, 1961.

Goffman, Erving. "The Interaction Order." *American Sociological Review* 48 (1983): 1–17.

Golden, Tim. "Was Illness at Bridges in the Minds of Workers?" *The New York Times,* March 12, 1990, pp. B1ff.

Goldfield, Michael. *The Decline of Organized Labor in the United States.* Chicago: University of Chicago Press, 1987.

Goldman, Ari L. "Mainstream Islam Rapidly Embraced by Black Americans." *The New York Times,* February 21, 1989a; pp. A1ff.

Goldscheider, Calvin, and Frances Kobrin Goldscheider. "Moving Out and Marriage: What Do Young Adults Expect?" *American Sociological Review* 52 (1987): 278–285.

Goldscheider, Frances Kobrin, and Linda J. Waite. "Sex Differences in the Entry into Marriage." *American Journal of Sociology* 92 (1986): 91–109.

Goldstein, Joshua. "How Military Might Robs an Economy." *The New York Times,* October 16, 1988, p. E3.

Goldthorpe, John H., ed. *Order and Conflict in Contemporary Capitalism.* New York: Oxford University Press, 1985.

Goode, William J. "A Theory of Role Strain." *American Sociological Review* 25 (1960): 483–496.

Goode, William J. *The Celebration of Heroes: Prestige as a Social System.* Berkeley: University of California Press, 1978.

Goodlad, J. I. *A Place Called School.* New York: McGraw-Hill, 1984.

Gordon, Linda. *Heroes of Their Own Lives: The Politics and History of Family Violence: Boston 1890–1960.* New York: Viking, 1988.

Gordon, Milton. *Human Nature, Class and Ethnicity.* New York: Oxford University Press, 1978.

Gorriti, A. Gustavo. "How to Fight the Drug War." *Atlantic Monthly* 283(1) (July 1989): 70–76.

Gottfried, Adele Eskeles, and Allan W. Gottfried, eds. *Maternal Employment and Children's Development: Longitudinal Research.* New York: Plenum, 1988.

Gove, Walter R. "Sex, Marital Status, and Mortality." *American Journal of Sociology* 79 (July 1973): 45–67.

Gove, Walter R., Suzanne T. Ortega, and Carolyn Briggs Styles. "The Maturational and Role Perspectives on Aging and the Self through the Adult Years: An Empirical Evaluation." *American Journal of Sociology* 94 (1989): 1117–1145.

Graber, Doris. *Processing the News: How People Tame the Information Tide.* New York: Longman, 1984.

Gramsci, Antonio. *The Modern Prince and Other Writings.* New York: International Publishers, 1959.

Gramsci, Antonio. *Prison Notebooks: Selections.* Quintin Moare and Geoffrey N. Smith (trans.). New York: International Publishers, 1971.

Grauerholz, Elizabeth, and Bernice Pescosolido. "Gender Representation in Children's Literature." *Gender & Society* 3 (1989): 113–125.

Greeley, Andrew M. *Religious Change in America.* Cambridge, MA: Harvard University Press, 1989.

Green, Richard. *The "Sissy Boy" Syndrome and the Development of Homosexuality.* New Haven, CT: Yale University Press, 1987.

Greenberg, Edward S. *Workplace Democracy: The Political Effects of Participation.* Ithaca, NY: Cornell University Press, 1986.

Greenblat, Cathy S. "Sexuality in the Early Years of Marriage." In James Henslin, *Marriage and the Family in a Changing Society,* 3rd ed. New York: Free Press, 1989, pp. 180–189.

Greeno, Catherine G., and Eleanor E. Maccoby. "How Different is 'The Different Voice'?" *Signs* 11(2) (1986): 310–316.

Greenwald, Mathew. "Bad News for the Baby Boomers." *American Demographics,* February 1989, pp. 34–37.

Grenier, Guillermo. *Inhuman Relations: Quality Circles and Anti-Unionism in American Industry.* Philadelphia: Temple University Press, 1988.

Griffin, Larry J., Michael E. Wallace, and Beth A. Rubin. "Capitalist Resistance to the Organization of Labor Before the New Deal: Why? How? Success?" *American Sociological Review* 51 (1986): 147–167.

Gunther, Barrie. *Dimensions of Television Violence.* New York: St. Martin's Press, 1985.

Gupta, Mahesh. "A Basis for Friendly Dyadic Interpersonal Relationships." *Small Group Behavior* 14(1) (February 1983): 15–33.

Gutek, Barbara A. *Sex and the Workplace: The Impact of Sexual Behavior and Harassment on Women, Men, and Organizations.* San Francisco: Jossey-Bass, 1985.

Guttmann, Allen. *From Ritual to Record: The Nature of Modern Sports.* New York: Columbia University Press, 1978.

Gwartney-Gibbs, Patrica A. "The Institutionalization of Premarital Cohabitation: Estimates from Marriage License Applications, 1970 and 1980." *Journal of Marriage and the Family* 48 (1986): 423–434.

Hagan, John and Alberto Pallioni. "Toward a Structural Criminology: Method and Theory in Criminological Research." *Annual Review of Sociology* (12) (1986): 431–449.

Haines, Herbert H. "Black Radicalization and the Funding of Civil Rights." *Social Problems* 32(1) (1984): 31–43.

Halaby, Charles N. "Worker Attachment and Workplace Authority." *American Sociological Review* 51 (1986): 634–649.

Hall, Edward. *The Silent Language.* Garden City, NY: Doubleday, 1959.

Hallinan, Maureen T., and Richard R. Williams. "Interracial Friendship Choices in Secondary Schools." *American Sociological Review* 54 (February 1989): 67–78.

Halloran, Richard. "Women, Blacks, Spouses Transforming the Military." *The New York Times,* August 25, 1986, pp. 1ff.

Halloran, Richard. "Military Women: Increasingly Indispensable." *The New York Times,* March 13, 1988a, p. E5.

Halloran, Richard. "The All-Volunteer Force is More Popular Than Ever." *The New York Times,* October 16, 1988b, p. E5.

Hammond, Philip E., ed. *The Sacred in a Secular Age.* Berkeley: University of California Press, 1985.

Hareven, Tamara K. "Historical Analysis of the Family." In Marvin B. Sussman and Suzanne K. Steinmetz (eds.), *Handbook of Marriage and the Family,* pp. 37–58. New York: Plenum, 1987.

Harkess, Shirley. "Women's Occupational Experiences in the 1970s: Sociology and Economics." *Signs* 10 (1985): 495–520.

Harlow, Harry F., and Margaret K. Harlow. "Effects of Various Mother-Infant Relationships on Rhesus Monkey Behaviors." In B. M. Foss (ed.), *Determinants of Infant Behavior.* Vol. 4, pp. 15–36. London: Methuen, 1977.

Harner, Michael J. "The Ecological Basis for Aztec Sacrifice." *American Ethnologist* 4 (1977): 117–135.

Harrington, Michael. *Socialism: Past and Future.* New York: Arcade, 1989.

Harris, Louis. *Crime Fear Decreasing: Harris Survey.* Orlando, FL: Tribune News Service, March 21, 1985.

Harris, Louis and Associates. *Inside America.* New York: Vintage Books, 1987.

Harris, Marvin. *Good to Eat: Riddles of Food and Culture.* New York: Simon & Schuster, 1985a.

Harrison, Bennett. "The Impact of Corporate Restructuring on Labor Income." *Social Policy,* Fall 1987, pp. 6–10.

Harrison, Bennett, and Barry Bluestone, *The Great U-Turn: Corporate Restructuring and the Polarizing of America.* New York: Basic Books, 1988.

Harrold, Francis B., and Raymond A. Eve, eds. *Cult Archaeology and Creationism: Understanding Pseudoscientific Beliefs About the Past.* Iowa City: University of Iowa Press, 1987.

Harry, Joseph. *Gay Couples.* New York: Praeger, 1984.

Hart-Nibbrig, Nand, and Clement Cottingham. *The Political Economy of College Sports.* Lexington, MA: D. C. Heath, 1986.

Hauser, Robert M., and David B. Grusky. "Cross-National Variation in Occupational Distributions, Relative Mobility Chances, and Intergenerational Shifts in Occupational Distributions." *American Sociological Review* 53 (1988): 723–741.

Hazelton, Lesley. "British Soccer: The Deadly Game." *New York Times Magazine,* May 7, 1989, p. 40ff.

Headland, Thomas N., and Lawrence A. Reid. "Hunter-Gatherers and Their Neighbors from Prehistory to the Present." *Current Anthropology* 30 (1989): 43–66.

Hechinger, Fred M. "How Should Colleges Pick Students?" *The New York Times,* June 24, 1986, p. C5.

Hendrix, Lewellyn, and Zakir Hossain. "Women's Status and Mode of Production." *Signs* 13 (1988): 437–460.

Henshaw, Stanley K., and Jennifer Van Vort. "Teenage Abortion, Birth and Pregnancy Statistics: An Update." *Family Planning Perspectives,* 21 (1989): 85–88.

Hentoff, Nat. "Child Abuse in the Schools." *Washington Post,* March 12, 1988, p. A25.

Herberg, Will. *Protestant, Catholic, Jew.* Garden City, NY: Doubleday, 1960.

Hertel, Bradley R., and Michael Hughes. "Religious Affiliation, Attendance, and Support for "Pro-Family" Issues in the United States." *Social Forces* 65 (1987): 858–882.

Hertz, Rosanna. *More Equal Than Others: Women and Men in Dual-Career Marriages.* Berkeley: University of California Press, 1986.

Hess, Beth B. "Beyond Dichotomy: Drawing Distinctions and Embracing Differences." Presidential address to the 59th annual meeting of the Eastern Sociological Society, Baltimore, March 1989. *Sociological Forum,* Vol. 5, No. 1, pp. 75–94, 1990.

Heyns, Barbara. "Educational Ethics: Issues in Conceptualization and Measurement." In John G. Richardson (ed.), *Handbook of Theory and Research for the Sociology of Education,* pp. 305–340. Westport, CT: Greenwood Press, 1986.

Higginbotham, Elizabeth, and Lynn Weber Cannon. "Women and Mobility: Integrating Race and Gender into an Analysis of Upward Mobility in America." Paper presented at the 81st annual meeting of the American Sociological Association, New York, August 1986.

Hill, Martha S., Sue Augustyniak, Greg J. Duncan, Gerald Gurin, Patrica Gurin, Jeffry K. Liker, James N. Morgan, and Michael Ponza. *Motivation and Economic Mobility.* Ann Arbor, MI: Institute for Social Research, 1985.

Hill, Richard J. "Potential Expansion of the Academic Job Market: Opportunities for Sociologists." *American Sociologist* 20 (1989): 144–153.

Hirsch, Paul M. "From Ambushes to Golden Parachutes: Corporate Takeovers as an Instance of Cultural Framing and Institutional Integration." *American Journal of Sociology* 91 (1986): 800–837.

Hirschhorn, Larry. *Beyond Mechanization: Work and Technology in a Post Industrial Age.* Cambridge, MA: Massachusetts Institute of Technology Press, 1984.

Hochfield, George. "Must SUNY at Buffalo Become a Pigskin Factory?" *New York Times,* May 3, 1986, p. 27.

Hochschild, Arlie Russell. "Emotion Work, Feeling Rules and Social Structure." *American Journal of Sociology* 85 (1979): 551–575.

Hochschild, Arlie Russell. *The Managed Heart: Commercialization of Human Feelings.* Berkeley: University of California Press, 1983.

Hochschild, Arlie Russell, and Anne Machung. *The Second Shift: Working Parents and the Revolution at Home.* New York: Viking, 1989.

Hochschild, Jennifer L. *The New American Dilemma: Liberal Democracy and School Desegregation.* New Haven, CT: Yale University Press, 1984.

Hodge, Bob, and David Tripp. *Children and Television.* Stanford, CA: Stanford University Press, 1986.

Hodson, Randy. *Workers' Earnings and Corporate Economic Structure.* New York: Academic Press, 1984.

Hoelter, Jon W. "Factorial Invariance and Self-esteem: Reassessing Race and Sex Differences." *Social Forces* 61 (1983): 834–846.

Hofferth, Sandra L., Joan R. Kahn, and Wendy Baldwin. "Premarital Sexual Activity among U.S. Teenage Women Over the Past Three Decades." *Family Planning Perspectives* 19 (1987): 46–53.

Hoge, Dean R., Jann Hoge, and Janet Wittenberg. "The Return of the Fifties: Trends in College Student Values Between 1952 and 1984." *Sociological Forum.* 2 (1987): 500–519.

Holden, Stephen. "Pop's Angry Voices Sound the Alarm." *The New York Times,* May 21, 1989; p. 2:1.

Homans, George C. *Social Behavior: Its Elementary Forms.* New York: Harcourt Brace Jovanovich, 1961.

Hood, Jane C. *Becoming a Two-Job Family.* New York: Praeger, 1983.

Hoose, Philip M. *Necessities: Racial Barriers in American Sports.* New York: Random House, 1988.

Hope, Christine A., and Ronald G. Stover. "Gender Status, Monotheism, and Social Complexity." *Social Forces* 65 (1987): 1132–1138.

Hope, Keith, "Vertical and Nonvertical Class Mobility in Three Countries." *American Sociological Review* 47 (1982): 99–113.

Hopper, Rex D. "The Revolutionary Process." *Social Forces* 28 (March 1950): 207–279.

Horowitz, Irving Louis. "Socialist Utopias and Scientific Socialists: Primary Fanaticisms and Secondary Contradictions." *Sociological Forum* 4 (1989): 106–113.

House, James S. "Social Support and Social Structure." *Sociological Forum* 2 (1987): 135–145.

Houseknecht, Sharon K. "Voluntary Childlessness." In Marvin B. Sussman and Suzanne K. Steinmetz (eds.). *Handbook of Marriage and the Family,* pp. 365–396. New York: Plenum, 1987.

Hout, Michael, and Andrew M. Greeley. "The Center Doesn't Hold: Church Attendance in the United States, 1940–1984." *American Sociological Review* 52 (1987): 325–345.

Howard, Robert. *Brave New Workplace.* New York: Viking, 1985.

Huber, Joan. "Trends in Gender Stratification, 1970–1985." *Sociological Forum* 1 (1986): 476–495.

Hudson, Barbara. *Justice through Punishment: A Critique of the Justice Model of Corrections.* New York: St. Martin's Press, 1987.

Hunter, James Davison. *Evangelicism: The Coming Generation.* Chicago: University of Chicago Press, 1987.

Hyman, Herbert H. "The Psychology of Status." *Archives of Psychology* 37 (1942): 15.

Imber, Jonathan B. *Abortion and the Private Practice of Medicine.* New Haven, CT: Yale University Press, 1986.

Inciardi, James. "The War On Drugs: Heroin, Cocaine, Crime and Public Policy." *The New York Times,* March 15, 1987, pp. 1ff.

Irwin, John. *The Jail: Managing the Underclass in American Society.* Berkeley: University of California Press, 1985.

Jackman, Mary R., and Robert W. Jackman. *Class Awareness in the United States.* Berkeley: University of California Press, 1983.

Jacobs, James. *Socio-Legal Foundations of Civil-Military Relations.* New Brunswick, NJ: Transaction Press, 1986.

Jacobs, Jerry A. "Long-Term Trends in Occupational Segregation by Sex." *American Journal of Sociology* 95 (1989): 160–173.

Jaffe, David "The Political Economy of Job Loss in the United States, 1970-1980." *Social Problems* 33 (1986): 297–315.

Janowitz, Morris. *The Professional Soldier: A Social and Political Portrait.* New York: Free Press, 1980.

Jansen, Sue Curry. *Censorship: The Knot That Binds Power and Knowledge.* New York: Oxford University Press, 1988.

Jeffery, C. R. "Criminal Behavior and Learning Theory." In Ronald A. Farrell and Victoria Lynn Swigert (eds.), *Social Deviance,* (2nd ed.). Philadelphia: Lippincott, 1978.

Jeffords, Susan. *The Remasculinization of America: Gender and the Vietnam War.* Bloomington: Indiana University Press, 1989.

Jeffreys-Jones, Rhodri. *The CIA and American Democracy.* New Haven, CT: Yale University Press, 1989.

Jencks, Christopher, Lauri Perman, and Lee Rainwater. "What Is a Good Job? A New Measure of Labor-Market Success." *American Journal of Sociology* 93 (1988): 1322–1357.

Jennings, M. Kent, and Gregory B. Markus. "Yuppie Politics." *ISR Newsletter,* Spring/Summer 1986, pp. 5–7.

Jiobu, Robert M. "Ethnic Hegemony and the Japanese of California." *American Sociological Review* 53 (June 1988): 353–367.

Johnson, Allen W., and Timothy Earle. *The Evolution of Human Societies: From Foraging Group to Agrarian State.* Stanford, CA: Stanford University Press, 1987.

Johnson, Norris R. "Panic at 'The Who Concert Stampede': An Empirical Assessment." *Social Problems* 34 (1987): 362–373.

Johnson, Stephen D., and Joseph B. Tamney, eds. *The Political Role of Religion in the United States.* Boulder, CO: Westview Press, 1986.

Johnstone, Ronald L. *Religion and Society in Interaction: The Sociology of Religion* (3rd ed.). Englewood Cliffs, NJ: Prentice-Hall, 1988.

Jones, Elsie F., Jacqueline Darroch Forrest, Noreen Goldman, Stanley K. Hensaw, Richard Lincoln, Jeannie I. Rosoff, Charles E. Westoff, and Dierdre Wulf. *Teenage Pregnancy in Industrialized Countries.* New Haven, CT: Yale University Press, 1987.

Kagan, Jerome. *The Nature of the Child.* New York: Basic Books, 1984.

Kagan, Jerome. *Unstable Ideas: Temperament, Cognition, and Self.* Cambridge, MA: Harvard University Press, 1989.

Kalish, Richard, and D. K. Reynolds. *Death and Ethnicity.* Los Angeles: University of Southern California Press, 1976.

Kamerman, Sheila, and Alfred J. Kahn. *The Responsive Workplace: Employers and a Changing Labor Force.* New York: Columbia University Press, 1987.

Kanter, Rosabeth Moss. *Men and Women of the Corporation.* New York: Basic Books, 1977.

Kaplan, E. Ann. *Rocking Round the Clock: Music Television, Postmodernism, and Consumer Culture.* New York: Methuen, 1987.

Karen, David, and Katherine E. McClelland. "Trends in Access to Higher Education: Class, Race, and Sex." Paper presented at the annual meeting of the American Sociological Association, Detroit, August 1983.

Katz, Daniel, and K. W. Braley. "Racial Stereotypes of 100 College Students." *Journal of Abnormal and Social Psychology* 28 (1933): 280–290.

Katzenstein, Mary Fainsod, and Carol McClurg Mueller, eds. *The Women's Movements in the U.S. and Western Europe: Feminist Consciousness, Political Opportunity and Public Policy.* Philadelphia: Temple University Press, 1987.

Kaufman, Robert L. "The Impact of Industrial and Occupational Structure on Black-White Employment Allocation." *American Sociological Review* 51 (1986): 310–323.

Kelling, George L. Robert Wasserman, and Hubert Williams. "Police Accountability and Community Policing." *Perspectives on Policing* 7 (November 1988) Washington, D.C.: U.S. Department of Justice, Office of Justice Programs, 1988.

Keller, Evelyn Fox. *Reflections on Gender and Science.* New Haven, CT: Yale University Press, 1985.

Kelly, Joan. *Women, History, and Theory: The Essays of Joan Kelly.* Chicago: University of Chicago Press, 1984.

Kennedy, Robert E. *Life Choices: Applying Sociology.* (2nd ed.). New York: Holt, Rinehart & Winston, 1989.

Kerckhoff, Alan C. "On the Social Psychology of Social Mobility Processes." *Social Forces* 68 (1989): 17–25.

Kertzer, David I. *Ritual, Politics, and Power.* New Haven, CT: Yale University Press, 1988.

Kertzer, David I., and Dennis P. Hogan. "Family Structure, Individual Lives, and Societal Change." In Matilda White Riley (ed.), *Social Structure and Human Lives,* Vol. 1, pp. 83–100. Newbury Park, CA: Sage, 1988.

Kilman, Ralph, Mary J. Saxton, Roy Serpa, and Associates, eds. *Gaining Control of the Corporate Culture.* San Francisco: Jossey-Bass, 1985.

Kimmel, Michael S. 'The 'Crisis' of Masculinity in Historical Perspective." Paper presented at the 81st annual meeting of the American Sociological Association, New York, August 1986.

Kimmel, Michael S., and Michael A. Messner, eds. *Men's Lives.* New York: Macmillan, 1989.

Kimura, Doreen. "Male Brain, Female Brain: The Hidden Difference," *Psychology Today,* November 1985, pp. 50–58.

Kingston, Paul William. "Theory at Risk: Accounting for the Excellence Movement." *Sociological Forum* 1 (1986): 632–656.

Kingston, Paul William, and Steven L. Nock. "Time Together among Dual-Earner Couples." *American Sociological Review* 52 (1987): 391–400.

Kinsey, Alfred C., Wardell Pomeroy, and Clyde Martin. *Sexual Behavior in the Human Male.* Philadelphia: Saunders, 1948.

Kinsey, Alfred C., Wardell Pomeroy, Clyde Martin, and Paul H. Gebhard. *Sexual Behavior in the Human Female.* Philadelphia: Saunders, 1953.

Kipnis, David. *The Powerholders.* Chicago: University of Chicago Press, 1976.

Kirsch, Irwin S., and Ann Jungeblut. *Literacy: Profiles of America's Young Adults.* Washington: National Assessment of Educational Progress, 1986.

Kitano, Harry. *Japanese Americans.* Englewood Cliffs, NJ: Prentice-Hall, 1976.

Kitzinger, Celia. *The Social Construction of Lesbianism.* Newbury Park, CA: Sage, 1988.

Klandermans, Bert, and Dirk Oegema. "Potentials, Networks, Motivations, and Barriers: Steps Toward Participation in Social Movements." *American Sociological Review* 52 (1987): 519–531.

Klapp, Orrin E. *Overload and Boredom: Essays on the Quality of Life in the Informational Society.* Westport, CT: Greenwood Press, 1987.

Klassen, Albert D., Colin J. Williams, and Eugene Levitt. *Sex and Morality in the U.S.: An Empirical Inquiry under the Auspices of the Kinsey Institute.* Middletown, CT: Wesleyan University Press, 1989.

Kleck, Gary. "Racial Discrimination in Criminal Sentencing: A Critical Evaluation of the Evidence with Additional Evidence on the Death Penalty." *American Sociological Review* 46 (1981): 783–805.

Kluegel, James R., and Eliot R. Smith. *Beliefs About Inequality: Americans' Views of What Is and What Ought to Be."* Hawthorne, NY: de Gruyter, 1986.

Knoke, David. "Incentives in Collective Action Organizations." *American Sociological Review* 53 (1988): 311–329.

Knottnerus, J. David. "Status Attainment Research and Its Image of Society." *American Sociological Review* 52 (1987): 113–121.

Koenig, Frederick. *Rumor in the Marketplace: The Social Psychology of Commercial Hearsay.* Dover, MA: Auburn House, 1985.

Koenig, Thomas, and Tracey Boyce. "Corporate Financing of the Christian Right." *Humanity and Society* 9(1) (1985): 13–28.

Kohlberg, Lawrence. *The Philosophy of Moral Development.* Vol. 1. *Essays on Moral Development.* New York: Harper & Row, 1981.

Kohn, Melvin L. "Bureaucratic Men: A Portrait and an Interpretation." *American Sociological Review* 36 (June 1971): 461–474.

Kohn, Melvin L., Atsushi Naoi, Carrie Schoenbach, Carmi Schooler, and Kazimierz M. Slomczynski. "Position in the Class Structure and Psychological Functioning in the United States, Japan, and Poland." *American Journal of Sociology* 95 (1990): 964–1008.

Kolata, Gina. "Gender Gap in Aptitude Tests is Narrowing, Experts Find." *The New York Times,* July 1, 1989, p. 1ff.

Konner, Melvin. "Homosexuality: Who and Why?" *The New York Times Magazine,* April 2, 1989, pp. 60–61.

Korpi, Walter. "Power, Politics, and State Autonomy in the Development of Social Citizenship: Social Rights During Sickness in Eighteen OECD Countries Since 1930." *American Sociological Review* 54 (1989): 309–328.

Koss, M. P. "Hidden Rape: Incidence, Prevalence, and Descriptive Characteristics of Sexual Aggression and Victimization in a National Sample of College Students." In Anne W. Burgess (ed.), *Sexual Assault,* Vol. 2. New York: Garland, 1988.

Kouzi, Anthony, and Richard E. Ratcliffe. "Politics and the Corporate Wallet: Political Contributions by Corporate Officers." Paper presented at the annual meeting of the Society for the Study of Social Problems, Detroit, August 1984.

Kozol, Jonathan. *Illiterate America.* New York: Anchor/Doubleday, 1986.

Krauze, Tadeusz, and Kazimierz M. Slomczynski. "How Far to Meritocracy? Empirical Tests of a Controversial Thesis." *Social Forces* 63 (1985): 623–642.

Krein, Shiela Fitzgerald, and Andrea H. Beller. "Educational Attainment of Children from Single-Parent Families: Differences by Exposure, Gender, and Race." *Demography* 25 (1988): 221–234.

Kretschmer, Ernst. *Physique and Character.* New York: Harcourt Brace, 1925.

Kuhn, Thomas S. *The Structure of Scientific Revolutions.* Chicago: University of Chicago Press, 1962.

Labarree, David F. "Academic Excellence in an Early U.S. High School." *Social Problems* 31(5) (1984): 558–567.

Lamb, Michael, ed. *The Father's Role: Applied Perspectives.* New York: Wiley, 1986.

Lamb, Stephen. "Cultural Consumption and the Educational Plans of Australian Secondary School Students." *Sociology of Education* 62 (1989): 95–108.

Landry, Bart. *The New Black Middle Class.* Berkeley and Los Angeles: University of California Press, 1987.

Lane, Christel. *The Rites of Rulers: Ritual in Industrial Society—The Soviet Case.* New York: Cambridge University Press, 1981.

Laner, Mary R. "Prostitution as an Illegal Vocation: A Sociological Overview." In Clifford D. Bryant (ed.), *Deviant Behavior: Occupational and Organizational Bases.* Chicago: Rand McNally, 1974.

Larkin, Ralph W. *Suburban Youth in Cultural Crisis.* New York: Oxford University Press, 1979.

Lasch, Christopher. *Haven in a Heartless World.* New York: Basic Books 1977.

Laudon, Kenneth C. *Dossier Society: Value Choices in the Design of National Information Systems.* New York: Columbia University Press, 1986.

Lawson, Annette. *Adultery: An Analysis of Love and Betrayal.* New York: Basic Books, 1988.

Leavitt, Robin Lynn and Martha Bauman Power. "Emotional Socialization in the Post-modern Era: Children in Day Care." *Social Psychology Quarterly* 52 (March 1989): 35–43.

Lechner, Frank J. "Fundamentalism Revisited." *Society,* January/February 1989; pp. 51–60.

Lee, Valerie E., and Anthony S. Bryk. "A Multilevel Model of the School Distribution of High School Achievement." *Sociology of Education* 62 (1989): 172–192.

Lehman, Edward C. *Women Clergy: Breaking Through the Gender Barriers.* New Brunswick, NJ: Transaction Press, 1985.

Leland, John. "Heavy Metal's Not-So-Obscure Objects of Desire." *The New York Times,* October 8, 1989, p. 27.

Lemert, Edwin M. *Human Deviance, Social Problems, and Social Control.* Englewood Cliffs, NJ: Prentice-Hall, 1967.

Lenski, Gerhard. *Power and Privilege: A Theory of Social Stratification.* New York: McGraw-Hill, 1966.

Lenski Gerhard, and Patrick D. Nolan. "Trajectories of Development: A Test of Ecological-Evolutionary Theory." Paper presented at the American Sociological Association annual meeting, Detroit, August 1983.

Leonard, W. and D. Reyman (1988), "Racism in Sports." In D. Stanley Eitzen and George H. Sage (eds.), *Sociology of North American Sport,* (4th ed.). Dubuque, IA: W. C. Brown, 1990.

Levine, Martin P. Personal Communication, 1989.

Levi-Strauss, Claude. *Elementary Structures of Kinship.* Boston: Beacon Press, 1969.

Levitan, Sara, and Isaac Shapiro. *Working but Poor: America's Contradiction.* Baltimore: Johns Hopkins University Press, 1988.

Levy, Frank. *Dollars and Dreams: The Changing American Income Distribution.* New York: Basic Books, 1988.

Lewis, Lionel S. "Working at Leisure." *Society* 19 (July–August 1982): 27–32.

Lewis, Oscar. *Four Families: Mexican Case Studies in the Culture of Poverty.* New York: Basic Books 1959.

Lewis, Robert A. and Robert E. Salt, eds. *Men in Families.* Beverly Hills, CA: Sage, 1986.

Lieberson, Stanley. *A Piece of the Pie: Black and White Immigrants Since 1880.* Berkeley and Los Angeles: University of California Press, 1981.

Lieberson, Stanley, and Mary C. Waters. *From Many Strands: Ethnic and Racial Groups in Contemporary America.* New York: Russell Sage Foundation, 1988.

Liebman, Robert C., and Robert Wuthnow (eds.). *The New Christian Right: Mobilization and Legitimation.* New York: Aldine, 1983.

Lin, Nan, and Walter M. Ensel. "Life Stress and Health: Stressors' and Resources," *American Sociological Review* 54 (June 1989): 382–399.

Lincoln, Bruce ed. *Religion, Rebellion, Revolution: An Interdisciplinary and Cross-Cultural Collection of Essays.* New York: St. Martin's Press, 1985.

Lindsey, Robert. "Isolated, Strongly Led Sects Growing in U.S." *The New York Times,* June 22, 1986, pp. 1ff.

Link, Bruce. "Reward System of Psychotherapy: Implications for Inequities in Service Delivery." *Journal of Health and Social Behavior* 24 (March 1983): 61–69.

Linton, Ralph. *The Study of Man.* New York: Appleton-Century 1936.

Lipset, Seymour Martin, and Earl Raab. "The Election and the Evangelicals." *Commentary* 71 (March 1981): 26–32.

Litwak, Eugene, and Peter Messeri. "Organizational Theory, Social Supports, and Mortality Rates: A Theoretical Convergence." *American Sociological Review* 54 (1989): 49–66.

Looker, E. Dianne, and Peter C. Pineo. "Some Social Psychological Variables and Their Relevance to the Status Attainment of Teenagers." *American Journal of Sociology* 88 (1983): 1195–1219.

Lorence, Jon and Jeylan Mortimer. "Work Experience and Political Orientation: A Panel Study." *Social Forces* 58 (1979): 651–676.

Lubeck, Sally. *Early Education in Black and White America—A Comparative Ethnography.* Philadelphia: Falmer Press, 1985.

Luhrmann, T. M. *Persuasions of the Witch's Craft: Ritual Magic in Contemporary England.* Cambridge, MA: Harvard University Press, 1989.

Luria, Zella, Susan Friedman, and Mitchell D. Rose. *Human Sexuality.* New York: J. Wiley and Sons, 1987.

Macklin, Eleanor D. "Nontraditional Family Forms." In Marvin B. Sussman and Suzanne K. Steinmetz (eds.), *Handbook of Marriage and the Family,* pp. 317–354. New York: Plenum, 1987.

MacLeod, Jay. *Ain't No Makin' It: Leveled Aspirations in a Low-Income Neighborhood.* Boulder, CO: Westview Press, 1987.

Magrass, Yale R. "The Boy Scouts, the Outdoors, and Empire." *Humanity and Society* 10 (February 1986): 37–57.

Makower, Joel. *Woodstock: The Oral History.* New York: Tilden Press/Doubleday, 1989.

Malamuth, Neil M., and Edward Donnerstein. "The Effects of Aggressive-Pornographic Mass Media Stimuli." In Leonard Berkowitz (ed.), *Advances in Experimental Social Psychology,* Vol. 15, pp. 103–136. New York: Academic Press, 1982.

Malinowski, Bronislaw. *Argonauts of the Western Pacific.* New York: Dutton, 1922/1955.

Malinowski, Bronislaw. "The Principle of Legitimacy: Parenthood, The Basis of Social Structure." In Rose Laub Coser (ed.), *The Family: Its Structure and Functions* (1929). New York: St. Martin's Press, 1964. (originally 1929).

Mamonova, Tatyana. *Russian Women's Studies: Essays on Sexism in Soviet Culture.* New York: Pergamon, 1989.

Marger, Martin N. "Social Movement Organizations and Response to Environmental Change: The NAACP, 1960–1973." *Social Problems* 32(1) (1984): 16–30.

Markoff, John "Computing in America: A Masculine Mystique." *The New York Times,* February 13, 1989a, pp. 1ff.

Marks, Gary. *Unions in Politics: Britain, Germany, and the United States in the Nineteenth and Early Twentieth Centuries.* Princeton, NJ: Princeton University Press, 1989.

Markson, Elizabeth W. "After Deinstitutionalization, What?" *Journal of Geriatric Psychiatry* 18(1) (1986): 37–56.

Markson, Elizabeth W. "Critical Age Period or Midlife Crisis? Theoretical and Empirical Issues." Paper presented at the annual meeting of the Eastern Sociological Society, Baltimore 1989.

Marland, Michael, ed. *Sex Differentiation and Schooling.* London: Heinemann Educational Books, 1984.

Marsden, Peter V., and Jeanne S. Hurlbert. "Social Resources and Mobility Outcomes: A Replication and Extension." *Social Forces* 66 (1988): 1038–1059.

Marshall, Jonathan, Peter Scott and Dale Hunter. *The Iran-Contra Connection: Secret Teams and Covert Operations in the Reagan Era.* Boston, MA: South End Press, 1989.

Martin, Patricia Yancey, and Roberta A. Hummer. "Fraternities and Rape on Campus." *Gender & Society* 3 (1989): 457–473.

Marwell, Gerald, N.J. Demerath, III, and Michael T. Aiken. "The Present Lives of 1960s Civil Rights Activists: The Dreamers Turn Forty." Paper presented at the 84th annual meeting of the American Sociological Association, San Francisco, August 1989.

Marx, Gary T. "The Iron Fist and the Velvet Glove: Totalitarian Potentials Within Democratic Structures." in James F. Short, Jr. (ed.), *The Social Fabric: Dimensions and Issues,* pp. 135–162. Newbury Park, CA: Sage, 1986.

Marx, Karl. *The German Ideology* (1846). New York: International Publishers. 1939.

Mason, Karen Oppenheim. "The Status of Women: Conceptual and Methodological Issues in Demographic Studies." *Sociological Forum* 1 (1986): 284–300.

Mason, Karen Oppenheim, and Yu-Hsia Lu. "Attitudes Toward Women's Familial Roles: Changes in the United States, 1977–1985." *Gender & Society* 2 (1988): 39–57.

Maurer, Suzanne B., and Richard E. Ratcliff. "Looking for Where the Buck Stops: In Search of Capitalist Investors Among Wealthy Americans." Paper presented at the annual meeting of the Eastern Sociological Society, Baltimore, March 1989.

Maynard, Douglas W. *Inside Plea Bargaining: The Language of Negotiation.* New York: Plenum, 1984.

McAdam, Doug. *Political Process and the Development of Black Insurgency: 1930–1970.* Chicago: University of Chicago Press, 1982.

McAdam, Doug. "Tactical Innovation and the Pace of Insurgency." *American Sociological Review* 48(5) (1983): 735–754.

McAdam, Doug. *Freedom Summer.* New York: Oxford University Press, 1988.

McAdoo, Harriette Pipes. *Black Families,* (2nd ed.). Newbury Park, CA: Sage, 1988.

McCarthy, John D., and Mayer N. Zald. "Resource Mobilization and Social Movements: A Partial

Theory." *American Journal of Sociology* 82(6) (May 1977): 1212–1241.

McCracken, Grant. *Culture and Consumption: New Approaches to the Symbolic Character of Consumer Goods and Activities.* Bloomington: Indiana University Press, 1988.

McLanahan, Sara, and Larry Bumpass. "Intergenerational Consequences of Family Disruption." *American Journal of Sociology* 94 (1988): 130–152.

McLean's. "A Growing Menace: Violent Skinheads are Raising Urban Fears." *McLean's,* January 23, 1989, pp. 43–44.

McNall, Scott G. *Road to Rebellion: Class Formation and Kansas Populism, 1865–1900.* Chicago: University of Chicago Press, 1988.

McNeil, Linda M. *Contradictions of Control: School Structure and School Knowledge.* New York: Routledge & Kegan Paul, 1986.

McPherson, J. Miller, and Lynn Smith-Lovin. "Homophily in Voluntary Organizations: Status Distance and the Composition of Face-to-Face Groups." *American Sociological Review* 52 (June 1987): 370–379.

McWhirter, David P., and Andrew A. Mattison. *The Male Couple: How Relationships Develop.* Englewood Cliffs, NJ: Prentice-Hall, 1984.

Mead, G. H. *Mind, Self, and Society.* Chicago: University of Chicago Press, 1934.

Mead, Lawrence M. *Beyond Entitlement: The Social Obligations of Citizenship.* New York: Free Press, 1986.

Mechanic, David. *Medical Sociology.* New York: Free Press, 1978.

Mechanic, David, and Stephen Hansell. "Divorce, Family Conflict and Adolescents' Well-Being." *Journal of Health and Social Behavior* 30 (1989): 105–116.

Merton, Robert K. *Social Theory and Social Structure.* New York: Free Press, 1957.

Merton, Robert K. "Manifest and Latent Functions." In *Social Theory and Social Structure,* (rev. ed.). New York: Free Press, 1968.

Messner, Steven F., and Judith R. Blau. "Routine Leisure Activities and Rates of Crime: A Macro-Level Analysis." *Social Forces* 65 (1987): 1035–1052.

Metz, Mary Haywood. *Different by Design: The Context and Character of Three Magnet Schools.* New York: Routledge & Kegan Paul, 1986.

Miall, Charlene E. "The Stigma of Involuntary Childlessness." *Social Problems* 33 (1986): 268–282.

Michels, Robert. *Political Parties* (1911). Translated by Edan and Cedar Paul, New York: Collier, 1962.

Mickelson. Roslyn Arlin. "Why Does Jane Read and Write So Well? The Anomaly of Women's Achievement." *Sociology of Education* 62 (1989): 47–63.

Milgram, Stanley. "Some Conditions of Obedience and Disobedience to Authority." *Human Relations* 18 (1965): 57–75.

Miller, Eleanor M. *Street Women.* Philadelphia: Temple University Press, 1986.

Miller, Karen, Stephen Kulis, Leonard Gordon, and Morris Axelrod, "Representation of Women in U.S. Sociology Departments." *ASA Footnotes,* April 1988: 3.

Miller, Lori B. "Only 9 States Spare the Rod." *The New York Times,* January 4, 1987, p. ED9.

Miller, Wesley E., Jr. "The New Christian Right and Its Preexistent Network: A Resource Mobilization Explanation." *Humanity and Society* 10 (May 1986): 179–195.

Mills, C. Wright. *The Power Elite.* New York: Oxford University Press, 1956.

Milner, Murray, Jr. "Theories of Inequality: An Overview and a Strategy for Synthesis." *Social Forces* 65 (1987): 1053–1089.

Mintz, Beth, and Michael Schwartz. *The Power Structure of American Business.* Chicago: University of Chicago Press, 1985.

Mintz, Morton. *At Any Cost: Corporate Greed, Women, and the Dalkon Shield.* New York: Pantheon Books, 1985.

Mintz, Steven, and Susan Kellogg. *Domestic Revolutions: A Social History of American Family Life.* New York: Free Press 1988.

Mirowsky, John. "Depression and Marital Power: An Equity Model." *American Journal of Sociology* 91 (1985): 557–592.

Mizruchi, Mark S. "Similarity of Political Behavior among Large American Corporations." *American Journal of Sociology* 95 (1989): 401–424.

Moen, Phyllis. *Working Parents: Transformations in Gender Roles and Public Policies in Sweden.* Madison: University of Wisconsin Press, 1989.

Money, John. Remarks before the American Psychological Association. Reported in *Psychology Today,* August 1987, p. 64.

Montero, Darrel. 'The Japanese Americans: Changing Patterns of Assimilation over Three Generations." *American Sociological Review* 46 (1981): 829–839.

Montgomery, David. *The Fall of the House of Labor: The Workplace, the State, and American Labor Activism, 1865–1925.* New York: Cambridge Unviersity Press, 1987.

Monthly Labor Review. "Labor Market Completes

Sixth Year of Expansion in 1988." *Monthly Labor Review,* February 1989, pp. 3–6.

Moore, Gwen. "Women in Elite Positions: Insiders or Outsiders?" *Sociological Forum* 3 (1988): 566–585.

Moore, Kristin A., Margaret C. Simms, and Charles L. Betsey. *Choice and Circumstance: Racial Differences in Adolescent Sexuality and Fertility.* New Brunswick, NJ: Transaction Press, 1986.

Moore, Mark H., and Robert C. Trojanowicz. *Policing and the Fear of Crime; Perspectives on Policing,* No. 3. Washington: U.S. Department of Justice, June 1988.

Moran, Theodore H., ed. *Multinational Corporations: The Political Economy of Foreign Direct Investment.* Lexington, MA: Lexington Books, 1985.

Morehouse, Ward, and David Dembo. *The Underbelly of the U.S. Economy: Joblessness and the Pauperization of Work in America.* New York: Council on International and Public Affairs, 1987.

Morello, Karen Berger. *The Invisible Bar: The Woman Lawyer in America, 1638 to the Present.* New York: Random House, 1986.

Moreno, J. L. *Who Shall Survive?* (1934). Boston: Beacon Press, 1953.

Morgan, S. Philip, and Linda J. Waite. "Parenthood and the Attitudes of Young Adults." *American Sociological Review* 52 (1987): 541–547.

Morgan, S. Philip, Diane N. Lye, and Gretchen A. Condran. "Sons, Daughters, and the Risk of Marital Disruption." *American Journal of Sociology* 94 (1988): 110–129.

Morris, Aldon. *The Origins of the Civil Rights Movement: Black Communities Organizing for Change.* New York: Free Press, 1984.

Morris, Michael, and John B. Williamson. "Workfare: The Poverty/Dependence Trade-Off." *Social Policy.* Summer 1987.

Mortimer, Jeylan T., and Jon Lorence. "Satisfaction and Involvement: Disentangling a Deceptively Simple Relationship." *Social Psychology Quarterly* 52 (1989): 249–265.

Moskos. Charles C. *A Call to Civic Service: National Service for Country and Community.* New York: Free Press, 1988.

Moss, Philip I. "Employment Gains by Minorities, Women in Large City Government, 1976–1983." *Monthly Labor Review* (November 1988): 18–24.

Moynihan, Daniel Patrick. *The Negro Family: The Case for National Action.* Washington: U.S. Dept. of Labor, 1965.

Mukenge, Ida Rousseau. *The Black Church in Urban America: A Case Study in Political Economy.* New York: University Press of America, 1983.

Mukerji, Chandra. *From Graven Images: Patterns of Modern Materialism.* New York: Columbia University Press, 1983.

Muller, Edward N. "Income Inequality, Regime Repressiveness, and Political Violence." *American Sociological Review* 50 (1985): 47–61.

Mydans, Seth. "20th-Century Lawsuit Asserts Stone-Age Identity." *The New York Times,* October 29, 1988, p. 4.

Mydans, Seth. "Evolution Theory's Foes Win Textbook Battle in California." *New York Times,* November 10, 1989, p. 1ff.

Myrdal, Gunnar. *An American Dilemma.* New York: Harper & Row, 1945.

Nagel, William. "Stream of Consciousness: A View of Prisonia." *Psychology Today* 14(3) (1980): 78.

Nakell, Barry and Kenneth A. Hardy. *The Arbitrariness of the Death Penalty.* Philadelphia: Temple University Press, 1987.

Nance, John. *Lobo of the Tasaday: A Stone Age Boy Meets the Modern World.* New York: Pantheon, 1982.

Nanda, Serena. *Cultural Anthropology,* 2nd ed. Belmont, CA: Wadsworth, 1988.

National Center for Education Statistics. *Digest of Education Statistics 1989.* Washington: U.S. Government Printing Office, 1989.

National Center for Health Statistics. *See* U.S. Department of Health and Human Services.

National Coalition for the Homeless. *Pushed Out: America's Homeless: Thanksgiving 1987.* Washington: National Coalition for the Homeless, 1987.

National Women's Political Caucus, *Newsletter,* 1989.

Natriello, Gary, Aaron M. Pallas, and Karl Alexander. "On the Right Track? Curriculum and Academic Achievement." *Sociology of Education* 62 (1989): 109–118.

Nature. "Half-hearted War on Drugs." 341 (September 7, 1989): 1–2.

Nelson, Joel I., and Jon Lorence. "Metropolitan Earnings Inequality and Service Sector Employment." *Social Forces* 67 (1988): 492–511.

Neugarten, Bernice L., and Gunhild Hagestad. "Age and the Life Course." In Robert H. Binstock and Ethel Shanas (eds.), *Handbook of Aging and the Social Sciences* (2nd ed.) New York: Van Nostrand, 1983.

Newcomb, Theodore. *Personality and Social Change: Attitude Formation in a Student Community.* New York: Dryden, 1943.

Newman, Katherine S. *Falling From Grace: The Ex-*

perience of Downward Mobility in the American Middle Class. New York: Free Press, 1988.

New Republic. "Nazi Retreat," *New Republic,* April 3, 1989; pp. 10–11.

Newsweek. "Skinheads on the Rampage," *Newsweek,* September 7, 1987; p. 22.

New York Times. "Third World Nations Finally Embracing Population Control." May 31, 1987, p. E30.

New York Times. "CBS News Poll of American Catholics, August, 1987." September 10 and 11, 1987.

New York Times. "Four Sisters' Death Pact Stirs South Korea." March 7, 1988, pp. 1ff.

New York Times. "Bill to Raise Minimum Wage Advances in a Ready Congress." March 28, 1988, p. 1ff.

New York Times "Redefining the Boundaries: Who May Come In." April 10, 1988, p. C5.

New York Times. "What a Minimum Wage Does to the Economy." August 21 1988, p. E5.

New York Times. "No-Smoking Policy Brings Rift in Kentucky." November 25, 1988, p. A25.

New York Times. "Jewish Feminists Prompt Protests of Wailing Wall." December 2, 1988, p. A10.

New York Times. "As Economy Grew Since '83, Closing and Layoffs Tool 9.7 Million Jobs." December 13, 1988, p. B12.

New York Times. "New Albany Audits Collect $28 Million from 12 Tax Cheats." February 2, 1989, p. 1.

New York Times. "Ranks of Black Men Shrink on U.S. Campuses." Feburary 5, 1989, p. 1ff.

New York Times. "In New York City, There Are Many Ways to Be Poor." March 5, 1989, p. E6.

New York Times. "White House Admits Censoring Testimony." May 9, 1989, p. C1.

New York Times. 'San Francisco Votes Legislation Recognizing Unmarried Partners." May 24, 1989, p. A20.

New York Times. "Sex Survey is Dealt a Setback." July 26, 1989, p. B6.

New York Times. "Suit Says Magnet Schools Bar Black Children." August 3, 1989, p. A14.

New York Times. "Struggle for Work and Family Fueling Women's Movement." August 22, 1989, p. 1ff.

New York Times. "Michigan Curtails New Rights Policy." August 23, 1989, B9.

Oakes, Jennie. *Keeping Track: How Schools Structure Inequality.* New Haven, CT: Yale University Press, 1985.

Ogburn, William T. *Social Change: With Respect to Culture and Original Nature.* New York: B. W. Huebsch, 1922.

Olneck, Michael R., and Ki-Seok Kim. "High School Completion and Men's Incomes: An Apparent Anomaly." *Sociology of Education* 62 (1989): 193–207.

Olson, Mancur, Jr. *The Logic of Collective Action.* Cambridge, MA: Harvard University Press, 1965.

Olzak, Susan. "Labor Unrest, Immigration, and Ethnic Conflict in Urban America." *American Journal of Sociology* 94 (1989): 1303–1333.

Olzak, Susan, and Elizabeth West. "Ethnic Conflicts and the New Immigrants." Paper Presented at the 84th annual meeting of the American Sociological Association, San Francisco, August 1989.

Omi, Michael, and Howard Winant. *Racial Formation in the United States: From the 1960s to the 1980s.* New York: Routledge & Kegan Paul, 1987.

Opp, Karl-Dieter. "Grievances and Participation in Social Movements." *American Sociological Review* 53 (1988): 853–864.

O'Rand, Angela M., and Vicky M. MacLean, "Labor Markets, Pension Rule Structure, and Retirement Benefits for Long-Term Employees," *Social Forces* 65 (1986): 134–141.

Oren, Dan A. *Joining the Club: A History of Jews and Yale.* New Haven, CT: Yale University Press, 1985.

Orfield, Gary, and Franklin Montford. "Racial Change and Desegregation in Large School Districts." Washington: National School Boards Association, 1988.

Orr, Donald. "Teens, Sex, and Self-Esteem." *Parents' Pediatric Report,* 6, 1989, p. 24.

Orwell, George. *Animal Farm.* New York: Harcourt 1954.

Orwell, George. *1984.* New York: Harcourt, 1948.

Ostrander, Susan. *Women of the Upper Class.* Philadelphia: Temple University Press, 1984.

Pace, Eric. "Women's Cults of Antiquity: The Veil Rises." *The New York Times,* April 30, 1985, pp. C1 ff.

Page, Ann L., and Donald Clelland. "The Kanawha County Textbook Controversy: A Study of Politics of Lifestyle Concerns." *Social Forces* 57(1) (1978).

Paludi, Michele A., and Lisa A. Strayer. "What's in an Author's Name? Differential Evaluations of Performance as a Function of Author's Name." *Sex Roles* 12 (1985): 353–361.

Pareles, Jon. "There's a New Sound in Pop Music: Bigotry." *New York Times,* September 10, 1989, Sect. 2. pp. 1ff.

Parkinson, C. Northcote. *Parkinson's Law* (1957). Boston: Houghton Mifflin, 1980.

Parrillo, Vincent N. "Arab American Immigrant Communities: Diversity and Parallel." Paper presented at the Eastern Sociological Society meeting. Baltimore, March 1983.

Parrillo, Vincent N. *Strangers to These Shores: Race and Ethnic Relations in the United States,* 3rd ed. New York: Macmillan, 1989.

Parsa, Misagh. "Theories of Collective Action and the Iranian Revolution." *Sociological Forum* 3 (1988): 44–71.

Parsons, Talcott. *The Social System.* New York: Free Press, 1951.

Pear, Robert. "Social Security Said to Bridge Gap in Income." *The New York Times,* December 28, 1988, pp. 1ff.

Pearce, Diana M. "Toil and Trouble: Women Workers and Unemployment Compensation." *Signs* 10 (1985): 439–459.

Pearce, Diana M. "On the Edge: Marginal Women Workers and Employment Policy." In Christine Bose and Glenna Spitze (eds.), *Ingredients for Women's Employment Policy,* pp. 197–210. Albany: State University of New York Press, 1987.

Peek, Charles W., Judith J. Fischer, and Jeannie S. Kidwell. "Teenage Violence Toward Parents: A Neglected Dimension of Family Violence." *Journal of Marriage and the Family* 47 (1985): 1051–1060.

Penner, Louis A. *Social Psychology: Concepts and Applications.* St. Paul, MN: West, 1986.

Perman, Lauri, and Beth Stevens. "Industrial Segregation and the Gender Distribution of Fringe Benefits." *Gender & Society* 3 (1989): 388–404.

Perrow, Charles. "Risky Systems: Inducing and Avoiding Errors." Paper delivered at the annual meeting of the American Sociological Association, September 1986.

Persell, Caroline Hodges. "Equal Opportunity for Academic Women." *Journal of Educational Equity and Leadership* 4(1) (1984): 17–26.

Pessen, Edward. *The Log Cabin Myth: The Social Background of the Presidents.* New Haven, CT: Yale University Press, 1984.

Peter, Lawrence, and R. Hull. *The Peter Principle.* New York: Morrow, 1969.

Petersilia, Joan, Susan Turner, and Joyce E. Peterson. *Prison versus Probation in California: Implications for Crime and Offender Recidivism.* Rand Corporation, 1987.

Petranek, Charles F. "Recruitment and Commitment." *Society,* January/February 1988, pp. 48–51.

Piliavin, Irving, Herb Westerfelt, and Elsa Elliott. "Estimating Mental Illness: The Effects of Choice-based Sampling." *Social Problems* 36 (5) (1989): 525–531.

Pincus, Fred L. "The False Promises of Community Colleges: Class Conflict and Vocational Education." *Harvard Educational Review* 50 (Aug. 1980): 332–361.

Pines, Maya. "The Civilizing of Genie." *Psychology Today* (Sept. 1981), pp. 28–34.

Piotrkowski, Chaya S., Robert N. Rapoport, and Rhona Rapoport. "Families and Work." In Marvin B. Sussman and Suzanne K. Steinmetz (eds.), *Handbook of Marriage and the Family,* pp. 251–284. New York: Plenum, 1987.

Piven, Frances Fox, and Richard A. Cloward. *Why Americans Don't Vote.* New York: Pantheon Books, 1988.

Plaskow, Judith, and Carol P. Christ, eds. *Weaving the Visions: New Patterns in Feminist Spirituality.* San Francisco: Harper & Row, 1989.

Pleck, Joseph. *Family Supportive Employer Policies and Men's Participation.* Washington: U.S. Government Printing Office, U.S. Department of Labor, Women's Bureau, 1989.

Pleck, Joseph H. *Working Wives/Working Husbands.* Beverly Hills: Sage, 1985.

Pollak, Lauren Harte and Peggy A. Thoits. "Processes in Emotional Socialization." *Social Psychology Quarterly* 52 (March 1989): 22–34.

Popora, Douglas U. *The Concept of Social Structure.* Westport. CT: Greenwood Press, 1987.

Population Reference Bureau, Inc. *1989 World Population Data Sheet,* Washington, D.C.: PRB, 1989.

Powell, Gary. *Women and Men in Management.* Newbury Park, CA: Sage, 1988.

Preston, James. *Mother Worship: Themes and Variations.* Chapel Hill.: University of North Carolina Press, 1983.

Price, Jerome. *The Antinuclear Movement.* Boston: Twayne, 1982.

Price, T. Douglas, and James A. Brown. *Prehistoric Hunter-Gatherers: The Emergence of Cultural Complexity.* New York: Academic Press, 1985.

Pruett, Kyle D. *The Nurturing Father: Journey Toward the Complete Man.* New York: Warner Books, 1987.

Przeworski, Adam, and John Sprague. *Paper Stones: A History of Electoral Socialism.* Chicago: University of Chicago Press, 1986.

Punch, Maurice. *Conduct Unbecoming: The Social Construction of Police Deviance and Control.* New York: Tavistock, 1985.

Pynoos, Jon. *Breaking the Rules: Bureaucracy and Reform in Public Housing.* New York: Plenum, 1986.

Quadagno, Jill, and Madonna Harrington Meyer. "Organized Labor, State Structures, and Social Policy Development: A Case Study of Old Age Assistance in Ohio, 1916–1940." *Social Problems* 36 (1989): 181–196.

Quinney, Richard. *Class, State, and Crime: On the Theory and Practice of Criminal Justice.* New York: David McKay, 1977.

Quinney, Richard, and John Wildeman. *The Problem of Crime* (2nd ed.). New York: Harcourt Brace Jovanovich, 1977.

Radelet, Michael I. "Racial Characteristics and the Imposition of the Death Penalty." *American Sociological Review* 46 (1981): 918–927.

Radelet, Michael I., ed. *Facing the Death Penalty: Essays on a Cruel and Unusual Punishment.* Philadelphia: Temple University Press, 1989.

Rank, Mark R. "Fertility among Women on Welfare: Incidence and Determinants." *American Sociological Review* 54 (1989): 296–304.

Raschke, Helen J. "Divorce." in Marvin B. Sussman and Suzanne K. Steinmetz (eds.) *Handbook of Marriage and the Family,* pp. 597–624. New York: Plenum, 1987.

Ravitch, Diane. *The Troubled Crusade: American Education, 1945–1980.* New York: Basic Books, 1983.

Rawlings, Steve W. "Single Parents and Their Children." In *Studies in Marriage and the Family,* Current Population Reports, Series P-23, No. 162, pp. 13–26. Washington: U.S. Government Printing Office, U.S. Bureau of the Census, June 1989.

Redfield, Robert. *The Folk Culture of Yucatan.* Chicago: University of Chicago Press, 1941.

Reese, William J. *Power and the Promise of School Reform: Grassroots Movements During the Progressive Era.* New York: Routledge & Kegan Paul, 1986.

Reiner, Robert. *The Politics of the Police.* New York: St. Martin's, 1985.

Reskin, Barbara F., and Heidi I. Hartmann. *Women's Work, Men's Work: Sex Segregation on the Job.* Washington: National Academy Press, 1986.

Reuss-Ianni, Elizabeth. *Two Cultures of Policing: Street Cops and Management Cops.* New Brunswick, NJ: Transaction Books, 1983.

Rice, Joy K., and Annette Hemmings. "Women's Colleges and Women Achievers: An Update." *Signs* 13 (1988): 546–559.

Riche, Martha. "Mysterious Young Adults." *American Demographics,* February 1987, pp. 38–43.

Riddlesperger, James W., and James D. King. "Elitism and Presidential Appointments." *Social Science Quarterly* 70 (1989): 902–910.

Riesman, David. *The Lonely Crowd.* New Haven, CT: Yale University Press, 1950.

Riley, Matilda White. "Age Strata in Social Systems." In Robert H. Binstock and Ethel Shanas (eds.), *Handbook on Aging and the Social Sciences* (2nd ed.), pp. 369–411. New York: Van Nostrand-Reinhold, 1985.

Rindfuss, Ronald R., S. Philip Morgan, and Gary Swicegood. *First Births in America: Changes in the Timing of Parenthood.* Berkeley: University of California Press, 1988.

Ringen, Stein. *The Possibility of Politics: A Study in the Political Economy of the Welfare State.* New York: Oxford University Press, 1987.

Risman, Barbara J. "Can Men 'Mother'? Life as a Single Father." *Family Relations* 35 (1986): 95–102.

Risman, Barbara J. "Intimate Relationships from a Microstructural Perspective: Men Who Mother." *Gender & Society* 1 (1987): 6–32.

Robbins, Thomas. *Cults, Converts and Charisma: The Sociology of New Religious Movements.* Newbury Park, CA: Sage, 1988.

Rodriguez, Noelie Maria. "A Successful Feminist Shelter: A Case Study of the Family Crisis Shelter in Hawaii." *Journal of Applied Behavioral Science* 24(3) (1989): 235–250.

Roebuck, Julian B., and Mark Hickson, III. *The Southern Redneck: A Phenomenological Class Study.* New York: Praeger, 1982.

Rogler, Lloyd, and Rosemary Cooney. *Puerto Rican Families in New York City: Integrational Processes.* Maplewood, NJ: Waterfront Press, 1986.

Rohner, Ronald P., and Evelyn C. Rohner. *The Kwakiutl: Indians of British Columbia.* New York: Holt, Rinehart & Winston, 1970.

Rohter, Larry. "From 6 New Benefactors, 425 College Dreams." *The New York Times,* June 21, 1986, pp. B1ff.

Rohter, Larry. "Isolated Desert Community Lives by Skinner's Precepts." *The New York Times,* November 7, 1989, pp. C1ff.

Rojek, Chris, ed. *Leisure for Leisure: Critical Essays.* New York: Routledge. 1989.

Roof, Wade Clark, and William McKinney. *American Mainline Religion: Its Changing Shape and Future.* New Brunswick, NJ: Rutgers University Press, 1987.

Rose, Peter I., Myron Glazer, and Penina Migdal Glazer. "In Controlled Environments: Four Cases of Intensive Resocialization." In Peter I. Rose (ed.), *Socialization and the Life Cycle,* pp. 320–338. New York: St. Martin's Press, 1979.

Rosenbaum, David E. "Bush and Congress Reach Accord Raising Minimum Wage to $4.25." *The New York Times,* November 1, 1989, pp. 1ff.

Rosenberg, Charles E. *The Care of Strangers: The Rise of America's Hospital System.* New York: Basic Books, 1988.

Rosenberg, Morris, and Howard B. Kaplan, eds. *Social Psychology of the Self-Concept*. Arlington Heights, IL: Harlan Davidson, 1982.

Rosenfeld, Jeffrey. "Intergenerational Wealth Study: Inferences from Estate Taxes." Paper presented at the 59th annual meeting of the Eastern Sociological Society, Baltimore, 1989.

Rossi, Alice S. "Gender and Parenthood." In Alice S. Rossi (ed.), *Gender and the Life Course*, pp. 161–191. New York: Aldine, 1985.

Rothman, Barbara Katz. "Reproduction." In Beth B. Hess and Myra Marx Ferree (eds.), *Analyzing Gender: A Handbook of Social Science Research*, pp. 154–170. Newbury Park, CA: Sage, 1987.

Rothschild, Joyce, and Raymond Russell. "Alternatives to Bureaucracy: Democratic Participation in the Economy." *Annual Review of Sociology* 12 (1986): 307–328.

Rothschild, Joyce, and J. Allen Whitt. *The Cooperative Workplace: Potentials and Dilemmas of Organizational Democracy and Participation*. New York: Cambridge University Press, 1987.

Rubin, Jeffrey Z., Frank J. Provenzano, and Zella Luria. "The Eye of the Beholder: Parents' Views on Sex of Newborns." In Juanita H. Williams (ed.), *Psychology of Women*, pp. 134–141. New York: W. W. Norton, 1979.

Rubinstein, Ruth. "The Sociology of Clothing." Paper presented at the annual meeting of the Eastern Sociological Society, Boston: 1985.

Ruether, Rosemary Radford. *Womanguides: Readings Toward a Feminist Theology*. Boston: Beacon Press, 1985.

Ruggles, Steven. *Prolonged Connections: The Rise of the Extended Family in Nineteenth Century England and America*. Madison: University of Wisconsin Press, 1987.

Rule, James B. "Biotechnology: Big Money Comes To the University." *Dissent*, Fall 1988, pp. 430–436.

Rumbaut, G. Rubén. "Southeast Asian Refugees in the United States: A Portrait of a Decade of Migration and Resettlement, 1975–1985." Paper presented at the 81st annual meeting of the American Sociological Association, New York, August 1986.

Russell, Diana E. H. *Sexual Exploitation: Rape, Child Sexual Abuse, and Workplace Harassment*. Beverly Hills, CA: Sage, 1984.

Russell, Graeme. *The Changing Role of Fathers*. Portland, OR: University of Queensland Press, 1983.

Ryan, Barbara. "Ideological Purity and Feminism: The U.S. Women's Movement from 1966 to 1975." *Gender & Society* 3 (1989): 239–257.

Ryan, John. *The Production of Culture in the Music Industry: The ASCAP-BMI Controversy*. Lanham, MD: University Press of America, 1985.

Ryan, William. *Blaming the Victim*. New York: Vintage, 1972.

Rytina, Steven, Peter M. Blau, Terry Blum, and Joseph Schwartz. "Inequality and Intermarriage: A Paradox of Motive and Constraint." *Social Forces* 66 (1988): 645–675.

Saint-Germaine, Michelle A. "Does Their Difference Make a Difference? The Impact of Women on Public Policy in the Arizona Legislature." *Social Science Quarterly* 70 (1989): 956–968.

Sanick, Margaret M., and Teresa Mauldin. "Single versus Two-Parent Families: A Comparison of Mothers' Time." *Family Relations* 35 (1986): 54–56.

Sapir, Edward. "Selected Writings of Edward Sapir." In David G. Mandelbaum (ed.), *Language, Culture and Personality*. Berkeley: University of California Press, 1949.

Sassen-Koob, Saskia, and S. Grover. "Unregistered Work in the New York Metropolitan Area." New York: Columbia University Graduate School of Architecture and Planning, 1986.

Scarf, Maggie. *Intimate Partners: Patterns in Love and Marriage*. New York: Random House, 1987.

Scheff, Thomas. *Being Mentally Ill: A Sociological Theory*. Chicago: Aldine, 1966.

Scheff, Thomas. "Shame and Conformity: The Difference-Emotion System." *American Sociological Review* 53 (June 1988): 395–406.

Schmidt, Annesley K. "Electronic Monitoring of Offenders Increases." *National Institute of Justice Reports* 212 (January/February 1989): 2–5.

Schnaiberg, Allan, and Sheldon Goldenberg. "From Empty Nest to Crowded Nest; The Dynamics of Incompletely-Launched Young Adults." *Social Problems* 36 (1989): 251–269.

Schneider, Beth E. "Gender, Sexuality, and AIDS: Social Responses and Consequences." In Berk, R. E. (ed.), *The Social Impact of AIDS in the U.S.*, Garden Grove, CA: ABT Books, 1989, pp. 15–36.

Schneider, Beth E., and Meredith Gould. "Female Sexuality: Looking Back into the Future." In Beth B. Hess and Myra Marx Ferree (eds.). *Analyzing Gender: A Handbook of Social Science Research*, pp. 120–153. Newbury Park, CA: Sage, 1987.

Schoen, Robert, John Wooldredge, and Barbara Thomas, "Ethnic and Educational Effects on Marriage Choice." *Social Science Quarterly* 70 (1989): 617–630.

Schudson, Michael. "The Giving of Gifts." *Psychology Today*, December 1986, pp. 27–29.

Schutt, Russell K. "Craft Unions and Minorities: De-

terminants of Change in Admission Practices."
Social Problems 34 (1987): 388–400.

Schwartz, Martin D., and Charles Ellison. "Criminal Sanctions for Corporate Misbehavior: A Call for Capitalist Punishment." *Humanity and Society* 6 (1982): 267–293.

Schwartz, Martin D. "Age and Spousal Assault Victimization." Paper presented at the 81st annual meeting of the American Sociological Association, New York, August 1986.

Schwartz, Martin D. "Censorship of Sexual Violence: Is the Problem Sex or Violence?" *Humanity & Society* 11 (1987): 212–243.

Schwartz, Michael, ed. *The Structure of Power in America: The Corporate Elite as a Ruling Class.* New York: Holmes & Meier, 1987.

Schwartz, Michael. *Radical Protest and Social Structure: The Southern Farmers' Alliance and Cotton Tenancy, 1880–1890.* Chicago: University of Chicago Press, 1988.

Sciolino, Elaine. "Report Urging End of Homosexual Ban Rejected by Military." *The New York Times,* October 22, 1989, pp. 1ff.

Sebold, Hans. "Adolescents' Shifting Orientation toward Parents and Peers: A Curvilinear Trend over Recent Decades." *Journal of Marriage and the Family.* February 1986, pp. 5–13.

Sedlak, Michael W., Christopher W. Wheeler, Diana C. Pullin, and Philip A. Cusick. *Selling Students Short: Classroom Bargains and Academic Reform in the American High School.* New York: Teachers College Press, 1986.

Seeman, Melvin. "The Signals of '68: Alienation in Pre-Crisis France." *American Sociological Review* 37(3) (1972): 385–402.

Segal, David R. *Recruiting for Uncle Sam: Citizenship and Military Manpower Policy.* Lawrence: University Press of Kansas, 1989.

Seltzer, Judith A., and Debra Kalmuss. "Socialization and Stress Explanations for Spouse Abuse." *Social Forces* 67 (1988): 473–491.

Shakeshaft, Carol. *Women in Educational Adminstration.* Newbury Park, CA: Sage, 1987.

Shank, Susan. "Women and the Labor Market: The Link Grows Stronger." *Monthly Labor Review,* March 1988, pp. 3–8.

Shavit, Yossi. "Segregation, Tracking, and the Educational Attainment of Minorities: Arabs and Oriental Jews in Israel." *American Sociological Review* 55 (1990): 115–126.

Sheffield, Carole J. "Sexual Terrorism: The Social Control of Women." In Beth B. Hess and Myra Marx Ferree (eds.), *Analyzing Gender: A Handbook of Social Science Research,* pp. 171–189. Newbury Park, CA: Sage, 1987.

Sheldon, William H. *Varieties of Delinquent Youth.* New York, Harper & Row, 1949.

Shelton, Beth Anne, and Juanita Firestone, "Household Labor Time and the Gender Gap in Earnings." *Gender & Society* 3 (1989): 105–112.

Shepelak, Norma J. "The Role of Self-Explanations and Self-Evaluations in Legitimating Inequality." *American Sociological Review* 52 (1987): 495–503.

Shibamoto, Janet S. "Japanese Sociolinguistics." *American Review of Anthropology* 16 (1987): 261–278.

Shils, Edward A. "Primary Groups in the American Army." In Robert K. Merton and Paul Lazarsfeld (eds.), *Continuities in Social Research.* Glencoe, IL: Free Press, 1950.

Shlapentokh, Vladimir. *The Politics of Sociology in the Soviet Union.* Boulder, CO: Westview Press, 1987.

Shostak, Arthur B. "Singlehood." In Marvin B. Sussman and Suzanne K. Steinmetz (eds.), *Handbook of Marriage and the Family,* pp. 355–368. New York: Plenum, 1987.

Shostak, Arthur. *Robust Unionism.* Ithaca, NY: ILR Press, 1990.

Shostak, Arthur, and David Skocik. *The Air Controllers' Controversy: Lessons from the PATCO Strike.* New York: Human Sciences Press, 1986.

Shupe, Anson, William A. Stacey, and Lonnie R. Hazelwood. *Violent Men, Violent Couples: The Dynamics of Domestic.* Lexington, MA: Lexington Books, 1987.

Shweder, Richard A., and Robert A. LeVine, eds. *Culture Theory: Essays on Mind, Self, and Emotion.* New York: Cambridge University Press, 1985.

Sieber, R. Timothy. "The Politics of Middle Class Success in an Inner-City School." *Journal of Education* 164(1) (1982): 30–47.

Siegel, Karolynn, Laurie J. Bauman, Grace H. Christ, and Susan Krown. "Patterns of Change in Sexual Behavior Among Gay Men in New York City." *Archives of Sexual Behavior* 17 (1988): 481–497.

Signs. "Common Grounds and Crossroads: Race, Ethnicity, and Class in Women's Lives." *Signs, Special Issue* 14 (Summer 1989).

Simmel, Georg. *The Sociology of Georg Simmel.* Translated by Kurt H. Wolff. New York: Free Press, 1950.

Simmons, J. L. *Deviants.* Berkeley, CA: Glendessary Press, 1969.

Simon, William, and John H. Gagnon. "Sexual Scripts: Permanence and Change." *Archives of Sexual Behavior* 15 (1986): 97–120.

Siu, Paul C. P. *The Chinese Laundryman: A Study of Social Isolation.* New York: New York University Press, 1987.

Sivard, Ruth Leger. *World Military and Social Expenditures 1989* (13th ed.). Washington: World Priorities, 1989.

Skocpol, Theda. *States and Social Revolutions: A Comparative Analysis of France, Russia, and China.* Cambridge: Cambridge University Press, 1979.

Skocpol, Theda, and Edwin Amenta. "States and Social Policies." *Annual Review of Sociology* 12 (1986): 131–157.

Skogan, Wesley. "Fear of Crime and Neighborhood Change." In Albert J. Reiss, Jr. and Michael Tonrey (eds.), *Communities and Crime.* Chicago: University of Chicago Press, 1986.

Skolnick, Jerome H. "Seven Crack Dilemmas in Search of an Answer." *New York Times,* May 23, 1989, p. A17.

Slomczynski, Kazimierz M., and Tadeusz K. Krauze. "Crossnational Similarity in Social Mobility Patterns: A Direct Test of the Featherman-Jones-Hauser Hypothesis." *American Sociological Review* 52 (1987): 598–611.

Slomczynski, Kazimierz, Joanne Miller, and Melvin Kohn. "Stratification, Work, and Values: A Polish-United States Comparison." *American Sociological Review* 46 (1981): 720–744.

Smart, Carol. *The Ties that Bind: Law, Marriage, and the Reproduction of Partriarchal Relations.* London: Routledge & Kegan Paul, 1984.

Smelser, Neil J. "Toward a General Theory of Social Change." In Neil J. Smelser (ed.), *Essays in Sociological Explanation,* Englewood Cliffs, NJ: Prentice-Hall, 1968.

Smith, Allen C., III, and Sherryl Kleinman. "Managing Emotions in Medical School: Students' Contacts with the Living and the Dead." *Social Psychology Quarterly* 52 (1) (1989): 56–69.

Smith, Audrey D., and William J. Reid. *Role-Sharing Marriage.* New York: Columbia University Press, 1986.

Smith, Douglas A. and G. Roger Jarjoura. "Household Characteristics. Neighborhood Composition and Victimization Risk." *Social Forces* 68 (2) (1989): 621–640.

Smith, Drake S. "Wife Employment and Marital Adjustment: A Cumulation of Results." *Family Relations* 34 (1985): 483–490.

Smith, J. Owens. *The Politics of Racial Inequality: A Systematic Comparative Macro-Analysis from the Colonial Period to 1970.* Westport, CT: Greenwood Press, 1987.

Smith, James P., and Michael P. Ward. *Women's Wages and Work in the Twentieth Century.* Santa Monica, CA: Rand Corporation, 1985.

Smith, Michael J. *Violence and Sport.* Toronto: Butterworth, 1983.

Snarey, John. "A Question of Morality." *Psychological Bulletin* 97 (1987): 202–232.

Snipp, C. Matthew, and Gary D. Sandefur. "Earnings of American Indians and Alaskan Natives: The Effects of Residence and Migration." *Social Forces* 66(4) (1988): 994–1008.

Snow, David A., Susan G. Baker, and Leon Anderson. "On the Precariousness of Measuring Insanity in Insane Contexts." *Social Problems* 35(2) (April 1988).

Society. "Social Science and the Citizen: Weapons, Crime and Violence," 19(4) (1982): 4–5.

Society. "Job Satisfaction Based on Generation, Not Class," November/December, 1989, p. 2.

Solomon, Barbara Miller. *In the Company of Educated Women: A History of Women and Higher Education in America.* New Haven, CT: Yale University Press, 1986.

Sorenson, Annemette, and Sara McLanahan. "Married Women's Economic Dependency, 1940–1980." *American Journal of Sociology* 93 (1987): 659–687.

Sorokin, Pitirim A. *The Crisis of Our Age.* New York: E. P. Dutton, 1941.

South, Scott J., and Glenna Spitze. "Determinants of Divorce Over the Marital Life Course." *American Sociological Review* 51 (1986): 583–590.

Spade, Joan Z. "Occupational Structure and Men's and Women's Parental Values." Paper presented at the 78th annual meeting of the American Sociological Association, Detroit, August 1983.

Spanier, Graham B., and Frank F. Furstenburg, Jr. "Remarriage and Reconstituted Families." In Marvin B. Sussman and Suzanne K. Steinmetz (eds.), *Handbook of Marriage and the Family.* pp. 419–434. New York: Plenum, 1987.

Spence, Gerry. *With Justice for None: Destroying an American Myth.* New York: Times Books, 1989.

Spencer, Herbert. *The Social Organism.* London: Greenwood, 1860.

Stacey, Judith, and Barrie Thorne. "The Missing Feminist Revolution in Sociology." *Social Problems* 32 (1985): 301–316.

Stage, F. K., and D. R. Hossler. "Differences in Family Influences on College Attendance Plans for Male and Female Ninth Graders." Paper presented at the annual meeting of the American Educational Research Association, New Orleans, 1988.

Staggenborg, Suzanne. "The Consequences of Professionalization and Formalization in the Pro-

Choice Movement." *American Sociological Review* 53 (1988): 586–606.

Standohar, Paul. *The Sports Industry and Collective Bargaining.* Ithaca, NY: ILR Press-Cornell University, 1986.

Staples, Robert, and Alfredo Mirandé. "Racial and Cultural Variations Among American Families." *Journal of Marriage and the Family* 42(4) (November 1980): 887–903.

Starhawk. *Dreaming the Dark: Magic, Sex, and Politics* (2nd ed.). Boston: Beacon Press, 1989.

Stark, Evan, and Anne H. Flitcraft. "Women and Children at Risk: A Feminist Perspective on Child Abuse." *International Journal of Health Services* 18 (1988): 97–118.

Starr, Paul. *The Transformation of American Medicine.* New York: Basic Books, 1982.

Statistical Abstracts of the United States. See: U.S. Bureau of the Census.

Stein, Arlene. "Three Models of Sexuality: Drives, Identities, and Practices." *Sociological Theory* 7 (1989): 1–13.

Stein, Peter J. "Men in Families." In Beth B. Hess and Marvin Sussman (eds.), *Women and the Family: Two Decades of Change.* New York: Haworth, 1984.

Stein, Peter J., and Steven Hoffman. "Sports and Male Role Strain." In Donald Sabo and Ross Runfola (eds.), *Jock: Sports and Male Identity,* pp. 53–74. Englewood Cliffs, NJ: Prentice-Hall, 1980.

Stein, Peter J. "The Diverse World of Single Adults." In James M. Henslin (ed.), *Marriage and the Family in the Modern World,* pp. 62–72. New York: Macmillan, 1989.

Steinberg, Ronnie. "Radical Challenges in a Liberal World: The Mixed Success of Comparable Worth." *Gender & Society* 1 (1987): 466–475.

Steinmetz, Suzanne K. "Family Violence: Past, Present, and Future." In Marvin B. Sussman and Suzanne K. Steinmetz (eds.), *Handbook of Marriage and the Family.* pp. 725–764. New York: Plenum, 1987.

Stirling, Kate J. "Women Who Remain Divorced: The Long-Term Economic Consequences." *Social Science Quarterly* 70 (1989): 549–561.

Stone, Christopher. *Where the Law Ends: The Social Control of Corporate Behavior.* New York: Harper & Row, 1985.

Stouffer, Samuel, et al. *The American Soldier: Combat and Its Aftermath—Social Studies in Social Psychology in World War II,* Vol. 2. Princeton, NJ: Princeton University Press, 1949.

Strathern, Andrew, (ed.) *Inequality in New Guinea Highlands Societies.* New York: Cambridge University Press, 1982.

Sumner, William Graham. *Folkways* (1906). Boston: Ginn, 1940.

Sutherland, Edwin H. *Principles of Criminology.* Philadelphia: Lippincott, 1939.

Swanson, Guy E. *Ego Defenses and the Legitimation of Behavior.* New York: Cambridge University Press, 1988.

Sweetser, Dorrian Appel. "Broken Homes, Stable Risk, Changing Reasons, Changing Forms." *Journal of Marriage and the Family* 47 (1985): 709–715.

Swidler, Ann. "Culture in Action: Symbols and Strategies." *American Sociological Review* 51 (April 1986): 273–286.

Synnott, Marcia. *The Half-Opened Door: Discrimination and Admissions at Harvard, Yale, and Princeton, 1900–1970.* New York: Greenwood, 1979.

Szasz, Thomas. *Insanity: The Idea and Its Consequences.* New York: WIley, 1987.

Szelenyi, Szonja. "Social Inequality and Party Membership: Patterns of Recruitment into the Hungarian Socialist Workers' Party." *American Sociological Review* 52 (1987): 559–573.

Tannenbaum, Frank. *Crime and the Community.* Boston: Ginn, 1938.

Taubman, Philip. "Classless Soviet Far Off, Paper Says." *The New York Times,* January 17, 1986, p. A4.

Taylor, Patricia A., Burke D. Grandjean, and Niko Tos. "Work Satisfaction Under Yugoslav Self-Management: On Participation, Authority, and Ownership." *Social Forces* 65 (1987): 1020–1034.

Teachman, Jay D. "Family Background, Educational Resources, and Educational Attainment." *American Sociological Review* 52 (1987): 548–557.

Teachman, Jay D., and Karen A. Polonko. "Marriage, Parenthood, and the College Enrollment of Men and Women." *Social Forces* 67 (1988): 512–523.

Teachman, Jay D., and Paul T. Schollaert. "Economic Conditions, Marital Status, and the Timing of First Births: Results for Whites and Blacks." *Sociological Forum* 4 (1989): 27–46.

Testart, Alain. "Game Sharing Systems and Kinship Systems among Hunter-Gatherers." *Man* 22 (1987): 287–304.

Theodore, Athena. *The Campus Troublemakers: Academic Women in Protest.* Galveston, TX: Cap and Gown, 1985.

Thoits, Peggy. "Multiple Identities: Examining Gender and Marital Status Differences in Distress." *American Sociological Review* 51 (1986): 259–272.

Thomas, George M., and Pat Lauderdale. "State Authority and National Welfare Programs in the World System Context." *Sociological Forum* 3 (1988): 383–399.

Thomas, William I. *The Unadjusted Girl.* Boston: Little Brown, 1927.

Thompson, Maxine Seaborn, Karl L. Alexander, and Doris R. Entwisle. "Household Composition, Parental Expectations, and School Achievement." *Social Forces* 67 (1988): 424–451.

Thompson, Maxine Seaborn, and Margaret E. Ensminger. "Psychological Well-Being Among Mothers with School Age Children: Evolving Family Structures." *Social Forces* 67 (1989): 715–730.

Thompson, Paul. *The Nature of Work: An Introduction to Debates on the Labor Process.* Atlantic Highlands, NJ: Humanities Press, 1984.

Thorne, Barrie. "Revisioning Women and Social Change: Where Are the Children?" *Gender & Society* 1 (1987): 85–109.

Thornton, Arland, and Deborah Freeman. *The Changing American Family.* Washington: Population Reference Bureau, 1983.

Thornton, Russell. *American Indian Holocaust and Survival: A Population History Since 1492.* Norman: University of Oklahoma Press, 1987.

Thurow, Lester. "The Task at Hand." *Wall Street Journal,* June 12, 1987, p. 46D.

Thurow, Lester. *The Zero Sum Society: Distribution and the Possibilities of Economic Change.* New York: Basic Books, 1980.

Tiano, Susan. "Gender, Work, and World Capitalism: Third World Women's Role in Development." In Beth B. Hess and Myra Marx Ferree (eds.), *Analyzing Gender: A Handbook of Social Science Research,* pp. 216–243. Newbury Park, CA: Sage, 1987.

Tienda, Marta, and Ding-Tzann Lii. "Minority Concentration and Earnings Inequality: Blacks, Hispanics, and Asians Compared." *American Journal of Sociology* 93 (1987): 141–165.

Tigges, Leann M. *Changing Fortunes: Industrial Sectors and Workers' Earnings.* New York: Praeger, 1987.

Tilly, Charles. *From Mobilization to Revolution.* Reading, MA: Addison-Wesley, 1978.

Tilly, Charles. *The Contentious French.* Cambridge, MA: Harvard University Press, 1986.

Time Magazine. "Onward, Women!" December 4, 1989: 80–89.

Tolbert, Charles M., Patrick M. Horan, and E. M. Beck. "The Structure of Economic Segmentation: A Dual Economy Approach." *American Journal of Sociology* 85(5) (March 1980): 1095–1116.

Tolchin, Martin. "Hospitals' Drive for More Nurses Brings Pay Rise," *The New York Times,* March 26, 1988a, p. L18.

Troeltsch, Ernst. *The Social Teachings of the Christian Churches.* New York: Macmillan, 1931.

Troiden, Richard R. *Gay and Lesbian Identity: A Sociological Analysis.* Dix Hills, NY: General Hall, 1988.

Trussell, Jamers. "Teenage Pregnancy in the United States." *Family Planning Perspectives* 20 (1988): 262–272.

Tumin, Melvin. "Some Principles of Stratification: A Critical Analysis." *American Sociological Review* 18 (Aug. 1953): 387–393.

Turnbull, Colin. *The Mountain People.* New York: Simon and Schuster, 1972.

Udry, J. Richard, and John O. G. Billy. "Initiation of Coitus in Early Adolescence," *American Sociological Review* 52 (1987): 841–855.

USA Today, "College Costs Climb." January 25, 1989, p. 6A.

U.S. Bureau of the Census. "Marital Status and Living Arrangements: March 1985." *Current Population Reports,* Series P-20, No. 410. Washington: U.S. Government Printing Office, November 1986.

U.S. Bureau of the Census. "Money Income and Poverty Status of Families and Persons in the United States: 1985 (Advance Data From the March 1986 Current Population Survey)." *Current Population Reports,* Series P–60, No. 154. Washington: U.S. Government Printing Office, August 1986.

U.S. Bureau of the Census. "Voting and Registration in the Election of November 1984." *Current Population Reports,* Series P-20, No. 405. Washington: U.S. Government Printing Office, March 1986.

U.S. Bureau of the Census. *Statistical Brief, Who's Minding the Children?* SB-2-87. Washington: U.S. Government Printing Office, May 1987.

U.S. Bureau of the Census, "Fertility of American Women: June 1988." *Current Population Reports,* Series. P-20, No. 436. Washington: U.S. Government Printing Office, 1989.

U.S. Bureau of the Census. *The Hispanic Population of the United States.* Washington: U.S. Government Printing Office, March 1989.

U.S. Bureau of the Census. "The Hispanic Population of the United States: March 1989." *Current Population Reports,* Series P-20. Washington, D.C.: U.S. Government Printing Office, 1990.

U.S. Bureau of Labor Statistics. 89–330, Washington: U.S. Department of Labor, July 1989, p. 2.

U.S. Bureau of Labor Statistics. *Labor Force Statistics Derived from the Current Population Survey,*

1948–87, Bulletin 2307. Washington: U.S. Departmnet of Labor, Bureau of Labor Statisics, August 1988.

U.S. Department of Health and Human Services. Monthly Vital Statistics Report, Vol. 38, No. 1. Washington: U.S. Government Printing Office, May 1989.

U.S. Department of Justice. *Criminal Victimization in the United States, 1986: A National Crime Survey Report.* Washington: U.S. Dept. of Justice, Bureau of Justice Statistics, 1988a.

U.S. Department of Justice. *Survey of Youth in Custody, 1987.* Washington: U.S. Dept. of Justice, 1988b.

U.S. News and World Report. "A Million Millionaires: How Ordinary People Get Rich." January 13, 1986, pp. 43–45.

U.S. Senate. *Developments in Aging: 1987. Vol. 1. Report of the Special Committee on Aging, United States Senate, 1987.* Washington: U.S. Government Printing Office, 1988.

Unnever, James D. "Direct and Organizational Discrimination in the Sentencing of Drug Offenders." *Social Problems* 30(2) (1982): 212–225.

Useem, Bert. "Disorganization and the New Mexico Prison Riot of 1980." *American Sociological Review* 50 (1985): 677–688.

Useem, Michael, and Jerome Karabel. "Pathways to Top Corporate Management." *American Sociological Review* 51(2) (1986): 184–200.

Vallas, Steven Peter. "The Labor Process as a Source of Class Consciousness: A Critical Examination." *Sociological Forum* 2 (1987): 237–256.

Van Gennep, Arnold. *The Rites of Passage* (1909). Chicago: University of Chicago Press, 1960.

Vanneman, Reeve, and Lynn Weber Cannon. *The American Perception of Class.* Philadelphia: Temple University Press, 1987.

Veblen, Thorstein. *The Theory of the Leisure Class.* New York: Macmillan, 1899.

Velez, William. "High School Attrition Among Hispanic and Non-Hispanic Youths." *Sociology of Education* 62 (1989): 119–133.

Verbrugge Lois M., and Patricia Madans. "Women's Roles and Health." *American Demographics* (March, 1985): 36–39.

Vernon, Raymond. "Ethics of Transnationalism." *Society,* March/April 1987, pp. 52–56.

Villers Foundation. *On the Other Side of East Street.* Washington: Villers Foundation, 1987.

Virginia Slims American Women's Opinion Poll, 1986. Storrs, CT: The Roper Organization, Inc. 1986.

Vladeck, Bruce. *Unloving Care.* New York: Basic Books, 1985.

Voydanoff, Patricia. *Work and Family Life.* Newbury Park, CA: Sage, 1987.

Wachs, Eleanor. *Crime-Victim Stories: New York City's Urban Folklore.* Bloomington: Indiana University Press, 1988.

Waite, Linda J., Frances Kobrin Goldscheider, and Christina Witsberger. "Nonfamily Living and the Erosion of Traditional Family Orientations Among Young Adults." *American Sociological Review* 51 (1986): 541–554.

Waite, Thomas L. "Those Who Rejected Vows Find New Roles in Church." *The New York Times,* February 27, 1989, p. B1.

Walker, Barbara. *The Crone: Women of Age, Wisdom, and Power.* New York: Harper & Row, 1985.

Walker, Henry A., Larry Rogers, and Morris Zelditch, Jr. "Legitimacy and Collective Action." *Social Forces* 67 (1988): 216–228.

Wallerstein, Immanuel. *The Modern World System.* New York: Academic Press, 1974.

Wallerstein, Judith S., and Sandra Blakesley. *Second Chances: Men, Women, and Children a Decade After Divorce.* New York: Ticknor & Fields, 1989.

Wall Street Journal. August 15, 1986, p. 1ff.

Walsh, Edward J. "The Role of Target Vulnerabilities in High-Technology Protest Movements: The Nuclear Establishment at Three Mile Island." *Sociological Forum* 1(2) (1986): 199–218.

Walsh, Edward J., and Marylee C. Taylor. "Occupational Correlates of Multidimensional Self-esteem: Comparisons Among Garbage Collectors, Bartenders, Professors, and Other Workers." *Sociology and Social Research* 66 (1982): 252–268.

Walters, Pamela Barnhouse, and Philip J. O'Connell. "The Family Economy, Work, and Educational Participation in the United States, 1890–1940." *American Journal of Sociology* 93 (1988): 1116–1152.

Wandersman, Abraham, Paul Florin, Robert Friedmann, and Ron Meier. "Who Participates, Who Does Not, and Why? An Analysis of Voluntary Neighborhood Organizations in the United States and Israel." *Sociological Forum* 2 (1987): 534–555.

Ward, Kathryn B. *Women in the World Economic System: Its Impact on Status and Fertility.* New York: Praeger, 1984.

Warner, Rebecca L., Gary R. Lee, and Janet Lee. "Social Organization, Spousal Resources, and Marital Power: A Cross-cultural Study." *Journal of*

Marriage and the Family 48 (1986): 121–128.

Warner, R. Stephen. *New Wine in Old Wineskins: Evangelicals and Liberals in a Small-Town Church.* Berkeley: University of California Press, 1988.

Warren, Carol A. B. *Madwives: Schizophrenic Women in the 1950s.* New Brunswick, NJ: Rutgers University Press, 1987.

Weber, Max. *The Social Psychology of the World Religions,* New York: Oxford University Press, 1922–23.

Weber, Max. *Economy and Society* (1922). New York: Bedminster Press, 1968.

Weber, Max. "Bureaucracy." In Hans H. Gerth and C. Wright Mills (eds.), *From Max Weber: Essays in Sociology,* pp. 196–244. New York: Oxford University Press, 1946.

Weber, Max. *Economy and Society* (1922). Excerpted in H. H. Gerth and C. Wright Mills (trans. and eds.), *From Max Weber: Essays in Sociology.* New York: Oxford University Press, 1958.

Weber, Max. "Some Consequences of Bureaucratization." In J. P. Mayer, *Max Weber and German Politics.* New York: Free Press, 1956.

Weber, Max. *The Protestant Ethic and the Spirit of Capitalism* (1904). New York: Scribners, 1958.

Weed, James. "The Life of a Marriage," *American Demographics,* February 1989, p. 12.

Weigert, Andrew J., J. Smith Teitge, and Dennis W. Teitge. *Society and Identity: Toward a Social Psychology.* New York: Cambridge University Press, 1986.

Weinberg, Joanna K. "Workfare—It Isn't Work, It Isn't Fair." *The New York Times,* August 19, 1988, p. 27.

Weitzman, Lenore J. *The Divorce Revolution: The Unexpected Social and Economic Consequences for Women and Children in America.* New York: Free Press, 1985.

Weitzman, Lenore J., Deborah Eifler, Elizabeth Hokado, and Catherine Ross, "Sex Role Socialization in Picture Books for Pre-School Children." *American Journal of Sociology* 77 (1972): 1125–1150.

Welch, Susan, and Lee Sigelman. "A Black Gender Gap?" *Social Science Quarterly* 70 (1989): 120–133.

Westoff, Charles F. "Fertility in the United States." *Science* 234 (1986): 554–559.

Westoff, Charles F. "Unintended Pregnancy in America and Abroad." *Family Planning Perspectives* 20 (1988): 254–261.

Wharton, Amy S. "Gender Segregation in Private-Sector, Public-Sector, and Self-Employed Occupations, 1950–1981." *Social Science Quarterly* 70 (1989): 923–940.

Whiddon, Beverly, and Patricia Yancey Martin. "Organizational Democracy and Work Quality in a State Welfare Agency." *Social Science Quarterly* 70 (1989): 667–687.

Whitam, Frederick L., and Robin M. Mathy. *Male Homosexuality in Four Societies: Brazil, Guatemala, the Philippines, and the United States.* New York: Praeger, 1986.

White, Michael D. "Conscription and the Size of Armed Forces." *Social Science Quarterly* 70 (1989): 772–781.

Whyte, William Foote, and Kathleen King Whyte. *Making Mondragon: The Growth and Dynamics of the Workers Cooperative Complex.* Ithaca, NY: ILR Press, 1988.

Wilkinson, Doris Y. "Ethnicity." In Marvin B. Sussman and Suzanne K. Steinmetz (eds.), *Handbook of Marriage and the Family,* pp. 183–210. New York: Plenum, 1987.

Wilkinson, Louise Cherry, and Cora B. Marrett, eds. *Gender Influences in Classroom Interaction.* Orlando, FL: Academic Press, 1985.

Williams, Robin, Jr. *American Society: A Sociological Interpretation,* (3rd ed.). New York: Alfred A. Knopf, 1970.

Williams, Terry, and William Kornblum. *Growing Up Poor.* Lexington, MA: Lexington, 1985.

Williams, Walter L. *The Spirit and the Flesh: Sexual Diversity in American Indian Culture.* Boston: Beacon, 1986.

Williams, Walter L. "Women, Men, and Others." *American Behavioral Scientist* 31 (1987): 135–141.

Willie, Charles, and Susan Greenblatt, eds. *Community Politics and Educational Change: Ten School Systems Under Court Order.* New York: Longman, 1981.

Willner, Ann Ruth. *The Spellbinders: Charismatic Political Leadership.* New Haven, CT: Yale University Press, 1984.

Wilson, Kenneth L., and Janet P. Boldizar. "Gender Segregation in Higher Education: Effects of Aspirations, Mathematics Achievement, and Income." *Sociology of Education* 63 (1990): 62–74.

Wilson, William Julius. *The Declining Significance of Race: Blacks and Changing America* (2nd ed.). Chicago: University of Chicago Press, 1980.

Wilson, William Julius. "The Black Community in the 1980s: Questions of Race, Class, and Public Policy." *Annals of the American Academy of Political and Social Science.* 454 (March 1981): 26–41.

Wilson, William Julius. *The Truly Disadvantaged: The Inner City, the Underclass, and Public Policy.* Chicago: University of Chicago Press, 1987.

Winter, Laraine. "The Role of Sexual Self-Concept in the Use of Contraceptives." *Family Planning Perspectives* 20 (1988): 123–127.

Wolfgang, Marvin, and Franco Ferrecuti. *The Subculture of Violence: Towards an Integrated Theory.* London: Tavistock, 1967.

Wright, Sam. *Crowds and Riots: A Study in Social Organization.* Beverly Hills, CA: Sage, 1978.

Wrong, Dennis. "The Oversocialized Conception of Man in Modern Sociology." *American Sociological Review* 26 (1961): 183–193.

Wuthnow, Robert. *Meaning and the Moral Order: Explorations in Cultural Analysis.* Berkeley: University of California Press, 1987.

Wuthnow, Robert. *The Restructuring of American Religion: Society and Faith Since World War II.* Princeton, NJ: Princeton University Press, 1988.

Wyatt, Gail Elizabeth, Stefanie Doyle Peters, and Donald Guthrie. "Kinsey Revisited. Part I. Comparisons of the Sexual Socialization and Sexual Behavior of White Women Over 33 Years." *Archives of Sexual Behavior* 17 (1988): 201–239.

Yegidis, Bonnie. "Date Rape and Other Forced Sexual Encounters Among College Students." *Journal of Sex Education and Therapy* 12 (1986): 51–54.

Yinger, J. Milton. "A Structural Examination of Religion." *Journal for the Scientific Study of Religion* 6 (1969): 88–99.

Yinger, J. Milton. *Countercultures.* New York: Free Press, 1982.

Zabin, Laurie Schwab, Marilyn B. Hirsch, Rosalie Strett, Mark R. Emerson, Morna Smith, Janet B. Hardy, and Theodore M. King. "The Baltimore Pregnancy Prevention Program for Urban Teenagers." *Family Planning Perspectives* 20 (1988): 182–192.

Zajonc, Robert B. "Family Configuration and Intelligence." *Science* 192 (1976): 227–236.

Zald, Mayer N., and Roberta Ash. "Social Movement Organizations." In Barry McLaughlin (ed.), *Studies in Social Movements.* pp. 461–485. New York: Free Press, 1969.

Zald, Mayer N., and John D. McCarthy, eds. *Social Movements in an Organizational Society.* New Brunswick, NJ: Transaction Press, 1987.

Zborowski, Mark. "Cultural Components in Response to Pain." *Journal of Social Issues* 8 (1952): 16–30.

Zeitz, Dorothy. *Women Who Embezzle or Defraud: A Study of Convicted Felons.* New York: Praeger Publishers, 1981.

Zelizer, Viviana. *Pricing the Priceless Child: The Changing Social Value of Children.* New York: Basic Books, 1985.

Zelnick, N., J. Kanter, and K. Ford. *Sex and Pregnancy in Adolescence.* Beverly Hills, CA: Sage Publications, 1981.

Zerubavel, Eviatar. *The Seven-Day Circle: The History and Meaning of the Week.* New York: Free Press, 1985.

Zimbardo, Philip, Curtis W. Banks, Craig Haney, and David Jaffe. "The Mind Is a Formidable Jailer." *The New York Times,* April 8, 1973.

Zimbardo, Philip, Ebbe B. Ebbesen, and Christine Maslach. *Influencing Attitudes and Changing Behavior.* Reading, MA: Addison-Wesley, 1977.

Zimmer, Lynn. "Tokenism and Women in the Workplace: The Limits of Gender-Neutral Theory." *Social Problems* 35 (1988): 64–77.

Zimmerman, Mary K. "The Women's Health Movement: A Critique of Medical Enterprise and the Position of Women." In Beth B. Hess and Myra Marx Ferree (eds.), *Analyzing Gender: A Handbook of Social Science Research.* Newbury Park, CA: Sage, 1987, pp. 442–472.

Zipp, John F. "Social Class and Social Liberalism." *Sociological Forum* 1 (1986): 301–329.

Zipp, John F., and Joel Smith. "A Structural Analysis of Class Voting." *Social Forces* 60 (1982): 738–759.

Zuboff, Shoshana. *In the Age of the Smart Machine: The Future of Work and Power.* New York: Basic Books, 1988.

Zweigenhaft, Richard L. "Recent Patterns of Jewish Representation in the Corporate and Social Elite." *Contemporary Jewry* 6 (1982): 36–46.

Photo Credits

Table and Line Art Credits

CHAPTER 4 Table 4-1: Skolnick, Arlene S. From *The Intimate Environment: Exploring Marriage and the Family,* 4/e. Copyright © 1987 by Arlene S. Skolnick. Reprinted by permission of HarperCollins Publishers.

CHAPTER 5 Table 5-1: Institute for Social Research at the University of Michigan. Table 5-2: Adapted from Merton, Robert K. *Social Theory and Social Structure.* Copyright © 1957 by the Free Press; copyright renewed 1985 by Robert K. Merton.

CHAPTER 6 Table 6-1: Davis, James A. and Tom W. Smith. *General Social Survey Cumulative File, 1972–1982.* Ann Arbor, MI: Inter-University Consortium for Political and Social Research, Distributor. Figure 6-1: Reprinted by permission of *The Wall Street Journal* © Dow Jones & Company, 1986. All rights reserved worldwide. Table 6-4: Kluegel, James R. "Macro-Economic Problems, Beliefs about the Poor and Attitudes toward Welfare Spending. © 1987 by the Society for the Study of Social Problems. Reprinted from *Social Problems,* Vol. 34, No. 1. Feb. 1987, pp. 82-99, by permission. Figure 6-5: Adapted from Blau, Peter and Otis Dudley Duncan. *The American Occupational Structure.* Copyright © 1967 by Peter M. Blau and Otis Dudley Duncan. Reprinted with permission of the Free Press, a Division of Macmillan, Inc.

CHAPTER 7 Tables 7-1 and 7-3: For this *Newsweek* poll, the Gallup Organization interviewed a national sample of 600 adults by telephone, September 14 and 15. The margin of error is + or − 4 percentage points. Some "don't know" and other answers are omitted. The *Newsweek* poll © 1989 by *Newsweek,* Inc. Table 7-2: Hofferth, Sandra L. et al. "Premarital Sexual Activity among U.S. Teenage Women over the Past Three Decades." *Family Planning Perspectives,* Vol. 19, No. 2, March/April 1987, p. 47. © The Alan Guttmacher Institute. Table 7-4: The National Information Bank on Women in Public Office (NIB), a service of the Center for the American Woman and Politics, Eagleton Institute of Politics, Rutgers University, 1989. Figure 7-5: Stanford Kay/Paragraphics. Table 7-5: Copyright © 1989 by the New York Times Company. Reprinted by permission.

CHAPTER 8 Table 8-2: Adapted from Olzak, Susan and Elizabeth West. Technical Report #88-13. Department of Sociology, Cornell University, Ithaca, New York. Figure 8-4: Data from Population Reference Bureau, Inc. *United States Population Data Sheet 1986.* Washington, D.C.: Population Reference Bureau, Inc., 1986. Graph from *The New York Times.* Copyright © 1988 by the New York Times Company. Reprinted by permission. Table 8-3: Adapted from Tidwell, Billy J. *Stalling Out: The Relative Progress of African Americans.* Washington, D.C.: National Urban League. Research Department, 1989. Published by permission. Figure 8-6: Population Reference Bureau, Inc. *United States Population Data Sheet 1985.* Washington, D.C.: Population Reference Bureau, Inc., 1985. Table 8-6: Archdeacon, Thomas J. *Becoming an American: An Ethnic History.* Copyright © 1983 by the Free Press, a Division of Macmillan, Inc.

CHAPTER 10 Table 10-2: Copyright © 1989 by the New York Times Company. Reprinted by permission. Figure 10-5: Copyright © 1988 by the New York Times Company. Reprinted by permission. Figure 10-9: Sivard, Ruth Leger. Reproduced with permission from *World Military and Social Expenditures 1989* by Ruth Leger Sivard. Copyright © 1989 by World Priorities, Washington, D.C., USA.

CHAPTER 11 Figure 11-1: Copyright © 1989 by the New York Times Company. Reprinted by permission.

CHAPTER 12 Figure 12-1: Coates, Vary T. "The Potential Impact of Robotics." *The Futurist,* February 1983, p. 80.

NAME INDEX

SUBJECT INDEX